D1571787

U.S. MERCHANT VESSEL
WAR CASUALTIES

U.S. MERCHANT VESSEL
WAR CASUALTIES
OF WORLD WAR II

Robert M. Browning Jr.

NAVAL INSTITUTE PRESS   Annapolis, Maryland

Library of Congress Cataloging-in-Publication Data.

Browning, Robert M. Jr., 1955–
    U.S. merchant vessel war casualties of World War II / by Robert M. Browning, Jr.
        p.   cm.
    Lists only those ships flying under the American flag that the Coast Guard and Navy documented
as receiving damage or were lost.
    Includes bibliographical references (p.   ) and index.
    ISBN 1-55750-087-8
    1. Merchant marine—United States—Registers. 2. World War, 1939–1945—Naval operations,
American. 3. Merchant ships—United States—Registers. 4. Armed merchant ships —United
States—Registers. 5. Shipwrecks—Registers. I. Title.
D810.T8B76 1995
940.54'5973—dc20   95-10711

Printed in the United States of America on acid-free paper ⊗

02 01 00 99 98 97 96   9 8 7 6 5 4 3 2

First printing

This book is dedicated to the forgotten men who sailed and fought on U.S. merchant ships during World War II.

CONTENTS

ILLUSTRATIONS

ABBREVIATIONS

DATA FIELD

D: date of attack
T: time of attack (ship's time)
Pos: ship's position when attacked
Ow: owner of vessel
Op: operator of vessel
M: master
A: armament

YB: year built
Tn: vessel's gross tonnage
Dr: draft when attacked
C: cargo when attacked
P: propulsion
S: speed in knots when attacked

TEXT

BBLS—Barrels
BWI—British West Indies
CAL—Caliber
CB—Construction Battalion
CTL—Constructive total loss
CZ—Canal Zone
FV—Fishing vessel
GMT—Greenwich Mean Time
GT—Gross Tons
GWT—German War Time
LBER—Pounder
MM—Millimeter
MS—Motor ship

MV—Merchant vessel
NWI—Netherlands West Indies
PI—Philippine Islands
POW—Prisoner of War
RAF—Royal Air Force
SS—Steamship
USAT—United States Army Transport
USCG—United States Coast Guard
USSR—Union of Soviet Socialist Republics
WSA—War Shipping Administration

CONVOYS

AS—United States to West Africa
AT—United States to United Kingdom, military
BA—Bombay to Red Sea ports
BB—Belfast to Bristol Channel
BT—Bahia to Trinidad
BTC—United Kingdom, coastal
BX—Boston to Halifax
CD—Capetown to Durban
CU—New York to United Kingdom, special
DN—Durban outwards to dispersal
EBC—English Channel
EMB—English Channel
EMC—English Channel
FS—Methil, Scotland, to Southend, England
GAT—Guantanamo to Trinidad
GUS—Port Said to North Africa to United States, slow
HS—Halifax to Sydney, Nova Scotia
HX—New York to United Kingdom
JW—Locke Ewe to Kola Fjord
KG—Key West to Guantanamo
KMF—United Kingdom to North Africa to Port Said, fast
KMS—United Kingdom to North Africa to Port Said, slow
KN—Key West to New York
KS—Norfolk to Key West
KW—Key West to Havana
MKF—Port Said to North Africa to United Kingdom, fast
MKS—Port Said to North Africa to United Kingdom, slow
NG—New York to Guantanamo
NV—Naples to Augusta
ON—Liverpool to New York
ONS—United Kingdom to North America, slow
PA—Persian Gulf to Aden
PB—Persian Gulf to Bombay and Karachi
PQ—Iceland to North Russia
QP—North Russia to Iceland
RA—Kola Fjord to Loche Ewe
SC—Halifax to United Kingdom
SG—Sydney, Nova Scotia, to Greenland
SNF—Italy to Algiers and Oran, fast
TA—United Kingdom to United States, military
TAG—Trinidad to Aruba to Guantanamo
TAW—Trinidad to Aruba to Key West
TB—United States to Sydney, Nova Scotia, military

TBC—United Kingdom, Coastal
TE—Trinidad east to dispersal point
TJ—Trinidad to Rio de Janeiro
UC—United Kingdom to New York, special
UGS—United States to North Africa to Port Said, slow
VN—Augusta to Naples
WB—Wabana, Newfoundland to Sydney, Nova Scotia
WS—United Kingdom to Middle East and India, military
XB—Halifax to Boston

MAJOR SOURCES USED IN THE NOTES

AG—Armed Guard Officer Voyage Reports to CNO, National Archives, Record Group 38, National Archives, Washington, DC.

DANFS—Dictionary of American Naval Fighting Ships.

NHC—Naval Historical Center, Washington, DC.

NSS—Summaries of Statements by Survivors. Operational Archives, Naval Historical Center, Washington, DC.

ONF—Official Number Files, These are found in three record groups: Records of the Bureau of Customs, Record Group 36, National Archives, Washington, DC; Records of the Bureau of Marine Inspection and Navigation, Record Group 41; National Archives, Washington, DC; and the most recent files are in the custody of the Coast Guard, Record Group 26.

RWCS—Records of the War Casualty Section, U.S. Coast Guard, Record Group 26, National Archives, Washington, DC.

RWSA—Records of the War Shipping Administration, Record Group 248, National Archives, Washington, DC.

TF—Tenth Fleet Records, Operational Archives, Naval Historical Center, Washington, DC.

USMMA—U.S. Merchant Marine Academy Cadet Voyage Reports 1941-1945, U.S. Merchant Marine Academy, King's Point, New York.

VSC—Vessel Status Card, U.S. Maritime Administration, Washington, DC.

WACR—War Action Casualty Reports, U.S. Coast Guard, Coast Guard Historian's Office, Washington, DC.

WCSR—U.S. Coast Guard, War Casualty Shipping Records 1941-45, Record Group 26, National Archives, Washington, DC.

WJ—War Journals of U-boats and U-boat Commands, Record Group 242, National Archives, Washington, DC.

ACKNOWLEDGMENTS

When I first began this project I did not have a full appreciation of the role that America's Merchant Marine played during World War II. While reading the thousands of documents necessary to write this book, I was moved by the mixture of heroism, sacrifice, and determination in almost every recorded incident. I also came to the conclusion that several books would be required to do real justice to the ships and men who made these voyages. Since this is beyond the scope of my work, I hope that this book, like the original documents, will provide the reader with some extra appreciation and knowledge of the war at sea.

In researching this book, I have attempted to review virtually every major source of information to provide a better accounting of the tremendous losses suffered by the American Merchant Marine during the war. Because of the nature of the records that remain, however, there are many discrepancies and likely a few omissions. Any mistakes and omissions are my own.

This book, as is the case with most books of this nature, could not have been written without the assistance, encouragement, and support of a large number of people, many institutions, and my family. Richard von Doenhoff and Barry Zerby, both of the National Archives, greatly aided my research, and without their help my project would have been a far lengthier one. I wish to give special thanks to Paul Branch who shared research notes and translated German documents for a book he is preparing on the Battle of the Atlantic. I am also indebted to Brian Whetstine who translated many of the German U-boat War Journals for my use. My sincerest thanks to Cathy Lloyd, Mike Walker, and John Hodges of the Operational Archives, Naval Historical Center, for their untiring efforts and guidance. John Reilly and the entire staff of the Ship's History Branch of the Naval Historical Center were always extremely helpful. I would like to extend my gratitude to Dana and Kay Gibson who so cheerfully provided me with information regarding Army Transports and other pertinent and related information. I appreciate the help of Dr. George J. Billy of the U.S. Merchant Marine Academy who made available the Cadet-generated records of World War II. I would like to thank Mike Bratton and Petty Officer Kurtis Riva for their help with the Coast Guard's War Casualty Shipping Records and Mrs.

Eleanor Fisher of the Vessel Documentation Branch, U.S. Coast Guard, for helping to document various ships in this study. Angie VanDereedt, Bill Sherman, and Aloha South were extremely helpful with the Coast Guard Records in the National Archives. Thanks are extended to Ann House of the Steamship Historical Society who provided great assistance with the photography in the book. I am also grateful to Dr. Jim Valle who gave me some guidance and Cherie Voris, the Archivist for Texaco, who furnished information from the company's archives. Thanks also go to Scott Price, Kevin Foster, Bob Cressman, Chris Wright, Jeff Ethell, Don Canney, Dr. Bill Armstrong, Dr. Carl Boyd, and Bob Scheina, who all helped with portions of the manuscript.

Last and most important is my family's support of this effort. Sheri, Bobby, and Holly all helped in their own special ways. Susan, of course, has been my major pillar of support. She has spent hundreds of hours typing and proofreading the manuscript and along with my children has shared her time with my work. These few words cannot express what I truly owe her.

INTRODUCTION

Great military commanders have always recognized the importance of wartime logistics, and the general principles of logistics have remained unchanged throughout history. The movement of supplies to support military operations is an essential part of warfare and, predictably, is exposed to enemy attack. This idea may have been stated best by the famous Civil War Confederate Cavalry leader John S. Mosby who wrote, "The line that connects an army with its base of supplies is the heel of Achilles—its most vital and vulnerable point."[1] This maxim is one of the most fundamental aspects of military logistics, yet the importance of logistics is frequently downplayed or overlooked. This oversight is even more pronounced when maritime logistics are involved.

World War II was fought on a global scale and the lines of supply stretched for incredible distances. These lengthy supply lines were extremely vulnerable and frequently interrupted. In fact, enemy submarine successes threatened the very continuance of the war in the first few years.

The obstacle of long supply routes could only be overcome in part by assembling and building a fleet to carry the necessary supplies, men, and war materiel to the front. The logistical demands of industrial nations fighting modern wars are astonishing. The Allies could not have fought a single foreign campaign without this military/civilian component. The nearly 500 large ocean-going vessels of the American merchant marine in 1941 grew more than tenfold during the war to the immense number of over 5,600 ships. The American merchant marine thus played a vital role in Allied victories during the war. This tremendous worldwide endeavor, however, cost the lives of thousands of men and the demise of more than 700 U.S. ships.

Historians have often overlooked the sealift capacity of this fleet. During the war, 203,522,000 tons of dry cargo, 64,730,000 tons of petroleum products, 1,000,000 vehicles, 24,000 aircraft, and over 7,000,000 troops and civilians were carried by American ships. The ability to move personnel and this amount

---

[1] John S. Mosby, *Mosby's War Reminiscences and Stuart's Cavalry Campaigns*, New York: Dodd, Mead & Company, 1887, p. 117.

of materiel over such long distances is staggering. It is also completely beyond today's capability. To put this operation in perspective, American ships delivered over 8,000 tons of cargo every hour of every day and every night during the entire war. This tremendous logistical effectiveness established the Allies' merchant marine as perhaps the most important strategic factor leading to the defeat of the Axis powers during the war.[2]

The construction, mobilization, and movement of this vital component were made necessary in part because of the early and extremely successful U-boat campaign off the American coast. Reacting to this campaign, the federal government nationalized the oceangoing merchant marine to ensure that all merchant vessel activity could be coordinated to win the war. On 7 February 1942, exactly two months after Pearl Harbor, President Franklin Roosevelt established the War Shipping Administration (WSA), using the powers granted to the president under the Merchant Marine Act of 1936. This act had created the United States Maritime Commission, and the president used these war emergency powers to requisition and put the American-flagged fleet under the WSA's control. The WSA designated cargoes for ships based on the logistical needs of the war. This agency organized, operated, chartered, provided insurance, administered repairs, and recruited and trained seamen for the entire fleet of American-flagged vessels. Under these provisions the WSA took all the risks.[3]

Even though the shipping companies surrendered control over their ships, as general agents they continued to oversee the normal seagoing and shoreside operations such as manning, berthing, provisioning, cargo handling, bunkering, repairing and overhauling, and hiring of tugs and pilots. The government paid steamship operators fixed amounts as operating agents of these vessels, as well as compensation for their use. What made this arrangement financially feasible to the shipping companies was the fact that the WSA provided war-risk insurance for vessels, cargoes, and crews. This insurance made it possible for shippers and cargo owners to risk operating in war zones without facing financial ruin. The shipping companies also managed vessels belonging to the U.S. Maritime Commission and the WSA. Qualified ship operators thereby

---

[2] *The United States Merchant Marine at War, Report of the War Shipping Administration to the President*, Washington, DC, 1946, pp. 4, 33, gives the figure of 1,340 vessels at the war's beginning. Eloise Engle and Arnold S. Lott, *America's Maritime Heritage*, Annapolis, Naval Institute Press, 1925, p. 306.

[3] Charles Dana Gibson, *Merchantman or Ship of War*, pp. 105-106; Daniel Levine and Sara Ann Platt, "The Contribution of the U.S. Shipbuilding and the Merchant Marine to the Second World War" from Robert A. Kilmarx, (ed.) *America's Maritime Legacy*, Westview Press, Boulder, CO, 1979, p. 205; *The United States Merchant Marine at War*, pp. 38-39.

became operating agents for the federal government. Paid a fixed rate each day, they could manage as many ships as they could effectively handle.[4]

In some instances vessels were requisitioned by the WSA and then released back to their owners for commercial service. All, however, were subject to immediate recall to the WSA to carry wartime cargoes. Vessels in coastwise and Caribbean service often entered and left government service under these arrangements.

In all cases the WSA's pool of merchant ships remained separate and distinct from those ships controlled by the Army and Navy. Some of the American vessels sailed under bareboat charters for the Army and Navy. When this happened, the military resumed full responsibility, including all expenses and manning. In emergency situations when a ship was hurriedly taken over by the Army, manning with a Civil Service crew was not always possible. At times such ships sailed under Army control with a merchant crew. If a ship was badly damaged while under charter to the military, the owner, whether it was a private line, the WSA, or the U.S. Maritime Commission, would be paid a predetermined price.[5]

Another common relationship was the sub-bareboat charter. In these cases, the WSA as the bareboat charterer of the vessel rechartered the ship to another party. Prior to late 1943, the WSA used this arrangement to transfer vessels to Army control, and in this situation the Army crewed and fully operated the ships in the same manner as would have been the case in a straight bareboat charter. Beginning in 1943, however, this practice was changed in favor of "allocating" these vessels to carry military cargoes. In this circumstance, the WSA remained the operator of the ship. The early emergencies created by the war often caused the Army to take vessels into service without formal paperwork. The *Portmar* is a perfect example. Some records erroneously list her as an Army transport in February 1942.

A third arrangement was a time charter. In these cases, the Army paid for the use of the ship, and furnished the fuel, and paid all port expenses. The crew and provision expenses were paid by the owner—thus the ship remained a merchant vessel by definition.[6]

This book does not include any ships placed under bareboat or sub-bareboat charters to the Army or Navy. Vessels like the *Cynthia Olsen* and *Malama* lost their status as merchant ships when the Army chartered them.

---

[4] *The United States Merchant Marine at War*, pp. 40, 74; John Gorley Bunker, *Liberty Ships*, New York, Arno Press, 1980, pp. 52, 54-55; Texas Company, *History of the Texas Company's Marine Department*, nd, pp. 27-28; Gibson, p. 108.

[5] Gibson, pp. 106-07.

[6] The U.S. Navy also operated cargo ships in the Naval Transport Service. The employment status of the crews on these vessels remains uncertain, and the status of the ships is sometimes questionable.

The Definition of a War Casualty

The ships included in this book are those American-flagged merchant ships that the Coast Guard and the Navy documented as either receiving damage or lost through some act of the enemy. A small number of vessels suffered damage prior to or in the early months of the war and have not been thoroughly documented by any government agency. Many were not even counted as war casualties in the official government lists. Because of such limited documentation, most could not be included in the narrative portion of the book. I have, however, listed these vessels in the appendix to provide a fuller accounting of all the ships lost during the war.

Previous works have used the U.S. Navy's Survivors Statements as the primary database. This collection of narratives is excellent but incomplete. The Coast Guard concurrently filed War Action Casualty Reports on almost every vessel damaged or sunk. I have used the Coast Guard's determination of a war casualty, even when the reported damage was minor, to define the entries in this book. This includes all types of active and passive weapons and covers casualties suffered after the hostilities ceased. There are dozens of ships, however, whose damage was so slight, either from shrapnel or from explosive concussions, that were never documented by the government and are not included in this study. There were also a number of ships listed as war casualties but whose damage was extremely minor or could not be ascertained. The *Watson C. Squire*, *Streator Seam*, *Stephen Furdek*, *George E. Merrick*, *Rock Springs Victory*, *Will R. Wood*, and *Simeon G. Reed* are among these.

I have included Philippine vessels in this study. At the outbreak of war the Philippines was not a sovereign nation but a commonwealth of the United States, thus these merchant vessels had a special and unique status. The United States did not document Philippine vessels or seamen but did have direct control and supervision of all Philippine foreign affairs including the regulation of its trade. During the war, these vessels were considered American ships but their losses are poorly documented in American sources. The plight of these vessels calls for further study.[7]

I have, however, purposely omitted ships such as the *Stanvac Calcutta*. This ship sailed with an American merchant crew and a U.S. Navy Armed Guard gun crew, but she sailed under a Panamanian flag. A number of ships owned by American companies sailed under this or other flags of convenience but do not appear in this study because they were not American-flagged vessels at the time of the attack.

---

[7] Correspondence relating to this issue can be found in the records of the Department of Commerce, Record Group 40, and the Department of State, Record Group 59.

About the Major Sources

The source material available for this study is dispersed throughout the archives of various government agencies. The most complete and extensive source, and the one used most often here, is the Summary of Statements of Survivors in the Operational Archives, Naval Historical Center. Prepared by the Office of Naval Intelligence, these statements comprise approximately 800 narratives prepared to disseminate intelligence data concerning attacks on the American and foreign merchant vessels. Overall, they are accurate, the most valuable source, and often the only remaining narrative of the event.

The Records created by the Coast Guard during the war are numerous. The Records of the War Casualty Section, Record Group 26, National Archives, include photographs and other documents concerning war casualties. There are two other groups of Coast Guard Records that researchers have neglected. The most valuable are the War Action Casualty Reports. In these, the Coast Guard interviewed survivors and used other records to complete a detailed form. The compiler answered sixty-one specific questions, some with multiple parts. The Coast Guard gathered this information to ascertain whether any changes might be necessary in lifesaving equipment or whether any of the crew neglected their duty. The questions were originally asked only of tanker casualties, but the survey was later extended to all merchant vessels. Because the questions explored facts not covered by the Office of Naval Intelligence's Statement of Survivors, the information often reveals data not found elsewhere. These reports at times contradict the Navy reports, particularly regarding such aspects as crew size and time of attack.

The U.S. Coast Guard War Casualty Shipping Records contain a medley of data including shipping articles, message traffic, newspaper clippings, consular reports and documents, press releases, affidavits and statements by the crews, and letters to families of deceased merchant mariners. These records embellish the story and also contain information that contradicts other sources.

Another source of material can be found at the U.S. Merchant Marine Academy. The Academy required its cadets to make a report to the Supervisor of the Cadet Corps when the enemy attacked their ship. These Cadet Voyage Reports are in narrative form and complement the Statements of Survivors. They sometimes contain unique information not found elsewhere.

The war journals of the various U-boats are another important source of information. These are found within the *Records of the German Navy 1850– 1945-Received from the United States Naval History Division*. These 4,200 rolls of microfilm are in the National Archives in Microfilm Publication T1022. The microfilm contains summaries of combat operations of the U-boats. Although these journals, like ship's logs, vary in detail, they do give a variety of information such as data on the weather, the distances traveled daily, radio communications, and the ships spotted and attacked. They are helpful in determining specific details of attacks, particularly when there were no survivors or other Allied witnesses. In these cases, the U-boat war journal is a crucial part of the story.

Finally, the Armed Guard reports add valuable details to the events. These reports are irregular, however; some are extensive while others are terse and of little value. They likewise frequently contain information not found elsewhere.

The largest body of records was, of course, those accounts maintained by the shipping companies and the WSA. Unfortunately, these have been lost or destroyed over the past several decades. Their loss has been costly in terms of providing details of the events that will never be recounted in other sources.

The Most Common Contradictions

Given the wide variety of sources used in this study, it was inevitable contradictions would occur. The most frequent contradictory information involves the time of the attack. This is due to the fact that these ships were attacked in time zones all around the world. When possible, times are listed in ship's time, but if the specific time zone is not known, another reference is used. All the times listed are approximate, but most of the differences within the sources vary by only a few minutes.

The recorded position of the attack is frequently contradictory because navigation fifty years ago was not as precise as it is today. I have listed the most plausible positions and have often cited others as a second reference. Jürgen Rohwer usually provided a position but sometimes used the U.S. Navy's coordinates.

The most confusing and conflicting information by far is the personnel data. The War Casualty Shipping Records contain the shipping articles for most of the war casualties. These documents are not always reliable, however, because they often show the crew only at the beginning of the voyage, even though the crew size frequently changed throughout the voyage. For one reason or another men failed to join the ship before sailing, they fell ill, and they transferred off the ship. Because of these changes, the number of men on board at the time of the attack is open to question. The Navy Summary of Survivors, the War Action Casualty Reports, and sometimes the Armed Guard Records are usually the only sources other than the shipping articles that relate this information. Foreign seamen and British gunners detailed to the Armed Guard Crew at times do not show up on the figures. The Masters often presented other evidence in their official statements. In counting the Armed Guard contingent on board, I have always included the Navy men assigned to communications duty.

U.S. MERCHANT VESSEL
WAR CASUALTIES

CITY OF RAYVILLE

D: 11-9-40   YB: 1920
T: 1938   Tn: 5,883

D: 11-9-40	YB: 1920
T: 1938	Tn: 5,883
Pos: 120 miles SW of Melbourne	Dr: 14 ft. 5 in.
Ow: U.S. Maritime Commission	C: general, lead ingots, wool, fruit
Op: U.S. Lines	P: diesel
M: Arthur P. Cronin	S: 10
A: unarmed	

The *City of Rayville* sailed from Adelaide to Melbourne, Australia. Six miles off Cape Otway the freighter struck a mine laid by the German auxiliary minelayer *Passat*. The explosion occurred off the starboard side forward of the midship house. The blast sent up red flames and hurled lead ingots through the superstructure. The *City of Rayville* began to sink rapidly. The cargo of ingots stowed in the #2, #3, and #4 holds, shifted forward and broke through the bulkheads as the ship settled. This caused the freighter to break in two, and the forward half of the ship sank immediately. The crew of nine officers and thirty men, with the exception of the third engineer, escaped in two lifeboats within ten minutes of the explosion. Fishermen from Apollo Bay towed the boats ashore. The after section of the ship disappeared beneath the water at 2030.

WACR; *The Herald* (Melbourne), 9 November 1940; Muggenthaler, p. 73.

ROBIN MOOR

D: 5-21-41	YB: 1919
T: 0625	Tn: 4,999
Pos: 6.28 N / 25.54 W	Dr: 23 ft. 6 in.
Ow: Seas Shipping Co. Inc.	C: 5,100 tons general
Op: Seas Shipping Co. Inc.	P: steam
M: Edward W. Myers	S: 11
A: unarmed	

The *Robin Moor* was surprised and stopped by blinker light by the *U-69* (Metzler) while en route from New York to Cape Town, South Africa. After questioning the chief mate, Metzler claimed he would have to sink the ship. He allowed the nine officers, twenty-nine crewmen, and eight passengers thirty minutes to abandon ship. The *U-69* fired a torpedo into the port side and then finished her with thirty-three shells from its 88-mm gun. The *Robin Moor* went to the bottom in about twenty minutes. Metzler provided rations to the survivors in the four boats. The boats managed to stay together for three days, but the #4 boat later became separated from the others. Thirteen days after the attack, a British ship bound for Cape Town spotted the three boats. The Brazilian

SS *Osorio* discovered the #4 boat and its eleven passengers eighteen days after the attack and landed them at Recife, Brazil. All hands survived the attack.

WACR; *The Evening Star* (Washington) 10 June 1941; Rohwer, p. 53, places the attack at 06.10 N / 25.40 W; Moore, p. 243

STEEL SEAFARER

D:	9-5-41	YB:	1921
T:	2338	Tn:	5,718
Pos:	27.20 N / 34.15 E	Dr:	22 ft. 5 in.
Ow:	Isthmian Steamship Co.	C:	7,000 tons general
Op:	Isthmian Steamship Co.	P:	steam
M:	John D. R. Halliday	S:	4
A:	unarmed		

The *Steel Seafarer*, on a voyage from New York to Suez, Egypt, came under aerial attack by a German plane in the Red Sea. Steaming at four knots, the vessel proceeded with her navigational lights lit in clear weather and rough seas. A large American flag painted on the side of the ship marked her nationality. The *Steel Seafarer* was struck by one bomb in the #5 double bottom tank, and the master immediately stopped the engines and ordered the ship to be abandoned. The crew launched three boats and the freighter sank in fifteen minutes. All nine officers and twenty-seven crewmen reached Egypt the next day. Five men received treatment ashore for injuries.

WACR; WCSR; *New York Times*, 10 September 1941.

LEHIGH

D:	10-19-41	YB:	1919
T:	0855	Tn:	4,983
Pos:	8.26 N / 14.37 W	Dr:	16 ft.
Ow:	U.S. Maritime Commission	C:	in ballast
Op:	United States Lines	P:	steam
M:	Vincent Patrick Arkins	S:	11
A:	unarmed		

The *Lehigh* departed Spain en route to Africa. Even though American flags marked her nationality, the *U-126* (Bauer) attacked the freighter seventy-five miles west of Freetown, Sierra Leone. The *U-126* fired a torpedo that struck at the #5 hold on the starboard side. After stopping the engines, the crew found the *Lehigh* could not be saved and abandoned her in a slight sea, thirty-five minutes after the torpedo struck. The ten officers, thirty crewmen, and four Spanish stowaways escaped in four lifeboats. The radio operator and two other men reboarded the vessel to send a message but were unsuccessful. The #1 and #2 boats, being faster, left the other two boats behind. British motor launches rescued the survivors in these boats. A British destroyer spotted the other two boats nearly two days after the attack. Five of the crew reported injuries, but all survived. The *Lehigh* sank stern first at 1019.

WACR; WCSR; Rohwer, p. 69.

ASTRAL

D:	12-2-41	YB:	1916
T:	0924 GWT	Tn:	7,542
Pos:	35.40 N / 24.00 W	Dr:	29 ft. (approximately)
Ow:	Socony-Vacuum Oil Co.	C:	78,200 bbls. gasoline and
Op:	Socony-Vacuum Oil Co.		kerosene
M:	Chris Alsager	P:	steam
A:	unarmed	S:	unknown

The *Astral*, en route from Aruba, NWI, to Portugal, was torpedoed by the *U-43* (Luth). On 1 December, in a full moon, Luth followed the tanker for several hours before maneuvering into a favorable position to attack. Luth missed with his first shot, but lookouts on board the *Astral* spotted the torpedo. The *Astral* immediately began steaming a zigzag course to escape. Luth followed the tanker throughout the night and the next day. He successfully put two torpedoes into her, one in the stern and another amidships. The tanker exploded into flames and quickly sank within minutes. The flaming cargo in the water burned for an hour longer. The flammable nature of the cargo contributed to the deaths of the entire crew of eight officers and twenty-nine men.

The *Astral* was first spotted by the *U-575* (Heydemann), and he tracked her for several hours. Noticing the American flag painted on the *Astral*'s side, he let her go. WACR; WCSR; WJ; Rohwer, p. 72.

SAGADAHOC

D:	12-3-41	YB:	1918
T:	1920	Tn:	6,275
Pos:	21.50 S / 07.50 W	Dr:	26 ft. 8 in.
Ow:	American South African Line	C:	5,800 tons general
Op:	American South African Line	P:	steam
M:	Frederick I. Evans	S:	10
A:	unarmed		

The *Sagadahoc* sailed from New York to South Africa and en route was stopped at sea by the *U-124* (Mohr). A search by the submarine's crew revealed that the merchantman had contraband on board. Mohr allowed the crew of eight officers, twenty-six men, and the one passenger to abandon ship. One crewman, however, failed to clear the vessel and perished when she sank. The *U-124* fired three torpedoes. One struck under the bridge, another demolished the engine room, and the last hit between hatches #4 and #5. The two boats with the survivors later became separated. An Allied merchant vessel rescued the men in one boat after six days and those in the other boat after seven days at sea. With the exception of an oiler, all hands survived.

WACR; WCSR; Rohwer, p. 72.

PRESIDENT HARRISON

D:	12-7-41	YB:	1921
T:	1400	Tn:	10,509
Pos:	31.20 N / 122.00 E	Dr:	22 ft.
Ow:	American President Lines	C:	none
Op:	American President Lines	P:	steam
M:	Orel A. Pierson	S:	15.5
A:	unarmed		

On 4 December, the *President Harrison* sailed from Manila, Philippine Islands, to embark the Marine detachments from Peking and Tientsin. The Marines had arrived at Chinwangtao, the nearest port. The master, after receiving word of the Japanese attack on Pearl Harbor, was pursued by a Japanese cruiser and aircraft. He intentionally grounded the *Harrison* off Swaweishan Island to tear her bottom out. The entire complement of 14 officers, 140 men, and 1 passenger escaped in seven boats, but 3 of these men drowned when their lifeboat was pulled into the *Harrison*'s screws. The Japanese captured the remaining crew members. The master spent six months in jail for wrecking the ship. The Japanese kept the deck and engineering officers as POWs and interned the crewmen in civilian camps. Twelve of these men died in captivity. The Japanese spent thirteen days salvaging the extensively damaged ship and later operated her as the *Kachidoki Maru*. On 12 September 1944, the USS *Pampanito* (SS-383) torpedoed the ship off Hainan, China.

WACR; WCSR; Morison, 3:155; Niven, pp. 148-49.

CAPILLO

D:	12-8-41	YB:	1920
T:	unknown	Tn:	5,135
Pos:	in Manila Bay	Dr:	24 ft.
Ow:	WSA	C:	6,020 tons general, wheat, flour
Op:	American Mail Line	P:	steam
M:	Karl Olag Dreyer	S:	anchored
A:	unarmed		

On 2 October, the *Capillo* sailed from Seattle, Washington, and arrived in Manila Bay on 6 November. On 6 December, while at anchor in Manila Bay, the *Capillo* was subjected to a Japanese aerial bombing attack. During this attack, bombs fell nearby, but the ship escaped damage. On 8 December, fifty-nine Japanese twin-engined bombers appeared from the south. The planes bombed and strafed the moored vessels and managed to hit the *Capillo* with machine gun fire her entire length. One bomb struck the freighter's deck at the #6 hatch, penetrated into the hold, and exploded. The cargo of wheat and flour absorbed the blast and limited the damage. Fire broke out immediately, but firefighting parties discovered that the firefighting equipment on board was inoperative. With no way to fight the flames, the crew abandoned the ship in the one good lifeboat. The damaged *Capillo* subsequently developed a bad list, and U.S. Army forces sank her with dynamite on 11 December. All of the eight officers and thirty-two crew members on board at the time of the attack survived. On 2 January 1942, Japanese forces captured these men and interned them at Santo Tomas Prison in Manila.

The complement figures are contradictory within the sources. NSS; WACR; WCSR; Moore, p. 41.

SAGOLAND

D:	12-10-41	YB:	1913
T:	unknown	Tn:	5,334
Pos:	Manila	Dr:	unknown
Ow:	Madrigal & Co.	C:	flour
Op:	Madrigal & Co.	P:	steam
M:	unknown	S:	unknown
A:	unarmed		

The *Sagoland* sailed from Union Bay for Manila, Philippine Islands. Japanese aircraft attacked and severely damaged the freighter on 10 December, and she sank the following day. The size of the crew and the number on board at the time of the attack are not related within the sources.

WCSR; Lloyd's, p. 320.

LAHAINA

D:	12-11-41	YB:	1920
T:	1340	Tn:	5,645
Pos:	27.42 N / 147.38 W	Dr:	11 ft. 6 in.
Ow:	Matson Navigation Co.	C:	1,050 tons general, molasses,
Op:	Matson Navigation Co.		scrap iron
M:	Hans Otto Heinrich Matthiesen	P:	steam
A:	unarmed	S:	10

On 4 December, the *Lahaina* sailed from Hawaii to San Francisco. At 1340 on 11 December, the *I-9* (Fujii) approached the *Lahaina* at approximately right angles to the starboard beam, from the direction of the sun. The submarine fired a warning shot across the freighter's bow, and the master passed the order to abandon ship after the confidential codes went overboard and the radio operator sent a distress message. The *I-9* fired about twenty-five rounds and hit the merchantman with eight shots on the starboard side and four on the port side. The mixture of explosive and incendiary shells set the vessel afire. The crew managed to launch only the starboard boat, the other having been destroyed by the gunfire. At 0900 the next day, the master returned to the vessel hoping to salvage her, but on boarding the *Lahaina* he found the fire out of control. The survivors secured food and water, and the eight officers and twenty-six crewmen set sail for Hawaii. On 12 December, the *Lahaina* capsized slowly to port and sank at 1230. For nine days the crew struggled to make land, facing heavy seas, short rations, and an overcrowded lifeboat. With the assistance of the USCG cutter *Tiger* (WPC-152), thirty men landed near Kahului, Maui, on 21 December. During the journey in the boat, two of the crew had jumped overboard and two died of exposure and shock.

NSS; WACR; WCSR; Rohwer, p. 278; Stindt, p. 118; *Ships in Gray*, p. 42.

VINCENT

D:	12-12-41	YB:	1919
T:	1907	Tn:	6,210
Pos:	22.40 S / 118.13 W	Dr:	28 ft.
Ow:	U.S. Maritime Commission	C:	8,300 tons wool, ore, tallow,
Op:	U.S. Lines		walnut logs
M:	Angus Mackinnon	P:	steam
A:	unarmed	S:	10

The *Vincent*, bound from Sydney, Australia, for Panama, was discovered by the Japanese merchant cruisers *Hokoku Maru* and *Aikoku Maru* in clear weather and moderate seas. The Japanese vessels started shelling the freighter at 1907 and fired a total of eight shells. The crew began abandoning ship in three boats within thirty minutes as fire broke out on board. The Japanese later fired a single torpedo that struck the merchantman and sent her to the bottom. All nine officers and twenty-seven crewmen survived the attack. The *Hokoku Maru* picked up the men, who then traveled with the raider for sixty-three days until interned as POWs in Japan. Two crew members later died in the POW camps.

WACR; WCSR; WCSR for *Malama*.

GOVERNOR WRIGHT

D:	12-12-41	YB:	1938
T:	unknown	Tn:	496
Pos:	12.55 N / 123.55 E	Dr:	unknown
Ow:	Visayan Trans. Co., Inc.	C:	unknown
Op:	Visayan Trans. Co., Inc.	P:	motor
M:	unknown	S:	unknown
A:	unarmed		

Japanese aircraft attacked the *Governor Wright* off Panay Island, Philippines, and sank her on 12 December. The size of the crew and the number on board at the time of the attack are not related within the sources.

Lloyd's, p. 326.

ADMIRAL Y. S. WILLIAMS

D:	12-12-41	YB:	1920
T:	unknown	Tn:	3,252
Pos:	at Kowloon, China	Dr:	20 ft.
Ow:	American Trading Co.	C:	4,076 tons rubber and tin
Op:	American Trading Co.	P:	steam
M:	Fred Nystrom	S:	docked
A:	unarmed		

On 19 September, the *Admiral Y. S. Williams* weighed anchor in Singapore for Los Angeles. Five days later the ship ran aground and went into dry dock in Kowloon, China. Here, to prevent her capture by the enemy, the British deliberately damaged her by dynamiting the end of the dry dock where she lay. The seven officers and twenty-seven crew members survived, with the exception of one messman who died from a gunshot wound. The Japanese took

twenty-one of the men as POWs and repatriated ten others; two escaped. The Japanese salvaged the ship and renamed her the *Tasutama Maru*.

WACR; WCSR; Moore, p. 2.

MANATAWNY

D:	12-13-41	YB:	1920
T:	unknown	Tn:	5,030
Pos:	Manila Harbor	Dr:	unknown
Ow:	Madrigal & Co.	C:	dynamite
Op:	Madrigal & Co.	P:	steam
M:	unknown	S:	unknown
A:	unarmed		

The tanker *Manatawny* sailed from Los Angeles, California, to Hong Kong via Seattle, Honolulu, and Manila. While in the harbor of Manila, she was attacked by Japanese bombers, and direct hits set her on fire. She sank sometime later. The size of the crew and the number on board at the time of the attack are unknown.

WCSR; Lloyd's, p. 322.

MANINI

D:	12-17-41	YB:	1920
T:	1840	Tn:	3,253
Pos:	17.46 N / 157.03 W	Dr:	20 ft. 6 in.
Ow:	Matson Navigation Co.	C:	2,700 tons general
Op:	Matson Navigation Co.	P:	steam
M:	George Sidon	S:	8
A:	unarmed		

The *Manini* sailed from Hawaii and en route to San Francisco was spotted by the *I-75* (Inoue) 180 miles south of Hawaii. The *I-75* fired a torpedo that struck the *Manini* on the port side between the #3 and #4 holds. The main topmast crashed to the deck, destroying the radio antenna and preventing the radio operator from sending a distress signal. She sank by the stern in about ten minutes. In rough seas the eight officers and twenty-five crewmen managed to escape the vessel and the floating wreckage in two boats. One man drowned trying to leave the freighter. The two boats became separated after the attack. On 28 December, a naval vessel and the USCG cutter *Tiger* (WPC-152) rescued the survivors in the #1 boat twenty-five miles south of Kauai. The *Patterson*

(DD-392) spotted the #2 boat the next day. On 26 December, a messman in this boat died of exposure and was buried at sea—the only casualty of the attack.

WACR; WCSR; The *I-75* was later renumbered as the *I-175;* Rohwer, p. 278; Stindt, p. 118.

PRUSA

D:	12-19-41	YB:	1919
T:	0530	Tn:	5,113
Pos:	16.45 N / 156.00 W	Dr:	25 ft.
Ow:	Lukes Bros. SS Co.	C:	6,720 tons chrome, copra, hemp,
Op:	Lukes Bros. SS Co.		mahogany
M:	George David Henry Roy	P:	steam
A:	unarmed	S:	10.5

On 16 December, the *Prusa* sailed from Honolulu to Baltimore and was torpedoed by the *I-172* (Togami) approximately 150 miles south of Hawaii. The ship was on a course almost due southeast when lookouts spotted a torpedo approaching about 100 yards away. The helmsman could not avoid the torpedo, and it struck the ship at the #5 hold and the shaft alley on the port side. The explosion fatally damaged the ship, blew out doors, ruptured steam lines, and knocked out the electrical system. The ship sank in about eight minutes. The crew of ten officers and twenty-four men began to abandon ship in the two lifeboats. These two boats got away with all but nine of the crew, eight of whom died in the explosion, and the radio operator who went down with the ship. The master remained in the vicinity of the sinking for three days and then, because of the prevailing winds, set a course for one of the Gilbert Islands, over 2,500 miles away. Thirty-one days later these eleven men were rescued by a Fiji Island government vessel and landed at Beruin Island. During the journey one man in this boat died of exposure. The thirteen men in the other boat, in charge of the first officer, remained at the site of the sinking and were rescued by the USCG cutter *Tiger* (WPC-152) on 27 December 1941.

NSS; WACR; WCSR; RWCS; *Pilot*, 20 February 1942, 1 May 1942, 15 May 1942; Rohwer, p. 278.

EMIDIO

D:	12-20-41	YB:	1921
T:	1345	Tn:	6,912
Pos:	40.34.30 N / 124.50 W	Dr:	16 ft. 7 in.
Ow:	Socony-Vacuum Oil Co.	C:	2-3-5-7-8 tanks ballasted
Op:	Socony-Vacuum Oil Co.	P:	steam
M:	Clarke Arthur Farrow	S:	13
A:	unarmed		

The *Emidio* departed Seattle, Washington, en route to Ventura, California. As the ship proceeded in squally weather and choppy seas, twenty miles off Blunts Reef, lookouts spotted the submarine *I-17* (Nishino). The master altered the *Emidio*'s course and increased speed, but the *I-17* gained rapidly and opened fire with its deck gun at a half mile, forcing the master to stop the vessel. The crew of eight officers and twenty-eight men began to abandon the freighter as the *I-17* continued firing. One shell struck the #3 boat as the crew lowered it, and two men were killed. Another boat capsized after getting caught in the discharge of the condenser. Within thirty minutes the survivors had cleared the ship in two lifeboats and one workboat. At 1435 a torpedo struck the ship on the starboard side at the stern. Both boats managed to make the Blunts Reef Lightship within fifteen hours. The USCG cutter *Shawnee* (WAT-54) carried the men from the lightship to Eureka, California. The crew left the tanker in a sinking condition with her stern submerged, but she managed to remain afloat and became stranded on the rocks at Crescent City—a total loss. One officer and four men died in the attack.

WACR; WCSR; Rohwer, p. 278; *War Action Casualties*, p. 2.

JUSTINE FOSS

D:	12-23-41	YB:	1930
T:	unknown	Tn:	39
Pos:	Wake Island	Dr:	unknown
Ow:	Foss Launch & Tug Co.	C:	none
Op:	Foss Launch & Tug Co.	P:	steam
M:	Tom McInnis	S:	unknown
A:	unarmed		

The tug *Justine Foss* was chartered by a construction company to tow barges of construction materials from ships anchored offshore to construction projects on Wake Island. When the Japanese captured Wake Island on 23 December, the tug and her crew of four fell into their hands. The Japanese executed the master and mate ashore and sent the other two to a POW camp. The Japanese used the *Justine Foss* to lighter cargo and later scuttled her. Engineers later blasted her hulk to clear the port.

The fifty-five foot diesel tug *Pioneer* was also at Wake Island, but her status and eventual disposition are unknown. Woodbury, pp. 246-passim; Dierdorff, pp. 502-passim; Moore, p. 160; Lloyd's, p. 959.

MONTEBELLO

D:	12-23-41	YB:	1921
T:	0540	Tn:	8,272
Pos:	35.35.30 N / 121.16.30 W	Dr:	29 ft. 10 in.
Ow:	Union Oil Co. of California	C:	75,346 bbls. crude oil
Op:	Union Oil Co. of California	P:	steam
M:	Olof Walfrid Ekstrom	S:	10.0
A:	unarmed		

On 23 December, the *Montebello* departed Port San Luis, California, en route to Vancouver, British Columbia. Lookouts spotted an enemy submarine approaching only hours out of port. The *I-21* (Matsumura) attacked the tanker four miles off Cambria, California, hitting her with a torpedo in the #2 hold. The crew mustered at their boat stations when the general alarm rang. Within fifteen minutes the crew of eight officers and thirty men abandoned the tanker in four lifeboats. Matsumura fired several shells from his deck gun to quicken the sinking. This forced the men to enter the boats on the other side of the vessel. The ship went down in just over an hour. One of the lifeboats became separated from the others and made port, while the other three were picked up not far from the attack by the launch *Alma* and a Standard Oil launch. All hands survived the attack.

WACR; WCSR; *Los Angeles Times*, 24 December 1941, 23 December 1941; Rohwer, p. 278.

ABSAROKA

D:	12-24-41	YB:	1918
T:	1040	Tn:	5,695
Pos:	34 N / 121 W	Dr:	25 ft. 2 in.
Ow:	Pope and Talbot Inc.	C:	7,519 tons general
Op:	McCormick SS Co. Div.	P:	steam
M:	Louis Prendle	S:	9
A:	unarmed		

The *Absaroka* sailed from Oregon to Los Angeles, California. About three miles off Point Vicente, California, the *I-19* (Narahara) attacked the *Absaroka*. One torpedo hit the freighter at the #5 hold causing extensive damage and blowing the cargo from the hold into the air. The crew of eight officers and twenty-six men immediately abandoned ship. One of their two lifeboats capsized, and the surviving thirty-three men managed to get away from the ship in a single lifeboat. This lifeboat was picked up at the scene eighty minutes after the attack, and the *Absaroka* was later reboarded by the Coast Guard and towed into San

Pedro. One of the crewmen died of injuries after being struck by the displaced cargo.

WACR; WCSR; Rohwer, p. 278.

DON JOSE

D:	12-29-41	YB:	1920
T:	unknown	Tn:	10,893
Pos:	14.35 N / 120.55 E	Dr:	unknown
Ow:	Madrigal & Co.	C:	flour, general deck cargo of
Op:	Madrigal & Co.		lumber
M:	unknown	P:	motor
A:	unarmed	S:	at anchor

The *Don Jose* sailed from Vancouver, British Columbia, Canada, for Manila, Philippine Islands. While anchored off the northeastern point of the North Harbor of Corregidor, the freighter was attacked by Japanese aircraft. Bombs struck the ship but did not severely damage her. The explosions, however, started a fire that eventually burned out of control and completely gutted the freighter. Port authorities, fearing that the ship would sink and block the channel, had her towed around to the south side of the island. The Japanese, after capturing the Philippines, had her towed to Hong Kong.

The sources do not relate the size of the crew, nor whether any casualties occurred. The date is also not completely clear within the sources. NSS; TF; Lloyd's, p. 333.

RUTH ALEXANDER

D:	12-31-41	YB:	1913
T:	0930	Tn:	8,135
Pos:	1.0 N / 119.10 E	Dr:	22 ft.
Ow:	American President Lines	C:	2,000 tons general
Op:	American President Lines	P:	steam
M:	Frederick P. Willarts	S:	14
A:	unarmed		

The *Ruth Alexander* was attacked by a Japanese four-engined amphibious reconnaissance plane while en route from Manila to Balikpapan, Borneo. Lookouts on the ship spotted the plane five miles astern, and the helmsman began steering a zigzag course. The bomber made one pass and then returned in line with the ship's heading. Flying at 2,000 feet, it came over the stern from starboard to port and dropped two bombs. Both missed by about twenty feet, but the concussions slightly damaged the engines. The plane then descended to 300 feet and dropped two larger bombs that struck on the after part of the pilot house on the port side. They passed through three decks, blew a ten-foot hole in the port side near the light load line, and knocked out the steering gear. The master ordered the crew to abandon ship at 0945. The crew of nine officers and forty men, with the exception of one man, got away in six lifeboats as the ship steamed in circles. A Dutch seaplane rescued the survivors at 1530 the same day and landed them at Tarakan, Indonesia. Dutch naval authorities reported that the *Ruth Alexander* sank on 2 January 1942.

NSS; WACR; WCSR.

MALAMA

D:	1-1-42	YB:	1919
T:	1440	Tn:	3,275
Pos:	26.21 S / 153.24 W	Dr:	21 ft.
Ow:	Matson Navigation Co.	C:	Army supplies and vehicles
Op:	Matson Navigation Co.	P:	steam
M:	Malcolm Rutherford Peters	S:	10
A:	unarmed		

On 29 November, the *Malama* sailed from San Francisco to Manila, Philippines, via Honolulu. She weighed anchor at Honolulu on 16 December, and two weeks later, at 0930, a Japanese float plane from the merchant cruiser *Aikoku Maru* circled and began strafing the *Malama*. Using international code, the plane ordered the ship to stop. The plane returned again at 1415, this time armed with bombs. As it circled over the ship, the master readied the crew to leave while the chief engineer prepared the ship for scuttling. At 1430 the eight officers, twenty-five crewmen, and five passengers left the ship in two lifeboats. After all hands escaped, the plane attacked and dropped four bombs, setting the ship on fire. At 1530 two Japanese merchant cruisers, the *Aikoku Maru* and the *Hokoku Maru*, hove into sight. The *Aikoku Maru* picked up all hands. The Japanese interned everyone in a POW camp, and all survived to be repatriated with the exception of two crewmen.

The U.S. Maritime Commission time chartered this vessel beginning 15 September 1941. WACR; WCSR; RWSA; Stindt, p. 118.

FRANCES SALMAN

D: 1-18-42   YB: 1919
T: 0044   Tn: 2,609
Pos: off Newfoundland   Dr: unknown, light
Ow: Canadian Gulf Line Ltd.   C: none
Op: Canadian Gulf Line Ltd.   P: steam
M: Rasmus Wathne   S: unknown
A: unarmed

The *Frances Salman*, steaming from St. Johns, Newfoundland, to Corner Brook, Newfoundland, was torpedoed and sunk by the *U-552* (Topp) at 0644 Central European Time. The U-boat made four unsuccessful attacks on the freighter. The *Salman* attempted to escape the U-boat, and the radio operator sent several distress messages. The fifth torpedo, fired from 500 yards, struck the after part of the ship. The *Salman* sank quickly and some of the eight officers and twenty crewmen managed to launch a boat in rough seas. The *Salman* sank by the stern within ten minutes, but the bow remained above the water for about twenty-five minutes before disappearing. Due to the state of the seas, none of the men in the boat survived.

WACR; WJ; Rohwer, p. 74.

ALLAN JACKSON

D: 1-18-42   YB: 1921
T: 0135   Tn: 6,635
Pos: 35.57 N / 74.20 W   Dr: 27 ft. 3 in.
Ow: Standard Oil Co. of N. J.   C: 72,870 bbls. crude oil
Op: Standard Oil Co. of N. J.   P: steam
M: Felix W. Kretchmer   S: 11
A: unarmed

The *Allan Jackson* was attacked by the *U-66* (Zapp) while en route from Cartagena, Colombia, to New York. The ship left port without routing instructions and proceeded independently. As the *Jackson* proceeded about fifty miles east of Cape Hatteras, Zapp fired two torpedoes at her. The first hit the starboard side forward of the bridge. The second, moments behind, hit the starboard side aft of the deckhouse. Flaming oil spewed from the *Jackson*'s side and spread over the water hundreds of feet around the tanker, making it hazardous for the crew to abandon the ship. Many of the men burned to death on the deck trying to get aft. The second torpedo broke the ship apart amidships, and she sank in five minutes. She sank so fast that only the #3 boat carrying eight men could be launched. Other survivors jumped into the water and clung to the wreckage. Of the eight officers and twenty-seven men aboard, five officers and seventeen men died and the rest were injured in some manner. The USS *Roe* (DD-418) rescued the survivors the next day and landed them at Norfolk, Virginia.

NSS; WACR; WCSR; WJ; *Life*, 2 February 1942, p. 16; Rohwer, p. 74; *War Action Casualties*, p. 4.

MALAY

D:	1-18-42	YB:	1921
T:	0320	Tn:	8,206
Pos:	35.25 N / 75.23 W	Dr:	15 ft. 6 in.
Ow:	Marine Transport Lines	C:	none, ballast
Op:	C. D. Mallory & Co., Inc.	P:	steam
M:	John M. Dodge	S:	10
A:	unarmed		

On 18 January, the *Malay* departed Philadelphia en route to Port Arthur, Texas, in water ballast. The *Malay*, showing only dim navigational lights, headed south in an unprotected convoy of five ships. Ten miles from the Wimble Shoals Lighted Whistle Buoy, the *U-123* (Hardegen) attacked. As the *U-123* advanced on the surface, her gun crew fired at the tanker's bridge. The shots, however, did only superficial damage. The submarine fired a total of ten rounds and struck the *Malay* five times from about 700 yards. The second shell destroyed a lifeboat, and the other three struck in the crew's quarters, killing one man. Hardegen, thinking he had fatally wounded the ship, left the burning tanker in search of other victims. He found and torpedoed the Latvian freighter *Ciltvaira* and later returned to finish the *Malay*. The passing freighter *Scania*, meanwhile, had come to help the *Malay* and passed firefighting equipment on board. The crew of eight officers and twenty-six men got the fire under control and again got the ship under way. The *U-123* returned at 0530 and fired its last torpedo, hitting the #7 starboard side tank, just aft of amidships. The crew manned their boat stations and launched three lifeboats. The #1 boat capsized, drowning four men, and the other two boats with fourteen men circled the ship for about an hour before returning to the tanker. Boats from the Chicamacomico Coast Guard Station removed the dead and badly injured. The *Malay* got under way and arrived in Hampton Roads, Virginia, on 19 January.

The figures for the ship's complement conflict within the sources. WACR; WCSR; RWCS; WJ; Gannon, pp. 258-65; Rohwer, p. 74, places the attack at 35.40 N 75.20 W; *War Action Casualties*, p. 5.

CITY OF ATLANTA

D: 1-19-42   YB: 1904
T: 0215   Tn: 5,269
Pos: 35.42 N / 75.21 W   Dr: 17 ft. 1 in.
Ow: Ocean SS Co.   C: 2,870 tons general
Op: Ocean SS Co.   P: steam
M: Lehman Chapman Urquhart   S: 12.0
A: unarmed

The *U-123* (Hardegen) began what was to be a productive night by spotting the navigational lights of the *City of Atlanta* en route from New York to Savannah. Approximately twelve miles south of the Wimble Shoals Buoy and about eight or ten miles offshore, the *U-123* fired one torpedo that struck the port side forward of the #3 hold. The ship quickly took a sharp list, making it difficult for the crew of eight officers and thirty-eight men to abandon ship. The vessel rolled over in about ten minutes before any of the four lifeboats could be lowered. The *U-123* surfaced on the starboard side, flashed a searchlight over the *City of Atlanta*, and then disappeared. Only one officer and two men survived by clinging to the wreckage. The SS *Seatrain Texas* picked up these men after six hours.

NSS; WACR; *Post*, 19 January 1942; Gannon, p. 256; *Life*, 2 February 1942, p. 16; Rohwer, p. 74.

NORVANA

D: 1-22-42   YB: 1920
T: 0539   Tn: 2,677
Pos: off coast of North Carolina   Dr: 24 ft. 5 in. (normal)
Ow: Merchants & Miners Trans. Co.   C: 3,980 tons ore
Op: North Atlantic & Gulf SS Co.   P: steam
M: Ernest Jefferson Thompson   S: 9.0
A: unarmed

On 14 January, the *Norvana* sailed from Nuvitas, Cuba, to Philadelphia. As part of the German Navy's Operation Paukenschlag (Drum Roll), the *U-123* (Hardegen) torpedoed the *Norvana* south of Cape Hatteras. From 800 yards the *U-123* fired a torpedo that did not run straight and instead sped behind the freighter. The U-boat maneuvered for a second shot and from 450 yards fired a second torpedo. Thirty seconds later it struck forward of the stack. A tremendous explosion sent large pieces of the freighter into the air, hitting the *U-123*, and she disappeared beneath the water in ninety seconds. Of the eight officers and twenty-one men on board the *Norvana*, no one survived. One of the ship's empty lifeboats was found by the Navy off Wimble Shoals.

WACR; WJ; Gannon, p. 254; Rohwer, p. 75, states she was bound from Curaçao to Baltimore. Rohwer also misidentifies the ship as the *Brazos*.

VENORE

D:	1-23-42	YB:	1921
T:	1948	Tn:	8,016
Pos:	34.50 N / 75.20 W	Dr:	34 ft.
Ow:	Ore SS Corp.	C:	8,000 tons iron ore
Op:	Ore SS Corp.	P:	steam
M:	Fritz Duurloo	S:	10
A:	unarmed		

The freighter *Venore* sailed from Chile for Sparrows Point, Maryland. About fifteen miles from the Diamond Shoals Buoy, the *U-66* (Zapp) attacked the freighter. The *U-66* had just finished attacking the British tanker SS *Empire Gem* two or three miles ahead when Zapp spotted the *Venore*'s dimmed running lights. At 1948 lookouts spotted the submarine about 150 yards away. Zapp fired two torpedoes. One struck amidships on the port side, forward of the boiler room, and the other missed. The *Venore* changed to a zigzag course while firefighting parties fought a fire caused by the explosion. As the freighter proceeded at hish speed, some of the crew of eight officers and thirty-three men panicked and launched three lifeboats without instructions from the master. Two of the boats disintegrated upon hitting the water, drowning more than a dozen men. Two fortunate men in the third boat survived. About forty minutes later the *U-66* put another torpedo into the port side of the #9 hold. Minutes after this explosion the remaining crew of twenty-one abandoned ship in the last boat. The *Venore* turned over and sank just over an hour later. At 1100 on 25 January, the SS *Tennessee* spotted the boat with twenty-one survivors about sixty-two miles north of Diamond Shoals and landed the men at Norfolk. The other boat with two men made port after forty-nine hours. On 25 January, the Texaco tanker *Australia* rescued another man. Two officers and fifteen men died.

NSS; WACR; WCSR; WJ; RWCS; Gannon, pp. 270-71; Moore, p. 284.

WEST IVIS

D:	1-26-42	YB:	1919
T:	approximately 0430	Tn:	5,666
Pos:	off Cape Hatteras	Dr:	25 ft.
Ow:	Pope and Talbot Inc.	C:	unknown
Op:	Pope and Talbot Inc.	P:	steam
M:	Alfred C. Larsen	S:	approximately 10
A:	1-4"; 4-50 cal.; 4-30 cal.		

The *West Ivis* sailed from New York on 24 January, bound for Trinidad. The *U-125* (Folkers) spotted the *Ivis* on 26 January. On this moonlit night Folkers had trouble maneuvering to attack. He missed with his first torpedo and tried again. The *Ivis* was traveling with lights on, but shortly before Folker's second try the crew turned them off. A second torpedo struck the ship under the stack and broke her in two, causing her to sink in fourteen minutes. Folkers mentions a lifeboat in his war journal, but all eight officers, twenty-eight crewmen, and a gun crew of nine perished.

The figures for the armed guards are contradictory. WACR; WCSR; WJ; AG; Rohwer, p. 76.

FRANCIS E. POWELL

D:	1-27-42	YB:	1922
T:	0235	Tn:	7,096
Pos:	37.45 N / 74.53 W	Dr:	25 ft. 5 in.
Ow:	Atlantic Refining Co.	C:	81,000 bbls. furnace oil,
Op:	Atlantic Refining Co.		gasoline
M:	Thomas J. Harrington	P:	steam
A:	unarmed	S:	10.5

The *Francis E. Powell* sailed from Port Arthur, Texas, to Providence, Rhode Island. The *U-130* (Kals) attacked the tanker about eight miles northeast of the Winter Quarter Light Vessel. The *Powell* was proceeding completely blacked out when the torpedo struck the port side aft of the midships house, between the #4 and #5 tanks. The explosion started a small fire in the ship's pump room. Lookouts then spotted the submarine a few hundred yards from the *Powell*. The destruction of the radio antenna spoiled the radio operator's attempt to send an SOS. The crew of eight officers and twenty-four men left the tanker in two lifeboats. The master was crushed to death when he slipped and fell between the boat and the ship. This same boat was lifted back on the ship by a wave, and the men had to launch another boat. The tanker *W. C. Fairbanks* picked up the seventeen men in the #3 boat after five hours and landed them at Lewes, Delaware. A Coast Guard boat from the Assateague Station spotted the #2 boat with eleven men and landed these survivors at Chincoteague, North Carolina.

Two officers and two men died as a result of the attack. The *Powell* sank at about 0700.

NSS; WACR; WCSR; RWCS; WJ; Rohwer, p. 76, places the attack at 38.05 N / 74.53 W; Washington *Star*, 28 January 1942; Virginia *Pilot*, 27 February 1942; *War Action Casualties*, p. 7.

FLORENCE LUCKENBACH

D:	1-29-42	YB:	1920
T:	1005	Tn:	5,237
Pos:	12.55 N / 80.33 E	Dr:	24 ft. 4 in.
Ow:	Luckenbach SS Co.	C:	3,500 tons general, 3,400 tons
Op:	Luckenbach SS Co.		manganese ore
M:	Thure Gottfid Eckart	P:	steam
A:	unarmed	S:	10

The *Florence Luckenbach* sailed from Madras, India, for New York, via Cape Town, South Africa. The *I-164* (Ogawa) attacked the freighter from a position directly between the sun and ship and was not seen until after the attack. The first torpedo struck the port side near the #1 hold along the waterline. The explosion blew the hatch covers and the beams onto the deck. Within ten minutes the crew of eight officers and thirty men had abandoned ship in one lifeboat, the other having been destroyed by the initial explosion. Ogawa then fired another torpedo after the boats cleared the ship. This struck amidships on the port side, sinking the freighter by the head in ten minutes. The survivors made their way back to Madras in nine hours. All hands survived.

NSS; WACR; WCSR; Rohwer, p. 259.

ROCHESTER

D:	1-30-42	YB:	1920
T:	1105	Tn:	6,836
Pos:	37.10 N / 73.58 W	Dr:	20 ft. 8 in.
Ow:	Socony Vacuum Oil Co.	C:	ballast
Op:	Socony Vacuum Oil Co.	P:	steam
M:	Alden S. Clark	S:	10.4
A:	unarmed		

The *Rochester* was attacked eighty-five miles east of the Chesapeake Light Vessel, while proceeding from New York to Corpus Christi, Texas, on a zigzag course. Off the mouth of the Chesapeake Bay, the *U-106* (Rasch) maneuvered into a favorable attack position. A torpedo struck aft in the engine room, and the explosion killed the officer and two men on watch below, stopped the engines, destroyed communications, and damaged the rudder and propeller. Orders were immediately passed to muster at the boat stations, and when the submarine surfaced nearby, the master ordered the crew of eight officers and twenty-seven men to abandon ship. Within fifteen minutes the crew lowered two boats. The *U-106* readied its deck guns for action but waited for both boats to clear the ship. The submarine fired eight rounds at the tanker from a range of about 500 yards. With the ship still afloat, the *U-106* moved on the surface to about 400 to 500 yards off the starboard bow and at 1145 fired a second torpedo that hit amidships. The *Rochester* immediately listed to starboard and sank at about 1220. The USS *Roe* (DD-418) rescued thirty-two survivors off the Virginia Capes after they had spent three hours in the boats, and landed them at Norfolk Navy Base the next morning.

The survivors stated that thirteen rounds were fired, but Rasch reports his gun jammed on the eighth round. NSS; WACR; WCSR; RWCS; WJ; *Star*, 31 January 1942; *Times Herald*, 31 January 1942; Rohwer, p. 76; *War Action Casualties*, p. 8. According to Moore, p. 243, a fireman later died of burns from the explosion.

W. L. STEED

D:	2-2-42	YB:	1918
T:	1245	Tn:	6,182
Pos:	38.25 N / 73.00 W	Dr:	26 ft. 6 in.
Ow:	Standard Oil Co. of N. J.	C:	65,936 bbls. crude oil
Op:	Standard Oil Co. of N. J.	P:	steam
M:	Harold G. McAvenia	S:	10.5
A:	unarmed		

On 23 February, the *W. L. Steed* cleared Cartagena, Colombia, for New York via Key West, Florida. The tanker maintained a zigzag course, and the *U-103* (Winter) intercepted her 100 miles off the New Jersey coast in broad daylight. In rough seas and overcast weather the *U-103* struck the *W. L. Steed* with a torpedo on the starboard side in the #3 tank. The ship caught fire, but the breaking seas extinguished it. The *U-103* waited while the crew of nine officers and twenty-nine men abandoned ship in four boats. With everyone off, the *U-103* began shelling the tanker with more than eighty shells and set her on fire once again. When a second torpedo struck the vessel, the *Steed* exploded, shooting fire 500 feet in the air. She settled by the head and sank approximately fifty minutes after the first explosion. The British SS *Hartlepool* discovered the #2 lifeboat on 6 February. This boat had started with sixteen men and all but two had died of exposure. The chief mate later died ashore. The Canadian Auxiliary cruiser *Alcantara* discovered the #3 boat with only three of its five men still alive. On 12 February, the British SS *Raby Castle* spotted the #4 boat. It had cleared the *Steed* with fourteen men but had only one man still alive. He, like his comrades, also died of exposure about three days later. The #1 boat, with three men, cleared the ship first. It may have been the boat found by the

Mexican tanker *Poza Rica* on 19 February, northwest of Cape Hatteras. Of the thirty-eight men in the lifeboats, only one officer and three men survived.

WACR; WCSR; RWCS; WJ; Rohwer, p. 77; *Times Herald*, 12 February 1942; *Post*, 12 February 942; *Ships of the Esso Fleet*, pp. 83-89; *War Action Casualties*, p. 9.

INDIA ARROW

D:	2-4-42	YB:	1921
T:	1859	Tn:	8,327
Pos:	38.48 N / 73.40 W	Dr:	28 ft. 6 in.
Ow:	Socony Vacuum Oil Co.	C:	88,369 bbls. diesel fuel
Op:	Socony Vacuum Oil Co.	P:	steam
M:	Carl Samuel Johnson	S:	10.5
A:	unarmed		

The *India Arrow* sailed from Corpus Christi, Texas, en route to Carteret, New Jersey. About thirty-five miles due east of Five Fathom Bank, the *U-103* (Winter) intercepted the tanker. The *India Arrow* was steering a nonevasive course when the torpedo struck the starboard quarter at about the #10 bunker. The ship caught fire and began to sink by the stern at a rapid rate. The radio operator sent a distress signal but not a position before the dynamo failed. Within three minutes the crew of nine officers and twenty-nine men began abandoning ship. Minutes later the *U-103* started shelling the vessel from a distance of approximately 250 yards. The submarine fired seven shells at two-minute intervals, setting the after portion of the ship afire. The crew managed to launch successfully only one of the ship's four lifeboats. In a sea of blazing oil two other boats swamped, and the rapidly sinking tanker pulled the #2 boat beneath the water. Only one officer and eleven men survived, rescued by the twenty-four foot fishing skiff *Gitana* twelve miles off Atlantic City. Two men died as a result of the shelling, and the remaining men apparently drowned when the two boats swamped.

NSS; WACR; WCSR; RWCS; WJ; *Times* (New York), 4 February 1942; *Star* (Washington), 7 February 1942; Rohwer, p. 77, places the attack at 38.48 N / 72.43 W; Moore, pp. 134-35.

CHINA ARROW

D:	2-5-42	YB:	1920
T:	1115	Tn:	8,403
Pos:	37.44 N / 73.18 W	Dr:	28 ft.
Ow:	Socony Vacuum Oil Co.	C:	81,773 bbls. fuel oil
Op:	Socony Vacuum Oil Co.	P:	steam
M:	Paul Hoffman Browne	S:	10.5
A:	unarmed		

Bound from Beaumont, Texas, for New York, the SS *China Arrow* was torpedoed off Winter Quarter Shoals by the *U-103* (Winter). While running on a zigzag course and blacked out, the ship was struck by two torpedoes. One struck the starboard side between the #8 and #9 tanks; the other hit between tanks #9 and #10. The explosions blew fuel oil 125 feet into the air and over the length of the ship. Fire immediately broke out in these tanks. The live steam firefighting equipment smothered the blaze in tanks #9 and #10 but could not put out the fire in the #8 tank. The master ordered the crew of nine officers and twenty-eight men to abandon ship. Three boats cast off at 1140. As the boats neared the water, the *U-103* surfaced to conning tower depth. The master and radio operator had stayed behind to send out a distress signal but scurried off the ship when the U-boat surfaced. As the *U-103* approached, it fired nearly fifty shots at the tanker. The *China Arrow* sank by the stern at 1230. Coast Guard planes spotted the survivors after they had spent fifty-seven hours in the boats, and the USCG cutter *Nike* (WPC-112) guided them to the Lewes, Delaware, Coast Guard Station. All hands survived.

NSS; WACR; RWCS; WJ; Rohwer, p. 77; *Star* (Washington), 9 February 1942; *Coast Guard at War*, p. 11.

MAJOR WHEELER

D:	2-6-42	YB:	1918
T:	approximately 0900	Tn:	3,431
Pos:	East Coast	Dr:	21 ft.
Ow:	Baltimore Insular Line	C:	4,611 tons sugar
Op:	Baltimore Insular Line	P:	steam
M:	Frank W. Losey	S:	9 approximately
A:	unarmed		

While en route from Fajardo, Puerto Rico, to Philadelphia, Pennsylvania, the freighter *Major Wheeler* was attacked by the *U-107* (Gelhaus). The *U-107* had spotted another steamer and then disengaged to follow the *Wheeler*. The U-boat fired a torpedo from over 700 yards, hitting the freighter amidships. The ship sank by the stern in two minutes. None of the eight officers and twenty-seven men survived.

WACR; WCSR; WJ; Rohwer, p. 77.

ARKANSAS

D:	2-16-42	YB:	1919
T:	0300	Tn:	6,452
Pos:	Eagle Dock, Aruba	Dr:	approximately 14 ft.
Ow:	Texas Co.	C:	none
Op:	Texas Co.	P:	steam
M:	Karl Karlson	S:	docked
A:	unarmed		

On 31 January, the *Arkansas* weighed anchor at Santos, Brazil, en route to Aruba, NWI. While laying at the Eagle dock in San Nicholas, the tanker and two other British ships were attacked by the *U-156* (Hartenstein). A torpedo struck the starboard side of the tanker between the #4 and #5 bunkers. The explosion created a large hole on the starboard side and smaller holes on the opposite side, causing extensive structural damage. The crew of eight officers and twenty-nine men remained on the vessel and later walked down to the dock. Three hours later the crew reboarded her to assess the damage. The crew suffered no casualties.

WACR; *Times Herald*, 17 February 1942, 18 February 1942; *Star*, 19 February 1942; Rohwer, p. 78.

MAUNA LOA

D:	2-16-42	YB:	1919
T:	1112	Tn:	5,436
Pos:	off Australian coast	Dr:	24 ft.
Ow:	Matson Navigation Co.	C:	general, 500 troops
Op:	Matson Navigation Co.	P:	steam
M:	Frederick R. Trask	S:	10
A:	unarmed		

On 21 November, the *Mauna Loa* departed San Francisco, California, bound for the Philippines. After stopping at Sydney, Australia, she sailed to Darwin. On 15 February 1942, the USAT *Meigs*, *Mauna Loa*, USAT *Tulagi*, and *Portmar* stood out at Darwin with five other ships escorted by the USS *Houston* (CA-30) and USS *Peary* (DD-226) bound for Koepang, Timor. On the 16th, two heavy four-motored Japanese sea planes appeared over the convoy, and the USS *Houston* successfully drove them away. At about 1115, on 16 February, four squadrons of Japanese planes approached the convoy in horizontal rows of nine planes each. The USS *Houston* began maneuvering at high speed and fired on the planes while the convoy scattered. The *Mauna Loa* steamed at a speed of ten knots while the helmsman threw the wheel hard to starboard or port as each succeeding wave released its bombs. After the attack it was discovered that all four ships had developed leaks resulting from the near misses. The *Mauna Loa*

received one glancing blow in the #2 hold. One man among the crew of eight officers and thirty men died as a result of this attack. The bomb also killed 1 of the 500 troops on board and wounded 18 others. The convoy was ordered back to Darwin, arriving there during the morning of 18 February 1942.

NSS; WACR; WCSR; RWSA; TF; Stindt, pp. 118-19; *Ships in Gray*, p. 44.

E. H. BLUM

D:	2-16-42	YB:	1941
T:	2033	Tn:	11,615
Pos:	off Cape Henry Light House	Dr:	15 ft. 7 in.
Ow:	Atlantic Refining Co.	C:	water ballast
Op:	Atlantic Refining Co.	P:	steam
M:	William L. Evans	S:	4
A:	unarmed		

On 15 February, the *E. H. Blum* sailed in ballast from Philadelphia to Hampton Roads, Virginia. In foggy weather the tanker hove to to pick up a pilot and to receive permission to enter the Chesapeake. While at slow speed she wandered into an American minefield 950 yards off the Cape Henry Lighthouse. The first explosion amidships at the engine room lifted the bow six feet into the air. About fifteen minutes later a second explosion ripped into the ship. The master ordered the crew of eight officers and thirty-two men to abandon ship. Using four lifeboats all hands successfully left the ship as she struck a third mine. After forty minutes, the ship broke in two at the pump room. The forward end of the vessel sank after an hour and fifteen minutes. After spending nearly four and a half hours in the boats, the forty survivors were picked up by the USCG cutter *Woodbury* (WPC-155) and taken to Little Creek, Virginia. The next day salvage crews boarded the after end and towed it into port. Salvors later floated the forward end and joined it with the after end. Only two men in the crew received injuries. The *E. H. Blum* returned to service on 27 August 1943.

WACR; WCSR; *Pilot*, 27 February 1942; *Times Herald*, 19 February 1942; *Coast Guard at War*, pp. 11-12; *War Action Casualties*, p. 13.

MOKIHANA

D:	2-18-42	YB:	1921
T:	2340	Tn:	7,460
Pos:	Port-of-Spain, Trinidad	Dr:	26 ft. 10 in.
Ow:	Matson Navigation Co.	C:	7,300 tons general
Op:	WSA	P:	steam
M:	Charles Porta	S:	anchored
A:	1-3"; 4-50 cal.; 2-30 cal.		

The *Mokihana* sailed from Baltimore, Maryland, to the Red Sea area with a full cargo of lend-lease material for the Middle East. While at anchor in Port-of-Spain, Trinidad, the *U-161* (Achilles) attacked. The *Mokihana* lay two miles from the wharf in forty feet of water with all anchor, cargo, and port lights burning and silhouetted against the lights on shore. The *U-161*'s torpedo struck the starboard side, just forward of the bridge. The explosion created a hole approximately thirty-five feet by forty-five feet. The crew of eight officers and twenty-eight men along with nine armed guards remained on board and suffered no casualties. On 2 May 1942, after making temporary repairs, the ship left Port-of-Spain, but had to be towed to the Virgin Islands and then to San Juan, Puerto Rico, by the U.S. Navy tugs *Partridge* (AM-18) and *Mankato* (YNT-8). After more repairs, she arrived at Galveston, Texas, on 15 June 1942.

NSS; WACR; WCSR; RWCS; AG; Rohwer, p. 79.

LAKE OSWEGA

D:	2-19-42	YB:	1918
T:	0453 GWT	Tn:	2,398
Pos:	43.14 N / 64.45 W	Dr:	unknown
Ow:	Ford Motor Co.	C:	general
Op:	Ford Motor Co.	P:	motor
M:	Karl E. Prinz	S:	unknown
A:	2-3"		

The *Lake Oswega* sailed from New York to Iceland via Halifax, Nova Scotia. Before midnight, the *U-96* (Lehmann-Willenbrock) intercepted the freighter at sea. Several hours earlier the British SS *Empire Sea*, three miles off the *Lake Oswega*'s port quarter, had been torpedoed by the same U-boat. From 500 yards the *U-96* fired a single shot at the zigzagging freighter. The torpedo struck the vessel about amidships and broke her in two, and she sank quickly by the bow. The German documents indicated that three lifeboats left the ship, but none of the American freighter's eight officers, twenty-two men, and seven armed guards survived.

WACR; WCSR; AG; WJ; Rohwer, p. 79.

DON ISIDRO

D:	2-19-42	YB:	1939
T:	0845	Tn:	3,263
Pos:	West Melville Island	Dr:	unknown
Ow:	De la Rama SS Co., Inc.	C:	rations, ammunition
Op:	De la Rama SS Co., Inc.	P:	motor
M:	Rafael J. Cirnoros	S:	unknown
A:	yes, but unknown		

The *Don Isidro* loaded rations and ammunition at Brisbane, Australia, to run the Japanese blockade into Corregidor, Philippine Islands. On 4 February she sailed from Fremantle to Soerabaja, Java, and left Java on the 14th. Five days later, as she steamed through the Timor Sea, Japanese aircraft discovered her and attacked. Five direct hits set the *Don Isidro* on fire, and her master beached her. Because the flames gutted the freighter, the owners abandoned her as a total loss. Most of the sixty-seven crew members, as well as the one Navy and sixteen Army passengers, safely abandoned ship and landed on Bathurst Beach. The Australian minesweeper *Warrnambol* (J-202) rescued the survivors. The attack killed eleven of the crewmen and one of the Army passengers. Two other men later died in the hospital at Port Darwin.

The *Don Isidro* was on a time or trip charter to the Army at a rate of $1,200 per day. TF; RWSA; WACS; Morton, pp. 393-95; Moore, p. 76.

ADMIRAL HALSTEAD

D:	2-19-42	YB:	1920
T:	0930	Tn:	3,289
Pos:	anchored off Darwin, Australia	Dr:	25 ft.
Ow:	Pacific Lighterage Corp.	C:	14,000 drums gasoline
Op:	Pacific Lighterage Corp.	P:	steam
M:	Edward E. Johnson	S:	unknown
A:	unarmed		

On 15 February, the *Admiral Halstead* and about a half dozen other ships escorted by the USS *Houston* (CA-30) and the USS *Peary* (DD-226) stood out of Port Darwin, Australia, bound for Koepang, Timor. Attacked twice by Japanese aircraft, the convoy turned back to Port Darwin and arrived on the morning of 18 February. The Japanese thus caught the Allies with a harbor full of ships, among them the two U.S. merchant ships, *Portmar* and *Mauna Loa*. At 0930 lookouts on the *Admiral Halstead* spotted seventy planes. During the ensuing attack, bombs struck near the *Halstead*. The concussions opened up the fuel oil tanks, and the ship began taking on water fore and aft. The crew abandoned the ship at about 1500. The *Halstead* was later repaired and put back in service. The master brought the ship to the boom defense jetty assisted by

engineers from the Australian depot ship *Platypus* and unloaded 8,000 drums of gasoline in the next five days. The crew reported no casualties after the attack.

The U.S. Maritime Commission time chartered this ship both in September and December 1941. WCSR; NSS; RWSA; Lloyds Register, 1941-1942.

MAUNA LOA

D:	2-19-42	YB:	1919
T:	1020	Tn:	5,436
Pos:	off Australian coast	Dr:	24 ft.
Ow:	Matson Navigation Co.	C:	general
Op:	Matson Navigation Co.	P:	steam
M:	Frederick R. Trask	S:	10
A:	unarmed		

On 21 November, the *Mauna Loa* departed San Francisco for the Philippines. On 16 December, authorities ordered her to Sydney and then to Darwin. The freighter had attempted to steam to Koepang, Timor, on the 15th, but the next day Japanese planes forced the small convoy of ships to return to port and slightly damaged the *Mauna Loa*. After returning to Darwin, she anchored to discharge her cargo, and on the 19th Japanese bombers attacked the harbor. During the attack, dive bombers placed two bombs into the #5 hatch. As the ship slowly sank, the master ordered all eight officers, twenty-nine men, and seven passengers off the ship. They left in a lifeboat and a workboat. All hands safely got ashore. The *Mauna Loa* sank at 1159.

Also see entry for 16 February. The *Mauna Loa* was apparently under a time charter to the U.S. Maritime Commission, but Army records often mistakenly claim her as a USAT. NSS; WACR; RWSA; Stindt, pp. 118-19; *Ships in Gray*, p. 44.

PORTMAR

D:	2-19-42	YB:	1919
T:	1045	Tn:	5,550
Pos:	12.34 S / 130.52 E	Dr:	12 ft. 5 in.
Ow:	Calmar SS Corp.	C:	2,000 tons general
Op:	Calmar SS Corp.	P:	steam
M:	Axel Michelson	S:	at anchor
A:	unarmed		

The *Portmar* departed San Francisco, California, en route to Manila, Philippine Islands. During the voyage, the Japanese attacked Pearl Harbor, so she deviated her voyage, sailing to Suva and then to Sydney, Australia. In Sydney the Army, without specific authority, virtually took her under their control. She proceeded to Brisbane and then to Port Darwin, where the *Portmar* loaded troops and

Army supplies. On the 15th, she sailed with a small convoy escorted by the USS *Houston* (CA-30) and the USS *Peary* (DD-226) to Koepang, Timor. The next day, four squadrons of Japanese aircraft attacked and slightly damaged the *Portmar* but forced all the ships to return to Darwin. On the 19th, two waves of Japanese planes attacked the ships in the harbor. The *Portmar* received a direct hit on the stern, and other near misses sent bomb shrapnel through the freighter's shell plating from amidships to the stern. The master beached her to prevent her from sinking. The crew of 8 officers and 26 men and the 300 troops on board abandoned ship directly into Allied vessels beginning about 1730. The explosions killed one seaman and two soldiers and injured another dozen men. The Army later salvaged the undamaged cargo and after making repairs in Brisbane, Australia, took her into service as a transport.

The Army considered this vessel a USAT, but she was under time charter to the U.S. Maritime Commission and her owner continued to man, victual, and supply her. Thus, by definition, she remained a merchant vessel. The Army took title to the *Portmar* on 17 November 1942. NSS; WACR; WCSR; RWSA; TF.

PAN MASSACHUSETTS

D:	2-19-42	YB:	1919
T:	1345	Tn:	8,201
Pos:	28.27 N / 80.08 W	Dr:	31 ft. 10 in.
Ow:	National Bulk Carriers, Inc.	C:	104,000 bbls. refined petroleum,
Op:	National Bulk Carriers, Inc.		gasoline, kerosene, oil
M:	Robert E. Christy	P:	steam
A:	unarmed	S:	13.5

On 15 February, the *Pan Massachusetts* sailed from Texas City to New York. In misty, squally weather and rough seas the *U-128* (Heyse) attacked the tanker. Heyse fired two torpedoes, striking the tanker amidships on the starboard side and rupturing the tanks and deck. The explosions sprayed the ship's cargo over the length of the ship, and thousands of gallons gushed out of the tanks. The cargo caught fire, turning the tanker into an inferno and immediately consuming the lifeboats before they could be used. Some men jumped into the water and swam underneath the flames to open spots. Other men went forward and escaped into the water by lowering a mooring line over the side. The flames accounted for twenty deaths—three of the nine officers died as well as seventeen of the twenty-nine crewmen. The British tanker SS *Elizabeth Massey* and the USCG *Forward* (WAGL-160) arrived to rescue the survivors. The *Massey* immediately put out a boat to save the men in the water, but the rough seas hampered the effort. The *Forward* took the *Massey*'s boat in tow and

moved among the wreckage to pick up the victims. The *Elizabeth Massey* carried all the survivors into Jacksonville, Florida.

NSS; WACR; WCSR; WJ; Rohwer, p. 79; *Pilot*, 27 February 1942; *Star*, 22 February 1942; *Coast Guard at War*, pp. 13-14.

FLORENCE D

D:	2-19-42	YB:	1919
T:	1410	Tn:	2,638
Pos:	10.56 S / 130.07 E	Dr:	unknown
Ow:	Cadwallader-Gibson Lumber Co.	C:	munitions, supplies
Op:	Cadwallader-Gibson Lumber Co.	P:	steam
M:	C. L. Manzano	S:	unknown
A:	unarmed		

On 14 February, the *Florence D* sailed from Soerabaja, Java, to run the Japanese blockade into Gingoog, Mindanao, Philippine Islands. She initially joined the *Don Isidro* and steamed east through the Timor Sea. At 0730, about sixty miles northwest of the coast of Bathurst Island, lookouts spotted Japanese planes en route to attack Port Darwin, Australia. One of the Japanese planes diverted to shoot down an American plane two miles from the freighter. The *Florence D* changed her course and rescued the eight Navy flyers. At 1300 a single bomber appeared and dropped two bombs that both missed. Before leaving, the plane strafed the decks. Just over an hour later seventeen Japanese bombers and fighters located the *Florence D* and attacked, dropping bombs all around the ship. Bombs struck the forward holds and midships sections, setting them ablaze. The order to abandon ship was passed to the crew of thirty-seven and the eight Navy passengers. Many of the men dove over the side after the first explosions. The freighter sank rapidly by the head until only the stern remained above the water. Some of the men reboarded the ship and cut loose two lifeboats. The survivors searched the area and picked up the men they could locate in the water. The boats later separated to find help. The Australian minesweeper *Warrnambool* (J-202) rescued one group of survivors and the mission boat *St. Francis* spotted the other group. Three of the crew and one of the Navy men died in the attack.

The *Florence D* was on time charter to the Naval Transport Service. NSS; TF; RWSA; Morton, pp. 393-95; Moore, p. 103; Mullins, pp. 129-130; Winslow, pp. 187-94.

DELPLATA

D: 2-20-42
T: 0530
Pos: 14.45 N / 62.10 W
Ow: Mississippi Shipping Co.
Op: Mississippi Shipping Co.
M: Roelaf Brouver
A: 1-4"; 4-50 cal.; 4-30 cal.

YB: 1920
Tn: 5,127
Dr: 24 ft. 9 in. (22 ft.)
C: 6,100 tons general
P: steam
S: 12.0

While steaming from Rio de Janeiro, Brazil, to St. Thomas, Virgin Islands, the *U-156* (Hartenstein) fired a single torpedo at the *Delplata*, hitting her on the starboard side aft of the #2 hatch. The explosion damaged the superstructure, the wheelhouse, the chart room, and the master's quarters. The freighter took an immediate list to starboard. The whistle cord become fouled and the whistle blew continuously, making it difficult to pass orders vocally. Most of the ten officers, thirty men, and thirteen armed guards left the vessel by the four lifeboats and the three life rafts. The master, seven merchant crew, and seven armed guards remained on board. The naval contingent manned the after gun. At about 1030 the *U-156* fired a second torpedo from the starboard side, and five minutes later a third torpedo struck the port side aft of the #2 hatch. The gun crew managed to fire about twelve shots in the direction of the submarine. At 1115 the master gave orders for the remaining men to abandon ship because of the ship's heavy list to port. The USS *Lapwing* (AVP-1) rescued the entire crew. Some of the crew returned to consider salvage possibilities and to recover belongings. The *Lapwing* sank the *Delplata* by shellfire after the boarding party determined that she could not be salvaged.

NSS; WACR; WCSR; RWCS; AG; *Pilot*, 27 February 1942; Rohwer, p. 79, places the attack at 14.55 N / 62.10 W.

AZALEA CITY

D: 2-20-42
T: 1024
Pos: 38.00 N / 73.00 W
Ow: Waterman SS Co.
Op: Waterman SS Co.
M: George Robert Self
A: unarmed

YB: 1920
Tn: 5,529
Dr: 26 ft.
C: 7,806 tons linseed
P: steam
S: 10.5

On 13 February, the freighter *Azalea City* departed Trinidad, BWI, for Philadelphia, Pennsylvania. In heavy seas, the *U-432* (Schultze) maneuvered into position and fired a shot that missed the freighter. The *U-432* then crossed behind the steamer to the port side. At 800 meters the U-boat fired a second torpedo, hitting her amidships. At 1142 a third shot forward of the bridge sent her to the bottom. The entire crew of eight officers and thirty men perished in the attack.

WACR; WJ.

J. N. PEW

D:	2-21-42	YB:	1921
T:	1855	Tn:	9,033
Pos:	12.40 N / 74.00 W	Dr:	29 ft.
Ow:	Sun Oil Co.	C:	104,270 bbls. fuel oil
Op:	Sun Oil Co.	P:	steam
M:	Thomas E. Bush	S:	11
A:	unarmed		

The *J. N. Pew* was torpedoed about 225 miles west of Aruba by the *U-67* (Müller-Stöckheim). On 20 February, the vessel sailed from Aruba, NWI, to the Panama Canal. While steaming on a zigzagging course and completely blacked out, the ship was struck by the first torpedo on the port side between the mainmast and the midships pump room. The explosion sprayed oil over the entire length of the vessel and set the midships house afire. The master ordered the ship abandoned as the fire began to consume the vessel. Fire destroyed two of the four lifeboats and two life floats. Two additional torpedoes, both striking aft, sank the vessel quickly. Survivors among the crew of eight officers and twenty-eight men got away in two lifeboats. Rough seas prevented the smooth launching of the two boats. The #4 boat cleared the ship with only two men in it, and it reached shore about thirty-five miles east of Riohacha, Colombia. The #3 lifeboat swamped when it hit the water. The eleven men in it managed to right the boat but set sail without water and little food. One by one the men died over the weeks. On 14 March, twenty-one days later, the Panamanian MS *Annetta I* rescued the single survivor off Cristobal, Canal Zone. Eight officers and twenty-five men perished in the attack.

NSS; WACR; WCSR; RWCS; Rohwer, p. 79; *War Action Casualties*, p. 15.

REPUBLIC

D:	2-21-42	YB:	1920
T:	2200	Tn:	5,287
Pos:	27.05 N / 80.15 W	Dr:	16 ft.
Ow:	American Republic Corp.	C:	water ballast
Op:	American Republic Corp.	P:	steam
M:	Alfred Hilderbrand Anderson	S:	10.5
A:	unarmed		

The tanker *Republic* was attacked by the *U-504* (Poske) approximately three and a half miles northeast of Jupiter Island Lighthouse off the coast of Florida. On 16 February the vessel sailed from Paulsboro, New Jersey, en route to Port Arthur, Texas. Two torpedoes struck almost simultaneously on the port side, thirty-five feet to fifty feet forward of the stern. The explosions destroyed the engine room and sprayed oil from the bunkers over the entire ship. As the vessel began to settle by the stern, the master ordered the ship abandoned. The surviving crew of seven officers and twenty-two men got away from the sinking vessel in two lifeboats. The #1 boat with eighteen survivors rowed to shore. The SS *Cities Service Missouri* spotted the second lifeboat with six survivors near the scene. The *Republic* eventually settled with a starboard list. The Coast Guard located the *Republic* the next day and found a large hole in the port side and the engine room and the #5 tank flooded. The *Republic* drifted on to reefs about five miles due east of Hobe Sound, Florida, and sank on the afternoon of 23 February. One officer and four crewmen perished, two by drowning and three while on watch below.

NSS; WACR; WCSR; WJ; *Pilot*, 27 February 1942; *Times Herald*, 25 February 1942; Rohwer, p. 80; *War Action Casualties*, p. 10.

CITIES SERVICE EMPIRE

D:	2-22-42	YB:	1918
T:	0425	Tn:	8,103
Pos:	28.00 N / 80.22 W	Dr:	27 ft. 6 in.
Ow:	Cities Service Oil Co.	C:	9,400 bbls. crude oil
Op:	Cities Service Oil Co.	P:	steam
M:	William Faucett Jerman	S:	10
A:	1-5"; 2-50 cal.; 2-30 cal.		

The *Cities Service Empire*, en route from Texas to Philadelphia, was torpedoed by the *U-128* (Heyse) about twenty-five miles North of Bethel Shoals off the Florida coast. The vessel maintained a nonevasive course in moderate to heavy seas. The *U-128* missed with four torpedoes before striking the vessel. Two torpedoes struck the vessel amidships at the after pump room deep in the ship's bowels on the starboard side. Fire broke out immediately, and within seconds the ship and the water around the tanker were ablaze. The intense heat drove the Navy gun crew from their guns. The master passed the order to abandon ship at 0435. The watch below stopped the ship's engines and reversed them immediately following the explosion. The fire consumed the lifeboats, and only two of the life rafts could be utilized. Most of the crew of eight officers, thirty-three men, and nine armed guards jumped overboard. The crippled vessel broke in two and sank at 0450. The USCG *Vigilant* (WPC-154) reached the burning vessel first. Pulling up to the blazing tanker, the cutter pulled off two survivors.

Just as these men boarded the cutter, the tanker exploded and showered the *Vigilant* with unignited oil. The USS *Biddle* (DD-151) also rescued some of the survivors and took them to Fort Pierce, Florida. The master, three armed guards, and ten merchant crewmen died in the attack.

NSS; WACR; WCSR; RWCS; WJ; AG; Rohwer, p. 80, places the attack at 28.25 N / 80.02 W; *Coast Guard at War*, p. 15.

W. D. ANDERSON

D:	2-22-42	YB:	1921
T:	1900	Tn:	10,227
Pos:	27.09 N / 79.56 W	Dr:	29 ft. 7 in.
Ow:	Atlantic Refining Co.	C:	133,360 bbls. crude oil
Op:	Atlantic Refining Co.	P:	steam
M:	Albert Benjamin Walters	S:	11.0
A:	unarmed		

The *W. D. Anderson* was torpedoed about twelve miles northeast of Jupiter Light, Florida, by the *U-504* (Poskc). The *W. D. Anderson* sailed from Texas to Philadelphia, Pennsylvania. Shortly after the ship passed the Jupiter Inlet Lighthouse, the lone survivor stated that he heard a dull thud and a booming explosion. Almost instantly a flame twenty or thirty feet high engulfed a huge area aft of the deckhouse. The lone survivor, on the fantail at the time, witnessed another seaman's hair catch on fire as he sat talking to him. The survivor immediately dove overboard, and while in the air a second explosion occurred. He got caught in the wash of the propeller but miraculously came to the surface astern of the ship. Flames quickly spread around the vessel for several hundred feet, making it impossible for other men to escape. The ship was seen to settle down to the stack. A small fishing boat picked up the survivor and later transferred him to a Coast Guard vessel. Eight officers and twenty-seven men perished in the attack.

The coordinates provided by the Navy were nearly two degrees further south. NSS; WACR; WCSR; WJ; Rohwer, p. 80; *Times Herald*, 28 February 1942; *Report on Lifeboat and Life Raft Performance for U.S. Tank Vessels Suffering War Casualties*, p. 16; *War Action Casualties*, p. 18.

WEST ZEDA

D:	2-22-42	YB:	1918
T:	2237	Tn:	5,658
Pos:	9.15 N / 59.04 W	Dr:	23 ft. 2 in.
Ow:	U.S. Maritime Commission	C:	6,500 tons general and
Op:	Isthmian SS Co.		manganese
M:	Ivar J. H. Rosequist	P:	steam
A:	unarmed	S:	10.5

The *West Zeda* sailed from Cape Town via Trinidad and then to Philadelphia, Pennsylvania. The *U-129* (Clausen) fired a torpedo that the third officer spotted about forty feet from the ship. Because it was too late for the ship to take evasive action, the torpedo struck the starboard side at the #2 hatch and blew the hatch into the air. The radio operator sent distress signals four times but received no reply. The crew of nine officers and twenty-six men abandoned ship in the two port lifeboats within ten minutes of the explosion. The *U-129* fired a second torpedo after the crew cleared the ship. This torpedo struck amidships, and the *West Zeda* sank about ten minutes later. At 0720 on 23 February, a Navy patrol plane sighted the lifeboats and directed the private schooner *Emeralda*, out of St. Vincent, to the boats. At noon the schooner rescued all hands and took them to Georgetown, British Guiana.

NSS; WACR; WCSR; RWCS; AG; Rohwer, p. 80, places the attack at 09.13 N / 59.04 W; *Times Herald*, 3 April 1942.

LIHUE

D:	2-23-42	YB:	1919
T:	0010	Tn:	7,001
Pos:	14.30 N / 64.45 W	Dr:	22 ft. 6 in.
Ow:	Matson Navigation Co.	C:	5,000 tons general
Op:	WSA	P:	steam
M:	W. G. Leithead	S:	10
A:	1-3"; 4-50 cal.; 2-30 cal.		

The SS *Lihue* was attacked and sunk by the *U-161* (Achilles) while en route from New York to Trinidad, BWI. The torpedo from the *U-161* struck the port side of the *Lihue* forward in the #1 hold. About fifteen minutes later the U-boat surfaced to attack. The *U-161* fired a few shots from its deck gun and then submerged. The armed guards returned the fire, and the helmsman managed to dodge a second torpedo. The crew abandoned the freighter nearly twelve hours after the attack began. Launching two lifeboats and three life rafts, the crew of eight officers, twenty-eight men and the gun crew of nine all safely left the ship. The British tanker SS *British Governor* later rescued all hands. A salvage crew from the Canadian armed merchant cruiser *Prince Henry* (F-70) boarded the *Lihue* to attempt to save her. The *Lihue*, however, sank on 26 February while being towed to St. Lucia by the minesweeper USS *Partridge* (AM-16).

WACR; WCSR; AG; Deck Log of *Partridge*, 23-26 February 1942; Rohwer, p. 80.

SUN

D:	2-23-42	YB:	1928
T:	0945	Tn:	9,002
Pos:	13.02 N / 70.41 W	Dr:	18 ft.
Ow:	Sun Oil Co.	C:	water ballast
Op:	Sun Oil Co.	P:	diesel
M:	Cornelius Van Gemert	S:	9.5
A:	unarmed		

The *Sun* sailed to Aruba, NWI, from Chester, Pennsylvania, and was torpedoed approximately fifty-four miles from her destination. The *U-502* (von Rosenstiel) fired a torpedo that struck the *Sun* on the port side. The explosion ripped the side and bottom almost completely out. The explosion was so violent that it twisted and tore out most of the inner structure and framework. Fortunately, the vessel did not catch fire because the tanks had been cleaned and were gas free. The explosion did blow oily ballast water over the master and officers on the bridge. The *Sun* began to list badly to port, and the crew calmly mustered at their stations. About thirty minutes after the explosion the crew of eight officers and twenty-eight men abandoned the ship in two lifeboats. The lifeboats followed in the wake of the *Sun*, which still had some way on. After sighting a plane the crew reboarded the vessel. The engineers got up steam, and the master proceeded cautiously and anchored near the Venezuelan coast until the following morning. The ship sailed to Aruba when an escort plane arrived. The vessel received some repairs at Aruba and then returned to Chester for complete repairs. All hands survived the attack.

NSS; WACR; WCSR; Rohwer, p. 80.

R. P. RESOR

D:	2-26-42	YB:	1935
T:	0025	Tn:	7,451
Pos:	39.47 N / 73.26 W	Dr:	30 ft.
Ow:	Standard Oil Co. of N. J.	C:	105,025 bbls. fuel oil
Op:	Standard Oil Co. of N. J.	P:	steam
M:	Fred Marcus	S:	12.5
A:	1-4"		

The *R. P. Resor* was torpedoed by the *U-578* (Rehwinkle) approximately twenty miles east of Manasquan Inlet, New Jersey. Traveling from Baytown, Texas, to Fall River, Massachusetts, the vessel steered a zigzag course and remained completely blacked out. A torpedo fired by the *U-578* struck just forward of amidships on the port side. The explosion blew oil over the entire length of the ship and into the water. The oil ignited and flames rapidly spread 500 feet around the ship as the eight officers, thirty-three men, and eight armed guards tried to abandon the vessel. One survivor witnessed a boat loaded with about thirty men launched successfully only to become engulfed in flames as it attempted to get away from the vessel. Other men perished trying to swim through the flames and oil. Of the forty-nine men on board, only one merchant crewman and one armed guard survived. The Coast Guard picket boat *CG-4344* rescued these men and landed them at the Manasquan Coast Guard Station. The *Resor* remained afloat and burning for several days. The tug *Sagamore* attempted to salvage her, but she rolled over and sank almost exactly forty-eight hours after the initial explosion.

NSS; WACR; WCSR; RWCS; AG; WJ; *Star*, 3 March 1942; *Post*, 28 February 1942; Rohwer, p. 81; *War Action Casualties*, p. 20; *Assistance*, 2:148.

MARORE

D:	2-26-42	YB:	1922
T:	2330	Tn:	8,215
Pos:	35.33 N / 74.58 W	Dr:	34 ft.
Ow:	Ore Steamship Corp.	C:	23,000 tons iron ore
Op:	Ore Steamship Corp.	P:	steam
M:	Charles E. Nash	S:	11
A:	unarmed		

While bound for Baltimore, Maryland, from Cruz Grande, Chile, the *Marore* was attacked by the *U-432* (Schultze) three and a half miles off Wimble Shoals. The *U-432* fired a torpedo from more than 800 yards away and struck the freighter amidships on the port side. As the *Marore* slowed, the crew of eight officers and thirty-one men mustered at their lifeboat stations. Fifteen minutes later, the men left in three lifeboats just as the *U-432* began to shell the vessel. The U-boat fired 100 shells and hit her ninety times. The German gunners continued firing as the vessel rolled over and sank in thirty minutes. A Coast Guard motor surfboat from the Big Kinnakeet Lifeboat Station helped the survivors in the #3 boat get ashore. The American SS *John D. Gill* discovered lifeboats #1 and #4 and landed the men at Norfolk. All hands survived the attack.

WACR; WCSR; RWCS; WJ; *Times Herald*, 3 March 1942; Rohwer, p. 82; *Coast Guard at War*, p. 19.

OREGON

D:	2-28-42	YB:	1920
T:	0415	Tn:	7,017
Pos:	20.44 N / 67.52 W	Dr:	27 ft.
Ow:	Texas Co.	C:	78,000 bbls. fuel oil
Op:	Texas Co.	P:	steam
M:	Ingvald C. Nilsen	S:	10
A:	unarmed		

The *Oregon* sailed from Aruba, NWI, to Melville, Rhode Island, maintaining a zigzag course and running completely blacked out. The *U-156* (Hartenstein) opened the attack on the tanker with its 105-mm deck gun. The first shell hit the starboard side in the master's quarters, and the second shell demolished the radio shack. The *U-156* initially concentrated on the midships section above the decks. Satisfied that the radio was unusable, the U-boat began to circle the tanker, firing at point blank range along the waterline. The tanker's crew of eight officers and twenty-eight men left the ship during the shelling, which lasted for seventy-five minutes. The shells' explosions started a fire on the bridge, in one of the fuel tanks, and at the stern of the ship. One of the boilers also exploded, but the cargo never caught fire. The *Oregon* sank stern first at about 0815. The men at their boat stations on the port side were strafed by machine gun fire and therefore left in the starboard #3 boat. Other men dove in the water and climbed onto a released raft. The twenty-six survivors in the #3 lifeboat landed near Puerto Plata, Dominican Republic, at noon on 4 March. The SS *Gulfpenn* rescued the four men on the raft five and a half days after the attack. Three officers and three men died during the attack.

NSS; WACR; WCSR; Rohwer, p. 82.

MARY

D:	3-3-42	YB:	1920
T:	1122	Tn:	5,104
Pos:	8.25 N / 52.50 W	Dr:	26 ft. 6 in.
Ow:	A. H. Bull SS Co.	C:	general (fully loaded)
Op:	A. H. Bull SS Co.	P:	steam
M:	Severin Broadwick	S:	10.0
A:	unarmed		

The *Mary* sailed from New York to Suez via San Juan, Puerto Rico, and had a full load of lend-lease cargo. As the *Mary* traveled in a nonevasive pattern approximately 165 miles off the north coast of Brazil, the *U-129* (Clausen) approached her from the port side, keeping between the ship and the sun. The first torpedo struck the port side at the #3 hold. This explosion blew a column of water over the bridge and wrecked the radio shack, preventing the radio operator from sending a distress message. A second torpedo struck about eight seconds later at the #4 lower hold. Most of the crew of eight officers and twenty-six men abandoned ship in two lifeboats after the second explosion. Seven or eight minutes later, and after the boats had cleared the ship, a third torpedo struck the port side at the #1 hold. At 1140 the *Mary* disappeared beneath the water. The submarine surfaced and approached the master's lifeboat. Clausen inquired in English the ship's name, tonnage, origin, destination, and the type of cargo. The two lifeboats sailed for six days, traveling 540 miles. The SS *Alcoa Scout* rescued the survivors about thirty-eight miles northeast of Georgetown, British Guiana, and took them to Port-of-Spain, Trinidad. One of the ship's crewmen failed to leave the ship and probably died in the initial explosion.

NSS; WACR; WCSR; RWCS; Rohwer, p. 82.

MARIANA

D:	3-5-42	YB:	1915
T:	0444	Tn:	3,109
Pos:	22.14 N / 71.23 W	Dr:	20 ft.
Ow:	Agwilines, Inc.	C:	sugar
Op:	NY and Puerto Rican SS. Co.	P:	steam
M:	Ivan Elroy Hurlstone	S:	unknown
A:	1-4"; 1-3"; 8-20 mm		

The *Mariana*, en route from Guanica, Puerto Rico, to Boston, was torpedoed by the *U-126* (Bauer) off Turks Island. The ship's position was given away by smoke on the horizon just after midnight. The *U-126* fired a torpedo that struck aft of the mast, and she sank in five minutes. The crew of eight officers and twenty-eight men all perished.

WACR; WJ; Rohwer, p. 82; The coordinates given by the Navy (27.45 N / 67.00 W) are hundreds of miles from those given in the WJ.

COLLAMER

D:	3-5-42	YB:	1920
T:	0630	Tn:	5,113
Pos:	44.18 N / 63.10 W	Dr:	24 ft. 7 in.
Ow:	U.S. Maritime Commission	C:	5,500 tons general, war supplies
Op:	Moore-McCormack Lines	P:	steam
M:	John M. Hultman	S:	9.0
A:	unarmed		

The *Collamer* sailed from Halifax, Nova Scotia, to Murmansk as part of Convoy HX-178. Having lost the convoy in heavy seas, unable to maintain convoy speed, and with damage to her deck cargo, the *Collamer* returned to Halifax. While traveling on a nonevasive course in rough seas, the *Collamer* was attacked by the *U-404* (von Bülow). The first torpedo struck the starboard side, amidships, causing the boilers to explode, and killed the engine room crew. The freighter began sinking fast by the stern, and the master ordered the ship abandoned. Survivors among the crew of seven officers and twenty-four men launched two lifeboats, but before they could get away from the vessel, they spotted the wake of a second torpedo. This torpedo struck the ship underneath the bridge just aft of the #2 hatch on the port side. A terrific explosion caused the ship to sink immediately stern first. The radioman managed to send an SOS to Halifax. After several hours, two planes spotted the lifeboats and signaled the British SS *Empire Woodcock*. Three officers and four men died in the attack.

NSS; WACR; WCSR; Rohwer, p. 82, places the attack at 41.19 N / 69.09 W.

STEEL AGE

D:	3-6-42	YB:	1920
T:	2205	Tn:	6,194
Pos:	06.45 N / 53.15 W	Dr:	28 ft. 6 in.
Ow:	Isthmian SS Co.	C:	ore
Op:	Isthmian SS Co.	P:	steam
M:	Ralph Jones	S:	11
A:	unarmed		

On 18 January, the *Steel Age* sailed independently from Calcutta, India, for New Orleans, Louisiana. Approximately 600 miles southeast of Trinidad the *U-129* (Clausen) fired two torpedoes that struck the starboard side. The first torpedo hit amidships, and the second struck between the #4 and the #5 hatches. Most of the ship's crew never had time to leave the ship. The ore cargo caused the ship to sink in two minutes. The sole survivor ran from the messroom when the first torpedo struck. When he reached the deck, it was already awash and he jumped on a nearby life float. None of the other eight officers or twenty-six crew members survived. The *U-129* picked up the survivor within twenty minutes. Interned in a POW camp, he was liberated in 1945.

NSS; WACR; WCSR; Rohwer, p. 83.

BARBARA

D:	3-7-42	YB:	1913
T:	0230	Tn:	4,637
Pos:	20.00 N / 73.56 W	Dr:	20 ft. 7 in.
Ow:	A. H. Bull Co.	C:	4,015 tons general
Op:	A. H. Bull Co.	P:	steam
M:	Walter Gwynn Hudgins	S:	12
A:	unarmed		

The *Barbara* was torpedoed about nine miles north northeast of West Tortuga Island, Dominican Republic. The *Barbara* sailed from Baltimore, Maryland, to San Juan, Puerto Rico, on an approved zigzagging course. In the moonlight, the *U-126* (Bauer) spotted the freighter and fired a torpedo that struck the port side of the ship amidships, penetrated deep, and exploded on the starboard side. The explosion caused a fire that spread rapidly, killed the watch below, damaged the engines, and within moments had the midships decks ablaze mast high. The fire bell rang, but the intense fire prevented the eight officers, fifty men, and twenty-seven passengers from launching any of the four lifeboats. The passengers and crew resorted to jumping or climbing into the water and then swimming to the life rafts that had floated astern. The *Barbara* burned for two and a half hours before sinking stern first sometime around 0500. One group of twenty-one persons landed on Tortuga Island after nearly three days at sea. A Navy plane rescued the survivors on another life raft. Four officers, fourteen crewmen, and eight passengers lost their lives in the attack.

The figures listed for the passengers and crew are extremely contradictory within the sources. NSS; WACR; WCSR; Rohwer, p. 83, places the attack at 20.10 N / 73.05 W.

CARDONIA

D:	3-7-42	YB:	1920
T:	0410	Tn:	5,104
Pos:	19.50 N / 73.25 W	Dr:	14 ft. 6 in.
Ow:	Lykes Bros. SS Co.	C:	81 tons general
Op:	Lykes Bros. SS Co.	P:	steam
M:	Gus W. Darnell	S:	13.5
A:	unarmed		

The *Cardonia* sailed from Ponce, Puerto Rico, to Guayabal, Cuba. The *U-126* (Bauer) attacked the freighter five miles west-northwest of the St. Nicholas Mole, Haiti. Only two hours earlier the watch on the *Cardonia* had witnessed the SS *Barbara* go up in flames, seven miles distant. The master altered the course of the *Cardonia* to approach closely to the Haitian coast and increased the speed of the vessel to nearly fourteen knots. Lookouts sighted the *U-126* on the surface one-half mile off the port (land) side. At the same time they also spotted the wakes of two torpedoes approaching the *Cardonia*. The master ordered hard right rudder, and the two torpedoes passed several feet astern. The helmsman maneuvered the vessel to keep her stern to the submarine and began a zigzagging course, while the watch below provided an improvised smoke screen. The *U-126* missed with two more torpedoes and then began firing shells. The first several shots fell short, but the German gunners soon found the *Cardonia*'s range. The U-boat fired about forty-five shots at the rate of one per minute. The shells killed one crew member, carried away the radio antenna and mainmast, damaged the steering gear, and set the ship on fire. At 0500 the master gave orders for the ten officers, twenty-six crewmen, and two passengers to abandon ship. As the survivors began clearing the ship, a torpedo hit just forward of amidships on the starboard side, causing the ship to sink by the stern at 0600. Twenty crew members and two passengers climbed into the only good lifeboat. The other fifteen crew members found safety in three life rafts. The lifeboat made landfall at Port St. Nicholas, Haiti, at about 1000. The USS *Mulberry* (AN-27) rescued the crew members on the life rafts on 8 March, at about 1100, and took them to the Naval Base at Guantánamo, Cuba. Shellfire caused the only casualty.

NSS; WACR; WCSR; RWCS; *Post*, 11 March 1942, 22 March 1942; Rohwer, p. 83, places the attack at 19.53 N / 73.27 W.

GULFTRADE

D:	3-10-42	YB:	1920
T:	0040	Tn:	6,776
Pos:	39.50 N / 73.52 W	Dr:	26 ft. 6 in.
Ow:	Gulf Oil Corp.	C:	80,000 bbls. bunker "C" oil
Op:	Gulf Oil Corp.	P:	steam
M:	Torger Olsen	S:	10.5
A:	unarmed		

The *Gulftrade* sailed from Port Arthur, Texas, to New York. During the trip, the ship's running lights and the masthead light had been turned on to avoid collision with several colliers in the vicinity. This allowed the *U-588* (Vogel) to easily spot the tanker three miles off Barnegat Light. A torpedo struck the starboard side of the tanker just forward of the mainmast and just aft of the bridgehouse and broke the ship in two. The explosion ripped up the decks and completely opened tanks #5, #6, and #7. The explosion sprayed oil and debris over the vessel from stem to stern, and she caught fire immediately. Fortunately, within less than a minute, the high seas washed over the vessel and extinguished the flames. The master immediately stopped the engines, and the crew of eight officers and twenty-six men began abandoning the ship. The high seas and the fact that oil lay several inches deep all about the deck and had filled the boats complicated the abandonment of the ship. Seven survivors remained on the stern half of the ship, and nine survivors abandoned ship in the #2 boat. Both the #3 and #4 boats with eighteen men swamped in the heavy seas, and the officer and seventeen crewmen in them drowned. The USCG cutter *Antietam* (WPC-128) arrived to take the men off the stern but suffered a breakdown, and the Navy tender *Larch* (AN-21) finished the job. The survivors who remained on the stern reported that the submarine surfaced five minutes after the attack, circled the stern section, and departed forty-five minutes later on a southerly course.

NSS; WACR; WCSR; RWCS; WJ; *Post*, 11 March 1942; Rohwer, p. 84; *Coast Guard at War*, p. 21.

TEXAN

D:	3-11-42	YB:	1902
T:	2035	Tn:	7,005
Pos:	21.32 N / 76.24 W	Dr:	30 ft. 3 in.
Ow:	American-Hawaiian Line	C:	10,915 tons general
Op:	Moore-McCormack SS Co.	P:	steam
M:	Robert Hugh Murphy	S:	11.8
A:	unarmed		

The *Texan* sailed from New York to Rio de Janeiro via Port-of-Spain, Trinidad. The freighter proceeded along a nonevasive course with all her lights extinguished. The *U-126* (Bauer) fired a torpedo, striking the port side bulkhead between the #6 and the #7 holds. The explosion left a large hole approximately ten feet below the waterline. About five minutes later the *U-126* began shelling the *Texan* from about three-quarters of a mile in an attempt to silence radio communication. The U-boat hit the vessel four times but not before three Florida stations received the SOS. Within eight minutes of the torpedo's explosion the crew of ten officers and thirty-seven men managed to launch two lifeboats. The suction of the ship, however, held them nearby, and both boats capsized. At daybreak ten men who had clung to one of the boats all night managed to right it. These men then picked up another twenty-eight men. About fifteen hours after the attack, the Cuban fishing boat *Yoyo* spotted the survivors approximately fifteen miles west-southwest of the position of the sinking and towed the boat to Nuevitas, Cuba. Three officers and six men perished in the attack.

The vessel was chartered to the U.S. Maritime Commission according to naval records. NSS; WACR; WCSR; RWCS; Rohwer, p. 84, places the attack at 21.34 N / 76.28 W.

CARIBSEA

D:	3-11-42	YB:	1919
T:	0202	Tn:	2,609
Pos:	34.40 N / 76.10 W	Dr:	24 ft. 6 in.
Ow:	Stockard SS Corp.	C:	3,600 tons manganese ore
Op:	Stockard SS Corp.	P:	steam
M:	Nicholas Manolis	S:	4.5
A:	unarmed		

The *Caribsea* departed Cuba for Baltimore, Maryland. About fourteen miles East of Cape Lookout Lighthouse the *U-158* (Rostin) attacked the ship while she steamed on a nonevasive course. The master received a message in Merchant Marine Code that routed the vessel to pass Cape Hatteras in daylight. He therefore reduced the ship's speed to four or five knots. When Rostin spotted the freighter, he thought she lay dead in the water. This mistake caused Rostin to miss with his first torpedo. The second torpedo hit the starboard bow at the #2 hatch. A second explosion thought to be another torpedo was likely the ship's boilers exploding. The *Caribsea* with her cargo of ore sank by the head in less than three minutes. This allowed no radio distress signal to be sent, and the crew of eight officers and twenty men had no chance to launch the lifeboats. The few survivors managed to climb onto two rafts that floated free of the sinking freighter. The survivors later observed the *U-158* within 100 yards of the torpedoed vessel. The SS *Norlindo* picked up the survivors, two officers and five crewmen, ten hours later and took them to the Cape Henry Lighthouse. The remaining six officers and fifteen crewmen died, some drawn under the water by the suction of the vessel.

The figures for the ship's complement are contradictory. NSS; WACR; WCSR; WJ; *Post*, 15 March 1942; *Times Herald*, 15 March 1942; Rohwer, p. 84.

OLGA

D:	3-12-42	YB:	1919
T:	0014	Tn:	2,496
Pos:	23.39 N / 77.00 W	Dr:	18 ft.
Ow:	Carter Coal Transportation	C:	none
Op:	Carter Coal Transportation	P:	steam
M:	William Dewey Graham	S:	10.5
A:	unarmed		

The *Olga* was torpedoed about seven miles east of Punta Maternillos Light, Camaguey, Cuba. The *Olga* sailed from Port Everglades, Florida, to Baracoa, Cuba, on a nonevasive course. A lookout observed a torpedo fired by the *U-126* (Bauer) but not in time for the helmsman to take avoiding action. The torpedo struck the port side at the #3 hold about five feet below the waterline. The blast destroyed the fireroom bulkhead, blew away the #4 hatch cover, and wrecked the wheelhouse and communication room. The loss of the radio prevented the radio operator from sending a distress signal. The engineer stopped the engines because he could not communicate with the bridge. With the vessel stopped, the crew of eight officers and twenty-five men began abandoning ship. Part of the crew launched the #1 lifeboat, while others jumped into the water and swam to two rafts. The *U-126* rescued two members of the crew from the water and placed them on one of the rafts. The *Olga* sank at 0045. Naval craft rescued the remaining thirty-two crewmen. One of the crew died from shock and exposure.

Coast Guard records indicate the torpedo struck the vessel on the starboard side. The complement figures of the ship are contradictory within the sources. NSS; WACR; Rohwer, p. 84, places the attack at 21.32 N / 76.24 W; *Post*, 22 March 1942.

COLABEE

D:	3-12-42	YB:	1920
T:	2140	Tn:	5,627
Pos:	22.14 N / 77.35 W	Dr:	24 ft. 2 in.
Ow:	Illinois-Atlantic Corp.	C:	38,600 bags of sugar
Op:	American Hawaiian Line	P:	steam
M:	Lee M. Morgan	S:	10
A:	unarmed		

The *Colabee* sailed from Port Tarafa, Cuba, to Baltimore, Maryland, and proceeded on a nonevasive course. Apparently the *U-126* (Bauer) fired a torpedo on the surface, abaft of the starboard beam, not more than 800 yards away. The torpedo struck the *Colabee* ten or twelve feet below the waterline on the starboard side at the after end of the #2 hold. The explosion created a large hole that varied from ten to twenty feet long from the #2 hatch coming to below the waterline. The explosion also extensively damaged the bridge, blew off the #2 hatch covers, and scattered bags of sugar about the deck. The explosion did not damage the engine room, but an overboard discharge line broke and flooded the engine spaces. Because of the flooding, the radio operator could not send an SOS. The chief engineer attempted to reverse the engines but failed and stopped them. The *Colabee* went aground shortly thereafter, and the master passed the order to abandon ship at 2155. The ship carried two lifeboats and no life rafts, but the torpedo explosion destroyed the starboard lifeboat. The crew of eight officers and twenty-nine men panicked, and only ten managed to get away in this boat. Others jumped overboard and many drowned. The *U-126* surfaced and the Germans helped one man into the lifeboat and questioned the survivors. This boat made its way to Key Verde, where the Cuban ship *Oriente* picked up these survivors. The first engineer and two men stayed with the ship and were rescued the next day at 1430 by the American tanker *Cities Service Kansas*. Four officers and nineteen men died. The *Oriente* later pulled the *Colabee* off the shoal and, with the assistance of the Cuban Navy, salvaged her. The *Colabee* was later towed into port and put back in service.

NSS; WACR; WCSR; RWCS; WJ; *Star*, 16 March 1942; Rohwer, p. 85. Other sources place the attack at 22.10 N / 70.35 W.

JOHN D. GILL

D:	3-12-42	YB:	1942
T:	2352	Tn:	11,641
Pos:	33.55 N / 77.39 W	Dr:	31 ft. 1 in.
Ow:	Atlantic Refining Co.	C:	141,981 bbls. of crude oil
Op:	Atlantic Refining Co.	P:	steam
M:	Allen D. Tucker	S:	15
A:	1-5"; 2-50 cal.; 2-30 cal.		

On 7 March, the SS *John D. Gill*, a new tanker completed in February 1942, sailed from Atreco, Texas, to Philadelphia, Pennsylvania. While steaming off Frying Pan Shoals, the vessel stopped zigzagging for approximately twenty minutes, the master flashed his running lights, and then the ship continued zigzagging. This allowed the *U-158* (Rostin) to get a clear shot at the tanker. The torpedo struck amidships on the starboard side under the mainmast in the #7 tank. The ship seemed to lift out of the water and move sideways. The explosion, however, did not ignite the oil. The oil was ignited when a seaman tossed overboard a life ring with a self-igniting carbide light. This life ring caught the oil on fire and turned the ship and sea into a blazing inferno. After the initial explosion, and with no power, the master passed the word to abandon ship. The armed guards manned their guns but could not locate the submarine. The crew of eight officers and thirty-four men abandoned the ship within eight minutes. The seven armed guards followed seven minutes later. While lowering one of the after lifeboats, the lines became fouled and dumped the occupants into the sea. The turning prop killed at least two of these men. The crew escaped in only one of the four lifeboats and one of the six life rafts. After the crew left the tanker, a series of terrific explosions rocked the ship as one tank after another ignited and exploded. Many of the men died in the sea of flames surrounding the tanker. A Coast Guard motor lifeboat, Coast Guard patrol boat No. 186, and the cutter *Agassiz* (WPC-126) rescued one group of survivors and landed them at Southport, North Carolina. The tanker *Robert H. Colley* picked up a second group and landed them at Charleston, South Carolina. The gutted ship sank on 13 March, at about 0900. Six officers, thirteen men, and four armed guards perished in the attack.

NSS; WACR; WCSR; RWCS; AG; WJ; *Washington Post*, 16 March 1942; Rohwer, p. 85; *Coast Guard at War*, pp. 21-23; *War Action Casualties*, p. 25.

ALBERT F. PAUL

D:	3-13-42	YB:	1917
T:	0120	Tn:	735
Pos:	26.00 N / 72.00 W	Dr:	14 ft.
Ow:	Albert Shipping Co.	C:	salt
Op:	Albert Shipping Co.	P:	sail
M:	William Mack Martino	S:	unknown
A:	unarmed		

The four-masted schooner *Albert F. Paul* sailed from Baltimore, Maryland, to Turks Island. In heavy seas the *U-332* (Liebe) spotted the vessel. Liebe considered using his deck gun to sink the schooner, but heavy seas prevented this. He fired a torpedo that passed under the bowsprit. A second torpedo struck under the third mast and the schooner sank immediately. The entire crew of eight perished in the attack.

WACR; WJ; Rohwer, p. 85.

LEMUEL BURROWS

D:	3-14-42	YB:	1917
T:	0200	Tn:	7,610
Pos:	39.18 N / 74.16 W	Dr:	29 ft. 6 in.
Ow:	Mystic SS. Co.	C:	12,450 tons coal
Op:	Mystic SS. Co.	P:	steam
M:	Grover Dale Clark	S:	9.5
A:	unarmed		

The *Lemuel Burrows* sailed from Norfolk, Virginia, to Boston, Massachusetts. The *U-404* (von Bülow) attacked the collier about five miles south-southwest of the Brigantine Gas Buoy off Atlantic City after spotting the vessel's silhouette against the city's bright lights. The U-boat initially fired two shots but both missed. The third torpedo hit the starboard side of the ship between the #2 and #3 holds. The master immediately ordered the ship abandoned, and the crew of eight officers and twenty-six men lowered one of the two lifeboats. Minutes later a second torpedo hit the port side amidships. This explosion threw all twenty-one men into the icy water. Only eight of these men managed to cling to the overturned boat, and two eventually slipped into the water and drowned. Other survivors swam to two rafts. The *U-404* surfaced and the Germans questioned the men about the ship's name before leaving the area. After drifting for six hours, the SS *Sewalls Point* and a boat from the SS *James Elwood Jones* rescued the survivors. Four officers and sixteen men died in the attack.

NSS; WACR; WCSR; RWCS; WJ; Rohwer, p. 85, places the attack at 39.21 N / 74.33 W.

OLEAN

D:	3-14-42	YB:	1919
T:	2305	Tn:	7,118
Pos:	34.24.30 N / 76.29.00 W	Dr:	18 ft.
Ow:	Socony-Vacuum Oil Co.	C:	water ballast
Op:	Socony-Vacuum Oil Co.	P:	steam
M:	Theodore Bockhoff	S:	11
A:	yes; unknown		

On 14 March, the *Olean* sailed from Norfolk, Virginia, to Beaumont, Texas. According to the master, the ship proceeded with all lights extinguished. One survivor, however, reported a dim masthead light burning. The *U-158* (Rostin) spotted the tanker and attacked her fifteen miles south of Cape Lookout. The first torpedo struck the port quarter in the machinery space, causing the vessel to veer out of control. The gun crew spotted the submarine but could not depress the gun enough to fire. The order to abandon ship was passed, and the eight officers, thirty men, and four armed guards began leaving at 2345. The ship still had headway, and the first boat capsized as it hit the water. These men transferred to the #3 boat. As the starboard #3 boat touched the water, a second torpedo hit the engine room, shattering this boat and killing six men (one officer and five men). The remaining seven officers, twenty-five men, and four armed guards managed to escape in the #2 lifeboat and by swimming to three rafts. The Cape Lookout and Fort Macon Lifeboat Stations each sent a motor lifeboat to rescue the survivors, and they arrived nine hours after the attack. They landed the men at Morehead City, North Carolina. The *Olean* was later towed to Hampton Roads and salvaged. Declared a CTL, she was rebuilt and renamed the *Sweep*.

NSS; WACR; WCSR; RWCS; WJ; *Albany Times Union*, 19 March 1942; Rohwer, p. 85, places the attack at 34.22 N / 76.29 W; *War Action Casualties*, p. 28; *Coast Guard at War*, p. 23.

ARIO

D:	3-15-42	YB:	1920
T:	0120	Tn:	6,952
Pos:	34.20 N / 76.39 W	Dr:	27 ft. 6 in.
Ow:	Socony-Vacuum Oil Co.	C:	water ballast
Op:	Socony-Vacuum Oil Co.	P:	steam
M:	Thorolf R. Hannenig	S:	10.5
A:	unarmed		

On 11 March, the *Ario* sailed from New York to Corpus Christi, Texas. Eleven miles southwest of the Cape Lookout Buoy, the *U-158* (Rostin) attacked the tanker. The *Ario* did not steer a zigzag course, and at about 0117 a small vessel crossed the port bow, whereby the helmsman changed the ship's direction. As

the *Ario* straightened her course, a torpedo struck the starboard side at the #9 tank. The master ordered the ship abandoned, and the radio operator sent a distress call and received an answer. Before any of the boats could be launched, the *U-158* began shelling the *Ario*. For thirty minutes the U-boat shelled the tanker while the crew of eight officers and twenty-six men cleared the ship. The *U-158* fired forty shells. One shell struck the #3 boat before it could reach the water and killed most of its occupants. The crew managed to launch another boat and picked up survivors from the water. The first assistant engineer remained on board until 0800 when he shoved off on a life raft. The *U-158* closed in to view the vessel and almost hit the lifeboat. The USS *Dupont* (DD-152) picked up the survivors at about 0800 and took them to Charleston. One officer and seven men died in the attack.

The ONI report mentions a second submarine shelling the tanker. This cannot be confirmed in the German records. NSS; WACR; RWCS; WCSR; WJ; *War Action Casualties*, p. 29.

AUSTRALIA

D:	3-16-42	YB:	1928
T:	1410	Tn:	11,728
Pos:	35.07 N / 75.22 W	Dr:	32 ft. 2 in.
Ow:	Texas Co.	C:	110,000 bbls. fuel oil
Op:	Texas Co.	P:	diesel
M:	Martin Ader	S:	11
A:	unarmed		

On about 10 March, the *Australia* sailed from Port Arthur, Texas, to New York. The *U-332* (Liebe) spotted the zigzagging tanker off the Diamond Shoals Lighted Buoy and within sight of the SS *William J. Salman* and several other ships. Lightning in the distance outlined the ship against the sky, making the tanker a better target. A torpedo struck the starboard side in the engine room about twelve feet below the waterline. The explosion sent flames and smoke through engine room skylights, destroyed the engine room fuel lines and auxiliary pipes, and killed the officer and three men on watch below. Water flooded into the compartment, extinguishing the blaze as the ship settled quickly by the stern. The surviving seven officers and twenty-nine men left the ship in three lifeboats. The SS *William J. Salman* picked them up within one hour and thirty-five minutes and delivered them to the USS *Ruby* (PY-21). On 17 March, the *Ruby* landed the survivors at Southport, North Carolina. The stern of the *Australia* rested on the bottom on an even keel with her bow afloat and all her cargo tanks intact. The total loss committee of the WSA sent a notice to the Texas Company that they could collect insurance for total loss by sinking the vessel, and she was sunk on 20 March.

NSS; WACR; WCSR; WJ; *Star*, 22 March 1942; *Post*, 22 March 1942; Rohwer, p. 85, places the attack at 35.43 N / 75.22 W; *War Action Casualties*, p. 30.

ACME

D:	3-17-42	YB:	1916
T:	1750	Tn:	6,878
Pos:	35.06 N / 75.23 W	Dr:	16 ft.
Ow:	Socony-Vacuum Oil Co.	C:	water ballast
Op:	Socony-Vacuum Oil Co.	P:	steam
M:	Sigsmund Schulz	S:	10.5
A:	unarmed		

On 15 March, the *Acme* departed New York en route to Corpus Christi, Texas. The *U-124* (Mohr) intercepted the tanker and torpedoed her one mile west of the Diamond Shoals Buoy. The *Acme* had proceeded completely blacked out and on a nonevasive course. Two tankers and two freighters lay ahead while astern near the buoy was the Greek merchantman SS *Kassandra Louloudis* and two other tankers. The USS *Dickerson* (DD-157) and the USCG cutter *Dione* (WPC-107) were two and four miles distant, respectively. At 1750 a torpedo struck directly aft of the stack. The explosion blasted through the engine room, killing the three men on watch below and eight others aft (one officer and ten men). The blast destroyed the engines completely. All the bulkheads forward of the engine room held, however, and the ship settled by the stern but did not sink. The remaining crew of six officers and fourteen men abandoned ship in two lifeboats at 1820. The *Dione* picked up the survivors within ten minutes and landed them at Norfolk, Virginia. The vessel was later towed to Norfolk, repaired, and put back into service.

NSS; WACR; WCSR; WJ; *Star*, 33 March 1942; Rohwer, p. 86, places the attack at 35.05 N / 75.20 W; *War Action Casualties*, p. 31.

E. M. CLARK

D:	3-18-42	YB:	1921
T:	0125	Tn:	9,647
Pos:	34.50 N / 75.35 W	Dr:	29 ft.
Ow:	Standard Oil Co. of N. J.	C:	118,000 bbls. heating oil
Op:	Standard Oil Co. of N. J.	P:	steam
M:	Hubert L. Hassell	S:	10.5
A:	unarmed		

Steaming from Baton Rouge, Louisiana, to New York, the *E. M. Clark* was torpedoed about twenty-two miles southwest of the Diamond Shoals Lighted Buoy. Although the tanker was completely blacked out, thunderstorms in the area generated enough light to silhouette her. In a moderately rough sea, the *U-124*'s (Mohr) first torpedo struck the port side amidships, eight to ten feet below the waterline. A terrific explosion destroyed the #2 lifeboat and brought down the radio antenna. The general alarm sounded and the engine room

signaled "full astern." The crew made an attempt to repair the antenna
equipment, but a second torpedo struck the port side at the forward hold and
doomed the ship. The master passed the order to abandon ship, and the crew
readied two lifeboats as the ship's jammed steam whistle continuously roared.
These boats successfully left as the tanker slowly settled in the water. Ten
minutes after the first torpedo struck, the tanker slipped beneath the waves with
the whistle still blaring. All but a messman in the crew of eight officers and
thirty-three men successfully got away. The Venezuelan tanker SS *Catatumbo*
picked up the #4 boat containing twenty-six men and landed them at Cape
Henry. The USS *Dickerson* (DD-157) rescued the fourteen men in the #1 boat.
A motor surfboat from the Ocracoke Coast Guard Station took these men
ashore.

NSS; WACR; WCSR; WJ; *New York Times*, 22 March 1942; Rohwer, p. 86; *Ships of the Esso
Fleet*, pp. 144-48; *War Action Casualties*, p. 32; *Assistance*, 2:151.

PAPOOSE

D:	3-18-42	YB:	1921
T:	2135	Tn:	5,939
Pos:	34.17 N / 76.39 W	Dr:	unknown (light)
Ow:	America Republic Corp.	C:	water ballast
Op:	America Republic Corp.	P:	steam
M:	Raymond Zalnick	S:	11
A:	unarmed		

On 15 March, the *Papoose* sailed from Providence, Rhode Island, via New York
for Corpus Christi, Texas. The *U-124* (Mohr) torpedoed the tanker about fifteen
miles southwest of Cape Lookout while the ship maintained a zigzag course in
moderately rough seas. The first torpedo struck the port side at the break of the
poop and entered the fuel bunker. The engine room and the fireroom quickly
flooded with oil and water, the engines stopped immediately, and the blast killed
the chief engineer and a fireman. The #3 boat got away five minutes after the
first torpedo hit. At 1805 a second torpedo slammed into the tanker just aft of
amidships on the starboard side and barely missed the lifeboat in the water. This
explosion tore a large hole near the waterline that extended eight feet above the
water. The #1 lifeboat got away five minutes after the second torpedo struck.
The USS *Stringham* (DD-83) rescued the surviving eight officers and twenty-
four men at 0730 on 19 March and took them to Norfolk. The *Papoose*
remained afloat for two days and sank on 20 March.

Documents in WCSR state that the tanker was owned by the Petroleum Navigation Co.; NSS;
WACR; WJ; Rohwer, p. 86; *War Action Casualties*, p. 34.

W. E. HUTTON

D:	3-18-42	YB:	1920
T:	2210	Tn:	7,076
Pos:	34.05 N / 76.40 W	Dr:	27 ft. 4 in.
Ow:	Pure Oil Co.	C:	64,000 bbls. #2 fuel oil
Op:	Pure Oil Co.	P:	steam
M:	Carl A. Flaathan	S:	10
A:	unarmed		

The tanker *W. E. Hutton* was torpedoed about twenty miles southeast of Cape Lookout by the *U-124* (Mohr). The tanker maintained a nonevasive course, having sailed on 12 March, from Smiths Bluff, Texas, to Marcus Hook, Pennsylvania. The *U-124* fired a torpedo from about 1,000 yards that the bridge lookout spotted fifty feet from the ship. The torpedo struck the starboard bow near the stem, and the explosion carried away the anchors, buckled the bow, and flooded the forepeak tanks. The master mustered the crew of eight officers and twenty-eight men on deck and ordered the lifeboats lowered about three-fourths of the way down. The radio operator sent distress signals and received an acknowledgment. As the master changed course to head his ship toward shore, the *U-124* fired a second torpedo that missed the tanker. Eight minutes after the first explosion, the *U-124* fired a third torpedo that struck amidships on the port side just aft of the bridge. The explosion vented up through the decks, buckled and overturned the pilot house, and sprayed oil over the entire length of the ship. The amidships section caught fire and became a blazing inferno for about ten minutes. As the fire raged, the remaining crew left the ship in two lifeboats and two rafts. The ship sank just an hour after the first torpedo struck. Twelve survivors left in one starboard lifeboat, and three in the other, while two life rafts each had four men. At daybreak the seven officers and sixteen men transferred into one lifeboat and began to row toward shore. On 19 March, at 1035, the British MV *Port Halifax* rescued the survivors and took them to the Savannah Sea Buoy, where they transferred into a pilot boat. One officer and twelve men died in the attack.

NSS; WACR; WCSR; WJ; *New York Times*, 29 March 1942; *New York Herald Tribune*, 29 March 1942; Rohwer, p. 86, places the attack at 34.25 N / 76.50 W; *Pilot*, 1 May 1942; *War Action Casualties*, p. 35.

LIBERATOR

D: 3-19-42   YB: 1918
T: 0905   Tn: 7,720
Pos: 35.05 N / 75.30 W   Dr: unknown
Ow: Lykes Bros. SS Co.   C: 11,000 tons sulphur
Op: Lykes Bros. SS Co.   P: steam
M: Albin Johnson   S: 10.5
A: 1-4"

The *Liberator* sailed from Galveston, Texas, to New York. The freighter had been steering a zigzag course but had discontinued it just before the attack. Three miles west of the Diamond Shoals Buoy the *U-332* (Liebe) fired a torpedo that struck about twenty feet below the waterline on the port side in the engine room. The explosion destroyed the engine room and vented upward through the deck, destroying the #4 boat and blowing off the #4 hatch cover. The crew made an effort to enter the engine room to look for survivors, but sulphur fumes overwhelmed them. The vessel quickly filled with black and bluish smoke, rolled to starboard, and then listed heavily to port. The survivors among the six officers, twenty-five men, and four armed guards left the ship within ten minutes in two boats. The *Liberator* sank on her port side at about 1040. The USS *Umpqua* (ATO-25), a witness to the sinking, picked up the survivors about an hour after the attack. The officers and crew landed at Morehead City, North Carolina. The watch below consisting of one officer and four men died in the torpedo explosion.

NSS; WACR; WCSR; AG; WJ; Rohwer, p. 86.

OAKMAR

D: 3-20-42   YB: 1920
T: 1425   Tn: 5,766
Pos: 36.21 N / 68.50 W   Dr: 28 ft.
Ow: Calmar SS Co.   C: 8,300 tons manganese ore, jute,
Op: Calmar SS Co.   rubber
M: Nolan Eugene Fleming   P: steam
A: unarmed   S: 11.2

The *Oakmar* sailed from Port-of-Spain, Trinidad, to Boston, Massachusetts. While the ship maintained a zigzag pattern in heavy seas, lookouts spotted the *U-71* (Flachsenberg) surfacing off the starboard quarter. Because of the weather, the *U-71* could not use its deck gun and advanced on the surface firing its machine gun into the bridge and superstructure of the freighter. The master ordered the ship stopped and the eight officers, twenty-seven men, and one passenger began to abandon ship in two boats. The *U-71* fired a torpedo that missed. A second torpedo struck forward of the bridge after the lifeboats reached the water. The Greek SS *Stavros* rescued the thirty survivors in the starboard lifeboat and landed them in Bermuda. The fate of the remaining two officers and four men is unknown. Two were seen in the water and could not be rescued because of the heavy seas. The other four lowered the port lifeboat and were never seen again. The *U-71* finished off the *Oakmar* with about thirty-five shells, and she sank at 1455.

NSS; WACR; WCSR; WJ; Rohwer, p. 86, places the attack at 36.22 N / 68.50 W.

ESSO NASHVILLE

D:	3-21-42	YB:	1940
T:	0015	Tn:	7,943
Pos:	33.35 N / 77.22 W	Dr:	29 ft. 2 in.
Ow:	Standard Oil Co. of N. J.	C:	106,718 bbls. fuel oil
Op:	Standard Oil Co. of N. J.	P:	steam
M:	Edward V. Peters	S:	13
A:	unarmed		

On 16 March, the tanker *Esso Nashville* departed Port Arthur, Texas, bound for New Haven, Connecticut. The *Esso Nashville* steamed to her destination on a nonevasive course. Off the Frying Pan Lightship Buoy, the *U-124* (Mohr) fired a torpedo from about 900 yards that struck the starboard side of the tanker forward of the crew quarters and about five feet from the stem. This torpedo did not detonate. The *U-124* fired a second torpedo a minute later that struck the tanker amidships about ten feet below the waterline. The explosion lifted the vessel out of the water, broke the tanker's back, and showered the deck with hot oil. Before abandoning ship, most of the crew of eight officers and twenty-nine men donned rubber lifesuits. They lowered all four lifeboats at 0030. On 21 March, the USS *McKean* (DD-784) picked up two lifeboats containing eight survivors and took them to Norfolk, Virginia. The USCG cutter *Tallapoosa* (WPG-52) rescued twenty-one crewmen and landed them in Savannah. The USCG cutter *Agassiz* (WPC-126) rescued the remaining eight survivors, including the master who had fallen into the water and climbed back on board the ship. These men landed at Southport, North Carolina. For several hours only deck plating and pipe lines held the ship together. After the vessel split completely in two, the after end of the tanker remained afloat and was towed to Morehead City by the fleet tug *Umpqua* (ATO-25). Fitted with a new bow, the tanker went back into service in March 1943. All hands survived the attack.

NSS; WACR; WCSR; RWCS; WJ; *Ships of the Esso Fleet*, pp. 155-60.

ATLANTIC SUN

D:	3-21-42	YB:	1941
T:	0245	Tn:	11,355
Pos:	33.32 N / 77.26 W	Dr:	31 ft.
Ow:	Sun Oil Co.	C:	156,840 bbls. crude
Op:	Sun Oil Co.	P:	diesel
M:	Robert Linwood Montague	S:	15
A:	1-5"; 4-30 cal.		

On 16 March, the *Atlantic Sun* departed Beaumont, Texas, en route to Marcus Hook, Pennsylvania. Off the Beaufort Sea Buoy, the *U-124* (Mohr) spotted the tanker but could not get into a favorable firing position because of the tanker's speed. As a last resort, the U-boat fired a torpedo at about 4,000 yards. This torpedo struck the tanker on the starboard side in the forward tank but did not severely damage the ship. The master managed to get his vessel to Beaufort, North Carolina, to receive temporary repairs. None of the crew of eight officers, thirty-two men, and five armed guards reported any injuries.

WACR; WCSR; WJ; AG; Rohwer, p. 86, places the attack at 33.34 N / 77.25 W; *War Action Casualties*, p. 36.

NAECO

D:	3-22-42	YB:	1918
T:	0315	Tn:	5,372
Pos:	33.59 N / 76.40 W	Dr:	26 ft.
Ow:	Pennsylvania Shipping Co.	C:	72,000 bbls. kerosene, heating
Op:	Pennsylvania Shipping Co.		oil
M:	Emil H. Engelbrecht	P:	steam
A:	unarmed	S:	10.5

On 16 March, the *Naeco* weighed anchor at Houston, Texas, en route to Seawarren, New Jersey. The *U-124* (Mohr) pursued the tanker after abandoning another attack. The first torpedo, fired from the bow tube, missed. Mohr fired his last torpedo from about 700 yards and struck the tanker just aft of the mast. The explosion created a fireball 100 yards high. Fire engulfed the entire amidships superstructure, and burning oil spurted out over the surrounding sea. The chief engineer shut off the engine and turned on the steam smothering system. Meanwhile, the remnants of the crew of eight officers and thirty men gathered on deck to abandon ship. The explosion and fire destroyed two of the four lifeboats. With headway still on the ship, crewmen launched the #4 lifeboat, but it swamped when it touched the water. The #3 lifeboat got away with ten survivors. The USCG *Dione* (WPC-107) rescued the ten men in the lifeboat and two more from the sea. The minesweeper USS *Osprey* (AM-56) rescued one seaman and four bodies from a life raft. A boatswain, who returned

to the ship, was taken off by the USS *Umpqua* (ATO-25). All the survivors landed at Morehead City, North Carolina. Five officers and nineteen men perished in the attack. The tanker broke in half and the stern section sank about 0830. The USS *Roper* (DD-147) then sank the bow section that afternoon.

NSS; WACR; WCSR; RWCS; WJ; *War Action Casualties*, p. 38.

MUSKOGEE

D:	3-22-42	YB:	1913
T:	1155	Tn:	7,034
Pos:	28.00 N / 58.00 W	Dr:	unknown
Ow:	Muskogee Steamship Corp.	C:	67,265 bbls. heavy crude oil
Op:	Standard Oil Co.	P:	steam
M:	William W. Betts	S:	unknown
A:	unarmed		

On 13 March, the *Muskogee* sailed from Trinidad, BWI, to Halifax, Nova Scotia. The *U-123* (Hardegen) intercepted the tanker and made the first attack with one of the stern tubes just after 1100. Missing with this shot, Hardegen maneuvered for a second shot but had difficulty lining up the steamer for an attack because of her zigzagging course and the moderately heavy seas. The *U-123*'s second shot hit the tanker deep in the engine room and caused the ship to sink rapidly within twenty minutes. A dozen or so men managed to climb on two rafts that floated free of the ship, and Hardegen questioned them before he left the scene. None of the seven officers and twenty-seven men, however, survived the attack. Those who managed to leave the ship were never seen again.

WACR; WCSR; WJ; Rohwer, p. 87; Gannon, p. 318; *War Action Casualties*, p. 33.

DIXIE ARROW

D:	3-26-42	YB:	1921
T:	0800	Tn:	8,046
Pos:	34.59 N / 75.33 W	Dr:	28 ft. 4 in.
Ow:	Socony-Vacuum Oil Co.	C:	86,136 bbls. crude oil
Op:	Socony-Vacuum Oil Co.	P:	steam
M:	Anders M. Johanson	S:	11
A:	unarmed		

The *Dixie Arrow* was torpedoed by the *U-71* (Flachsenberg) about twelve miles off the Diamond Shoals Lighted Buoy while en route from Texas City, Texas, to Paulsboro, New Jersey. The tanker proceeded on a zigzag pattern with 45° tacks. The *U-71* fired two torpedoes; one hit amidships and the second struck between the mast and the smokestack. The first torpedo destroyed the deckhouse, killing all the deck officers and several other men. The second torpedo broke the ship in half. The engine room suffered no damage except the extinguishing of the lights. The forward part of the ship became enveloped in flames almost at once, and the master ordered the engines stopped. The helmsman then turned the ship into the wind to allow the eight men on the forecastle to escape the flames and to jump overboard. The helmsman stayed at his post long enough to allow these men to escape, but he died when the flames blew back toward the bridge. Fire destroyed the #1 and #2 boats and the #3 boat swamped. The last boat got away with eight men. The USS *Tarbell* (DD-142) picked up these eight men and fourteen others in the water and landed them at Morehead City, North Carolina. The ship's complement consisted of eight officers and twenty-five men. Four officers and seven men either burned to death or drowned in the attack. The *Dixie Arrow* sank at 0950.

The helmsman, Oscar G. Chappell, won the Merchant Marine Distinguished Service Medal. NSS; WACR; WCSR; The WJ of *U-71* states that two torpedoes were fired and the casualty reports state three. *New York Times*, 29 March 1942; *New York Herald Tribune*, 29 March 1942; Rohwer, p. 87, places the attack at 34.55 N / 75.02 W; *War Action Casualties*, p. 39.

CITY OF NEW YORK

D:	3-29-42	YB:	1930
T:	1245	Tn:	8,272
Pos:	35.16 N / 74.25 W	Dr:	25 ft.
Ow:	American South African Line	C:	6,612 tons ore, wool, skins,
Op:	American South African Line		asbestos
M:	George T. Sullivan	P:	diesel
A:	1-4"; 4-50 cal.; 4-30 cal.	S:	14

The *City of New York* sailed from Cape Town, South Africa, via Port-of-Spain, Trinidad, to New York. The *U-160* (Lassen) intercepted the freighter forty miles east of Cape Hatteras, while she steamed in twenty-foot seas on a nonevasive course. Lookouts spotted the *U-160*'s first torpedo that struck the #3 hold just below the bridge on the port side at the waterline. The helmsman brought the ship into the wind, and the watch below secured the engines. The armed guards loaded the four-inch gun on the poop, trained it, and fired twelve shots at the U-boat's periscope. The submarine circled the stern at a distance of about 250 yards, and off the starboard quarter fired a second torpedo that struck the starboard side at the #4 hold, sinking the ship within minutes. The master ordered the thirteen officers, seventy men, nine armed guards, and forty-one passengers on board to abandon ship. They left the freighter in four boats, and the gun crew jumped off the ship as water reached the after deck. The USS *Roper* (DD-147) and the USS *Acushnet* (ATO-63) picked up three boats and took the survivors to Norfolk. A plane spotted the fourth boat with nine passengers and crew members, including two bodies, and they were brought into

Lewes, Delaware, by a naval vessel fourteen days after the attack. The dead included one armed guard, sixteen of the ship's crew, and seven passengers.

The figures for the ship's complement and casualties conflict within the sources. NSS; WACR; WCSR; RWCS; AG; WJ; Rohwer, p. 87.

EFFINGHAM

D:	3-30-42	YB:	1919
T:	2230	Tn:	6,421
Pos:	70.28 N / 35.44 E	Dr:	26 ft. 2 in.
Ow:	Lykes Bros. SS Co.	C:	4,672 tons general, explosives
Op:	Lykes Bros. SS Co.	P:	steam
M:	Charles H. Hewlett	S:	6.5
A:	1-4"; 4-50 cal.; 4-30 cal.		

The *Effingham* sailed from Boston, Massachusetts, to Murmansk, USSR, via Reykjavik, Iceland. After the freighter joined Convoy PQ-13 in Iceland, heavy weather caused her to straggle ninety miles behind the formation. The *U-435* (Strelow) spotted the lone vessel in a snow squall. The U-boat missed with the first two torpedoes; however, the third torpedo struck the freighter amidships on the port side at the #4 hold. The complement of eight officers, twenty-six men, and nine armed guards immediately began to abandon the ship. In the rough seas the crew launched the #1 and #3 lifeboats from the lee side of the ship. The explosion started a fire that left the ship completely ablaze. Nearly two hours later the fire reached one of the holds carrying ammunition, causing the ship to explode and sink. The two boats carried all but two of the crew, both of whom drowned trying to escape the ship. The minesweeper HMS *Harrier* (N-71) picked up the #1 lifeboat with the master, the chief mate, and fifteen men, after thirty-two hours. Six men in this boat later died of exposure. Sixty-five hours after the attack a Russian patrol boat discovered the #3 lifeboat containing eleven men and three of the armed guards. Four men in this boat also died of exposure. The total number of dead included one armed guard and eleven of the ship's crew. All the survivors landed in Murmansk.

WACR; WCSR; WJ; AG; Rohwer, p. 197.

MENOMINEE

D:	3-31-42	YB:	1919
T:	0210	Tn:	441
Pos:	37.34 N / 75.25 W	Dr:	16 ft.
Ow:	Southern Transportation Co.	C:	none
Op:	Southern Transportation Co.	P:	steam
M:	Leslie F. Haynie	S:	5.0
A:	unarmed		

The tug *Menominee* sailed from Norfolk, Virginia, to Stamford, Connecticut, towing three barges with a cargo of 2,959 tons of coal and 441,000 board feet of dunnage. About fifty miles from the mouth of the Chesapeake Bay, the *U-754* (Oestermann) surprised the tug and her tow, the barges *Allegheny*, *Barnegat*, and *Ontario*. The submarine was first spotted coming from the port bow of the tug. At about fifty feet, the *U-754* fired three rounds: one entered the captain's cabin through a window and destroyed the ship's telephone and radio equipment, then passed through the starboard bulkhead without exploding. The tug immediately cut loose the barges and tried to escape at eleven knots. The submarine came along the port side of the barges and fired three or four rounds at each barge, then went up the starboard side of the barges and down the port side, again firing as it went. By this time the tug had steamed about one mile astern of the last barge. The submarine then turned to chase the tug, firing its deck gun and missing with eight shots. The *U-754* increased its speed to about sixteen knots and overhauled the tug. The tug's master ordered the engines stopped, hoping his crew would be allowed to abandon ship. The submarine fired four shells. The last one exploded amidships near the paint locker, blowing the tug out of the water and setting her afire. The crew cut loose two rafts and abandoned ship by jumping overboard; seven men swam to one raft, but only two of them survived. After the *Menominee* sank, the U-boat returned to the barges, firing about a dozen more shells. The tug *Menominee* and the barges *Allegheny* and *Barnegat* all sank. The barge *Ontario*, because of the cargo of dunnage, remained afloat. The *Ontario*'s crew of three men abandoned the barge. The Coast Guard motor lifeboat #4063 from the Metomkin Inlet Lifeboat Station picked them up one mile offshore. The other barge crews abandoned their barges and boarded the *Ontario* and were likewise taken off by this motor lifeboat. The Coast Guard boat took the nine survivors to Norfolk on 1 April. The tanker *Northern Sun* landed the two survivors from the tug at the Lewes, Delaware, Coast Guard station. Only two of the tug's crew of five officers and thirteen men survived. All nine men on the barges survived the attack.

NSS; WACR; WCSR; WJ; *Coast Guard at War*, p. 23; Rohwer, p. 88.

T. C. McCOBB

D:	3-31-42	YB:	1936
T:	1615	Tn:	7,451
Pos:	07.10 N / 45.20 W	Dr:	20 ft.
Ow:	Standard Oil Co. of N. J.	C:	water ballast
Op:	Standard Oil Co. of N. J.	P:	steam
M:	Robert Overbeck	S:	12
A:	unarmed		

The *T. C. McCobb*, steaming on a zigzag pattern, was attacked by the Italian submarine *Pietro Calvi* (Olivieri) en route from Buenos Aires, Argentina, to Caripito, Venezuela. A shot from the *Calvi*'s deck gun came from five miles dead astern before lookouts even spotted the enemy. The master ordered all speed possible in an attempt to outrun the submarine. The radio operator sent distress signals, and the master emptied the ship's water ballast. The submarine began firing at the rate of once every two minutes for about one-half hour and then stopped for about forty minutes to close the distance between the two. Gaining on the tanker, the submarine resumed fire. When the Italian gunners found the range, they began firing one shot per minute. The *Calvi* fired about twenty-eight rounds before the tanker's crew abandoned ship. At this point only five shells had struck the tanker. The submarine approached close aboard on the starboard quarter and fired four torpedoes. Two struck in the engine room aft while two hit amidships, and the *T. C. McCobb* sank at about 2100. The crew of eight officers and thirty-one men left the ship in three boats, but the #2 boat sank after launching because of shrapnel damage. Five of the men transferred to the #3 boat, and the #1 boat later took the remaining men out. At least three others found a raft. The #3 lifeboat with fifteen men made sail for Surinam. On 8 April, the Panamanian SS *Santa Monica* rescued the survivors in the #3 boat. The Norwegian SS *Marpesia* rescued the nineteen survivors in the #1 lifeboat off Surinam two days later. The raft with three men landed after forty-six days at sea. Only one man survived the ordeal; the other two died of exposure. A total of two officers and two men died in the attack. Two died of exposure, one died from shellfire, and the last drowned.

NSS; WACR; WCSR; RWCS; Rohwer, p. 88; *War Action Casualties*, p. 40.

TIGER

D:	3-31-42	YB:	1917
T:	2318	Tn:	5,992
Pos:	36.50 N / 75.49 W	Dr:	28 ft. 9 in.
Ow:	Socony-Vacuum Oil Co.	C:	64,321 bbls. #1 Navy fuel oil
Op:	Socony-Vacuum Oil Co.	P:	steam
M:	Rein S. Schnore	S:	8
A:	unarmed		

On 21 March, the *Tiger* sailed from Aruba, NWI, to Norfolk, Virginia. She had just reduced speed, turned on her dimmed running lights, and signaled with blinkers to pick up a pilot. The *U-754* (Oestermann) fired a three-torpedo spread, and all missed the tanker. The lookouts on board the *Tiger* shortly thereafter spotted the submarine on the surface, and the master ordered hard left rudder and increased speed to full speed ahead. The *U-754* fired a fourth torpedo from the surface because the water was shallow. The torpedo struck as the vessel swung, hitting the tanker on the starboard side just aft of amidships and well below the waterline. The explosion blew oil over the entire ship. The stern began to settle immediately, and the crew of eight officers and twenty-eight men, as well as six passengers (a Navy gun crew in transit), abandoned ship. The explosion killed one of the firemen on watch below. The remaining persons on board abandoned the ship in three lifeboats in orderly fashion and were rescued two hours later by the *YP-52*, which landed them at Norfolk. A salvage crew boarded the *Tiger* the next day. Later the Navy tug *Relief* (SP-2170) and the USCG cutter *Jackson* (WPC-142) took her in tow, but she sank on 2 April, before reaching Norfolk.

NSS; WACR; WCSR; RWCS; WJ; *New York Herald Tribune*, 5 April 1942; Rohwer, p. 88; *War Action Casualties*, p. 41; *Assistance*, 2:153.

LIEBRE

D:	4-2-42	YB:	1921
T:	0022	Tn:	7,057
Pos:	34.11 N / 76.08 W	Dr:	13 ft. 1 in.
Ow:	Socony-Vacuum Oil Co.	C:	water ballast
Op:	Socony-Vacuum Oil Co.	P:	steam
M:	Frank C. Girardeau	S:	10.5
A:	unarmed		

On 30 March, the *Liebre* sailed from New York to Beaumont, Texas. As she steamed on a zigzag course, the *U-123* (Hardegen) missed with its first torpedo and surfaced for an attack. The German gun crew began shelling the vessel from the port side. The submarine fired between twenty and thirty rounds and hit the tanker with about ten shells. Several of these shells hit the midships house, crew

quarters, and deck gear. Three shells penetrated the hull, and one of these hit the generator. When the attack began, the general alarm sent the crew to their stations, and fifteen minutes later the master had the engines secured and ordered the crew to abandon ship. The radio operator sent an SOS and received an acknowledgment. The appearance of the British motor torpedo boat MTB-332 hastened the departure of the *U-123* without finishing off the tanker. Most of the crew of eight officers and twenty-six men abandoned the ship in two lifeboats. The #1 boat contained the master and fifteen men, and the #4 boat held the chief engineer and nine more men. A Coast Guard boat towed the boats back to the ship, and the crew reboarded her at 0825. The tug *Resolute* and the British trawler *St. Zeno* (FY-280) towed the *Liebre* into Morehead City, North Carolina, arriving there on 4 April. One officer and eight men perished. Seven drowned when they dove overboard and two died of shrapnel injuries.

The *Liebre* became the USS *Meredosia* (IX-193). NSS; WACR; WCSR; WJ; *War Action Casualties*, p. 42; Gannon, p. 332; DANFS, 4:334.

DAVID H. ATWATER

D:	4-2-42	YB:	1919
T:	2115	Tn:	2,438
Pos:	37.37 N / 75.10 W	Dr:	23 ft. 5 in.
Ow:	Atwacoal Transportation Co.	C:	3,911 tons coal
Op:	Atwacoal Transportation Co.	P:	steam
M:	William Keith Webster	S:	9.0
A:	unarmed		

The *U-552* (Topp) attacked the freighter *David H. Atwater* east of Chincoteague Inlet, Virginia, while she was en route from Norfolk to Fall River, Massachusetts. In order to attack the ship at night, Topp followed her underwater, surfaced, and began to shell the freighter without warning, never allowing the crew to abandon ship. At 600 yards Topp fired ninety-three shots at the helpless freighter, struck her over fifty times, and set her on fire. The *Atwater* sank in forty-five minutes. The crew of eight officers and nineteen men were unable to abandon ship in the boats, and most jumped in the water and drowned. All the officers died, and only three men who dove overboard and swam to an empty lifeboat survived the attack. Coast Guard boat #218 rescued these men and took them to Chincoteague Inlet.

WACR; WCSR; WJ.

EXHIBITOR

D: 4-3-42   YB: 1940
T: 1220   Tn: 6,736
Pos: Beaumont Cut near Calcutta   Dr: 24 ft.
Ow: American Export Lines   C: 6,153 tons general, tea
Op: American Export Lines   P: steam
M: Ebert C. Wilson Jr.   S: 7
A: 1-4"; 4-50 cal.

On 3 April, the *Exhibitor* weighed anchor and entered Beaumont Cut, near Calcutta, India, en route to Colombo, Ceylon. At about 1220, a Japanese flying boat approached on the port side at 4,500 feet and dropped two bombs. The first bomb fell ten yards off the port quarter, and the second pierced the #6 hatch and exploded against the tween deck hatch coaming. This latter explosion caused a fire and tore a hole two feet by three feet in the ship's starboard side. The crew managed to put out the fire in about twenty minutes. The plane returned, flying low from the starboard quarter. As it neared the ship, the gunners opened fire with the .50 caliber machine guns and drove the plane away. Only four of the complement of eight officers, thirty-five men, and nine armed guards reported any injury during the attack. After emergency repairs the ship steamed back to Calcutta.

NSS; WACR; WCSR; AG; McCoy, *Nor Death Dismay*, p. 40, states the crew was forty-six merchant crew and twelve naval gun crew; Carse, pp. 43-46.

OTHO

D: 4-3-42   YB: 1920
T: 0554   Tn: 4,839
Pos: 36.25 N / 71.57 W   Dr: 24 ft.
Ow: American-West African Lines   C: 6,446 tons palm oil, tin,
Op: American-West African Lines   manganese ore
M: John Makkinje   P: steam
A: 1-4"; 4-50 cal.   S: 9.5

The *Otho* was torpedoed by the *U-754* (Oestermann) while en route from Takoradi, Gold Coast, to Philadelphia, Pennsylvania. The ship proceeded on a nonevasive course in moderately rough seas. The *U-754* approached and fired a single torpedo that struck the starboard side directly below the stack at the bulkhead between the #3 tank and the engine room. The explosion severely damaged the vessel and owing to the nature of the cargo she sank within eleven minutes. Most of the *Otho*'s ten officers, twenty-six men, ten armed guards and seven passengers left the ship in five minutes in three boats and a raft. The USS *Zircon* (PY-16) rescued three officers, nine men, one armed guard, and three passengers five days after the attack. Twenty-two days later, the Norwegian

MV *Gallia* picked up six other survivors (one seaman and five of the naval gun crew) on a raft. The gun crew ensign, who was among these men, died hours after the rescue. The other boat was never found. Seven officers, sixteen men, four armed guards, and four passengers died.

NSS; WACR indicates the owner and operator of the vessel was the Barber SS Line; WCSR; RWCS; AG; WJ; *Pilot*, 12 June 1942; Rohwer, p. 88, places the attack at 36.25 N / 72.22 W.

WEST IRMO

D:	4-3-42	YB:	1919
T:	1935	Tn:	5,775
Pos:	2.10 N / 5.50 W	Dr:	20 ft.
Ow:	American-West African Line	C:	3,800 tons general
Op:	American-West African Line	P:	steam
M:	Torleif C. Selness	S:	7
A:	1-5"; 4-30 cal.		

The *West Irmo* departed from Marshall, Liberia, en route to Takoradi, Gold Coast. The vessel proceeded under escort but did not zigzag as directed by the escorting vessel, the HMS *Copinsay* (T-147). The *Copinsay*, about two miles off the starboard quarter, ordered the *West Irmo* to reduce speed to allow the escort vessel to close. Thirty-five minutes later a torpedo fired from the *U-505* (Loewe) struck the port side at the #1 hold. The blast tore the bow off the vessel and created a hole twenty feet long and eighteen feet wide and killed ten African longshoremen seated on the #1 hatch. The watch below secured the engines immediately, and the helmsman turned the rudder hard right. The *West Irmo*'s complement of nine officers, twenty-seven men, and eight armed guards, along with the fifty-five surviving African longshoremen, abandoned ship at 2005. Launching four boats, all ninety-nine survivors were taken on board the *Copinsay* at 2130. On 4 April, the *Copinsay* made an effort to tow the *West Irmo* stern first. The escort abandoned the effort when the ship settled to her fore deck and her rudder and propeller protruded from the water. As the water claimed the vessel, the *Copinsay* dropped a depth charge to hasten her sinking. The only casualties came from the initial explosion, which killed the ten longshoremen seated on the hatch.

NSS; WACR; WCSR; AG; Rohwer, p. 88, places the attack at 02.10 N / 05.35 W.

COMOL RICO

D: 4-4-42   YB: 1919
T: 1506   Tn: 5,034
Pos: 20.46 N / 66.46 W   Dr: 25 ft. 2 in.
Ow: Commercial Molasses Corp.   C: 8,068 tons bulk molasses
Op: Commercial Molasses Corp.   P: steam
M: Peter Hansen Lang   S: 9
A: 1-4"; 2-50 cal.; 2-30 cal.

On 3 April, the *Comol Rico* sailed from Humacoa, Puerto Rico, to Boston, Massachusetts. The tanker proceeded on a nonevasive course, making an easy target for the *U-154* (Kölle). Lookouts spotted a torpedo 150 feet from the tanker. The helmsman put the wheel over hard left, but it struck amidships and the tanker began to sink quickly. The gun crew failed to offer any defensive fire because the ship sank in seven minutes. The surviving members of the complement of eight officers, twenty-eight men, and six armed guards got away in one lifeboat and on three rafts within minutes. A second torpedo struck just as the boats left. The blast from the torpedoes blew away the whole side and killed an officer and two men on watch below. The survivors spotted a passenger ship and sent up flares. The ship, however, when about three miles off, turned and steamed in the opposite direction. On 6 April, a Navy patrol plane spotted the survivors and directed the USS *Sturtevant* (DD-240) to pick them up. The thirty-nine survivors landed at San Juan, Puerto Rico.

The men criticized the company's policy requiring its ships to steam with one boiler under natural draft. Although this saved operating expenses, it naturally made more smoke for a submarine to spot. NSS; WACR; WCSR; AG; *Pilot*, 29 Mary 1942; Rohwer, p. 88; *War Action Casualties*, p. 43.

BYRON D. BENSON

D: 4-4-42   YB: 1921
T: 2140   Tn: 7,953
Pos: 36.08 N / 75.32 W   Dr: 28 ft. 3 in.
Ow: Tide Water Associated Oil Co.   C: 91,500 bbls. crude oil
Op: Tide Water Associated Oil Co.   P: steam
M: John MacMillan   S: 6.0
A: unarmed

On 27 March, the *Byron D. Benson* sailed from Port Arthur, Texas, to Bayonne, New Jersey, in consort with another tanker, the *Gulf of Mexico*, and two escort vessels. About eight miles off Currituck Inlet, the *U-552* (Topp) fired a torpedo at 1,000 yards distance, hitting the vessel amidships between the #7 and #8 tanks. The explosion sent burning oil hundreds of feet in the air and all over the after part of the ship. The crew of eight officers and twenty-nine men began abandoning the ship without orders. The fire caused a great deal of panic among the crew as they tried to leave the burning ship. The engines, however, were never secured, and the boats went into the water with the vessel still moving at six knots. With flaming oil spewing out of the ship's side, two lifeboats got away. One, with about ten persons in it including the master, drifted into flaming water. Four officers and twenty-four men of the crew got away in the #4 port lifeboat and a raft. The USS *Hamilton* (DMS-18) rescued the men in the boat, and the HMS *Norwich City* (FY-229) rescued a single man on a raft. All the survivors landed at Norfolk, Virginia. Four officers and five men perished in the inferno caused by the burning oil. The tanker did not sink until three days later.

NSS; WACR; WCSR; RWCS; WJ; Rohwer, p. 88; *War Action Casualties*, p. 44.

CATAHOULA

D:	4-5-42	YB:	1920
T:	1725	Tn:	5,030
Pos:	19.16 N / 68.12 W	Dr:	26 ft. 6 in.
Ow:	Cuba Distilling Co.	C:	molasses, full load
Op:	Cuba Distilling Co.	P:	steam
M:	Gunvald B. Johannesen	S:	10.5
A:	1-4"; 4-50 cal.; 2-30 cal.		

On 4 April, the SS *Catahoula* sailed from San Pedro de Macorís, Dominican Republic, to Wilmington, Delaware. The *U-154* (Kölle) attacked the tanker about 100 miles into the voyage. The first torpedo hit the ship on the port side at the #4 cargo hatch. A terrific explosion blew molasses over the length of the vessel. The blast ripped up deck plates, destroyed the catwalk to the poop deck, and damaged the engine room bulkhead, causing this compartment to flood. The explosion also destroyed the #4 lifeboat and the #4 raft. The master ordered the helmsman to turn the wheel hard right and sounded general quarters while the radio operator sent an SOS. The Navy gun crew raced to their battle stations, manned the machine guns, and shot at the submarine's periscope. Four minutes after the first torpedo struck, a second torpedo hit the tanker about ten feet forward of the bridge on the starboard side. The ship sank about a minute later. The starboard boats, not away from the ship, swamped as the ship rolled over. Twenty-five men in the complement of eight officers, thirty men, and seven armed guards managed to successfully launch the #2 port lifeboat. Thirteen others cleared the ship on a life raft. Two of the crew died in the initial blast and five drowned. A bomber sighted the survivors on 5 April, and the next day the USS *Sturtevant* (DD-240) rescued the surviving seven officers, seven gun crew, and twenty-four men.

The number of armed guards conflicts within the sources. NSS; WACR; WCSR; AG.

BIDWELL

D:	4-6-42	YB:	1920
T:	0120	Tn:	6,837
Pos:	34.25 N / 75.57 W	Dr:	27 ft. 1 in.
Ow:	Sun Oil Co. of N. J.	C:	83,144 bbls. fuel oil
Op:	Sun Oil Co. of N. J.	P:	diesel
M:	S. Berg Hegglund	S:	10.5
A:	unarmed		

On 29 March, the *Bidwell* departed Corpus Christi, Texas, en route to New York. About thirty miles east of Cape Lookout, the *U-160* (Lassen) attacked the ship as she proceeded up the coast on a zigzagging course. A single torpedo hit the port side amidships near the waterline. The explosion sent up a column of flame 150 feet in the air, tore a hole approximately 20 feet in diameter through the side and deck, and ripped open the #7 and #8 tanks and the summer tanks below them. The blast threw oil over the entire length of the ship, but it burned for only a short period. After being showered with burning oil, the second mate on the bridge jumped overboard. To escape oil burning on the surface, the chief engineer kept the engines running. The explosion also damaged the steering gear so that the ship ran in circles for nearly an hour. The chief engineer stopped some of the men aft from lowering the #3 boat to abandon ship. Thirty minutes later he had the auxiliary steering gear working. Because of the destroyed communications and the steam that obscured their view, the master and five men lowered a boat to drift aft. They also hoped to have the engines stopped in order to rescue the second mate. At about 0300, two destroyers appeared astern and offered assistance, but by this time the crew had the ship under control. The captain's boat returned, having had no luck finding the second mate. All of the ship's complement of eight officers and twenty-five men, with the exception of the second mate, survived. The ship proceeded to Hampton Roads at eight knots under her own power and, after discharging her cargo, was repaired and returned to service.

NSS; WACR; WJ; Rohwer, p. 88; *War Action Casualties*, p. 48.

BIENVILLE

D:	4-6-42	YB:	1920
T:	0640	Tn:	5,492
Pos:	17.50 N / 84.50 E	Dr:	26 ft. 3 in.
Ow:	Waterman SS Corp.	C:	2,500 tons manganese ore, 5,000
Op:	American Export Lines		tons jute gunnies, general cargo
M:	Robert Spearing	P:	steam
A:	unarmed	S:	9.5

About thirty-five miles off the coast of India two Japanese airplanes and a Japanese cruiser attacked the *Bienville* as she steamed from Calcutta, India, to Colombo, Ceylon. The cruiser with an aircraft carrier astern and two destroyers on each beam closed on the freighter. At 0618 lookouts spotted two planes approaching at about 1,500 feet. They dropped four bombs: one struck the forward port corner of the #2 hatch and set the cargo afire, another struck close alongside, and two more missed completely astern. At 0640 the cruiser moved toward the vessel and opened fire from a distance of about one mile. The cruiser fired five turret salvos at the rate of one every two or three minutes and hit the ship five times. The radio operator sent distress signals but received no reply. While under attack, the engineer unsuccessfully tried to lay a smoke screen from the stack. The crew of nine officers and thirty-two men abandoned the vessel about forty-five minutes after the attack began. By this time shellfire had destroyed three of the lifeboats and the fourth fell into the water. The shells killed many of the men as they tried to abandon the ship. The crew began jumping into the sea as the ship sank. Three of the four rafts floated free, allowing many to save their lives. The survivors drifted for three hours until fishing craft rescued them and put them ashore. Five officers and nineteen men died from the shellfire, with five of these men dying after being rescued.

The casualty and crew numbers conflict within the sources. NSS; WACR; WCSR.

SELMA CITY

D:	4-6-42	YB:	1921
T:	0645	Tn:	5,686
Pos:	17.40 N / 83.20 E	Dr:	17 ft. 10 in.
Ow:	Isthmian SS Co.	C:	311 tons general, 150 tons case
Op:	Isthmian SS Co.		oil and lube oil
M:	John Michael Griffin	P:	steam
A:	unarmed	S:	10.0

Japanese bombers attacked the *Selma City* in the Bay of Bengal while en route from Colombia to Calcutta, via Vizagapatam, India. About twenty-five miles off Vizagapatam, a single-engined amphibian Japanese plane approached and released two bombs. One bomb missed off the starboard side; the other hit near the engine room uptake, pierced the deck and exploded over the engine room storeroom. Fire broke out and spread rapidly, while the engine room slowly flooded. The plane made a second low-level pass and dropped a bomb on the starboard side that damaged the boiler room and other equipment. The crew of eight officers and twenty-one men fought the fire by forming a bucket brigade. At 1130 the master ordered the ship abandoned. As the men climbed into the four boats, two Japanese planes began circling the ship. One plane dropped two bombs: one hit the wheelhouse and the other struck the ship forward. The second plane dropped four bombs, but all missed. A burst of machine gun fire in the general direction of the loaded lifeboats signaled them to leave. The motor lifeboat towed the others about twenty miles to Vizagapatam, where they landed at 1850. All hands survived, and only two reported slight injuries from bomb fragments. The crew left the ship ablaze and sinking. She sank forty hours after the initial attack began.

NSS; WACR; WCSR.

EXMOOR

D:	4-6-42	YB:	1919
T:	0915	Tn:	4,986
Pos:	19.53 N / 86.30 E	Dr:	25 ft. 1 in.
Ow:	American Export Lines	C:	3,800 tons manganese ore and
Op:	American Export Lines		jute
M:	Ragnar F. Eklund	P:	steam
A:	unarmed	S:	11.5

The *Exmoor* proceeded with five other vessels in convoy, en route from Calcutta, India, to Colombo, Ceylon. When only a few hours from the Hooghly River, 250 miles south southwest of Calcutta, the ships were spotted by a Japanese seaplane, which then strafed two of the vessels in the group. At 0850 a force of three cruisers hove in sight on the northern horizon and opened fire at a range of three miles. The cruisers concentrated their fire on the armed merchantmen and within fifteen minutes put them out of action. The cruisers' shells struck the unarmed *Exmoor* with eight ten-inch and ten five-inch shells, while the vessels in the convoy attempted to hide and escape in a hastily devised smoke screen. The first salvo struck the bridge and blew the master off the deck. He returned and stayed on the bridge until the forward deck became submerged. Altogether the cruisers fired seventy or more rounds at the six victims and sank all the ships. The *Exmoor* was the last to receive their attention. Within fifteen minutes after the first shot struck the *Exmoor*, the crew of eight officers and twenty-nine men had abandoned the ship. The cruisers sailed through the ships to confirm the sinkings. All hands escaped in the #2 and #4 boats and reached Ceylon safely.

NSS; WACR; WCSR.

WASHINGTONIAN

D: 4-6-42
T: 1555
Pos: 07.25 N / 73.05 E
Ow: American-Hawaiian Line
Op: American-Hawaiian Line
M: Colman Raphael
A: unarmed

YB: 1919
Tn: 6,300
Dr: 11 ft.
C: 180 tons general, German tanks
P: steam
S: 12

The *Washingtonian* sailed from Suez to Colombo, Ceylon, via Calcutta, India. The ship was on a zigzag course when the *I-5* (Utsuki) attacked. Lookouts spotted a torpedo 500 yards away bearing down on the port side. The master ordered "Hard Right," but the slow merchantman did not answer fast enough. Two torpedoes struck the port side, at the #2 and #3 holds, six feet below the waterline. The torpedoes immediately set fire to the fuel tanks, and flames spread rapidly throughout the ship. At 1605 with the ship listing 25° to port, ten officers, twenty-nine men, and two passengers on board immediately cleared the ship in the two lifeboats. In less than a day they rowed to the Maldive Islands. They made two trips in native dhows to Male. On 20 April, all hands arrived safely at Cochin, India, where most of the men were hospitalized.

NSS; WACR; WCSR; Rohwer, p. 261.

OKLAHOMA

D: 4-8-42
T: 0200
Pos: 31.18 N / 80.59 W
Ow: Texas Co.
Op: Texas Co.
M: Theron P. Davenport
A: unarmed

YB: 1940
Tn: 9,264
Dr: 29 ft.
C: 105,000 bbls. refined oils
P: steam
S: 16

The *Oklahoma* was torpedoed twelve miles off Brunswick, Georgia, by the *U-123* (Hardegen). The ship sailed from Port Arthur, Texas, to Providence, Rhode Island, on the inshore route. Because the *Oklahoma* was proceeding on a nonevasive course at high speed, the *U-123* had trouble catching the tanker. Hardegen fired from 500 yards away, and the torpedo struck the tanker in the engine room. The ship quickly settled by the stern in water forty feet deep. The vessel's bow remained afloat for approximately forty-five minutes as the ship drifted about one mile to the northeast before settling on the bottom. When the stern touched bottom she listed about 3° to starboard, and the bow remained above the water. Eighteen of the crew of eight officers and twenty-nine men abandoned ship in three lifeboats. Hearing screams on board, the master and three others reboarded the ship. They found one of the officers critically wounded but could not reach the eighteen men apparently trapped below. The wounded officer subsequently died. While on board, the radio operator sent another SOS and the men abandoned the ship again. Hardegen, meanwhile, left the scene, caught and torpedoed the *Esso Baton Rouge*, and returned. He fired twelve rounds at the *Oklahoma*, striking the vessel five times. The tanker sank, but salvors later refloated her and towed her to port. After repairs at Chester, Pennsylvania, she returned to service. The eighteen men who initially abandoned ship were the only survivors, and they landed in Brunswick, Georgia, with the help of a Coast Guard boat.

NSS; WACR; WCSR; WJ; Rohwer, p. 89; Gannon, pp. 335-36.

ESSO BATON ROUGE

D:	4-8-42	YB:	1938
T:	0250	Tn:	7,989
Pos:	31.13 N / 80.05 W	Dr:	29 ft. 6 in.
Ow:	Standard Oil Co. of N. J.	C:	89,398 bbls. heating and
Op:	Standard Oil Co. of N. J.		lubricating oil
M:	James S. Poché	P:	steam
A:	unarmed	S:	13.5

The *Esso Baton Rouge* sailed from Baytown, Texas, to New York on an inshore route. The ship proceeded on a zigzagging course, but the bright moon silhouetted the tanker for the *U-123* (Hardegen). About fifteen miles northeast of St. Simons Island, Georgia, the U-boat fired a torpedo that struck the starboard side between the after bunkers and the engine room. A cloud of smoke and flame shot upwards, and the engine room and the crew's quarters flooded immediately. The vessel rapidly sank by the stern in forty feet of water and settled with the stern resting on the bottom. Most of the ship's eight officers and thirty-one men rushed to their lifeboat stations after the explosion and abandoned the vessel in lifeboats #1 and #3. The explosion killed two men in the engine room. A third man jumped overboard in a rubber suit and was never found. The men rowed until morning and met the survivors of the SS *Oklahoma*. Together they headed for the Georgia coast. The next morning a Coast Guard boat took them in tow and landed them at Brunswick. Hardegen had pronounced the ship a "total loss." The *Esso Baton Rouge*, however, was not finished. The salvage tug *Resolute* floated the vessel and with the help of the salvage tug *Willet* (ARS-12) towed the tanker to St. Simon Sound. She went back in service in November 1942.

NSS; WACR; WCSR; WJ; *Ships of the Esso Fleet*, pp. 177-185; Rohwer, p. 89, places the attack at 31.02 N / 80.53 W; *War Action Casualties*, p. 51.

ESPARTA

D: 4-9-42
T: 0115
Pos: 30.46 N / 81.11 W
Ow: United Fruit SS Corp.
Op: United Fruit SS Corp.
M: Alfred L. Case
A: unarmed

YB: 1904
Tn: 3,365
Dr: 19 ft. 1 in.
C: 1,450 tons bananas, coffee,
    general
P: steam
S: 12.5

The *Esparta* departed Puerto Cortés, Honduras, en route to New York. Fourteen miles south of Brunswick, Georgia, the *U-123* (Hardegen) attacked the freighter. The U-boat fired a torpedo that struck the starboard side at the #4 hatch. The explosion blew off the #3 and #4 hatch covers, damaged both sides of the ship, and released 1,200 pounds of ammonia gas used in the ship's refrigerating system. The escaping fumes forced several men to jump overboard. A small fire burned at the point of impact. The ship quickly listed 15° to starboard and began to sink rapidly by the stern. The radio operator sent distress signals and received acknowledgments. Ten minutes after the explosion most of the crew of eleven officers and twenty-nine men abandoned the ship in the #1 and #3 starboard lifeboats and the forward life raft. The master and radio operator left last, jumping overboard into a waiting life raft and later transferring to a lifeboat. A Navy patrol boat, the USS *Tyrer* (WIX-339), rescued thirty-nine members of the crew seven hours later. One crew member panicked after the explosion and jumped overboard to his death. The freighter's bow remained afloat and finally sank at 0315.

NSS; WACR; WCSR; WJ; Rohwer, p. 89.

MALCHACE

D: 4-9-42
T: 0158
Pos: 34.28 N / 75.56 W
Ow: Solvay Process Co.
Op: Solvay Process Co.
M: Arnt Magnusdale
A: unarmed

YB: 1920
Tn: 3,515
Dr: 20 ft.
C: 6,628 tons soda ash
P: steam
S: 10.7

The *Malchace* was torpedoed fifty miles from Cape Hatteras while en route from Baton Rouge, Louisiana, to Hopewell, Virginia. The *U-160* (Lassen) spotted the freighter's silhouette while she steamed a nonevasive course. The first torpedo fired by the U-boat struck the port side forward of the #4 hatch and just below the waterline. Fortunately, the cargo of soda ash cushioned the blast, and this lessened the effect of the explosion. The master stopped the engines,

The tanker *Dixie Arrow,* her back broken and burning, sinks twelve miles off the Diamond Shoals Lighted Buoy after being torpedoed by the *U-71.*

The *Esparta,* a United Fruit Company refrigeration ship, had accommodations for eighteen passengers. Used for the fruit trade, she could carry 45,000 stems of bananas. She met her untimely end when the *U-123* torpedoed her off Brunswick, Georgia.

and most of the crew of eight officers and twenty-one men mustered on deck. The master put the engines in reverse, and the fuel oil and steam lines were shut off from the deck. The explosion damaged the radio equipment, preventing the radio operator from sending a distress message. The conning tower of the *U-160* emerged about 300 feet dead astern about ten minutes after the first torpedo explosion. Lassen slowly circled the vessel waiting for the crew to abandon ship. The crew eventually left in the one good lifeboat and made fast a raft to this boat. Lassen then fired a second torpedo that did not detonate. A third torpedo hit the port side just below the waterline and aft of the #3 hatch, just as the last men prepared to leave the ship. This explosion blew four men off the poop deck into the water. Twenty-eight of the crew of twenty-nine abandoned the ship safely. One member of the crew drowned after diving overboard. The Mexican tanker *Faja De Oro* rescued the survivors about seven hours after the attack. The *Malchace* sank at approximately 0345.

NSS; WACR; WCSR; WJ; *Pilot,* 1 May 1942.

ATLAS

D:	4-9-42	YB:	1916
T:	0250	Tn:	7,137
Pos:	34.27 N / 76.16 W	Dr:	27 ft. 6 in.
Ow:	Socony-Vacuum Oil Co.	C:	84,239 bbls. gasoline
Op:	Socony-Vacuum Oil Co.	P:	steam
M:	Hamilton Gray	S:	11.0
A:	unarmed		

On 1 April, the *Atlas* sailed from Houston, Texas, to Seawarren, New Jersey. The *Atlas* steered a nonevasive course but after hearing a diesel engine swung her stern toward the sound. With the moon rising, the *U-552* (Topp) fired a torpedo at 2,000 meters that struck the starboard side of the ship amidships at the #6 tank. The explosion threw up a cloud of smoke and water but did not ignite the cargo. The engines were stopped after the first explosion, and the crew of eight officers and twenty-six men abandoned the ship in three lifeboats in an orderly manner. The *U-552* crept closer and fired a second torpedo that created a fireball and caused the ship to burn from stem to stern. One lifeboat drifted into the burning gasoline on the water, and the master ordered the men overboard as the fire swept over them. One officer and a utilityman drowned trying to escape the flames. Coast Guard boats picked up the remaining thirty-two men on 9 April and took them to Morehead City, North Carolina.

NSS; WACR; WCSR; RWCS; WJ; Rohwer, p. 89; *War Action Casualties,* p. 52.

EUGENE V. R. THAYER

D:	4-9-42	YB:	1920
T:	2120	Tn:	7,137
Pos:	02.20 S / 39.30 W	Dr:	16 ft.
Ow:	Sinclair Refining Co.	C:	water ballast
Op:	Sinclair Refining Co.	P:	steam
M:	Bodvar F. Svenson	S:	12
A:	unarmed		

The *Eugene V. R. Thayer* was attacked by the Italian submarine *Pietro Calvi* (Olivieri) as she sailed from Buenos Aires, Argentina, to Caripito, Venezuela. As the *Thayer* steamed a nonevasive course with her running lights on, the submarine approached the starboard side, parallel to the tanker, and by some accounts fired a torpedo that struck the vessel. A star shell exploded shortly thereafter, initiating a chase. The *Thayer* tried to keep the submarine astern while the *Calvi* peppered the vessel with its deck gun and machine guns. The *Thayer*'s radio operator sent continuous SOS signals as the submarine fired on the vessel. Unknown to the master, during the lengthy attack, ten members of the crew panicked and attempted to launch the after port lifeboat without orders. Shrapnel may have killed one or two of these men while they readied a boat to clear the ship. When they launched the boat, the tanker was still proceeding at top speed and the lifeboat swamped when it hit the water. All the men in this boat drowned. The master ordered the ship abandoned at 2245 after efforts to elude the submarine failed. The remaining crew of eight officers and nineteen men abandoned ship in two lifeboats. The *Calvi* fired about thirty rounds before the crew abandoned the tanker, and the ship caught fire after ninety minutes of shelling. At noon the next day two planes spotted one lifeboat with thirteen survivors. One landed and took them to Natal, Brazil. Thirty-six hours after the attack thirteen additional survivors made their way to the coast, seven miles north of Aracatí, Brazil. The *Eugene V. R. Thayer* sank two days later. One officer and ten men died in the attack.

NSS; WACR; WCSR; RWCS; *Pilot*, 8 May 1942; Rohwer, p. 89, places the attack's beginning at 02.12 S / 39.55 W.

TAMAULIPAS

D:	4-9-42	YB:	1919
T:	2320	Tn:	6,943
Pos:	34.25 N / 76.00 W	Dr:	27 ft. 1 in.
Ow:	Mexican Trading & Shipping Co.	C:	70,000 bbls. furnace oil
Op:	Mexican Trading & Shipping Co.	P:	steam
M:	Allan Victor Falkenberg	S:	10.0
A:	unarmed		

On 2 April, the *Tamaulipas* sailed from Tampico, Mexico, to New York. The tanker sailed without routing instructions and steered a zigzag course during her journey. The *U-552* (Topp) intercepted the ship and fired one torpedo that struck on the starboard side about fifteen feet abaft the midships house at the #5 tank. The explosion wrecked the bridge, folded the ship in the middle, and broke her back. The flammable oil immediately began to burn, prompting the master to stop the engines. Damage to the radio transmitters prevented the sending of a distress signal. The ship's complement of eight officers and twenty-nine men left the ship in two lifeboats. Two men died when they jumped overboard and drowned. The British trawler HMS *Norwich City* (FY-229) picked up the thirty-five survivors about two hours later and landed them at Morehead City, North Carolina. The tanker sank early the next morning.

NSS; WACR; WCSR; RWCS; WJ; Rohwer, p. 89.

GULFAMERICA

D:	4-10-42	YB:	1942
T:	2220	Tn:	8,081
Pos:	30.14 N / 81.18	Dr:	29 ft. 8 in.
Ow:	Gulf Oil Corporation	C:	101,500 bbls. furnace oil
Op:	Gulf Oil Corporation	P:	steam
M:	Oscar Anderson	S:	13.5
A:	1-4"; 2-50 cal.		

The *Gulfamerica* was torpedoed and shelled by the *U-123* (Hardegen) while on her maiden voyage from Port Arthur, Texas, to New York. Illuminated by the lights of the Jacksonville Beach resort, the tanker had stopped steaming a zigzag course only twenty minutes before the attack. The *U-123* fired one torpedo that struck at the #7 tank and caused a tremendous explosion and fire. The explosion shattered the after mainmast, and the master immediately ordered the engines stopped and the ship abandoned as the radio operator sent radio distress calls. The armed guards manned the four-inch after gun but for some reason did not fire on the U-boat. The abandonment by the crew of eight officers and thirty-three men, along with the seven armed guards, proceeded in an orderly manner until the *U-123* began shelling the tanker. Hardegen, not satisfied the tanker would sink, began shelling her engine room on the port side. He fired approximately twelve shells in addition to spraying the vessel with machine gun fire directed toward the mainmast and the radio antenna. In the resulting confusion, the #4 lifeboat capsized. The master and ten crewmen got away in one boat in ten minutes, but only three men got away in another boat ten minutes later. About twenty-five men jumped overboard, and three men abandoned the tanker on a life raft and then picked up two other seamen from the water. Fourteen men died of drowning, and the shellfire or the torpedo blast killed five more. A total of two officers, two armed guards, and fifteen crewmen perished. Coast Guard craft rescued the survivors and took them to Mayport, Florida. The tanker turned over and sank six days later.

Most American sources state that two torpedoes were fired. This is not substantiated by the U-boat's war diary. NSS; WACR; WCSR; AG; WJ; *Pilot*, 8 May 1942; Rohwer, p. 89, places the attack at 30.10 N / 85.15 W; *War Action Casualties*, p. 56.

HARRY F. SINCLAIR JR.

D:	4-11-42	YB:	1931
T:	0621	Tn:	6,151
Pos:	34.25 N / 76.30 W	Dr:	24 ft. 6 in.
Ow:	Sinclair Refining Co.	C:	66,000 bbls. gasoline
Op:	Sinclair Refining Co.	P:	steam
M:	William Collegan	S:	13.5
A:	unarmed		

While steaming on a zigzag course seven miles south of Cape Lookout, the *Harry F. Sinclair Jr.* was torpedoed by the *U-203* (Mützelburg). On 5 April, the tanker sailed from Houston, Texas, to Norfolk, Virginia. While not attached to a convoy, she had a U.S. destroyer and a Coast Guard boat off the port quarter. The torpedo struck under the pump room on the port side between the #4 and #5 tanks. The blast immediately created a blazing inferno amidships, and the crew of eight officers and twenty-eight men cleared the ship in the #2, #3, and #4 lifeboats. Twenty-five men left the ship in the #3 and #4 lifeboats and two dove overboard. The men in the #2 boat perished in the flames while trying to escape the ship. A total of four officers and six men died. Two and one-half hours later the British armed trawler HMS *Hertfordshire* (FY-176) rescued the survivors in the lifeboats. The USS *Herbert* (DD-160) rescued the two men on the raft. All the survivors landed in Morehead City, North Carolina. Neither the radio operator nor any of the deck officers survived the intense fire. The trawler HMS *Senateur Durhamel* (FY-327) towed the *Harry F. Sinclair* into Morehead City, and she later returned to service as the *Annibal*.

NSS; WACR; WCSR; WJ; Moore, p. 360; Rohwer, p. 89; *War Action Casualties*, p. 57.

DELVALLE

D:	4-12-42	YB:	1919
T:	0030	Tn:	5,032
Pos:	16.51 N / 72.25 W	Dr:	23 ft. 7 in.
Ow:	Mississippi Shipping Co.	C:	5,165 tons general cargo
Op:	Mississippi Shipping Co.	P:	steam
M:	Edgar F. Jones	S:	13
A:	1-4"; 2-30 cal.		

The *Delvalle* sailed from New Orleans, Louisiana, to Buenos Aires via St. Thomas. The freighter proceeded on a nonevasive course in an effort to increase the ship's speed. On 11 April, at 1000 a passenger plane spotted the *U-154* (Kölle) off the vessel's port quarter and advised the vessel of this discovery. At about 1730 lookouts spotted a submarine's periscope about 500 yards from the ship. The master changed the ship's course in an effort to ram the U-boat, but it submerged and escaped. At 0030 ship's time, two torpedoes struck the starboard side almost simultaneously about fifteen feet below the waterline and just forward of amidships. The explosions extensively damaged the ship and destroyed the lifeboats on the starboard side. As the vessel rapidly sank, the launching of the #2 and #4 boats proved difficult because of the ship's severe list. As the crew abandoned the ship, a third torpedo struck. The gun crew did not fire a shot because they never spotted the submarine and the vessel's list prevented the aiming of the gun. The ship sank only fifteen minutes after the initial explosion. The freighter's complement of nine officers, forty-five men, five passengers, and a gun crew of four all successfully left the ship, with the exception of the ship's doctor who drowned. The boats and two rafts, remained together until daybreak. The motor launch left the other survivors behind to try and reach the coast for help. On 12 April, a patrol plane sighted the boat and rafts and one hour later the Canadian armed merchant cruiser *Prince Henry* (F-70) rescued these men. The motor launch with part of the crew landed at Jacmel, Haiti.

NSS; WACR; WCSR; RWCS; AG; *New York Herald Tribune*, 23 April 1942; Rohwer, p. 90.

ESSO BOSTON

D:	4-12-42	YB:	1938
T:	1320	Tn:	7,698
Pos:	21.42 N / 60.00 W	Dr:	28 ft. 9 in.
Ow:	Standard Oil Co. of N. J.	C:	105,400 bbls. crude oil
Op:	Standard Oil Co. of N. J.	P:	steam
M:	Lohn Ludwig Johnson	S:	14.0
A:	unarmed		

The *Esso Boston* was torpedoed by the *U-130* (Kals) while en route from Güiria, Venezuela, to Halifax, Nova Scotia. The tanker, on a zigzag course when attacked, had just made a right turn. A torpedo struck between the #2 and #3 tanks on the starboard side, ten feet below the waterline, and blew open the forward deck. The watch below immediately put the engines into reverse to stop the ship's headway. The crew of eight officers and twenty-nine men lowered the #2 and #4 boats. The submarine surfaced about five minutes later and began shelling the ship as the crew got away. The shellfire spread fire the entire length of the vessel. The *U-130* then came alongside one of the boats. The Germans questioned the men about the ship, offered them food and water, and provided directions to the nearest convoy and land. Early on 13 April, the chief engineer and a fireman reboarded the tanker. A cursory inspection by the men revealed that the ship could have been salvaged, but with no salvage equipment the prospect for saving the vessel seemed slim. The riddled tanker sank shortly thereafter. The USS *Biddle* (DD-151) picked up the survivors at 1600 on 13 April and landed them at San Juan, Puerto Rico.

NSS; WACR; RWCS; *Ships of the Esso Fleet*, pp. 189-92; *War Action Casualties*, p. 58.

LESLIE

D:	4-12-42	YB:	1919
T:	2322	Tn:	2,609
Pos:	28.37 N / 80.25 W	Dr:	24 ft. 6 in.
Ow:	Worth SS Corp.	C:	3,225 tons raw sugar
Op:	Grace SS Line	P:	steam
M:	Albert Eriksson	S:	6
A:	2-30 cal.		

The *Leslie* was torpedoed by the *U-123* (Hardegen) about three miles southeast of the Hetzel Shoals Gas Buoy while en route from Antilla, Cuba, to New York via Havana. In rough seas the *U-123* fired its last torpedo, striking the starboard side abaft of amidships at the #3 hold. The explosion blew open the bulkheads, disabled the radio, ruptured tanks, and flooded the shaft alley with sugar and water. The master ordered the ship abandoned and had the engine reversed and then stopped. The ship listed heavily to starboard and then settled by the stern, leaving the deck awash in fifteen minutes. The survivors of the crew of nine officers, twenty-two men, and one consular passenger managed to launch two lifeboats and landed north of the Cape Canaveral Lighthouse the next day. The *Esso Bayonne* rescued one other seaman and put him ashore at Key West on 14 April. Four men died in the attack.

NSS; WACR; WCSR; WJ; AG; Rohwer, p. 90, places the attack at 28.35 N / 80.19 W.

MARGARET

D:	4-14-42	YB:	1916
T:	1400	Tn:	3,352
Pos:	off the East Coast	Dr:	22 ft.
Ow:	A. H. Bull SS Co.	C:	4,508 tons sugar
Op.:	A. H. Bull SS Co.	P:	steam
M:	Leonard Logren Davis	S:	unknown
A:	unarmed		

On 28 March, the *Margaret* departed San Juan, Puerto Rico, bound for Philadelphia, Pennsylvania. The *U-571* (Möhlmann) spotted the sugar freighter and maneuvered to attack. At 600 yards, the *U-571* fired a single torpedo that hit the vessel in the stern and ripped the hull to the upper deck. The steamer settled stern first and rapidly sank in five minutes. Some of the crew of eight officers and twenty-one men managed to get one boat and several rafts in the water. None of the crew, however, survived the attack.

In the *U-571*'s war journal, Möhlmann recorded observing several explosions on board, probably the *Margaret*'s boilers exploding as she sank. WACR; WJ; Rohwer, p. 90.

ROBIN HOOD

D:	4-15-42	YB:	1919
T:	2142	Tn:	6,886
Pos:	38.39 N / 66.38 W	Dr:	27 ft.
Ow:	Seas Shipping Co.	C:	8,725 tons chrome ore, asbestos,
Op:	Seas Shipping Co.		concentrates, etc.
M:	John A. O'Pray	P:	steam
A:	unarmed	S:	11.0

The *Robin Hood* sailed from Trinidad, BWI, to Boston, Massachusetts. The ship proceeded in rough seas on a zigzag course with all lights extinguished. Earlier in the day the *U-575* (Heydemann) fired a torpedo spread that missed the freighter. Pushing after the steamer, the U-boat caught her about five hours later. The *U-575* fired two torpedoes that both hit the vessel within seconds. The first struck the starboard side amidships at the fireroom and caused the boilers to explode, which lifted the deck up and folded it over. A second torpedo struck forward of the first and blew the hatch covers off the #1 and #2 holds and carried away the foremast. The vessel flooded rapidly, and water covered the well deck within one minute of the first explosion. Immediately the master gave the order to abandon ship. The freighter settled evenly, then broke in half at the #3 hatch and both sections rapidly sank. Most of the crew of nine officers and twenty-nine men abandoned ship in the #2 lifeboat. The officer and two men on watch below died. Three other officers and eight more men never left the ship. On 23 April, the USS *Greer* (DD-145) picked up the survivors and landed them at Hamilton, Bermuda.

The NSS report mentions a second U-boat; however, this cannot be confirmed. The survivors also claim that the U-boat used its deck gun and that a third torpedo hit the vessel. The war journal of the *U-575* speaks of only two torpedoes and mentions no use of its deck gun. As the vessel broke in two, the sharp reports made by the ship breaking apart gave some the impression that the U-boat shelled the vessel. NSS; WACR; WCSR; WJ; *New York Herald Tribune*, 1 May 1942; *Pilot*, 15 May 1942; Rohwer, p. 90, places the attack at 38.45 N / 66.45 W.

ALCOA GUIDE

D:	4-16-42	YB:	1919
T:	2150	Tn:	4,834
Pos:	35.34 N / 70.08 W	Dr:	25 ft. 5 in.
Ow:	Alcoa Steamship Co.	C:	5,890 tons general Army
Op:	Alcoa Steamship Co.		supplies
M:	Samuel Leroy Cobb	P:	steam
A:	unarmed	S:	10.0

The *Alcoa Guide* sailed alone from New York to Point a Pitre, Guadeloupe. The *U-123* (Hardegen) spotted the freighter and pursued her for hours. Lacking torpedoes, the *U-123* attacked with incendiary shells. The first warning came when a shell struck the starboard side of the saloon deck. The submarine bore two points off the starboard bow on a parallel course. The master ordered the helmsman to throw the wheel hard to starboard to try and ram the U-boat. Moments later a shell hit the bridge, fatally injuring the master and jamming the rudder. With the engines still running, the vessel began circling out of control. The *U-123* continued firing at the ship as she raced in a circle. A damaged ammonia condenser kept men from reaching the engine room to stop the engines. The *U-123* halted the fusillade and allowed the crew of eight officers and twenty-six men to get off the ship. With the ship still running at high speed, six officers and twenty-two men, exhibiting remarkable seamanship, managed to launch two boats. The *U-123* continued the shelling after the crew escaped and finally sent the freighter to the bottom at 2250. On 19 April, the USS *Broome* (DD-210) located the boats and rescued twenty-seven survivors. The master and a seaman had died from their wounds. Four other survivors got away on a raft and became separated from the boats. The British SS *Hororata* located this raft thirty-two days later, but only one seaman was still alive. A total of two officers and four men died in the attack.

NSS; WACR; WCSR; WJ; *Pilot*, 15 May 1942; *Tribune*, 25 April 1942; Rohwer, p. 90.

AXTELL J. BYLES

D:	4-18-42	YB:	1927
T:	1835	Tn:	8,955
Pos:	35.32 N / 75.19 W	Dr:	29 ft. 7 in.
Ow:	Tide Water Associated Oil Co.	C:	57,000 bbls. crude oil and
Op:	Tide Water Associated Oil Co.		27,000 bbls. #6 fuel oil
M:	John D. Baldwin	P:	steam
A:	unarmed	S:	9.5

On 11 April, the *Axtell J. Byles* departed Port Arthur, Texas, for New York City. The tanker sailed from Cape Lookout Light in a convoy of six other tankers and

a freighter. Four small Coast Guard boats, the USCG *Dione* (WPC-107), and an airplane escorted the convoy. The convoy steamed at 9 1/2 knots but did not zigzag. The *Axtell J. Byles* took station as the lead ship in the seaward column of the two-column convoy. The *U-136* (Zimmerman) spied the convoy and fired a four-torpedo spread. The escorting plane discovered the track of one of the torpedoes, dipped its wings and dove toward the torpedo, alerting the ship's crew. The helmsman turned the wheel hard left, and the master gave orders for evasive actions. The whistle blared a warning for the other ships to give way, and the *Byles* increased speed by one knot. The slow merchantman, however, could not move fast enough, and the torpedo struck her just forward of the bridge on the starboard side at the #2 tank. The explosion blew a large hole in the starboard side, both above and below the waterline. It also vented upward and severely damaged the bridge and the midships house. The ship settled by the bow and all the tanks forward of the #6 tank flooded, but she did not sink. The vessel arrived at Hampton Roads under her own power the next day. The crew of eight officers and thirty-one men reported no injuries.

NSS; WACR; WCSR; WJ; *War Action Casualties*, p. 60.

STEEL MAKER

D:	4-19-42	YB:	1920
T:	2232	Tn:	6,176
Pos:	33.05 N / 70.36 W	Dr:	28 ft. 2 in.
Ow:	Isthmian SS Co.	C:	7,660 tons war supplies
Op:	Isthmian SS Co.	P:	steam
M:	Leonard Duks	S:	11.0
A:	1-4"; 2-50 cal.; 2-30 cal.		

The *Steel Maker* sailed from New York to Abadan, Iran, via Cape Town, South Africa. As the freighter maintained a zigzag course, the *U-654* (Forster) fired two torpedoes. The first torpedo missed the vessel; the second struck the port side in the #5 after cargo hold. The explosion ripped a large hole in the ship's side, spewing cargo and wreckage into the water. The master stopped the engines and ordered the ship abandoned. The armed guards mustered at their battle stations, but the *U-654* did not come to the surface until after the ship sank. The vessel filled with water rapidly and sank in fifteen minutes. The nine officers, twenty-eight men, nine armed guards, and one passenger got away in two lifeboats in less than ten minutes. The U-boat officers questioned the master, asking the name of the ship, tonnage, destination, and cargo. An officer then stated, "I am sorry to have to sink you and do this to you but this is war. You will be rescued, do not worry, I shall send your position out by radio." The next day the two boats came together and redistributed their loads. On 22 April, the USS *Rowan* (DD-405) rescued eighteen survivors, including five armed guards, in one boat. These men landed in Norfolk. On 29 April, the British SS

Pacific Exporter picked up twenty-seven additional survivors off Frying Pan Shoals and transferred them to a Coast Guard boat. They landed at Morehead City, North Carolina. The radio operator managed to grasp onto a raft as the vessel sank, and by combining the emergency supplies of several rafts he lived comfortably for twenty-nine days until being picked up by a rescue craft. Only the steward died in the attack.

NSS; WACR; WCSR; RWCS; AG; WJ; *Times Herald,* 3 May 1942; Rohwer, p. 91, places the attack at 33.48 N / 70.36 W.

WEST IMBODEN

D:	4-20-42	YB:	1919
T:	2248	Tn:	5,751
Pos:	41.14 N / 65.54 W	Dr:	24 ft.
Ow:	Seas Shipping Co.	C:	7,357 tons general
Op:	Seas Shipping Co.	P:	steam
M:	Anton Anderson	S:	9.8
A:	unarmed		

The *West Imboden* departed Trinidad, BWI, en route to Boston, Massachusetts, and had approached to within 200 miles of the Nantucket Lightship. During the trip, an accumulation of carbon caused a fire in the stack. Sparks spewed on the deck and the tarpaulin hatch covers, and the smoke turned the ship into a beacon. This attracted the attention of the *U-752* (Schroeter). The *U-752* fired two torpedoes, both passing ahead of the steamer. A second pair also missed. The U-boat then fired two single shots; one passed ahead of the ship and a lookout and the master spotted the track of the sixth torpedo off the starboard beam about 150 feet before it struck the ship. The torpedo hit forward of the #1 hold on the starboard side. The *U-752* then surfaced and began shelling the freighter. Two rounds struck the vessel before she could be abandoned. All members of the crew of eight officers and twenty-seven men safely left the ship in two lifeboats. The *U-752* maintained a slow rate of fire; the German gun crew shot about one round every two minutes. Schroeter shelled the vessel for nearly two hours, putting over thirty-five shells into the ship and setting her ablaze. After the shelling, the *U-752* came alongside one of the lifeboats and inquired about casualties. Upon learning there were none, the officer on the U-boat's conning tower replied, "That's good," and the submarine disappeared into the darkness. The USS *Bristol* (DD-453) rescued all hands late on the 22nd and took them to Portland, Maine.

NSS; WACR; WCSR; WJ; Rohwer, p. 91, places the attack at 41.14 N / 65.55 W.

PIPESTONE COUNTY

D:	4-21-42	YB:	1919
T:	1305	Tn:	5,102
Pos:	37.35 N / 66.20 W	Dr:	26 ft.
Ow:	Seas Shipping Co.	C:	6,700 tons general
Op.:	Robin Line	P:	steam
M:	Richard E. Hocken	S:	9
A:	1-4"; 4-50 cal.; 4-30 cal.		

The *Pipestone County* sailed from Trinidad, BWI, to Boston, Massachusetts, and was intercepted by the *U-576* (Heinicke). The *U-576* fired a torpedo from 300 meters, and it struck in the #1 hold. Realizing the engine room bulkhead had not given way and the vessel still had steam up, Heinicke put a coup de grâce shot in the #2 hold. The freighter filled with water quickly and sank in less than twenty minutes. The entire crew of nine officers and twenty-seven men, as well as the nine armed guards, got away safely in four lifeboats and one raft. Officers on the *U-576* questioned the crew and gave one of the boats some provisions before leaving the scene. Because of rain and moderate seas, the boats became separated after the attack. The British SS *Tropic Star* rescued the survivors in two boats, one twenty-eight hours after the attack and the other two hours later, and landed them in Boston. On 7 May the USCG cutter *Calypso* (WPC-104) rescued the men in the third boat, while, a plane out of Elizabeth City spotted the remaining boat and led the fishing vessel *Irene and May* to rescue the men on 8 May. All hands survived.

WACR; WCSR; RWCS; AG; RWSA records indicate the ship was bareboat chartered to WSA until October 1942. Rohwer, p. 91, places the attack at 37.43 N / 66.16 W; Moore, p. 223.

SAN JACINTO

D:	4-21-42	YB:	1903
T:	2130	Tn:	6,069
Pos:	31.10 N / 70.45 W	Dr:	20 ft. 5 in.
Ow:	Agwilines Inc.	C:	3,200 tons general
Op:	New York & Puerto Rico SS Co.	P:	steam
M:	Robert W. Hart	S:	13.5
A:	unarmed		

The *U-201* (Schnee) intercepted and attacked the *San Jacinto*, en route from New York to San Juan, Puerto Rico. The officer of the deck sighted the U-boat on the surface only 300 feet off the port beam just before a torpedo hit. The torpedo struck slightly aft of amidships in the #5 hold near the waterline. The force of the blast vented upwards, tore up the deck, and demolished staterooms, recreation halls, the radio room, and the boat deck. The damaged engines stopped and the lighting and power shut down. The 8 officers, 71 men, and 104 passengers mustered at their abandon ship stations. As the men readied the boats for departure, the *U-201* began firing its 88-mm deck gun. Before the vessel sank, the U-boat fired about seventy-five rounds. Six lifeboats and several life rafts were launched quickly and in good order, considering the number of passengers the ship carried. Nine passengers, one officer, and four men died in the attack. The crew carried a portable radio transmitter in one of the lifeboats, but they did not use it until morning fearful the U-boat would attack. The survivors secured the boats together with lines, and they managed to stay together. The USS *Rowan* (DD-782) rescued passengers and crew at about noon the next day.

NSS relates the vessel was chartered to the U.S. Maritime Commission. WACR; WCSR. According to the survivors, two U-boats began shelling the *San Jacinto* with incendiary shells, firing about forty rounds before the crew abandoned ship. The survivors continually related how the U-boats signaled as the passengers and crew left the *San Jacinto*. The second submarine cannot be confirmed. RWCS; WJ; *New York Herald Tribune*, 26 April 1942; *Pilot*, 1 May 1942; Rohwer, p. 91.

CONNECTICUT

D:	4-23-42	YB:	1938
T:	0210	Tn:	8,684
Pos:	23.50 S / 19.50 W	Dr:	28 ft.
Ow:	Texas Co.	C:	84,200 bbls. gas, airplane engine
Op.:	Texas Co.		oil, heating oil
M:	Thomas A. Petersen	P:	steam
A:	1-4"; 1-3"; 4-50 cal.; 2-30 cal.	S:	13.0

On 31 March, the *Connecticut* departed Port Arthur, Texas, en route to Cape Town, South Africa. On the night of 22 April, Captain Helmuth Von Ruckteschell of the German raider *Michel* had his torpedo boat *LS-4*, named *Esan*, hoisted overboard. After spotting the tanker some hours later, the *Esan* fired a torpedo that struck the tanker in the #15 tank on the port side amidships. The torpedo created a violent explosion and sent a huge cloud of gas into the air, but the ship did not ignite. Quickly the men began abandoning ship and had successfully launched three boats when a second torpedo struck. This explosion ignited the cargo, creating an inferno on the ship and in the water as flaming oil and gas surrounded the tanker. Two of the lifeboats had just come around the stern rowing into the wind, but they could not get away from the flames and were engulfed. The *Connecticut* burned for nearly six hours before sinking. The crew consisted of eight officers, thirty-five men, and a gun crew of eleven men. The entire gun crew perished, as did four officers and twenty men from the freighter—all burned to death in the fire. The raider took the survivors on board. One man died on the raider, and Ruckteschell transferred the remaining men to

a supply ship. Eighteen survivors entered a Japanese prison camp at Fukouka, Japan. Sixteen men lived to be repatriated after the war.

WACR; WCSR; AG; Muggenthaler, pp. 210-11.

LAMMOT DU PONT

D:	4-23-42	YB:	1914
T:	1520	Tn:	5,102
Pos:	27.10 N / 57.10 W	Dr:	24 ft. 13 in.
Ow:	International Freighting Co.	C:	6,812 tons linseed, general
Op:	International Freighting Co.	P:	steam
M:	Robert Cameron Housten	S:	9.5
A:	1-4"; 2-30 cal.		

The *Lammot Du Pont* sailed from Buenos Aires to New York independently and proceeded on a nonevasive course. The *U-125* (Folkers) fired a torpedo that struck approximately fifteen feet below the waterline on the port side between the #4 hatch and the engine room. The explosion blew the booms at the #4 and #5 hatches onto the deck and threw a large column of water and linseed from the #4 hatch. The vessel listed rapidly to port and within five minutes rolled over completely on her side. The gun crew manned the gun for several minutes but never spotted the submarine. Only one lifeboat and three rafts could be launched by the nine officers, thirty-seven men, and nine armed guards on board. Four of these men never left the ship. The lifeboat, which contained thirty-one men, remained adrift for twenty-three days. Eight of these men died before the USS *Tarbell* (DD-142) spotted them. The Swedish MV *Astri* rescued fifteen men on two of the rafts after two days afloat and they were transferred to the USS *Omaha* (CL-4). Two of the men abandoned ship on a broken raft. The other survivors attempted unsuccessfully to reach these men in the heavy seas, but they drifted away and were never found. Three others later died in a San Juan hospital. Eight armed guards, eight ship's officers, and twenty-two of the crew survived the attack.

NSS; WACR; WCSR; Rohwer, p. 91.

ALCOA PARTNER

D:	4-26-42	YB:	1919
T:	0130	Tn:	5,513
Pos:	13.32 N / 67.57 W	Dr:	26 ft. 2 in.
Ow:	Alcoa SS Co.	C:	8,500 tons bauxite ore
Op:	Alcoa SS Co.	P:	steam
M:	Ernest Henke	S:	10.5
A:	unarmed		

The *Alcoa Partner* was torpedoed and shelled about eighty miles northeast of Bonaire, NWI, while bound from Trinidad, West Indies, for Mobile, Alabama. The *U-66* (Zapp) spotted the zigzagging freighter and fired a torpedo that struck the port side at the #2 hatch. Zapp's gun crew also immediately fired one shell that struck the poop deck. Because of the nature of the cargo, the *Alco Partner* sank in less than three minutes after being hit. The crew of seven officers, twenty-seven men, and one workaway found themselves in the water, never having enough time to launch any of the ship's four lifeboats. The starboard lifeboat with one man on board floated free of the sinking ship. Twenty-four other men managed to reach this boat. The survivors remained in the vicinity until after dawn searching for the ten missing men. The lifeboat made landfall in Bonaire thirty-seven hours after the attack. One officer, eight men, and the workaway died.

NSS; WACR; WCSR; Rohwer, p. 91.

MOBILEOIL

D:	4-29-42	YB:	1937
T:	0228	Tn:	9,925
Pos:	26.10 N / 66.15 W	Dr:	30 ft. 9 in.
Ow:	Socony-Vacuum Oil Co.	C:	water ballast
Op:	Socony-Vacuum Oil Co.	P:	steam
M:	Ernest V. Farrow	S:	14.0
A:	1-4"; 2-50 cal.; 2-30 cal.		

On 16 April, the *Mobileoil* sailed from New York bound for Caripito, Venezuela, via Norfolk. The master had orders to await a convoy, but when the vessels did not arrive at the appointed hour, he proceeded alone. As the *Mobileoil* maintained course at high speed, the *U-108* (Scholtz) fired a single torpedo from 2,000 yards and missed. A second torpedo struck between the #1 and #2 tanks on the starboard side and blew a large hole in the bow. Just as the torpedo hit, the *U-108* began shelling the tanker and hit the vessel at least three times. When the attack began, the master had the tanker swing around to bring her stern to the submarine, shift some ballast, and continue toward Bermuda. The armed guards manned the four-inch stern gun and four machine guns. The gunners fired twelve four-inch rounds at the flashes from the submarine's guns. The *U-108* fired a third torpedo that struck at 0415 on the starboard side of the #4 tank. The explosion destroyed the lifeboats, part of the superstructure, and the gyro compass. The *U-108* maneuvered to fire a fourth torpedo that struck the ship at 1030 between the #7 and #8 tanks on the port side. This became the coup de grâce and broke the ship in two. The crew of eight officers and thirty-five men, along with the nine armed guards, launched three lifeboats. Eighty-six hours after the attack the USS *PC-490* rescued all hands and landed them at San

Juan, Puerto Rico. The master was later convicted of violating convoy routing orders.

NSS; WACR; WCSR; WJ; AG; Rohwer, p. 92, places the attack at 25.35 N / 66.18 W; *War Action Casualties*, p. 62.

FEDERAL

D:	4-30-42	YB:	1901
T:	1215	Tn:	2,882
Pos:	21.13 N / 76.05 W	Dr:	21 ft. 6 in.
Ow:	Petroleum Navigation Co.	C:	water ballast
Op:	Petroleum Navigation Co.	P:	steam
M:	Walter Furst	S:	8.0
A:	unarmed		

On 27 April, the *Federal* sailed from Tampa, Florida, to Banes, Cuba, to obtain a cargo of molasses. Carrying only water ballast in tanks #1, #3, and #5, she maintained a zigzag course until a lookout spotted the *U-507* (Schact) three miles away on the horizon. The master changed the ship's course and headed for land, and the U-boat submerged. At 1210 the submarine again surfaced and from a range of about 450 yards fired a shell that went through the crew's quarters. The U-boat fired approximately thirty rounds at the rate of three to four rounds per minute before the crew abandoned ship. The shellfire destroyed the #3 boat and was so heavy the men found it impossible to launch the #2 boat. The *U-507* approached the tanker close on the port side and put more than 100 additional rounds into the vessel. The shellfire set the wooden bridge on fire and killed four men before they could abandon ship. The survivors of the crew of eight officers and twenty-five men managed to launch only one lifeboat and two rafts as the ship sank. The ship settled on an even keel and then listed to port and sank stern first an hour after the attack began. Fourteen men left in the #1 lifeboat, and fifteen others clung to the two rafts. A Navy plane arrived on the scene about one hour after abandonment, and a second plane followed twenty minutes later. They unsuccessfully searched for the submarine and other survivors. At 1515 the U.S. Army transport *Yarmouth* circled the survivors several times and steamed away. Fishing craft from Gibara, Cuba, picked up the men on the rafts two and a half hours after the attack. The lifeboat followed the craft to shore. A fifth member of the crew died from wounds after reaching shore.

NSS lists the vessel's owner as American Republics Corp. and the operator as Pennsylvania Shipping Co.; WACR; WCSR; RWCS; Rohwer, p. 92; *War Action Casualties*, p. 64.

EASTERN SWORD

D:	5-4-42	YB:	1920
T:	0345	Tn:	3,785
Pos:	07.10 N / 57.58 W	Dr:	15 ft. 9 in.
Ow:	Sword SS Line	C:	1,550 tons general
Op:	Alcoa SS Co.	P:	steam
M:	Julius Niels Lars Jensen	S:	under 9.0
A:	unarmed		

The *Eastern Sword* departed Trinidad, BWI, for Georgetown, British Guiana. About twelve miles off the Georgetown Light the *U-162* (Wattenberg) intercepted the freighter. Two torpedoes struck in quick succession at the #4 hold. The ship settled rapidly by the stern, and within two minutes water had reached the decks. She settled on an even keel with fifteen feet of her mainmast above water. The explosion destroyed the radio shack, preventing the radio operator from sending a distress message. Twelve of the crew of seven officers and twenty-three men got away in one lifeboat and landed the next day at Georgetown. At 1400 on 6 May, the fishing boat *Ocean Star* rescued one other crew member from a raft and landed him in Georgetown. Four officers and seven men died, five of these on watch below.

NSS; WACR; WCSR; *Pilot*, 12 June 1942, claims the vessel was on a zigzag pattern; Rohwer, p. 93.

NORLINDO

D:	5-4-42	YB:	1920
T:	1040	Tn:	2,686
Pos:	24.57 N / 84.00 W	Dr:	14 ft.
Ow:	M & M Transportation Co.	C:	water ballast
Op:	North Atlantic & Gulf SS Co.	P:	steam
M:	Clesson E. Pierce	S:	10.0
A:	unarmed		

The *U-507* (Schacht) attacked the *Norlindo* about 200 miles northeast of Havana while she was en route from Mobile, Alabama, to Havana, Cuba. Two oil tankers, *Joseph M. Cudahy* and *Munger T. Ball*, lay in view, one about ten miles to the east and the other just over the horizon. A torpedo struck aft on the starboard side between the #3 and #4 hatches, causing the mainmast to fall. The tanker began sinking quickly, listed to starboard, and settled by the stern. Having no time to launch the ship's lifeboat, the master ordered the crew to jump over the side. Only twenty-three of the crew of seven officers and twenty-one men reached the life rafts as the ship went down. Five members of the crew, working in the after hold, never escaped. Officers on the *U-507* asked the survivors the name of the ship and her tonnage and then provided them with supplies. The SS *San Blas* rescued the twenty-three survivors two days later and landed them at Cristobal, Canal Zone, on 11 May.

The records are contradictory concerning the number of men on board; some say 28, others say 29. NSS; WACR; WCSR; Rohwer, p. 93.

TUSCALOOSA CITY

D:	5-4-42	YB:	1920
T:	1521	Tn:	5,686
Pos:	18.25 N / 81.35 W	Dr:	25 ft. 2 in.
Ow:	Isthmian SS. Co.	C:	7,916 tons ore, rubber, jute,
Op:	Isthmian SS. Co.		shellac
M:	Harold W. Hendrickson	P:	steam
A:	unarmed	S:	12

The *U-125* (Folkers) torpedoed the *Tuscaloosa City* as she was en route from Calcutta, India, to New Orleans, Louisiana. The first torpedo struck on the starboard side at the #2 hatch, broaching the surface twenty seconds before striking the ship. A second torpedo exploded twenty seconds later just before striking at the #4 hatch. The body of this torpedo landed on deck. The watch below failed to secure the engines after the second torpedo struck, and when the crew of ten officers and twenty-four men attempted to launch the lifeboats, the ship still had a nine-knot headway. As the #4 boat touched the water, it was smashed to bits, spilling five men into the sea. The *U-125* fired a third torpedo as a coup de grâce to quicken the sinking, and the ship sank twenty-five minutes later. The crew managed to successfully launch one boat and pick the other survivors out of the water. Before leaving, the officers on board the *U-125* questioned the crew, gave directions to the nearest land, and then wished them luck. The SS *Falcon* rescued all hands about seven hours after the attack and landed them at Cartagena, Colombia.

NSS; WACR; WCSR; RWCS; Rohwer, p. 93.

MUNGER T. BALL

D:	5-4-42	YB:	1920
T:	1845	Tn:	5,104
Pos:	25.17 N / 83.57 W	Dr:	28 ft.
Ow:	Sabine Transportation Co.	C:	65,000 bbls. gasoline
Op:	Sabine Transportation Co.	P:	steam
M:	Karl Ragnar Olsen	S:	10.0
A:	unarmed		

On 1 May, the *Munger T. Ball* sailed from Port Arthur, Texas, to Norfolk, Virginia. The *U-507* (Schacht) observed the tanker traveling on a nonevasive course and fired a torpedo from 500 yards, striking on the port side amidships. Thirty seconds later a second torpedo struck farther aft near the engine room. After the first explosion, the vessel immediately burst into flames. The *U-507* came to the surface on the port side after the second explosion and began to rake the vessel with its machine gun from stem to stern. The men tried to launch the #4 boat, but the boat could not be freed. Only four men of the crew of eight officers and twenty-six men managed to abandon the tanker by jumping overboard or by climbing down lines and swimming away from the ship. Burning gasoline immediately spread on the water, creating a deathtrap on board. Survivors in the water saw several of the officers going forward trying to escape the flames. The four survivors swam to a life raft, and the Norwegian MV *Katy* rescued the men about four hours later and landed them at Key West, Florida. Nine officers and twenty-four men perished in the attack.

The small arms fire is not mentioned in the WJ. The sources conflict on crew size. NSS; WACR; WCSR; WJ; Rohwer, p. 93, places the attack at 25.24 N / 83.46 W; *War Action Casualties*, p. 65.

JOSEPH M. CUDAHY

D:	5-4-42	YB:	1921
T:	2128	Tn:	6,949
Pos:	25.57 N / 83.57 W	Dr:	27 ft.
Ow:	Sinclair Refining Co.	C:	77,444 bbls. crude and
Op:	Sinclair Refining Co.		lubricating oils
M:	Walter Edmund Reed	P:	steam
A:	unarmed	S:	11.0

On 2 May, the *Joseph M. Cudahy* sailed from Houston, Texas, to Marcus Hook, Pennsylvania. Two days later seventy-four miles northwest of the Dry Tortugas Light, lookouts spotted the tanker *Munger T. Ball* nine miles to the south in flames. The master altered course and headed for Tampa in a zigzag pattern. The *U-507* (Schact), however, had observed the tanker and began maneuvering for an attack. The third officer spotted the *U-507*'s conning tower and a moment later saw the track of a torpedo about twenty feet from the vessel. The torpedo struck at the waterline on the starboard side at the #4 main tank. The explosion blew a large hole in the ship's side and started a fire in the midships house. The master put the wheel hard right and into the wind to allow the crew of eight officers and twenty-nine men to launch the lifeboats. The master and eight men, who were forward at time of the attack, managed to lower the #2 lifeboat. Ten minutes later a Navy PBY plane came into sight. A fishing schooner offered to help the men, but they declined. At 0900 on 5 May, a Navy PBY plane picked up these men and took them to Key West, Florida. Another Navy PBY plane

rescued one other survivor the same morning and also landed him at Key West. Three officers and twenty-four men died in the attack. On 7 May, the USS *Coral* (PY-15) sighted the tanker completely gutted and still burning. Since the tanker was beyond salvage and a menace to navigation, the *Coral* sank her by gunfire.

The vessel sank at 24.57 N / 84.10 W. NSS; WACR; WCSR; RWCS; Rohwer, p. 93; *War Action Casualties*, p. 66.

DELISLE

D:	5-4-42	YB:	1919
T:	2200	Tn:	3,478
Pos:	27.02 N / 80.03 W	Dr:	22 ft. 8 in.
Ow:	Baltimore Insular Line	C:	2,800 tons general
Op:	A. H. Bull SS Co.	P:	steam
M:	William Washington Callis	S:	9.0
A:	unarmed		

The *Delisle* sailed from Baltimore, Maryland, to San Juan, Puerto Rico, carrying a general cargo that included a deck cargo of camouflage paint in steel drums. The freighter proceeded on a nonevasive course, and the *U-564* (Suhren) attacked her about fifteen miles off Jupiter Inlet. The first mate saw the wake of the torpedo but too late for the helmsman to take evasive action. The torpedo hit amidships on the starboard side, and the explosion created a hole approximately twenty feet by thirty feet at the engine room, about five feet below the main deck. The blast killed two men on watch below. The master ordered the ship abandoned, and the surviving members of the crew of eight officers, twenty-four men, and four stowaways left in one lifeboat and a raft. The thirty-four men reached shore just after midnight. The crew reboarded the ship at 0400 the next day and prepared her to be towed into Miami by a Navy tug. After repairs she went back in service and was later mined and sunk in October 1943.

NSS; WACR; RWCS; WJ; Rohwer, p. 93, places the attack at 27.06 N / 80/03 W.

AFOUNDRIA

D:	5-5-42	YB:	1920
T:	1623	Tn:	5,010
Pos:	19.59 N / 73.26 W	Dr:	25 ft. 3 in.
Ow:	Waterman SS Corp.	C:	7,700 tons general
Op:	Waterman SS Corp.	P:	steam
M:	William A. Sillars	S:	11.0
A:	unarmed		

The *U-108* (Scholtz) intercepted the *Afoundria* eight miles due north of Le Male Light, Haiti, while she was en route from New Orleans, Louisiana, to San Juan, Puerto Rico. The vessel had a general cargo that included aerial demolition bombs, dynamite, frozen foodstuffs, road-building machinery, and lumber. Lookouts spotted the torpedo's wake just before it struck well below the waterline between the #4 and #5 holds on the starboard side. The explosion ripped a large hole in the ship and immediately flooded the after holds. The ship lost way at once and could not be maneuvered. The radio operator sent distress signals and received a reply from Guantánamo. The ship settled by the stern and sank in fifty minutes. The crew of eight officers and thirty men together with eight American passengers abandoned the ship in an orderly manner in three lifeboats. The USS *Mulberry* (AN-27), dispatched from Guantánamo, rescued all hands seventeen hours after the attack.

NSS; WACR; WCSR; AG; Rohwer, p. 92, places the attack at 20.00 N / 73.30 W.

JAVA ARROW

D:	5-5-42	YB:	1921
T:	2330	Tn:	8,327
Pos:	27.30 N / 80.08 W	Dr:	22 ft. 6 in.
Ow:	Socony-Vacuum Oil Co.	C:	water ballast, 1,300 drums lube
Op:	Socony-Vacuum Oil Co.		oil
M:	Sigrard J. Hennichen	P:	steam
A:	1-4"; 4-30 cal.	S:	11.0

On 28 April, the *Java Arrow* departed New York and traveled to Cape Town via Curaçao, NWI. The *U-333* (Cremer) maneuvered into a favorable position and fired a torpedo that struck the port side about fifteen feet above the keel at the #5 tank, just aft of the bridge. Approximately one minute later, a second torpedo struck the port side about ten feet above the keel and demolished the engine room. The gun crew took no defensive action. The first boat, at the order of the master, left the ship approximately twenty minutes after the first explosion. The second boat left the side of the ship ten minutes later. The USS *PC-483* and a U.S. Coast Guard craft picked up the two boats, with seven officers, thirty-two men, and six armed guards. They landed the men at Miami and Ft. Pierce, Florida. Two officers died when the second torpedo struck the engine room. A Coast Guard officer boarded the tanker to ascertain the damage and concluded she could be saved. He allowed the master and four men to return to the ship. For ninety hours the tugs *Ontario* and *Bafshe,* escorted by Coast Guard vessels,

towed the *Java Arrow* to reach Port Everglades, Florida. After repairs were completed, she was renamed the *Kerry Patch*.

The Navy reports relate that the second torpedo struck the starboard side, but the owners and the Coast Guard later determined that the second torpedo struck the port side. NSS; WACR; WCSR; *Coast Guard at War*, *Assistance*, 2:31; Rohwer, p. 93; *War Action Casualties*, p. 67; Cremer, p. 70.

JOHN ADAMS

D:	5-5-42	YB:	1942
T:	2305	Tn:	7,180
Pos:	23.11 S / 165.08 E	Dr:	18 ft.
Ow:	U. S. Maritime Commission	C:	2,000 tons gasoline in drums
Op:	Sudden & Christenson	P:	steam
M:	Conrad Peterson	S:	12.0
A:	1-4"; 4-50 cal.		

The *John Adams* was torpedoed by the *I-21* (Matsumura) eighty-five miles from Amadee Lighthouse, New Caledonia, while en route from Nouméa, New Caledonia, to Brisbane, Australia. As the vessel sailed on a nonevasive course, a torpedo struck the port side sixty feet abaft the beam in the #4 hold. The torpedo caused a low rumbling explosion that shook the ship and ripped a large hole nearly twenty feet wide in the #4 hold. Fire broke out immediately, consumed the after end of the ship, and spread to the deckhouse. Burning oil and gasoline shooting mast high spread over the ship and into the water around her. The vessel did not answer the helm, and the engines were finally stopped. As the ship quickly lost way, the eight officers, thirty-one men, and eleven armed guards abandoned ship in three lifeboats ten minutes after the torpedo struck. The Navy gun crew could not get forward because of the fire and had to jump overboard. Five of these men drowned and were the only casualties. One boat was picked up at sea, and the other two made port at Nouméa, both four days after the attack.

NSS; WACR; WCSR; AG; Rohwer, p. 279, places the attack at 22.30 S / 164.35 E.

GREEN ISLAND

D:	5-6-42	YB:	1937
T:	0730	Tn:	1,946
Pos:	18.25 N / 81.30 W	Dr:	12 ft. 4 in.
Ow:	Ford Navigation Co.	C:	2,704 tons general
Op:	Atlantic Barge Carrier Co.	P:	motor
M:	Josef Anderson	S:	7.7
A:	unarmed		

The *U-125* (Folkers) torpedoed the *Green Island* as she steamed on a nonevasive course from New Orleans, Louisiana, to Aruba, NWI. The torpedo struck at the #2 bulkhead between the #4 and #5 hatches about six feet below the waterline. The explosion nearly broke the ship in half. The radio operator sent no distress signals because the blast knocked out the radio. The crew of eight officers and fourteen men abandoned the vessel in two lifeboats. At 1300, five of the crew reboarded the ship to inspect the damage and concluded she could not be saved. The *Green Island* sank almost six hours later. The next day at 0535, the British SS *Fort Quappelle* rescued all hands and landed them at Kingston, Jamaica.

NSS; WACR; WCSR; *Post*, 18 May 1942; Rohwer, p. 93.

HALSEY

D:	5-6-42	YB:	1920
T:	0455	Tn:	7,088
Pos:	27.14 N / 80.03 W	Dr:	27 ft. 3 in.
Ow:	Maritime Transport Line	C:	40,000 bbls. naphtha and 40,000
Op:	Halsey Corp.		bbls. heating oil
M:	Henrik K. Johnson	P:	steam
A:	unarmed	S:	10.5

On 30 April, the *Halsey* sailed from Corpus Christi, Texas, to New York. The tanker proceeded on a nonevasive course in bright moonlight. The *U-333* (Cremer) waited for the freighter and fired two torpedoes that struck close together on the port side at the #2 and #3 main tanks. The explosions ripped a hole in the side sixty feet long. The master stopped the engines and then putting the vessel hard to port, headed toward the shore. The explosion felled the antenna, and the radio operator sent no distress signal. The entire crew of eight officers and twenty-four men abandoned the tanker in the #3 and #4 lifeboats fifteen minutes after the explosions. At 0540 an unidentified tanker came alongside the lifeboats and offered assistance. The survivors declined the offer, and the tanker continued on her course. The survivors recounted that the calcium lights on the lifebuoys ignited the naphtha two hours later. The *Halsey* exploded amidships, broke in two, and burst into flames both fore and aft. At the time of the explosion a Coast Guard patrol boat, the *PC-451*, had approached the survivors but had to immediately investigate what was probably the sighting of the conning tower of the *U-333*. Two fishermen later took the lifeboats in tow and brought them to the Gilbert Bar Lifeboat Station. All hands survived the attack.

The Maritime Transport Line was part of the Halsey Corp. NSS claims the owner was the American Petroleum Transportation Corp. WACR; WCSR; WJ; VSC; Rohwer, p. 93, places the attack at 27.20 N / 80.03 W; *War Action Casualties*, p. 68; Cremer, p. 71.

The tanker *Java Arrow* lays in port after being struck by two torpedoes fired by the *U-333*. The explosion amidships, deep under the vessel, has ripped the shell plating like paper.

The naphtha cargo of the tanker *Halsey* burns on the surface of the water. The *U-333* torpedoed the *Halsey* northeast of Jupiter Inlet, Florida, on 6 May 1942.

ALCOA PURITAN

D:	5-6-42	YB:	1941
T:	1155	Tn:	6,759
Pos:	28.40 N / 88.22 W	Dr:	28 ft. 3 in.
Ow:	Alcoa SS Co.	C:	9,700 tons bauxite
Op:	Alcoa SS Co.	P:	steam
M:	Yngvar Axelstein Krantz	S:	16.5
A:	unarmed		

The *U-507* (Schacht) attacked the *Alcoa Puritan* as she was en route from Port-of-Spain, Trinidad, to Mobile, Alabama. The *Puritan* steered a nonevasive course, and at 1155 lookouts spotted a torpedo passing approximately fifteen feet astern. The master immediately ordered full speed and swung the ship to keep the submarine dead astern to present as small a target as possible. The submarine surfaced at once and at a speed of eighteen to twenty knots began to overtake the freighter on the starboard side. At 1200 the *U-507* opened fire with both deck guns from a distance of one mile. In the next forty minutes, the submarine fired approximately seventy-five rounds at the *Alcoa Puritan*, at a rate of one to two rounds per minute. Scoring about fifty hits on the freighter, the U-boat managed to disable the steering gear. The master then gave orders to abandon ship. Some of the ten officers, thirty-seven crewmen, and seven passengers on board abandoned the ship in one lifeboat, but most jumped overboard and scrambled onto two life rafts. At 1245 the *U-507* came up on the port beam and fired one torpedo that struck below the #4 hatch. The *Alcoa Puritan* sank stern first in eight minutes. The *U-507* then approached to within 100 yards of the survivors, and a German officer with a megaphone shouted, "Sorry we can't help you--hope you get ashore," and waved as the U-boat sailed away. At 1605 on 6 May, the USCG cutter *Boutwell* (WPC-130) rescued all hands. Two members of the crew suffered minor shrapnel injuries. The crew and passengers landed at the Burrwood Section Base, Burrwood, Louisiana.

NSS; WACR; WCSR; *New Orleans State*, 9 May 1942; Other sources list the attack at 28.35 N / 88.22 W; Rohwer, p. 93.

OHIOAN

D:	5-8-42	YB:	1919
T:	1214	Tn:	6,078
Pos:	26.31 N / 79.58 W	Dr:	24 ft. 8 in.
Ow:	American-Hawaiian SS Co.	C:	7,800 tons manganese, ore,
Op:	American-Hawaiian SS Co.		wool, licorice root
M:	Frank H. Roberts	P:	steam
A:	unarmed	S:	14.5

The *Ohioan* sailed from Bombay, India, via Port Elizabeth, South Africa, and San Juan, Puerto Rico, to Baltimore, Maryland. As the freighter steamed four and a half miles off the coast of Florida on a nonevasive course, the *U-564* (Suhren) fired a torpedo that struck on the starboard side at the #4 hold. The ship immediately developed a list, sank within three minutes by the stern, and rolled over. The ship sank so rapidly that none of the eight officers and twenty-nine men had a chance to get the lifeboats away. The #1 boat swamped as it touched the water, and the #2 boat's falls were cut, but it did not float after hitting the water. The men jumped into the water and climbed on the six life rafts that had broken loose as the ship went down. Only seven officers and fifteen men survived. The Coast Guard brought the survivors to West Palm Beach, and four entered a local hospital. The suction created as the ship sank caused the majority of the deaths.

NSS; WACR; WCSR; RWCS; WJ; *Pilot*, 15 May 1942; Rohwer, p. 94.

GREYLOCK

D:	5-8-42	YB:	1921
T:	2115	Tn:	7,460
Pos:	44.14 N / 63.33 W	Dr:	29 ft. 4 in.
Ow:	Seas Shipping Co.	C:	8,530 tons general
Op.:	Seas Shipping Co.	P:	steam
M:	Charles Herbert Whitmore	S:	10.0
A:	1-4"; 4-50 cal.; 4-30 cal.		

The *Greylock*, en route from New York to the USSR via Halifax, Nova Scotia, was torpedoed by the *U-588* (Vogel). The submarine attacked in a fog about ten miles from the Sambro Lightship outside Halifax Harbor. Lookouts spotted the torpedoes as they approached from astern. Two missed the vessel and the third struck the freighter at the stern. The explosion blew off a section of the stern frame. The ten officers, thirty-one crewmen, and a gun crew of eleven did not abandon ship and brought the freighter into Halifax under her own power.

WACR; AG; Rohwer, p. 94.

AURORA

D: 5-10-42   YB: 1920
T: 0230   Tn: 7,050
Pos: 28.35 N / 90.00 W   Dr: 15 ft.
Ow: Socony-Vacuum Oil Co.   C: water ballast
Op.: Socony-Vacuum Oil Co.   P: diesel
M: William H. Sheldon   S: 10.0
A: 1-5"; 2-30 cal.

The *Aurora*, en route from New York to Beaumont, Texas, was intercepted and torpedoed by the *U-506* (Würdemann). The first torpedo struck aft of the bridge in the #6 tank on the starboard side. The tanker immediately took a list to starboard, but by shifting ballast she returned to an even keel. The master proceeded and kept most of the men on deck near the lifeboats. Ninety minutes later a second torpedo hit just aft of the first, in tank #8, and a third torpedo struck at the #4 tank. The *U-506* then surfaced and began shelling the tanker, and a fire broke out in the paint locker. The armed guards on board never returned the fire. Shrapnel wounded the chief mate and the radio operator as they tried to abandon ship. All hands (nine officers, twenty-nine men, and the gun crew of twelve) cleared the ship in two boats and three rafts. The *U-506* departed thinking the tanker was finished. The master, who launched a boat by himself, reboarded the ship at daybreak. At 1000 the diesel yacht USS *Onyx* (PYc-5) and the USS *YP-157* rescued the survivors. All hands lived except the chief mate who died from shrapnel wounds on one of the life rafts. The USCG tug *Tuckahoe* (WYT-89) arrived and sent a rescue party on board with fire hose and extinguishers. Later, with the assistance of the tug *Robert W. Wilmot*, she took the *Aurora* in tow to Algiers, Louisiana. After repairs the *Aurora* returned to service as the *Jamestown*.

The *Aurora* later became the USS *Mariveles* (IX-197). WACR; WCSR; RWCS; Moore, p. 342, claims there were only seven armed guards on board; *War Action Casualties*, p. 70; *Assistance*, 2:160; DANFS, 4:244-45.

VIRGINIA

D: 5-12-42   YB: 1941
T: 1506   Tn: 10,731
Pos: 28.53 N / 89.29 W   Dr: 31 ft.
Ow: National Bulk Carriers   C: 150,000 bbls. gasoline
Op: National Bulk Carriers   P: steam
M: Bengt H. Larson   S: stopped
A: unarmed

The *Virginia* hove to one and a half miles off the entrance to Southwest Pass, Mississippi River, to await a pilot. The tanker sailed from Baytown, Texas, bound for Baton Rouge, Louisiana. The *U-507* (Schacht) spotted the tanker at the pilot buoy in broad daylight with its three flag code hoist flying. A torpedo struck the #8 tank port side, about twelve feet below the water. Two minutes later a second and a third torpedo struck the port fire and engine rooms. The first torpedo created no fire, but the second and third immediately engulfed the entire stern of the tanker in flames. Burning gasoline poured from the ship's side and quickly spread out around the ship for fifty feet on the starboard side and a greater distance on the port side. Flames spread so quickly that none of the lifeboats or life rafts could be launched. The crew of eight officers and thirty-three men tried to escape the flames by jumping overboard. All the survivors, two officers and twelve men, managed to jump into the water from the windward side within minutes of the explosions. They swam away from the tanker until being picked up by *PT-157* thirty minutes later and landed at Burrwood, Louisiana. Several crewmen exhibited bravery by saving the lives of men who had severe burns and could not swim.

NSS; WACR; WCSR; RWCS; *New Orleans Daily States* 16 May 1942; Rohwer, p. 95; *War Action Casualties*, p. 71.

ESSO HOUSTON

D:	5-12-42	YB:	1938
T:	2035	Tn:	7,698
Pos:	12.12 N / 57.24 W	Dr:	30 ft.
Ow:	Standard Oil Co. of N. J.	C:	81,701 bbls. fuel oil
Op:	Standard Oil Co. of N. J.	P:	steam
M:	Trafton Fletcher Wonson	S:	11.5
A:	1-4"		

On 9 May, the *Esso Houston* departed Aruba, NWI, for Montevideo, Uruguay. About 150 miles east of Barbados, lookouts spotted the *U-162* (Wattenberg) crossing the bow of the tanker. Moments later lookouts observed the wake of a torpedo, and the helmsman put the wheel over hard right. With the ship swinging, the torpedo hit on the port side instead of the starboard side. The torpedo struck about twenty-five feet aft of the bridge at the #6 hatch and blew oil over the after part of the ship. Fortunately, the oil did not ignite. The master sounded the general alarm, stopped the engines, and surveyed the damage. He realized that the explosion broke the ship's back and blew the signal to abandon ship. The armed guards mustered at the gun, but the tanker took an extreme list preventing them from using it. At 2045, the crew of eight officers and thirty men, along with the four armed guards, abandoned the ship in three lifeboats and one raft. Twenty minutes after the first torpedo fatally wounded the tanker, Wattenberg put another torpedo amidships into the vessel to finish her off. The *U-162* surfaced near the lifeboats, and Wattenberg questioned the crew and offered assistance. He returned to let the master know that one of the lifeboats

was in a sinking condition near the tanker's stern. The Norwegian SS *Havprins* rescued the eighteen men in the #4 lifeboat forty hours later. These survivors transferred to the Latvian SS *Everagra* and landed at St. Thomas, Virgin Islands. The #3 lifeboat carrying twenty-three men made landfall five days later on St. Vincent Island. One armed guard died from injuries.

NSS; WACR; WCSR; AG; Rohwer, p. 95; *Ships of the Esso Fleet*, pp. 212-18; *War Action Casualties*, p. 72.

GULFPRINCE

D:	5-13-42	YB:	1921
T:	0600	Tn:	6,560
Pos:	28.32 N / 91.00 W	Dr:	27 ft.
Ow:	Gulf Oil Co.	C:	71,000 bbls. crude oil
Op:	Gulf Oil Co.	P:	steam
M:	Peter J. Sigona	S:	10.0
A:	unarmed		

The *Gulfprince* sailed from Port Arthur, Texas, to New York. En route, lookouts spotted a U-boat's periscope one mile astern. The *U-506* (Würdenmann) attacked the zigzagging tanker about six miles south of the Ship Shoals Sea Buoy. The tanker *Gulfpenn* could be seen about five miles ahead. The master maneuvered the ship skillfully and evaded two pairs of torpedoes, two passing ahead and two passing astern. One of the third pair struck the *Gulfprince* a glancing blow on the starboard side aft and abreast of the #8 main cargo tank. After glancing off, it jumped into the air about three feet and then submerged again. The collision sprung hull plates, and four feet of oil leaked from the tank. The master put his ship under full steam and continued on a zigzag course to escape. After being piloted into New Orleans and her cargo discharged, she went into dry dock for repairs and later returned to service. The attack injured none of the eight officers and thirty-four men on board.

NSS; WACR; WCSR; RWCS; WJ; RWSA; The *U-506* was operating in this area and torpedoed the *Gulfpenn* hours later; *War Action Casualties*, p. 75.

NORLANTIC

D:	5-12-42	YB:	1919
T:	2120	Tn:	2,606
Pos:	12.13 N / 66.30 W	Dr:	24 ft. 11 in.
Ow:	Norlasco SS Co.	C:	3,800 tons general, cement, steel pipe
Op:	North Atlantic & Gulf SS Co.		
M:	Rodger John O'Sullivan	P:	steam
A:	unarmed	S:	11.0

The *U-69* (Gräf) attacked the *Norlantic* as she was en route from Pensacola, Florida, to Puerto La Cruz, Venezuela. After lookouts sighted the U-boat, the master altered course, turned the ship's stern to the submarine, and began to zigzag. At fifteen knots the *U-69* overtook the vessel on the port quarter in twenty minutes. At a range of 150 yards the submarine began shelling the freighter. The first shell destroyed the mast and antenna. After this shot the master ordered the engines stopped and signaled the submarine by flashlight that his crew would abandon ship. The *U-69*'s gunners, however, continued to fire as the crew abandoned ship. They fired approximately eight rounds from the deck gun and peppered the ship with machine gun fire. The *U-69* then fired a torpedo that struck on the port side at the boiler room, sinking the vessel within five minutes. Twenty-seven of the seven officers and twenty-two men mustered to abandon the ship in two lifeboats and two rafts. Two men had perished in the engine room, and four others died trying to launch the boats. One severely wounded crew member died of wounds in the lifeboat. Late in the afternoon of 16 May, the Netherlands trading schooners *India* and *Mississippi* sighted the lifeboats. The latter towed the lifeboat with seventeen survivors to the Island of Bonaire, where they landed on the morning of 17 May. On 24 May, ten days after the attack, the SS *Marpesia* picked up two survivors from one of the rafts and landed them at Port-of-Spain. The tug *Crusader Kingston* picked up three other men thirty-seven days later and 1,000 miles from the sinking. A total of seven men died in the attack.

NSS; WACR; WCSR; RWCS; *Times Herald*, 5 June 1942; Rohwer, p. 95.

GULFPENN

D:	5-13-42	YB:	1921
T:	1450	Tn:	8,862
Pos:	28.29 N / 89.12 W	Dr:	28 ft. 4 in.
Ow:	Gulf Oil Corp.	C:	104,181 bbls. fuel oil
Op:	Gulf Oil Corp.	P:	steam
M:	Arthur S. Hodges	S:	12.5
A:	unarmed		

The *Gulfpenn* was torpedoed by the *U-506* (Würdemann) while en route from Port Arthur, Texas, to Philadelphia, Pennsylvania. The tanker proceeded on a zigzagging course in irregular patterns. The *Gulfprince* could be seen astern about five miles. The torpedo struck aft in the engine room on the starboard side, killed all on watch below, and immediately stopped the engines. Twenty-six of the crew of eight officers and thirty men shoved off in the #1 and #2 lifeboats. One crewman later died in the #1 lifeboat. One officer and eleven men died in the explosion or went down with the ship; two of these died trying to retrieve personal papers. The ship made a half-circle and then plunged stern first within five minutes. A Coast Guard plane directed the Honduran ship *Telde* to rescue the survivors three hours later. The survivors landed at Pilottown, Louisiana.

NSS; WACR; WCSR; WJ; Rohwer, p. 95, places the attack at 28.29 N / 89.17 W; *War Action Casualties*, p. 76.

DAVID McKELVY

D:	5-13-42	YB:	1921
T:	2245	Tn:	6,820
Pos:	28.30 N / 89.55 W	Dr:	27 ft. 4 in.
Ow:	Tide Water Associated Oil Co.	C:	81,000 bbls. crude oil
Op:	Tide Water Associated Oil Co.	P:	steam
M:	Carl A. Zwicker	S:	10.0
A:	1-4"; 2-50 cal.		

On 11 May, the *David McKelvy* sailed from Corpus Christi, Texas, to New York City. About thirty-five miles south of the mouth of the Mississippi River, the *U-506* (Würdemann) attacked the zigzagging vessel. A torpedo struck amidships on the port side at about the #4 tank. A huge explosion set the vessel on fire, and the water around the ship quickly became covered with burning oil. All the deck officers perished as the bridge crumpled in the flames. The intense fire kept the gun crew from manning the guns. Twenty-three men among the eight officers, twenty-nine men, and five armed guards abandoned ship at 2305 in the #3 lifeboat, and the others jumped overboard and swam to two rafts. After the attack, Würdemann examined the vessel for ten minutes and left without trying to do further damage. The USCG *Boutwell* (WPC-130) rescued the survivors in the boats and took them to the section base at Burrwood, Louisiana. The chief engineer and the pumpman also survived by standing in the fresh water tanks of the ship's double bottom until the fire burned out. The Norwegian ship *Norsol* rescued these men the next day and took them to Key West, Florida. Four officers, twelve men, and one armed guard died in the attack. A salvage crew reboarded the ship on the 29th and prepared her to be towed to the beach. After beaching, she was declared a CTL because the damage was judged so extensive.

The sources conflict on the size of the crew. NSS; WACR; WCSR; RWCS; AG; *Coast Guard at War*, 14: vol. II, 39; Rohwer, p. 95; *War Action Casualties*, p. 77.

YAKA

D:	5-15-42	YB:	1920
T:	2115	Tn:	5,432
Pos:	Murmansk, USSR	Dr:	17 ft.
Ow:	Waterman SS Co.	C:	none
Op.:	WSA	P:	steam
M:	Oscar Pederson	S:	0
A:	1-3"; 2-30 cal.		

While anchored in Murmansk, USSR, the *Yaka* came under an air attack from about ten German aircraft. A single bomb struck the ship just aft of amidships, passed through the ship's side, struck the boiler, and passed out the deep tank, exploding under the vessel. The explosion extensively damaged the freighter and flooded the machinery space. The ship was towed and beached to prevent further damage. None of the eight officers, thirty men, and eleven armed guards reported any injuries and never abandoned ship. After being repaired, the ship went back in service and was attacked again on 13 June 1942.

WACR; WCSR; AG.

NICARAO

D:	5-15-42	YB:	1920
T:	2115	Tn:	1,445
Pos:	25.20 N / 74.19 W	Dr:	16 ft. 8 in.
Ow:	United Fruit Co.	C:	500 tons fruit, bananas,
Op:	United Fruit Co.		coconuts, charcoal
M:	Cecil Desmond	P:	steam
A:	1-4"; 2-30 cal.	S:	10.0

The *Nicarao* sailed from Kingston, Jamaica, BWI, to Jacksonville, Florida. The *U-751* (Bigalk) attacked the freighter just north of San Salvador, Bahamas. The master saw the track of the torpedo about twenty feet from the ship approaching at an angle of about 40°. The torpedo struck the starboard side five feet below the waterline and just forward of amidships. The force of the explosion vented upward, ruptured the deck plates, tore a hole in the ship's side, and broke her back. She sank by the bow not more than three minutes after the explosion. Eight officers, twenty-seven crewmen, and the four armed guards attempted to launch the two boats, but both swamped. The men managed to right one and bailed it out the next morning. Most of the crew abandoned ship by jumping overboard and swimming to three of the four rafts carried by the freighter. The MS *Esso Augusta* picked up thirty-one survivors twenty-one hours later and brought them to Hampton Roads. One officer and seven men drowned trying to get on board the rafts.

NSS; WACR; WCSR; RWCS; AG; Rohwer, p. 96.

SUN

D:	5-16-42	YB:	1928
T:	0403	Tn:	9,002
Pos:	28.41 N / 90.19 W	Dr:	18 ft. 2 in.
Ow:	Sun Oil Co.	C:	water ballast
Op:	Sun Oil Co.	P:	diesel
M:	John Peter Bakke	S:	11.0
A:	1-4"; 4-30 cal.		

The *Sun* was torpedoed by the *U-506* (Würdemann) while en route from Chester, Pennsylvania, to Beaumont, Texas. A lookout on the forecastle head sighted a torpedo's wake at a distance of about 150 feet from the ship but stood entranced until the torpedo struck the bow. The torpedo threw up a column of water and black smoke and created a rectangular hole approximately thirty feet by twenty feet, beginning eight feet from the bow. Some of the plates on the opposite side of the vessel bulged out severely, and the blast ruptured the lower deck in several places. The engineer immediately stopped the engines according to the master's standing orders. The master countermanded this and ordered them to be started again. The helmsman immediately put the wheel hard over right to position the U-boat dead astern, and the tanker worked up to full speed. The armed guards manned the four-inch gun, while the balance of the crew not on watch mustered at their boat stations and swung the boats out ready for launching. All eight officers, twenty-nine men, and five armed guards survived. The tanker steamed to New Orleans under her own power and after repairs returned to service.

The sources conflict over the armament of this ship. NSS; WACR; AG; Rohwer, p. 96.

WILLIAM C. McTARNAHAN

D:	5-16-42	YB:	1941
T:	0412	Tn:	7,306
Pos:	28.52 N / 90.20 W	Dr:	16 ft. 9 in.
Ow:	National Bulk Carriers	C:	water ballast
Op.:	National Bulk Carriers	P:	diesel
M:	John G. Leech	S:	11.1
A:	1-4"		

The *William C. McTarnahan* sailed from New York via Charleston, South Carolina, to Port Isabel, Texas. The tanker departed Charleston on 10 May, and approximately thirty-five miles east of the Ship Shoal Light, Louisiana, the *U-506* (Würdemann) attacked. The tanker proceeded on a nonevasive course and made an easy target. The chief officer spotted two torpedo tracks 200 yards away and had time only to shout, "Hard right" to the quartermaster. The first torpedo struck the starboard side at the #2 cargo tank and flooded this compartment immediately. The second torpedo struck aft an instant later and damaged the after peak tank, the main engine room, and the steering engine room. The engine stopped at once and a fire broke out, killing all the men in the after part of the vessel. The vessel's fuel bunkers ignited shortly thereafter. The blast also destroyed the main and auxiliary antennas, preventing the radio operator from sending a distress signal. The explosion put the four-inch gun out of action, and the flames drove away the gun crew so that they took no action against the U-boat. Taking advantage of this, Würdemann opened fire fifteen minutes after the torpedo explosions. Three shells struck the ship before the crew could abandon her. The *U-506* then closed to 400 yards and fired twelve to fifteen shells in half-minute intervals. Most of the nine officers, twenty-nine men, and seven armed guards abandoned the ship in two lifeboats and three life rafts. Three officers and fifteen men died. The shrimp trawlers *Defender*, *Pioneer*, and *Viscali* and an unknown boat took the survivors ashore four hours after the attack and landed them at Houma, Louisiana. The *U-506* left thinking the tanker would sink. The Coast Guard tug *Tuckahoe* (WYT-89), with the assistance of the commercial tug *Baranca*, towed the vessel to the entrance of Southwest Pass. She returned to service under the name *St. James*.

The complement and casualty figures conflict within the sources. NSS; WACR; WCSR; Rohwer, p. 96; *War Action Casualties*, p. 79.

RUTH LYKES

D: 5-16-42
T: 1624
Pos: 16.37 N / 82.27 N
Ow: Lykes Bros. SS Co.
Op: Lykes Bros. SS Co.
M: Gosta M.C. Carlson
A: unarmed

YB: 1919
Tn: 2,612
Dr: 22 ft.
C: 39,136 bags coffee
P: steam
S: 10

The *U-103* (Winter) fired a torpedo at the *Ruth Lykes* as she steered a zigzag course from Barranquilla, Colombia, to Houston, Texas. The torpedo struck amidships on the port side, failed to explode, and glanced off the ship. Five minutes later lookouts spotted a periscope aft. The master turned the ship, putting the stern directly toward the submarine. Before the *U-103* completely surfaced, at a range of one and a half miles, it began shelling the freighter. Two dozen shots heavily damaged the superstructure and rigging, and the master had the engines stopped and put full astern. The ship began to list to port and sank at 1644. Most of the eight officers, twenty-one crewmen, and three passengers cleared the ship in two lifeboats, while several others jumped overboard and swam to a raft. The *U-103* picked up one crewman who had injured himself by falling on wreckage as he jumped overboard. Winter ordered a lifeboat alongside, placed the crewman on board, and stated, "You can thank Mr. Roosevelt for this. I am sorry." While alongside the U-boat, one of the ship's officers asked for bandages and received four packages of bandages and two packs of cigarettes. The Norwegian MV *Somerville* picked up twenty-seven survivors twelve hours after the attack and landed them at Key West, Florida. Three officers and two crewmen died on the *Ruth Lykes*, and one crew member died on the rescuing vessel.

NSS; WACR; WCSR; RWCS; Rohwer, p. 96, places the attack at 16.37 N / 82.25 W.

GULFOIL

D:	5-16-42	YB:	1912
T:	2241	Tn:	5,188
Pos:	28.08 N / 89.46 W	Dr:	24 ft. 4 in.
Ow:	Gulf Oil Corp.	C:	54,000 bbls. diesel oil, gas
Op:	Gulf Oil Corp.		enrichment, bunker oil
M:	Henry Rowe	P:	steam
A:	1-4"; 2-30 cal.	S:	9.5

The *Gulfoil* departed Port Arthur, Texas, and sailed to New York, via Key West. The *U-506* (Würdemann) intercepted the tanker about seventy-five miles southwest of the Mississippi River Delta. The ship had maintained a zigzagging course up to 2200 that day. The mate on watch spotted the first torpedo before it hit the starboard side amidships at the #4 tank. The explosion blew the catwalk away from the mainmast to the midships house. A second torpedo hit the starboard side fifteen seconds later and struck the engine room, killing the three men on watch below. The first torpedo caused the vessel to list about 40° to starboard. When the second torpedo struck, the vessel partially righted herself, then sank by the stern in two minutes with a heavy starboard list. The ship sank so rapidly that the crew had no time to launch the boats. Only five officers and fourteen men out of eight officers, twenty-eight men, and the four-man gun crew managed to leave the ship. These men swam to two life rafts, and they stayed within sight of each other for thirty-five hours. At dawn on 18 May, the SS *Benjamin Brewster* rescued the men and brought them to Galveston, Texas.

NSS; WACR; WCSR; AG; Rohwer, p. 96; *War Action Casualties*, p. 80.

CHALLENGER

D: 5-17-42
T: 0357
Pos: 12.11 N / 61.18 W
Ow: American South African Line
Op: U.S. Maritime Commission
M: John G. Waller
A: 1-4"; 1-3"; 6-50 cal.

YB: 1918
Tn: 7,668
Dr: 29 ft. 9 in.
C: 8,400 tons general
P: diesel
S: 8.5

The *Challenger*, en route from New York to Cape Town, South Africa, broke down after leaving New York and steamed to Savannah for repairs. With no facilities available there, she limped to Trinidad. The *U-155* (Piening) caught the ship on a slow zigzagging course and fired a torpedo that struck the #3 tank amidships on the starboard side. A second torpedo struck five seconds later, abaft the #5 hold on the starboard side. This torpedo caused the after magazine to explode, destroyed the entire stern section of the ship, and blew the four-inch gun completely off its mounting. The master stopped the engines and sent an SOS, but he received no reply. Spotting a light off the port beam, the gun crew opened fire with the forward three-inch gun at 3,000 yards. They fired eighteen rounds with no effect. The light eventually crossed the bow of the freighter and disappeared to the southwest. The ship carried nine officers, thirty-two men, eleven armed guards, and twelve passengers. Fifty-six men managed to get off the ship in the two port lifeboats. The USS *Turquoise* (PY-19) picked them up eleven hours later and landed them at Trinidad. The ship sank by the stern at 0458. Eight persons died on the ship—two armed guards, one passenger, and five of the vessel's crew.

NSS; WACR; WCSR; *Virginia Pilot*, 12 June 1942; Rohwer, p. 96.

FOAM

D: 5-17-42
T: 1220
Pos: 43.20 N / 63.08 W
Ow: General Seafoods Corp.
Op: General Seafoods Corp.
M: Daniel Joseph Maher
A: unarmed

YB: 1919
Tn: 324
Dr: 16 ft. 6 in.
C: none
P: steam
S: 8.0

The trawler *Foam* was shelled by the *U-432* (Schultze) about eighty-five miles south of Halifax, Nova Scotia, while en route from Boston, Massachusetts, to the fishing banks of Nova Scotia. Crewmen on the trawler sighted the submarine on the surface at the same time a shell passed over the bow. The master immediately stopped the boat. The second shell hit the bow, and the master rang the emergency alarm to call the crew out on deck. The *U-432* began shelling the trawler, firing approximately twenty-nine shots before the crew abandoned ship, and approximately fifteen more shots afterwards. The shells did not explode and passed through the vessel. The crew of two officers and nineteen men abandoned the trawler ten minutes after the *U-432* fired the first shot. Seventeen men left in a lifeboat and four on board a raft. One of the men on the raft later died as a result of the shellfire. The lifeboat steered for land and arrived at the Sambro Light Ship thirty hours after the attack. A Canadian patrol boat took them off and landed them at Halifax. The Canadian corvette *Halifax* (K-237) rescued the other three survivors from the raft two days after the attack and landed them at Boston.

NSS; WACR; WCSR; WJ; Rohwer, p. 96.

DEER LODGE

D:	5-18-42	YB:	1919
T:	1123	Tn:	6,178
Pos:	Anchored at Kola Inlet	Dr:	24 ft. 6 in.
Ow:	WSA	C:	none
Op:	Moore McCormack Lines	P:	steam
M:	Alexander Smith Henry	S:	anchored
A:	1-4"; 4-50 cal.		

The *Deer Lodge* was attacked three times by German dive bombers beginning at 1123 on 18 May, again at 1000 on 27 May, and finally on 29 June at 1545. The first attack came while at anchor in Kola Inlet, North Russia. The latter two attacks occurred when the ship lay beached at nearby Rosta. On the 18th, after having discharged cargo and while laying at anchor in Kola Inlet, the ship was attacked by six German dive bombers. Numerous bombs fell close to the stern, and the explosions bodily lifted the stern out of the water, buckling and twisting the vessel with each explosion. As she settled quickly by the stern, the chief engineer rushed below to close the watertight door that led from the shaft alley. By doing this, he saved the vessel. A survey by the master and the chief engineer showed that the #5 hold and the after peak tank flooded to the level of the tween deck, but the #4 hold remained dry. They agreed that the vessel should be moved to a shallow anchorage. At about 1300 Russian naval engineers came alongside and put a diver overboard. After a short survey the diver reported a hole in the vessel approximately twelve feet long by ten feet wide. A large rip in the ship's side extended from the hole to the garboard strake under the counter. The explosion had severely damaged the crew's quarters aft and had broken the furniture loose. It also broke the pipelines for the sanitary system, as well as the steam and fresh water pipes. At 1445 the crew weighed anchor and the vessel proceeded, with the aid of two tugs, to an anchorage opposite Rosta. On 27 May at about 1045 seven German planes again attacked the vessel. They dropped bombs all around, but luckily none did any serious damage. A survey showed that 700 square feet of shell plating on the port side had been blown inboard. In the center of this area the blast had created a hole approximately ten feet square and had torn a large gash about eight feet long. On 25 July, after some repairs, the ship moved, aided by two tugs, to the repair yard. During the last attack on 29 June, a bomb landed off the port bow and only slightly injured the ship. There were no casualties among the seven officers, twenty-seven men, and eleven armed guards in any of the three attacks.

See 17 February 1943 for another attack. NSS; WACR; AG.

MERCURY SUN

D:	5-18-42	YB:	1931
T:	0004	Tn:	8,893
Pos:	20.02 N/ 84.25 W	Dr:	28 ft. 11 in.
Ow:	Sun Oil Co.	C:	93,607 bbls. Navy oil
Op:	Sun Oil Co.	P:	diesel
M:	Willard Davis Jr.	S:	8.5
A:	unarmed		

On 13 May, the *Mercury Sun* sailed from Beaumont, Texas, to Pearl Harbor via Cristobal, Canal Zone. The tanker had steered a zigzag course throughout the day. The *U-125* (Folkers) fired two torpedoes that struck in quick succession on the port side at the #4 and #5 tanks and broke the ship's back. The tanker's carbon dioxide smothering system successfully kept the cargo from igniting after the first torpedo explosion. When the second torpedo hit, however, the vessel burst into flames. The watch below secured the engines when the second torpedo exploded. Twenty-nine men of the crew of nine officers and twenty-six men managed to abandon ship in two lifeboats. A third torpedo struck the vessel on the starboard side in the #8 tank as the last boat cleared the ship. The lifeboats stood by the burning vessel until daybreak and then proceeded under sail. Nearly forty hours after the attack the SS *Howard* rescued twenty-eight survivors and landed them at Mobile, Alabama. One seriously injured crew member was transferred to a Coast Guard boat at the Tampa Sea Buoy. Three officers and three men perished on the ship. The tanker, with her bow sagging, sank at 0300.

NSS; WACR; WCSR; RWCS; WJ; Rohwer, p. 96, places the attack at 20.01 N / 84. 26 W; *War Action Casualties*, p. 81.

QUAKER CITY

D: 5-18-42   YB: 1920
T: 0440   Tn: 4,962
Pos: 15.47 N / 53.12 W   Dr: 22 ft.
Ow: U.S. Maritime Commission   C: 4,500 tons manganese ore
Op: U.S. Maritime Commission   P: steam
M: Edward A. Richmond   S: 9.5
A: unarmed

The *Quaker City* sailed from Cape Town, South Africa, to Norfolk, Virginia. Three hundred miles east of Barbados the *U-156* (Hartenstein) intercepted and attacked the freighter. A single torpedo struck the stern near the waterline. The explosion shattered the propeller, the rudder, and the after part of the ship and killed ten men. The ship sank in less than ten minutes. The *U-156* surfaced about five minutes later but did not fire. The survivors of the crew of ten officers and thirty men immediately abandoned the freighter in four lifeboats. The *U-156* approached the boat containing the master. After asking the ship's name, cargo, and destination, Hartenstein gave the master directions to Barbados. The USS *Blakeley* (DD-150) picked up seven survivors and landed them at Trinidad. Nearly a week after the attack eight survivors landed at Dominica, and the remaining fifteen men landed in Barbados. An oiler later died ashore from injuries received during the blast.

The NSS places the sinking at 14.55 N / 51.40 W; WACR; WCSR; RWCS; Rohwer, p. 96.

WILLIAM J. SALMAN

D: 5-18-42   YB: 1919
T: 1455   Tn: 2,616
Pos: 20.08 N / 83.47 W   Dr: unknown
Ow: Stockard SS Corp.   C: 2,730 tons building material
Op.: Stockard SS Corp.   P: steam
M: Charles D. Bryant   S: 10
A: unarmed

The *William J. Salman* was torpedoed by the *U-125* (Folkers) as she was en route from New Orleans, Louisiana, to Antigua, BWI. The torpedo struck at the #3 hatch on the starboard side, nearly splitting the vessel in two. The explosion lifted the stern five or six feet into the air, rocked the masts violently, and knocked the antenna to the deck. The freighter flooded rapidly and sank stern first within two minutes. The crew, trying to reach the deck, had to pass through gas fumes that burned their eyes and throats. The ship sank so fast that none of the crew of eight officers and twenty men successfully launched any of the boats. Two overturned boats floated free of the sinking vessel and were later righted by the men. Two officers and four men never left the ship. The survivors set sail for the Cuban coast. Twenty hours after the attack the Latvian SS *Kegums* rescued the men and landed them at Key West, Florida.

NSS; WACR; WCSR; RWCS; Rohwer, p. 97, places the attack at 20.08 N / 83.46 W.

HEREDIA

D:	5-19-42	YB:	1908
T:	0200	Tn:	4,732
Pos:	27.32 N / 91 W	Dr:	23 ft.
Ow:	United Fruit SS Co.	C:	1,500 tons bananas, coffee
Op:	United Fruit SS Co.	P:	steam
M:	Erwin F. Colburn	S:	13.5
A:	1-3"; 2-30 cal.		

The *U-506* (Würdemann) attacked the *Heredia* two miles southeast of the Ship Shoal Buoy as she neared the end of her journey from Puerto Barrios, Guatemala, to New Orleans, Louisiana. Three torpedoes struck the vessel, causing her to plunge stern first within three minutes. The *Heredia* had not performed any evasive maneuvers, making her an easy target for the *U-506*. The first and second torpedoes struck the port quarter aft at the #3 and #4 holds. The third torpedo struck amidships on the starboard side. The explosions blew the decks up and destroyed the #3 and the #4 lifeboats and two life rafts. The survivors of the crew of eleven officers and thirty-seven men, the eight passengers, and the six armed guards had no time to launch the boats. Only two rafts got away from the vessel. The shrimp trawlers *Papa Joe*, *Conquest*, *J. Edwin Treakle*, and *Shellwater* rescued twenty-three survivors. They landed these men at Morgan City, Louisiana. A seaplane picked up three other survivors and landed them at New Orleans. Six officers, twenty-four men, one passenger, and five of the armed guards died in the attack.

NSS; WACR; WCSR; *Pilot*, 26 June 1942; Rohwer, p. 97, places the attack at 28.53 N / 91.03 W.

ISABELA

D:	5-19-42	YB:	1911
T:	0445	Tn:	3,109
Pos:	17.50 N / 75.00 W	Dr:	17 ft. 10 in.
Ow:	Agwilines Inc.	C:	1,950 tons general cargo, cars
Op.:	Agwilines Inc.	P:	steam
M:	Reginald J. Dexter	S:	10
A:	unarmed		

The *U-751* (Bigalk) attacked the *Isabela* thirty-five miles south of Navassa Island Light, as she steamed from New York to San Juan, Puerto Rico. The torpedo entered a coal bunker at the waterline slightly abaft the bridge on the starboard side. The explosion caused extensive damage and brought the ship to an immediate halt. The blast collapsed all the partial bulkheads on the main deck and above, and jarred the galley range off its foundation, causing it to fall through the tremendous hole in the various decks at least to the bottom of the ship, and perhaps right on through the bottom. The *U-751* immediately came to the surface and began to shell the vessel off the port side from a range of 350 yards. The master directed the clearing of the lifeboats and rafts. The U-boat fired four shots before the crew abandoned ship and three shots after abandonment. The shelling hastened the *Isabela*'s sinking, and she went down in thirty minutes. Two firemen and a coal passer died on watch below. The surviving thirty-four men, consisting of eight officers and twenty-six men, abandoned the ship in two lifeboats and three rafts. The boats took the men off the rafts the next morning, and they rowed to Cape Briton, Haiti. One boat made landfall in eighteen hours, the other in thirty hours.

NSS; WACR; WCSR; Rohwer, p. 97.

OGONTZ

D:	5-19-42	YB:	1919
T:	1329	Tn:	5,037
Pos:	23.30 N / 86.37 W	Dr:	24 ft. 7 in.
Ow:	Intercoastal Packing Co.	C:	7,660 tons nitrate
Op.:	Chile Nitrate Sales Corp.	P:	steam
M:	Adolph M. Wennerlund	S:	11.5
A:	1-4"; 4-50 cal.; 4-30 cal.		

The *Ogontz* sailed from Chile en route to Panama City, Florida. The ship maintained a zigzag course and had been followed by the *U-103* (Winter) for sixty miles. A torpedo struck the starboard side below the navigating bridge, at the bulkhead separating the fireroom and the engine room. The engines were immediately secured, and the radio operator sent distress signals but received no answer. The ship plunged to the bottom bow first within five minutes. Before leaving the ship, the gun crew managed to fire a single desperate shot from the stern gun. Surviving members of the seven officers, thirty men, and the four armed guards abandoned ship in two lifeboats and two life rafts. A falling mast struck the lifeboat commanded by the master and caused most of the casualties. The *U-103* took two of the crew on board for questioning for a few minutes. After learning the name and tonnage of the vessel, dressing a wound, and giving the men cigarettes, the Germans placed them back in a lifeboat. The master, sixteen men, and two armed guards died in the attack. The SS *Esso Dover* rescued the survivors the following day and landed them at New Orleans, Louisiana, on 22 May.

NSS; WACR; WCSR; RWCS; AG; Rohwer, p. 97.

HALO

D:	5-20-42	YB:	1920
T:	0020	Tn:	6,986
Pos:	28.42 N / 90.08 W	Dr:	26 ft. 8 in.
Ow:	Cities Service Oil Co.	C:	64,103 bbls. crude oil
Op:	Cities Service Oil Co.	P:	steam
M:	Ulrich Fred Moller	S:	10.4
A:	unarmed		

The *Halo* sailed from Tampico, Mexico, to New Orleans, Louisiana, via Galveston, Texas. On 19 May, the tanker weighed anchor at Galveston and proceeded on a rapidly changing zigzag pattern. The *U-506* (Würdemann) attacked the *Halo* about fifty miles from the Southwest Pass of the Mississippi River. The first torpedo struck on the starboard side, under the bridge, and completely destroyed this part of the ship. Ten seconds later a second torpedo hit the starboard side, aft of the bridge but forward of the engine room. This torpedo tore the ship apart, ignited the cargo, and caused her to plunge bow first with her propeller still turning. The crew consisted of eight officers and thirty-four men, but only twenty-three managed to leave the ship, most of these from the after part of the tanker. While still under way the crew managed to launch only one life raft. Explosions and fire destroyed the four lifeboats and three other rafts. The men grabbed life preservers, jumped over the side, and swam away from the ship as she went down. The survivors huddled together clinging to wreckage in the water near the sunken ship throughout the night and the next day. Two men managed to cling to a half-burned life raft and stayed on it for seven days without food or water. The British tanker SS *Orina* rescued these two men. The others in the water near the wreck began dying from exposure and injuries. On the third day wreckage ascended from the tanker, and the seven remaining survivors tied boards together with strips of canvas torn from their life preservers. Crude oil also floated to the surface forming a layer four inches thick. On the fifth day a Mexican cargo ship, the *Oaxaca*, picked up the three remaining survivors, but one of these men died at sea. On the 28th the two survivors arrived at a Tampico hospital; however, only one of them lived. Thus, only one officer and two men lived through the incident.

NSS; WACR; WCSR; Rohwer, p. 97; *War Action Casualties*, p. 82.

GEORGE CALVERT

D:	5-20-42	YB:	1942
T:	1311	Tn:	7,191
Pos:	22.55 N / 84.26 W	Dr:	30 ft.
Ow:	U.S. Maritime Commission	C:	9,116 tons general
Op:	A. H. Bull & Co., Inc.	P:	steam
M:	Severin Broadwick	S:	11
A:	1-4"; 4-50 cal.; 2-30 cal.		

The fully loaded *George Calvert* was torpedoed by the *U-752* (von Mannstein) while en route from Baltimore, Maryland, to Bandar Shahpur, Iran, via Cape Town, South Africa. The ship had traveled with a convoy and left the formation about eleven miles off the Dry Tortugas. As the ship steered a zigzag course, a torpedo hit the #3 hold about five or six feet below the waterline. A second torpedo struck the freighter twenty feet forward of the stern. This explosion set off the magazine, blew the stern gun overboard, and killed three armed guards. A third torpedo hit amidships and broke the ship in half. The *Calvert* sank almost immediately after the third torpedo struck. Following the first explosion, the master sounded the general alarm and the entire complement of eight officers, thirty-three men, and ten armed guards mustered at their boat stations. Forty-eight men abandoned the ship in three lifeboats. While still near the freighter, the German officers questioned some of the survivors, asking the name of the ship, her tonnage, and cargo. The boats reached shore about six hours later but waited to land at Dimas, Cuba, the next day.

The complement figures are contradictory within the sources. NSS; WACR; WCSR; AG; RWCS; Rohwer, p. 97.

CLARE

D:	5-20-42	YB:	1915
T:	2146	Tn:	2,139
Pos:	21.35 N / 84.43 W	Dr:	21 ft.
Ow:	U.S. Maritime Commission	C:	3,000 tons general
Op:	A. H. Bull Co. Inc.	P:	steam
M:	William Tausendschoen	S:	10
A:	1-4"; 2-30 cal.		

The *Clare* departed from Baltimore, Maryland, en route to San Juan, Puerto Rico. About forty miles off the coast of Cuba the *U-103* (Winter) spotted the freighter and attacked. A torpedo struck at the foremast between cargo holds #1 and #2, about six feet below the waterline. The blast created a hole about fifteen feet in diameter, demolished the entire front of the ship, and scattered the cargo below and above decks. The ship lost way rapidly and sank thirty minutes later, listing to port about 25° and then going down quickly by the head. The radio operator sent an SOS four times but received no answer. The Navy gun crew had no opportunity to use any of the guns because the U-boat remained submerged. The entire complement of eight officers, twenty-five men, and seven armed guards abandoned the ship in one lifeboat and three rafts. The lifeboat made Cape Corrientes, Cuba, in eight hours, and a Cuban gunboat picked up the three rafts at sea. All hands survived.

The figures for the armed guards conflict. NSS; WACR; WCSR; AG; Rohwer, p. 98.

ELIZABETH

D:	5-20-42	YB:	1915
T:	2215	Tn:	4,727
Pos:	21.36 N / 84.48 W	Dr:	23 ft.
Ow:	WSA	C:	3,500 tons trucks and
Op:	A. H. Bull Co.		construction material
M:	Walter G. Hudgins	P:	steam
A:	1-4"; 2-30 cal.	S:	11

The *Elizabeth* sailed from New York City to San Juan, Puerto Rico. From about 400 yards the *U-103* (Winter) brought the zigzagging freighter to with a star shell across her bow. Three minutes later the U-boat hit the stack with a shell. At 2231, the *U-103* fired a torpedo that struck the port side between the #3 hatch and the engine room. The explosion killed the three men on watch in the engine room and destroyed the main steam line, the condenser, the shelter deck, and the radio shack. The severely damaged freighter quickly came to a dead stop. The radio operator sent distress signals and received acknowledgments. The armed guard contingent manned the after gun and fired two shots. At 2255, with the freighter sinking, the surviving members of the complement of eight officers, twenty-seven men, and seven armed guards abandoned the ship in one lifeboat and one raft. The freighter sank stern first ten minutes later. The three men who got away on the raft were never seen again. The remaining thirty-six crewmen landed twenty-one hours after the attack on the western Cuban coast.

NSS; WACR; WCSR; AG.

PLOW CITY

D:	5-21-42	YB:	1920
T:	1430	Tn:	3,282
Pos:	39.08 N / 69.57 W	Dr:	23 ft.
Ow:	Hedger SS Corp.	C:	4,971 tons bauxite ore
Op:	Alcoa SS Co.	P:	steam
M:	George Hazeleaf	S:	8
A:	unarmed		

The *Plow City* sailed from Port-of-Spain, Trinidad, to New York. About 0900 a lookout spotted what appeared to be a lifeboat with a sail. The master investigated and mistook a lifeboat from the British SS *Peisander* for a submarine. He turned the freighter's stern and fled the area on a zigzag course. The *U-588* (Vogel) spotted the freighter's smoke and chased her for over four hours to maneuver into a firing position. The *U-588's* first torpedo missed ahead by about five feet. A second torpedo struck almost immediately thereafter on the port side aft of the #2 hold at the waterline. The explosion cut off communications to the engine room, and the watch below secured the engines. The master ordered the ship abandoned, and most of the crew of eight officers and twenty-three men climbed immediately into the two lifeboats. The radio operator stayed behind to send distress messages. With the crew safely off the ship, the *U-588* moved to the starboard side and fired a torpedo into the engine room and she sank stern first within minutes. The *U-588* then took one crew member on board for questioning and returned him along with rations of cigarettes and rum. The U-boat crew also helped to right one of the boats that capsized during launching. The USS *Sapphire* (PYc-2) picked up the survivors after five days. The second mate, the only casualty, died when he was blown off the bridge by the second torpedo.

NSS; WACR; WCSR; RWCS; WJ; Rohwer, p. 98; *Assistance*, 2:162-63.

WILLIAM BOYCE THOMPSON

D:	5-22-42	YB:	1921
T:	1805	Tn:	7,061
Pos:	16.26 N / 76.55 W	Dr:	13.05 ft.
Ow:	Sinclair Refining Co.	C:	water ballast
Op:	Sinclair Refining Co.	P:	steam
M:	Hjalmus V. Rasmussen	S:	10.5
A:	unarmed		

The *U-558* (Krech) discovered the *William Boyce Thompson* sailing from New York to Curaçao, NWI. Although the freighter steered on a nonevasive course, a single torpedo from the *U-558* struck about ten feet below the waterline on the starboard side. The explosion ripped a twenty-foot hole in the hull at the #4 tank and created several small holes on the port side and the weather deck. The #4 and #3 tanks flooded, while the main pump room filled slowly. After the explosion, the master ordered the helmsman to begin a zigzag course, and the ship headed north at full speed. The tanker sent distress messages and her position but received no reply. The tanker made port under her own power. The eight officers, twenty-nine crewmen, and two Navy signalmen on board reported no injuries.

NSS; WACR; Rohwer, p. 98, places the attack at 16.26 N / 77.51 W.

SAMUEL Q. BROWN

D:	5-23-42	YB:	1921
T:	0140	Tn:	6,624
Pos:	20.15 N / 84.38 W	Dr:	27 ft. 2 3/4 in.
Ow:	Tide Water Associated Oil Co.	C:	80,000 bbls. Navy #6 fuel oil
Op:	Tide Water Associated Oil Co.	P:	steam
M:	Aksel Andersen	S:	10
A:	1-4"; 4-20 mm; 2-30 cal.		

The *Samuel Q. Brown* sailed from New Orleans, Louisiana, to Honolulu, Hawaii, via the Yucatan Channel. The tanker had discontinued her zigzagging course at sunset. A torpedo fired by the *U-103* (Winter) struck the port side at the bulkhead between the #9 main cargo tank and the after fuel tanks. Flames immediately engulfed the vessel. The ship's engineers reversed the engines from full ahead to slow astern to stop the tanker. The explosion destroyed the mainmast and the aerial, preventing the radio operator from sending a distress signal. The burning oil kept the gun crew from manning the guns, and the master immediately ordered the boats to be launched. The flames advanced so quickly that the master ordered all hands to jump over the side to save themselves. The initial explosion killed two crew members from the complement of eight officers, thirty-one men, and sixteen armed guards. The remaining men swam to the two ship's boats and two rafts and managed to escape the flames. The submarine surfaced about twenty minutes after the attack, and officers inquired about the name of the ship and her cargo. Later in the morning the men on the rafts transferred into the two boats. On 23 May, a patrol plane from Naval Air Station, Upham, Canal Zone, rescued five injured men and took them to a hospital at Key West. The next day the USS *Goff* (DD-247) rescued the remaining forty-eight and took them to Cristobal. The blazing hulk of the *Brown* remained afloat until sunk by gunfire from the *Goff* at 2120 on 25 May.

Other sources place the attack at 20.15 N / 84.37 W. NSS; WACR; WCSR; RWCS; Rohwer, p. 98; *War Action Casualties*, p. 84.

BEATRICE

D: 5-24-42
T: 1940
Pos: 17.23 N / 76.58 W
Ow: A. H. Bull SS Lines
Op: U.S. Maritime Commission
M: Charles Hendrickx
A: unarmed

YB: 1917
Tn: 3,450
Dr: 21 ft. 2 in.
C: 4,549 tons raw sugar
P: steam
S: 9.5

The *Beatrice* departed Mayagüez, Puerto Rico, en route to Pensacola, Florida. In moderate seas the *U-558* (Krech) fired a torpedo that struck the ship but failed to explode. Krech decided to sink the vessel with gunfire and surfaced directly astern. Lookouts spotted the U-boat a few minutes before the Germans opened fire. The *Beatrice* began to zigzag in an attempt to keep the U-boat astern. The *U-558* opened fire at a range of about a mile and fired about thirty shells from its forward 88-mm gun. The 20-mm machine gun in the conning tower also peppered the ship. Once the shells began striking the *Beatrice*, the master concluded he could not escape and ordered the ship abandoned. The crew of eight officers and twenty-two men began leaving the ship in one lifeboat and three rafts. One of the rafts drifted into the shellfire of the U-boat and presumably one man was killed. At about 2105 a PBY appeared, circled the submarine, and dropped depth charges, but the *U-558* escaped. The boat carrying twenty-one men sailed to Pigeon Island, Jamaica. The British patrol boat *Hauken* picked up the nine remaining survivors from one raft and landed them at Kingston, Jamaica. The survivors last saw the *Beatrice* afloat and burning. She sank at about 0440 the next day.

NSS; WACR; WCSR; Rohwer, p. 98, places the attack at 17.21 N / 76.07 W.

CARLTON

D: 5-25-42
T: 1600
Pos: approx. 65.00 N / 10.00 W
Ow: Lykes Bros. Inc.
Op: Lykes Bros. Inc.
M: Ragnavald Hansen
A: 1-4"; 2-50 cal.; 2-30 cal.

YB: 1919
Tn: 5,127
Dr: 24 ft.
C: 5,500 tons explosives, tanks,
      ammunition
P: steam
S: 7.0

On 20 May, the *Carlton* sailed in Convoy PQ-16 from Reykjavik, Iceland, to Murmansk, USSR. Five days out of port, about 300 miles off North Cape, lookouts spotted about twenty-eight aircraft preparing to attack the convoy. On one of the bombing runs a plane flew over the stern and released bombs at an estimated height of 300 yards. One stick of charges hit ten feet from the ship and lifted her stern into the air. The concussion opened up the steel plating, penetrated the #5 and the #6 double bottoms, damaged a main steam pipe, and ruptured other piping systems. After dropping from the convoy, a British escort vessel indicated she would torpedo the *Carlton* if repairs could not be made within an hour. The master asked the convoy commodore for more time and received it. The escort held the *Carlton*'s head into the sea, and the engineers made repairs in ten hours. The *Carlton* left the convoy to return to Reykjavik in tow of the British trawler *Northern Spray* (FY-129). The following day German planes attacked again but inflicted no additional damage. The ship returned to Reykjavik under her own power on 30 May. None of the eight officers, twenty-seven men, or the eleven armed guards reported injuries.

NSS; WACR; AG; Irving, pp. 18-20.

ALCOA CARRIER

D:	5-25-42	YB:	1919
T:	2115	Tn:	5,588
Pos:	18.45 N / 79.50 W	Dr:	25 ft.
Ow:	Alcoa SS Co.	C:	6,500 tons general
Op:	Alcoa SS Co.	P:	steam
M:	Victor L. Parsons	S:	11
A:	unarmed		

The *Alcoa Carrier* was torpedoed and shelled by the *U-103* (Winter) while en route from Mobile, Alabama, to Kingston, Jamaica. The ship had discontinued her zigzagging course because of cloudy weather. A torpedo struck the #2 hatch on the starboard side at a depth of about twenty feet below the waterline. As the compartment flooded, the master had the engines stopped and the damage surveyed. The explosion crippled the radio, preventing the radio operator from sending a distress signal. The *U-103* surfaced twenty minutes after the torpedo struck and fired about twenty-three rounds at the freighter from a position 400 yards away. Seventeen shells hit in the area of the bridge and started a fire. The crew of eight officers and twenty-seven men abandoned ship in two lifeboats. Winter asked the freighter's captain the name and the speed of the vessel, and if all the crew had been accounted for; he then gave the crew a package of cigarettes. The *U-103* put a second torpedo into the ship amidships at about 2215 and left the area after the ship sank. Five days later, a Cuban gunboat picked up thirty-three men and took them to Havana, Cuba. A Navy plane rescued the remaining two men and took them to Key West. The ship finally sank bow first three hours after the attack.

NSS; WACR; WCSR; WJ.

SYROS

D:	5-26-42	YB:	1920
T:	0100	Tn:	6,191
Pos:	72.35 N / 05.30 E	Dr:	28 ft.
Ow:	Lykes Brothers	C:	6,390 tons general war cargo
Op:	Lykes Brothers	P:	steam
M:	Cornelius A. Holmes	S:	11
A:	yes but unknown		

The *Syros* sailed from Philadelphia to Murmansk via Reykjavik, Iceland, in Convoy PQ-16. About 200 miles southwest of Bear Island, at 0500 local time, a submarine signal sounded in column one. The master ordered the crew to general quarters and posted extra lookouts. At about 0057 a torpedo fired by the *U-703* (Bielfeld) sped past the port quarter astern of column three. It traveled at a right angle to the convoy from port to starboard. The ships in the rear of the convoy opened fire at the torpedo but failed to hit it. This torpedo struck the *Syros* abreast of her stack in the engine room, on the port side. A moment later a second torpedo hit at the #2 hatch, causing the ammunition on board to explode. The ship began to sink on an even keel after the first explosion. The second explosion broke the ship in two, and she sank within eighty seconds. The explosions blew off the two lifeboats on the port side, and the other boats could not be launched. The eight officers, twenty-nine crewmen, and two Navy signalmen on board managed to launch three rafts before going into the water. Thirty survivors clung to the rafts until rescued by the minesweeper HMS *Hazard* (N-02). Two of these men died of exposure and were buried at sea. The remaining five officers, twenty-two men, and one Navy signalman landed at Murmansk.

The personnel numbers are contradictory within the sources. NSS; WACR; WCSR; Rohwer, p. 198.

CARRABULLE

D:	5-26-42	YB:	1920
T:	0400	Tn:	5,030
Pos:	26.18 N / 89.21 W	Dr:	26 ft.
Ow:	Cuba Distilling Co.	C:	42,307 bbls. liquid asphalt
Op:	International Freighting Corp.	P:	steam
M:	Norris T. Ela	S:	10.5
A:	unarmed		

The *U-106* (Rasch) stopped the *Carrabulle* at sea by a signal from a siren and a shot across her bow. The tanker had departed from Good Hope, Louisiana, on 25 May, and had steered a zigzagging course while en route to San Juan, Puerto Rico. The second mate observed the U-boat at 0350, a ship's length away from the starboard beam. The *U-106* began firing shells at the bridge and superstructure, and the master immediately ordered the ship abandoned. The radio operator remained behind to continue sending distress signals. The crew of eight officers and thirty-two men, with the exception of the radio operator, left in two lifeboats. One boat held twenty-four men, including the master and first mate. At the moment this boat reached the water, a torpedo struck just below the waterline on the port side and blew the boat to pieces. Only two men, one of them the second mate, survived; the other twenty-two died instantly. Fifteen members of the crew left in the other boat. They later took the radio operator off the ship and picked up the two living men from the first lifeboat. The SS *Thompson Lykes* rescued the three officers and fifteen men fifteen hours after the attack and brought them to New Orleans, Louisiana. The tanker sank stern first at 0555.

Some survivors claimed that Rasch asked if all the men had gotten clear of the ship. Receiving a negative answer, he reportedly laughed and fired the second torpedo that killed twenty-two men. NSS; WACR; WCSR; *War Action Casualties*, p. 85; Rohwer, p. 99.

ATENAS

D:	5-26-42	YB:	1908
T:	2209	Tn:	4,639
Pos:	25.50 N / 89.05 W	Dr:	unknown
Ow:	United Fruit Co.	C:	general
Op:	United Fruit Co.	P:	steam
M:	Trygve Angell	S:	12.5
A:	1-4"; 2-30 cal.		

The *Atenas* was shelled by the *U-106* (Rasch) while en route from New Orleans, Louisiana, to Cristobal, Canal Zone. At 1300, lookouts sighted a periscope about one point off the port beam. It moved slowly at first and then disappeared a few times. When the periscope moved toward the vessel, the master changed course so that the stern gun could be cleared and fired. The first and second salvo exploded near the periscope. The fourth salvo exploded on top of the periscope and it disappeared. The *Atenas* then resumed a southerly course in a zigzagging pattern. At 2209, the *U-106* began rapidly shelling the freighter from about 2,000 yards for about two minutes. The *U-106* evidently tried unsuccessfully to bring down the radio antenna. Seven shells hit the port side and started two small fires but did little damage. The master sounded the general alarm, and the helmsman again swung the ship's stern toward the submarine. With the stern toward the U-boat, the gunners opened fire. After one shot the

U-106 dove and disappeared. None of the ten passengers and eight armed guards or the crew of eight officers and forty-six men reported any injuries.

The figures for the ship's crew and armament are contradictory within the sources. NSS; WACR; AG; Only the *U-106* was in the area but did not make out an attack report. The *U-558* reportedly attacked a Soviet vessel but saw her sink. Rohwer, p. 99.

ALAMAR

D:	5-27-42	YB:	1916
T:	0010	Tn:	5,688
Pos:	100 miles SE of Bear Island	Dr:	unknown
Ow:	Calmar SS Corp.	C:	6,762 tons munitions, foodstuffs,
Op:	Calmar SS Corp.		tanks, fuel, truck bodies
M:	Ragnar Emanuel Nystrom	P:	steam
A:	1-4"; 2-50 cal.; 2-30 cal.	S:	9

On 20 March, the *Alamar* departed Philadelphia bound for Murmansk, via Reykjavik. Sailing as part of Convoy PQ-16, she was bombed and sunk 100 miles southeast of Bear Island. During an air raid, a bomb struck the ship at the after end of the #4 hatch on the port side. The ship immediately caught fire and began to settle rapidly. The corvette HMS *Starwort* (K-20), the trawler HMS *St. Elstan* (FY-240), and the submarine HMS *Trident* (N-52) picked up the eight officers, twenty-eight crewmen, and nine armed guards in four lifeboats twelve hours later. About twenty-five minutes after abandonment, the British submarine sank the freighter to prevent her from becoming a menace to navigation.

WACR; WCSR; AG.

ALCOA BANNER

D:	5-27-42	YB:	1919
T:	0630	Tn:	7,800
Pos:	200 miles SW Bear Island	Dr:	24 ft. 5 in.
Ow:	Alcoa SS. Co.	C:	10,000 tons general
Op:	Alcoa SS. Co.	P:	steam
M:	Magnus Emanuel Wiklund	S:	7.5
A:	5-30 cal.		

The *Alcoa Banner* sailed in Convoy PQ-16 en route from Reykjavik, Iceland, to Murmansk, USSR. About 200 miles southwest of Bear Island, German bombers attacked the convoy. Bomb fragments from near misses ruptured the shell plating of the *Alcoa Banner* at the #5 hold. None of the eight officers, thirty-six men, and two armed guards reported being injured. The gun crew claimed to have downed one plane with its armament of .30 caliber machine guns—just installed in Iceland.

WACR; AG.

CITY OF JOLIET

D:	5-27-42	YB:	1920
T:	1520	Tn:	6,167
Pos:	73.50 N / 26.06 E	Dr:	21 ft.
Ow:	Lykes Brothers	C:	7,000 tons war materiel
Op:	U.S. Maritime Commission	P:	steam
M:	Albert Miller	S:	8
A:	1-4"; 2-50 cal.; 2-30 cal.		

German aircraft attacked the *City of Joliet* while she was traveling with Convoy PQ-16, en route from Boston, Massachusetts, to Murmansk, USSR. On 25 May, eight torpedo planes and eighteen dive bombers attacked the convoy from off the starboard beam. The convoy commodore signaled "Repel Aircraft," and the convoy broke formation during the attack. The dive bombers dove at angles and released three to five bombs from a height of 1,000 feet. The splash from the misses rose seventy-five feet in the air. Meanwhile, the torpedo planes attacked in two groups. Flying about forty feet above the water, they released their torpedoes 3,000 yards off the starboard side of the convoy. The *City of Joliet* escaped unharmed from the attacks. On 27 May, a total of 108 German planes attacked the convoy. The planes approached the convoy from the starboard beam. High level bombers flew in "V" formation and released their bombs from a height of about 12,000 feet. They scored three hits on the other ships, and several near misses fell off the starboard side of the *City of Joliet*. The *Joliet* received no direct hits, but a near miss just off the starboard side sprung her hull. The pumps could not keep up with the incoming water, and the crew abandoned her in the Barents Sea the next day. At 0542 the ship's complement of nine officers, twenty-eight men, and eleven Navy men left in two lifeboats. The trawler HMS *St. Elstan* (FY-240) and the French corvette *Roselys* picked up the survivors and landed them in Murmansk. The freighter sank fifteen minutes later.

NSS; WACR; WCSR; AG; The NSS mentions 200 passengers on board. This is not confirmed in the WACR.

MORMACSUL

D:	5-27-42	YB:	1920
T:	1230	Tn:	5,481
Pos:	approx. 73.00 N / 20.00 W	Dr:	23 ft.
Ow:	U.S. Maritime Commission	C:	5,600 tons tanks, trucks,
Op:	Moore-McCormack		ammunition
M:	John Helge Nygren	P:	steam
A:	1-4"; 2-50 cal.; 2-30 cal.	S:	7

Enemy aircraft subjected the *Mormacsul* to intermittent attacks from 25 May to 27 May off the Norwegian coast. As part of Convoy PQ-16 bound from Philadelphia, Pennsylvania, for Murmansk, USSR, the *Mormacsul* sank at 1255 on 27 May, approximately 250 miles due west of North Cape and fifty miles due south of Bear Island. Seven enemy aircraft dove from the sun off the port beam and released four bombs from 5,000 feet. Three bombs landed nearby off the port side. Two of these bombs landed close enough to damage the hull. A single bomb struck the ship on the port side. The near misses ruptured the hull, killed one officer and two men on watch below, and caused her to sink. The surviving members of the crew of ten officers and twenty-nine men, along with the nine armed guards, launched three lifeboats and three rafts. One of the lifeboats capsized, but the corvette HMS *Starwort* (K-20) and a British trawler rescued the forty-five men thirty minutes after they abandoned ship.

NSS; WACR; WCSR; AG.

ALCOA PILGRIM

D:	5-27-42	YB:	1941
T:	2130	Tn:	6,759
Pos:	16.28 N / 67.37 W	Dr:	28 ft. 2 in.
Ow:	Alcoa SS Line	C:	9,500 tons bauxite ore
Op:	Alcoa SS Line	P:	steam
M:	Leon Roar Petersen	S:	13.5
A:	unarmed		

The *Alcoa Pilgrim* sailed from Port-of-Spain, Trinidad, BWI, to Mobile, Alabama. The *U-502* (von Rosenstiel) spotted the zigzagging freighter and fired a torpedo that hit the starboard side just below the waterline in the engine room. The blast extensively damaged the ship, and she sank in ninety seconds. The crew of nine officers and thirty-one men had no time to launch a boat, and only nine managed to get on board two life rafts. After the ship sank, the *U-502* came alongside one of the rafts, and an officer inquired about the ship's name, her nationality, tonnage, and cargo. The officer also asked if the rafts had sails and wished the men luck. The SS *Thomas Nelson* picked up the surviving three officers and six men six days later and landed them at Port-of-Spain on 5 June.

The WACR reports that the ship carried 5,500 tons of cargo. NSS; WACR; WCSR; RWCS; Rohwer, p. 99.

NEW JERSEY

D:	5-28-42	YB:	1921
T:	0510	Tn:	6,414
Pos:	18.32 N / 82.28 N	Dr:	27 ft. 5 1/4 in.
Ow:	The Texas Co.	C:	water ballast
Op:	The Texas Co.	P:	steam
M:	Trygue Lehland	S:	10.5
A:	1-4"; 2-30 cal.		

On 20 May, the *New Jersey* sailed from Norfolk, Virginia, bound for Aruba, NWI, in water ballast. The *U-103* (Winter) found the vessel an easy target as she plied a nonevasive course. The first torpedo struck the port side behind the bridge at the #5 or #6 tank about four feet below the waterline. The second torpedo hit at the #8 tank, also four feet below the waterline. The explosions created holes about twenty feet in diameter. The master stopped the ship after the first explosion, and most of the eight officers, twenty-eight crewmen, and the five armed guards abandoned the ship in two lifeboats. The master and steward remained on board. The steward went aft and attempted to fire the four-inch gun after the submarine surfaced. Unsuccessful, he and the master then abandoned the ship. After these men left, the *U-103* fired approximately twenty rounds at the ship and set the after housing on fire. The ship sank stern first at 0600. Thirty-three hours later the USS *Tattnall* (DD-125) picked up twenty-six men, including three armed guards, and landed them at Kingston, Jamaica, BWI. The USS *Biddle* (DD-151) rescued the other fifteen men, including two armed guards, in the other boat and landed them four days later. All hands survived the attack.

NSS; WACR; WCSR; AG; Rohwer, p. 99, places the attack at 19.10 N / 81.50 W; *War Action Casualties*, p. 86.

ALCOA SHIPPER

D:	5-30-42	YB:	1920
T:	0425	Tn:	5,490
Pos:	37.49 N / 65.15 W	Dr:	26 ft. 2 in.
Ow:	Alcoa SS Co.	C:	8,340 tons bauxite ore
Op:	Alcoa SS Co.	P:	steam
M:	Alderman Logan Scott	S:	10.5
A:	unarmed		

The *Alcoa Shipper* was torpedoed by the *U-404* (von Bülow) while en route from Port-of-Spain, Trinidad, BWI, to New York City. The ore carrier had proceeded using two different zigzag plans. Just as a torpedo struck, lookouts spotted the *U-404* breaking the surface 1,000 yards off the starboard quarter. The torpedo struck the starboard side at the fireroom and caused the boiler to explode. The vessel immediately stopped, and the general alarm rang signaling the crew to abandon ship. The vessel settled within five minutes, so fast in fact that the two boats being launched became fouled and went down with the ship before they could be cleared. Twenty-five out of a total crew of eight officers and twenty-four men abandoned ship on three rafts that released themselves. The U-boat approached the survivors, and the Germans inquired about the ship's name, destination, and cargo. They then gave the survivors several bottles of rum, cigarettes, and a pair of dungarees for a man who had escaped with little clothing. Fifty-six hours after the attack the Norwegian SS *Margrethe Bakke* picked up the twenty-five survivors and landed them in New York. The explosion killed three on watch below, and four others went down with the ship—three officers and four men.

NSS; WACR; WCSR; RWCS; WJ; Rohwer, p. 99.

HAMPTON ROADS

D:	6-1-42	YB:	1919
T:	0440	Tn:	2,689
Pos:	23.00 N / 85.42 W	Dr:	24 ft.
Ow:	Polar SS Co.	C:	3,620 tons phosphate rock
Op:	U.S. Maritime Commission	P:	steam
M:	William Hanson Lane	S:	6
A:	unarmed		

The *Hampton Roads* sailed from Tampa, Florida, to San Juan, Puerto Rico, maintaining a zigzag course according to routing instructions. At 0535 the *U-106* (Rasch) suddenly surfaced astern of the ship and approached the freighter at high speed. When approximately 300 yards off the starboard quarter, the U-boat fired two warning shots across the stern. The master sounded the alarm to abandon ship, and the radio operator began sending distress signals. The crew of eight officers and twenty men abandoned the ship immediately. Sixteen men managed to launch the port lifeboat that picked up two men from the water and five men off a raft. The surfaced U-boat then fired one torpedo that struck the freighter at the #3 hatch. The torpedo exploded deep in the bowels of the ship and caused extensive damage. The ship sank one minute later. Four men apparently died when the torpedo struck the ship near their lifeboat. The SS

Alcoa Pathfinder picked up twenty-three survivors seven hours later and landed them at Curaçao. Three officers and two men died in the sinking.

NSS; WACR; WCSR; Rohwer, p. 100, places the attack at 22.45 N / 85.13 W.

WEST NOTUS

D:	6-1-42	YB:	1919
T:	0600	Tn:	5,492
Pos:	34.10 N / 68.20 W	Dr:	25 ft.
Ow:	McCormick SS Co.	C:	7,400 tons flaxseed
Op:	International Freighting Corp.	P:	steam
M:	Hans Gerner	S:	10.0
A:	1-5"; 4-30 cal.		

The *West Notus* sailed from Port-of-Spain, Trinidad, BWI, to New York, steering on a nonevasive course. The *U-404* (von Bülow) approached the freighter from the stern and from about two miles distant opened fire. The *U-404* fired its 88-mm gun for forty-five minutes and using a combination of explosive and incendiary shells, registered about twenty hits all over the vessel. Eventually the gunfire shot the steering controls away, causing the vessel to circle. When this happened, the crew stopped the engines. The radio operator sent no distress signals because the gunfire had knocked the radio out of commission. The armed guards fired the thirty-caliber guns and seven five-inch rounds but with no effect. An hour and a half after the attack began, the master ordered the ship abandoned. Thirty-six of the complement of eight officers, twenty-seven crewmen, and the five armed guards left in the #2 and #4 lifeboats. The master, two officers, and the radio operator died from the shellfire. The *U-404* came alongside one lifeboat, and the crew rendered aid to some of the survivors, including distributing bottled Perrier mineral water and giving directions to Hatteras. Afterwards, the vessel resumed shelling the freighter for several hours. The Greek SS *Constantinos H* rescued one boat with eighteen survivors two days later and landed them in Bermuda. The Swiss SS *Saentis* spotted the other boat on 4 June and landed the men in New York the next day. The freighter remained afloat until early the next morning when men from the *U-404* placed an explosive charge on the ship's hull and sank her.

NSS; WACR; WCSR; AG; WJ; Rohwer, p. 100.

KNOXVILLE CITY

D: 6-1-42
T: 2057
Pos: 21.15 N / 83.50 W
Ow: Isthmian SS Co.
Op: U.S. Maritime Commission
M: George P. Shanahan
A: 1-5"; 4-20 mm; 2-30 cal.

YB: 1921
Tn: 5,686
Dr: 25 ft. 3 in.
C: 7,585 tons general
P: steam
S: 10

The *Knoxville City* departed New York for Suez in convoy and later left the convoy to sail alone to Trinidad for refueling. As the ship steamed on a zigzagging course, a torpedo fired by the *U-158* (Rostin) struck at the engine room on the starboard side, twenty feet below the waterline. The explosion killed two men on watch below, likely caused the boilers to explode, and stopped the engines immediately. The ship lost way completely in two minutes. The explosion carried away the two starboard lifeboats and the radio antenna. The radio operator used the emergency radio to send distress signals but received no answer. Within five minutes, the master gave orders to abandon ship. The armed guards manned the guns, but the U-boat never surfaced. Most of the nine officers, twenty-eight men, fourteen armed guards, and four passengers on board abandoned ship within twenty minutes in two lifeboats. The *U-158* put a second torpedo in the vessel one hour after the initial attack, and she sank ten minutes later. The Brazilian ship *Jamaica* offered to take the survivors to New Orleans, but they declined the offer because she was dimly lit and they thought the submarine might still be nearby. The survivors made landfall at La Calina, Cuba, forty-eight hours after the attack, with the help of the Cuban gunboat *Donativo*.

NSS; WACR; WCSR; AG; Rohwer, p. 100, places the attack at 21.25 N / 83.50 W.

ILLINOIS

D: 6-1-42
T: 2100
Pos: 24.00 N / 60.00 W
Ow: States Steamship Co.
Op: Isthmian SS Co.
M: Hans Mathiesen
A: 1-4"; 2-30 cal.

YB: 1920
Tn: 5,447
Dr: 27 ft.
C: 8,000 tons manganese ore
P: steam
S: 10

The *Illinois* was torpedoed by the *U-172* (Emmermann) while en route from Cape Town, South Africa, to Baltimore, Maryland. The freighter maintained no evasive course, making her an easy target. Two torpedoes hit amidships, just aft of the bridge, about thirty seconds apart. The ship sank so fast that no distress signal could be sent. Of the crew of eight officers and thirty men, only one officer and five men managed to jump into the water and right a capsized lifeboat. These men remained in the vicinity for nearly twenty hours but never found any other survivors, boats, or rafts. Setting a southwesterly course, the SS *Esso Montpelier* picked them up six days after the attack and landed them at Port-of-Spain, Trinidad.

NSS; WACR; WCSR; AG; Rohwer, p. 100.

DOMINO

D:	6-2-42	YB:	1919
T:	0505	Tn:	3,170
Pos:	entrance to Nuevitas Bay	Dr:	unknown
Ow:	American Sugar Refining Co.	C:	ballast
Op:	U.S. Maritime Commission	P:	steam
M:	John E. Ellison	S:	stopped
A:	1-4"; 2-30 cal.		

The *Domino* was attacked by machine gun fire from a surfaced submarine while en route from Port Everglades, Florida, to Nuevitas, Cuba. Traveling in a Puerto Rico-bound convoy, the *Domino* hove to outside the Port of Nuevitas, drifting with engines stopped, waiting for daylight to proceed into port. Lookouts spotted a submarine approaching directly astern at high speed. The master sounded the general alarm and engaged the engines. The helmsman put the wheel over hard right to keep the stern gun on the U-boat. The surfaced submarine apparently never saw the drifting ship until it was too late to fire a torpedo. After sighting the *Domino*, the submarine opened fire with its machine gun. At over 100 yards the U-boat fired 150 rounds and about 30 struck the freighter, doing little damage. The ship's gun crew returned fire with its four-inch gun, firing three rounds. Within two minutes after the first shots, the submarine dove about 500 feet from the ship.

NSS; AG; ONF.

CITY OF ALMA

D:	6-2-42	YB:	1920
T:	2210	Tn:	3,446
Pos:	23.00 N / 62.30 W	Dr:	26 ft. 1 in.
Ow:	U.S. Maritime Commission	C:	7,400 tons manganese ore
Op:	Waterman SS Corp.	P:	steam
M:	James Joshua Baker	S:	9.5
A:	unarmed		

The *City of Alma* was likely torpedoed by the *U-159* (Witte) while en route from Port-of-Spain, Trinidad, to Baltimore, Maryland. The "Hog Island" type freighter proceeded along a nonevasive course in moderate seas. One torpedo hit the vessel between the #3 port hatch and the fireroom. The explosion blew the hatches off the #3 hatch and ripped a hole about forty feet long in the side. The freighter sank within three minutes, so quickly that the radio operator did not send a message and died on board. Few of the crew of eight officers and twenty-eight men survived. Twenty-six died, including the master, the second mate, and all the engineering officers. The ten survivors (two officers, eight men) found a lifeboat that had floated free of the ship. The patrol boat *YP-67* picked up the men on the raft and took them to San Juan four days later.

NSS; WACR; WCSR; Rohwer, p. 100

M. F. ELLIOTT

D:	6-3-42	YB:	1921
T:	1558	Tn:	6,940
Pos:	11.58 N / 63.33 W	Dr:	16 ft.
Ow:	Standard Oil Co. of N. J.	C:	water ballast 2-4-6-8 tanks
Op:	Standard Oil Co. of N. J.	P:	steam
M:	Harold I. Cook	S:	10.0
A:	1-4"; 1-3"; 2-50 cal.; 2-30 cal.		

On 19 May, the *M. F. Elliott* departed Newport News en route to Caripito, Venezuela, via Trinidad in convoy. Off the Florida Keys the vessel left the convoy and proceeded with the tanker *C. O. Stillman*. These two later separated, and the *Elliott* proceeded alone on a zigzagging course. A torpedo fired from the *U-502* (von Rosenstiel) struck the starboard quarter well below the waterline. The explosion wrecked the fuel bunker and the fireroom. Fuel oil covered the surface of the sea but did not catch fire. The radio operator sent a distress signal to a Navy PBY patrol plane seen earlier in the day. The *Elliott* listed to starboard, settled by the stern, and plunged bow up within six minutes. The armed guards stood by until water covered the gun muzzle but never sighted the enemy. The ship plunged to the bottom so quickly that the eight officers, thirty crewmen, and the seven armed guards never had time to get away safely. Three lifeboats capsized before they could clear the ship. The men swam to four life rafts that had floated free. The patrol plane remained in contact with the life rafts throughout the night. The USS *Tarbell* (DD-142) picked up twenty-seven men at dawn the next day and later pulled three others from the water. These men landed at Port-of-Spain. Before leaving, the *U-502* picked up two men and questioned them. A patrol plane forced the U-boat to submerge and take the men with them. The Germans later released these two men and put them in a life raft with provisions. The Brazilian tanker SS *Santa Maria* picked them up five

days later and landed them at Santos, Brazil. Four officers and nine men died—six from drowning and seven from the torpedo explosion.

NSS; WACR; WCSR; AG; *Times Herald*, 21 July 1942; Rohwer, p. 100; *War Action Casualties*, p. 87.

BEN AND JOSEPHINE

D:	6-3-42	YB:	1941
T:	1600	Tn:	102
Pos:	43.07 N / 66.51 W	Dr:	12 ft.
Ow:	Benjamin Curcurn	C:	none
Op:	Guiseppe Ciaramitaro	P:	diesel
M:	Guiseppe Ciaramitaro	S:	10
A:	unarmed		

The fishing vessels *Ben and Josephine* and *Aeolus* were intercepted by the *U-432* (Schultze) 170 miles east by south of Thatchers Island. Both had sailed from Gloucester, Massachusetts, to Sea Island, Nova Scotia. The U-boat surfaced and allowed the *Ben and Josephine*'s crew of two officers and six men to leave safely. After the crewmen had abandoned the ship in two dories, the *U-432* sank the fishing vessel by gunfire. Forty-five shells riddled the vessel, and she caught fire and sank thirty minutes later. The crew safely arrived at the Mt. Desert Coast Guard Light Station thirty-six hours later.

WACR; WCSR; WJ; RWSA; Rohwer, p. 100, places the attack at 43.50 N / 67.00 W.

AEOLUS

D:	6-3-42	YB:	1922
T:	1630	Tn:	41
Pos:	43.07 N / 66.51 W	Dr:	8 ft.
Ow:	John O. Johnson	C:	none
Op:	John O. Johnson	P:	diesel
M:	John O. Johnson	S:	8.5
A:	unarmed		

The dragger *Aeolus*, en route from Gloucester, Massachusetts to Sea Island, Nova Scotia, was shelled and sunk by the *U-432* (Schultze). The U-boat caught both the *Ben and Josephine* and the *Aeolus* simultaneously. The submarine sank the *Ben and Josephine* first. Schultze then fired seventeen shots into the smaller *Aeolus*, and she sank in twenty minutes. The crew of two officers and four men made their way back with the survivors of the *Ben and Josephine* and landed at the Mt. Desert Coast Guard Light Station thirty-six hours after the attack.

WACR; WCSR; WJ; RWSA; Rohwer, p. 100, places the attack at 43.50 N / 67.00 W.

STEEL WORKER

D:	6-3-42	YB:	1920
T:	2000	Tn:	5,686
Pos:	Kola Inlet, Murmansk	Dr:	25 ft.
Ow:	Isthmian SS Co.	C:	7,250 tons Army equipment,
Op:	Isthmian SS Co.		food
M:	William E. Green	P:	steam
A:	yes; unknown	S:	11

The *Steel Worker* struck a mine while moving to her anchorage in Kola Inlet, Murmansk, USSR. The ship sailed from Philadelphia, Pennsylvania, to Murmansk, and had discharged her 375 tons of ammunition. While proceeding from the ammunition dock to another anchorage, she struck a mine. The explosion occurred under the #4 hold. The ship settled on an even keel and then broke in two and sank stern first forty-five minutes later. The authorities at Murmansk theorized that an enemy airplane had dropped the mine, it had become embedded in the mud, and had worked loose. They had found several similar mines in the harbor. Eight officers, twenty-eight men, and the two Navy signalmen safely abandoned ship in four lifeboats. Other vessels anchored nearby picked up the men and took them to Murmansk.

NSS; WACR; WCSR; AG.

VELMA LYKES

D:	6-4-42	YB:	1920
T:	2135	Tn:	2,572
Pos:	21.21 N / 86.36 W	Dr:	25 ft.
Ow:	Lykes Bros. SS. Co.	C:	3,629 tons general
Op:	Lykes Bros. SS. Co.	P:	steam
M:	Hans G. Beck	S:	8.6
A:	1-3"; 2-30 cal.		

The *Velma Lykes* sailed from Galveston, Texas, to Cristobal, Canal Zone. The ship changed course after dark and had stopped zigzagging one hour before the *U-158* (Rostin) attacked. A lookout reported seeing a submarine's conning tower and spotted the wake of the torpedo off the starboard beam. Within seconds the torpedo struck at the #3 hatch just below the surface of the water. The explosion blew out a large section of the ship's side at the #3 and #4 holds and killed three men on watch below. The ship lost way immediately, listed slightly to starboard, and sank by the stern in one minute, leaving no time to fire the guns or to send distress signals. The eight officers, twenty crewmen, and four armed guards had no time to clear any of the lifeboats. The master, third officer, and helmsman attempted to lower the port lifeboat, but the boat jammed in the falls. The three men then stepped into the after port life raft just as the ship went under. The remaining survivors swam to two rafts that had released when the ship sank. About thirty-six hours later, the survivors sighted a PBY plane and signaled their plight with flags. On the 6th, the British MV *Ardenvohr* picked up the surviving four officers, nine men, and four armed guards on the rafts. On 10 June, the *U-68* torpedoed the *Ardenvohr*, but the seventeen men all survived and eventually landed at Cristobal.

NSS; WACR; WCSR; Rohwer, pp. 101-02.

DELFINA

D:	6-5-42	YB:	1918
T:	0010	Tn:	3,480
Pos:	22.22 N / 67.08 W	Dr:	22 ft.
Ow:	Bull SS Co.	C:	raw sugar
Op:	Bull SS Co.	P:	steam
M:	Jake Jacobs	S:	9.5
A:	unarmed		

On 4 June, the *Delfina* departed San Juan, Puerto Rico, for Charleston, South Carolina. A torpedo from the *U-172* (Emmermann) struck the ship between the #3 hold and the boiler room on the port side. The radio operator sent a distress message and received an acknowledgment from a San Juan radio station. The inexperienced crew of eight officers and twenty-three men abandoned ship in a chaotic manner. They launched a single boat but put it into the water in such a way that it filled half-way with water. The men in the boat then quickly pulled away from the ship without waiting for others, fearing that the submarine would shell the freighter. Twelve other crew members got off in two rafts. The patrol boat *PC-67* picked up these men eighteen hours after the attack. The fifteen in the boat landed at Montecristi, Dominican Republic. The first assistant engineer, chief mate, third mate, and the radio operator died.

NSS; WACR; WCSR; Rohwer, p. 100, places the attack at 20.20 N / 67.07 W.

L. J. DRAKE

D:	6-5-42	YB:	1918
T:	0130	Tn:	6,693
Pos:	17.30 N / 68.20 W	Dr:	25 ft. 2 in.
Ow:	Standard Oil Co. of N. J.	C:	72,961 bbls. gasoline
Op:	Standard Oil Co. of N. J.	P:	steam
M:	Peder Nielsen	S:	10
A:	1-4"; 1-3"; 2-50 cal.; 2-30 cal.		

On 4 June, the *L. J. Drake* sailed from Aruba, NWI, en route to San Juan, Puerto Rico. Earlier in the night the *U-68* (Merten) sank the Panamanian vessel *C. O. Stillman*. While attacking the *Stillman*, Merten spotted the *Drake* and decided to finish the *Stillman* first. After midnight, from a range of 700 yards, the *U-68* put three torpedoes into the *L. J. Drake*. The tanker exploded in flames, and afterwards nothing remained but pieces of wreckage. Men in the *Stillman*'s lifeboats saw the tremendous glow over the horizon. The entire crew of eight officers and twenty-seven men, along with the six armed guards, died in the explosion and fire that resulted.

WACR; WCSR; AG; WJ; *Ships of the Esso Fleet*, pp. 252-54.

GEORGE CLYMER

D:	6-6-42	YB:	1942
T:	2000	Tn:	7,176
Pos:	14.28 S / 18.37 W	Dr:	24 ft.
Ow:	U.S. Maritime Commission	C:	7,600 tons general
Op:	American Mail Line	P:	steam
M:	Edward F. Ackerman	S:	2.0
A:	1-4"; 4-50 cal.; 2-30 cal.		

The *George Clymer* sailed from Portland, Oregon, en route to Cape Town, South Africa, with a full cargo and a deck load of twenty-four planes. Unfortunately, the main shaft and thrust block bearings split, and the ship drifted for over seven days. The crippled ship lay in an area where air cover was possible but unavailable. The German raider *Michel* (Ruckteschell) intercepted an SOS sent by the vessel and took advantage of this predicament. Sending the torpedo boat *Esan* to the Liberty ship, she put two torpedoes into the hapless freighter. One struck the engine room and the other at the after end of the #1 hold. The crew abandoned the vessel so quickly that they left the armed guards and several of the merchant crew on board. The next day the master and the crew reboarded the ship. On the 8th, the British armed merchant cruiser *Alacantara* (F-88) took off the survivors among the nine officers, thirty men, sixteen armed guards, and two passengers on board. One fireman died in the engine room. A party from the British ship boarded the *Clymer* and decided the ship could be towed to port. A higher authority, however, ordered the vessel sunk. The *Alacantara* used gunfire and depth charges and even launched her plane to sink the ship. Fire eventually gutted the *Clymer*, and she overturned after being subjected to more gunfire and depth charges. On 12 June, the *Alacantara* had to leave with the vessel still afloat.

WACR; WCSR; AG; Muggenthaler, pp. 212-13; Moore, p. 109.

MELVIN H. BAKER

D: 6-6-42
T: 0240
Pos: 21.44 S / 36.38 E
Ow: National Gresum Co.
Op: Waterman SS. Co.
M: Demosthenis Helmis
A: 1-4"

YB: 1919
Tn: 4,999
Dr: 25 ft. 3 in.
C: 6,825 tons manganese ore, jute
P: diesel
S: 10

Forty-five miles from the coast of Mozambique, the *Melvin H. Baker* was torpedoed by the *I-10* (Kayahara) while en route from Bombay, India, to New York via Cape Town, South Africa. Several hours before the attack sparks from the stack and glowing soot on the stack's spark screen may have revealed the ship's position. A torpedo from the *I-10* hit the starboard side at the #4 hatch. The ship flooded immediately, and she sank by the stern within ten minutes with a slight list to port. The explosion blew out the lights, severed communications between the bridge and the four-inch gun, knocked down the radio antennae, and damaged the radio transmitter. The commanding officer of the armed guards decided to abandon his gun rather than fire at the surfaced submarine. He feared the submarine would shell the lifeboats. All hands in the crew of eight officers and twenty-six men, as well as the eight passengers and the six armed guards, abandoned the ship in two lifeboats and one life raft. Those on the life raft later climbed into the boats. Six of the passengers were survivors of the SS *Bienville*. Ten hours later the British SS *Twickenham* rescued all hands and landed them at Mombasa, Kenya.

NSS; WACR; WCSR; AG.

COAST TRADER

D: 6-7-42
T: 1410
Pos: 48.19 N / 125.40 W
Ow: Coastwise Line SS Co.
Op: Coastwise Line SS Co.
M: Lyle G. Havens
A: 2-37 mm; 4-50 cal.; 2-30 cal.

YB: 1920
Tn: 3,286
Dr: 15 ft. 6 in.
C: 1,250 tons newsprint
P: steam
S: 10

The *Coast Trader* sailed from Port Angeles, Washington, to San Francisco, California. About thirty miles from the Strait of Juan de Fuca the *I-26* (Yokota) attacked the ship as she steered a nonevasive course. A torpedo blasted a six-foot hole in the starboard side beneath the #4 hatch in the stern. The explosion blew the #4 hatch cover forty feet in the air, and scattered bits of paper from the 2,000-pound newsprint rolls over the decks. The engines immediately stopped and the hold filled with steam. The gun crew offered no counter offensive. Ammonia fumes leaking from the ship's refrigeration unit overcame some of the crew as they mustered at their boat stations. The men managed to launch one lifeboat and two rafts. The fishing vessel *Virginia I* towed the lifeboat to Neah Bay thirty hours after the attack. Ten hours later the Canadian corvette *Edmundston* (K-106) picked up the rafts carrying nine officers, twenty-eight men, and nineteen armed guards and landed them at Port Angeles. One man died from exposure before being rescued. The freighter sank stern first at 1435.

NSS; WACR; WCSR; AG; TF; *Coast Guard at War*, p. 45; Rohwer, p. 279, places the attack at 48.15 N / 125.40 W.

EDITH

D:	6-7-42	YB:	1915
T:	1530	Tn:	3,382
Pos:	14.33 N / 74.35 W	Dr:	17 ft. 5 in.
Ow:	A. H. Bull Lines	C:	1,700 tons general
Op:	A. H. Bull Lines	P:	steam
M:	Samuel M. Houston	S:	10.9
A:	unarmed		

On 30 May, the *Edith* sailed from Tampa, Florida, to Mayagüez, Puerto Rico, via Puerto Castilla, Honduras. A torpedo fired by the *U-159* (Witte) from close in, at an angle of 90°, struck the starboard side of the zigzagging freighter about fifteen feet below the main deck between the #4 hold and the engine room. The ship sank stern first in minutes and prevented the radio operator from sending a distress signal. All but two of the crew of eight officers and twenty-three men abandoned ship using one lifeboat and two rafts. The Germans made several inquiries of the crew, gave them directions to land, and then picked up floating case goods before submerging and leaving the scene. Most of the survivors later transferred into the lifeboat, and seven remained on a single raft. Almost seven days later they arrived at Black River, Jamaica.

NSS; WACR; WCSR; RWCS; The radio operator and an oiler died in the attack. Rohwer, p. 262.

SUWIED

D:	6-7-42	YB:	1920
T:	2330 GCT	Tn:	3,250
Pos:	20.00 N / 84.48 W	Dr:	24 ft.
Ow:	Hedger SS Co.	C:	4,970 tons bauxite ore
Op:	Alcoa SS Co.	P:	steam
M:	Bernard Roosevelt Davis	S:	9.0
A:	unarmed		

The *U-107* (Gelhaus) torpedoed the *Suwied* as she steamed from Kingston, Jamaica, to Mobile, Alabama. The freighter made an easy target as she plied a nonevasive course. The torpedo struck aft of the engine room on the port side and killed two men on watch below. The ship settled so quickly that the radio operator had no chance to send a distress signal. The *U-107* surfaced after firing the torpedo and witnessed the sinking. The ship carried eight officers, twenty-four men, and one passenger. Twenty-seven men abandoned the ship in one boat and one raft. The USCG cutter *Nemesis* (WPC-111) rescued these men after nineteen hours in the water. Two officers and four men died in the attack.

NSS; WACR; WCSR; Rohwer, p. 102, places the attack at 20.05 N / 85.35 W.

FRANKLIN K. LANE

D:	6-8-42	YB:	1920
T:	1815	Tn:	6,589
Pos:	11.12 N / 69.38 W	Dr:	27 ft. 11 in.
Ow:	Standard Oil Co. of N. J.	C:	73,000 bbls. crude oil
Op:	Standard Oil Co. of N. J.	P:	steam
M:	Warner Edgar Loeffler	S:	11.0
A:	1-4 in.		

On 1 June, the *Franklin K. Lane* departed Trinidad in Convoy TA-5, en route to Aruba, NWI. Thirty-five miles northeast of Cape Blanco the tanker received signals to change position in the convoy. Just as the ship began to move, the *U-502* (von Rosenstiel) attacked. The first torpedo missed, but the second struck the tanker in the #7 tank on the starboard side aft of the bridge. The explosion created a large column of smoke, and a geyser of oil rained on the poop deck. The ship buckled at the point of impact, and fire quickly enveloped the bridge and spread on the water. The explosion and fire also damaged two of the lifeboats. Thirty-seven men of the eight officers, twenty-seven men, and six armed guards on board cleared the tanker in two lifeboats and one raft. Three hours later the destroyer HMS *Churchill* (I-45) picked up the survivors. The next morning the *Churchill* sank the tanker with about twenty shells, concluding that she would be a hazard to navigation. The master, the chief mate, and two crewmen perished in the fire. The survivors landed in Curaçao, NWI.

NSS; WACR; WCSR; AG; *Ships of the Esso Fleet*, pp. 274-76; *War Action Casualties*, p. 89; Rohwer, p. 102, places the attack one minute farther west.

HAGAN

D: 6-10-42   YB: 1919
T: 2010   Tn: 6402
Pos: 22.00 N / 77.30 W   Dr: 20 ft.
Ow: Paco Tankers   C: 22,676 bbls. molasses
Op: WSA   P: steam
M: Brazier B. Calaway   S: 10.5
A: 1-4"; 4-50 cal.; 2-30 cal.

On the morning of 10 June, the *Hagan*, proceeding on a nonevasive course, sailed with a partial load of black strap molasses from Antilla, Cuba, to Havana. The *U-157* (Henne) fired a torpedo that struck the starboard quarter below the waterline at the engine room. The blast destroyed the engines and caused at least one boiler to explode. About one minute later a second torpedo struck the port fuel bunkers, blowing fuel oil all over the ship. The tanker started to sink fast, plunging by the stern. After the first torpedo struck, the master had the wheel put hard to port but could not maneuver the ship because the engines had stopped. The radio operator sent a distress signal; however, he never received a reply because the explosion had damaged the receiver. The gun crew stood at their stations throughout the attack but took no offensive action, having never sighted the enemy. The master finally ordered them to abandon ship. Of the complement of eight officers, twenty-seven men, and nine armed guards, only thirty-eight managed to abandon the *Hagan* in the #1 and #3 lifeboats. Both boats drifted to shore, one reaching Cayo Verde and the other making landfall at Cape Roman, Cuba, thirteen hours after the attack. Two officers and four men died, four of these men while on watch below.

The WACR reports the armament at one four-inch and 4-30 cal. NSS; WACR; WCSR; AG; Rohwer, p. 102; *War Action Casualties*, p. 90.

AMERICAN

D: 6-11-42   YB: 1916
T: 1004   Tn: 4,846
Pos: 17.58 N / 84.28 W   Dr: 25 ft. 6 in.
Ow: American Hawaiian SS Co.   C: 6,500 tons ore, coffee, jute, oil
Op: U.S. Maritime Commission   P: steam
M: Robert M. Pierce   S: 12
A: unarmed

The *American* sailed from Santos, Brazil, to New Orleans, Louisiana. As she prepared to alter her zigzag course, the *U-504* (Poske) attacked. The first torpedo struck the after peak tank on the starboard side, about five feet below the waterline. The explosion demolished the after part of the ship, the rudder, and the propeller. The *U-504* immediately fired a second torpedo that struck the starboard side at the mainmast in the #4 hold. At 1015 the U-boat fired a third torpedo that hit the fireroom on the starboard side and caused the boilers to explode. The radio antenna crashed to the deck, and water crippled the generators, preventing the radio operator from sending distress signals. The ship sank in twenty-five minutes, listing to starboard and then capsizing. The crew of eight officers and thirty men immediately lowered the #1 and the #3 lifeboats. Some men, trapped by the first explosion, finally reached the deck and launched the #4 lifeboat. The SS *Kent* rescued the survivors six hours later and landed them at Cristobal, Canal Zone. Three men died in the explosion and one later died on the *Kent*.

The sources conflict concerning the crew size. NSS; WACR; WCSR; Rohwer, p. 103.

F. W. ABRAMS

D:	6-11-42	YB:	1920
T:	0640	Tn:	9,310
Pos:	34.55 N / 75.50 W	Dr:	29 ft. 9 in.
Ow:	Standard Oil Co. of N. J.	C:	90,000 bbls. fuel oil
Op:	Standard Oil Co. of N. J.	P:	steam
M:	Anthony J. Coumelis	S:	10.0
A:	unarmed		

The *F. W. Abrams* in poor visibility lost sight of her Coast Guard escort, *CG-484*, and wandered into the Hatteras minefield while en route from Aruba, NWI, to New York. The British, unaware of the minefield, had issued the routing instructions, and the master continued on course. The first explosion occurred on the starboard bow twelve feet from the stem and halfway between the keel and waterline. The explosion damaged the anchor, and it would not drop. The ship drifted until she hit a second mine forward of the pump room on the starboard side at the #5 tank about thirty-five minutes later. A third explosion occurred just twelve minutes after the second. This mine struck the port side between the bow and the bridge at the #4 tank. The tanker settled to the bottom with her forward half submerged. Heavy seas eventually caused the tanker to settle until she lay just partially above the water. The radio operator sent distress messages and the ship's whistle was blown until steam was exhausted, but no assistance came. About an hour after the first explosion, the tanker's crew of eight officers and twenty-eight men abandoned ship in four boats. All reached the beach near Morehead City, North Carolina. A crew from the salvage tug *Relief* later boarded the vessel and after three days of work considered her too damaged to salvage and sank her on 15 June.

NSS; WACR; WCSR; *Ships of the Esso Fleet*, pp. 288-91.

CITIES SERVICE TOLEDO

D:	6-12-42	YB:	1918
T:	0150	Tn:	8,192
Pos:	29.02 N / 91.59 W	Dr:	29 ft.
Ow:	Cities Service Oil. Co.	C:	84,000 bbls. crude
Op:	Cities Service Oil. Co.	P:	steam
M:	Kosti F. Toivola	S:	9.0
A:	1-5"; 2-50 cal.; 2-30 cal.		

On 10 June, the *Cities Service Toledo* weighed anchor at Corpus Christi, Texas, to steam to Portland, Maine. The tanker made an easy target for the *U-158* (Rostin) as she plied a nonevasive course. Twenty miles east of the Trinity Shoals Gas Buoy, the *U-158* fired two torpedoes that struck two seconds apart on the starboard side amidships in the #6 and #7 tanks. The vessel rapidly took a starboard list. Five minutes later two more torpedoes struck the starboard side about amidships at the #4 and #5 tanks. The last torpedo caused the vessel to burst into flames. The Navy gun crew stayed with the ship as long as possible and fired three rounds from the five-inch gun at a light thought to be the submarine. When the gun's gears broke, the nine armed guards abandoned ship with the rest of the crew of eight officers and twenty-eight men. The explosion and fire consumed the life rafts and two of the boats. The crew launched a third boat, but they could not clear the flames and had to jump in the water. Seventeen men abandoned the tanker in the remaining lifeboat. The Norwegian tanker SS *Belinda* rescued the men in the lifeboat several hours later. Eight hours after the attack the tanker SS *Gulf King* and the SS *San Antonio* rescued the surviving thirteen men in the water. All the survivors landed at Burwood, Louisiana. The fifteen who died included one officer, ten crewmen, and four armed guards.

NSS; WACR; WCSR; AG; Rohwer, p. 103; *War Action Casualties*, p. 92.

SIXAOLA

D:	6-12-42	YB:	1911
T:	2115	Tn:	4,693
Pos:	09.54 N / 81.25 W	Dr:	24 ft.
Ow:	United Fruit Company	C:	900 tons Army cargo, trucks,
Op:	United Fruit Company		trailers
M:	William H. Fagan	P:	steam
A:	1-3"; 2-50 cal.	S:	12.5

The *Sixaola* sailed from Cristobal, Canal Zone, to New Orleans, Louisiana, via Puerto Barrios, Guatemala. As the *Sixaola* made a righthand zigzag, the *U-159* (Witte) attacked. The first torpedo hit five feet below the waterline on the starboard bow. A minute later a second torpedo struck the middle of the #2 hold. After the first explosion the master put the engines full speed astern and then stopped them. The master ordered the ship abandoned two minutes after the second torpedo struck. The ship had an unusually large number on board, consisting of 8 officers, 79 men, 6 armed guards, and 108 passengers. The crew and passengers abandoned ship in five lifeboats and six rafts. Just after the master and the chief mate abandoned the ship, the boiler exploded. The *U-159* remained in the area to question the crew about the ship and her cargo. The SS *Carolinian* rescued thirty-two people in the #2 boat and transferred them to the USS *Niagara* (PG-52). The *Niagara* later picked up seventy-five persons in boats #4 and #5 and landed them all at Cristobal. The Army tug *Shasta* rescued twenty-three persons in boat #3. Forty-two others beached their lifeboat in Panama after four days at sea and were rescued by the *PC-460* and landed at Cristobal. Twenty-nine of the ship's crew died in the explosions; most of these men lay sleeping in the bow of the vessel.

The complement figures conflict within the sources. NSS; WACR; WCSR; AG; Rohwer, p. 103, places the attack at 09.41 N / 81.10 W.

SOLON TURMAN

D:	6-13-42	YB:	1941
T:	1340	Tn:	6,762
Pos:	10.45 N / 80.24 W	Dr:	25 ft.
Ow:	Lykes Bros. SS. Co.	C:	5,100 tons naval stores,
Op:	U.S. Maritime Commission		explosives, construction
M:	Frederick Ulstad		equipment
A:	1-4"; 4-50 cal.	P:	steam
		S:	14.5

The *Solon Turman* sailed in a six-ship convoy from Quonset Point, Rhode Island, to Bora Bora, Society Islands, via the Panama Canal. On 12 June, the *Turman* left the convoy and proceeded on a zigzagging course. The next day a torpedo fired by the *U-159* (Witte) struck the port quarter at the #5 hold. About three minutes later a second torpedo struck at the #4 hold. Both caused tremendous explosions. The gun deck split, the after mast snapped, the radio antenna fell, and the cargo of pontoons, tanks, and other deck cargo flew into the air. The armed guards manned the gun immediately after first torpedo hit, and the second explosion blew one member of the gun crew overboard. The ship had ten officers, thirty-four men, and nine armed guards on board. They abandoned the quickly sinking ship in two lifeboats minutes after the torpedoes struck. The *U-159* surfaced and officers questioned the survivors and offered food, water, medical supplies, and cigarettes. On the 14th, the Colombian schooners *Envoy* and *Zaroma* rescued all hands and later transferred them to U.S. patrol boat #458. They landed at Cristobal, Canal Zone. The only casualty occurred when the second assistant engineer accidentally fell overboard from the rescue schooner *Envoy* and drowned.

NSS; WACR; WCSR; USMMA; AG; Rohwer, p. 103.

YAKA

D:	6-13-42	YB:	1920
T:	2115	Tn:	5,432
Pos:	anchored at Murmansk	Dr:	14 ft.
Ow:	Waterman SS Co.	C:	none
Op:	WSA	P:	steam
M:	Oscar Pederson	S:	anchored
A:	1-3"; 2-30 cal.		

Seven German aircraft attacked the ships that were anchored in Murmansk, and the *Yaka* suffered damage from several near misses. The gun crew fought back with no apparent success. One stick of bombs fell from stern to bow and put fourteen holes in the port side. Concussions from near misses opened the deep tanks and ruptured hull plates near the engine room, causing this space to flood. The damage was repaired without drydocking, and the eight officers, thirty crewmen, and eleven armed guards reported no injuries.

The *Yaka* went through 156 air raids while in Murmansk. WACR; AG.

LEBORE

D:	6-14-42	YB:	1923
T:	0250	Tn:	8,289
Pos:	12.53 N / 80.40 W	Dr:	26 ft. 6 in.
Ow:	Ore SS Corp.	C:	10,145 tons coal
Op:	U.S. Maritime Commission	P:	steam
M:	John William Jimmyer	S:	10.4
A:	1-4"; 2-50 cal.; 2-30 cal.		

The *U-172* (Emmermann) attacked the *Lebore* as she steamed from Newport News, Virginia, to Cruz Grande, Chile, via the Panama Canal. The vessel had maintained no evasive course for four hours prior to the attack. A lookout spotted the torpedo's wake 400 feet from the ship. The helmsman had no time to avoid the torpedo, and it struck at the #6 hatch on the starboard side. The explosion opened the #3 wing tank to the sea. The tank rapidly filled with water and caused the ship to list 45° to starboard. The master ordered the engines full speed astern, but the freighter continued to make way. The explosion jammed the four-inch gun's gearing, and the rapid listing of the vessel prevented the gun crew from getting the gun into action. The crew of seven officers and thirty-two men, along with the six armed guards and forty-nine survivors of the SS *Crijnssen* who had been rescued by the *Lebore* on 11 June, abandoned the freighter in three lifeboats and three rafts. The USS *Tattnall* (DD-125) and USS *Erie* (PG-50) rescued most of the survivors and landed them at Cristobal. One of the boats made landfall on San Andres Island. The only casualty was the first assistant engineer who failed to leave the ship.

NSS; WACR; WCSR; AG; Rohwer, p. 103.

SCOTTSBURG

D:	6-14-42	YB:	1919
T:	1900	Tn:	8,001
Pos:	11.51 N / 62.56 W	Dr:	31 ft. 6 in.
Ow:	Lykes Bros. SS. Co.	C:	10,500 tons general, tanks,
Op:	Lykes Bros. SS. Co.		planes
M:	Gustaf Adolph Olofson	P:	steam
A:	1-5"; 4-20 mm; 2-30 cal.	S:	7.0

The *U-161* (Achilles) attacked the *Scottsburg* en route from New York to Basra, Iraq, via Trinidad and Cape Town. As the *Scottsburg* steamed on a nonevasive course, a torpedo struck the port side, deep in the engine room and killed two men on watch below. A second torpedo struck at the after end of the #2 hatch and burst steam pipes and threw cargo all over the ship. The ship was ordered abandoned and the ten officers, thirty crewmen, and eleven armed guards escaped on one raft and in two lifeboats. The master and radio operator went down with the ship trying to send distress signals. A total of three officers and two crewmen died in the attack. The SS *Kahuku* rescued forty-six men on 15 June, eighteen hours after the attack. Six of these men died on the *Kahuku*, when the *U-126* torpedoed her two days later.

NSS; WACR; WCSR; AG; Rohwer, p. 103.

CHANT

D:	6-15-42	YB:	1938
T:	0720	Tn:	5,601
Pos:	36.25 N / 11.40 E	Dr:	25 ft. 6 in.
Ow:	WSA	C:	7,600 tons general
Op:	American President Lines	P:	diesel
M:	Viggo Aage Vernum	S:	12.0
A:	1-4"; 15 anti-aircraft guns		

The *Chant* was a Danish ship taken over by the U.S. Government when war began. The ship took a cargo over to Belfast and was armed and loaded in

Glasgow by the British. The *Chant* became part of the small, heavily protected Convoy WS-19Z bound for Malta. The *Chant* had a cargo of aviation gasoline in five-gallon cans, a deck cargo of coal, and two Royal Air Force rescue boats. During the trip, the convoy was shelled by Italian cruisers and destroyers, but the *Chant* escaped damage. On the morning of the 14th, fifty high and medium level bombers and torpedo planes attacked the convoy. The *Chant* also escaped this attack without serious injury. The next day, however, a bomber released a stick of bombs that struck the ship; one landed near the engine room and another landed in the #4 hold. The bombs demolished the superstructure, felled the mainmast, blew off the hull plating, and started fires in the cargo of aviation gasoline. The intense, quickly spreading flames caused ammunition on board to start exploding. With the ship rapidly sinking, most of the men jumped overboard. The *Chant* sank in flames at 0730. The ship carried nine officers, forty-three men, eleven armed guards, and twenty-five Royal Navy and British Army, the last put on board to man the extra guns. Only one lifeboat and a workboat along with two rafts were used to escape. The British minesweeper *Rye* (J-76) rescued the survivors. One man from the American gun crew and three merchant crewmen died in the attack.

The vessel was "taken over by the British Ministry of War," but she seems to have remained an American-flagged vessel. WACR; WCSR; AG; RWSA; ONF; Gleichauf, pp. 272-73.

WEST HARDAWAY

D:	6-15-42	YB:	1919
T:	1415	Tn:	5,702
Pos:	11.50 N / 62.15 W	Dr:	25 ft. 11/16 in.
Ow:	Isthmian SS Co.	C:	7,000 tons steel and coal
Op:	U.S. Maritime Commission	P:	steam
M:	Karl W. Jaenicke	S:	6
A:	1-4"; 4-20 mm; 2-30 cal.		

The *West Hardaway* sailed from Baltimore, Maryland, to Suez, Egypt, and proceeded on a zigzagging course. The *U-502* (von Rosenstiel) fired four torpedoes: one passed ahead and another passed astern. The third torpedo hit on the starboard bow in the #1 hold. The radio operator immediately sent distress calls and received answers from three stations. The gun crew mustered at their battle stations and fired five shots at a "slick" at a range of about 800 yards. The two shells exploded in the "slick," but the gunners never spotted the U-boat. Within minutes after the initial explosion the ten officers, twenty-seven men, and thirteen armed guards abandoned the ship in four lifeboats and four rafts. Twenty minutes later the gun crew, the second mate, and two crewmen reboarded the ship. The armed guards fired another round at a "slick" at a range of 1,200 yards, but this shell did not explode. The *U-502* then fired another torpedo that struck the vessel just abaft of the first in the #2 hold. The sixteen men left the ship a second time. The ship sank about an hour later. All hands survived and landed at Margarita Island off the coast of Venezuela forty-three hours after the attack. The Venezuelan steamer *Maracaibo* transported them to Trinidad.

NSS; WACR; WCSR; AG; Rohwer, p. 104.

ROBERT C. TUTTLE

D:	6-15-42	YB:	1940
T:	1704	Tn:	11,615
Pos:	36.51.20 N / 75.51.15 W	Dr:	30 ft. 6 in.
Ow:	Atlantic Refining Co.	C:	152,000 bbls. crude oil
Op:	Atlantic Refining Co.	P:	steam
M:	Martin Johansen	S:	5.0
A:	1-5"; 4-30 cal.		

The *Robert C. Tuttle* was damaged by a mine laid by the *U-701* (Degan) within sight of Virginia Beach, Virginia. The tanker sailed from Port Arthur, Texas, to Philadelphia, Pennsylvania, and held the last position in the port column of the two-column Convoy KN-109. The mine struck at the #2 tank on the starboard side about 100 feet from the stem. The blast sprayed oil over the length of the tanker and blew the second assistant engineer overboard to his death. The master stopped the engines, and she swung out of line as all the forward compartments flooded. The vessel went down by the head in about ten minutes and rested on the bottom. Minutes after the explosion the eight officers, thirty-three crewmen, five armed guards, and one Navy signalman minus the engineer abandoned ship in three lifeboats. The survivors rowed for six miles, and at 1750 the *PC-474* took the boats in tow. The *Robert C. Tuttle* was later salvaged and repaired but considered a CTL.

NSS; WACR; WCSR; AG; Rohwer, p. 104; *War Action Casualties*, p. 93.

ESSO AUGUSTA

D:	6-15-42	YB:	1940
T:	1730	Tn:	11,237
Pos:	36.52 N / 75.51.30 W	Dr:	29 ft. 10 in.
Ow:	Standard Oil Co. of N. J.	C:	119,000 bbls. diesel oil
Op:	Standard Oil Co. of N. J.	P:	diesel
M:	Eric Robert Blomquist	S:	16.0
A:	1-5"; 1-3"; 4-50 cal.; 2-30 cal.		

The *Esso Augusta* was damaged by a mine laid by the *U-701* (Degan) less than one-half mile due south of the Chesapeake Bay Entrance Lighted Whistle Buoy.

On 4 June, the tanker sailed from Texas City, Texas, to the United Kingdom. The tanker traveled in the two-column Convoy KN-109 in the lead position, port column. The master received a message from the convoy commodore to reduce speed to five knots. At 1704 a mine struck the *Robert C. Tuttle*. Thinking a U-boat had torpedoed the *Tuttle*, the helmsman put the wheel of the *Esso Augusta* hard right, and the master ordered full speed ahead and general quarters rung. The tanker proceeded on a fast zigzag and for safety headed toward the Chesapeake Bay. As the vessel made a large circle to the right, while still on her zigzag course, an explosion occurred about ten feet off the port quarter. The blast disabled the main engines and the steering gear of the ship, blew off the rudder and stern post, burst steam and fuel lines, and broke auxiliary foundations. The radio operator requested that a tug be sent to tow the ship in. Three hours later the tug *Keshena* arrived to take the tanker in tow. The tug *Coyote* later arrived to help the *Keshena*, and at 0100, 16 June, a third tug arrived alongside. None of the crew of eight officers and thirty-six men, or the thirteen armed guards, reported serious injuries. The vessel returned to service on 7 November 1942.

NSS; WACR; WCSR; AG; Rohwer, p. 104; *Ships of the Esso Fleet*, pp. 296-99.

ARKANSAN

D:	6-15-42	YB:	1921
T:	2029	Tn:	6,997
Pos:	12.54 N / 63.47 W	Dr:	26 ft. 11 in.
Ow:	American Hawaiian Line	C:	9,000 tons general and coffee
Op:	American Hawaiian Line	P:	steam
M:	Paul R. Jones	S:	13.0
A:	unarmed		

The *Arkansan* was torpedoed by the *U-126* (Bauer) about seventy miles west of Grenada while en route from Port-of-Spain, Trinidad, to New Orleans, Louisiana. The freighter had discontinued her zigzag course about forty-five minutes before when lookouts sighted a U-boat on the surface three points forward of the port beam. The master ordered full right rudder and increased speed in an attempt to put the ship's stern toward the submarine. Within a minute, two torpedoes hit the vessel amidships. The explosions wrecked the radio antenna and prevented the radio operator from sending a distress signal. Most of the crew of ten officers, twenty-eight men, and two workaways abandoned the ship in an orderly fashion in one lifeboat. They encountered some difficulties caused by the extreme port list and the fact that the ship was still moving at seven knots. The *Arkansan* sank in just over twenty minutes. One officer and three men could not be accounted for after the attack. The USS *Pastores* (AF-16) picked up the survivors and landed them at Trinidad.

NSS; WACR; WCSR; Other sources place the attack at 12.07 N / 62.51W; Rohwer, p. 104.

KAHUKU

D:	6-15-42	YB:	1920
T:	2120	Tn:	6,062
Pos:	11.54 N / 63.07 W	Dr:	25 ft. 6 in.
Ow:	Matson SS Co.	C:	7,000 tons cranes, tractors,
Op:	Matson SS Co.		equipment
M:	Eric Herbert Johanson	P:	steam
A:	1-4"; 2-20 mm; 2-50 cal.;	S:	9.5
	1-30 cal.		

The *Kahuku* was attacked by the *U-126* (Bauer) while steaming from New York to Trinidad, BWI. As the ship proceeded on a zigzagging course, the lookouts spotted the wake of the torpedo about twenty yards away from the ship. The torpedo struck abaft the bridge about eight feet below the waterline in the engine room. The ship carried an unusually large number of people, eight officers, twenty-eight men, ten armed guards, and sixty-three survivors from the *Scottsburg* and *Cold Harbor*. As soon as the torpedo struck, the men began abandoning ship. The armed guards fired a few shots from the after gun and then joined those leaving the ship. Some chaos resulted because of the extra men, but most got away in two lifeboats and three rafts. The *U-126* surfaced and used its deck gun on the bridge and radio room and fired approximately thirty shells, one striking the after magazine. The *U-126* fired a second torpedo into the vessel at midnight, and she sank at 0030. The submarine later picked men out of the water and put them on rafts. One man stayed on the U-boat for three days. Bauer later placed him on board the Venezuelan vessel *Minataora* for repatriation. The USS *Opal* (PYc-8) and the *YP-63* rescued ninety-one survivors and landed them at Trinidad. Two officers, four men, three armed guards, and nine of the passengers died.

NSS; WACR; WCSR; AG; Rohwer, p. 104; Moore, p. 163; Stindt, p. 119.

CHEROKEE

D:	6-15-42	YB:	1925
T:	2330	Tn:	5,896
Pos:	42.11 N / 69.25 W	Dr:	17 ft.
Ow:	Clyde Mallory Lines	C:	350 tons sand ballast
Op:	Clyde Mallory Lines	P:	steam
M:	Twiggs E. Brown	S:	8.0
A:	1-4"; 2-50 cal.; 2-30 cal.		

In a gale, the *U-87* (Berger) attacked the *Cherokee* fifty miles east of Boston while the tanker was en route from Halifax, Nova Scotia, to Boston in Convoy XB-25. The first torpedo hit the port side under the bridge and lifted the ship out of the water. The blast destroyed the chart house, and incoming water gave the ship a sharp list to port. The *Cherokee* increased speed and the helmsman turned the rudder hard right, but a second torpedo struck the port bow ninety seconds later. The damage from the two torpedoes was so extensive that the ship sank in about six minutes. The lifeboats could not be launched because of the extreme list and the rough seas. The crew cut seven life rafts loose, and some survivors clung to the wreckage while others jumped into the water. The ship carried 9 officers, 103 crew, 11 armed guards, and 46 passengers. The SS *Norlago* picked up forty-four survivors in the same vicinity. The USCG cutter *Escanaba* (WPG-77) rescued thirty-nine men. Three officers, sixty-two men, twenty passengers, and one armed guard died as a result of the explosions or drowning.

Other sources place the attack at 42.25 N / 69.10 W. NSS; WACR; WCSR; AG; Rohwer, p. 104.

TILLIE LYKES

D:	6-15-42	YB:	1920
T:	unknown	Tn:	2,572
Pos:	19.00 N / 85.00 W	Dr:	24 ft.
Ow:	Lykes Bros. SS. Co.	C:	2,705 tons food, machinery
Op:	Lykes Bros. SS. Co.	P:	steam
M:	Gus Warren Darnell	S:	unknown
A:	1-3"; 2-30 cal.		

The *Tillie Lykes* independently sailed from Galveston, Texas, to San Juan, Puerto Rico. The *U-502* (von Rosenthiel) is believed to have torpedoed the freighter about 150 miles east southeast of Punta Herrero, Mexico. Authorities never received any distress messages or discovered any wreckage. The eight officers, twenty-one crewmen, and four armed guards all perished.

WACR; AG; Rohwer, pp. 104-05. The *U-502* claimed three vessels on the 15th and 16th. The *U-158* was also in the area but did not make a report and was later lost.

COLUMBIAN

D:	6-17-42	YB:	1913
T:	0005	Tn:	4,964
Pos:	7.18 N / 41.03 W	Dr:	25 ft.
Ow:	American-Hawaiian SS Co.	C:	general
Op:	American-Hawaiian SS Co.	P:	steam
M:	Edwin E. Johnson	S:	12
A:	1-4"; at least 2-20 mm		

The *Columbian*, en route from New York to Basra, Iraq, was attacked by an unknown submarine. The master of the *Columbian* spotted a submarine before dark and maneuvered to escape. Minutes after midnight lookouts spotted the U-boat off the port beam, and a hard right turn by the *Columbian* put the submarine astern. The submarine opened fire and the ship's armed guard contingent immediately returned fire with the freighter's four-inch stern gun. The master maneuvered the ship skillfully to evade the submarine while the gun crew prepared to open fire. The first shot from the gun reportedly struck the submarine's conning tower, and 20-mm machine gun fire also peppered the submarine. A second hit by the freighter's stern gun caused the submarine to abandon the attack. The *Columbian* was slightly damaged all over by shell fragments and machine gun fire. One life raft caught fire from the bursting shells. None of the nine officers, thirty-three men, and seventeen armed guards reported injuries.

WACR; WCSR; Morison, 1:395; *Washington Post*, 2 April 1943.

MILLINOCKET

D:	6-17-42	YB:	1910
T:	1705	Tn:	3,274
Pos:	23.12 N / 79.58 W	Dr:	24 ft.
Ow:	A. H. Bull SS Co.	C:	4,300 tons bauxite ore
Op:	U.S. Maritime Commission	P:	steam
M:	Lewis Wesley Callis	S:	9.1
A:	1-6 lber.; 2-30 cal.		

The *Millinocket* was torpedoed by the *U-129* (Witt) while en route from St. Thomas, Virgin Islands, to Mobile, Alabama. While proceeding on a nonevasive course, the ship was struck by a torpedo between the #4 and the #5 hatches about twelve feet below the waterline. The explosion opened a large hole in the freighter's side and blew some men into the water. Because of the nature of the cargo the ship sank rapidly, settling on an even keel and then plunging beneath the water in three minutes. The radio operator had no time to send a distress message, and the armed guards never manned the guns. Only one lifeboat and two rafts cleared the ship, while some men jumped into the water to escape. The ship carried seven officers, twenty-two men, and six armed guards. The eleven casualties (four officers, five men, and two armed guards) resulted from drowning, with the exception of the chief gunner who apparently died in the explosion. Witt questioned the second assistant engineer concerning the name of the ship, tonnage, cargo, origin, and destination. The engineer asked for and received a first aid kit for the wounded men. A Cuban motor boat and two Cuban fishing boats rescued the twenty-four survivors thirteen hours later and landed them at Isabela de Sagua, Cuba.

NSS; WACR; WCSR; AG; RWCS; Rohwer, p. 105, places the attack at 23.12 N / 79.28 W.

SANTORE

D:	6-17-42	YB:	1918
T:	0745	Tn:	7,117
Pos:	36.52 N / 75.51 W	Dr:	29 ft. 10 in.
Ow:	Ore SS Co.	C:	11,095 tons coal
Op:	Ore SS Co.	P:	steam
M:	Eric Nyborg	S:	7.5
A:	1-4"; 2-50 cal.; 2-30 cal.		

The collier *Santore* presumably struck a mine laid by the *U-701* (Degan) while en route from Norfolk, Virginia, to Cristobal, Canal Zone. The collier was one of fourteen vessels maneuvering for position in Convoy KS-511. The mine struck the port side, and the explosion extensively damaged the #1, #2, and #3 side tanks and the #1 and #2 holds. The ship quickly flooded, listed to port, and sank. The master ordered the eight officers, twenty-nine crewmen, and nine armed guards to abandon ship, but because of the extreme list, they could not launch the lifeboats. The crew managed to free only one raft, and most of the men jumped overboard. Coast Guard vessels picked up the survivors within twenty or thirty minutes and landed them at Little Creek, Virginia. Three of the ship's crew died in the mishap.

NSS; WACR; AG; *Washington Daily News*, 23 June 1942.

SEATTLE SPIRIT

D:	6-18-42	YB:	1919
T:	0130	Tn:	5,627
Pos:	50.23 N / 42.25 W	Dr:	24 ft. 7 in.
Ow:	U.S. Maritime Commission	C:	ballast
Op:	Seas Shipping Co.	P:	steam
M:	Edward W. Myers	S:	8.0
A:	1-4"; 4-50 cal.; 4-30 cal.		

The *Seattle Spirit* sailed in Convoy ON-102, from Murmansk to New York via Reykjavik. In rough seas the *U-124* (Mohr) managed to get off a good shot at the zigzagging freighter. The ship traveled in convoy station #112, on the starboard side of the convoy. The torpedo struck amidships on the port side at the fire and engine rooms and rapidly flooded the ship. The machinery stopped immediately, and it is believed the boiler exploded. The master ordered the ship abandoned because of her complete disability. The radio operator sent no distress signals, and the gun crew offered no counter offensive before leaving the ship. The crew consisted of nine officers and twenty-eight men, and the ship carried seven passengers and eleven armed guards. One officer and two men died on watch below. A fourth man died of exposure after jumping into the water. A motorboat from the SS *Perth* and the Canadian corvette *Agassiz* (K-129) picked up the fifty-one survivors in two lifeboats. Four hours after the attack, an officer from the *Agassiz* boarded the freighter and determined she could not be salvaged. The corvette then sank the vessel with gunfire.

NSS; WACR; WCSR; AG; Rohwer, p. 104.

CHEERIO

D:	6-19-42	YB:	1893
T:	0800	Tn:	35
Pos:	18.02 N / 67.40 W	Dr:	unknown
Ow:	Antilles Shipping Corporation	C:	mahogany
Op:	Antilles Shipping Corporation	P:	sail
M:	Felix Hernandez	S:	2.5
A:	unarmed		

The schooner *Cheerio* was intercepted by the *U-161* (Achilles) eight miles southeast of Mona Island, West Indies. The *U-161* shelled and set the schooner on fire. The crew of nine abandoned the *Cheerio* about fifteen minutes after the first shots struck the vessel. During the attack, a patrol plane forced the U-boat to submerge but not before it fatally wounded the schooner, which sank at about 0900. A second patrol plane alerted the Coast Guard cutter *CG-459* of the position of the survivors. The cutter found the survivors clinging to driftwood, rescued all hands, and landed them at Mayagüez, Puerto Rico.

The WJ entry for this attack is misleading. NSS; WCSR; Rohwer, p. 105; *Assistance*, 2:167.

WEST IRA

D: 6-20-42   YB: 1919
T: 2215   Tn: 5,681
Pos: 12.04 N / 57.35 W   Dr: 26 ft. 10 in.
Ow: McCormick SS Co.   C: 6,418 tons general cargo
Op: Isthmian SS Co.   P: steam
M: Peter G. Winsens   S: 7.5
A: 1-4"; 4-20 mm; 2-30 cal.

The *West Ira* sailed from New York to the Persian Gulf via Cape Town, South
Africa. While steaming in rough seas on a nonevasive course, the ship was
attacked by the *U-128* (Heyse). A torpedo struck the freighter in the #2 hold, on
the starboard side, and she sank in ten minutes. The radio operator immediately
sent out distress signals, but the ship received no reply. On the master's orders
the crew of eight officers and twenty-eight men, along with the thirteen armed
guards, abandoned ship in four boats and one raft. The boats took three to five
days to make land. One lifeboat arrived at Trinidad. The Dutch SS *Macuba*
picked up another boat and landed the men at Barbados. The remaining twenty-
five survivors arrived at Barbados three days later. All hands were alive and
accounted for when the radio operator washed ashore on a raft eleven days after
the attack.

NSS; WACR; WCSR; AG; Rohwer, p. 105, places the attack at 12.28 N / 57.05 W.

ALCOA CADET

D: 6-21-42   YB: 1919
T: 1503   Tn: 4,823
Pos: at anchor, Kola Inlet, USSR   Dr: 15 ft.
Ow: Alcoa SS. Co.   C: 1,220 tons sand ballast
Op: Alcoa SS. Co.   P: steam
M: John Luther Martino   S: anchored
A: yes but unknown

A mine struck the *Alcoa Cadet* while she lay anchored at Kola Inlet, Murmansk,
USSR. The freighter sailed from Boston, Massachusetts, to Murmansk and had
safely discharged a cargo of war supplies and foodstuffs and had loaded 1,220
tons of sand ballast for the return trip. The authorities at Murmansk speculated
that an enemy mine had been dropped in the harbor by aircraft and eventually
had worked loose, surfaced, and struck the ship. The explosion occurred under
the #4 hold and broke the ship into at least two sections. The nine officers,
twenty-five men, and ten passengers on board abandoned the ship in one
lifeboat and two rafts. Several other ships anchored nearby rescued the men and

landed them at Murmansk. The explosion killed one member of the crew and injured several others.

NSS; WACR; WCSR.

E. J. SADLER

D:	6-22-42	YB:	1921
T:	1557	Tn:	9,638
Pos:	15.36 N / 67.52 W	Dr:	28 ft. 10 in.
Ow:	Standard Oil Co. of N. J.	C:	149,003 bbls. kerosene
Op:	Standard Oil Co. of N. J.	P:	steam
M:	Leslie Dean Cushman	S:	8.4
A:	unarmed		

On 21 June, the *E. J. Sadler* departed San Nicolaas, Aruba, for New York. The tanker, thirty-six hours out of port, did not steam an evasive course. The *U-159* (Witte) managed to fire a shot from its deck gun at about four miles away before being seen. The master swung the tanker's stern toward the submarine, and the radio operator began sending distress signals. The first ten rounds from the U-boat's 105-mm forward gun scored eight hits before the tanker was abandoned. The crew of eight officers and twenty-eight men abandoned the tanker in four lifeboats. The *U-159* then put seventy-five rounds from the deck gun and 175 rounds from its 37-mm gun into the *Sadler* at close range. The ship caught fire soon thereafter. The next morning PBYs spotted the survivors and directed the USS *Biddle* (DD-151) to the scene. She rescued all hands twenty hours after the attack and landed them at Mayagüez, Puerto Rico. A German boarding party with demolition charges sank the *Sadler* at about 2000.

NSS; WACR; WCSR; *Ships of the Esso Fleet*, pp. 302-05; Rohwer, p. 105; *War Action Casualties*, p. 99.

RAWLEIGH WARNER

D:	6-22-42	YB:	1912
T:	2300	Tn:	3,663
Pos:	28.53 N / 89.15 W	Dr:	23 ft. 6 in.
Ow:	Sabine Transportation Co. Inc.	C:	38,909 bbls. gasoline
Op:	Sabine Transportation Co. Inc.	P:	steam
M:	Jewel Homer Levingston	S:	unknown
A:	unarmed		

The *Rawleigh Warner* departed Smiths Bluff, Texas, on 21 June en route to Port St. Joe, Florida. About forty miles south of South Pass, Louisiana, the *U-67* (Müller-Stöckheim) fired a torpedo that hit the ship and caused a huge explosion. The tanker's gas cargo immediately burst into flames and engulfed the entire length of the ship. According to an eye witness, the ship sank in less than ten minutes and no boats left the ship. The entire crew of eight officers and twenty-five men perished in the attack.

NSS; WACR; WCSR; WJ.

JOHN R. WILLIAMS

D:	6-24-42	YB:	1913
T:	1605	Tn:	397
Pos:	38.45 N / 74.55 W	Dr:	15 ft. 6 in.
Ow:	Great Lakes Dredge & Dock Co.	C:	none
Op:	Moran Towing Co.	P:	steam
M:	Leroy Herbert Allen	S:	11.5
A:	unarmed		

The ocean tug *John R. Williams* struck a mine while returning to Cape May, New Jersey, from a towing assignment off the Delaware Capes. The tug worked out of the Cape May Naval Base for rescue and salvage. The *U-373* (Loeser) laid the mine about two weeks earlier. The mine struck the port side just forward of amidships and blew the ship apart; she sank instantly. Only two officers and two crew members, who were sitting on the fantail when the explosion occurred, survived. They managed to find a life raft that had blown free of the tug. The *YP-334* rescued these men about forty minutes after the explosion and landed them at Lewes, Delaware. Four officers and ten men died in the attack.

NSS; WACR; WCSR; Rohwer, p. 105.

MANUELA

D:	6-24-42	YB:	1934
T:	1927	Tn:	4,773
Pos:	34.30 N / 75.40 W	Dr:	24 ft. 6 in.
Ow:	A. H. Bull SS. Co.	C:	6,500 tons sugar
Op:	U.S. Maritime Commission	P:	steam
M:	Conrad G. Nilsen	S:	11.5
A:	1-4"; 2-30 cal.		

The *Manuela* sailed in convoy from San Juan, Puerto Rico, to New York. She took station as the second ship in the center column of a three-column convoy of ten ships. At 1923 a torpedo struck the Panamanian SS *Nordal*, about 1,000 yards off the *Manuela*'s starboard bow. The master ordered the ship's speed increased and the ship's course changed about 25° to port. Moments later a torpedo from the *U-404* (von Bülow) hit amidships between the engine room and the boiler room, on the starboard side. The blast tore a large hole in the ship, and both compartments flooded quickly. The explosion also wrecked the starboard lifeboat and threw a column of water and oil higher than the masthead. The freighter developed a pronounced list to starboard and prevented the gun crew from offering any counteroffensive. The crew of eight officers and twenty-eight men, along with six armed guards, abandoned ship within seven minutes. Twenty-three crewmen, including the master, entered the port lifeboat. The British armed trawler *Norwich City* (FY-229) picked up the survivors in this boat approximately thirty minutes later. Sixteen others, including the six members of the naval gun crew, abandoned ship by jumping over the side and swimming to three life rafts. The USCG escort vessel *CG-483* rescued these men and brought them to the Naval Operating Base at Norfolk, Virginia. One officer and two men on watch below died in the attack. The *Manuela* remained afloat, and the following day a salvage crew readied her to be towed. She sank while in tow to Morehead City, North Carolina, almost exactly twenty-four hours after the initial explosion.

NSS; WACR; WCSR; AG; WJ; Rohwer, p. 105.

POLYBIUS

D:	6-27-42	YB:	1919
T:	0950	Tn:	7,041
Pos:	11.00 N / 57.30 W	Dr:	26 ft. 6 in.
Ow:	U.S. Maritime Commission	C:	7,671 tons manganese ore and
Op:	American South African Line		general cargo
M:	Ole P. Stender	P:	steam
A:	unarmed	S:	9.0

The *Polybius* sailed from Bombay, India, to Norfolk, Virginia, via Cape Town and Trinidad. The *U-128* (Heyse) attacked the freighter as she maintained a nonevasive course. A lookout noticed a column of water about 100 feet off the stern that was rising about 3 feet from the surface and rapidly approaching the ship. It was too late to take action, and the torpedo struck abaft the #5 hatch directly under the living quarters, blowing off the stern. The ship settled rapidly by the stern and sank in less than ten minutes. The general alarm was sounded when the torpedo hit, and the surviving crewmen began lowering all four of the ship's lifeboats. The ship's complement comprised eight officers and thirty-six men. Officers aboard the *U-128* questioned the master, asking him only the name of his ship, and then the submarine steamed away. The next day the Dutch SS *Dracos* picked up seven men in one boat and landed them in Georgetown, British Guiana. Three days after the attack the SS *Clarona* rescued another twelve men and landed them at Trinidad. An Allied vessel picked up the final two boats two days after the attack and landed the men in Trinidad. The explosion killed ten crewmen in the living quarters of the ship.

NSS; WACR; WCSR; Rohwer, p. 106, places the attack 10.55 N / 57.40 W.

POTLATCH

D:	6-27-42	YB:	1920
T:	1552	Tn:	6,560
Pos:	19.20 N / 53.18 W	Dr:	27 ft. 2 in.
Ow:	Weyerhaeuser SS Co.	C:	7,500 tons Army supplies,
Op:	Weyerhaeuser SS Co.		trucks, tanks
M:	John Joseph Lapoint	P:	steam
A:	1-4"; 4-20 mm; 2-30 cal.	S:	7.0

The *Potlatch* sailed from New York to Suez, Egypt, via Trinidad, BWI. The *U-153* (Reichmann) attacked the freighter about 850 miles east of Puerto Rico. The freighter did not steer a zigzag course during her journey because of heavy smoke coming from the stack. She had stopped several times during the day to check the water content in the fuel oil. A torpedo struck on the port quarter, near the engine room about ten feet below the waterline. The explosion blew a hole through the deck and threw the deck cargo of tank cars and trucks into the air, buckled the deck plates, and damaged the steering gear. The ship immediately began settling on an even keel and sank within five minutes, plunging by the bow. The armed guards manned their stations, but the *U-153* did not surface until the after gun was awash. The seven officers, thirty-two crewmen, and sixteen armed guards abandoned the ship on the master's orders. Only one lifeboat could be launched; the other survivors jumped overboard and reached four life rafts and two doughnut rafts. The *U-153* surfaced, and the Germans questioned the crew concerning the ship and her cargo and gave them cigarettes. All the survivors left in the single twenty-five foot lifeboat. The forty-seven survivors remained at sea thirty-two days with little food or water and finally made landfall on the Bahama Islands. They landed on Great Inagua and found some water but had to sail to Little Inagua for more water. They then set sail to Aklins Island and went on to Nassau on board the *Vergermere*, arriving there on 1 August. One officer and five men died on board the *Potlatch*, and two other men died (one from exposure and one from an infected shark bite) while in the lifeboat.

NSS; WACR; WCSR; AG; Rohwer, p. 106. Some survivors suggest that two torpedoes struck the ship.

RAPHAEL SEMMES

D:	6-28-42	YB:	1920
T:	0433	Tn:	6,020
Pos:	29.30 N / 64.30 W	Dr:	27 ft. 6 in.
Ow:	U.S. Maritime Commission	C:	7,500 tons ore, tobacco, licorice,
Op:	Isthmian SS Co.		wool, rugs
M:	Harold Goron Eaton	P:	steam
A:	unarmed	S:	9.0

The *Raphael Semmes* sailed from Bombay, India, to New York via Trinidad. The ship was not zigzagging when two torpedoes fired from the *U-332* (Liebe) hit the freighter on the starboard side ten seconds apart. One struck at the #2 hatch below the surface and the other at the #4 hatch near the waterline. The explosives thoroughly destroyed the ship's watertight integrity, and she sank in two minutes. The ship's complement of nine officers and twenty-six men, as well as the two passengers, had little time to get off the freighter. Some of the crew attempted to launch boats, but the *Semmes* sank under them before they could do so. At least eighteen men managed to jump overboard and swim away from the ship. They clung to wreckage and eventually climbed onto three life rafts. The *U-332* circled the wreck, picking up some of the survivors. The Germans dressed their wounds and gave them tobacco, cigarettes, water, and food. Eighteen days after the attack the SS *Explorer* picked up the eighteen survivors and landed them at Jersey City. Seven officers, eleven men, and one passenger died in the attack.

NSS; WACR; WCSR; RWCS; Rohwer, p. 106.

SAM HOUSTON

D:	6-28-42	YB:	1942
T:	0945	Tn:	7,116
Pos:	19.21 N / 62.22 W	Dr:	28 ft.
Ow:	Waterman Agency Ltd.	C:	10,000 tons Army supplies
Op:	Waterman Agency Ltd.	P:	steam
M:	Robert Perry	S:	11
A:	1-4"; 4-20 mm		

The *Sam Houston* sailed on her maiden voyage from Mobile, Alabama, to Bombay, India, via Cape Town. A torpedo fired by the *U-203* (Mützelburg) struck the bulkhead between the engine room and the #4 deep tank. A tremendous explosion started fires in the ship's cargo. The #4 hold and the engine room quickly flooded and the engines stopped. After listing slightly at first, the ship righted herself and floated on an even keel with the deck only two feet above the water. The complement of eight officers, twenty-nine men, and nine armed guards abandoned the ship in three lifeboats, fifteen minutes after the initial explosion. The *U-203* then surfaced and sank the *Sam Houston* with gunfire. During the shelling, the ammunition on board ignited and exploded. The U-boat crew took the master on board for questioning. The submarine's crew reportedly knew the name of the ship and the master even though the master had been replaced only hours before sailing. Three men died while on watch below, and four others died later in the lifeboats from burns received at the time of attack. The minesweeper *Courier* (AMC-72) picked up the survivors two days later and landed them at St. Thomas. One of these men died of burns while in the hospital ashore. A total of one officer and seven men perished in the attack.

NSS; WACR; WCSR; AG; Rohwer, p. 106.

WILLIAM ROCKEFELLER

D:	6-28-42	YB:	1921
T:	1216	Tn:	14,054
Pos:	35.07 N / 75.07 W	Dr:	31 ft. 6 in.
Ow:	Standard Oil Co. of N. J.	C:	135,000 bbls. fuel oil
Op:	Standard Oil Co. of N. J.	P:	steam
M:	William R. Stewart	S:	9.2
A:	1-3"		

On 19 June, the *William Rockefeller* departed Aruba, NWI, bound for New York. The tanker had anchored overnight near Ocracoke Lighthouse and sailed north with a Coast Guard escort. The master proceeded without zigzagging because he had received instructions not to zigzag while steaming under ten knots. About sixteen miles east northeast of Diamond Shoals, a torpedo fired by the *U-701* (Degan) struck amidships on the port side about ten feet below the waterline at the pump room. The explosion created a hole about twenty feet in diameter and sprayed oil over the ship. The pump room and the #5 tank flooded, and the cargo began to burn. The men used the deck valve controls to secure the engines, and the radio operator sent an SOS but received no answer. The gun crew manned the three-inch gun but never saw the U-boat. Flames engulfed the whole after end of the vessel. When smoke and steam cut off communication with the after section of the ship, some of the crew of nine officers, thirty-five men, and six armed guards hastily lowered the #2 and #4 boats without orders. Others abandoned the ship on two rafts. The USCG escort vessel *CG-470* picked the men up within twenty minutes and landed them at the Ocracoke Coast Guard Station the same afternoon. All hands survived. Both a Coast

Guard plane and the *CG-470* attacked the *U-701* with no positive results. The tanker drifted fifteen miles before sinking about eleven hours after the attack.

NSS; WACR; WCSR; AG; *Coast Guard at War*, pp. 45-46; *Ships of the Esso Fleet*, pp. 321-22; Rohwer, p. 106; *War Action Casualties*, p. 101.

SEA THRUSH

D:	6-28-42	YB:	1920
T:	1303	Tn:	3,447
Pos:	22.40 N / 61.20 W	Dr:	26 ft. 2 in.
Ow:	Shepherd Line	C:	6,800 tons general
Op:	Shepherd Line	P:	steam
M:	Arthur C. Hunt	S:	10.5
A:	1-4"; 4-20 mm; 2-30 cal.		

The *Sea Thrush* sailed from Philadelphia, Pennsylvania, to Cape Town, South Africa, via Trinidad. The *U-505* (Loewe) fired a torpedo that struck forward of the collision bulkhead on the port side. The crew of eight officers and thirty-four men, together with eleven armed guards and fourteen Army officers and technicians as passengers, abandoned ship in four lifeboats. Just under an hour after the first torpedo struck, the *U-505* fired a second torpedo that hit the starboard side in the #2 hold. The explosion broke the ship in two, and she sank immediately. Forty-eight hours after the attack, the gunboat *Surprise* (PG-63) rescued the men in three of the boats and landed them in San Juan, Puerto Rico. A patrol plane spotted the other boat with sixteen survivors, and it made landfall at St. Thomas about five days after the initial attack. All hands survived the attack.

WACR; WCSR; AG; *New York Herald Tribune*, 19 July 1942; Moore, p. 257; Rohwer, p. 106, places the attack at 22.38 N / 60.59 W.

RUTH

D:	6-28-42	YB:	1919
T:	2255	Tn:	4,833
Pos:	21.44 N / 74.05 W	Dr:	22 ft.
Ow:	A. H. Bull SS Co.	C:	5,000 tons manganese ore
Op:	Isthmian SS Co.	P:	steam
A:	1-4"; 2-30 cal.	S:	10.5
M:	Robert Melville Callis		

The *U-153* (Reichmann) attacked the *Ruth* as she was en route from Rio de Janeiro to Baltimore via Port-of-Spain, Trinidad. As she steered a zigzag course, the *Ruth* was hit by a torpedo that struck the magazine in the stern. The whole after part of the ship disappeared in the blast. The vessel listed to port and sank by the stern within two minutes. The *Ruth* sank so quickly that the seven officers, twenty-seven men, and four armed guards on board had no time to launch any boats or even get off the ship. Four of the crew found themselves in the water, and three of these men managed to get on board a raft that floated free of the sinking freighter. The *U-153* rescued the fourth man and later placed him on the raft. The *U-153* apparently cruised around the area looking for survivors and after finding none, left. The USS *Corry* (DD-463) picked up the four crewmen six days later and landed them at Trinidad. Seven officers, twenty-three men, and the entire armed guard contingent died.

NSS; WACR; WCSR; AG; Rohwer, p. 107.

THOMAS McKEAN

D:	6-29-42	YB:	1942
T:	0723	Tn:	7,191
Pos:	22.00 N / 60.00 W	Dr:	26 ft. 6 in.
Ow:	Calmar SS Co.	C:	9,000 tons food, general
Op:	Isthmian SS Co.		supplies, 11 planes
M:	Mellin E. Respess	P:	steam
A:	1-4"; 4-20 mm; 2-30 cal.	S:	10

The *U-505* (Loewe) attacked the *Thomas McKean* as she was en route from New York to the Persian Gulf via Cape Town, South Africa, on her maiden voyage. The steamer had just changed her zigzag course when a torpedo hit aft of the #5 hold. The explosion knocked the stern gun out of action and killed three armed guards. Because of the extensive damage, the master ordered the ship abandoned. The eight officers, thirty-one crewmen, sixteen armed guards, and four passengers on board abandoned ship in four boats. Twenty minutes after the explosion the *U-505* surfaced about one and a quarter miles distant and immediately began to shell the ship. The U-boat fired fifty-seven shells and set the freighter on fire. She began to burn violently and sank about an hour after the torpedo struck. Crew members from the *U-505* boarded the lifeboats and administered first aid treatment before leaving the area. Two boats carrying twenty-nine survivors arrived at St. Thomas on 4 July; one boat with twelve survivors arrived at Antigua on 12 July; and the remaining boat with thirteen survivors and one dead landed at Micheson, Dominican Republic, on 14 July. Three armed guards and one crewman lost their lives in the attack.

The official documents disagree on the number of men on board the freighter. NSS; WACR; WCSR; AG; Rohwer, p. 107.

EXPRESS

D: 6-30-42	YB: 1940
T: 0030	Tn: 6,736
Pos: 23.30 S / 37.30 E	Dr: 27 ft. 8 in.
Ow: American Export Lines Inc.	C: 7,655 tons manganese ore, jute,
Op: American Export Lines Inc.	leather, general
M: William Kuhne	P: steam
A: 1-5"; 2-50 cal.; 2-30 cal.	S: 16.5

On 18 June, the *Express* sailed from Bombay, India, to Cape Town, South Africa. While steaming almost due south on a zigzagging course, she was attacked by the *I-10* (Kayahara). The *I-10* fired a single star shell seconds before two torpedoes hit the ship. The first torpedo struck at the waterline at the #7 hatch on the starboard side. A second torpedo struck five seconds later at the #5 hatch. The explosion damaged the steering apparatus, wrecked the guns, blew off the after hatch covers, and damaged the radio gear, preventing the radio operator from sending a distress signal. The vessel immediately flooded and began plunging stern first. The gun crew could not defend the ship because of the quickness of the sinking and the fact that the explosions had wrecked the guns. The ship's complement of ten officers, thirty-five men, and ten armed guards began launching two lifeboats. The master and several men launched a small workboat, but it swamped because the ship was still under way. The #1 boat carrying two armed guards and eleven men also swamped in the long swells, and none of these men survived. The #2 boat picked a few men out of the water, and the forty-one survivors in this boat landed on the coast of Mozambique six days later. One crew member abandoned the ship on a raft and later moved to a water-filled lifeboat. A Dutch tanker later rescued him and landed him at Cape Town.

WSS; WACR; WCSR; AG; McCoy, pp. 81-96; Rohwer, p. 262.

CITY OF BIRMINGHAM

D: 6-30-42	YB: 1923
T: 1930	Tn: 5,861
Pos: 35.04 N / 70.46 W	Dr: 21 ft.
Ow: Ocean SS Co.	C: 2,400 tons general
Op: Alcoa SS Co.	P: steam
M: Lewis P. Borum	S: 11
A: 1-4"; 2-30 cal.	

The *City of Birmingham* was torpedoed by the *U-202* (Linder) while en route from Norfolk, Virginia, to Bermuda. The minesweeper USS *Stansbury* (DMS-8) escorted the ship and took station a mile distant. About ten minutes before the attack, the *Stansbury* signaled by flags and blinkers for a change of course. Shortly thereafter two torpedoes hit in quick succession on the port side. The first torpedo struck about 100 feet abaft the bow in the #1 hatch. The second struck under the bridge. A third torpedo missed, passing ahead of the ship. The second explosion caused all the sections in the forward part of the ship to flood. The ship quickly listed 45° to port and sank within five minutes. Most of the 10 officers, 103 crew, 263 passengers, and 5 armed guards on board abandoned the ship in an orderly fashion in five lifeboats, five rafts, and seven floats. The armed guards left last and leapt into the sea. The *Stansbury* quickly came to the stricken vessel after dropping depth charges. A total of 372 survived. The *Stansbury* took the last passengers on board by 2200. Two passengers and six of the crew could not be accounted for, and one of the crew later died on board the *Stansbury*.

NSS; WACR; WCSR; AG; *Times Herald*, 21 July 1942; Rohwer, p. 107, places the attack at 35.10 N / 70.53 W.

WARRIOR

D:	7-1-41	YB:	1920
T:	1245	Tn:	7,551
Pos:	10.54 N / 61.01 W	Dr:	30 ft.
Ow:	Waterman SS Co.	C:	10,080 tons general war
Op:	Isthmian SS Line		supplies, fuel
M:	William Raymond MacDonough	P:	steam
A:	1-4"; 1-3"; 4-50 cal.; 2-30 cal.	S:	8

The *U-126* attacked the *Warrior* as she steamed from New York to Bandar Shahpur, Iran. The ship had just passed through a squall north of Trinidad and altered course when two torpedoes struck the vessel on the port side. Both hit below the waterline: the first hit abaft the bridge and the second struck in the #5 hatch, breaking the main shaft. The ship sank rapidly by the stern and disappeared in five minutes. Despite the rapid descent, the forward gun crew fired four rounds from the three-inch gun. On board, the eight officers, thirty-four men, and fourteen armed guards had time to launch only two lifeboats. All survived except three crewmen and the four members of the forward gun crew. An Allied ship picked up the survivors four hours after the attack and landed them in Trinidad.

NSS; WACR; WCSR; Rohwer, p. 107, places the attack one minute farther west.

EDWARD LUCKENBACH

D:	7-1-42	YB:	1916
T:	2150	Tn:	7,934
Pos:	24.56 N / 81.53 W	Dr:	33 ft.
Ow:	Luckenbach Line	C:	11,646 tons ore and wool
Op:	Grace Line	P:	steam
M:	Richard F. Kelly	S:	9.5
A:	1-4"; 4-50 cal.; 4-30 cal.		

The *Edward Luckenbach* accidentally wandered into an American minefield five miles off Smith Shoal Light, while en route from Kingston, Jamaica, to Texas City, Texas. The ship's master received faulty routing instructions from British officials in Kingston, Jamaica, who never mentioned the area as being restricted. The first mine struck the port side just forward of the engine room. Three minutes later another explosion occurred just slightly forward of the first. The ship settled immediately on an even keel with the superstructure above the water. The ship's complement of eight officers, thirty-four men, and twelve armed guards all survived, except for the third assistant engineer believed killed by the first explosion. Most of the survivors abandoned the ship in three lifeboats. The armed guards dove in the water and were picked up by the three boats. The lifeboats remained close to the ship throughout the night. The crew reboarded the ship at about 1000 the next day, and a patrol craft picked them up and took them to Key West.

NSS; WACR; WCSR; AG.

GULFBELLE

D:	7-3-42	YB:	1936
T:	0015	Tn:	7,104
Pos:	11.43 N / 60.35 W	Dr:	20 ft.
Ow:	Gulf Oil Corp.	C:	water ballast
Op:	Lago Oil Corp.	P:	steam
M:	Charles Wahl	S:	11.0
A:	1-5"		

The *Gulfbelle* was torpedoed by the *U-126* (Bauer) twenty-one miles north of Tabago while en route from Belém, Brazil, to Aruba, NWI. A torpedo hit the zigzagging tanker on the starboard quarter, fifteen feet below the waterline. The explosion ripped a hole forty feet square in the bottom, wrecked the engine room, and caused the turbine to fall out of the ship. The engine room flooded, but the master successfully righted the ship by shifting water ballast forward. The *U-126* surfaced for about five minutes and crossed the tanker's stern. The gun crew fired one round from the five-inch after gun at a range of 300 yards.

The shell passed over the submarine, which then submerged. Most of the ship's crew of eight officers and thirty-three men abandoned ship about five minutes after the explosion. The master had ordered the crew to stand by their abandon ship stations. They did not clearly understand the order and lowered three boats, two of which drifted away in the choppy seas. The master, four crewmen, and the eight-man gun crew remained on board. The crew in the #4 boat later reboarded the ship and subsequently transferred on board the destroyer HMS *Warwick* (D-25). The *Warwick* towed the tanker to Port-of-Spain, Trinidad. An oiler and the second assistant engineer died on watch below.

NSS; WACR; WCSR; Rohwer, p. 107, places the attack at 11.40 N/ 60.39 W.

ALEXANDER MACOMB

D:	7-3-42	YB:	1942
T:	0630	Tn:	7,192
Pos:	41.40 N / 66.52 W	Dr:	28 ft. 2 in.
Ow:	U.S. Maritime Commission	C:	9,000 tons military equipment,
Op:	A. H. Bull & Co.		tanks, planes, explosives
M:	Carl Monsen Froisland	P:	steam
A:	1-4"; 1-3"; 4-20 mm; 2-30 cal.	S:	10.5

The Liberty ship *Alexander Macomb*, on her maiden voyage, sailed as part of Convoy BA-2 en route from New York to Archangel, USSR, via Woods Hole, Massachusetts, and Halifax. During the night heavy fog and a fear of collision caused the ship to fall astern of the forty-one ship convoy. The master maintained an intermittent zigzag course and was attempting to catch the convoy in the daylight when the *U-215* (Hoeckner) attacked. The *Alexander Macomb* had reached the rear of the convoy and had about seven ships and an escort vessel in sight when a torpedo struck between the #4 and #5 holds. The torpedo caused the explosives stowed in the after part of the ship to ignite and burst into flames. The eight officers, thirty-three crewmen, and twenty-five armed guards began to abandon ship immediately. No one had secured the engines, but even with the ship still under way, the men managed to launch three lifeboats and one raft. One of the boats, however, capsized. Other survivors jumped into the water and hung onto pieces of wreckage. The ship sank by the stern at 0700. The trawler HMS *Le Tiger* (FY-243) rescued thirty-one men and brought them to Woods Hole. The Canadian corvette *Regina* (K-234) rescued another twenty-five. Six armed guards and four crew members perished in the attack.

NSS; WACR; WCSR; AG; Rohwer, p. 107, places the attack at 41.48 N / 66.35 W.

NORLANDIA

D:	7-3-42	YB:	1919
T:	2140	Tn:	2,689
Pos:	19.33 N / 68.39 W	Dr:	13 ft. 6 in.
Ow:	Merchants & Miners Trans. Co.	C:	ballast
Op:	North Atlantic & Gulf SS. Co.	P:	steam
M:	Herbert Elvin Callis	S:	11.0
A:	unarmed		

The *Norlandia* was attacked and sunk by the *U-575* (Heydemann) while en route from San Juan, Puerto Rico, to Neuvitas, Cuba. The U-boat fired a torpedo that struck between the engine room and the #3 hatch on the starboard side. The explosion caused extensive damage, tore up the deck, jammed the machinery, and flooded the ship rapidly. The ship dove beneath the water stern first in fifteen minutes. Fumes from the explosion severely affected the men, causing partial paralysis at first and afterwards, nausea and vomiting. The blast also destroyed the radio room, preventing the sending of a distress signal. The U-boat's skipper, Heydemann, expressed some surprise that the ship had no cargo and seemed concerned over the welfare of the crew. He handed down a bottle of German brandy for the survivors before leaving the scene. Twenty-one of the eight officers and twenty-two men abandoned the vessel in two lifeboats. One boat with fourteen survivors arrived at Samaná, Dominican Republic, in eighteen hours. The other boat with seven men arrived twelve hours later. Authorities presumed that the nine crew members who failed to leave the ship drowned after being overcome by the fumes.

NSS; WACR; WCSR; Rohwer, p. 107.

WILLIAM HOOPER

D:	7-4-42	YB:	1942
T:	1845	Tn:	7,177
Pos:	75.57 N / 27.14 E	Dr:	27 ft. 9 in.
Ow:	American South African Line	C:	8,600 tons war cargo, trucks,
Op:	U.S. Maritime Commission		tanks, ammunition
M:	Edward Lester Graves	P:	steam
A:	1-4"; 1-3"; 4-50 cal.; 2-30 cal.	S:	8.0

German aircraft attacked the *William Hooper*, on her maiden voyage, while in Convoy PQ-17 en route to Archangel, USSR, from Philadelphia, Pennsylvania. The *Hooper* sailed in a convoy of thirty-seven ships proceeding in nine columns. The *Hooper* took station as the stern ship in the port column, leaving her exposed to enemy attacks. Late in the day, German torpedo bombers attacked in formation from out of the clouds. The leader of the formation made a run up the center of the convoy to the starboard side of the *Hooper*. The remaining three veered close astern. One of these bombers passed over the *Hooper*, abaft the starboard beam, and released two torpedoes. The master ordered hard left rudder, but one hit the starboard side in the main engine room. The explosion blew parts of the engines and steering gear up through the stack and the engine room skylight. Fire broke out instantly in the settling tank and the ship began sinking immediately. The freighter's gun crew opened fire at 4,000 yards and set the port engine of one plane afire. The crew of eight officers and thirty-one men, together with the fifteen armed guards, abandoned the ship in a disorderly manner. Three of the merchant crew and four of the gun crew jumped overboard immediately, and the master personally had to stop the lowering of lifeboats until the ship had lost way. The only casualties, one officer and two crewmen, occurred on watch below. The British rescue ships *Rathlin* and *Zamalek* picked up the survivors and took them to the USSR. A British escort shelled the *Hooper*, but she did not immediately sink. Several hours later the *U-334* (Siemon) spotted the freighter and fired two torpedoes to finish her off.

NSS; WACR; WCSR; Irving, pp. 51, 52, 115, 144, 154; Rohwer, p. 198, places the attack one minute farther east.

CHRISTOPHER NEWPORT

D:	7-4-42	YB:	1942
T:	0250	Tn:	7,191
Pos:	75.49 N / 22.15 E	Dr:	27 ft.
Ow:	U.S. Maritime Commission	C:	8,200 tons war materiel
Op:	Calmar SS Corp.	P:	steam
M:	Charles Ernest Nash	S:	8.5
A:	1-4"; 4-50 cal.; 2-30 cal.		

German aircraft attacked the Liberty ship *Christopher Newport* 200 miles northeast of Bear Island while she was en route to Archangel, USSR, from Baltimore, Maryland. The freighter took station as the lead ship in the eighth column (#81) of Convoy PQ-17. The convoy had just begun to disperse when German torpedo bombers appeared. One plane launched two torpedoes about one-half mile away. The helmsman put the slow freighter hard aport to avoid the torpedo, but she did not answer the helm quickly enough. The torpedoes passed by two other American ships, the *Carlton* and the *Samuel Chase*, and struck the *Christopher Newport* amidships on the starboard side. The ship's gunners were unable to fire on the attacking plane because it flew in a direct line of fire of another ship in the convoy. The explosion tore a large hole in the hull, completely flooded the engine room, and destroyed the steering gear. After the torpedo struck, she continued veering to port, crossed the bows of ships in two other columns, and headed in the opposite direction before being stopped. Most of the eight officers, thirty-one men, and eleven armed guards began abandoning ship in the two port lifeboats. The rescue ship *Zamalak* rescued the men within fifteen minutes and took them to Archangel. A British escort unsuccessfully attempted to sink the *Newport* by riddling her with gunfire. The *U-457* (Brandenburg) found her at 0808 (GWT) the next day and put a torpedo in her as a coupe de grâce. One officer and two men died on watch below as a result of the torpedo explosion.

NSS; WACR; WCSR; Irving, pp. 94, 98; Rohwer, p. 198.

CARLTON

D:	7-5-42	YB:	1919
T:	0810	Tn:	5,127
Pos:	72.50 N / 24.35 E	Dr:	24 ft.
Ow:	Lykes Bros. Inc.	C:	5,500 tons tanks, TNT,
Op:	Lykes Bros. Inc.		ammunition, food
M:	Ragnvald Hansen	P:	steam
A:	1-4"; 2-50 cal.; 2-30 cal.	S:	10

On 27 June, the *Carlton* sailed from Reykjavik, Iceland, to Archangel, USSR, in Convoy PQ-17. On 4 July, German aircraft attacked the ships in the convoy, and at 2000 that day the convoy commodore ordered the formation to scatter. The *U-88* (Bohmann) spotted the freighter the next day and pursued her for three hours. The first torpedo struck the ship but failed to detonate. The second struck the ship's starboard side, entering the tank containing 5,000 bbls. of Navy special fuel oil and ignited the cargo. The blast collapsed the forward fireroom bulkhead and the after bulkhead of the #2 hold. The explosion also destroyed the two starboard lifeboats and blew the #3 hatch covers off, dispersing the cargo of flour in this hold all over the deck. With the ship sinking rapidly and enveloped in flames, the master ordered her abandoned. She sank on an even keel by the bow within ten minutes. Survivors slid down ropes or falls and jumped into the water. They also made use of four rafts and the #4 lifeboat. The total complement on board was eight officers, twenty-six men, and eleven armed guards. Two died on watch in the engine room. The lashed the four rafts and the boat together. A German seaplane landed on the water and took two men ashore about ten hours after the attack. Three more trips by German aircraft reduced the number in the boat to seventeen. On 9 July, a British plane dropped food for these survivors. On 13 July, the *U-376* (Marks) offered the men medical assistance, which the men declined. The Germans did give the men biscuits, water, blankets, and cigarettes. They eventually made landfall at North Cape, Norway, nineteen days after the attack. Before landing, the first assistant

engineer died of exposure. The Germans captured these men and put all forty-three survivors in a POW camp near Bremen.

The *Carlton*'s survivors provided valuable information to the Germans regarding the convoy and the cargoes carried by the ships. This proved to be quite a propaganda coup for the Germans. NSS; WACR; WCSR; RWCS; Irving, pp. 158-60, 176-78; *The Washington Post*, 22 February 1945; Rohwer, pp. 198-99.

PETER KERR

D:	7-5-42	YB:	1920
T:	1450	Tn:	6,476
Pos:	74.30 N / 35.00 E	Dr:	23 ft.
Ow:	Pacific-Atlantic SS Co.	C:	6,700 tons food, trucks, steel,
Op:	Pacific-Atlantic SS Co.		bombers
M:	William Hall Butler	P:	steam
A:	1-4"; 2-50 cal.; 2-30 cal.	S:	11.5

The *Peter Kerr* sailed with Convoy PQ-17 en route from Hoboken, New Jersey, to Murmansk, USSR. The convoy commodore dispersed the convoy on the 4th, and the *Peter Kerr* proceeded with the SS *Earlston Smiles*. On 5 July, at about 1300, lookouts spotted seven torpedo planes and four dive bombers flying from the southeast. The *Peter Kerr* began to zigzag at eight knots as the torpedo planes dropped thirteen torpedoes in succession. By changing course, speed, and zigzag plan, the master successfully avoided damage. The dive bombers then began their attack at an altitude of 4,000 feet. The planes dropped thirty-six bombs; three of these hit the freighter and set fire to the #3 hatch, the radio shack, and the deck cargo. The explosions also destroyed the steering gear as well as instruments and steam lines on the bridge. The ship began to flood because of a near miss off the port bow. The master had the engines secured five minutes after the first bomb hit. Bombs later struck at the #5 and #6 hatches and set fire to the cargo in the holds. When the fire became uncontrollable, the ship's complement of six officers, twenty-nine men, and eleven armed guards began to abandon ship in good order in two lifeboats. The vessel burned for eleven hours, then exploded and sank. The survivors remained in the lifeboats, and seven days later a Russian PT boat rescued all hands and landed them in Murmansk.

NSS; WACR; WCSR; AG.

DANIEL MORGAN

D: 7-5-42	YB: 1942
T: 1500	Tn: 7,177
Pos: 75.08 N / 44.10 E	Dr: 26 ft.
Ow: American South African Line	C: 8,200 tons steel, food,
Op: U.S. Maritime Commission	explosives, tanks
M: George T. Sullivan	P: steam
A: 1-4"; 1-3"; 4-50 cal.	S: 13.0

The *Daniel Morgan* sailed from Baltimore, Maryland, to Archangel, USSR, as part of the ill-fated PQ-17 convoy. After the dispersement of the convoy, the *Daniel Morgan* traveled with four other ships in an effort to escape and reach Archangel. The *Daniel Morgan* unsuccessfully fought the German bombers that later sank the *Fairfield City* three miles away. Five German bombers attacked the *Morgan* for over one hour, dropping approximately eighty-one bombs. The zigzagging freighter suffered thirty near misses. Three of these hit in the vicinity of the #4 and #5 holds, causing the holds to flood and the ship to list to starboard. As the crippled vessel still tried to escape, the *U-88* (Bohmann) fired a torpedo into her port side amidships. Minutes later the U-boat fired a second torpedo into the engine room. The eight officers, thirty-one men, and fifteen armed guards on board all abandoned the vessel in three lifeboats. One of the lifeboats capsized, however, killing two men. A third man died from a concussion. Bohmann questioned the master and men and told them to follow the submarine, which they did for some time before the *U-88* pulled away. The Russian tanker *Donbass* rescued the survivors and took them to Archangel.

The sources do not agree on the ship's complement. NSS; WACR; WCSR; Irving, pp. 168-70; Rohwer, p. 199, places the attack at 75.08 N / 45.00 E.

WASHINGTON

D: 7-5-42	YB: 1919
T: 1550	Tn: 5,564
Pos: 76.25 N / 33.41 E	Dr: 25 ft.
Ow: States SS Co.	C: 5,500 tons war materiel
Op: U.S. Maritime Commission	P: steam
M: Julius Richter	S: 11.5
A: 1-4"; 2-50 cal.; 4-30 cal.	

In a bombing attack that lasted twenty-two hours, the *Washington* was sunk by enemy aircraft 175 miles east-northeast of Bear Island. The freighter sailed in Convoy PQ-17 en route from Philadelphia, Pennsylvania, to Archangel, USSR. Falsely believing a German battle fleet threatened the convoy, the ships had been ordered dispersed for their safety. Enemy aircraft attacked the *Washington* on 3 and 4 July. During the attacks the freighter developed leaks as a result of several near misses off the starboard side. The *Washington* joined the *Paulus Potter* and *Bolton Castle* hoping the small convoy would bolster their chances of escape. At 1300 on 5 July a single plane appeared and circled the ships. Dive bombers later arrived and attacked from different directions. After sinking the other two vessels, they concentrated on the *Washington*. The planes released approximately twenty bombs that weighed between 200 and 500 pounds. Several bombs exploded close enough to disable the steering apparatus. The leaks in the hull now developed to a point where the pumps could not handle the water. The master ordered the main engines shut down, and the radio operator sent an SOS. The *Olopana* replied to the message and arrived two hours later. The ship's complement of eight officers, twenty-eight men, and nine armed guards abandoned the ship in two lifeboats after it became apparent the vessel would sink. Several planes strafed the ship after abandonment and set her on fire. When the *Olopana* appeared, the survivors decided that they would be safer in the lifeboats than on another ship. The *Olopana* was subsequently sunk by a torpedo attack the next day. The survivors rowed along the coast of Novaya Zemlya, boarding the grounded *Winston-Salem* for provisions, their first real meal in ten days. On 12 July, a Russian whaler rescued all hands and placed them on board the *Empire Tide* on 17 July. They landed in Archangel on 24 July. One crewman died of exposure after being ashore for four days.

The *Winston Salem*'s crew ran her aground and abandoned her. The freighter was later refloated and brought undamaged into Molotovsk. NSS; WACR; WCSR; AG.

HONOMU

D:	7-5-42	YB:	1919
T:	1558	Tn:	6,999
Pos:	75.05 N / 38.00 E	Dr:	28 ft.
Ow:	Matson Navigation Co.	C:	7,000 tons food, steel,
Op:	Matson Navigation Co.		ammunition, tanks
M:	Fredrik Anderson Strand	P:	steam
A:	2-30 cal.	S:	10.5

The *Honomu* was torpedoed by the *U-456* (Teichert) while en route to Archangel, USSR, from Philadelphia, Pennsylvania. The vessel, once part of the dispersed PQ-17 convoy, was sailing alone trying to escape to Archangel. The *U-456*'s first torpedo hit the vessel at the #3 hold on the starboard side. The explosion destroyed the fireroom and shut off all power. As the ship began to settle, a second torpedo struck at the #4 hold, causing the ship to sink by the stern in ten minutes. Nineteen of the seven officers, twenty-eight men, four British armed guards, and two Navy signalmen on board managed to launch a boat, and twenty-two others scrambled onto four rafts. The Germans took the master off the #5 raft and into the U-boat as a POW. The men on the *U-456* handed out meat and bread to the men. After drifting for thirteen days a British minesweeper and another escort vessel rescued the survivors on the rafts 360 miles from Murmansk and took them to Scotland. The nineteen men in the #2 boat did not fare well. They drifted for twenty-three days, until a U-boat picked up the survivors and took them as POWs to Norway. Two officers, eight men, and one of the British armed guards died of exposure in the boat.

The figures for the complement conflict within the sources. NSS; WACR; WCSR; AG; RWSA; Rohwer, p. 198; Irving, pp. 170-71.

PAN KRAFT

D:	7-5-42	YB:	1919
T:	1600	Tn:	5,644
Pos:	76.50 N / 38.00 E	Dr:	22 ft. 6 in.
Ow:	Waterman SS Corp.	C:	7,800 tons aircraft parts,
Op:	Waterman SS Corp.		bombers, TNT
M:	Jacob Jacobson	P:	steam
A:	1-4"; 2-50 cal.; 2-30 cal.	S:	11.5

The *Pan Kraft* sailed from New York to Archangel, USSR, as part of the PQ-17 convoy. The convoy dispersed on 4 July, by order of the convoy commodore, to avoid any confrontation with the German fleet thought to be in the vicinity. The master rang general quarters when lookouts heard enemy planes approaching. At 1500 three German bombers each dropped a bomb as they crossed over the ship. Three just missed the vessel, landing twenty feet close aboard to the port side of holds #1, #3, and #4 in that order. The concussions ruptured the steam and oil connections. The watch below secured the main engines in ten minutes, and the master gave orders to abandon ship. The second mate remained behind to supervise the abandonment as the eight officers, twenty-eight crewmen, and eleven armed guards began leaving the ship in four lifeboats. The second mate died of bullet wounds, and a seaman died of shrapnel wounds while in the lifeboat. Within an hour the corvette HMS *Lotus* (K-93) rescued the survivors of the crew. The corvette put three or four shells in the *Pan Kraft*, but these did not sink her and the corvette left the freighter behind, burning and sinking. The ship finally blew up and sank nine hours after the attack.

The time of the sinking is listed between nine and thirty-six hours later. NSS; WACR; WCSR; AG; Irving, pp. 204-05, 207.

FAIRFIELD CITY

D:	7-5-42	YB:	1921
T:	1615	Tn:	5,686
Pos:	74.40 N / 39.45 E	Dr:	25 ft.
Ow:	Isthmian SS Co.	C:	7,400 tons war supplies
Op:	Isthmian SS Co.	P:	steam
M:	Leon E. Walters	S:	12.0
A:	2-30 cal.		

The *Fairfield City* sailed from Iceland to Murmansk, USSR, as part of Convoy PQ-17. When the convoy commodore dispersed the ships, the freighter traveled as part of a group of four American vessels and a few British escorts. Just after 1500 three Junkers 88s found the group and began attacking the *Fairfield City*. The first stick of bombs fell close aboard. A second bomber released bombs that struck the afterdeck, and the third plane's bombs hit the bridge, killing two officers and six men but sparing the helmsman. The ship's complement consisted of ten officers, twenty-six men, and six armed guards. The surviving men abandoned ship in the #1, #2, and #3 lifeboats and a raft. The #1 boat, which had a motor, took the others in tow toward Novaya Zemlya. The thirty-four men made landfall nearly four days later. On 12 July, the trawler HMS *Ayrshire* (FY-225) rescued the men and placed them on board several ships for repatriation at Matochin Straight.

WACR; WCSR; AG; Irving, pp. 166, 168, 294.

RICHARD HENRY LEE

D:	7-5-42	YB:	1942
T:	2055	Tn:	7,191
Pos:	69.39 N / 22.33 W	Dr:	unknown
Ow:	U.S. Maritime Commission	C:	unknown
Op:	Calmar SS Line	P:	steam
M:	Johann P. Johansen	S:	approximately 7.5
A:	1-3"; 2-30 cal.		

On 26 June, the *Richard Henry Lee* sailed from Murmansk, USSR, for New York in Convoy QP-13. Because of poor visibility and fog, the convoy commodore failed to get a good navigational fix, and the convoy ran into a British minefield near Iceland. The *Richard Henry Lee* "sheared out to port" and found herself with several other ships in the minefield. According to Navy records, the freighter suffered some minor damage and remained in Iceland for three weeks before sailing for New York. The entire complement of eight officers, twenty-six crewmen, and nine armed guards survived the incident.

Some documents also indicate that the WSA was the owner. WCSR; TF; AG; VSC.

MASSMAR

D:	7-5-42	YB:	1920
T:	2056	Tn:	5,828
Pos:	66.39 N / 22.33 W	Dr:	unknown
Ow:	Calmar SS Corp.	C:	ballast
Op:	Calmar SS Corp.	P:	steam
M:	Albert Charles Leimback	S:	7.5
A:	1-4"; 2-50 cal.; 2-30 cal.		

The *Massmar* sailed from Murmansk to New York via Iceland as part of the ill-fated QP-13 convoy. The freighter along with three other American flagged vessels mistakenly steamed into an Allied minefield near Iceland because of poor visibility and foul weather. The *Massmar* suffered one explosion aft of the #5 hold and another near the #4 hold. The ship had a large number of men on board: eight officers, twenty-eight men, nine armed guards, and forty-five passengers from the *Alamar*, sunk in the eastbound PQ-16 convoy. In heavy seas they managed to launch three boats and three rafts. Two of the lifeboats capsized, however, including one with sixty men on board. The French corvette *Roselys* picked up survivors within thirty minutes as the ship disappeared beneath the waves. There was an incredible loss of life due to drowning and exposure. Twenty-two men from the *Alamar* died, along with four from the *Alamar*'s gun crew. The *Massmar* lost seven officers, ten men, and five armed guards, for a total of forty-eight dead. All survivors landed at Reykjavik.

The losses and the crew size are contradictory within the sources. WACR; WCSR; AG.

HYBERT

D:	7-5-42	YB:	1920
T:	2100	Tn:	7,776
Pos:	66.39 N / 22.33 W	Dr:	unknown
Ow:	Lykes Bros. SS. Co.	C:	ballast
Op:	Lykes Bros. SS. Co.	P:	steam
M:	Joseph Leonidas Dalton	S:	7.5
A:	1-4"; 2-50 cal.; 2-30 cal.		

On 27 June, the *Hybert* sailed from Murmansk, USSR, bound for Ireland as part of Convoy QP-13. Although the convoy had been attacked several times, the *Hybert* had not suffered any major damage. Twenty miles off North Cape, in poor visibility and foul weather, the convoy escort commander could not get a good fix on the position of the ships, and the convoy thus wandered into an Allied minefield. At about 2100, a mine struck one of the ships in the convoy. The convoy escort commander believed a U-boat had torpedoed this ship and ordered the convoy to disperse. Minutes later an explosion rocked the *Hybert* on

the port side. The explosion blew debris, water, and hatch covers fifty feet in the air; broke the propeller shaft; and destroyed the steering gear. The ship began filling rapidly and settled by the stern. The ship's complement of ten officers, twenty-nine men, and eleven armed guards, as well as the twenty-six passengers from the *Syros*, began to abandon ship and lowered four boats. Twenty minutes after the first explosion, as the final lifeboat came down the falls, the vessel struck another mine forward of the bridge at the #2 hatch. The British trawler *Lady Madeleine* (FY-283) and the French corvette *Roselys* rescued the survivors. All hands survived the attack.

The *Hybert* suffered minor damage to her hull and framing during attacks by German aircraft from 27 May until 30 May. WACR; WCSR; AG.

JOHN RANDOLPH

D:	7-5-42	YB:	1942
T:	2118	Tn:	7,191
Pos:	66.39 N / 22.33 W	Dr:	14 ft.
Ow:	U.S. Maritime Commission	C:	ballast
Op:	Union Sulphur Co.	P:	steam
M:	Paul Clements Mugge	S:	8.0
A:	1-4"; 2-50 cal.; 2-30 cal.		

The *John Randolph* was one of four unfortunate ships that ran into an Allied minefield in thick weather off the northwest coast of Iceland. On 27 June, the *Randolph* sailed from Murmansk to Iceland as part of Convoy QP-13, but the convoy commander could not get a navigational fix and navigated the ships into the minefield. The master observed the ship ahead swing at a 90° angle and ordered the helmsman to follow that ship. He thought he saw gunfire, but more likely the ship ahead had struck a mine. He then swung his vessel back to her original course, and an explosion occurred on the starboard side at the #3 hatch. The master ordered the engines stopped and directed the crew to clear the boats. While doing this, another explosion occurred abreast the #4 hatch. The first explosion blew the hatch beams, covers, and ballast into the air. The second explosion broke the ship in two at the bridge deck. The ship's complement of eight officers, thirty men, and twelve armed guards, along with twelve passengers, abandoned ship in two lifeboats and two rafts. Two officers and three crewmen died. Various escort vessels in the convoy picked up the survivors within two and a half hours. The stern sank in ten minutes and the bow remained afloat. An Icelandic trawler towed the bow of the *John Randolph* into port, and the Navy later used it for storage.

The figures for the ship's complement are contradictory. WACR; WCSR; AG; Morison, 1:178.

HEFFRON

D:	7-5-42	YB:	1919
T:	2125	Tn:	7,611
Pos:	66.39 N / 22.33 W	Dr:	15 ft.
Ow:	Weyerhaeuser SS Co.	C:	80 tons general
Op:	Weyerhaeuser SS Co.	P:	steam
M:	Edward Dick Geddes	S:	8.0
A:	2-30 cal.		

On 27 June, the *Heffron* sailed with Convoy QP-13 en route from Murmansk, USSR, to New York via Iceland. Because of poor visibility and rough weather, the convoy strayed into an Allied minefield twenty miles off the northeast tip of Iceland. Through the fog and mist the master observed the other vessels of the convoy steaming in all directions and a nearby corvette began blinking a signal. At that moment the freighter struck a mine on the starboard side at the #2 hatch. The explosion carried away the main steam line in the engine room and stopped the engines. Minutes later a second explosion occurred at the #5 or #6 hatch. The freighter began to settle rapidly to starboard. All nine officers, twenty-eight men, two Navy signalmen, and twenty-three passengers abandoned ship after the master passed the order. The rough seas complicated the launching of the boats, but the men managed to clear the ship in four boats. As the second boat touched the water, a third explosion ripped another hole in the hull near the engine room and knocked two men out of the boat and into the water. The crew also lowered an injured man into one of the ship's rafts. The French corvette *Roselys* picked up the survivors four hours later. The *Heffron* sank sometime after midnight. Only the third assistant engineer died when he injured himself and fell into the water.

The *Heffron* had suffered punctured hull plates from enemy bombs while docked in Murmansk. The passengers were seamen from four other ships being repatriated. The ship's complement figures conflict within the sources. WACR; WCSR; AG.

JOHN WITHERSPOON

D:	7-6-42	YB:	1942
T:	1440	Tn:	7,191
Pos:	72.05 N / 48.30 E	Dr:	29 ft.
Ow:	U.S. Maritime Commission	C:	8,575 tons tanks, ammunition
Op:	Seas Shipping Co.	P:	steam
M:	John Stewart Clark	S:	12.8
A:	1-4"; 4-50 cal.; 2-30 cal.		

The *John Witherspoon* was torpedoed by the *U-255* (Reche) about twenty miles from the shore of Novaya Zemlya. The freighter sailed in Convoy PQ-17 from Baltimore, Maryland, to Archangel, USSR. From 1 July to 6 July, the

Witherspoon had successfully avoided attacks by aircraft, and after the convoy dispersed, the *Witherspoon* made a dash to the White Sea. The *U-255* spotted the lone ship and attacked. One torpedo hit the starboard side between the #4 and #5 holds, and a second struck a minute later underneath the bridge. A third torpedo exploded amidships on the port side. It broke the ship in two and she sank within minutes. After the second torpedo explosion, the master ordered the ship's complement of eight officers, thirty-one men, and eleven armed guards to abandon the freighter. They left in three lifeboats and one raft. The *U-255* surfaced and approached the boat containing the master. The Germans asked about the cargo and promised to send a message for the survivors. Then the U-boat left. Fifty-three hours later in a heavy fog, the Panamanian ship *El Capitan* rescued the three armed guards and sixteen crew members in the #4 lifeboat. German bombers later set the *El Capitan* on fire, and the crew had to abandon ship again. The trawler HMS *Lord Austin* (FY-220) rescued them the second time and took them to Archangel. On 9 July, the HMS *La Malouine* (K-46) rescued the remaining armed guards and merchant crew. A seaman who drowned abandoning ship was the only man lost in the attack.

NSS; WACR; WCSR; RWCS; AG; Irving, pp. 267-68, 279-80.

PAN ATLANTIC

D:	7-6-42	YB:	1919
T:	1615	Tn:	5,411
Pos:	271 mi. off Cape Kanin, USSR	Dr:	25 ft.
Ow:	Waterman SS Co.	C:	8,000 tons TNT, tanks, food,
Op:	U.S. Maritime Commission		steel
M:	John Oscar Sieber	P:	steam
A:	1-4"; 4-50 cal.; 2-30 cal.	S:	12.0

The *Pan Atlantic* sailed from Philadelphia, Pennsylvania, to Archangel, USSR, via Reykjavik with Convoy PQ-17. After dispersement of the convoy, the master struck out alone toward the ice fields so that his crew could paint the ship white for camouflage. As the *Pan Atlantic* proceeded at full speed, a single German bomber dropped two bombs that struck forward of the well deck at the #2 hatch. The 3,000 tons of TNT in the hold ignited, blew the entire bow off, and caused the freighter to sink in three minutes. The complement of eight officers, twenty-nine men, and eleven armed guards abandoned ship in one lifeboat and two rafts. Both the *U-88* (Bohmann) and the *U-703* (Bielfeld) had followed the ship and surfaced to salvage the flotsam, particularly the provisions. Officers of one of the submarines questioned the survivors before leaving the scene. Seven of the gun crew and eighteen crewmen perished. The corvette HMS *Lotus* (K-93) rescued the survivors 170 miles north of Cape Kanin and landed them at Archangel.

The *Bellingham* carried the survivors for repatriation and was sunk by the *U-435*. See entry for *Bellingham*. WACR; WCSR; AG; Irving, p. 230.

OLOPANA

D:	7-7-42	YB:	1920
T:	2310	Tn:	6,069
Pos:	72.10 N / 51.00 E	Dr:	25 ft.
Ow:	Matson Navigation Co.	C:	6,000 tons explosives, gasoline,
Op:	Matson Navigation Co.		trucks
M:	Mervyn Clement Stone	P:	steam
A:	5-30 cal.	S:	9.6

The *Olopana* was torpedoed by the *U-255* (Reche) approximately ten miles west of Moller Bay, Novaya Zemlya, while en route from Philadelphia, Pennsylvania, to Archangel, USSR, in Convoy PQ-17. After the convoy scattered, the *Olopana* headed for Novaya Zemlya, with hopes of escaping to Archangel. A single torpedo struck the vessel on the port side in the engine room. The torpedo's warhead did not immediately engage, and the delayed explosion blew in all the bulkheads. The vessel settled immediately but did not sink. With the engines secured, the crew of eight officers and twenty-eight men, as well as the five armed guards, abandoned the ship on four rafts. The *U-255* surfaced and began shelling the *Olopana* from 200 yards, firing forty shells— twenty on each side. After shelling the freighter, the U-boat cruised among the lifeboats and the Germans questioned the officers. One ship's officer, two armed guards, and four crewmen died during the attack. Three of these men died while on watch in the engine room. The survivors made landfall on Novaya Zemlya Island at Moller Bay more than two days later. A Russian patrol plane took them to Archangel.

NSS; WACR; WCSR; RWSA; Rohwer, p. 199; Stindt, p. 119; Irving, pp. 233-passim.

ALCOA RANGER

D:	7-7-42	YB:	1919
T:	0735	Tn:	5,116
Pos:	71.38 N / 49.35 E	Dr:	24 ft.
Ow:	Alcoa SS Co.	C:	7,200 tons steel, armor plate,
Op:	U.S. Maritime Commission		flour, tanks
M:	Vernon Lancelot Jubb	P:	steam
A:	2 anti-aircraft guns, 1-30 cal.	S:	12.5

The *Alcoa Ranger* was torpedoed and shelled by the *U-255* (Reche) while en route from Philadelphia, Pennsylvania, to Archangel, USSR. The freighter sailed with Convoy PQ-17 and had survived numerous torpedo and bomber attacks. After the convoy dispersed on 4 July, the vessel steamed independently in an effort to escape. A torpedo struck the starboard side at the #2 hold, opening a large hole and causing the vessel to list heavily to starboard. The eight officers, twenty-six men, and six armed guards on board abandoned ship in three lifeboats fifteen minutes after the torpedo struck. The *U-255* surfaced, the Germans questioned the crew, and then from about 100 yards the submarine fired at least sixty shells at the freighter. The *Ranger* finally sank by the head at 0900. On the 7th, the #2 and #3 lifeboats landed at Novaya Zemlya, and seven days later the #4 boat landed at Cape Kanin. Russian patrol boats rescued all hands and landed them at Archangel.

Some survivors stated the *U-255* fired as many as 150 shells. NSS; WACR; WCSR; RWCS; AG; Rohwer, p. 199, places the attack at 71.20 N / 51.00 E.

PAUL H. HARWOOD

D:	7-7-42	YB:	1918
T:	0320	Tn:	6,610
Pos:	29.26 N / 88.38 W	Dr:	15 ft. 6 in.
Ow:	Standard Oil Co. of N. J.	C:	water ballast in tanks 2-5-7
Op:	Standard Oil Co. of N. J.	P:	steam
M:	George Rasmussen	S:	12.0
A:	1-4"; 1-3"; 4-20 mm		

On 24 June, the *Paul H. Harwood* departed New York bound for Port Arthur, Texas. The tanker and three other ships steamed abreast while being escorted by a destroyer. A single torpedo fired by the *U-67* (Müller-Stöckheim) struck abaft amidships on the port side at the #6 tank. The explosion blew a hole fifteen feet by twelve feet at the waterline and flooded tanks #5, #6, and #7. The master counterflooded the forward tanks to stabilize the tanker and rang full speed ahead. The vessel continued on her course, making ten knots into Southwest Pass to Burwood, Louisiana. None of the eight officers, thirty-two men, and sixteen armed guards on board reported an injury. The vessel returned to service on 28 September.

NSS; WACR; WCSR; AG; *Ships of the Esso Fleet*, pp. 329-32; Rohwer, p. 108.

J. A. MOFFETT JR.

D:	7-8-42	YB:	1921
T:	0020	Tn:	9,788
Pos:	24.45 N / 80.42 W	Dr:	20 ft.
Ow:	Standard Oil Co. of N. J.	C:	water ballast in tanks 3-5-7
Op:	Standard Oil Co. of N. J.	P:	diesel
M:	Patrick Sarsfield Mahony	S:	8.5
A:	1-4"; 2-30 cal.		

On 4 July, the *J. A. Moffett* departed Wilmington, North Carolina, en route to Port Arthur, Texas. Three miles southwest of Tennessee Reef, the *U-571* (Möhlmann) attacked. The first torpedo hit the #1 tank on the port side. The watch below secured the engines, and as the tanker began to lose way, Captain Mahony, in an attempt to beach her, had the helmsman swing the wheel hard to starboard. Most of the crew of eight officers and twenty-nine men began to abandon ship in two lifeboats and three rafts. The six-man gun crew remained on board to defend the ship. At 0035 a second torpedo hit the #8 tank on the port side before the gun crew could find the submarine. The disabled tanker now drifted in a semicircle until going aground on Tennessee Reef. At this point the rest of the gun crew left the ship. As the #2 boat was launched, the master's arm got caught in the falls and was amputated. He died of a loss of blood. The *U-571* surfaced at 0050 and began shelling the hapless tanker for five minutes, setting the midships house afire. The Coast Guard Auxiliary crafts *Mary Jean* and *Southbound* picked up the survivors within three hours. The USCG cutter *Nike* (WPC-112) saved another man. All survivors landed at Craig, Florida. In 1943 a salvage crew pulled the tanker off the reef and towed her to Galveston where she was declared a CTL.

The figures for the naval gun crew are contradictory. NSS; WACR; WCSR; AG; *Coast Guard at War*, p. 33; *Ships of the Esso Fleet*, pp. 335-40; Rohwer, p. 108, places the attack at 24.47 N / 80.42 W.

HOOSIER

D:	7-9-42	YB:	1920
T:	2145	Tn:	5,060
Pos:	69.45 N / 39.35 E	Dr:	24 ft.
Ow:	Hoosier Marine Corp.	C:	5,029 tons machinery,
Op:	U.S. Maritime Commission		explosives, tanks
M:	Julius Holmgren	P:	steam
A:	1-4"; 4-50 cal.; 2-30 cal.	S:	10.0

The *Hoosier* sailed as part of Convoy PQ-17 from Philadelphia, Pennsylvania, to Archangel, USSR, via Reykjavik. After the convoy had dispersed, the *Hoosier* sailed in company with a small group of other escorts and merchantmen. The group was attacked by about fifty-five German bombers, and about sixteen bombs straddled the *Hoosier*, exploding close aboard. The first stick of bombs did no damage. The second stick hit five feet from the boat deck and the third twenty yards away. These explosions damaged the steam pipes and oil lines, sprung some of the ship's hull plates, and disabled the engines. The master concluded that the engines could not be repaired and ordered the vessel abandoned. The crew of eight officers and thirty-four men, along with eleven armed guards, abandoned the ship in four lifeboats within minutes and boarded the corvette HMS *Poppy* (K-213). The commanding officer of the French corvette *La Malouine* (K-46) decided to tow the freighter. He put a salvage crew back on board that included the *Hoosier*'s engineers. When lookouts spotted the *U-255* four miles astern, the French corvette expeditiously dropped the tow and recovered the boarding party. As the freighter settled slightly, the *Poppy* tried to no avail to sink her with gunfire. The *U-376* (Marks) later fired a coup de grâce torpedo into the vessel, and she sank at 0105 on the 10th. All hands survived.

NSS; WACR; WCSR; AG; Irving, pp. 274-75; Rohwer, p. 199, places the sinking at 69.25 N / 38.35 E.

SANTA RITA

D:	7-9-42	YB:	1941
T:	8,379	Tn:	8,379
Pos:	26.11 N / 55.40 W	Dr:	26 ft.
Ow:	U.S. Maritime Commission	C:	7,000 tons chrome ore and
Op:	Grace Line		general
M:	Henry Stephenson	P:	steam
A:	1-5"; unknown number of 50- cal. and 30-cal.	S:	16

On 24 June, the *Santa Rita* departed Cape Town, South Africa, en route to Charleston, South Carolina, and proceeded on a nonevasive course. Seven hundred miles northeast of Puerto Rico lookouts sighted a torpedo's wake. This torpedo, fired by the *U-172* (Emmermann), struck between the #3 hatch and the engine room. The explosion wrecked the engines, created a hole thirty feet in diameter, and filled the #3 hold with water almost immediately. Ten minutes after the attack most of the eight officers, forty-four men, two passengers, and nine armed guards on board abandoned the ship without orders in the #3 and #4 lifeboats. Ten minutes later, the master, chief officer, and ten men left the ship in the #1 boat. The *U-172* surfaced and fired machine gun bursts to warn the crew away from the vessel and then fired four shells into the superstructure. A German officer questioned the master and then took him on the U-boat as a POW. Crewmen from the *U-172* also boarded the freighter and searched her. They secured some foodstuffs and returned to the submarine after two hours. The *U-172* put seven more shells into the freighter, and she sank on an even

keel, rolling over and disappearing at 1520. The USS *Livermore* (DD-429) and *Mayo* (DD-422) picked up most of the survivors and landed them at Port-of-Spain, Trinidad. A crash boat picked up the remaining survivors and landed them in Puerto Rico. Two men and an officer died on watch below, and one crewman drowned while getting into one of the lifeboats. The master returned to the United States in February 1945.

NSS; WACR; WCSR; AG; Rohwer, p. 108.

BENJAMIN BREWSTER

D: 7-9-42
T: 2335
Pos: 29.05 N / 90.05 W
Ow: Standard Oil Co. of N. J.
Op: Standard Oil Co. of N. J.
M: Peter George J. Hammel
A: 1-5"; 2-30 cal.

YB: 1917
Tn: 5,950
Dr: 27 ft. 6 in.
C: 70,578 bbls. aviation gas, lubricating oil
P: steam
S: at anchor

On 8 July, the *Benjamin Brewster* sailed from Baytown, Texas, to Tampa, Florida, and stopped for the night off the coast of Louisiana. The tanker anchored sixty miles west of Southwest Pass close into shore in about six fathoms of water. The *U-67* (Müller-Stöckheim) spotted the anchored tanker and fired two torpedoes that hit the port side about ten seconds apart. One struck at the bridge and the other aft, causing the ship to immediately burst into flames from the bridge forward. The wind fortunately kept the flames forward, but burning oil and gasoline covered the surface of the water for some distance around the vessel. The crew of eight officers and twenty-seven men, together with the five armed guards, tried to hastily leave the ship. The survivors jumped into the water from the stern as the ship rapidly sank. Only one partially burned boat managed to make it into the water. Six officers and nineteen crewmen died, most of them from burns. The survivors made landfall at Grand Isle, Louisiana, three hours later. A fishing boat picked them up and then transferred them to a Coast Guard vessel that took them to Burrwood, Louisiana.

NSS; WACR; WCSR; *Ships of the Esso Fleet*, pp. 343-46; Rohwer, p. 108; *War Action Casualties*, p. 105.

The *U-404* torpedoed the *Manuela* off the coast of North Carolina. She sank while under tow to Morehead City.

The *Santa Rita* was a U.S. Maritime Commission C2 type freighter. These ships had a cargo capacity of over 500,000 cubic feet, and three of these ships were built specifically for Grace Lines. The *U-172* sank the *Santa Rita* with a torpedo and gunfire north of Puerto Rico.

TACHIRA

D:	7-12-42	YB:	1920
T:	1650	Tn:	2,325
Pos:	18.15 N / 81.54 W	Dr:	21 ft.
Ow:	Grace Line	C:	2,100 tons cacao, dividivi,
Op:	Grace Line		coffee
M:	Sverre Mordale Gram	P:	steam
A:	1-3"	S:	11.0

The *Tachira* sailed from Baranquilla, Colombia, to New Orleans, Louisiana. While the *Tachira* maintained a zigzag course, the *U-129* (Witt) fired a torpedo that struck on the starboard side at the #4 hatch. The explosion severely damaged the ship, and she sank within three minutes. The eight officers, twenty-four crewmen, and six armed guards abandoned ship in one lifeboat and three rafts. Officers of the *U-129* questioned the survivors concerning the nature of the cargo and the ship's tonnage. They provided a bandage for one of the wounded men and gave directions to the nearest land. One officer, three crewmen, and one armed guard died. The survivors combined into one boat and landed at Punta Herrero, Mexico, four days later.

NSS; WACR; WCSR; AG; RWCS; Rohwer, p. 109, places the attack at 18.15 N / 81.45 W.

ANDREW JACKSON

D:	7-12-42	YB:	1920
T:	2112	Tn:	5,990
Pos:	23.32 N / 81.02 W	Dr:	14 ft.
Ow:	Waterman SS Corp.	C:	ballast
Op:	WSA	P:	steam
M:	Frank Lewis Murdock	S:	11.0
A:	1-4"; 4-50 cal.; 2-30 cal.		

About twenty miles off Cardenas Light, Cuba, the *Andrew Jackson* was attacked by the *U-84* (Uphoff). The *Jackson* sailed independently from Cristobal, Canal Zone, to Key West, Florida, on a nonevasive course. The *U-84* fired a double shot at the ship, but only one of these shots struck, just aft of amidships. The blast destroyed the engines and vented through the deck above the engine room, collapsing portions of the stern. The radio operator sent distress signals as the ship lost way. The eight officers, thirty crewmen, and eleven armed guards abandoned the ship before a second torpedo struck. Three men died on watch below. The survivors landed at Vavendaro on the north coast of Cuba in three lifeboats twelve hours after the attack.

NSS; WACR; WCSR; AG; WJ; Rohwer, p. 109.

ONEIDA

D:	7-13-42	YB:	1920
T:	1210	Tn:	2,309
Pos:	20.17 N / 74.06 W	Dr:	13 ft. 1 in.
Ow:	Ford Motor Co.	C:	ballast
Op:	Agwilines, Inc.	P:	steam
M:	Walter Franklin Deal	S:	10.0
A:	unarmed		

On 7 July, the freighter *Oneida* cleared San Juan, Puerto Rico, en route to Punta Gorda, Cuba. She sailed with Convoy NG-359 but straggled from the formation. About two miles north of Cape Maysi the *U-166* (Kuhlmann) attacked. The master saw the wake of the torpedo too late to take evasive action. The torpedo struck amidships at the waterline just aft of the engine room. The explosion extensively damaged the ship, and the *Oneida* sank three minutes later. The crew of eight officers and twenty-one men had no time to launch boats and abandoned the freighter in two rafts. Two officers and four men died in the attack—three of them on watch below. The survivors reached the coast of Cuba in several hours.

Another document states that Lykes Bros. were the operators. The status of this ship is uncertain, but she probably sailed under time charter to the Army—thus still a merchant vessel. NSS; WACR; WCSR; RWSA; VSC; Rohwer, p. 109.

R. W. GALLAGHER

D:	7-13-42	YB:	1938
T:	0140	Tn:	7,989
Pos:	28.32 N / 90.59 W	Dr:	29 ft. 3 in.
Ow:	Standard Oil Co. of N. J.	C:	80, 855 bbls. bunker "C" fuel oil
Op:	Standard Oil Co. of N. J.	P:	steam
M:	Aage Petersen	S:	12.5
A:	1-5"; 1-3"; 2-50 cal.; 2-30 cal.		

On 10 July, the *R. W. Gallagher* departed Baytown, Texas, en route to Port Everglades, Florida. Eighty miles from Southwest Pass, Mississippi, the *U-67* (Müller-Stöckheim) attacked the tanker. A torpedo struck the starboard side at the #3 tank just forward of amidships, and the second struck five seconds later abaft the midships house between the #8 tank and the pump room. The explosion buckled parts of the ship and started a fire that quickly spread the length of the vessel and into the water. The ship immediately took a 30° list to starboard and later capsized and sank at 0315. With the steam whistle jammed, the crew of eight officers and thirty-two men and the twelve armed guards abandoned the ship in the #4 lifeboat and one raft and by jumping into the water. The fire consumed the other boats and rafts before they could be

launched. The master remained on the bow for forty minutes until the flames forced him into the water. The USCG cutter *Boutwell* (WPC-130) began picking up the survivors within an hour. A Coast Guard plane removed three of the most seriously wounded and flew them to New Orleans for hospitalization. Two officers, six crewmen, and two armed guards perished in the flames. Two others died ashore after reaching the hospital.

NSS; WACR; WCSR; AG; *Coast Guard at War*, p. 53; *Ships of the Esso Fleet*, pp. 356-59; Rohwer, p. 109, places the attack at 28.50 N / 91.05 W; *War Action Casualties*, p. 106.

ARCATA

D:	7-14-42	YB:	1919
T:	2015	Tn:	2,722
Pos:	53.35 N / 157.40 W	Dr:	15 ft.
Ow:	Hammond Lumber Co.	C:	ballast
Op:	WSA	P:	steam
M:	Christian Evensen	S:	10.5
A:	unarmed		

In fog and choppy seas, the *Arcata* was attacked by the *I-7* (Koizumi) while en route from Bethel, Alaska, to Seattle, Washington. The master kept the vessel on a nonevasive course until the *I-7* surfaced and started shelling the freighter. The helmsman then began changing course rapidly, and the ship temporarily evaded the submarine. Ten minutes later the *I-7* reappeared and began shelling the freighter again. The *I-7* fired over twenty-five shots, and at least eleven struck the freighter. The gunfire eventually damaged the steering engine and set the forecastle bridge and poop afire. About an hour and thirty minutes after the first shell struck, the ship hove to and the men on board abandoned her. Seven officers, twenty-two men, three Navy men, and a passenger began leaving the ship in one lifeboat and four rafts. The *I-7* fired on the life rafts and fatally wounded one crewman. Two officers and six men perished. The USS *Kane* (DD-235) rescued eleven men on a raft, and the halibut boat *Yukon* rescued the remaining fourteen men in the lifeboat.

The sources conflict on the crew size. NSS; WACR; WCSR; Rohwer, p. 280, places the attack at 53.41 N / 157.45 W.

PENNSYLVANIA SUN

D:	7-15-42	YB:	1938
T:	0145	Tn:	11,394
Pos:	24.05 N / 83.42 W	Dr:	30 ft. 2 in.
Ow:	Sun Oil Co.	C:	107,500 bbls. Navy fuel
Op:	WSA	P:	diesel
M:	Frederick Lyall	S:	14.0
A:	1-5"; 1-3"; 4-20 mm; 2-30 mm		

The *Pennsylvania Sun* sailed from Port Arthur, Texas, to Belfast, Ireland. At 0130, one hundred and twenty-five miles west of Key West, Florida, an aircraft illuminated the tanker to identify her. The mate on watch ran up the appropriate flag hoist. He then returned to the wheelhouse to change the ship's zigzag course when a torpedo fired by the *U-571* (Möhlmann) struck amidships on the port side between the #5 and #6 tanks. The explosion blew away the port wing of the bridge, and flames immediately engulfed the ship. The master had the vessel steered southeast for five minutes and then ordered the engines stopped. The radio operator meanwhile sent distress signals and received a reply. The nine officers, thirty-three crewmen, and seventeen armed guards left the tanker in three lifeboats. They rowed away from the tanker and put out sea anchors to wait for a rescue vessel. The Quartermaster and a seaman died in the explosion. The USS *Dahlgren* (DD-187) picked up the survivors three and one-half hours after the attack and landed them at Key West. The next evening, the master, three officers, and the crew of the Navy salvage tug *Willet* (ARS-12) returned to the ship and helped extinguish the flames. The *Willet* later towed the vessel to port, and after repairs at Chester, Pennsylvania, she went back in service.

NSS; WACR; WCSR; AG; Rohwer, p. 109; *War Action Casualties*, p. 107.

CHILORE

D:	7-15-42	YB:	1923
T:	1620	Tn:	8,310
Pos:	34.45 N / 75.29 W	Dr:	22 ft. 5 in.
Ow:	Ore SS Co.	C:	ballast
Op:	Ore SS Co.	P:	steam
M:	George P. Moodie	S:	8.0
A:	1-5"; 2-50 cal.; 2-30 cal.		

The *Chilore* was torpedoed by the *U-576* (Heinicke) thirty-three miles south by east of Cape Hatteras while en route from Baltimore, Maryland, to Trinidad, BWI, in Convoy KS-520. A torpedo hit well below the waterline on the port side beneath the port hawse pipe. This reduced the ship's speed to five knots as the forepeak flooded. The master ordered the helmsman to steer a zigzagging course as the *Chilore* dropped out of the convoy. The Panamanian-flagged freighter *J. A. Mowinckel* and the Nicaraguan ship *Bluefield* joined the exodus after the *U-576* torpedoed them. The *Chilore*, unfortunately, wandered to the edge of the Cape Hatteras minefield. A blimp warned the master, but he thought that the flares dropped by the blimp indicated the presence of a submarine and he proceeded. Two mines hit the port side wing tanks at the #2 and #4 hatches. After these explosions part of the ship's complement of eight officers, thirty-four men, and nine armed guards tried to abandon the ship before ordered to do so by the master. The only deaths occurred when two men fell out of one of the lifeboats and drowned. The remaining men abandoned ship at 2100, and Coast Guard craft picked them up and landed them at Ocracoke. A Navy salvage crew later prepared the ship to be towed, but during the trip she capsized and sank at the entrance to the Chesapeake Bay.

The ship's complement is contradictory within the sources. NSS; WACR; WCSR; AG; *Ships of the Esso Fleet*, pp. 364-71; Rohwer, p. 109, places the attack at 34.47 N / 75.22 W.

FAIRPORT

D:	7-16-42	YB:	1942
T:	0945	Tn:	6,6163
Pos:	27.12 N / 64.30 W	Dr:	26 ft. 8 in.
Ow:	Waterman SS Co.	C:	8,000 tons war material and
Op:	Waterman SS Co.		tanks
M:	George F. Hancock	P:	steam
A:	1-4"; 4-50 cal.; 2-30 cal.	S:	13.0

The *Fairport* sailed in the six-ship Convoy AS-4 from New York to the Persian Gulf. The convoy consisted of six other vessels and three destroyers. The *Fairport* proceeded in station #12, the second ship in the port column of the convoy. A torpedo from the *U-161* (Achilles) struck the zigzagging freighter in the #4 hold on the port side. Ten seconds later a second torpedo struck the #1 hold on the port side about twelve feet below the waterline. The first torpedo started a fire that incoming sea water quickly extinguished. The second torpedo opened up a large hole thirty feet long by twenty-five feet wide in the hull. The watch below secured the engines immediately, and the gun crew fired one shot to indicate the direction of the torpedo. Five minutes after the initial explosion, the master ordered the crew of ten officers and thirty-three men, as well as the fourteen armed guards and sixty-six passengers, to abandon ship. The *Fairport* sank ten minutes later, plunging by the stern. The men launched two lifeboats and also used five rafts to clear the ship. The USS *Kearny* (DD-432) picked up the survivors after dropping depth charges. All hands survived the attack.

NSS; WACR; WCSR; Moore, p. 101; Rohwer, p. 109, places the attack at 27.10 N / 64.33 W.

GERTRUDE

D:	7-16-42	YB:	1902
T:	0430	Tn:	16
Pos:	23.32 N / 82.00 W	Dr:	6 ft. 6 in.
Ow:	Crosland Fish Co.	C:	20 tons onions
Op:	Crosland Fish Co.	P:	diesel
M:	Walter Broward Crosland	S:	7.5
A:	unarmed		

The fishing vessel *Gertrude* sailed from Miami, Florida, to Havana, Cuba. About thirty miles northeast of Havana, an officer on the *U-166* (Kuhlmann) hailed the *Gertrude* in English and then asked the crew to abandon ship. The three-person crew immediately left in a fourteen-foot motorboat. It is thought that the crew from the submarine boarded the vessel and sank her with a timed charge or fired one shell. The motorboat with the survivors ran out of fuel before reaching shore and drifted for seventy-eight hours before being spotted by an aircraft about three miles south of Alligator Lighthouse. A boat out of Whale Harbor brought the three men ashore.

The *U-166* was lost on patrol and never filed a written report of the attack. NSS; WACR; WCSR; Rohwer, p. 109.

WILLIAM F. HUMPHREY

D:	7-16-42	YB:	1921
T:	2137	Tn:	7,982
Pos:	05.37 S / 00.56 E	Dr:	19 ft. 6 in.
Ow:	Tidewater Associated Oil Co.	C:	water ballast in tanks 2-4-6-8-10
Op:	Tidewater Associated Oil Co.	P:	steam
M:	Richard Schwarz	S:	9.5
A:	1-5"		

The *William F. Humphrey* was attacked and sunk by the German raider *Michel* (von Schack) while en route from Cape Town, South Africa, to Trinidad, BWI. After spotting lights, the master, thinking it was a U-boat, turned at a 90° angle and proceeded at full speed away from the vessel. Minutes later, the *Michel* illuminated the area with star shells and then began firing salvos at the *Humphrey*. The raider fired about sixty shots and created an inferno on the tanker's decks, shattering the deckhouse and the boats. The gun crew feebly returned fire with the five-inch gun until it was put out of action after the third round. As small arms fire from the raider raked the tanker, a torpedo launch put three torpedoes into the ship. One struck the stern, and a second struck at the #5 tank on the starboard side. A third torpedo hit the bow and finished off the tanker, causing her to sink stern first at 2207. The surviving eight officers, thirty-one men, six armed guards, and one passenger on board abandoned ship in the #2 and #4 lifeboats and three rafts. Remarkably, with all the firepower aimed at the ship, only two armed guards, one officer, two men, and the passenger died. The raider took twenty-six of the merchant crew and three armed guards as prisoners. The master and ten other men in a boat managed to avoid capture and sailed 450 miles in five days. The Norwegian freighter *Triton* rescued them and they landed at Freetown, Sierra Leone. One of the armed guards on board the *Michel* later died, and three of the merchant crew perished in the POW camp.

The sources for the casualties and POWs conflict. NSS; WACR; WCSR; RWCS; AG; Muggenthaler, pp. 223-24; *War Action Casualties*, p. 110.

KESHENA

D:	7-19-42	YB:	1919
T:	1630	Tn:	427
Pos:	35.00 N / 75.45 W	Dr:	15 ft. 6 in.
Ow:	Southern Transportation Co.	C:	none
Op:	Southern Transportation Co.	P:	steam
M:	Oscar Johnson	S:	stopped
A:	unarmed		

The tug *Keshena* struck a mine while engaged in salvage operations in a minefield east of Ocracoke Island, North Carolina. The *Keshena* was working under the stern of the Panamanian-flagged ship *J. A. Mowinckel* that had previously been torpedoed and mined. A mine struck the tug aft of the engine room, and most of the crew of five officers, eleven men, and one woman abandoned her immediately by boarding a raft. Within ten minutes a small launch rescued the survivors, and they landed at the Ocracoke Coast Guard Station. Two men on watch below died in the explosion.

NSS; WACR; WCSR.

COAST FARMER

D:	7-21-42	YB:	1920
T:	0210	Tn:	3,290
Pos:	35.23 S / 151.00 E	Dr:	18 ft.
Ow:	Coastwise Line	C:	3,500 tons asphalt, tin, wood,
Op:	WSA		Army stores
M:	John Anton Mattson	P:	steam
A:	2 machine guns	S:	10

The *Coast Farmer* was torpedoed by the *I-11* (Hachiji) while en route from Sydney to Melbourne, Australia. As the ship maintained a nonevasive course, lookouts spotted the track of a torpedo on the port beam. The torpedo struck amidships and sent a sheet of water over the bridge, blew off the #3 hatch cover, and shattered steam lines. The explosion was so severe that the port side of the vessel amidships disappeared. The blast also disabled the radio equipment, preventing the radio operator from sending a distress signal. The master ordered the survivors among the nine officers, twenty-seven men, and five armed guards to abandon ship ten minutes after the explosion. Thirty-eight men escaped in a lifeboat, and two others dove overboard and climbed onto a raft. One man perished in the fireroom. A Royal Australian Air Force crash boat picked up the survivors ten hours later and landed them at Jarvis Bay.

Records indicate that the *Coast Farmer* was probably under time charter to the Army at the time of her sinking. NSS; WACR; WCSR; RWSA; Rohwer, p. 280.

WILLIAM CULLEN BRYANT

D:	7-21-42	YB:	1942
T:	0308	Tn:	7,176
Pos:	24.08 N / 82.23 W	Dr:	28 ft. 4 in.
Ow:	James Griffith & Sons	C:	10,962 tons sugar
Op:	WSA	P:	steam
M:	L. C. Perry	S:	10.5
A:	1-4"; 1-3"; 4-50 cal.; 2-30 cal.		

The Liberty ship *William Cullen Bryant* sailed from Hilo, Hawaii, to Philadelphia, Pennsylvania, in a convoy. On 17 July, she departed from Guantánamo, Cuba, in Convoy TAW-4J. Lookouts spotted the track of a torpedo fired by the *U-84* (Uphoff) pass across the ship's bow. Moments later a second torpedo struck the #1 hold nineteen feet below the waterline on the starboard side. The explosion opened a hole about eight feet in diameter, and the plates beneath the midships house buckled upwards. The ten officers, thirty men, twelve armed guards, and two Navy signalmen on board abandoned ship and then returned an hour and forty-five minutes later. The salvage tugs *Moran* and USS *Willet* (ARS-12) towed the freighter to Key West. She arrived at Key West on the 23rd, and tugs later towed her to Tampa. She returned to service in 1944. All hands survived the attack.

The armed guard figures contradict within the sources. NSS; WACR; WCSR; AG; TF; Rohwer, p. 110.

WILLIAM DAWES

D: 7-22-42   YB: 1942
T: 0518   Tn: 7,176
Pos: 36.47 S / 150.16 E   Dr: 27 ft. 9 in.
Ow: Weyerhaeuser SS Co.   C: 7,000 tons ammunition, trucks,
Op: WSA   army supplies
M: John Arvid Froberg   P: steam
A: 1-4"; 1-3"; 4-50 cal.; 2-30 cal. S: 10.0

The *William Dawes* departed on a coastwise trip from Adelaide to Brisbane, Australia. About halfway through the journey, lookouts spotted the *I-24* (Hanabusa) surface 200 yards from the ship. Seconds later a torpedo struck the after magazine, and the resulting explosion tore the whole stern off the ship and instantly flooded the engine room. The armed guard contingent could not fire on the submarine because the after gun had disappeared and the forward gun would not bear on the *I-24*. At 0602 the ship's complement of eight officers, thirty-two men, and fifteen armed guards, as well as five Army passengers, abandoned ship in four lifeboats and two rafts. Four of the armed guards and one of the Army detail died in the initial explosion. Two hours after the first torpedo struck, the *I-24* placed another torpedo into the ship just aft of the amidships. The *William Dawes* began to burn fiercely and sank the next day. The survivors had remained near the *Dawes* until the second torpedo hit the ship. Realizing the vessel could not be saved, they rowed to land, and local fishing vessels towed the boats the final few miles.

There were several Japanese submarines operating in this area; the most likely to have sunk the *William Dawes* is the *I-24*. NSS; WACR; WCSR; AG; Rohwer, p. 280, places the attack at 35.45 S / 150.20 E.

HONOLULAN

D: 7-22-42   YB: 1921
T: 1614   Tn: 7,494
Pos: 08.41 N / 22.12 W   Dr: 28 ft. 10 in.
Ow: American Hawaiian SS Co.   C: 8,350 tons manganese ore, jute
Op: U.S. Maritime Commission   P: steam
M: Charles Nathaniel Bamfort   S: 9.6
A: unarmed

The *Honolulan* sailed from Cape Town, South Africa, to Baltimore, Maryland, via Trinidad. The *U-582* (Schulte) sighted the ship on a nonevasive course and fired a torpedo that struck the starboard side at the #5 hatch and fatally wounded the ship. With the steam whistle jammed, the radio operator sent distress signals as the ship rapidly sank. Most of the crew of eleven officers and twenty-eight men abandoned ship in three lifeboats. The master, the first mate, and the radio operator stayed behind until a second torpedo struck the ship between the #2 and #3 hatch at 1628. With the decks awash, these men jumped into the water to be picked up by one of the boats. With the whistle still blowing, the freighter slipped beneath the water at 1830. The crew of the *U-582* offered the men cigarettes and asked about the ship and her cargo before the U-boat disappeared southward over the horizon. The British MV *Winchester Castle* rescued the entire complement six days later and landed them in New York. This included an extra man found by the crew floating on a hatch board on the second day out.

The times of the attack conflict within the sources. NSS; WACR; WCSR; RWCS; Rohwer, p. 110, places the attack at 08.41 N / 22.04 W.

ONONDAGA

D:	7-23-42	YB:	1920
T:	1630	Tn:	2,309
Pos:	22.40 N / 78.44 W	Dr:	20 ft.
Ow:	Ford Motor Co.	C:	full cargo of magnesium ore
Op:	U.S. Maritime Commission	P:	steam
M:	George Dewey Hodges	S:	8.5
A:	unarmed		

The *Onondaga* was torpedoed five miles north of Cayo Guillermo while en route from Nuevitas, Cuba, to Havana. The ship proceeded along a nonevasive course, until a torpedo fired by the *U-129* (Witt) struck the port side amidships. The ship sank in one minute, forcing the eight officers, twenty-five crewmen, and the one passenger to abandon the ship by jumping overboard. The survivors swam to two rafts that had floated free of the ship. Six officers and thirteen men perished. The passenger, the master of the torpedoed *Thomas McKean*, also died. A Cuban fishing boat, the *Laventina*, picked up the fourteen survivors the next morning and took them to Punta San Juan, Cuba.

NSS; WACR; WCSR; WJ; RWSA; Rohwer, p. 110.

STELLA LYKES

D:	7-27-42	YB:	1941
T:	0455	Tn:	6,801
Pos:	06.46 N / 24.55 W	Dr:	18 ft. 6 in.
Ow:	Lykes Bros. SS Co.	C:	ballast
Op:	U.S. Maritime Commission	P:	steam
M:	S. Charles Wallace	S:	15.4
A:	1-4"; 4-50 cal.; 4-30 cal.		

The *U-582* (Schulte) attacked and sank the *Stella Lykes* while the freighter was en route from Bombay, India, to Trinidad, Surinam. While steering a zigzagging course, the *Stella Lykes* was struck by a torpedo on the starboard side between the engine room and the #4 hatch. The ship immediately burst into flames from the mainmast to just forward of the bridge, but the fire lasted for only three minutes before going out. The explosion wrecked the entire starboard side of the vessel. The crew began to muster at their boat stations while the radio operator sent distress signals and the gun crew manned the guns. At 0520 the ship's complement of ten officers, thirty-three men, and nine armed guards left in one lifeboat and three rafts. Minutes after the men abandoned the ship, a second torpedo struck the vessel on the port side amidships. The *U-582* then surfaced and began circling the ship, firing over 160 rounds into the freighter. The Germans took the master and the chief engineer as POWs and offered the men in the boats cigarettes and first aid supplies. Men from the U-boat boarded the *Lykes* and sank the ship with demolition charges. The fifty survivors boarded the single lifeboat and sailed for ten days, landing at Portuguese Guinea. One man died on watch below and constituted the only casualty.

The second explosion may have been a boiler explosion. NSS; WACR; WCSR; RWCS; AG; WJ; Rohwer, p. 111, places the attack at 06.40 N / 25.05 W.

EBB

D:	7-28-42	YB:	1929
T:	0400	Tn:	259
Pos:	43.18 N / 63.50 W	Dr:	16 ft.
Ow:	General Sea Foods	C:	38 tons fish, ice, general
Op:	unknown	P:	diesel
M:	Philip Colbert	S:	9
A:	unarmed		

The trawler *Ebb* sailed from Boston bound for the Western Bank, part of the Sable Island Bank. Forty-five miles southeast of Cape Sable the *U-754* (Oestermann) shelled and sank the vessel. A lookout sighted the submarine off the starboard quarter steering parallel to the *Ebb*. The *U-754* opened fire from just over fifty yards away, and the master hove to. The U-boat continued to fire with its 88-mm and 20-mm guns, as the crew of four officers and thirteen men abandoned ship. The master and four men died as a result of the shelling, and the gunfire wounded seven others. The U-boat eventually fired about fifty shots into the fishing vessel before she sank. The destroyer HMS *Witherington* (I-76) rescued the surviving three officers and nine men fourteen hours later and landed them in Boston.

NSS; WACR; WCSR; Rohwer, p. 111.

CRANFORD

D:	7-30-42	YB:	1919
T:	1415	Tn:	6,096
Pos:	12.17 N / 55.11 W	Dr:	27 ft. 6 in.
Ow:	Lykes Bros. SS Co.	C:	8,500 tons chrome ore, cotton
Op:	Lykes Bros. SS Co.	P:	steam
M:	James Henry Donlon	S:	8.6
A:	1-3"; 4-50 cal.; 2-30 cal.		

Proceeding from Cape Town, South Africa, to Trinidad, BWI, the *Cranford* was torpedoed and sunk by the *U-155* (Piening). The master proceeded on a nonevasive course because of a lack of fuel and daylight conditions. About 300 miles east of Barbados, a single torpedo struck the vessel on the starboard side between the #2 and #3 holds. The nature of the cargo caused the ship to sink within three minutes. The armed guard contingent manned the gun, but the stern rose so rapidly that they could not take any offensive action. The ship's complement of ten officers, twenty-seven men, and eleven armed guards began leaving the ship within two minutes of the explosion. The survivors managed to launch one boat, and others swam to two rafts after diving overboard. The *U-155* surfaced close to the ship and circled the boats and rafts. The Germans asked if they could do anything for the crew and questioned them about the ship and cargo. They also treated two injured men on board the U-boat and gave the survivors water, supplies, and directions to land before leaving. The Spanish tanker *Castillo Alemenara* rescued the survivors several hours after the sinking. Six officers, three men, and two of the gun crew died in the attack.

NSS; WACR; WCSR; RWCS; AG; Rohwer, p. 112.

ROBERT E. LEE

D:	7-30-42	YB:	1925
T:	1631	Tn:	5,184
Pos:	28.40 N / 88.30 W	Dr:	16 ft. 3 in.
Ow:	Eastern SS Co.	C:	47 tons general and personal
Op:	Alcoa SS Co.		effects
M:	William C. Heath	P:	steam
A:	1-3"	S:	16.3

The *Robert E. Lee* sailed from Port-of-Spain, Trinidad, BWI, to New Orleans, Louisiana, escorted by the *PC-566*. Lookouts spotted a torpedo fired by the *U-166* (Kuhlmann) 200 yards before it struck just aft of the engine room. The explosion destroyed the #3 hold and vented through the B and C decks and wrecked the engines, the radio equipment, and the steering gear. The *PC-566* began dropping depth charges as the ship plunged stern first in fifteen minutes.

The complement of 8 officers, 122 men, and 6 armed guards, as well as 268 passengers, the last mostly survivors of other sinkings, abandoned ship in six lifeboats, eight life rafts, and five life floats. One officer, nine of the merchant crew, and fifteen passengers died. The *PC-566*, the *SC-519*, and the tug *Underwriter* rescued the survivors and landed them in Venice, Louisiana.

The vessel's original destination was Tampa, Florida, but she could not secure a pilot and was directed to go to New Orleans with the *PC-566* as an escort. The casualty figures are contradictory within the sources. NSS; WACR; WCSR; USMMA; AG; Rohwer, p. 111, places the attack at 28.40 N / 88.42 W.

WAWALOAM

D:	8-6-42	YB:	1918
T:	1600	Tn:	342
Pos:	39.18 N / 55.44 W	Dr:	13 ft.
Ow:	Louis Kennedy	C:	700 puncheons of molasses
Op:	Louis Kennedy	P:	motor and sail
M:	Louis Kennedy	S:	6
A:	unarmed		

The schooner *Wawaloam* was shelled and sunk by the *U-86* (Schug) while en route from Bridgetown, Barbados, to St. Johns, Newfoundland. The *U-86* spotted the schooner and missed with its first torpedo. The *U-86* then surfaced and opened fire at a range of five miles. The schooner hove to after the first shot, and the two officers, four men, and one passenger on board immediately abandoned ship in two dories. As the submarine advanced toward the schooner, it continued firing its deck gun. Approaching to within a mile, it fired two torpedoes meant to be coup de grâce shots. One passed ahead and one passed astern. The *U-86* then set the schooner afire by firing eight shells at close range and hitting drums of diesel fuel on deck, which set the ship on fire. She sank about three hours later. German officers tried to question the crew, but the moderate seas made conversation difficult and the master was ordered on board the submarine. After providing the name of the vessel, the master received flares and went back into a dory. The survivors spent five and a half days in the boats weathering a tremendous storm that capsized one of the dories. The SS *Irish Rose* rescued all hands and later transferred them to the corvette HMS *Campanula* (K-18), and they landed in Argentia, Newfoundland.

NSS; WACR; WCSR; WJ; Rohwer, p. 113.

KAIMOKU

D:	8-8-42	YB:	1919
T:	1332	Tn:	6,367
Pos:	56.32 N / 32.15 W	Dr:	26 ft. 9 in.
Ow:	Matson Navigation Co.	C:	5,560 tons general and steel
Op:	Matson Navigation Co.	P:	steam
M:	Theodore Henry Cunningham	S:	7.0
A:	1-4"; 4-50 cal.; 4-30 cal.		

The *Kaimoku* sailed in Convoy SC-94 en route from New York to Liverpool, England. German U-boats attacked the convoy for several days during the trip. The *U-379* (Kettner) fired two torpedoes that struck the freighter amidships. The first torpedo caused the ship to shudder, and the second torpedo sent flames and oil over the mast. The ship settled rapidly and sank in four minutes. The freighter's complement of eight officers, twenty-eight men, and fourteen armed guards managed to launch only one lifeboat and two rafts. Two of the gun crew, the second assistant engineer, and a fireman in the engine room died. The Canadian corvette *Battleford* (K-165) picked up the survivors within forty-five minutes and landed them in Gourock, Scotland.

WACR; WCSR; AG; RWSA; Washington *Star*, 13 September 1942; Rohwer, pp. 113-14, places the attack at 56.30 N / 32.14 W.

R. M. PARKER JR.

D:	8-13-42	YB:	1919
T:	0050	Tn:	6,779
Pos:	28.37 N / 90.48 W	Dr:	15 ft.
Ow:	Hartol SS Co.	C:	water ballast
Op:	Continental SS Co.	P:	steam
M:	Walter Ord Peters	S:	10.0
A:	1-5"; 2-50 cal.		

The *R. M. Parker Jr.* was torpedoed and sunk by the *U-171* (Pfeffer) while en route from Baltimore, Maryland, to Port Arthur, Texas. Lookouts spotted the two phosphorescent wakes of the torpedoes but too late to alarm the bridge. The two torpedoes struck almost simultaneously on the port side amidships at tanks #5 and #6. The two blasts opened a large hole and immediately flooded the tanks and buckled the decks, causing a severe list. The explosions also toppled the mainmast. The crew shut off the engines from the deck valve aft, and the helmsman turned the ship's wheel to starboard to cut the ship's speed and allow the easier launching of the lifeboats. The radio operator meanwhile sent a distress signal on the auxiliary transmitter. The gun crew mustered at their boat stations without firing a shot owing to the ship's heavy list. On the master's orders the *Parker*'s eight officers, twenty-nine men, and seven armed guards abandoned the tanker in three boats. The *U-171* then surfaced and fired five shells into the ship. The first shell struck the five-inch gun's ready ammunition box and caused it to explode. The other four shots struck the midships house. The tanker sank by the stern and rested on the bottom with the bow above the water for eight hours before finally disappearing. The ex-shrimp lugger and Coast Guard Auxiliary craft *Pioneer* rescued all hands eight hours later and landed them in Morgan City, Louisiana. All hands survived the attack.

NSS; WACR; WCSR; Rohwer, p. 116, places the attack at 28.50 N / 90.42 W; *War Action Casualties*, p. 111.

CRIPPLE CREEK

D:	8-13-42	YB:	1919
T:	0249	Tn:	6,378
Pos:	04.55 N / 18.30 W	Dr:	26 ft. 8 in.
Ow:	Lykes Bros. SS. Co.	C:	7,500 tons war supplies
Op:	Lykes Bros. SS. Co.	P:	steam
M:	Matello N. Olsen	S:	8.5
A:	1-4"; 2-50 cal.; 2-30 cal.		

The *Cripple Creek* was torpedoed by the *U-752* (Schroeter) while en route from New York to the Persian Gulf via Trinidad. The first torpedo struck the ship at the #3 hatch, venting upward through the deck. With the ship rapidly sinking and her forward deck awash, the master ordered the engine stopped and the men into the boats. Less than twenty minutes after the first explosion, the *U-752* surfaced and fired a second torpedo that struck the port side at the #4 hatch, causing the ship to sink one minute later. The freighter sank so rapidly that the armed guards never had an opportunity to use the guns. All but one of the ten officers, twenty-nine men, and thirteen armed guards on board abandoned the ship in three lifeboats. The three boats later became separated, but the trawler HMS *St. Wistan* (4-105) managed to round up all the boats on the 16th. An oiler on deck when the second torpedo struck died in the explosion. All the survivors landed in Freetown, Sierra Leone.

NSS; WACR; WCSR; AG; Rohwer, p. 115.

ALMERIA LYKES

D:	8-13-42	YB:	1939
T:	0350	Tn:	7,773
Pos:	36.40 N / 11.35 E	Dr:	28 ft. 4 in.
Ow:	Lykes Bros. SS Co.	C:	9,750 tons general and
Op:	WSA		ammunition
M:	William Henderson	P:	steam
A:	1-3"; 4-20 mm; 2-30 cal.	S:	15.0

The *Almeria Lykes* was involved in a sixty-hour battle with enemy planes and E-boats as part of Convoy WS-19Z bound from the River Clyde, Scotland, for Malta. The ship's lookouts remained at their stations for four days, sleeping when possible. By 12 August, a number of the convoy's escorts had been sunk or damaged. The freighter steamed astern two destroyers when a torpedo from a German E-boat struck at the #1 hold, port side. Miraculously, the torpedo did not set off the bombs in the hold but did split the ship from the forepeak bulkhead to the strakes below the main deck. As the ship began to settle by the head, the master ordered the nine officers, forty-two men, fifteen armed guards, and thirty-nine passengers off the ship. All hands remained close to the freighter in three lifeboats during the night. At daybreak, feeling the ship might be saved, the master called for volunteers to reboard her. The crew feared aircraft could return and sink the vessel, so only the master, an Engine Cadet, and a British naval officer reboarded the ship. They set an explosive charge at the forward bulkhead of the #3 hold. The explosion flooded the engine room, and the ship sank by the head in forty-five minutes. The destroyer HMS *Somali* (F-33) rescued all hands and landed them at Gibraltar just over three hours later.

Coast Guard documents relate that this ship may have been chartered or allocated to the British Ministry of War Transport. NSS; WACR; AG; RWSA.

DELMUNDO

D:	8-13-42	YB:	1919
T:	0356	Tn:	5,032
Pos:	19.55 N / 73.49 W	Dr:	25 ft. 4 1/2 in.
Ow:	Mississippi Shipping Co.	C:	5,457 tons general
Op:	Mississippi Shipping Co.	P:	steam
M:	Henry Peter Smith	S:	9.3
A:	1-4"; 2-30 cal.		

The *Delmundo* sailed as the commodore's flagship in Convoy TAW-12 bound from Buenos Aires for New York via Trinidad and Key West. The *U-600* (Zurmühlen) fired a spread of three torpedoes that missed their original targets and one struck the *Delmundo* in the stern. The torpedo hit the port side between the deep tank and the engine room. The blast extensively damaged the ship and caused the boilers to explode. The *Delmundo* sank in five minutes, little time for the ship's nine officers, thirty-two men, nine armed guards, and eight passengers, including two women, to abandon ship. The torpedo explosion damaged two of the lifeboats, and the #1 boat fouled while launching and capsized. The survivors managed to escape in one boat and two rafts. Two officers, three men, and three passengers died. The destroyer HMS *Churchill* (I-45) picked up the fifty survivors ninety minutes after the attack. The master later died in a hospital from his wounds.

NSS; WACR; WCSR; AG; Rohwer, p. 115.

SANTA ELISA

D: 8-13-42   YB: 1941
T: 0517   Tn: 8,379
Pos: 36.20 N / 11.28 E   Dr: 26 ft. 2 1/2 in.
Ow: U.S. Maritime Commission   C: 6,800 tons gasoline and general
Op: Grace Line   P: steam
M: Vlad Cernesco   S: 15.5
A: unknown, includes 4-20 mm

On 26 July, the *Santa Elisa* sailed in Convoy WS-21S bound from Newport, England, for Malta via Greenock, Scotland, as part of Operation *Pedestal*. The freighter separated from the convoy, and twenty-five miles southeast of Cape Bon, Tunisia, she was attacked and torpedoed by an E-boat. The ship had suffered two bomb hits aft of the bridge and other damage from strafing during previous aircraft attacks. Two E-boats located the ship in the darkness. One closed on the freighter and managed to get alongside before being seen. It approached and sprayed the decks with machine gun fire, but the freighter's guns reportedly sank this boat. As the E-boat burst into flames, a single torpedo fired from the other torpedo boat struck the ship on the starboard side near the #1 hatch. The cargo of aviation gasoline immediately burst into flames, and the eleven officers, forty-five men, ten armed guards, and thirty-three passengers abandoned ship. Explosions killed four of the passengers on board, but the rest of the men cleared the ship in three lifeboats and one raft. The British destroyer HMS *Penn* (G-77) picked up the survivors in just an hour and landed them at Malta. The vessel sank at 0722.

The Navy Survivor's Report states that two torpedoes struck the ship; the master in his report to the Coast Guard recalls only one. NSS; WACR; WCSR; USMMA; RWSA; Moore, p. 254, lists Theodore R. Thompson as the master. The shipping articles list him as the chief officer.

CALIFORNIA

D:	8-13-42	YB:	1920
T:	1750	Tn:	5,441
Pos:	09.24 N / 33.02 W	Dr:	24 ft. 6 in.
Ow:	States SS Co.	C:	7,100 manganese ore, jute,
Op:	U.S. Maritime Commission		gunnies, general
M:	Gregor Johnson	P:	steam
A:	unarmed	S:	9.5

The Italian submarine *Reginaldo Giuliani* (Bruno) attacked the *California* while she was en route from Cape Town, South Africa, to New York via Trinidad. The first torpedo fired by the submarine struck the ship but failed to explode. The master rang up full speed, and the helmsman began steering a zigzag course in an attempt to elude the submarine. Finding it impossible, the master had the engines reversed and then secured. The *Giuliani* then surfaced about one and a half miles away and began shelling the ship. The submarine fired approximately fifty shells all over the ship but most in the vicinity of the wheelhouse and the radio shack. The submarine continuously shelled the ship as the crew of eight officers and thirty men abandoned the freighter in the #1 and #2 lifeboats, each with nineteen men. At 1820, just before leaving, the *Giuliani* fired a second torpedo that struck at the #1 hold on the port side and blew off the hatch covers. A squall on the night of 15 August separated the boats. On 4 September, a German submarine surfaced beside the #2 boat and the Germans questioned the men. The U-boat's chief officer gave them brown bread, water, rum, and tobacco, and also checked the boat's compass, but he refused to give the boat a tow. After twenty-three days at sea the British SS *City of Capetown* spotted the #2 boat. These men landed in New York. The Norwegian SS *Talisman* discovered the #1 boat thirty-two days after the attack and landed the men at Takoradi, Gold Coast. The only casualty was the chief engineer who died of exposure in the later boat.

The Export Lines served as agent for the *California*. NSS; WACR; WCSR; Rohwer, p. 116, places the attack at 09.21 N / 34.35 W.

BALLADIER

D:	8-15-42	YB:	1919
T:	0145	Tn:	3,279
Pos:	55.00 N / 25.00 W	Dr:	22 ft. 6 in.
Ow:	WSA	C:	4,000 tons lumber, pipes,
Op:	Parry SS Co.		general
M:	Ernest G. Hellsten	P:	steam
A:	1-4"; 2-20 mm; 4-30 cal.	S:	9.0

The *Balladier* sailed in Convoy SC-95, which consisted of four freighters, a destroyer, and the USCG cutter *Campbell* (WPG-32) bound from New York for Reykjavik, Iceland. Lookouts on board the *Balladier* first spotted the *U-705* (Horn) four hours earlier, and the gun crew forced the submarine to dive with 20-mm gunfire. With determination, Horn continued to stalk the freighter, and about 550 miles southeast of Iceland, a torpedo struck the engine room on the starboard side. The ship sank so rapidly with a heavy starboard list that the gun crew had no chance to fire on the U-boat. The second officer sounded the general alarm, and the ship's complement of eight officers, twenty-six men, and eleven armed guards abandoned ship in one lifeboat, two rafts, and a float. The SS *Norluna* witnessed the attack and in spite of the danger rescued the survivors. They left the dead first mate in the lifeboat, and two others died on the *Norluna*. A total of three officers, eight men, and two armed guards died in the attack.

NSS; WACR; WCSR; AG; Rohwer, p. 116, places the attack at 55.23 N / 24.32 W.

LOUISIANA

D:	8-17-42	YB:	1937
T:	1000	Tn:	8,588
Pos:	07.24 N / 51.33 W	Dr:	28 ft. 7 in.
Ow:	Texas Co.	C:	92,514 bbls. gasoline and gas oil
Op:	Texas Co.	P:	motor
M:	Joel A. Swanson	S:	10
A:	1-4"; 2-50 cal.		

The tanker *Louisiana* sailed from Areno, Aruba, NWI, to Rio de Janeiro, Brazil. The *U-108* (Scholtz) attacked the zigzagging freighter 200 miles from Paramaribo, Dutch Guiana. The U-boat chased the tanker at high speed to reach a favorable firing position. During this time, the *U-108* signaled another U-boat nearby and continued the chase. From 2,000 yards the U-boat fired three torpedoes at the tanker. One struck forward of the bridge, but the *Louisiana* increased speed and tried to escape. The *U-108* surfaced and the officers could smell the gasoline fumes coming from the damaged tanker. The armed guards opened fire on the U-boat, and the radio operator sent distress signals. At least one raft with three men on board left the ship. It took nearly seven hours for the *U-108* to forge ahead of the tanker. The *U-108* fired two more torpedoes. The first struck the tanker at the forward edge of the bridge. When the second struck, the tanker caught fire and "leaping flames" covered the entire length of the ship. The three men that cleared the ship on the raft were spotted by a plane that attacked the *U-108* during the chase, but rescue vessels failed to find them. The entire complement of eight officers, thirty-three men, and eight armed guards perished in the attack.

WACR; WCSR; WJ; AG; Rohwer, p. 116, places the attack at 07.24 N / 52.33 W.

JOHN HANCOCK

D:	8-18-42	YB:	1942
T:	0312	Tn:	7,167
Pos:	19.27 N / 76.48 W	Dr:	27 ft. 6 in.
Ow:	U.S. Maritime Commission	C:	10,517 tons sugar
Op:	Lykes Bros. SS Co.	P:	steam
M:	Levi Johnson Plesner	S:	5.0
A:	1-4"; 4-30 cal.		

The *John Hancock*, attached to Convoy TAW-13, sailed from the Panama Canal Zone to Philadelphia, Pennsylvania. Lookouts spotted a torpedo fired by the *U-553* (Thurmann) seconds before it struck the vessel. The torpedo hit between the #2 and #3 holds on the port side and flooded both holds rapidly, causing the *Hancock* to sink in five minutes. All eight officers, thirty men, and eleven armed guards on board successfully abandoned ship in four lifeboats. A British corvette rescued all hands after nearly three hours in the water and landed them at Santiago, Cuba.

The ship's complement and the time of sinking vary with the different sources. NSS; WACR; WCSR; AG; Rohwer, p. 117, places the attack at 19.41 N / 76.50 W.

WEST CELINA

D:	8-18-42	YB:	1919
T:	2240	Tn:	5,722
Pos:	11.45 N / 62.30 W	Dr:	25 ft.
Ow:	U.S. Maritime Commission	C:	7,000 tons mica, rubber,
Op:	American Export Line		manganese ore, 250 monkeys
M:	Bernard Mirkin	P:	steam
A:	unarmed	S:	5.5

On 18 August, the *West Celina* sailed in Convoy TAW-15 en route from Trinidad to Guantánamo Bay, Cuba. The freighter took station in the center of the first column of five ships. About fifty miles off the coast of Venezuela, the *U-162* (Wattenberg) fired a torpedo that struck the ship on the port side deep under the #2 hatch. The explosion blew the covers off the hatch and destroyed the port wing of the bridge, collapsing it onto the deck. The engineers secured the engines within two minutes. Some of the ship's crew of eight officers, thirty-one men, and the convoy commodore and his staff of four, began to abandon

ship. Only twelve men remained on board, and five more men later came back to the ship. Around midnight, just after the master made the decision to restart the engines and try to get the ship to port, a second torpedo struck the vessel at the #3 hold on the starboard side. The ship sank rapidly after this explosion, sinking bow first within three minutes. The survivors finally got away in three lifeboats and two rafts. One boat with nineteen survivors landed at Manzanillo Bay, Venezuela, two days later. The other two boats with twenty-four survivors made landfall the following day. All hands survived with the exception of the convoy commodore.

The Coast Guard records indicate the ship sank on the 19th at 1300. NSS; WACR; WCSR; TF; Rohwer, p. 117.

ARLYN

D:	8-27-42	YB:	1919
T:	2130	Tn:	3,304
Pos:	51.53 N / 55.48 W	Dr:	20 ft. 6 in.
Ow:	A. H. Bull & Co.	C:	3,000 tons gas, trucks,
Op:	U.S. Maritime Commission		explosives, etc. general
M:	Eyolf Wennesland	P:	steam
A:	1-4"; 4-20	S:	7.5

The *Arlyn* sailed from New York to Hudson Bay, Canada, with Convoy SG-6, which was made up of five other ships and three escorts. The *Arlyn* took station on the port side of a three-ship column with the *Laramie* (AO-16) to starboard. A single torpedo fired by the *U-165* (Hoffman) struck amidships at the engine room on the port side. The explosion destroyed the boilers and immediately stopped the engines. The ship settled by the stern but then leveled off and remained afloat with decks awash. When the master ordered the eight officers, twenty-six crewmen, and the one passenger to abandon ship, some of the men panicked and jumped into the water without waiting to launch a boat. Those who waited launched a single lifeboat and those in the water swam to two rafts. The fourteen armed guards manned the guns until the last moment, but they never had a target and jumped overboard from the stern and swam to the boats. Three officers and nine men died in the attack. The SS *Harjurand* rescued some of the survivors the next day, and others rowed the ten miles to shore. The *Arlyn* remained afloat until the *U-517* (Hartwig) sunk her with a coup de grâce torpedo six hours later.

The number of armed guards cited in the various sources is contradictory. NSS; WACR; WCSR; AG; Rohwer, p. 119.

CHATHAM

D: 8-27-42   YB: 1926
T: 0846   Tn: 5,649
Pos: 51.51 N / 55.49 W   Dr: 17 ft. 4 in.
Ow: Merchants & Miners Trans. Co.   C: 150 tons food supplies,
Op: Agwilines, Inc.   passengers
M: Edward A. Anderson   P: steam
A: 1-4"; 1-3"; 4-20 mm   S: 9.0

The *Chatham* was torpedoed by the *U-517* (Hartwig) while en route from Sydney, Nova Scotia, to Greenland. The ship sailed with Convoy SG-6 with the USCG cutter *Mojave* (WPG-47) 1,200 yards ahead. A single torpedo struck the *Chatham* on the starboard side slightly forward of amidships. The explosion wrecked the ship through five decks, destroyed the boilers, and threw them through the deck. The blast also damaged the generators and the steering engines and blew up all but two of the starboard boats next to the stack. The ship remained on an even trim and sank within thirty minutes. On board the vessel were 10 officers, 96 men, 28 armed guards, and 428 passengers, mostly construction personnel. They abandoned the ship through choking smoke in twelve lifeboats and nine rafts. The majority of the survivors rowed ashore. The USCG *Mojave* (WPG-47), USS *Bernadou* (DD-153), and the Canadian corvette *Trail* (K-174) picked up the survivors on the rafts. Of the total of 562 persons on board, 7 crewmen and 7 passengers perished.

The status of this vessel is not clear, but it appears she sailed under a time charter to the Army. NSS; WACR; WCSR; AG; Rohwer, p. 119, places the attack at 51.53 N / 55.48 W.

ESSO ARUBA

D: 8-28-42   YB: 1931
T: 0043   Tn: 8,773
Pos: 17.54 N / 74.47 W   Dr: 28 ft. 6 in.
Ow: Standard Oil Co. of N. J.   C: 104,170 bbls. diesel fuel
Op: Standard Oil Co. of N. J.   P: steam
M: Frank Pharr   S: 8.0
A: 1-5"; 2-50 cal.

On 23 August, the *Esso Aruba* sailed in the twenty-five ship Convoy TAW-15 en route from Güiria, Venezuela, to New York via Trinidad. About 120 miles south southeast of Guantánamo, Cuba, the *U-511* (Steinhoff) attacked the tanker. Nearly two hours earlier the escorts had begun battling U-boats as they attempted to attack in the bright moonlight. The *U-511* finally broke through the cordon and torpedoed three vessels including the *Esso Aruba*. The convoy commodore was on board when the torpedo struck on the port side between the #5 and #6 tanks. The explosion tore up the deck and blew it twenty feet into the air. It also destroyed pipelines but failed to damage the engines or steering gear. The master rang the general alarm and ordered the engines stopped. The eight officers, thirty-three men, thirteen armed guards, and the convoy commodore and five of his staff, calmly proceeded to the lifeboats. When the chief engineer reported the machinery in good order, the master ordered the engines restarted and the ship resumed her course. In danger of breaking in two, the tanker remained with the convoy and made Guantánamo Bay at 1600 on 28 August. The remaining 60,000 bbls. of oil were offloaded into the *Cities Service Missouri*. After temporary strengthening, the tanker proceeded to Galveston, Texas, for a complete overhaul. After repairs, the *Esso Aruba* returned to service in February 1943. All hands survived the attack.

NSS; WACR; WCSR; AG; *Ships of the Esso Fleet*, pp. 393-97; Rohwer, p. 119, places the attack at 18.09 N / 74.38 W; *War Action Casualties*, p. 113.

TOPA TOPA

D:	8-28-42	YB:	1920
T:	2100	Tn:	5,356
Pos:	10.16 N / 51.30 W	Dr:	24 ft. 8 in.
Ow:	Waterman SS Corp.	C:	6,500 tons general and gasoline
Op:	Barber Line	P:	steam
M:	Clarence Edward McCoy	S:	12
A:	1-5"; 1-3"; 4-50 cal.; 2-30 cal.		

The *Topa Topa* sailed independently from Trinidad bound for Takoradi, Gold Coast. The ship had recently abandoned her zigzagging course because of a rain squall. In quick succession the *U-66* (Markworth) fired two torpedoes that struck the vessel on the starboard side. The first struck at the #2 hatch, and the explosion blew off the starboard side of the bridge. The second struck a minute later in the #5 hatch. The gasoline cargo caught fire and the drums began to explode, engulfing the entire ship in flames. The freighter sank about ninety minutes later. Survivors among the eight officers, thirty-four crewmen, three passengers, and fifteen armed guards on board immediately abandoned the ship in three lifeboats. The Germans took the chief officer from the lifeboat, questioned him, and returned him to his boat. The thirty-five survivors (five officers, nineteen men, eight gun crew members, and three passengers) remained in the area for some time searching for other survivors. The British SS *Clan MacInnes* rescued the survivors and took them to Port-of-Spain, Trinidad.

NSS; WACR; WCSR; AG; Rohwer, p. 119.

JACK CARNES

D:	8-30-42	YB:	1942
T:	2158	Tn:	10,907
Pos:	42.00 N / 28.05 W	Dr:	22 ft.
Ow:	Sinclair Refining Co.	C:	62,000 bbls. water ballast
Op:	WSA	P:	steam
M:	Theodore Roosevelt Merritt	S:	14.5
A:	1-4"; 1-3"; 4-20 mm; 2-30 cal.		

On 25 August, the *Jack Carnes* departed Swansea, Wales, on an independent voyage to Aruba, NWI. While the helmsman steered the prescribed zigzag course, lookouts spotted a submarine about five miles away. The *U-705* (Horn) immediately began shelling the tanker as she tried to escape. The submarine fired ten shots from its deck gun, but none struck the *Carnes*. Three exploded close enough, however, to slightly damage the ship and scatter shrapnel on the decks. The tanker's gunners answered with eight rounds from the forward three-inch gun and thirteen rounds from the after four-inch gun, forcing the U-boat to submerge. About sixteen hours later, at 2358, the *U-516* (Wiebe) torpedoed the ship on the starboard side forward of the bridge. Immediately the master ordered the helm to be swung to starboard. Unfortunately, the watch below erroneously secured the undamaged engines. As the ship lost way she exposed her port side to the U-boat, and a second torpedo hit this side in the #4 tank four minutes after the initial explosion. A third torpedo struck the starboard side amidships after the nine officers, thirty-three men, and fourteen armed guards began abandoning ship. A fourth torpedo struck the starboard side aft of the midships house, a fifth hit the starboard side bunker tanks, and a sixth struck amidships at 0135. The tanker broke in two and sank, bow and stern rising into the air. The entire crew got away divided evenly between two boats. The survivors set sail together in a southerly direction, but a storm on the night of the 31st reached gale force and separated the boats. The #4 boat with the chief mate, four other officers, four armed guards, and nineteen men landed on Terceira Island, Azores, six days later. The #2 boat containing the master, three other officers, fourteen men, and ten armed guards was never seen again.

NSS; WACR; WCSR; AG; Rohwer, p. 119, places the attack at 41.35 N / 29.01 W; *War Action Casualties*, p. 115.

STAR OF OREGON

D:	8-30-42	YB:	1941
T:	0230	Tn:	7,176
Pos:	11.48 N / 59.45 W	Dr:	27 ft. 1 in.
Ow:	U.S. Maritime Commission	C:	9,000 tons military equipment,
Op:	States SS Co.		manganese ore, general
M:	Ellis Penryn Thomas	P:	steam
A:	2-3"; 8-30 cal.	S:	11.4

The freighter *Star of Oregon* sailed independently from Durban, South Africa, to Trinidad, BWI. The ship had steered three different zigzag patterns during her trip when a torpedo fired by the *U-162* (Wattenburg) struck the starboard side in the #4 hold. The explosion blew the hatch covers off the #4 and #5 holds and threw cargo into the air. The master ordered the ship abandoned as she settled by the stern. The gun crew mustered at the guns and fired five rounds from the three-inch gun without ever sighting the submarine. Most of the complement of eight officers, thirty men, fourteen armed guards, and one workaway abandoned ship in four lifeboats within minutes after the explosion. At 0255 the *U-162* surfaced and the Germans questioned the men about the ship, the cargo, and whether anyone remained on board. Receiving a negative reply, the U-boat began shelling the port side of the ship. At 500 yards the German gun crew put eighteen shots into the freighter. The ship sank stern first at 0330, and the *U-162* left shortly thereafter. An American patrol boat rescued the survivors and landed them at Port-of-Spain the next day. The workaway, a seaman being repatriated, lay sleeping on the #4 hatch cover. He was blown overboard and never found.

NSS; WACR; WCSR; AG; Rohwer, p. 119.

WEST LASHAWAY

D:	8-30-42	YB:	1918
T:	1410	Tn:	5,637
Pos:	10.30 N / 55.10 W	Dr:	27 ft.
Ow:	American West African Line	C:	7,670 tons tin, copper, cocoa
Op:	American West African Line		beans, palm oil
M:	Benjamin Bogdan	P:	steam
A:	1-4"; 2-30 cal.	S:	7.0

The *West Lashaway* sailed independently from Takoradi, Gold Coast, to New York via Trinidad. About 375 miles east of Trinidad, the *U-66* (Markworth) observed the vessel steering a zigzagging course and attacked. Lookouts spotted a torpedo, and the emergency alarm sounded as the master put the ship under full speed and the helmsman swung her to port. The torpedo struck deep in the starboard side amidships, forward of the fireroom. A second torpedo struck nearby, blowing off the #3 hatch and causing extensive internal damage. The ship immediately rolled to starboard and sank in one minute. The ship's complement consisted of ten officers, twenty-eight men, and nine armed guards. The freighter also carried nine passengers, including a woman missionary and four children. The ship went down so rapidly that no boats could be launched. Only forty-two persons were seen to leave the vessel and reach the four rafts. The rafts remained together for three days until heavy weather separated them. On 13 September a plane sighted one raft with nineteen survivors and dropped supplies. The following day the survivors sighted a destroyer, but the lookouts on the destroyer never spotted the raft. On the 18th, a convoy and three planes again sighted the raft. The destroyer HMS *Vimy* (I-33) left the convoy to investigate. Thinking the raft was a submarine in disguise, the destroyer began firing and fortunately missed with all sixteen attempts. The survivors cut the sail down and the *Vimy* picked them up. This raft contained some of the passengers including the woman missionary and four children. The *Vimy* transferred the survivors to the Dutch SS *Prins William Van Oranje*, and they landed at Barbados. Two on this raft died of exposure before being rescued. Twenty-five days after the attack a West Indian fisherman picked up one raft with two survivors on board. Only one of these men lived. None of the other survivors or rafts were ever seen again. Only eighteen persons survived the attack—one officer, one armed guard, eleven of the ship's crew, and five passengers.

The sources conflict on the ship's complement and the number of survivors. NSS; WACR; WCSR; AG; *Washington Post*, 17 February 1945; Rohwer, p. 119.

AMERICAN LEADER

D:	9-10-42	YB:	1941
T:	1940	Tn:	6,778
Pos:	34.26 S / 02.00 E	Dr:	27 ft.
Ow:	U. S. Lines	C:	6,500 tons rubber, 300 bbls. fuel
Op:	U. S. Lines		on deck
M:	Haakon Andrew Pedersen	P:	diesel
A:	1-4"; several machine guns	S:	14.5

On 22 August, the *American Leader* departed Colombo, Ceylon, en route to Newport News, Virginia, via Cape Town. The freighter sailed alone from Cape Town on 6 September. About 800 miles west of the Cape of Good Hope, the German raider *Michel* (Ruckteshell) intercepted her. Lookouts sighted the *Michel* looming in the darkness, but the officers thought her to be another merchantman. Suddenly the raider opened fire from about 500 yards. Shells smashed the starboard lifeboat and the upper works of the vessel, and set fire to barrels of fuel on deck. The ship's whistle sounded general quarters and shrieked until the vessel went under, twenty-five minutes after the attack began. Some of the ten officers, thirty-nine men, and nine armed guards on board attempted to

launch the port boat, but the gunfire destroyed it. With the boat shot away, the men began releasing the four rafts and jumped into the water. After shelling the ship for twenty minutes, the raider fired two torpedoes that struck the freighter in the engine room on the port side, causing her to quickly sink by the stern. Just as many of the crew readied the rafts, the freighter capsized to port and sank. The *Michel* picked up eight officers, thirty-one men, and eight of the gun crew and landed them in Singapore to be interned in a Japanese prison camp. Fourteen of these men died in the POW camps.

WACR; WCSR; Muggenthaler, pp. 230-31; Moore, p. 485.

PATRICK J. HURLEY

D:	9-12-42	YB:	1941
T:	2035	Tn:	10,864
Pos:	22.59 N / 46.15 W	Dr:	31 ft. 3 in.
Ow:	Sinclair Refining Co.	C:	135,000 bbls. gasoline and diesel
Op:	WSA		oil
M:	Carl Strongren	P:	steam
A:	1-4"; 1-3"; 2-50 mm; 2-20 mm	S:	15.0

On 7 September, the *Patrick J. Hurley* sailed from Aruba, NWI, to Belfast, Ireland. A lookout spotted the *U-512* (Schultze) 125 yards off the starboard bow and running parallel to the ship. Immediately the *U-512* attacked with its large and small deck guns. The gunfire smashed the midships cabins, destroyed the radio antenna, wrecked the lifeboats, and destroyed the forward three-inch gun. The 105-mm shells hit the engine room and holed the ship at the waterline, opening the cargo tanks and starting a fire. The master increased the ship's speed to about seventeen knots and tried to evade the U-boat but to no avail. The naval contingent on the ship returned fire with six rounds from the four-inch stern gun and from the smaller caliber weapons. Within ten minutes the U-boat's gunfire had the ship ablaze from stem to stern. The submarine fired about thirty shells before the ten officers, thirty-four men, and eighteen armed guards began abandoning ship. The survivors abandoned ship in the #2 and #4 lifeboats and two rafts while the ship was still under way and later redistributed into the two boats. The Swedish SS *Etna* picked up the #2 lifeboat with twenty-two men seven days after the attack. The British SS *Loch Dee* rescued the #1 lifeboat with twenty-three men twenty days after the attack. Four officers, nine men, and four armed guards lost their lives.

NSS; WACR; WCSR; AG; *War Action Casualties*, p. 116.

OLIVER ELLSWORTH

D:	9-13-42	YB:	1942
T:	0930	Tn:	7,191
Pos:	75.52 N / 07.55 E	Dr:	29 ft.
Ow:	Agwilines	C:	7,200 tons ammunition, planes
Op:	WSA	P:	steam
M:	Otto Ernest Buford	S:	8.0
A:	1-4"; 1-3"; 8-20 mm; 2-30 cal.		

The Liberty ship *Oliver Ellsworth*, en route from New York to Archangel, USSR, was torpedoed in a general action against the forty-merchant ship Convoy PQ-18. During the trip the *U-589* (Horrer) and several other U-boats stalked the convoy. About 100 miles southwest of Spitsbergen, the *U-589* sighted the escort carrier HMS *Avenger* (D-14) and fired a two-torpedo spread. The first torpedo, however, struck the Russian SS *Stalingrad*. The helmsman on the *Oliver Ellsworth* put the rudder hard left to avoid the sinking *Stalingrad*. Moments later a second torpedo struck the *Oliver Ellsworth* between the #4 and #5 holds. The watch below immediately secured the engines, and the crew mustered at the boat stations. The ship's complement of eight officers, thirty-four men, and twenty-eight armed guards cleared the ship in four lifeboats within fifteen minutes after the explosion. With a great deal of headway still upon the freighter, both starboard boats swamped, and one of the port side boats struck a raft and sank. Despite the large number of men in the water, only one armed guard died in the action. The SS *Copeland* and the trawler HMS *St. Kenan* (FY-264) picked up the survivors within an hour and landed them at Archangel. The HMS *St. Kenan* sank the *Ellsworth* with gunfire, and she disappeared stern first at 1030.

NSS; WACR; WCSR; AG; Rohwer, p. 200.

JOHN PENN

D:	9-13-42	YB:	1942
T:	1545	Tn:	7,177
Pos:	67.00 N / 10.15 E	Dr:	28 ft.
Ow:	U.S. Maritime Commission	C:	7,000 tons lend-lease, cargo,
Op:	U.S. Maritime Commission		tanks
M:	Albin Johnson	P:	steam
A:	1-4"; 1-3"; 8-20 mm	S:	8.0

The *John Penn*, part of Convoy PQ-18, was torpedoed by aircraft while en route from Boston, Massachusetts, to Archangel, USSR. The freighter took station #73 in the convoy. While under attack from about fifty German bombers and torpedo planes, the ships and escorts maintained a scathing fire on the enemy aircraft. Two torpedoes struck the *John Penn* in quick succession, one at the bow and the other amidships at the engine room. Both severely damaged the ship and the second destroyed the engines. As the *Penn* began to settle rapidly, the survivors among the eight officers, thirty-two men, and twenty-five armed guards on board abandoned ship in an erratic manner. Three boats and four rafts got away, but they left twelve men on board, including some wounded. Eventually, the #2 boat returned to take off the remaining men. Three men, including one officer, died in the engine room. The destroyer HMS *Eskimo* (F-75) and the minesweeper HMS *Harrier* (N-71) rescued the survivors within two hours and landed them in Archangel. Escorts sank the ship with gunfire, and she went down by the head at about 1745.

The ship's complement varies within the different sources. NSS; WACR; WCSR; AG.

OREGONIAN

D:	9-13-42	YB:	1919
T:	1557	Tn:	4,862
Pos:	76.00 N / 09.30 E	Dr:	28 ft. 4 in.
Ow:	American Hawaiian SS Line	C:	6,700 tons tanks, steel, planes,
Op:	U.S. Maritime Commission		food
M:	Harold Willard Dowling	P:	steam
A:	1-4"; 4-20 mm; 4-30 cal.	S:	7.0

The *Oregonian* sailed with Convoy PQ-18, en route from New York to Archangel, USSR. At 1515 the commodore's ship alerted the rest of the convoy that enemy aircraft were approaching. The *Oregonian* maintained her convoy station as the first ship in the starboard wing of the formation. The attacking aircraft successfully flew through the covering fire and hit the freighter with three torpedoes. The torpedoes struck simultaneously, forward of the bridge, amidships, and aft of the bridge on the starboard side. The explosions virtually blew away the whole side of the vessel, damaging her so severely that she capsized and sank in two minutes. The ship's complement of ten officers, thirty crewmen, and fourteen armed guards had no chance to launch lifeboats. Most of the survivors jumped overboard and swam to two rafts. An escort vessel picked them out of the water quickly, but only twenty-nine men survived—three officers, eighteen crewmen, and eight armed guards.

The sources conflict on the number of casualties and the ship's complement. NSS; WACR; WCSR; AG.

MARY LUCKENBACH

D:	9-14-42	YB:	1918
T:	1415	Tn:	5,049
Pos:	76.00 N / 10.00 E	Dr:	26 ft.
Ow:	Luckenbach SS Co.	C:	5,219 tons general including
Op:	Luckenbach SS Co.		1,000 tons TNT
M:	John Klemm Chadwick	P:	steam
A:	1-4"; 1-3"; 8-22 mm; 2-30 cal.	S:	8.0

The *Mary Luckenbach*, part of Convoy PQ-18, was completely destroyed by an aerial torpedo while en route from Scotland to Murmansk, USSR. German torpedo and high level bombers attacked the convoy consisting of forty merchant vessels and thirty-nine escort vessels, the best-defended convoy to this date. The Germans sank thirteen of the convoy's vessels, eight of them American. One eyewitness reported seeing a bomber crash on the foredeck of the freighter. A second witness reported that the lead plane in the second attacking wave burst into flames and dropped "its entire load of torpedoes on the forward deck of the *Mary Luckenbach*." The torpedoes set off her cargo of TNT and with a huge explosion, fire and debris flew a thousand feet into the air. The ship disintegrated and took with her the attacking aircraft. The debris rained on the *Nathanael Greene* and the *Lafayette*, and the concussion knocked out the engines of the *Wacosta*. The entire complement of nine officers, thirty-two men, and twenty-four armed guards died in the explosion.

WACR; WCSR; AG; Morison, 1:362-64.

NATHANAEL GREENE

D:	9-14-42	YB:	1942
T:	1415	Tn:	7,176
Pos:	76.00 N / 10.00 E	Dr:	27 ft. 7 7/8 in.
Ow:	WSA	C:	5,200 tons general
Op:	U. S. Line	P:	steam
M:	George Arlington Vickers	S:	11
A:	1-4"; 1-3"; 4-50 cal.		

The *Nathanael Greene* sailed as part of Convoy PQ-18 from Loch Ewe, Scotland, to North Russia. In convoy station #72, steaming 200 yards away, the *Mary Luckenbach* was hit by an aerial torpedo and disintegrated. The explosion blew an immense amount of wreckage onto the deck of the *Nathanael Greene*, and the concussion damaged bulkhead doors. The crew on board the *Greene* thought their ship had been torpedoed and began going to their boat stations. The blast injured eleven of the crew, and the British destroyer *Onslaught* (G-04) took off five of the most critically wounded men. The freighter was also slightly damaged by bombs during the other attacks but made port at Molotovsk and discharged all her cargo. The ship's complement during the trip consisted of ten officers, thirty-two men, and twelve armed guards. A messman was reported missing, having been blown over the side from the forecastle head. During the aerial attack on 14 September, the naval gunners were credited with shooting down five enemy planes.

The complement numbers conflict within the sources. NSS; WACR; WCSR; AG; Morison, 1:362-364.

WACOSTA

D:	9-14-42	YB:	1920
T:	1530	Tn:	5,433
Pos:	76.05 N / 06.10 E	Dr:	25 ft. 3 in.
Ow:	U.S. Maritime Commission	C:	8,804 tons war supplies, tanks
Op:	Waterman SS Co.	P:	steam
M:	Jens Jensen	S:	10.0
A:	1-4"; 2-50 cal.; 2-30 cal.		

The *Wacosta* sailed with Convoy PQ-18 en route from Philadelphia, Pennsylvania, to Archangel, USSR. Fifty torpedo planes and high altitude bombers attacked the convoy and eventually sank thirteen vessels. An aerial torpedo struck the *Mary Luckenbach* steaming ahead of the *Wacosta*, and the *Luckenbach*'s cargo of ammunition violently exploded. The concussion from the blast ruptured steam valves and oil lines, destroyed instruments, and disabled the engine on board the *Wacosta*. While lying helplessly in the water, a torpedo plane approached and dropped its torpedo short. The torpedo landed and exploded on the #2 hatch and blew a large hole in the deck and on the starboard side, causing the vessel to sink by the head. The entire complement of seven officers, thirty-one men, and eleven armed guards abandoned ship in two lifeboats and two life rafts. The cruiser HMS *Scylla* (98) and the minesweeper HMS *Harrier* (N-71) rescued all hands and landed them at Scapa Flow.

The sources for the number of men on board conflict. NSS; WACR; WCSR; AG.

COMMERCIAL TRADER

D:	9-16-42	YB:	1919
T:	0505	Tn:	2,606
Pos:	10.30 N / 60.16 W	Dr:	25 ft.
Ow:	Moore & McCormack SS Co.	C:	3,400 tons ore and caster seed
Op:	Moore & McCormack SS Co.	P:	steam
M:	James Wilbur Hunley	S:	9.0
A:	1-3"; 2-30 cal.		

The *Commercial Trader* cleared Fortaleza, Brazil, independently bound for Trinidad, BWI. The vessel did not steer a zigzagging course but had changed her direction several times during the night. A torpedo fired by the *U-558* (Krech) struck the starboard side in the #2 hold and blew the hatch off, collapsed the starboard side of the bridge, and threw some men into the water. The explosion damaged the fireroom's forward bulkhead and flooded that compartment. Water also poured in the skylight over the engine room. The throttle became inaccessible, and the watch below could not secure the engines. Most of the crew of eight officers and twenty-one men, along with the nine armed guards, abandoned ship in one lifeboat and a raft. The ship sank bow first in two minutes, so quickly, in fact, that no other boat could be launched. All the survivors transferred into the single boat, set sail for Tobago, and arrived twelve hours later. Two officers, five men, and three armed guards died, including one man who later died in a hospital ashore.

NSS; WACR; WCSR; AG; Rohwer, p. 124.

MAE

D:	9-17-42	YB:	1918
T:	0015	Tn:	5,607
Pos:	08.03 N / 58.13 W	Dr:	15 ft. 3 in.
Ow:	A. H. Bull SS Co.	C:	water ballast
Op:	Alcoa SS Co.	P:	steam
M:	Willard R. Hudgins	S:	10
A:	1-4"; 2-30 cal.		

The *Mae* departed Trinidad en route to Georgetown, British Guiana, steering a zigzag course. Forty-one miles north of the Georgetown Beacon, and just after midnight, a lookout spotted a blinking light on the port side. Within moments a torpedo fired by the *U-515* (Henke) struck on the starboard side at the after bulkhead of the #5 hold. The explosion carried away the hatch covers and the well deck bulkhead, destroyed the living quarters, ruptured steam lines, flooded the #4 and #5 holds, and damaged the steering gear. The seven officers, twenty-five crewmen, and nine armed guards began abandoning ship without orders from the master. They escaped in three boats in less than ten minutes. The *U-515* then surfaced, passed astern, and began shelling the starboard side of the vessel, expending sixteen shells at 200 yards. The *Mae* sank by the stern at 0150. Officers on the *U-515* questioned the survivors before the U-boat departed. The Norwegian SS *Sorwangen* rescued the survivors about six hours later and transferred them at the Demerara Beacon to the Canadian SS *Gypsum*

King. A launch carried the wounded into Georgetown, and the *Gypsum King* landed the remaining survivors. The shellfire killed one man during the attack.

NSS; WACR; WCSR; AG; Rohwer, p. 123.

KENTUCKY

D:	9-18-42	YB:	1921
T:	1035	Tn:	5,446
Pos:	off Cape Kanin	Dr:	23 ft. 8 in.
Ow:	States SS Co.	C:	6,200 tons general
Op:	States SS Co.	P:	steam
M:	Richard Penual Child	S:	7.5
A:	1-4"; 2-50 cal.; 2-30 cal.		

The *Kentucky* was the final American ship sunk as a result of the attacks on Convoy PQ-18. The freighter sailed from Loch Ewe, Scotland, to Archangel, USSR. At 0725, thirty-five miles west southwest of Cape Kanin, lookouts spotted ten aircraft attacking the port side of the convoy. The master maneuvered the freighter to avoid one torpedo, but another torpedo struck the sluggish merchantman forward of the bridge on the starboard side. The master ordered the crew to take cover, and the explosion blew the #2 hatch cover into the rigging, damaged the port side of the bridge, and started a fire in the officer's quarters. The watch below secured the engines, and the master ordered them topside. As the ship slowly sank, the ship's complement of eight officers, thirty men, and sixteen armed guards left the vessel in two lifeboats and one raft. The *Kentucky* sank at 1200. Two British minesweepers rescued all hands within twenty minutes and landed them at Archangel.

The sources conflict on the size of the crew. The *Kentucky* had suffered some bomb damage aft of the bridge during an earlier attack. NSS; WACR; WCSR; AG.

WICHITA

D:	9-19-42	YB:	1920
T:	0648 GWT	Tn:	6,174
Pos:	15.00 N / 54.00 W	Dr:	approx. 28 ft.
Ow:	WSA	C:	unknown
Op:	U. S. Lines	P:	diesel
M:	Herman Swain Chessman	S:	11.5
A:	1-4"; 4-50 cal.		

The *Wichita* was torpedoed and sunk by the *U-516* (Wiebe) while en route from Takoradi, Gold Coast, to St. Thomas, Virgin Islands. The freighter left Takoradi on 1 September, and the *U-516* intercepted the zigzagging ship about 300 miles northwest of Barbados. The U-boat missed with its first three torpedoes. At 400 yards the *U-516* fired a torpedo that struck between the forward mast and the bridge. After being hit, the ship went down in less than one minute. The U-boat's report mentions no boats, and the entire complement of ten officers, thirty men, and ten armed guards perished.

WACR; WCSR; AG; WJ; Rohwer, p. 124.

SILVER SWORD

D:	9-20-42	YB:	1921
T:	1720	Tn:	4,937
Pos:	75.41 N / 03.12 E	Dr:	24 ft. 1 in.
Ow:	U.S. Maritime Commission	C:	5,000 tons wood, hides, chrome
Op:	Sword Line	P:	steam
M:	Clyde Wellington Colbeth	S:	8.0
A:	1-4"; 2-50 cal.; 2-30 cal.		

The *U-255* (Reche) torpedoed the *Silver Sword* as she traveled with Convoy QP-14 en route from Archangel, USSR, to New York. The first torpedo struck the ship on the port bow, and the tremendous explosion that followed also damaged the bridge. A second torpedo immediately hit the stern, blowing off the stern post, the propeller, and the rudder. Shortly afterwards the after magazine exploded. The engineer on watch sent a fireman topsides to learn of the damage and then secured the engines. The crew of seven officers and twenty-five men, as well as the eighteen passengers and eleven armed guards, abandoned ship in two lifeboats and one raft. The rescue ships *Rathlin* and *Zamelek* rescued all hands and took them to Scotland. An oiler later died on one of the rescue vessels, the only casualty. An escort sank the freighter with gunfire thirty minutes after the initial explosions, and she sank by the stern at 1759.

The passengers were survivors of the *Peter Kerr* and *Honomu*. The complement figures are contradictory within the sources. NSS; WACR; WCSR; AG; Rohwer, p. 200, places the attack at 75.52 N / 00.20 E.

ESSO WILLIAMSBURG

D:	9-22-42	YB:	1941
T:	0116 (GWT)	Tn:	11,237
Pos:	53.12 N / 41.00 W	Dr:	unknown
Ow:	WSA	C:	110,043 bbls. special Navy fuel
Op:	Standard Oil Co. of N. J.		oil
M:	John Tweed	P:	motor
A:	1-5"; 1-3"; 2-50 cal.; 2-30 cal.	S:	unknown

The *Esso Williamsburg* sailed from Aruba, NWI, to Reykjavik, Iceland. About 500 miles south of Cape Farewell, Greenland, the *U-211* (Hauser) spotted the tanker and attacked. Two torpedoes struck the tanker's port side. In poor visibility the tanker got under way again and temporarily evaded the U-boat. The *U-211* reportedly dove to use its listening gear to find the tanker. About ten hours later, the submarine again had the tanker in sight. From 2,000 yards, the *U-211* put a torpedo into the tanker's starboard side amidships, and the *Williamsburg* caught fire. At 0105 the coup de grâce shot struck amidships, and smoke and flames from the explosion rose nearly 500 feet in the air. The tanker broke in two, and the after section continued to burn as both halves sank. The U-boat's war journal gave no mention of any of the eight officers, thirty-four men, and eighteen armed guards abandoning ship. It does, however, mention the ship sending a weak distress signal. A shore station received the message but an extensive air and sea search failed to find any survivors or wreckage. All hands perished in the attack.

NSS; WACR; WCSR; AG; WJ; *Ships of the Esso Fleet*, pp. 406-08; Rohwer, p. 124.

BELLINGHAM

D:	9-22-42	YB:	1920
T:	0617	Tn:	5,345
Pos:	71.23 N / 11.03 W	Dr:	24 ft.
Ow:	Waterman SS Co.	C:	6,100 tons general and ore
Op:	U.S. Maritime Commission	P:	steam
M:	Soren Mortensen	S:	8.0
A:	1-4"; 4-50 cal.; 2-30 cal.		

The *Bellingham* sailed from Archangel, USSR, to New York, as part of Convoy QP-14. The freighter maintained station on the starboard wing, first line of the convoy. Forty-five miles west of Jan Mayen Island a torpedo from the *U-435* (Strelow) struck at the #4 hold on the starboard side. The watch below secured the engines and the crew abandoned ship. The eight officers, thirty-one men, ten armed guards, and twenty-six passengers on board cleared the ship in three lifeboats and one life raft. Miraculously no one was killed or injured. Escort vessels rescued all hands within minutes and landed them in Glasgow. The ship sank by the stern at 0715.

The *Bellingham* was struck by a dud torpedo but survived the disastrous PQ-17 convoy. She had waited two months in Archangel for a cargo. The passengers on board were the survivors from the *Pan Kraft* and *Pan Atlantic*. NSS; WACR; WCSR; AG; Rohwer, p. 200.

PAUL LUCKENBACH

D:	9-22-42	YB:	1913
T:	1846	Tn:	6,606
Pos:	10.03 N / 63.42 E	Dr:	27 ft. 4 in.
Ow:	Luckenbach SS Co.	C:	9,200 tons oil refinery supplies,
Op:	Luckenbach SS Co.		tanks, airplanes
M:	Frank A. Snow	P:	steam
A:	1-4"; 1-3"; 4-20 mm; 2-30 cal.;	S:	12.5
	2-50 cal.		

The *Paul Luckenbach* departed New York en route to the Persian Gulf via Cape Town, South Africa. A torpedo fired by the *I-29* (Izu) struck the vessel on the port side at the #1 hatch. The huge explosion also damaged the #2 hatch. The master had the engines immediately secured, and the ship turned around to reduce headway. The crew remained on the ship until a second torpedo struck the starboard side at the #3 hatch over an hour later. The damage from the second torpedo caused the ship to sink by the stern at 2051. After the second explosion the complement of eight officers, thirty-six men, and seventeen armed guards abandoned the freighter in four lifeboats. Two days later the boats all became separated in their 800-mile trip to India. One boat landed in Pallikere, one at Cannanore, one at Mangalore, and the last landed at Calicut, India. All the boats remained at sea between eighteen and twenty-six days without any casualties.

NSS; WACR; WCSR; AG; Rohwer, p. 263.

ANTINOUS

D:	9-23-42	YB:	1920
T:	0502	Tn:	5,554
Pos:	08.58 N / 59.33 W	Dr:	16 ft. 6 in.
Ow:	Waterman SS Corp.	C:	550 tons bauxite ore
Op:	Waterman SS Corp.	P:	steam
M:	Hamilton Powell	S:	12.0
A:	1-4"; 4-50 cal.; 2-30 cal.		

The *Antinous* sailed independently from Trinidad, BWI, to Georgetown, British Guiana. As the ship steered a nonevasive course, lookouts spotted the conning tower of the *U-515* (Henke) about 900 yards away. Moments later lookouts spotted the wake of a torpedo 100 yards off the port bow. Before the helmsman could take avoiding action, a torpedo struck the port side in the #2 hold about ten feet forward of the bridge. The explosion blew off the #2 hatch covers and opened a hole fourteen feet by eighteen feet in the port side. Torpedo fragments also punched holes in the starboard side. As the ship took a 20° list, the watch below secured the engines. The gun crew fired seven shots from the four-inch stern gun and drove the U-boat under water. At 0525 the ship's complement of eight officers, twenty-seven men, and sixteen armed guards abandoned ship in three lifeboats and two rafts. At about 0800 a volunteer crew reboarded the ship, but the engines could not be restarted. All hands came back on board the next morning, and at 1400 the rescue tug HMS *Zwaarte Zee* (W-163) took the ship in tow. After making five miles, the tug stopped to adjust the tow. The tug HMS *Busy* also came alongside to assist. The *U-512* (Schultze) took advantage of the pause and fired a torpedo that struck the freighter in the #1 hold. The ship began settling immediately. The gun crew fired seven more shells but to no effect. Fifteen minutes after the explosion the crew once again abandoned the ship in three lifeboats, and the tugs rescued all hands. The *Antinous* finally sank by the bow at 1510 on the 24th.

NSS; WACR; WCSR; AG; Rohwer, p. 125.

PENMAR

D:	9-23-42	YB:	1920
T:	2151	Tn:	5,868
Pos:	58.12 N / 34.35 W	Dr:	27 ft. 11 1/2 in.
Ow:	Calmar SS Corp.	C:	7,500 tons steel, food, trucks
Op:	WSA	P:	steam
M:	Sigmund Charles Krolikowski	S:	9.0
A:	1-4"; 1-3"; 4-20 mm; 4-50 cal.; 2-30 cal.		

The *Penmar* sailed with Convoy SC-100 from Halifax, Nova Scotia, to the United Kingdom. During the trip the ship suffered mechanical difficulties and straggled from the convoy. The freighter proceeded toward Cape Farewell for repairs. The *U-432* (Schultze) spotted the lone vessel and fired a torpedo that missed because of the heavy seas. The U-boat fired three more shots, one of which struck the port side thirty feet from the bow at the forepeak oil tank. A lookout spotted one of the two torpedoes passing under the ship. The watch below put the engines astern without orders from the bridge. The ship began to settle by the bow rapidly, and the ship's complement of eight officers, thirty-one men, and twenty-two armed guards abandoned ship in one lifeboat and two rafts. One man died after being crushed between a life raft and the ship. The USCG cutter *Bibb* (WPG-31) rescued sixty men and landed them in Reykjavik, Iceland.

One armed guard had previously washed overboard in a storm. NSS; WACR; WCSR; AG; WJ; Rohwer, p. 125, places the attack at 58.25 N / 32.15 W.

JOHN WINTHROP

D:	9-24-42	YB:	1942
T:	1910 (GWT)	Tn:	7,176
Pos:	56.00 N / 31.00 W	Dr:	27 ft. 9 in. (normal loaded draft)
Ow:	WSA	C:	unknown
Op:	United Fruit Co.	P:	steam
M:	Charles Malcolm Robertson	S:	unknown
A:	1-5"; 4-20 mm; 2-30 cal.		

The *John Winthrop* was torpedoed by the *U-619* (Makowski) while en route from Glasgow, Scotland, to New York. The freighter sailed as part of Convoy ON-131 but straggled from the convoy on the night of 21 September. The U-boat struck the ship with five torpedoes and she broke in two. The *U-619* then surfaced and sank the halves with gunfire. None of the seven officers, thirty-two men, and thirteen armed guards on board survived.

The sources conflict on the armed guard's complement. WACR; WCSR; AG; WJ; Rohwer, p. 125.

WEST CHETAC

D:	9-24-42	YB:	1919
T:	0330	Tn:	5,627
Pos:	08.06 N / 58.12 W	Dr:	25 ft. 6 in.
Ow:	U.S. Maritime Commission	C:	6,097 tons general war supplies
Op:	Seas Shipping Co.	P:	steam
M:	Frank Mathew Jasper	S:	7.5
A:	1-4"; 2-30 cal.; 4-20 mm		

The *West Chetac* sailed from Trinidad, BWI, to Basra, Iraq, via Aruba, in Convoy TAW-14. The convoy had dispersed less than seven hours earlier, and at 0315 lookouts spotted a wake from the conning tower of the *U-175* (Bruns). Fifteen minutes later a torpedo struck the port side in the #2 hold. The explosion blew off the hatch covers, and the freighter settled immediately by the bow. The gun crew went to battle stations but never spotted the U-boat. The master ordered the ship abandoned about two minutes after the explosion. The ship's complement of nine officers, thirty crewmen, and eleven armed guards attempted to get off the ship in heavy seas. Suction caused by the vessel's rapid sinking and the heavy seas capsized all the boats. Only nineteen men managed to swim to four of the rafts—three officers, fourteen men, and two armed guards. The rest presumably drowned when their boats capsized. The *U-175* surfaced after the attack and the Germans questioned the men on the rafts. Eight and a half days later the USS *Roe* (DD-418) picked up the survivors twenty miles off Trinidad and landed them at Port-of-Spain, Trinidad.

NSS; WACR; WCSR; AG; TF; Rohwer, p. 125, places the attack at 08.45 N / 57.00 W.

LOSMAR

D:	9-24-42	YB:	1919
T:	0558	Tn:	5,550
Pos:	08.00 N / 74.20 E	Dr:	23 ft.
Ow:	Calmar SS Corp.	C:	3,000 tons salt ballast
Op:	American Export Lines	P:	steam
M:	Valdemar Clifton Farrell	S:	9.5
A:	1-4"; 4-20 mm; 4-30 cal.		

The *Losmar* was torpedoed by the *I-165* (Torisu) while en route from Aden to Calcutta, India, via Colombo. Lookouts sighted a torpedo's track just in time for the helmsman to put the wheel over hard to port and to ring the general alarm. A single torpedo struck the ship aft of the bridge and above the engine room. The explosion blew off all the after hatches and buckled the deck. The watch below never secured the engines, and the ship continued making headway as she rapidly sank stern first within two minutes. Survivors among the eight officers, twenty-nine men, and eleven armed guards on board had no time to clear the lifeboats for launching and had to jump over the sides and swim to the rafts blown clear of the ship. Three officers, nine men, and nine armed guards swam to two rafts. They fastened the two rafts together with floating timbers and dunnage to make one large raft and removed food and water from the other rafts. These two rafts remained together for six days. On 30 September, the men decided to go separate ways, and they divided the rations. The master's raft with six other men landed on the west coast of Ceylon twenty-three days after the attack. On 5 October, the British SS *Louise Moller* discovered the other raft with fourteen men and landed the men in Aden.

NSS; WACR; WCSR; AG; Rohwer, p. 263.

STEPHEN HOPKINS

D:	9-27-42	YB:	1942
T:	0930	Tn:	7,181
Pos:	28.08 S / 20.01 W	Dr:	under 29 ft.
Ow:	WSA	C:	ballast
Op:	Luckenbach SS Co.	P:	steam
M:	Paul Buck	S:	12.0
A:	1-4"; 2-37 mm; 4-50 cal.; 2-30 cal.		

On 18 September, the *Stephen Hopkins* sailed from Cape Town, South Africa, to Paramaribo, Dutch Guiana. Several days out of Cape Town the radio operator received a message warning of German raiders. On the morning of the 27th a lookout spotted two ships in the haze flying signal flags. They were in reality

the German 5,000-ton raider *Stier* (Gerlach) and the 7,800-ton blockade runner *Tannenfels* (Haase). Both immediately began firing on the Liberty ship, and what ensued was one of the most remarkable surface engagements of the war. Captain Paul Buck immediately turned the *Hopkins'* stern to the raiders. The armed guards manned the four-inch stern gun to defend the ship. The gun crew fired as rapidly as possible on the smaller raider. Fire from the *Stier* killed the gun crew one by one, and volunteers replaced those who had fallen. At the same time the *Tannenfels* remained at a distance, raking the *Hopkins* with machine gun fire that was returned by the *Hopkins*. The *Stier* had a fire control system that enabled her to fire salvos and hit the Liberty ship repeatedly. One shell hit one of the main boilers, reducing the speed of the *Stephen Hopkins* to one knot. Shells struck the *Hopkins* near the waterline, and incendiary shells eventually set fire to the main deckhouse as the ship slowly sank. The *Stier*, however, had paid for attacking the *Stephen Hopkins*. The *Hopkins'* gun crew had repeatedly struck the smaller raider, now in flames and in a sinking condition. After about twenty minutes of fierce firing the master sounded the ship's whistle to abandon ship. In one last act of defiance Cadet Midshipman Edwin O'Hara fired the five remaining shells from the four-inch gun, and all struck the *Stier*. A salvo aimed at the gun killed O'Hara after he fired the last round. The able-bodied men helped place the wounded in the only undamaged lifeboat. This boat searched for two hours picking up survivors. The ship's complement originally consisted of eight officers, thirty-three men, and fifteen armed guards, but only nineteen men cleared the ship. Only fifteen of these men survived—five gunners, one officer, and nine men. After a thirty-one day trip they made landfall at a small fishing village on the coast of Brazil.

NSS; WACR; WCSR; AG; Morison, 1:398-99; Muggenthaler, p. 242; *Times Herald*, 10 December 1943.

ALCOA MARINER

D:	9-28-42	YB:	1919
T:	0550	Tn:	5,590
Pos:	08.57 N / 60.08 W	Dr:	14 ft.
Ow:	Alcoa SS. Co.	C:	ballast
Op:	Alcoa SS. Co.	P:	steam
M:	John Luther Martino	S:	9.0
A:	1-4"; 4-20 mm; 2-30 cal.		

The *Alcoa Mariner* was torpedoed by the *U-175* (Bruns) while en route from Trinidad, BWI, to Georgetown, British Guiana, to load bauxite ore. The freighter sailed alone and had not steered an evasive course. Twenty miles off the Orinoco River, Venezuela, one of the armed guards spotted the wake of a torpedo. The master ordered the helmsman to give the ship hard right rudder, and the torpedo passed fifteen feet astern. Three minutes later a torpedo struck the port side just forward of the poop deck. The explosion opened a crack three feet wide across the deck, destroyed the ship's interior compartments, and flooded the engine room. The stern dropped 30°, apparently held in place by the shaft. The crew secured the engines, and the eight officers, thirty-three men, and thirteen armed guards abandoned ship in four lifeboats and by jumping overboard. An hour after the crew abandoned the freighter, the *U-175* put a second torpedo into the ship aft of the engine room on the port side. The *Mariner* sank rapidly by the stern and disappeared at 0705. Six hours later the Canadian MS *Turret Cape* rescued all hands and landed them in Georgetown.

NSS; WACR; WCSR; AG; Rohwer, p. 126; Moore, p. 8.

ALCOA TRANSPORT

D:	10-2-42	YB:	1918
T:	0235	Tn:	2,084
Pos:	09.03 N / 60.10 W	Dr:	12 ft.
Ow:	Alcoa SS Co.	C:	ballast
Op:	Alcoa SS Co.	P:	steam
M:	Clement Hunter	S:	9.0
A:	1-3"; 2-30 cal.		

The *Alcoa Transport*, sailing alone, departed Trinidad, BWI, for Georgetown, British Guiana, to load bauxite ore. Lookouts observed a flashing red light at 0100, so the ship changed course. An hour and a half later a torpedo fired by the *U-201* (Rosenberg) struck the starboard side at the after end of the engine room. The explosion tore away the bulkhead between the #3 hold and the engine room, demolished the engine, broke steam lines, and blew off the #3 hatch covers. Concrete blocks used for ballast also shot through the port side and hastened the sinking. The survivors among the eight officers, twenty-three men, and five armed guards on board immediately abandoned ship in one lifeboat. They attempted to launch the life rafts, but the nips on the pelican hooks proved to be too tight and none could be released. The ship sank in four minutes, but 100 feet of her bow remained out of the water for several hours. The *PC-490* rescued seven officers, nineteen men, and the five armed guards at about 1500 and landed them at Port-of-Spain, Trinidad. The three crewmen on watch below died, and the chief engineer later died in a hospital ashore.

NSS; WACR; WCSR; RWCS; Rohwer, p. 126.

CAMDEN

D:	10-4-42	YB:	1921
T:	0655	Tn:	6,653
Pos:	43.42 N / 124.52 W	Dr:	27 ft.
Ow:	Charles Kurz & Co. Inc.	C:	76,000 bbls. diesel and fuel oil
Op:	Shell Oil Co.	P:	steam
M:	Donald M. Davidson	S:	stopped
A:	1-4"; 4-30 cal.		

On 30 September, the *Camden* sailed from San Pedro, California, to Portland, Oregon. The tanker developed engine trouble and stopped to make repairs at sunrise. The officers on the bridge observed a torpedo fired by the *I-25* (Tagami) cross the bow of the vessel. Five seconds later a second torpedo hit ten feet aft of the stem. A sheet of flame immediately appeared from the forepeak tank. The tanker began settling by the head until water reached the decks from the bow to the bridge and the propeller had lifted out of the water. The radio operator sent a distress message, and the master sounded the general alarm and ordered the men to the boats. The crew of eight officers and thirty-one men, along with the nine armed guards, abandoned ship in three lifeboats and several doughnut life rafts. One of the crew drowned after jumping in the water. The Swedish MS *Kockaburra* rescued the forty-seven survivors nearly four hours later. At 0915 the next day, a salvage crew boarded the tanker, and the tug *Kenai* put her under tow. Although the *Camden* was destined to go to Portland for repairs, the salvors discovered the bar too shallow to admit the bow of the vessel over the Columbia River Bar. They then attempted to tow her stern first to Seattle. On 10 October, the tanker suddenly burst into flames and sank fifteen minutes later.

She sank at 46.46.38 N / 124.31.15 W; NSS; WACR; WCSR; AG; *Seattle Star*, 13 October 1942; Rohwer, p. 281, places the attack at 43.43 N / 124.54 N; *War Action Casualties*, p. 117.

ROBERT H. COLLEY

D:	10-4-42	YB:	1938
T:	1640	Tn:	11,651
Pos:	59.06 N / 28.18 W	Dr:	29 ft.
Ow:	Atlantic Refining Co.	C:	120,273 bbls. Navy fuel oil
Op:	WSA	P:	steam
M:	James Joseph McCaffrey	S:	10.0
A:	1-5"; 1-3"; 4-20 mm; 2-30 cal.		

The *Robert H. Colley* sailed in Convoy HX-209 en route from New York to the United Kingdom. The convoy consisted of thirty-six merchant ships and six escort vessels. The *U-254* (Loewe) fired a torpedo that struck forward of the mainmast on the starboard side in the #6 tank and broke the vessel in two.

Extremely rough seas and a seventy-five mph gale made abandoning ship difficult for the ten officers, thirty-four men, and seventeen armed guards on board. The men on the forward part of the vessel managed to launch two lifeboats. Eight men in one boat and one in another rode beside the ship searching for more occupants until the painters parted and swept the boats away. These men were never seen again. The four officers, twenty men, and nine armed guards on the after section of the vessel remained until daybreak. At 0600 the corvette HMS *Borage* (K-120) came to rescue the men. Three men launched a workboat and seven more got off in a raft. Twenty-three others jumped into the sea. The forward part of the vessel sank hours after the attack, and the *Borage* sank the stern section with gunfire and depth charges. The corvette landed the men in Londonderry, North Ireland.

The complement figures conflict within the sources, but the Coast Guard records are consistent with the shipping articles. WACR; WCSR; AG; *War Action Casualties*, p. 118.

CARIBSTAR

D:	10-4-42	YB:	1919
T:	0505	Tn:	2,592
Pos:	08.30 N / 59.37 W	Dr:	14 ft.
Ow:	Stockard & Co.	C:	none—ballast
Op:	Alcoa SS Corp.	P:	steam
M:	Fred Gomez Velez	S:	9.5
A:	1 6-lber.; 2-30 cal.		

The *Caribstar* was torpedoed and sunk by the *U-175* (Bruns) while en route from Trinidad, BWI, to Georgetown. British Guiana. The freighter steamed a zigzag course, and off the mouth of the Orinoco River the master sighted the track of a torpedo fifty yards away. He shouted "hard right" and the helmsman put the sluggish freighter's helm over. The torpedo struck the port side amidships in the boiler room and destroyed the boilers, ruptured steam lines, and killed three men on watch below. The freighter listed to starboard and then to port. A few minutes later a second torpedo struck the starboard side just aft of amidships and caused a huge explosion, probably magnified by the ship's ammunition being ignited. The ship went down by the stern but remained afloat with 100 feet of her bow out of the water for three hours before finally sinking. The seven officers, twenty-two men, and six armed guards on board abandoned ship in one lifeboat and two rafts. The *PC-469* rescued six officers, nineteen men, and six armed guards fourteen hours later. One man died on board the *PC-469*, and the second assistant engineer later died ashore from burns. The patrol boat landed the survivors at Port-of-Spain, Trinidad.

NSS; WACR; WCSR; AG; Rohwer, p. 127, places the attack at 08.35 N / 59.37 W.

WILLIAM A. McKENNEY

D:	10-5-42	YB:	1916
T:	0010	Tn:	6,153
Pos:	08.35 N / 59.20 W	Dr:	17 ft.
Ow:	Mystic SS Co.	C:	3,118 tons general and bauxite
Op:	Alcoa SS Corp.		ore
M:	James Franklin Lusby	P:	steam
A:	1-4"; 2-30 cal.	S:	11.5

The *William A. McKenney* sailed independently from Georgetown, British Guiana, to Trinidad, BWI. The *U-175* (Bruns) intercepted the ship less than 100 miles out of port. The freighter had been instructed to steam on a nonevasive course. A torpedo struck the port side just aft of the engine room bulkhead, exploding in the #3 hold. The explosion opened up a hole about twenty feet in diameter at the waterline and blew off the #3 hatch covers. With the crew still on the ship, the submarine surfaced and began shelling the freighter from the port side from one-half mile away. The *U-175* fired about seven rounds into the hull and the bridge house, setting fire to the fuel in the settling tanks. The majority of the complement of eight officers, twenty-three men, and four armed guards abandoned ship in two lifeboats and one float. As the master and two other men left the ship, the *U-175* again began to shell the *McKenney,* firing an additional ten rounds. Only one man died during the attack. The USS *Blakely* (DD-150) rescued the survivors fourteen hours after the attack and landed them at Trinidad.

The Eastern Gas & Fuel Associates were also co-owners. NSS; WACR; WCSR; AG; Rohwer, p. 127.

LARRY DOHENY

D:	10-5-42	YB:	1921
T:	2207	Tn:	7,038
Pos:	42.20 N / 125.02 W	Dr:	26 ft. 6 in.
Ow:	Richfield Oil Corp.	C:	66,000 bbls. fuel oil
Op:	Richfield Oil Corp.	P:	steam
M:	Olaf Breiland	S:	10.4
A:	1-5"; 2-30 cal.		

On 3 October, the *Larry Doheny* departed Long Beach, California, en route to St. John, Oregon. At 2120 lookouts reported observing the wakes of two torpedoes. The third mate discounted both sightings. Just after 2200, however, a torpedo fired by the *I-25* (Tagami) struck the port side below the waterline at the #2 tank. Both the #2 and #3 tanks exploded, shooting flames high into the air and creating a hole fourteen feet in diameter. The violent explosion buckled the starboard side outward and destroyed the steering gear. The *Doheny* lost

headway in a few minutes, and the surviving eight officers, twenty-six men, and ten armed guards on board began to abandon ship within fifteen minutes in the #3 and #4 lifeboats. The USS *Coos Bay* (AVP-25) picked up one boat seven hours after the attack and located the other boat two hours later. The *Coos Bay* remained in the area looking for survivors until after the *Doheny* sank bow first at 1100 the next day. Two officers and four armed guards died in the attack. The survivors landed at Orford, Oregon.

The *Larry Doheny* was also unsuccessfully attacked by the *I-17* (Nishino) on 24 December 1941. The submarine fired its deck gun, but the *Doheny* escaped with no damage. NSS; WACR; WCSR; AG; Los Angeles *Times*, 24 December 1942; Rohwer, p. 281, places the attack at 41.30 N / 125.22 W; *War Action Casualties*, p. 119.

CHICKASAW CITY

D:	10-7-42	YB:	1920
T:	0502	Tn:	6,196
Pos:	34.00 S / 17.16 E	Dr:	17 ft.
Ow:	Isthmian SS Co.	C:	1,400 tons chrome ore, coffee,
Op:	Isthmian SS Co.		hides
M:	John Walker Monton	P:	steam
A:	1-4"; 4-20 mm; 4-30 cal.	S:	9.0

The *Chickasaw City* steamed from Cape Town, South Africa, to Port-of-Spain, Trinidad. About eighty-five miles south southwest of Cape Town, the *U-172* (Emmermann) spotted the freighter with dim navigation lights burning and steaming on a nonevasive course. Two torpedoes struck the starboard side and ruptured the double bottoms and the after deck. The watch below secured the engines as the ship rapidly sank in three minutes. The ship's complement of ten officers, twenty-seven men, eleven armed guards, and one passenger managed to launch one boat, two rafts, and two floats. The submarine commander questioned the survivors about the cargo before leaving. The corvette HMS *Rockrose* (K-51) rescued forty-two survivors thirty-eight hours later and landed them at Cape Town. Five men, one armed guard, and the passenger died.

Forty-one of the survivors of this attack were repatriated on the Dutch vessel *Zaandam*. She was torpedoed and eighteen more (twelve crew and six armed guards) died. The records concerning the deaths on the *Zaandam* are contradictory. NSS; WACR; WCSR; RWCS; AG; Rohwer, p. 263, places the attack at 34.15 S / 17.11 E.

JOHN CARTER ROSE

D:	10-7-42	YB:	1942
T:	2130	Tn:	7,191
Pos:	10.27 N / 45.37 W	Dr:	27 ft.
Ow:	WSA	C:	7,979 tons drummed gasoline
Op:	Barber West African Lines Inc.		and general
M:	Magnus Leknes	P:	steam
A:	1-5"; 1-3"; 4-20 mm	S:	11

The *John Carter Rose* was attacked by the *U-201* (Rosenberg) and the *U-202* (Poser) while en route from New York to Freetown, Sierra Leone, via Trinidad. The *U-201* fired a dud torpedo that struck the vessel and failed to explode. The master turned the vessel so that the stern gun would bear on the submarine. The freighter's gun crew fired four rounds at the U-boat before it submerged, and the ship began zigzagging to escape. Just over twenty-four hours later the *U-202* spotted the freighter and fired two torpedoes that struck her aft between the #2 and #3 holds. The explosion blew the hatch covers off and ignited the cargo of gasoline. The explosion did little structural damage, but it spread the fire from the bridge to the stack. The ship continued on course for twenty minutes before the master had the engines secured and ordered the crew to abandon the ship. Because of the fire, the ship's complement of eight officers, thirty-three men, and twenty armed guards had difficulty leaving the ship. After they had abandoned the vessel in three lifeboats, the *U-201* returned and fired a second dud torpedo and then fired seven shots into the vessel to hasten the sinking. The U-boat officers questioned the survivors and then handed them cigarettes, first aid supplies, and bread. The three lifeboats became separated that night. On 13 October, the American SS *West Humhaw* picked up one boat of eighteen survivors and landed them at Freetown. The Argentinean tanker *Santa Cruz* picked up the other boats containing thirty-five men and landed them at Recife, Brazil. Three of the gun crew and five men died in the attack.

NSS; WACR; WCSR; RWCS; AG; USMMA; Rohwer, p. 127.

SWIFTSURE

D:	10-8-42	YB:	1921
T:	2150	Tn:	8,206
Pos:	34.40 S / 18.25 E	Dr:	26 ft.
Ow:	Marine Transport Lines	C:	70,000 bbls. diesel oil
Op:	WSA	P:	steam
M:	Marion Jackson Mathews Jr.	S:	7.0
A:	2-30 cal.		

The *Swiftsure* was torpedoed twenty-five miles southeast of the Cape of Good Hope by the *U-68* (Merten). The tanker sailed independently from Abadan Island, Persia, to Cape Town, South Africa. Lookouts sighted a torpedo off the starboard side, and it struck at the #8 hold. The explosion ripped the hold open and the vessel caught fire. The master had the engines immediately secured as the crew raced to fight the flames. The crew battled the fire for thirty minutes and then abandoned ship. The eight officers and twenty-five men left the ship in the #1, #3, and #4 lifeboats. The boats remained near the *Swiftsure* for several hours with hopes they could return to the ship. The master and part of the crew returned the next day to determine whether the vessel could be salvaged, but she was still burning fiercely. At 0900 a British minesweeper rescued the men and took them to Cape Town. An attempt to tow the ship failed, and the *Swiftsure* sank about sixty-two hours after the initial torpedo struck. All hands survived the attack.

Fifteen men of the *Swiftsure*, while being repatriated, lost their lives on the Dutch MV *Zaamdam* when she was torpedoed and sunk on 2 November. NSS; WACR; WCSR; AG; Rohwer, p. 264; *War Action Casualties*, p. 120.

COLORADAN

D:	10-9-42	YB:	1921
T:	1055	Tn:	6,567
Pos:	35.47 S / 14.34 E	Dr:	28 ft. 2 in.
Ow:	American Hawaiian SS Co.	C:	2,500 tons manganese, gold ore,
Op:	U.S. Maritime Commission		general
M:	Robert Hugh Murphy	P:	steam
A:	1-4"; 1-6 lber.; 4-20 mm; 2-30 cal.	S:	10.0

The *Coloradan* sailed independently from Bandar Shahpur, Persia, to Port-of-Spain, Trinidad. The ship had maintained a zigzag course for over four days, but the *U-159* (Witte) worked its way into a favorable firing position and struck the ship with a torpedo between the #5 and #6 hatches. The explosion destroyed the bulkhead between the two holds, blew out the double bottom, and damaged the shaft alley. The watch below secured the main engines as the ship quickly sank. In minutes water splashed across the decks, and the ship plunged stern first beneath the waves in four minutes. The ship's complement consisted of nine officers, thirty men, and fifteen armed guards. Six of the ship's crew never reached the lifeboats and died. The survivors managed to launch two lifeboats and all four rafts, but two of the rafts drifted away before they could be used. The *U-159* surfaced and motioned the #1 boat to come over. The third mate answered questions concerning the ship and cargo. A German officer, thought to be the captain, gave the men in the boat their coordinates and wished them a "pleasant voyage and good liberty." The two lifeboats took the men off the rafts, and the survivors divided equally among the two boats. The chief mate had twenty-five men in boat #1 and the master had twenty-three men in boat #2. The boats sailed together but became separated on the afternoon of 10 October. The destroyer HMS *Active* (H-14) rescued the men in the #2 lifeboat on 11 October. A fishing boat towed the other boat to Thorne Bay, South Africa, on 19 October.

Six of the men of the *Coloradan* were lost on the *Zaamdam* while being repatriated. NSS; WACR; WCSR; AG; TF; Rohwer, p. 264.

EXAMELIA

D:	10-9-42	YB:	1920
T:	0348	Tn:	5,081
Pos:	34.52 S / 18.30 E	Dr:	25 ft.
Ow:	American Export Lines	C:	5,776 tons chrome ore, jute,
Op:	American Export Lines		hemp
M:	Andrew Tulenko	P:	steam
A:	1-4"; 4-20 mm; 2-30 cal.	S:	10.0

The *Examelia* sailed independently from Colombo, Ceylon, to Cape Town, South Africa, and proceeded in complete darkness on a nonevasive course. Twenty miles south of the Cape of Good Hope a torpedo fired by the *U-68* (Merten) struck on the starboard side amidships. The torpedo struck at the bulkhead between the fireroom and the engine room. The blast stopped the engines immediately and damaged the hull so extensively that the ship sank in seven minutes. Forty-three of the eight officers, thirty men, and thirteen armed guards on board left the ship in two lifeboats, four rafts, and two floats. The #2 lifeboat could not be successfully launched and went down with the ship, taking two men along. The #4 boat also capsized because of the ship's rapid sinking, and another man drowned. The remaining forty men in the #1 boat righted the #4 boat and distributed the men between the two. The officers in the *U-68* questioned the men in the boats and rafts before leaving. The SS *John Lykes* rescued these men and took them to Port Elizabeth, South Africa. Two officers, six men, and three armed guards died in the attack. Fifteen of the forty men from *Examelia*, being repatriated on the ore carrier *Zaamdam*, died when the *U-174* torpedoed her.

The figures of deaths on the *Zaamdam* are extremely contradictory within the sources. NSS; WACR; WCSR; RWCS; AG; TF; McCoy, pp. 127-137; Rohwer, p. 264.

STEEL SCIENTIST

D:	10-11-42	YB:	1921
T:	1912	Tn:	5,688
Pos:	05.48 N / 51.39 W	Dr:	20 ft.
Ow:	Isthmian SS Co.	C:	200 tons general, 1,800 tons salt
Op:	Isthmian SS Co.		ballast
M:	Karl O. Bornson	P:	steam
A:	1-4"; 4-20 mm; 2-30 cal.	S:	11.0

On 22 September, the *Steel Scientist*, bound from Cape Town, South Africa, for Paramaribo, Surinam, was struck by a torpedo fired by the *U-514* (Auffermann). The torpedo hit the zigzagging ship on the starboard side in the #4 hold. The explosion carried away the radio antennas, stopped the engines, started a fire on the poop deck, and caused the vessel to settle rapidly. The master ordered the men to their abandon ship stations. The chief engineer reported to the bridge that the engine room could not be entered because ammonia fumes were leaking from the destroyed ice machinery. With this knowledge, the master ordered the ship abandoned at 1925. Three boats and the master's gig got away successfully. All but one of the ten officers, twenty-eight men, and nine armed guards escaped. The boilers exploded at 1930 showering the gig with debris. Less than twenty minutes later the *U-514* put a second torpedo in the ship aft of the bridge, and she plunged bow first beneath the water at 2000. The master and the radio operator in the sixteen-foot gig did not join the other three boats. On 19 October, they landed near New Amsterdam, British Guiana, eight days after the attack. The other three boats made landfall in Paramaribo, British Guiana, on the 20th.

NSS; WACR; WCSR; AG; TF; Rohwer, p. 128, places the attack at 05.48 N / 51.50 W.

PAN GULF

D:	10-12-42	YB:	1918
T:	1417	Tn:	5,599
Pos:	10.01 N / 61.50.16 W	Dr:	16 ft.
Ow:	Pan Atlantic SS Co.	C:	none
Op:	Pan Atlantic SS Co.	P:	steam
M:	James Watson Blackwood	S:	9.5
A:	1-4"; 4-20 mm; 4-50 cal.; 2-30 cal.		

On 2 November, the *Pan Gulf* sailed from Trinidad, BWI, to Fort Amsterdam, Dutch Guiana. While proceeding in Convoy TAG-18-S, she struck a mine. The vessel veered out of the swept channel and struck an American mine on the port side. The explosion broke steam lines and extensively damaged the #2 oil tank

and the forward hold. The eight officers, thirty men, and twenty-one armed guards on board did not abandon ship, and the extensively damaged freighter returned to Port-of-Spain, Trinidad, under her own power.

WACR; WCSR; AG; TF.

SUSANA

D:	10-13-42	YB:	1914
T:	2010	Tn:	5,929
Pos:	53.41 N / 41.23 W	Dr:	unknown
Ow:	Madrigal and Co.	C:	unknown
Op:	Madrigal and Co.	P:	steam
M:	Jose Ayesa	S:	6.0
A:	1-4"; 4-50 cal.; 2-30 cal.		

The *Susana* sailed in Convoy SC-104 bound from New York for Cardiff, Wales. In rough seas the *U-221* (Trojer) fired a torpedo that struck the starboard side, forward of the #5 hatch. The stern rapidly settled, preventing the armed guards from manning the stern gun. The crew of forty-two merchant crewmen and the sixteen armed guards had to immediately leave the ship, which sank within minutes. Six armed guards managed to launch one boat, and the remaining men jumped into the water. The rough seas prevented the British rescue ship SS *Gothland* from launching a boat. The rescue vessel maneuvered carefully to pull the men from the water. The *Gothland* saved six of the armed guards and fifteen of the merchant crew within an hour.

NSS; AG; Rohwer, p. 128.

WINONA

D:	10-16-42	YB:	1919
T:	1520	Tn:	6,197
Pos:	11.00 N / 61.10 W	Dr:	27 ft. 7 in.
Ow:	Weyerhaeuser SS Co.	C:	8,000 tons coal
Op:	WSA	P:	steam
M:	John Beale Rynbergen	S:	8.0
A:	yes but unknown		

The *Winona* sailed in convoy from Port-of-Spain, Trinidad, to Rio de Janeiro, Brazil. While steaming among sixteen other merchant vessels, she took station in the center line, station #72, directly astern the commodore's ship. Just to starboard of the *Winona* a torpedo struck the bow of the British SS *Castle Harbour*. About thirty seconds later a torpedo fired by the *U-160* (Lassen) struck the starboard side of the *Winona* at the #2 hold. The explosion blew the hatch covers off and created a hole sixty-eight feet by twenty-eight feet. The #1 and #2 holds flooded and the #3 hold had a slight leak. The master immediately went to his cabin to secure confidential documents. When he returned to the bridge, he discovered that the man at the helm had abandoned his station, causing the ship to veer out of line. The master stopped the engines immediately and took the helm. The convoy had executed a turn to port, and the master found his ship heading toward the port quarter of the SS *Austvangen*. The *Winona*'s bow grazed the stern of this ship and fortunately did no serious damage to either. The master soon discovered the vessel could make port and restarted the engines. None of the freighter's complement of eight officers, thirty-three men, and fifteen armed guards abandoned ship. The *Winona*, listing badly and down by the head, reached Port-of-Spain the next day. All hands survived the attack.

NSS; WACR; WCSR; TF; Rohwer, p. 129.

ANGELINA

D:	10-17-42	YB:	1934
T:	2145	Tn:	4,772
Pos:	49.39 N / 30.20 W	Dr:	16 ft.
Ow:	A. H. Bull SS Co.	C:	1,500 tons sand ballast
Op:	U.S. Maritime Commission	P:	steam
M:	William Duncan Goodman	S:	6.0
A:	1-4"; 4-20 mm; 2-30 cal.		

The *Angelina* sailed from Liverpool, United Kingdom, to New York in Convoy ON-137. The freighter straggled from the convoy, and heavy weather delayed her return to the formation. With a Canadian corvette in view, a torpedo fired from the *U-618* (Baberg) struck the *Angelina* on the starboard side of the #4 hold well below the waterline. The explosion disabled the engines, and the ship began to list to starboard. In heavy seas most of the eight officers, thirty men, and seventeen armed guards abandoned ship in the port lifeboat and two life rafts. The torpedo explosion had destroyed all the other boats and rafts. Twenty minutes after the first explosion a second torpedo entered the starboard side of the magazine and caused a violent explosion. Tremendous seas washed over the rafts and boats and swept men into the water. More than five hours after abandoning ship, the British rescue vessel *Bury* picked up six men on a raft and three others from the water. One of these men later died. Only one officer, three men, and four armed guards survived the attack.

NSS; WACR; WCSR; Rohwer, p. 129.

STEEL NAVIGATOR

D: 10-19-42
T: 1338
Pos: 49.20 N / 32.00 W
Ow: Isthmian SS. Co.
Op: Isthmian SS. Co.
M: Lars Jorgensen
A: 1-5"; 4-20 mm

YB: 1921
Tn: 5,718
Dr: 18 ft.
C: 2,000 tons sand ballast
P: steam
S: 10.5

On 9 October, the *Steel Navigator* departed Liverpool, United Kingdom, for New York in the thirty-six ship Convoy ON-137. On 17 October, foggy weather and a fear of collision prompted the master to drop out of the convoy. The ship encountered a raging storm for about two days that caused the sand ballast to shift and gave the ship a 40° list. The Navy gun crew later joined by the merchant crew shifted ballast for two days to correct the list to 12°. On the 19th, at 0730, the third mate sighted the *U-610* (von Freyberg) 400 yards off the starboard beam. After sounding the general alarm, the master turned the ship so that the submarine lay astern, and the gun crew fired two shots before the *U-610* disappeared. Eight hours later a torpedo struck between the #1 and #2 hatches, and the vessel rapidly settled by the head and sank in three minutes. Immediately the master ordered the eight officers, twenty-eight men, and sixteen armed guards to abandon ship. The men hastily launched the motor boat, and it swamped in the heavy seas. The #3 lifeboat could not get away before the ship plunged to the bottom and it also capsized, spilling in the water thirty-five men, including some of the gun crew. Eighteen of these men climbed onto a raft. The #2 boat got clear of the ship and picked several men out of the water. Officers on board the *U-610* questioned the survivors in the #2 boat before leaving the scene. Late that night the survivors righted the #3 boat and redistributed, leaving the #2 boat with seventeen men and the #3 boat with ten men. The lifeboats remained in the vicinity of the sinking until daylight as the storm continued. The boats eventually became separated. Seven days after the attack the destroyer HMS *Decoy* (H-75) sighted the #3 boat containing sixteen survivors (two officers, eight men, and six gun crew, one other man having died in the boat). The #2 boat was never found. A total of six officers, twenty men, and ten armed guards died.

The times given for the attack vary within the sources. NSS; WACR; WCSR; AG; TF; Rohwer, p. 129, places the attack at 49.45 N / 31.20 W.

REUBEN TIPTON

D:	10-23-42	YB:	1940
T:	0107	Tn:	6,829
Pos:	14.33 N / 54.51 W	Dr:	28 ft.
Ow:	Lykes Bros. SS Co.	C:	8,300 tons chrome ore, rubber,
Op:	WSA		general
M:	Giles Warren Hatch	P:	steam
A:	1-4"; 4-50 cal.; 2-30 cal.	S:	13.0

The *Reuben Tipton* sailed independently from Port Elizabeth, South Africa, to Trinidad, BWI. In rough seas the *U-129* (Witt) attacked the freighter. The first torpedo struck the starboard side of the #1 hold. The explosion blew off the hatch covers and buckled the deck. The watch below immediately secured the engines, and the armed guards went into action. The gun crew fired twenty rounds in the direction of the U-boat but never sighted it. The radio operator sent distress signals and received a reply. The ship settled by the head, but once the master determined the ship would not sink, he had the engines restarted and began steering a zigzag course. Proceeding at only three knots, the *U-129* had ample opportunity to maneuver for another attack. Four hours after the initial torpedo struck, the *U-129* launched two more torpedoes that hit the port side— one in the engine room and one in the #4 hold. These torpedoes demolished the midsection of the ship. The survivors of the nine officers, thirty-four men, and ten armed guards on board managed to launch one lifeboat and a raft even though the ship sank in about two minutes. The master and a seaman climbed on the raft, and a Navy patrol plane picked them up two days later and took them to Trinidad. The following day a British motor torpedo boat rescued seven officers, thirty-two men, and all the armed guards and landed them at Barbados. One officer and two men died on watch below.

NSS; WACR; WCSR; AG; RWSA.

DANIEL BOONE

D:	10-25-42	YB:	1942
T:	0832	Tn:	7,176
Pos:	off Panama	Dr:	25 ft.
Ow:	U.S. Maritime Commission	C:	5,000 tons general
Op:	American-Hawaiian Lines	P:	steam
M:	D. W. Hassell	S:	10.0
A:	1-4"; 1-3"; 4-50 cal.		

The *Daniel Boone* was proceeding from a Panamanian port to join her convoy when she struck a mine. The mine exploded at the stern causing slight damage but enough to end her voyage. The eight officers, thirty-four men, and eleven armed guards did not abandon ship, and the freighter was towed into port, repaired, and placed back in service. The *Daniel Boone* was transferred to the Navy in December 1943, and was commissioned the *Ara* (AK-136).

WACR; ONF; AG; TF; DANFS, 1:54.

ANNE HUTCHINSON

D:	10-26-42	YB:	1942
T:	1903	Tn:	7,176
Pos:	33.12 S / 29/03 E	Dr:	17 ft.
Ow:	WSA	C:	ballast, 8,000 bbls. oil
Op:	Sudden & Christenson Inc.	P:	steam
M:	John Wilhelm Stenlund	S:	12
A:	1-4"; 4-20 mm; 2-30 cal.		

The *Anne Hutchinson* sailed from Aden to Cape Town, South Africa, via Suez. As the ship steamed a zigzag course, lookouts spotted a torpedo fired by the *U-504* (Poske) that passed twenty yards ahead of the vessel. A second torpedo struck the starboard side abaft the engine room in the #4 hold. The explosion created a hole fourteen feet by sixteen feet, knocked out the electrical systems, broke the main shaft, and stopped the engines. The explosion, however, did not destroy the watertight bulkheads on either side of the hold. The blast also killed three men sitting on the #4 hatch. The *U-504* placed a second torpedo into the fireroom, causing the boilers to explode. The U-boat surfaced and fired a single shot at the freighter's midships house to hasten the crew to their boat stations. The surviving eight officers, twenty-nine crewmen, and seventeen armed guards abandoned the freighter in four lifeboats. The SS *Steel Mariner* rescued ten men in one boat six hours after the attack. On 28 October, the other three boats landed at Port Alfred, South Africa. The vessel stayed afloat and men from the South African Navy boarded her. A minesweeper and harbor tug attempted to tow the *Hutchinson*, but they did not have enough power to do so. The salvage crew dynamited the freighter to break her in two. The after part sank and the trawler HMS *David Haigh* (T-13) towed the forward half to Port Elizabeth on 1 November.

NSS; WACR; WCSR; RWCS; AG; Rohwer, p. 264, places the attack at 33.10 S/ 28.30 E.

PRESIDENT COOLIDGE

D: 10-26-42
T: 0935
Pos: Espíritu Santo, New Hebrides
Ow: American President Lines
Op: WSA
M: Henry Nelson
A: 1-5"; 4-3"; 12-20 mm

YB: 1931
Tn: 21,900
Dr: 32 ft.
C: 10,000 tons general
P: electric
S: 15.0

The *President Coolidge* sailed from Nouméa to Lunganville Bay, Santos Island, and accidentally wandered into a minefield. The ship communicated outside the harbor, and the master received no navigating instructions from a destroyer. The master did not wait for the pilot who was scheduled to take his ship around the mined area. As the ship approached, a signal station sent word for the *President Coolidge* to stop. The master tried to back engines but because of the vessel's high speed he was unsuccessful. The first mine struck the vessel on the port side amidships at the after fireroom under the double bottom. A second struck the ship thirty seconds later on the bottom at the engine room. The vessel had enough headway for the master to beach her, and she slowly sank. The master ordered the crew and passengers to abandon ship. Besides the cargo, the vessel had on board 5,050 U.S. troops, along with the ship's complement of 19 officers, 271 men, and 51 armed guards. The men utilized all twenty lifeboats and eight life rafts to abandon ship. Some of the men swam the short distance to shore. Four of the passengers and one of the crew died during the mishap. The ship gradually filled with water and slipped off the side of the reef into deep water at 1045.

The master's papers were suspended and a Court of Inquiry cleared him of any wrongdoing. NSS; WACR; WCSR; AG; RWSA; Cameron, pp. 18-20.

GURNEY E. NEWLIN

D: 10-27-42
T: 1910
Pos: 54.51 N / 30.06 W
Ow: Union Oil Co. of Cal.
Op: WSA
M: Herman Leon Dahllof
A: 1-4"; 1-3"; 2-20 mm; 2-50 cal.;
     2-30 cal.

YB: 1942
Tn: 8,225
Dr: 28 ft. 6 in.
C: 92,000 bbls. gasoline and
     kerosene
P: steam
S: 8.5

The *Gurney E. Newlin* sailed with the forty-seven ship Convoy HX-212 en route from New York to Manchester, England. The *U-436* (Seibicke) attacked the convoy with a five-torpedo spread. One of these torpedoes struck the *Newlin*'s engine room on the port side, and she immediately began to settle by the stern.

The ship's complement of eight officers, thirty-two crewmen, and nineteen armed guards left the ship within twenty minutes in the #1, #2, and #4 lifeboats and two rafts. All got away except the officer and two men on watch in the engine room. Despite the nature of the cargo, the ship did not catch fire. The Canadian corvette *Alberni* (K-103) rescued the master and eleven other men in the #2 boat. The Canadian SS *Bic Island* picked up the other forty-four survivors within thirty minutes. The following day the *U-606* (Döhler) sank the tanker with a coup de grâce shot. Thirty-one of the crew and thirteen armed guards died when the *Bic Island* was torpedoed by the *U-224* (Kosbadt) in the same convoy and was sent down with all hands.

NSS; WACR; WCSR; AG; Rohwer, p. 130, places the attack at 54.32 N / 31.02 W; *War Action Casualties*, p. 123.

PAN NEW YORK

D:	10-29-42	YB:	1938
T:	0120	Tn:	7,701
Pos:	53.30 N / 23.00 W	Dr:	28 ft.
Ow:	Pan American Petroleum Co.	C:	104,740 bbls. aviation gasoline
Op:	Pan American Petroleum Co.	P:	steam
M:	Hedley Vernon Thompson	S:	8.0
A:	1-5"; 1-3"; 6-20 mm; 2-30 cal.		

On 18 October, the *Pan New York* departed New York for Glascow, Scotland, in Convoy HX-212. The *U-624* (Graf von Soden-Fraunhofen) torpedoed the tanker while she steamed in convoy station #43. The torpedo struck the #3 tank on the port side and blew flaming gasoline all over the after part of the vessel. The wind, coming from the port bow, blew the flames over nearly the entire length of the tanker, and the ventilators aft sucked the fire down below to the engine room and crew's quarters. As the vessel lost power she swung around and the flames spread forward. Gasoline also poured into the sea, leaving the water ablaze on the leeward side of the vessel. The flames destroyed or made inaccessible nearly all the lifeboats and rafts, and the heavy seas prevented the remaining boat from being launched. With the general alarm ringing, the remnants of the eight officers, thirty-one crewmen, and seventeen armed guards, fourteen in all, remained aft in the messroom. For more than nine hours they waited, and at daylight they jumped into the water with a corvette 500 feet off the starboard side. The Canadian corvette *Rosthern* (K-169) rescued thirteen men, but one of these later died. The Canadian corvette *Summerside* (K-141) rescued two other men. Only one member of the gun crew, one officer, and twelve men survived the ordeal. The escorts sank the *Pan New York* with gunfire and depth charges. She disappeared beneath the waves at 1204.

NSS; WACR; WCSR; RWCS; AG; Rohwer, p. 130, places the attack at 53.58 N / 23.56 W; *War Action Casualties*, p. 124.

WEST KEBAR

D:	10-29-42	YB:	1920
T:	1915	Tn:	5,620
Pos:	14.57 N / 53.37 W	Dr:	25 ft. 2 in.
Ow:	American West African Line	C:	7,750 tons manganese ore, palm
Op:	WSA		oil, rubber, mahogany
M:	Dwight A. Smith	P:	steam
A:	1-4"; 4-20 mm; 2-30 cal.	S:	9.0

The *West Kebar* sailed independently from Freetown, Sierra Leone, to St. Thomas, Virgin Islands. The ship, steaming on a nonevasive course, made an easy target for the *U-129* (Witt). A torpedo struck the starboard side amidships in the #3 deep tank. The explosion blew a hole twenty-five feet by thirty feet in the bulkhead, destroyed the starboard lifeboats, cut the power, and stopped the engines. The ship's complement of nine officers, twenty-nine men, and eleven armed guards as well as eight passengers left the freighter in two lifeboats and one life raft within twenty minutes. The #4 boat had thirty-four survivors, the #2 boat had eight, and the life raft had twelve. The *U-129* fired a second torpedo into the port side, causing the vessel to break in two and sink rapidly. In a heavy rain the *U-129* surfaced, and an officer first questioned crewmen and then hailed the master over to the submarine for questioning. The #2 boat had to be bailed for two hours but pulled away immediately from the *Kebar*. After nine days, this boat landed on a small island off Guadeloupe. A small boat took the survivors to Guadeloupe the next day. Twelve days after the attack, a British patrol boat spotted the #4 lifeboat seven miles north of Barbados. The men on the raft were not rescued until 18 November, by the Spanish SS *Campero*. Despite the attack and the subsequent ordeal faced by the men in the boats and the raft, only the officer and two men on watch below died.

The sources conflict regarding the ship's complement. NSS; WACR; WCSR; RWCS; AG.

GEORGE THATCHER

D:	11-1-42	YB:	1942
T:	1905	Tn:	7,175 tons
Pos:	01.45 S / 07.30 E	Dr:	28 ft. 6 in.
Ow:	WSA	C:	4,005 tons vehicles, Army cargo,
Op:	Moore-McCormick Lines		gasoline, road building
M:	Henry Olin Billings		equipment
A:	1-4"; 1-3"; 4-20 mm	P:	steam
		S:	8.2

On 13 September, the *George Thatcher* departed Charleston, South Carolina, bound for Point Norre, French Equatorial Africa, via Freetown and Takoradi.

The freighter had two Free French corvettes as escorts, and for two days submarines shadowed the group. One-half hour after sunset a torpedo fired by the *U-126* (Bauer) struck the starboard side between the #2 and #3 hatches. A second torpedo struck a minute later at the #4 hatch, setting fire to the gasoline stored in the after holds, destroying the #3 boat, and blowing the rafts overboard. The men hurried to their abandon ship stations, and thirty minutes after the initial explosion the master ordered the ship abandoned. The freighter, still under way, took a sharp list to starboard and began to settle by the head as she traveled in circles. The *Thatcher* later righted herself, facilitating the launching of the #1, #2, and #4 boats. The ship's complement consisted of eight officers, thirty-one men, and fifteen armed guards, along with twelve Army passengers. Two officers, three enlisted men, five armed guards, and eight Army passengers failed to abandon ship. The corvettes picked up the survivors, including two men in the water, and landed them at Point Noire on 3 November. The *Thatcher* continued burning but did not sink until 3 November at 0800.

NSS; WACR; WCSR; AG; Rohwer, p. 132, places the attack at 01.45 S / 07.40 W.

HAHIRA

D:	11-3-42	YB:	1920
T:	0745	Tn:	6,855
Pos:	54.15 N / 41.57 W	Dr:	27 ft
Ow:	Atlantic Refining Company	C:	8,985 tons fuel oil
Op:	Atlantic Refining Company	P:	steam
M:	James Bronna Elliott	S:	4.0
A:	1-4"; 1-3"; 4-20 mm; 2-30 cal.		

On 24 October, the *Hahira* sailed from New York bound for the United Kingdom as part of the eastbound Convoy SC-107. Four hundred miles south of Cape Farewell the *U-521* (Bargsten) attacked and sank the tanker. The *Hahira* was one of fifteen vessels attacked and sunk by the fifteen submarine group "Violet" that stretched from south of Greenland to Newfoundland. The *Hahira* took station #82 on the outboard starboard column of the convoy and later took station #81 when a U-boat torpedoed the leading ship. After three days of attacks, lookouts on the tanker spotted a torpedo track pass ten yards forward of the bow and another pass off the stern. A third torpedo struck the vessel on the starboard side in the #9 tank. The explosion virtually blew the after part of the ship away and sprayed blazing fuel oil over the after part of the vessel. The fire suppressant system managed to put out most of the fire, allowing the crew to abandon ship. With the engines secured, the ship's complement of eight officers, thirty crewmen, and eighteen armed guards began leaving the ship five minutes after the torpedo struck. Using three lifeboats and a raft, the crew, with the exception of two men and one armed guard, safely got away. Forty-five minutes later the British rescue vessel SS *Stockport* rescued the men and landed them in

Reykjavik. The *U-521* laid off at 800 yards and fired two more torpedoes to finish off the tanker.

The escorts also claim to have sunk the ship by gunfire. Records indicate that the British Admiralty chartered the vessel in some way (time or trip charter), but she evidently still remained an American-flagged vessel. NSS; WACR; WCSR; AG; RWSA; Rohwer, p. 133; Waters, pp. 16, 21-77; *War Action Casualties*, p. 125.

EAST INDIAN

D:	11-3-42	YB:	1918
T:	1650	Tn:	8,159
Pos:	37.23 S / 13.34 E	Dr:	29 ft. 6 in.
Ow:	Ford Motor Co.	C:	9,600 tons manganese ore, tea,
Op:	U.S. Maritime Commission		general
M:	Ovide L. St. Marie	P:	diesel
A:	1-4"; 2-50 cal.; 2-30 cal.	S:	11.5

The *East Indian*, en route from Cape Town, South Africa, to New York via Punta Arenas, was torpedoed and sunk by the *U-181* (Lüth) 300 miles southwest of the Cape of Good Hope. The *U-181* followed the zigzagging freighter for some time before putting two torpedoes in the starboard side at the after bulkhead of the engine room. The crew never had the chance to secure the engines, and the ship sank in two minutes while still under way. The ship had eight officers, thirty-nine men, fifteen armed guards, and twelve passengers on board. Seventeen of these men managed to launch the #4 lifeboat, while thirty-four others jumped overboard and swam to four rafts. The master, fifteen crewmen, and seven passengers never left the ship. At 1700, the *U-181* surfaced and the German officers questioned the third mate. At the end of the questioning, one German officer offered the men water and gave them a course to Cape Town. The British SS *Durando* spotted the #4 boat 135 miles south of Cape Town thirteen days after the attack. The men on the rafts, however, were never seen again. The radio operator, one of the survivors in the boat, later died ashore from shock and exposure. A total of six officers, twenty-eight men, eleven armed guards, and ten passengers died.

The sources conflict on the complement. The Isthmian SS Co. acted as agents during the voyage. NSS; WACR; WCSR; RWCS; AG; Rohwer, p. 265.

JOHN H. B. LATROBE

D:	11-4-42	YB:	1942
T:	0900	Tn:	7,176
Pos:	74.37 N / 02.00 E	Dr:	26 ft.
Ow:	U.S. Maritime Commission	C:	general
Op:	Calmar SS Corp.	P:	steam
M:	A. L. Hodgdon	S:	11
A:	1-5"; 1-3"; 8-20 mm; 2-30 cal.		

The *John H. B. Latrobe*, sailing independently from New York to Archangel, USSR, via Reykjavik, Iceland, was attacked and damaged by German aircraft. Eight German torpedo planes sighted the freighter. The master successfully maneuvered the ship to avoid the torpedoes, but during the attack the planes sprayed the ship with machine gun fire all over the superstructure. Only slightly damaged, the freighter returned to Reykjavik on the advice of the armed guard officer. The ship's complement consisted of nine officers, thirty-one men, and twenty-five armed guards. Three of the armed guards were injured by the gunfire.

NSS; WACR; WCSR; AG; ONF.

WILLIAM CLARK

D:	11-4-42	YB:	1942
T:	1158	Tn:	7,176
Pos:	71.05 N / 13.20 W	Dr:	24 ft.
Ow:	U.S. Maritime Commission	C:	6,337 tons aircraft, tires, tanks,
Op:	Isthmian SS Co.		ammunition
M:	Walter Edmund Elian	P:	steam
A:	1-5"; 1-3"; 8-20 mm	S:	10.5

The *William Clark*, en route from Hvalfiord, Iceland, to Murmansk, USSR, was torpedoed by the *U-354* (Herbschleb). The ship had steamed in Convoy BX-35 from Boston to Halifax and then became part of Convoy SC-99 from Halifax to Iceland. The freighter then traveled alone, one of ten vessels selected to sail without escort to Murmansk. The tremendous losses of the earlier convoys prompted the Allies to try this, but none of the ten vessels arrived at their destination. Lookouts on the *Clark* spotted no escorts, even though the master had been advised they would be in contact every five hours. The first torpedo struck the port side amidships at the engine room, filling the machinery space with water. The complement of eight officers, thirty-three men, and thirty armed guards abandoned the Liberty ship in three lifeboats. The three boats with sixty-six men on board remained together, with the motorboat towing the other two. In moderate seas, the tow lines later had to be cast off because of the danger of swamping and the boats became separated. The trawler HMS *St. Elstan* (FY-240) rescued twenty-six survivors after three days, and the trawler HMS *Cape Palliser* (FY-256) rescued fifteen more with two dead. The #1 boat containing the master and twenty-two other men was never seen again. A total of four officers, fourteen men, and thirteen armed guards perished.

NSS; WACR; AG; Moore, p. 305; Rohwer, p. 201, puts the attack at 71.02 N / 13.05 W.

METON

D:	11-5-42	YB:	1919
T:	0310	Tn:	7,027
Pos:	12.25 N / 69.20 W	Dr:	28 ft.
Ow:	Paco Tankers Inc.	C:	66,000 bbls. bunker C fuel oil
Op:	Pennsylvania Shipping Co.	P:	steam
M:	Victor Axel Hagstrom	S:	8
A:	1-4"; 4-30 cal.		

On 4 November, the *Meton* departed Curaçao, NWI, en route to Cienfuegos, Cuba. Sailing as part of the twenty-five ship Convoy TAG-18, the *Meton* took station as the lead ship in the outside column, starboard side. Three torpedoes fired by the *U-129* (Witt) struck the tanker in quick succession. They struck at the #4, the #6, and the #9 tanks. The first two explosions started fires, but when the last torpedo hit, the explosion extinguished the flames. The ship settled slowly, allowing the eight officers, thirty men, and twelve armed guards ample time to leave the ship. The explosions had wrecked three of the lifeboats and all the rafts, so the crew left the ship loaded into one lifeboat. The Dutch motor torpedo boat #23 rescued the survivors and landed them at Curaçao. One of the merchant crew died in the attack. The *Meton* sank ten hours later.

The armed guards figures are contradictory within the sources. NSS; WACR states 10; WCSR; AG; Rohwer, p. 134; *War Action Casualties*, p. 126.

NATHANIEL HAWTHORNE

D:	11-7-42	YB:	1942
T:	2340	Tn:	7,176
Pos:	11.34 N / 63.26 W	Dr:	29 ft.
Ow:	U.S. Maritime Commission	C:	7,576 tons bauxite ore
Op:	Pacific Atlantic SS Co.	P:	steam
M:	Richard C. Brannan	S:	10
A:	1-4"; 1-3"; 4-50 cal.; 2-30 cal.		

While en route from Trinidad, BWI, to New York, the *Nathaniel Hawthorne* was struck by two torpedoes fired by the *U-508* (Staats). Traveling in Convoy

TAG-19, the freighter had steamed ahead and to port of her assigned position when a torpedo struck the port side at the #1 hold. Fifteen seconds later a second torpedo struck the same side in the engine room. The extensive damage amidships caused the ship to fill rapidly with water, settle by the bow, and sink within a minute. As the ship sank, the acetylene supply or refrigerator gas also exploded. The survivors among the ship's eight officers, thirty-two men, ten armed guards, and two passengers swam to four released life rafts, since there was no time to launch the boats. Only three from the gun crew, ten merchant seamen, and one passenger survived. The USS *Biddle* (DD-151) saved the survivors thirty-nine hours later, some 150 miles from the attack. The survivors landed at Trinidad.

NSS; WACR; WCSR; AG; Rohwer, p. 134. The armed guard officer Lt. Kenneth Muir won the Navy Cross for Valor by directing his men to safety as the ship sank.

LA SALLE

D:	11-7-42	YB:	1920
T:	2250 GWT	Tn:	5,462
Pos:	40.00 S / 21.30 E	Dr:	25 ft. 6 in.
Ow:	Waterman SS Corp.	C:	6,116 tons trucks, steel,
Op:	WSA		ammunition
M:	William Arthur Sillars	P:	steam
A:	1-4"; 4-20 mm; 2-30 mm	S:	unknown

The *La Salle* sailed from Balboa, Canal Zone, to Cape Town, South Africa, via Cape Horn. About 450 miles southeast of Cape Town, the *U-159* (Witte) torpedoed the freighter. The *U-159* followed the *La Salle* for five hours. At 2119 the U-boat fired and missed from one of the stern torpedo tubes. A second shot at 2250 atomized the ship. The resulting explosion created a fireball hundreds of yards high and completely destroyed the ship. The submarine's war diary states that bits of wreckage fell on the *U-159* for minutes afterwards and wounded three men on the submarine's conning tower. The explosion could be heard over 300 miles away. The destruction was so complete that not one of the eight officers, thirty-two men, and twenty armed guards on board survived the blast.

WACR; WCSR; AG; WJ.

EDGAR ALLEN POE

D:	11-8-42	YB:	1942
T:	1947	Tn:	7,176
Pos:	56 mi. SE Amadeé Light, Nouméa	Dr:	18 ft. 6 in.
Ow:	U.S. Maritime Commission	C:	6,000 tons general war cargo
Op:	Weyerhaeuser SS Co.	P:	steam
M:	Jack Edgerton	S:	12
A:	1-4"; 1-3"; 4-50 cal.; 2-30 cal.		

The *Edgar Allen Poe* sailed from Nouméa, New Caledonia, to Espirítu Santo Island. The *I-21* (Matsumura) fired a torpedo that hit the zigzagging ship on the port side and opened a hole twenty-eight feet by forty feet. The explosion destroyed the engine room and caused the boilers to explode. The damage was localized to this spot, and no water leaked into the cargo spaces. The *I-21* surfaced six minutes after the torpedo exploded. At 300 yards the armed guards opened fire with the ship's guns, firing two shots from the forward three-inch gun and one shot from the four-inch stern gun. One shot from each gun reportedly hit the submarine. At 2005 some of the ship's eight officers, thirty-two men, thirteen armed guards, and eighteen passengers left the ship in two lifeboats and a raft. The master, the rest of the crew, and the armed guards remained behind. The lifeboats towed the raft away from the ship, and they drifted during the night. Twenty-two hours later a plane sighted the men, and the USS *Russell* (DD-414) rescued the survivors and landed them at Nouméa. The ship stayed afloat and with the partial crew on board was later towed to Nouméa by the New Zealand minesweeper *Matai* and trawler *Kiwi* (T-102). Declared a CTL, the *Poe* was later used by the Navy as a storeship. One officer and one merchant seaman died on watch below.

NSS; WACR; WCSR; AG; Rohwer, p. 281; Moore, p. 82.

WEST HUMHAW

D:	11-8-42	YB:	1918
T:	2300	Tn:	5,527
Pos:	04.21 N / 02.42 W	Dr:	24 ft. 2 in.
Ow:	American West African Line	C:	5,915 tons lubricating oil,
Op:	American West African Line		general, trucks
M:	Torleif Christian Selness	P:	steam
A:	1-4"; 4-20 mm; 2-30 cal.	S:	8.5

On 8 November, the *West Humhaw* sailed in a three-ship convoy from Freetown, Sierra Leone, to Takoradi, Gold Coast, and was torpedoed by the *U-161* (Achilles). The torpedo struck the starboard side near the #3 hatch and blew a hole twenty-five feet by fifteen feet in the vessel. The master continued

on course and sent the crew to ascertain the damage as the ship slowly settled by the bow. Satisfied that the ship was mortally wounded, the master ordered the engines secured. The eight officers, thirty men, sixteen armed guards, and five passengers launched four lifeboats. The British motor launch #281 picked up the crew within forty-five minutes and landed them at Takoradi, Gold Coast. All hands survived the attack. The *West Humhaw* sank bow first at 2330.

NSS; WACR; WCSR; AG; TF; Rohwer, 135.

EXCELLER

D:	11-8-42	YB:	1941
T:	1642	Tn:	6,597
Pos:	Surcouf Beach, Algiers	Dr:	unknown
Ow:	American Export Lines	C:	anti-aircraft guns, trucks, army
Op:	American Export Lines		supplies, ammunition
M:	Hugh Smitzer	P:	steam
A:	1-4"; 2-20 mm; 2-50 cal.; 2-30 cal.	S:	at anchor

The *Exceller* sailed from the United States to Algeria and anchored one-half mile off Surcouf Beach east of Algiers. During an air attack two bombs struck near the freighter, one about 100 feet off the port beam and a second 20 feet off the starboard quarter. The last bomb exploded underneath the #6 hold, bodily lifted the vessel out of the water several feet, and sprayed the entire length of the deck with water. The concussion broke the stern post, buckled plates in the after peak tank, and damaged the shaft. Two feet of oil leaked from the after peak tank into the #6 hold. The vessel had carried a merchant crew of 32, 19 armed guards, 30 Coast Guardsmen, and 160 troops. All had disembarked except the ship's crew and the armed guards. None of these men reported an injury. By 13 November, the crew discharged all the remaining cargo. The vessel entered dry dock in Glasgow, Scotland, on 29 November, completed temporary repairs by 4 December, and sailed to New York two days later.

WACR; AG; McCoy, pp. 186-97.

MARCUS WHITMAN

D:	11-9-42	YB:	1942
T:	2120	Tn:	7,176
Pos:	05.45 S / 32.40 W	Dr:	16 ft.
Ow:	WSA	C:	none, ballast
Op:	Matson Navigation Co.	P:	steam
M:	Joseph Carl Pierce	S:	12.5
A:	1-4"; 4-50 cal.; 3-30 cal.		

On 27 October, the *Marcus Whitman* sailed alone from Cape Town, South Africa, to Dutch Guiana, South Africa. The Italian submarine *Leonardo Da Vinci* (Gazzana) struck the freighter with a torpedo in the ballasted #5 hold. The explosion blew the propeller and rudder away and buckled the deck. Without a means to steer, the ship turned completely around. The gun crew fired two shots from the four-inch gun and then secured the gun, not wanting to give away the ship's location in the dark. At 2135 the eight officers, thirty-three men, and eleven armed guards left the ship in four lifeboats. After abandonment a second torpedo struck the ship on the starboard side amidships, causing the boilers to explode. The *Da Vinci* then surfaced and fired twenty shells from its deck gun. The motor lifeboat, carrying fifteen men, reached the port of Natal forty-six hours after the attack. The other three boats, under sail, all landed within the next four hours with no casualties among the crew or the armed guards.

NSS; WACR; WCSR; AG; TF; Rohwer, p. 135.

EXCELLO

D:	11-13-42	YB:	1919
T:	0715	Tn:	4,969
Pos:	32.23 S / 30.07 E	Dr:	14 ft. 10 in.
Ow:	American Export Lines	C:	none
Op:	American Export Lines	P:	steam
M:	Maurice Almond Kent	S:	9
A:	1-4"; 4-20 mm; 2-30 cal.		

The *Excello*, en route from Port Said, Egypt, to Cape Town, South Africa, was torpedoed and sunk by the *U-181* (Lüth). The freighter proceeded on a nonevasive course until a torpedo struck the port side at the #5 hold. There seemed to be two explosions from the single torpedo. The blast brought down the mainmast, blew the hatch covers off the #4 and #5 holds, unseated the winches, and threw wreckage all over the boat deck. The engine room began to flood within three minutes, and the watch below secured the engines. The ship's complement of eight officers, thirty men, and thirteen armed guards abandoned the ship in three lifeboats. The falls of the #1 boat jammed, forcing several men to jump into the water and climb on board rafts. The ship sank stern first in under twenty minutes. The *U-181* surfaced and German officers questioned the men before the U-boat left. The boats became separated sometime shortly after the attack. On 14 November, one of the boats made landfall at Port St. John and another landed the following day. The British hospital ship *Atlantis* discovered the third boat with thirteen survivors after seven days at sea and landed the survivors at Cape Town. The explosion killed one armed guard, and the first engineer died from shock and suffocation after swallowing fuel oil.

NSS; WACR; WCSR; AG; Rohwer, p. 265; McCoy, pp. 164-77.

STAR OF SCOTLAND

D:	11-13-42	YB:	1887
T:	0815	Tn:	2,290
Pos:	26.30 S / 00.20 E	Dr:	12 ft. 3 in.
Ow:	East Asiatic Co.	C:	800 tons sand ballast
Op:	East Asiatic Co.	P:	sail
M:	Constantin Flink	S:	6
A:	unarmed		

The six-masted schooner *Star of Scotland* cleared Cape Town, South Africa, en route to Paranaguá, Brazil. The *U-159* intercepted the sailing vessel at sea and fired a warning shot over her from two miles abaft the port beam. A second shot fell short, but a third shot struck the ship and started a fire. The master immediately ordered the sails struck, and the crew began to abandon ship. The U-boat continued to shell the ship as the crew launched a boat. The master remained on board to save the ship's accounts as well as a sextant, a chronometer, and other gear. He then launched a second boat. The officers of the *U-159* questioned the crewmen, while two men in a rubber boat from the submarine boarded the schooner for provisions. After loading the provisions, they also took the clothing, accounts, and instruments from the master's boat. The *U-159* fired a total of thirty shells at the schooner. She sank on an even keel and plunged bow first at 1530. All the survivors transferred their gear into one lifeboat and set sail for Angola. On 1 December, they landed at Santa Maria Lighthouse, having made a voyage of 1,040 miles. Of the crew of seventeen, all survived except one man who drowned abandoning ship.

NSS; TF; Rohwer, p. 265.

LUCY EVELYN

D:	11-15-42	YB:	1917
T:	2150	Tn:	374
Pos:	12.00 N / 75.00 W	Dr:	11 ft. 1 in. (depth)
Ow:	Everett C. Lindsey	C:	unknown
Op:	Everett C. Lindsey	P:	sail
M:	Arthur Henry Gray	S:	unknown
A:	unarmed		

The American schooner *Lucy Evelyn* was reportedly shelled by an enemy submarine. None of the crew of seven was injured. The schooner (no damage indicated) made port at Barranquilla, Colombia.

WACR.

PARISMINA

D:	11-18-42	YB:	1908
T:	0305	Tn:	4,732
Pos:	54.07 N / 38.26 W	Dr:	25 ft.
Ow:	United Fruit SS Co.	C:	200 tons sand ballast
Op:	U.S. Maritime Commission	P:	steam
M:	Edward T. Davidson	S:	6.5
A:	1-4"; 4-20 mm; 2-30 cal.		

The *Parismina* sailed from the United Kingdom to Boston, Massachusetts, via Reykjavik. The freighter took station #74 in the thirty-two ship, nine-column Convoy ON-144. A torpedo fired by the *U-624* (Graf von Soden-Fraunhofen) struck the starboard side between the #2 hold and amidships. The explosion caused extensive damage because there was no cargo and no transverse bulkhead separated the #1 and #2 holds. The explosion also started a fire in the forward part of the ship. The survivors among the eight officers, forty men, twelve armed guards, and fifteen passengers on board found that the rough seas complicated the launching of the lifeboats. Two of the four boats swamped, and only two of the four life rafts were usable after the explosion. The British rescue ship *Perth* and the Netherlands corvette *Rose* (K-102) rescued only fifty-five survivors. Four officers, eleven men, two armed guards, and three passengers perished in the attack.

Fourteen of the passengers were the survivors of the *Hahira*; NSS; WACR; WCSR; AG; Rohwer, p. 137.

BRILLIANT

D:	11-18-42	YB:	1930
T:	0503	Tn:	9,131
Pos:	50.42 N / 45.50 W	Dr:	28 ft. 5 in.
Ow:	Standard-Vacuum Oil Co.	C:	90,704 bbls. fuel oil
Op:	WSA	P:	diesel
M:	Soren Sorensen	S:	9.5
A:	1-4"; 1-3"; 4-20 mm; 2-30 cal.		

On 9 November, the *Brilliant* departed New York bound for Belfast, Ireland. She took station as the third ship in the seventh column (#73) of Convoy SC-109. The *U-43* (Schwantke) fired a four-torpedo spread, two at another freighter; the third missed the *Brilliant* and the fourth struck the starboard side between the #5 tank and the pump room. The watch below immediately secured the engines. The explosion extensively damaged the ship, opening a hole about forty feet in diameter in the side and destroying three tanks and causing leaks in three other tanks on the port side. The blast set the cargo on fire, and the whole ship abaft the bridge began to burn. The master, three other officers, three men, and two armed guards lowered a boat intending to stay with the tanker. The rough seas and the ship's headway caused this boat to swamp, tossing the men in the water. The rescue ship HMS *Bury* rescued these men. The surgeon on board the *Bury* denied the master's request to return to his ship, and these men later landed in Glasgow, Scotland. The men remaining on the *Brilliant*, in the charge of the junior third officer, put out the flames and at three knots brought the tanker into Buena Vista Bay, Newfoundland. The entire complement of nine officers, thirty-three men, and eighteen armed guards survived the attack. The *Brilliant* survived, but on 20 January 1943, while en route from St. John's, Newfoundland, to Halifax, she broke in two and sank after encountering heavy gales. Three officers, four men, and three armed guards died in this accident.

The junior third officer earned the Merchant Marine Distinguished Service Medal for bringing the ship into port. NSS; WACR; WCSR; AG; Rohwer, p. 138, gives the ship's position at 50.45 N / 45.53 W; *War Action Casualties*, p. 127.

YAKA

D:	11-18-42	YB:	1920
T:	0515	Tn:	5,432
Pos:	54.25 N / 29.30 W	Dr:	12.5 ft.
Ow:	Waterman SS Co.	C:	ballast
Op:	WSA	P:	steam
M:	Frank Lewis Murdock	S:	6.5
A:	1-3"; 4-20 mm; 2-50 cal.; 2-30 cal.		

The *Yaka* was torpedoed by the *U-522* (Schneider), while en route from Reykjavik, Iceland, to Halifax, Nova Scotia. Steaming in station #63 in Convoy ONS-144, the *Yaka* was struck by a torpedo on the starboard side between the #2 hold and the bridge. The explosion caused the foremast and the jumbo boom to fall across the deck and blew fragments of scrap iron ballast through the port side. The complement of eight officers, thirty-three men, and eleven armed guards abandoned the ship in three lifeboats, the fourth boat having been smashed by the explosion. One of the remaining boats jammed in the falls, then broke clear twenty feet above the water and luckily landed upright. The British corvette HMS *Vervain* (K-190) rescued all hands and landed them at St. John's, Newfoundland. The *U-522* sank the *Yaka* with a coup de grâce shot two hours after the initial attack.

NSS; WACR; WCSR; AG; Rohwer, p. 137. German records place the sinking at 54.07 N / 58.26 W. The *U-624* (Graf von Soden-Fraunhofen) also claimed the *Yaka*, but according to Rohwer the *U-522* sank the freighter.

PIERCE BUTLER

D: 11-20-42
T: 1340
Pos: 29.40 N / 36.35 E
Ow: U.S. Maritime Commission
Op: Calmar SS Co.
M: George Patullo Moodie
A: 1-5"; 1-3"; 4-20 mm

YB: 1942
Tn: 7,191
Dr: 26 ft. 10 in.
C: 8,900 tons general
P: steam
S: 11

The *Pierce Butler* sailed independently from Cape Town, South Africa, to Suez. As it steered on a nonevasive course, two torpedoes fired by the *U-177* (Gysae) struck the starboard side, one forward of the engine room and the second aft at the #5 hatch. The radio operator immediately sent distress signals and received a reply. The gun crew fired eight rounds from the forward three-inch gun and seven rounds from the five-inch after gun in order to keep the U-boat submerged. The watch below secured the engines after ten minutes, and the eight officers, thirty-three men, and twenty-one armed guards on board cleared the ship at 1405 in the four lifeboats. The ship plunged stern first about five minutes later. Officers in the *U-177* questioned the third mate after the attack. The destroyer HMS *Fortune* (H-70) rescued all hands twenty hours later and landed them at Durban, South Africa.

NSS; WACR; WCSR; RWCS; AG; Rohwer, p. 265, places the attack at 29.40 N / 35.35 E.

ALCOA PATHFINDER

D: 11-22-42
T: 0140
Pos: 26.41 S / 33.08 E
Ow: Alcoa SS Co.
Op: WSA
M: Frederick Ferdinand Dumke
A: 1-5"; 4-20 mm; 2-30 cal.

YB: 1941
Tn: 6,796
Dr: 27 ft. 5 in.
C: 7,200 tons chrome ore and
        general
P: steam
S: 15

On 20 November, the *Alcoa Pathfinder* departed Beira, Mozambique, bound for Port Elizabeth, South Africa. The *U-181* (Lüth) spotted the ship silhouetted by a full moon and managed to get a clear shot that struck the port side abreast the engine room. The explosion blew debris nearly 200 feet into the air. The severe damage and the nature of the cargo caused the vessel to sink by the stern in three minutes. The ship, still under way, was making nearly four knots when she sank. Five members of the gun crew remained at the after gun until the last minute. Unable to fire a shot and with water rising, they went over the stern into the sea. The other crew members managed to launch one lifeboat and two rafts. Most of the ten officers, thirty-five men, fifteen armed guards, and one passenger safely got away from the ship. One officer and two men died on watch below. The passenger and one crewman failed to leave the ship, and the radio operator died from electrical shock trying to send distress signals. The survivors landed on the coast of Mozambique eighteen hours after the attack.

NSS; WACR; WCSR; AG; Rohwer, p. 265, places the attack at 26.45 S / 33.10 E.

CADDO

D:	11-23-42	YB:	1942
T:	0250	Tn:	10,172
Pos:	42.25 N / 48.27 W	Dr:	30 ft. 2 in.
Ow:	Socony-Vacuum Oil Co.	C:	105,000 bbls. fuel oil, 300
Op:	Socony-Vacuum Oil Co.		drums gasoline
M:	Paul B. Muller	P:	steam
A:	1-4"; 1-3"; 4-20 mm; 2-30 cal.	S:	12.5

On 11 November, the tanker *Caddo* sailed from Baytown, Texas, for Iceland. The tanker maintained a zigzag course, changing every six to nine minutes. From a distance of 500 yards, lookouts spotted a torpedo fired by the *U-518* (Wißßmann). The helmsman put the helm over hard to starboard, but the torpedo struck the port side at the pump room, just forward of the after bulkhead. The explosion ripped up the deck, tore a huge hole in the ship's side, flooded the pump room, and destroyed a lifeboat and a raft. The tanker began to settle by the stern, and the watch below immediately secured the engines. The survivors of the ship's complement of ten officers, thirty-two men, and seventeen armed guards boarded three lifeboats and three rafts thirty minutes after the initial explosion. The ship plunged stern first at 0420. The *U-518* surfaced ten minutes after the ship sank and took the master and chief officer as prisoners. Seventeen men sailed for land in the #1 boat, while the #2 and #3 boats had forty men between them. The #1 boat capsized twice during the night of 7 December, drowning seven men. Four other men in this boat died at sea. On 8 December, the Spanish MS *Motomar* rescued three crewmen and three armed guards. The #2 and #3 lifeboats were never seen again. Only two officers,

three men, and three armed guards lived through the ordeal. The master, however, died in a POW camp, and the chief officer was repatriated in 1945.

NSS; WACR; WCSR; RWCS; Rohwer, p. 139.

JEREMIAH WADSWORTH

D:	11-27-42	YB:	1942
T:	1725	Tn:	7,176
Pos:	39.25 S / 22.23 E	Dr:	31 ft.
Ow:	Marine Transport Lines Inc.	C:	8,008 tons war materiel, trucks
Op:	Isthmian SS Lines	P:	steam
M:	Arnt Magnusdal	S:	11.4
A:	1-4"; 1-3"; 4-20 mm		

About 270 miles south of Cape Agulhas, South Africa, the *U-178* (Ibbeken) attacked and sank the *Jeremiah Wadsworth*, which was sailing from New Orleans, Louisiana, to Bombay, India. The first torpedo struck the zigzagging ship on the starboard side at the #5 hold, and a second struck her seconds later at the #3 hold. A third torpedo missed, passing under the fantail. A fourth torpedo struck well forward of the bridge in the #1 hold. The explosions fatally wounded the ship and blew the #1 and #3 rafts and the #1 boat overboard. The officer on the bridge ordered the engines to be secured, but a jammed valve prevented this. The first two lifeboats launched by the crew swamped because of the ship's headway. The ship circled out of control until she plunged by the bow with the screws still revolving. While the ship circled at seven knots, the armed guards fired three "wild" shots from the four-inch gun, and one of the 20-mm guns on the bridge also fired at a periscope. Fifteen minutes after the explosions, the ship's complement of eight officers, thirty-five men, and fourteen armed guards abandoned the ship in three lifeboats and two rafts. The officers on the *U-178* questioned the ship's crew briefly, then the U-boat cruised away. All the survivors eventually combined into the three boats. Later that night the boats became separated. Eight days later the U.S. freighter *John Lykes* rescued nineteen men and landed them in Bermuda. An Allied ship picked up twenty men in a second boat and took them to Cape Town. The British Armed merchant cruiser *Alcantara* (F-88) rescued eighteen more in the third boat the next day and landed them at Simonstown, South Africa. All hands survived the attack.

The various sources give conflicting numbers for the ship's complement. NSS; WACR; WCSR; RWCS; Rohwer, p. 262.

ALASKAN

D:	11-28-42	YB:	1918
T:	0450	Tn:	5,364
Pos:	02.38 N / 28.58 W	Dr:	16 ft.
Ow:	American Hawaiian Line	C:	800 tons chrome ore
Op:	WSA	P:	steam
M:	Edwin Earle Greenlaw	S:	13.0
A:	1-5"; 1-3"; 4-20 mm; 2-30 cal.		

While en route from Cape Town, South Africa, to New York, the *Alaskan* was sunk by the *U-172* (Emmermann) with a torpedo and gunfire. The freighter maintained a zigzag course in heavy rain, and one of the ship's lookouts spotted wakes from two torpedoes. One of the torpedoes struck the vessel amidships on the port side; the second missed. The explosion destroyed the main engines and both port side lifeboats. It also knocked down both aerial antennas and the topmast and buckled the deck, destroying some of the deck gear and machinery. The ship quickly listed to port but did not sink. Twenty-five minutes after the initial explosion, the master ordered the ten officers, thirty-two men, and sixteen armed guards to abandon ship. The #3 lifeboat swamped when it reached the water and four men drowned. The other survivors left the ship in two boats and four rafts. The *U-172* surfaced and began shelling the ship at the rate of one shot a minute. The German gun crew fired about sixty rounds, hitting the ship about forty times. With the superstructure on fire, the ship rolled over and sank bow first at 0545. A German officer questioned the survivors and said, "Sorry we sank you, but this is war. Why don't you tell America to get out of the war." German sailors took the master onto the submarine and questioned him on the port side of the conning tower out of hearing range. On 13 December, the Spanish SS *Cilurum* rescued eleven merchant seamen and three armed guards and landed them at Las Palmas, Canary Islands. Twenty-nine others landed at Salinas, Paraguay. One armed guard later died in a hospital. After the sinking, nine men in a raft commanded by the master later transferred to a swamped lifeboat. They righted the boat and survived for thirty-nine days, making landfall 2,000 miles away in French Guiana. Two officers, four men, and one armed guard lost their lives.

The ship's complement numbers and casualty figures are contradictory within the sources. Also the sources conflict on the number of torpedoes that struck the freighter. NSS; WACR; WCSR; RWCS; AG; WJ; Rohwer, p. 139, puts the attack at 03.58 N / 26.19 W; Cook, pp. 21-25.

SAWOKLA

D:	11-29-42	YB:	1920
T:	2037	Tn:	5,882
Pos:	approx. 28.06 S / 54.00 E	Dr:	31 ft.
Ow:	WSA	C:	8,500 tons jute and gunnies
Op:	American Export Lines, Inc.	P:	diesel
M:	Carl Wink	S:	10.2
A:	1-4"; 4-20 mm; 2-30 cal.		

On 21 November, the *Sawokla* departed Colombo, Ceylon, bound for Cape Town, South Africa. The German raider *Michel* (Ruckteschell) spotted the freighter five hours before she made any attempt to attack. Ruckteschell put two torpedo boats into the water and forged ahead of his quarry. The freighter maintained a zigzagging course in hazy weather and choppy seas. The raider opened fire after the freighter showed a green light and began a new leg of her zigzagging course. Thinking the vessel was showing a recognition signal, Ruckteschell opened fire. The first salvo struck the bridge, killed the master and several other men, and destroyed the radio shack. As the raider continued firing on the hapless vessel, one of the torpedo boats came into range, circled the *Sawokla*, and sprayed the decks with machine gun fire. One member of the gun crew put up a feeble fight with a 20-mm gun until gunfire killed him. Although the attack lasted only about five minutes, shellfire from the raider had ignited the freighter from stem to stern. The *Sawokla* capsized and sank in eight minutes. The survivors among the eight officers, thirty-three men, thirteen armed guards, and five passengers on board had to jump overboard because shellfire had destroyed all the rafts and boats. The *Michel* rescued five officers, twenty men, five of the gun crew, and the five passengers, most within hours of the attack. The next day the raider rescued four armed guards. All went to prison camps after they landed in Singapore eighty-one days following the attack.

The casualties numbers conflict within the sources. NSS; WACR; WCSR; AG; Muggenthaller, pp. 246-49.

COAMO

D:	12-2-42	YB:	1925
T:	2018 GWT	Tn:	7,057
Pos:	near Bermuda	Dr:	24 ft. 8 1/4 in.
Ow:	Agwilines, Inc.	C:	unknown
Op:	WSA	P:	steam
M:	Nels Helgesen	S:	17.5
A:	1-4"; 2-3"; 6-20 mm		

On 11 November, the *Coamo* departed Gibraltar in Convoy MKF-3 en route to New York. On 1 December, 150 miles west of Ireland, she left the convoy and,

on orders of the British Admiralty, proceeded independently. Off Bermuda, the *U-604* (Höltring) maneuvered into a favorable position and fired a torpedo from 800 yards, striking the vessel under the bridge. The *Coamo* sank in about five minutes. The ship had 11 officers, 122 men, 37 armed guards, and 16 Army passengers on board. A few men escaped the ship in rafts, but the survivors were likely killed in the gale that swept the area for three days beginning on 3 December. All 186 men on board lost their lives. This was the greatest loss of merchant mariners on a U.S.-flagged merchant vessel during the war.

This ship had previously been time chartered by the U.S. Army Transport Service. The merchant vessel status of this ship is extremely confusing but is included. WACR; WCSR; WJ; RWSA; Washington *Post*, 19 February 1943; Rohwer, p. 139.

JAMES McKAY

D: 12-7-42   YB: 1941
T: 0139 GWT   Tn: 6,762
Pos: 57.50 N / 23.10 W   Dr: 28 ft. 5 in.
Ow: Lykes Bros. SS Co.   C: 12,790 tons general
Op: Lykes Bros. SS Co.   P: steam
M: Herman N. Olsen   S: unknown
A: 1-4"; 4-20 mm; 1-30 cal.

On 3 December, the *James McKay* cleared Waban, Newfoundland, for Belfast, Ireland. She received instructions to join Convoy HX-217 at sea east of Newfoundland. Because a heavy gale developed, the freighter never managed to meet the convoy. Instead, the *U-600* (Zurmühlen) spotted the *James KcKay* and torpedoed her before midnight ship's time. Three torpedoes struck the ship—the first amidships under the stack and the other two seconds behind. The radio operator sent distress signals, the freighter immediately stopped, and two boats cleared the ship. Forty minutes later, the *U-600* moved to the ship's opposite side and put a coup de grâce shot into the ship. The blast threw smoke and water 300 feet high. The *McKay* remained afloat, however, and the *U-600* fired another torpedo at the ship seven minutes later, but it misfired. At 0219 GWT two heavy explosions occurred on the freighter and she sank. The entire ship's complement of ten officers, thirty-eight men, and fourteen armed guards perished in the attack. The survivors probably died in the gale that swept the area for several days.

The figures for the ship's complement are contradictory. WACR; WCSR; AG; WJ.

ALCOA RAMBLER

D:	12-14-42	YB:	1919
T:	2106	Tn:	5,500
Pos:	03.51 S / 33.08 W	Dr:	25 ft. 1 in.
Ow:	Alcoa SS Co.	C:	7,243 tons coal
Op:	Alcoa SS Co.	P:	steam
M:	Ernest Henke	S:	11
A:	1-5"; 4-20 mm		

On 5 December, the *Alcoa Rambler* sailed in convoy from Trinidad, Spain, to Santos, Brazil. She left the convoy to proceed independently and steered a zigzag course continuously for four days. The *U-174* (Thilo) fired a torpedo that struck the port side at the #3 hold. The explosion destroyed the bulkhead between this hold and the fireroom, and the ship developed an immediate list to port. Within five minutes the ship's complement of eight officers, thirty-two men, and fifteen armed guards began abandoning ship in two lifeboats and four rafts. The armed guards had no chance to fire at the submarine, and nine of these men jumped into the water. After the crew departed, the *U-174* fired another torpedo into the port side amidships. The latter explosion broke the ship in two and sent flames 100 feet in the air. One lifeboat with twenty-five survivors, commanded by the master, reached Natal on 17 December. The second lifeboat with twenty-nine men arrived eleven hours later. The only death was a seaman who jumped overboard and drowned.

NSS; WACR; WCSR; TF; Rohwer, p. 141.

DONA AURORA

D:	12-25-42	YB:	1939
T:	0730	Tn:	5011
Pos:	02.02 S / 35.17 W	Dr:	25 ft. 3 in.
Ow:	De La Rama SS Corp.	C:	hides, manganese ore, coffee,
Op:	U.S. Maritime Commission		wool
M:	Natalio C. Ventoso	P:	steam
A:	1-4"; 2-50 cal.; 2-30 cal.	S:	11.5

About 200 miles off the coast of Brazil the Philippine-registered and American-flagged vessel *Dona Aurora* was torpedoed and sunk by the Italian submarine *Enrico Tazzoli* (Fecia di Cassato). The ship sailed from Cape Town, South Africa, to Baltimore, Maryland. As the vessel steamed a zigzagging course, lookouts on board spotted a torpedo's wake. The master ordered hard aport, but the torpedo struck the engine room, disabling the ship. Fatally damaged, the ship began sinking rapidly and slid beneath the water in fifteen minutes. The ship's complement consisted of seven officers, forty men, twelve armed guards, along with twelve passengers. Most of the crew managed to get away in one boat and three rafts. The Italian submarine surfaced near the lifeboat containing the master and some other officers. An officer on the submarine selected two passengers to come on board. The *Tazzoli* later rescued an armed guard out of the water. These three men were held as POWs. A patrol plane spotted the boat with fifty survivors, and the British SS *Testbank* rescued them on 27 December. On 3 January, the USS *Humbolt* (AVP-21) rescued ten more men. Five other survivors reached the mouth of Pacatuba River in Brazil after thirty days on a raft. One of the men on the raft drowned trying to swim ashore. A total of three men and one armed guard died.

The figures for the number of casualties and POWs conflict within the sources. The status of the vessel is confusing but it appears that WSA time chartered the vessel and then chartered it back to the De La Rama Company. NSS; AG; WCSR; RWSA; VSC; McCoy, pp. 179-81; Rohwer, p. 142.

ARTHUR MIDDLETON

D:	1-1-43	YB:	1941
T:	1430	Tn:	7,176
Pos:	8 miles off Oran, Algeria	Dr:	25 ft.
Ow:	WSA	C:	6,412 tons general and
Op:	Lykes Bros. SS Co.		explosives
M:	John V. Smith	P:	steam
A:	1-4"; 9-20 mm	S:	5

On 12 December, the *Arthur Middleton*, sailing from New York to Oran, North Africa, was torpedoed and sunk by the *U-73* (Deckert). The freighter had steamed within a few miles of her destination in Convoy UGS-3. At Casablanca eleven ships in this convoy, including the *Arthur Middleton*, broke away to proceed toward Oran and began to form a single line to enter the harbor. Before the ships could form the line, two separate explosions occurred in quick succession at the *Middleton*'s bow. The explosions lifted the bow of the freighter, ignited portions of the cargo, and sent water, hull plates, parts of the ship, and flames 1,000 feet into the air. The ship disintegrated from the #5 hatch to the bow. The after part of the freighter remained afloat. Of the ship's complement of nine officers, thirty-five men, twenty-seven armed guards, and twelve passengers, only three of the armed guards survived. These three men jumped overboard from the stern and were rescued by the British destroyer HMS *Boreas* (H-77) twenty-five minutes later.

There are some indications in the Army records that this vessel may have been chartered to the Army, but they are not conclusive and the evidence seems more likely that Lykes Bros. was the operator for the voyage. NSS; WACR; WCSR; AG; RWSA; Rohwer, p. 241.

WILLIAM WIRT

D:	1-7-43	YB:	1942
T:	1810	Tn:	5,190
Pos:	off Bougie, Africa	Dr:	20 ft.
Ow:	International Freighting Corp.	C:	16,000 cases 100 octane gas,
Op:	International Freighting Corp.		general
M:	Cameron Dudley Simmons	P:	steam
A:	1-5"; 1-3"; 4-20 mm	S:	7

Enemy aircraft attacked and damaged the *William Wirt*, while she was en route from Liverpool, England, to Phillipsville, Algeria, in Convoy KMS-7. Enemy reconnaissance aircraft first spotted the convoy on 7 January, and two hours later, seventy miles west of Phillipsville, torpedo planes and dive bombers began the attack. The *William Wirt* in convoy station #43 opened fire and claimed four planes. One plane dove on the ship from the port beam, and at 300 yards the gunners opened fire, striking the plane's wing and engine. Bursting into flames, the plane banked and attempted to drop its bombs on the freighter. One of the bombs struck the ship's side at the #1 hold, four feet above the waterline. The bomb entered the hold containing gasoline and TNT, but fortunately it failed to explode. Water eventually filled up this hold to the level of the hole in the hull plates. The vessel arrived in Phillipsville on the 9th, and after repairs were made, she sailed again on the 19th. The ship had on board eight officers, thirty-three men, twenty-one armed guards, and thirty-five passengers, none of whom reported an injury.

On 7 February 1943, near misses from enemy aircraft damaged the *Wirt*'s shaft and she had to return to Liverpool for repairs before sailing to the United States. NSS; WACR; WCSR; AG.

BROAD ARROW

D:	1-8-43	YB:	1918
T:	2340	Tn:	7,718
Pos:	07.21 N / 55.43 W	Dr:	29 ft.
Ow:	Socony-Vacuum Oil Co.	C:	85,111 bbls. diesel and fuel oil
Op:	Socony-Vacuum Oil Co.	P:	steam
M:	Percy Louis Mounter	S:	8
A:	1-5"; 2-30 cal.		

On 5 January, the *Broad Arrow* sailed in Convoy TB-1 from Port-of-Spain, Trinidad, to Rio de Janeiro, Brazil. As the ship proceeded in convoy station #31, the *U-124* (Mohr) fired a torpedo that struck the tanker on the port side at the after magazine. The explosion tore open the entire after end of the vessel, and she flooded rapidly and settled by the stern. Moments later a second torpedo struck forward of amidships and set the cargo on fire. The tanker began to settle more evenly but did not sink immediately. The crew, trying to escape the

flames, abandoned the tanker within five minutes without orders. Some of the crew of eight officers and thirty-one men left the vessel in two lifeboats and two rafts. The initial explosion probably killed seven of the eight armed guards. The men abandoned the ship so hastily that a number remained stranded on the ship and in the water. The *PC-577* picked up one armed guard, three officers, and twenty-two men about ten hours after the attack and landed them at Paramaribo, Surinam. One officer and one crewman later died in a hospital ashore. The ship finally plunged stern first at 0200 the next day.

NSS; WACR; WCSR; AG; Rohwer, p. 145, places the attack at 07.35 N / 55.45 W; *War Action Casualties*, p. 129.

BIRMINGHAM CITY

D:	1-8-43	YB:	1920
T:	2341	Tn:	6,194
Pos:	07.12 N / 55.37 W	Dr:	28 ft. 2 in.
Ow:	Isthmian SS Co.	C:	10,000 tons general
Op:	WSA	P:	steam
M:	Michael Francis Barry	S:	6
A:	1-4"; 1-3"; 4-50 cal.		

The *Birmingham City* sailed from Trinidad, BWI, to Rio de Janeiro, Brazil, and served as the convoy commodore's flagship in Convoy TB-1. At 2340, a torpedo struck the American tanker *Broad Arrow*, off the *Birmingham City*'s port beam, and the resulting fire lit up the entire convoy of twelve vessels and four escorts. A minute later a torpedo fired from the *U-124* (Mohr) struck the *Birmingham City* on the port side amidships at the #3 hatch. The *Birmingham City* likewise began to blaze, adding to the brilliance of the night sky. The explosion blew the port lifeboats off the ship, destroyed the fireroom bulkhead, and caused her to sink on an even keel in three minutes. The surviving nine officers, twenty-nine men, and eighteen armed guards on board immediately abandoned ship as she rapidly settled. The #1 lifeboat (motorboat) capsized on launching, pitching men into the water and contributing to the drowning of several crewmen. Survivors also left the ship in the #3 lifeboat, and others jumped from the freighter and swam to several rafts. The men later righted the #1 boat and emptied the rafts. The USS *PC-577* rescued the survivors ten hours after the attack. Three officers, two crewmen, and five armed guards died, most from drowning. The survivors landed at Paramaribo, Surinam.

NSS; WACR; WCSR; RWCS; AG; Rohwer, p. 145, places the attack at 07.23 N / 55.48 W.

COLLINGSWORTH

D:	1-9-43	YB:	1920
T:	0059	Tn:	5,125
Pos:	07.12 N / 55.37 W	Dr:	26 ft.
Ow:	U.S. Maritime Commission	C:	8,000 tons oil, steel, coal
Op:	American Mail Line	P:	steam
M:	Barney Kirschbaum	S:	6.5
A:	1-4"; 1-3"; 8-20 mm		

The *Collingsworth* sailed in Convoy TB-1 en route from Trinidad, BWI, to Rio de Janeiro, Brazil. The convoy consisted of twelve ships and four escorts. An armed guard lookout reported an object resembling a submarine thirty minutes before seeing the tracks of a torpedo that passed close astern. Moments later a second torpedo fired by the *U-124* (Mohr) struck the port side between the #1 and #2 holds. The helmsman spotted a third torpedo and swung the ship hard aport, and it missed by ten feet. With engines secured, the crew surveyed the ship and found no serious damage other than flooding to the compartments. The torpedoes, however, had mortally wounded the *Collingsworth,* and she began to settle fast, sinking by the head four minutes after the attack. The ship's whistle signaled the crew to abandon ship, and the eight officers, thirty-five crewmen, and twenty-four armed guards began to leave almost immediately. The #1 boat got away with twenty-one men, but the #3 boat fouled while launching, forcing the men to jump into the sea. Some clung to wreckage while others climbed onto a raft. The USS *PC-577* picked up thirty-four men from the wreckage and the raft thirteen hours later. The Norwegian SS *Dalvanger* spotted the #3 boat with twenty-one men thirty-six hours after the attack. Two officers, six enlisted men, and four armed guards did not survive the attack.

NSS; WACR; WCSR; AG; Rohwer, p. 145.

MINOTAUR

D:	1-9-43	YB:	1918
T:	0100	Tn:	4,553
Pos:	07.12 N / 55.37 W	Dr:	25 ft.
Ow:	WSA	C:	4,400 tons coal, 12,000 bbls. oil
Op:	Waterman SS Co.	P:	steam
M:	Jens Jensen	S:	8
A:	2-3"; 2-50 cal.		

The *Minotaur* sailed from Trinidad, BWI, to Rio de Janeiro, Brazil, as part of Convoy TB-1 and became the fourth victim of the *U-124* (Mohr). One torpedo passed beside the American freighter *Collingsworth* and was seen about 200 yards from the *Minotaur*. The helmsman put the wheel hard to port, but the torpedo struck the port side in the #1 hold. The blast opened a large hole and flooded the compartment rapidly. The master had the engines put full speed astern and then ordered them secured. The eight officers, twenty-eight crewmen, fifteen armed guards, and one naval medical officer began to abandon ship in two boats. The *Minotaur* sank by the bow in four minutes, fouling one boat and capsizing another before they could be launched properly. The men thrown in the water swam to three life rafts that floated free of the ship. Later that day the USS *PC-577* rescued the survivors. Two officers and four men drowned while abandoning ship. The survivors landed at Paramaribo, Surinam, later that day.

NSS; WACR; WCSR; AG; Rohwer, p. 145.

LOUISE LYKES

D:	1-9-43	YB:	1941
T:	2025 GWT	Tn:	6,155
Pos:	58.55 N / 23.40 W	Dr:	unknown
Ow:	Lykes Bros. SS Co.	C:	munitions
Op:	Lykes Bros. SS Co.	P:	steam
M:	Edwin J. Madden	S:	15
A:	1-4"; 2-3"; 8-20 mm		

The *Louise Lykes*, en route from New York to Belfast, Ireland, was torpedoed and sunk by the *U-384* (von Rosenberg-Gruczszynski). As the *Louise Lykes* proceeded on a zigzagging course, her lookouts spotted the U-boat, and the armed guards opened fire, nearly hitting the submarine. The *U-384* fired four torpedoes from 2,000 yards. Two struck the vessel. Minutes later the *Lykes* exploded with a terrible blast. The complement of ten officers, forty-one men, and thirty-two armed guards all perished in the attack.

WACR; WCSR; AG; WJ; Rohwer, p. 146.

MOBILUBE

D:	1-18-43	YB:	1939
T:	2006	Tn:	10,222
Pos:	33.57 S / 157.20 E	Dr:	19 ft.
Ow:	Socony-Vacuum Oil Co.	C:	water ballast
Op:	Socony-Vacuum Oil Co.	P:	steam
M:	Archie W. Pope	S:	12.5
A:	1-4"; 4-50 cal.		

On 18 January, the *Mobilube* sailed independently from New South Wales, Australia, to San Pedro, California. A single torpedo fired by the *I-21*

(Matsumura) struck the tanker on the port quarter at the engineering spaces. The explosion killed an officer and two men on watch and disabled the engines. The master ordered the surviving ten officers, thirty-two crewmen, and eleven armed guards to abandon ship. The gun crew fired a few shots even though they never spotted the submarine. The master felt that only a skeleton crew should remain on board, and all hands, with the exception of the master and nine others, cleared the ship in the four lifeboats. The #1 boat swamped and threw nine men into the sea. Seven of these men climbed up nets back onto the ship; the others swam to a life raft released by the chief mate. The Australian minesweeper *Kapunda* (J-218) reached the *Mobilube* forty-five minutes after the explosion. The minesweeper rescued the men in the three boats and those on the raft. Since the ship sailed in ballast, the master, with the other sixteen men, managed to shift ballast and decrease the draft aft, putting her on an even keel. The salvage tug *St. Aristell* towed the ship into Sydney the following day. The *Mobilube* was later declared a CTL.

NSS; WACR; WCSR; AG; Rohwer, p. 282; *War Action Casualties*, p. 130.

WALT WHITMAN

D:	1-20-43	YB:	1942
T:	0555	Tn:	7,176
Pos:	36.55 N / 03.07 E	Dr:	15 ft.
Ow:	U.S. Maritime Commission	C:	none
Op:	Weyerhaeuser SS Co.	P:	steam
M:	Oscar Wilhelm Carlson	S:	8
A:	1-4"; 1-3"; 4-20 mm; 2-30 cal.		

During the 100-mile trip from Bougie, Algiers, to Algiers, Algeria, the *Walt Whitman* was attacked by German torpedo planes. On 20 January, the ship sailed as part of the fifteen-ship Convoy MKS-6 en route to the United Kingdom. While off Algiers, a torpedo launched by one of the planes struck the Liberty ship aft at the #5 hold and caused extensive damage. The explosion blew overboard four members of the gun crew at the after gun. Quick thinking crewmen released two rafts, and an escort vessel picked up the men within fifteen minutes. The *Whitman* proceeded to Algiers under her own power and arrived on 25 January. After making repairs she returned to service in August. The complement of ten officers, thirty men, and seventeen armed guards all survived.

WACR; WCSR; AG; TF.

PETER H. BURNETT

D:	1-22-43	YB:	1942
T:	2155	Tn:	7,176
Pos:	32.54 S / 159.32 E	Dr:	21 ft. 9 in.
Ow:	U.S. Maritime Commission	C:	18,154 bales of wool
Op:	American President Line	P:	steam
M:	Charles Adolphus Darling	S:	11
A:	1-5"; 1-3"; 4-20 mm; 4-50 cal.		

The *Peter H. Burnett*, homeward bound from her maiden voyage, was severely damaged while en route from Newcastle, Australia, to San Francisco, California. As the *Burnett* steamed on a nonevasive course, a torpedo fired from the *I-21* (Matsumura) struck the ship on the starboard side at the #5 hatch. The explosion blew out the entire side of this hold, threw wool and the hatch covers high into the air, and damaged the main shaft. The watch below secured the engines and drew the boiler fires. Ten minutes after the explosion, the master ordered the eight officers, thirty-two men, twenty-six armed guards, and eight passengers to the lifeboats, thinking the vessel might be torpedoed a second time. The naval gunnery officer and the communications officer asked to remain on board. Two engineers and two cadets also remained on the Liberty ship. The rest of the crew launched five lifeboats. Four of the boats stayed by the ship during the night, and all these men reboarded the freighter the next day. The #3 boat with the master and several other men drifted ninety miles southeast, where they were rescued by the USS *Zane* (DMS-14) two days later. The *Zane* towed the *Burnett* to Sydney, Australia, for repairs. The explosion injured one of the armed guards on watch at the five-inch gun, and he later died from his injuries.

The ship was later put into service as the USS *P. H. Burnett* (IX-104) and used for floating dry cargo stowage for advanced bases in the Pacific. NSS; WACR; WCSR; AG; DANFS, vol. 5, pp. 197-98; Rohwer, p. 282; Sawyer, Mitchell, p. 64.

BENJAMIN SMITH

D:	1-23-43	YB:	1942
T:	0200	Tn:	7,177
Pos:	04.05 N / 07.50 W	Dr:	28 ft. 5 in.
Ow:	WSA	C:	8,000 tons war supplies
Op:	South Atlantic SS Co.	P:	steam
M:	George W. Johnson	S:	11
A:	1-5"; 9-20 mm		

The *Benjamin Smith* sailed from Charleston, South Carolina, to Takoradi, Gold Coast, via Trinidad and Liberia. In almost a full moon the vessel sailed from Marshall, Liberia, without escort because the escort vessel's orders had been misforwarded and she arrived a day late. The freighter proceeded on a nonevasive course. About fifty miles off the Ivory Coast, a torpedo fired by the *U-175* struck between the #1 and #2 holds. The explosion shorted the radio antenna but did not severely damage the ship. The watch below secured the engines as the *Benjamin Smith* took a starboard list. After the water equalized in the holds the ship righted herself. Within five minutes the master had the engines restarted, and the ship began a zigzag pattern while working up to six knots. A second torpedo struck at 0220 on the starboard side about ten feet aft of the engine room. The crew again secured the engines, and the master ordered the ship abandoned. The complement of eight officers, thirty-five crewmen, and twenty-three armed guards abandoned the ship in three lifeboats and a raft. Shortly after they got away from the ship a third torpedo struck the port side amidships, causing her to sink quickly by the stern. The U-boat officers questioned the men in one of the boats, and after receiving the appropriate answers the German officers directed the survivors to the nearest land. At dawn the men abandoned the raft, and the motorized lifeboat towed the other two boats into Sassandra, French Ivory Coast, on the 24th. All hands survived the attack.

NSS; WACR; WCSR; RWCS; AG; Rohwer, p. 147.

STEPHEN JOHNSON FIELD

D:	1-23-43	YB:	1942
T:	0600	Tn:	7,176
Pos:	Milne Bay, New Guinea	Dr:	18 ft.
Ow:	WSA	C:	2,200 tons general, ammunition,
Op:	American Hawaiian SS Co.		gas
M:	Pierce A. Powers Jr.	P:	steam
A:	1-4"; 1-3"; 4-50 cal.; 2-30 cal.	S:	docked

The *Stephen Johnson Field* was bombed while lying beside Gili Gili dock in Milne Bay, New Guinea. The vessel sailed with 8,000 tons of war supplies. Stevedores had unloaded most of the cargo when an air alert from the shore station warned the crew, who quickly extinguished the cargo lights. Eight bombs fell along both sides of the vessel. Fragments pierced the port side shell plating and punched five holes below the waterline and thirty above it. The armed guards fired at the attacking aircraft with the ship's three-inch gun. Bomb fragments injured one armed guard and two merchant seamen. All eight officers, thirty-four men, and eighteen armed guards survived the attack.

NSS; WACR; AG; ONF.

CITY OF FLINT

D: 1-25-43   YB: 1918
T: 1915   Tn: 4,963
Pos: 34.47 N / 31.30 W   Dr: 23 ft.
Ow: U.S. Maritime Commission   C: war cargo, tanks, planes, jeeps
Op: Moore & McCormick Inc.   P: steam
M: John B. MacKenzie   S: 11
A: 1-4"; 1-3"; 6-20 mm

On 13 January, the *City of Flint* sailed from New York to Casablanca, Morocco, as part of Convoy UGS-4. While en route she encountered a storm that caused her deck cargo to shift, and she straggled from the convoy. The freighter maintained a zigzag course while trying to catch the other ships. The *U-575* (Heydemann) intercepted the freighter and fired a torpedo that struck the port side at the #1 hold and ignited the oil and gasoline stored there. As the vessel settled by the head, flames engulfed the forward section of the ship. With the engines secured, the crew abandoned the flaming freighter in rough water within ten minutes. Most of the ten officers, thirty crewmen, twenty-four armed guards, and one passenger left in the ship's four lifeboats, while others had to jump in the water to avoid the flames. A second torpedo struck the port side aft of the bridge, and the ship sank bow first at 2005. Three of the boats stayed in the area of the sinking for two days before setting sail for the Azores. The following day the Portuguese destroyer *Lima* rescued forty-eight men and landed them in the Azores. On 28 January, the destroyer HMS *Quadrant* (G-11) rescued the fourth boat carrying ten survivors and landed them at Gibraltar. The *U-575* rescued the chief cook and interned him in a POW camp. Two crewmen and four armed guards died in the attack.

NSS; WACR; WCSR; AG; *Sunday Star*, 21 March 1943; Rohwer, p. 147, places the attack at 34.47 N / 31.10 W.

CAPE DECISION

D: 1-27-43   YB: 1942
T: 0451   Tn: 5,106
Pos: 23.00 N / 46.40 W   Dr: 23 ft. 6 in.
Ow: Waterman SS Co.   C: 5,700 tons mines, ammunition,
Op: Waterman SS Co.   trucks, aircraft
M: Holger Emile Sorensen   P: diesel
A: 1-4"; 1-3"; 8-20 mm   S: 14.5

The *Cape Decision* sailed independently from Charleston, South Carolina, to Freetown, South Africa. As the ship steered a zigzag course in clear weather and moderate seas, two torpedoes fired by the *U-105* (Nissen) hit the vessel less than ten seconds apart. Striking between the #4 and #5 hatches, the explosions did not do much visual damage but quickly stopped the vessel. The blasts damaged the ship throughout and knocked out the electrical system, which halted the engines. As the ship settled by the stern, the general alarm sounded and the order to abandon ship was passed by the master and the chief mate. The ship's complement of nine officers, thirty-six men, and twenty-six armed guards, as well as the six passengers, abandoned ship in the two lifeboats and two of the four rafts. Some of the armed guards remained at their guns until the last moment and left the ship by diving into the water. With the crew off the ship, the *U-105* moved around the stern at periscope depth. At 0522 the *U-105* fired a third torpedo at the starboard side. It struck at the waterline in the engine room. The vessel listed to port and sank five minutes later at 0532. The submarine surfaced and officers called alongside the boat with the master. After questioning the men, the German officers directed them to the nearest land. The survivors distributed the men evenly between the two boats. The master's boat with forty men arrived at Barbados nine days after the sinking, and the chief mate's boat with thirty-seven men arrived at Saint Barthelemy, French West Indies, fourteen days after the attack. All hands survived the attack.

NSS; WACR; WCSR; RWCS; AG; Rohwer, p. 147, places the attack at 22.57 N / 47.28 W.

CHARLES C. PINCKNEY

D:	1-27-43	YB:	1942
T:	1945	Tn:	7,177
Pos:	36.37 n / 30.55 w	Dr:	22 ft.
Ow:	U.S. Maritime Commission	C:	ammunition, war supplies,
Op:	American South African Line		mechanized equipment
M:	Frank Theoron Woolverton Jr.	P:	steam
A:	1-4"; 1-3"; 8-20 mm	S:	12

On 13 January, the *Charles C. Pinckney* left New York in Convoy UGS-4 en route for North Africa. Eight days later, in heavy weather, the freighter straggled from the convoy. Early on the 27th lookouts spotted a submarine. The master changed course and increased the ship's speed, while the armed guards fired at the U-boat. Later that night lookouts spotted a torpedo 750 yards away approaching the ship off the port bow. The helmsman spun the wheel hard right, but the ship did not answer the helm. The torpedo, launched from the *U-514* (Auffermann), struck just abaft the stem. The explosion ignited a portion of the cargo, and the blast blew the bow off forward of the #1 hold and created a pillar of flame that shot skyward. The master immediately had the engines secured and gave the order to abandon ship. The ship's nine officers, thirty-two crewmen, twenty-seven armed guards, and two passengers launched four lifeboats and released a raft. A portion of the gun crew and the gunnery officer remained on board. The *U-514* surfaced 200 yards from the ship. The gun crew held its fire and then hit the submarine several times, driving it away. The crew

reboarded the ship at 0700 the next morning. During the inspection the chief engineer discovered he could not get steam up. Thirty minutes later the *U-514* resurfaced, and the crew with the exception of the six dead abandoned the ship a second time. The German officers questioned the men in the boats, and then the U-boat sank the vessel with gunfire. She went down bow first at 0830. The survivors set sail in the four lifeboats, but during the night of 28 January, they became separated. On 8 February, the Swiss vessel *Caritasi* picked up a boat carrying one officer, four men, and nine armed guards and landed them in the Azores. The fifty men in the other three boats were never found. Eight officers, twenty-eight men, and eighteen armed guards perished.

NSS; WACR; WCSR; RWCS; AG; Rohwer, p. 147.

JULIA WARD HOWE

D:	1-28-43	YB:	1942
T:	1350	Tn:	7,176
Pos:	35.29 N / 29.10 W	Dr:	27 ft.
Ow:	U.S. Maritime Commission	C:	8,000 tons, 60 tanks, food,
Op:	Barber-American West African		clothing, railroad cars
M:	Andrew Anthony Hammond	P:	steam
A:	1-5"; 1-3"; 8-20 mm	S:	11

In heavy weather the *Julia Ward Howe* straggled from Convoy UGS-4 while en route from New York to North Africa. In daylight, a torpedo from the *U-442* (Hesse) struck the Liberty ship on the starboard side between the #3 hold and the deckhouse. The explosion blew off the #3 hatch cover, wrecked two lifeboats, destroyed the radio equipment, and brought down the radio antenna. The ship immediately took a 15° list but flooded slowly afterwards and gradually righted herself on an even keel. The gun crew fired three shots from the five-inch gun in the direction of the submarine. The surviving men among the eight officers, thirty-six crewmen, twenty-nine armed guards, and one passenger on board cleared the ship in two boats and two rafts. The men then secured the rafts to the lifeboats. Forty minutes after the initial explosion a second torpedo struck amidships and broke the ship in two. The *U-442* surfaced and her officers questioned the crew, taking the second mate on board for closer examination. The mate was then released. The survivors hoisted sail for the Azores. Fifteen hours later, and 330 miles southwest of the Azores, the Portuguese destroyer *Lima* rescued the survivors and landed them at Ponta Delgada, Azores. The master died in the explosion, and the chief engineer died on the rescue vessel. In addition, one armed guard and the Army passenger died on the ship.

NSS; WACR; WCSR; AG; Rohwer, p. 147.

SAMUEL GOMPERS

D: 1-30-43   YB: 1942
T: 0348   Tn: 7,176
Pos: 24.28 S / 166.20 E   Dr: 22 ft. 10 in.
Ow: WSA   C: 4,600 tons chrome ore
Op: Weyerhaeuser SS Co.   P: steam
M: John Joseph Lapoint   S: 11.5
A: 1-3"; 5-20 mm; 2-30 cal.

In heavy seas, on a voyage from Nouméa, New Caledonia, to New Castle, Australia, the *Samuel Gompers* was torpedoed by the *I-10* (Yamada) 115 miles from Amedea Lighthouse, New Caledonia. One torpedo struck aft of the bridge on the port side, and a second hit in the #4 hold at the deep tanks. The explosions threw hatch beams, deck gear, and cargo everywhere and sprayed fuel oil forty feet in the air and all over the superstructure and the lifeboats. The survivors among the complement of eight officers, thirty-five men, and seventeen armed guards mustered at their boat stations to abandon ship. The men managed to launch the two starboard boats, but they had to cut loose the port boats on the windward side and they both capsized. The Liberty ship went down by the stern within five minutes. Survivors later righted the #4 boat. The three boats searched for seven hours for other survivors and then set sail north by east. The #3 boat landed on a small island off New Caledonia almost four days later, and French fishermen rescued the men the next morning. The #1 boat landed on New Caledonia, and the Army crash boat *P-111* rescued the men in the #4 boat. One armed guard and three men died in the attack.

NSS; WACR; WCSR; AG; Rohwer, p. 282, places the attack at 24.21 S / 166.12 E.

JEREMIAH VAN RENSSALAER

D: 2-2-43   YB: 1943
T: 0200   Tn: 7,177
Pos: 54.50 N / 28.55 W   Dr: 28 ft.
Ow: U.S. Maritime Commission   C: 9,000 tons Army cargo
Op: Agwilines   P: steam
M: Lucius Whitfield Webb   S: 10.0
A: 1-4"; 1-3"; 8-20 mm

The *Jeremiah Van Renssalaer* sailed with Convoy HX-224 bound from New York for the United Kingdom. She took station as the last vessel in the extreme port column. The *Van Renssalaer* had performed poorly keeping station in the convoy and had kept her station about once in seven nights. She managed to catch up in the daytime, and consequently her convoy position changed from #11 to #45. Two torpedoes fired from the *U-456* (Teichert) struck almost

simultaneously on the port side in the #1 hold. The blast created a hole eight feet
by thirty feet, blew the hatch cover off and strewed cargo overboard, and started
a fire. A third torpedo struck the port side at the #4 hatch. It blew a truck
secured on deck into the water and also started a small fire. The watch below
secured the engines within two minutes. Some of the eight officers, thirty-four
men, twenty-eight armed guards, and one passenger on board panicked and
abandoned the ship in a hasty and disorganized fashion. They tried to launch
three boats, but two capsized in the rough seas. A number of men got off in a
single lifeboat, while others jumped into the water and tried to make their way
to the three rafts. One man never left the ship and the escort took him off. Only
one officer, six crewmen, and seventeen of the gun crew survived. Most of the
deaths can be attributed to the harsh weather and the 36° water that caused the
men to die from exposure. The British rescue ship *Accrington* rescued the
survivors five hours after the attack. A crew from the escort vessel later boarded
the freighter and noted that she could have been saved. The watch below left the
boiler fires lit, which burned the boilers out. The vessel was then sunk by
gunfire at 1200.

NSS; WACR; WCSR; AG; Rohwer, p. 148, places the attack at 55.13 N / 28.53 W.

DORCHESTER

D:	2-3-43	YB:	1926
T:	0055	Tn:	5,649
Pos:	59.22 N / 48.42 W	Dr:	20 (mean)
Ow:	Merchants-Miner Trans. Co.	C:	1,069 tons general, lumber, mail,
Op:	Agwilines		troops
M:	Hans Jorgen Danielsen	P:	steam
A:	1-4"; 1-3"; 4-20 mm	S:	10

The *Dorchester* sailed from St. John's, Newfoundland, to Narsarssuak,
Greenland. The *U-223* (Wächter) attacked the sixty-four ship Convoy SG-19,
firing five single shots at three ships. One of the first shots struck the *Dorchester*
on the starboard side in the machinery spaces. The explosion stopped the
engines, and the vessel swung to starboard, losing way. Six blasts from the
ship's whistle indicated to the rest of the convoy that the *Dorchester* had been
torpedoed. Three minutes after the explosion the master ordered the ship
abandoned, but a lack of steam prevented him from completing the abandon
ship signal on the ship's whistle. The ship's complement consisted of 7 officers,
123 men, and 24 armed guards. The ship also carried 705 troops and passengers.
The explosion damaged three of the ship's fourteen lifeboats, and the crew
managed to successfully launch only two more overcrowded boats. The USCG
cutters *Escanaba* (WPG-77) and *Commanche* (WPG-75) began rescuing the
survivors within minutes. Rescue swimmers from the *Escanaba* jumped into the
icy water with lines tied about them to pull incapacitated men out of the water.

The *Escanaba* rescued fifty-one survivors in the #6 boat, and the *Commanche* rescued the forty-one survivors in the #13 boat. Thirty-three men survived on rafts. The cutters pulled another 104 men from the water. Tragically 4 officers, 98 crewmen, 15 armed guards, and 558 troops and passengers died, most from hypothermia.

The four Army chaplains on board aided the survivors in abandoning the ship. Their calm attitude and sacrifice were later acknowledged by Congress, which voted to posthumously award them a medal of heroism. NSS; WACR; WCSR; AG; *The Sinking of the Escanaba*, pp. 2-4; Rohwer, p. 148.

GREYLOCK

D:	2-3-43	YB:	1921
T:	1348	Tn:	7,460
Pos:	70.50 N / 00.48 W	Dr:	29 ft. 10 in.
Ow:	Seas Shipping Co.	C:	1,130 tons calcium phosphate
Op:	WSA		ballast
M:	Charles Herbert Whitmore	P:	steam
A:	1-4"; 1-3"; 8-20 mm; 2-30 cal.	S:	7.5

The *Greylock* began a journey from Murmansk, USSR, to the United States via Iceland in the eleven-ship Convoy RA-52. Six hundred miles northeast of Iceland, in smooth seas and broad daylight, a lookout spotted a torpedo fired from the *U-255* (Reche) 300 yards off the port side. The helmsman put the wheel over hard to avoid the torpedo but to no avail. The torpedo struck the ship between the #5 and #6 holds, creating a large hole below the waterline and also locking the steering gear. A second torpedo missed the bow by seventy-five yards. The ship immediately flooded and took a starboard list. The order to abandon ship was passed fifteen minutes after the initial explosion. The complement of ten officers, thirty-five men, and twenty-five armed guards left the ship in four boats, and the escort trawler HMS *Lady Madeleine* (FY-283) quickly rescued the men. All hands survived and landed at Belfast and Gourock. A British escort sank the *Greylock* with gunfire, and she plunged stern first at 1418.

NSS; WACR; WCSR; Rohwer, p. 202, places the attack at 70.52 N / 00.21 W.

WEST PORTAL

D:	2-5-43	YB:	1920
T:	1300	Tn:	5,376
Pos:	53.00 N / 36.00 W	Dr:	25 ft. 11 1/4 in.
Ow:	Pope and Talbot Inc.	C:	6,000 tons general
Op:	WSA	P:	steam
M:	Oswald Joseph Griffin	S:	unknown
A:	1-4"; 1-3"; 8-20 mm		

A straggler from Convoy SC-118, the *West Portal* was torpedoed by the *U-413* (Poel) while en route from New York to the United Kingdom. The freighter proceeded on a zigzagging course, and the U-boat fired a four-torpedo spread at over 3,500 yards. The third torpedo struck forward of the bridge, and the ship took an immediate list. The *U-413* quickly maneuvered for a coup de grâce shot and missed with the first torpedo. A second torpedo struck the after part of the freighter and fatally damaged her. Survivors among the eight officers, thirty-two men, twenty-five armed guards, and twelve passengers got off the ship in lifeboats. The radio operator managed to send a distress signal after the attack began. The British destroyer *Vanessa* (D-29), one of the SC-118 escorts, picked up the message but did not know the freighter's position. The *Vanessa* searched for survivors but found no trace and all hands perished.

One source states that Pope and Talbot were also the operators. WACR; WCSR; AG; WJ; VSC; Rohwer, p. 148.

ROBERT E. HOPKINS

D:	2-7-43	YB:	1921
T:	0048	Tn:	6,624
Pos:	55.14 N / 26.39 W	Dr:	25 ft. 6 in.
Ow:	Tide Water Assoc. Oil Co.	C:	68,000 bbls. Admiralty fuel oil
Op:	WSA	P:	steam
M:	Rene Blanc	S:	7.5
A:	1-4"; 1-3"; 4-20 mm; 2-50 cal.		

On 12 January, the tanker *Robert E. Hopkins* departed New York en route to Glasgow, Scotland. During the trip she became another casualty in Convoy SC-118 while proceeding as the fifth ship in the eleventh column. The *U-402* (von Forstner) fired two torpedoes at the *Hopkins* and missed. The *U-402* then quickly turned and fired a torpedo from the stern tube that struck the starboard side forward of the #1 tank in the dry cargo hold. The ship immediately lost maneuverability, and the crew secured the engines. Ten minutes later a second torpedo struck the engine room on the starboard side. This explosion tore away large portions of the hull, destroyed the boilers and the engines, and caused the ship to sink by the stern in three minutes. Survivors among the seven officers,

thirty-one crewmen, and nineteen armed guards left the ship in the only surviving lifeboat. Heavy weather had previously claimed one of the boats, and the explosions destroyed the other two. Other survivors swam to one life raft that floated free of the ship. The HMS *Mignonette* (K-38) rescued forty-two men and landed them in Londonderry, Northern Ireland. One officer and fourteen men died in the attack.

This vessel may have been allocated to the British Ministry of War Transport. NSS; WACR; WCSR; AG; RWSA; Waters, p. 148; Rohwer, p. 148, places the attack at 55.13 N / 26.22 W; *War Action Casualties*, p. 132.

HENRY R. MALLORY

D:	2-7-43	YB:	1916
T:	0400	Tn:	6,063
Pos:	55.30 N / 29.33 W	Dr:	22 ft. 3 in.
Ow:	Agwilines	C:	clothing, food, trucks, tanks
Op:	Clyde Mallory Lines	P:	steam
M:	Horace Rudolf Weaver	S:	6
A:	1-4"; 2-3"; 8-20 mm		

The *Henry R. Mallory* left New York in Convoy SC-118 en route to Iceland. As the freighter steamed in convoy station #33, the *U-402* (von Forstner) fired a torpedo that struck the #3 hold on her starboard side. The explosion damaged the main steam line, destroyed the oil pump and engine room gauges, and blew off the #4 hatch covers. The stern settled quickly, but when the water reached the deck, the rate of the sinking slowed. The master did not immediately give the order to abandon ship but communicated with the watch below to secure the engines. Over the next thirty minutes the ship gradually began to list to port, and he ordered the ship abandoned. The men poured from below, clad mostly in nightclothes. The freighter had ten lifeboats to accommodate the 9 officers, 68 crewmen, 34 armed guards, and 383 passengers. The torpedo explosion damaged two of the ten boats, a third could not be launched, and two more on either side capsized in the rough seas. The men left the ship with as many as seventy-five men per boat. Only 175 men cleared the ship in the boats. Many others jumped in the water or onto the balsa doughnut-type rafts. None of the other ships in the convoy knew the *Mallory* had been attacked, and four hours later the USCG cutter *Bibb* (WPG-31) discovered a boat of survivors. Later joined by the USCG *Ingham* (WPG-35), the two ships rescued 227 persons from the 50° water, but five of these died while on board the cutters. A total of 7 officers, 42 men, 15 armed guards, and 208 passengers died—most from exposure.

NSS; WACR; WCSR; RWCS; AG; Waters, pp. 152-60; Rohwer, p. 149, places the attack at 55.18 N / 26.24 W.

ROGER B. TANEY

D:	2-7-43	YB:	1942
T:	2250	Tn:	7,191
Pos:	22.00 S / 07.00 W	Dr:	unknown
Ow:	U.S. Maritime Commission	C:	none
Op:	Waterman SS Co.	P:	steam
M:	Thomas James Potter	S:	11
A:	1-4"; 1-3"; 4-50 cal.; 2-30 cal.		

On 31 December, the *Roger B. Taney* departed Suez en route to the United States via Bahia, Brazil. She sailed with Convoy ON-3 bound from Saldanha Bay, South Africa. The ship continued with the convoy for three days, then proceeded alone to Bahia. At about 2200 on the 7th, a lookout on board the *Taney* sighted a torpedo fired from the *U-160* (Lassen) that passed twenty yards ahead of the bow. The freighter made a 90° turn to avoid the submarine. Forty-five minutes later a torpedo struck the vessel on the starboard side at the engine room. The explosion ruptured the steam lines, stopped the engines, started a fire, and destroyed two lifeboats. The armed guards manned the guns and fired five rounds in the direction of the torpedo track. The merchant crew of eight officers and twenty-nine men, along with one passenger, abandoned ship about twenty minutes after the initial explosion; the 19 armed guards remained on board. The *U-160* fired a second torpedo at 2320, striking the #4 hold and causing a tremendous explosion. With the ship sinking, the armed guards abandoned her in two rafts they had fashioned in the emergency. The merchant crew picked these men up at dawn. Shortly after the second explosion the *U-160* surfaced and officers questioned the survivors before leaving. The lifeboats stayed within sight of each other for a day and a half before becoming separated. On 21 March, twenty-one days after the attack, the British SS *Penrith Castle* discovered the #2 boat with fifteen merchant crewmen and thirteen armed guards. The Brazilian SS *Baje* located the #4 boat under command of the master with twenty-six men forty-one days after the attack. They had sailed to within ten miles of the coast of Brazil. The third engineer, one fireman, and an oiler on watch below died from the initial explosion.

NSS; WACR; WCSR; RWCS; AG; *Star*, Washington, DC, 14 April 1944; Rohwer, p. 149, places the attack at 22.00 S / 07.45 W.

STARR KING

D: 2-10-43
T: 0613
Pos: 34.15 S / 154.20 E
Ow: WSA
Op: McCormick SS Co.
M: Gustav Winsens
A: 1-5"; 4-20 mm; 2-30 cal.

YB: 1942
Tn: 7,176
Dr: 22 ft. 11 in.
C: 9,747 tons Army and
commercial cargo
P: steam
S: 10

On 8 February, the *Starr King* left Sydney, Australia, en route to Nouméa, New Caledonia. The next day the *I-21* (Matsumura) sighted the freighter as she steered a zigzag course at about the same time lookouts spotted the submarine's periscope. The master tried to outrun the *I-21* and put the ship's stern toward the submarine. At twelve midnight the master began steering a nonevasive course in an effort to put distance between his ship and the submarine. The following morning lookouts spotted three torpedoes. The first torpedo crossed the bow. The second torpedo struck the starboard side in the #4 hold, blew covers and beams from the #4 hatch, ruptured steam lines, and started a fire in the tween decks. The third torpedo passed astern. The engineers immediately stopped the engines, and the crew put out the fire. The master ordered a few men to lower the lifeboats and to lay off and await orders. The chief mate, however, unsuccessfully attempted to countermand this order. With the boats lying at a safe distance from the ship, a fourth torpedo passed between and under the lifeboats and struck the ship between the #3 and #5 holds. The explosion ruptured the ship's bunkers and blew oil over the length of the vessel. The men remaining on the freighter climbed into the waiting boats, and the armed guards jumped onto rafts as the freighter settled in the water. The four lifeboats remained in the vicinity, and the Australian destroyer *Warramunga* (I-44) spotted them later that day. With the *Starr King* still afloat, a boarding party went back on board to pass a tow line to the destroyer. Unfortunately, the towing cable fouled the port screw of the *Warramunga*, so they abandoned the tow until morning to await a salvage tug then en route. The *Starr King*, however, sank later that night. All seven officers, thirty men, sixteen armed guards, and two passengers on board survived.

NSS; WACR; WCSR; AG; Rohwer, p. 282.

ATLANTIC SUN

D:	2-15-43	YB:	1941
T:	1000	Tn:	11,355
Pos:	51.0 N / 41.0 W	Dr:	20 ft.
Ow:	Sun Oil Co.	C:	water ballast
Op:	Sun Oil Co.	P:	motor
M:	William B. Longtin	S:	15
A:	1-5"; 1-3"; 8-20 mm		

On 8 February, the *Atlantic Sun* left Reykjavik, Iceland, in Convoy ON-165 bound for New York. The tanker developed engine trouble and straggled from the convoy. The *U-607* (Mengersen) spotted the vessel 150 miles off Cape Race trying to catch up and fired two torpedoes, striking the vessel on the port side. One explosion split the ship in half abaft the midships house, and the other blew a large hole in the bow. The forward section sank in twenty minutes. The after section, after examination, appeared sound enough to be taken into port under power. After the ship broke in two, twenty-two men led by the chief officer abandoned the after section. They returned at 1200 and reboarded the after part of the ship, going below to change clothing. At 1230, with the men still below, the *U-607* fired a third torpedo that struck near the stern post, causing the stern portion to sink thirty minutes later. After the third torpedo struck, a lifeboat with eight men cleared the ship half-swamped and without oars. Others went over the side into the sea just before the ship turned over keel up and sank. The *U-607* picked up one of the survivors and took him to Saint-Nazaire, France, and he eventually went to Milar Prison Camp. Those who remained behind faced moderate seas and 25° weather. None of the ten officers, thirty-six men, nineteen armed guards, and one passenger on board survived except William Golobich, the deck hand picked up by the *U-607*.

NSS; WACR; WCSR; RWCS; AG; Rohwer, p. 86; *War Action Casualties*, p. 133.

DEER LODGE

D:	2-16-43	YB:	1919
T:	2352	Tn:	6,178
Pos:	33.46 S / 26.57 E	Dr:	23 ft.
Ow:	WSA	C:	6,400 tons including oil, steel,
Op:	Moore-McCormack Lines		4 locomotives, 4 tenders
M:	Irving Dana Jensen	P:	steam
A:	1-4"; 6-20 mm	S:	6

The *Deer Lodge* sailed on an independent route from Baltimore, Maryland, to Suez via Durban, South Africa. About sixty miles east of Port Elizabeth, the *U-516* (Wiebe) spotted the freighter and followed her on the surface. Lookouts sighted the U-boat and the master attempted to escape by zigzagging, but the steering gear broke. The *U-516* maneuvered into a favorable position and fired a torpedo that struck the vessel on the port side at the #2 hold. The explosion threw up a tremendous column of water, tore up the decks, blew the deck cargo off the ship, and flooded the hold. Twenty minutes later a second torpedo struck at approximately the same location extending the damage to the ship. After this explosion the master stopped the engines, and the complement of ten officers, twenty-nine men, and eighteen armed guards abandoned ship in the three lifeboats and three rafts. The *U-516* surfaced beside the boats, and the German officers questioned the merchant seamen. The *Deer Lodge* sank bow first at 0156. The boats remained in the area picking up men out of the water, and the following morning the crew redistributed into three boats and one raft. The South Africa minesweeper *Africana* (T-01) picked up thirteen men; the London trawler *Havorn* rescued another thirty-two. The hospital ship *Atlantis* rescued ten more on the 20th. One seaman died when the davit from the #4 lifeboat broke off and fell on him. The only other casualty was a steward listed as missing.

NSS; WACR; WCSR; RWCS; USMMA; AG; Rohwer, p. 266.

ROSARIO

D:	2-21-43	YB:	1920
T:	1842	Tn:	4,659
Pos:	50.13.N / 24.48 W	Dr:	unknown
Ow:	A. H. Bull Co.	C:	sand and slag ballast
Op:	A. H. Bull Co.	P:	steam
M:	Gustav J. A. Larsen	S:	6
A:	1-5"; 5-20 mm; 2-30 cal.		

The *Rosario* sailed with Convoy ON-167 in station #11 from Avonmouth, England, to New York. The *U-664* (Graef) spotted the freighter and fired a double shot. The first torpedo struck the starboard side at the #2 hold, and twenty seconds later the other torpedo struck the #5 hold. The explosions blew off both hatch covers and threw sand and slag into the air. The ship took an immediate 35° list, and eventually listed to 45°. The master stopped the engines immediately, and the complement of eight officers, thirty-six crewmen, and nineteen armed guards abandoned the ship in great confusion. The tremendous list of the ship prevented the men from getting a good footing or from launching the boats or rafts. The ship went down in three minutes, capsizing before she went under. The men had to jump into the water and remained there for nearly two hours before being rescued by a lifeboat from the torpedoed Panamanian SS *H. H. Rodgers*, also sent to the bottom by the *U-664*. One raft and two life floats floated free of the sinking ship, allowing some of the men to get out of the water. The British rescue ship *Rathlin* rescued the surviving officer, thirteen men, and seventeen armed guards three hours later. Thirty-three men died—all but one through drowning and exposure.

NSS; WACR; WCSR; AG; Rohwer, p. 150, places the attack at 50.30 N / 24.38 W.

CHATTANOOGA CITY

D:	2-22-43	YB:	1921
T:	1920	Tn:	5,686
Pos:	46.54 N / 34.30 W	Dr:	21 ft.
Ow:	Isthmian SS Co.	C:	3,500 tons sand ballast
Op:	WSA	P:	steam
M:	Robert C. Forbes	S:	9.5
A:	1-4"; 1-12 lber.; 6-20 mm		

The *Chattanooga City* sailed from Liverpool, England, to New York as part of Convoy ON-166. The *U-606* (Döhler) fired a torpedo that struck the freighter in the center of the #4 hold. The explosion bodily lifted the ship out of the water, blew off the hatch covers of the #3 and #4 holds, tore deck booms away, and probably severed the main shaft. The ship quickly listed to starboard and settled rapidly. Two minutes after the explosion the master gave the order to abandon ship, and water reached the welldeck one minute later. The vessel sank by the stern in about fifteen minutes. The ship's complement of ten officers, twenty-seven men, and twenty-one armed guards cleared the ship in four lifeboats and one raft. The Canadian corvette *Trillium* (K-172) rescued the survivors three hours later. Ten of the gun crew transferred to the USCG *Spencer* (WPG-36) and landed in Argentia, Newfoundland. The rest landed at St. Johns. All hands survived the attack.

NSS; WACR; WCSR; AG. The forty-six ship Convoy ON-166 lost fifteen vessels. Shortly after attacking the convoy, the *U-606* was sunk by the USCG *Campbell* (WPG-32) and the Polish destroyer *Burza*. See Waters, pp. 178-94, for an account of the convoy battle. Rohwer, p. 150, places the attack at 46.53 N / 34.32 W. The armament for this ship is not clear in the various sources.

EXPOSITOR

D:	2-22-43	YB:	1920
T:	1930	Tn:	4,959
Pos:	46.52 N / 34.26 W	Dr:	17 ft.
Ow:	American Export Line	C:	water and slag ballast
Op:	American Export Line	P:	steam
M:	Linford Horace Seybert	S:	10
A:	1-4"; 1-3"; 2-50 cal.; 2-30 cal.; 4-20 mm		

The *Expositor* sailed in Convoy ON-166, en route from Belfast, Northern Ireland, to New York. The convoy commander had just ordered a turn when the ship directly astern suffered an explosion. The master sounded general quarters, and six minutes later a torpedo fired from the *U-606* (Döhler) struck the "Hog Islander" on the port side at the #3 hatch. This explosion caused the boiler to explode moments later and sent steam everywhere. The ship took an immediate list to starboard and then righted herself after settling by the stern. At 1940 the master ordered the ship abandoned. Most of the ship's complement of eight officers, thirty-one men, and twenty-one armed guards escaped in the single undamaged lifeboat and three rafts. The Canadian corvette *Trillium* (K-172) rescued seven officers, twenty-seven men, and all the armed guards. One officer died on the corvette, and an engineer later died in a hospital in St. Johns. The *Expositor* remained afloat, and the *Trillium* blew off the stern with depth charges three hours after the initial attack. The tough freighter eventually had to be sent to the bottom by a coup de grâce shot from the *U-303* (Heine).

NSS; WACR; WCSR; AG; RWSA. Earlier the *Expositor* had been under time charter to the U.S. Maritime Commission. Rohwer, p. 150, places the attack at 46.53 N / 34.32 W.

HASTINGS

D:	2-23-43	YB:	1920
T:	0435	Tn:	5,401
Pos:	46.30 N / 36.23 W	Dr:	17 ft.
Ow:	Waterman SS Co.	C:	1,500 tons coal slag ballast
Op:	WSA	P:	steam
M:	Richard O. West	S:	9.5
A:	1-4"; 2-30 cal.; 4-20 mm		

The *Hastings* became another victim of German submarines in Convoy ON-166. The freighter departed Milford Haven, Wales, en route to New York in station #12 in the convoy. A lookout spotted a torpedo fired from the *U-186* (Hesemann) just before it struck the port side at the #5 hold. The explosion flooded the engine room, sprung bulkheads between the #4 and #5 holds, destroyed the steering gear, and cut the ship's power. The master had the main engines secured immediately. The ten officers, thirty-one men, twenty armed guards, and one passenger on board began to abandon ship in three boats and two rafts. The ship plunged stern first seven minutes after being struck. The Canadian *Chilliwack* (K-131) picked up all the gun crew, nine officers, twenty-three men, and the passenger and landed them at St. Johns, Newfoundland. One officer and eight men perished in the attack.

NSS; WACR; WCSR; AG; Rohwer, p. 151, places the attack at 46.30 N / 36.30 W.

A close-up of the damage inflicted by a torpedo. This is the bow of the *William Cullen Bryant* torpedoed by the *U-84* in July 1942.

The Hog Island freighter *Expositor* sailed with Convoy ON-166 and was sunk by torpedoes fired by the *U-606* and *U-303*.

ESSO BATON ROUGE

D:	2-23-43	YB:	1938
T:	1920	Tn:	7,989
Pos:	31.15 N / 27.22 W	Dr:	18 ft.
Ow:	Standard Oil Co. of N. J.	C:	water ballast
Op:	Standard Oil Co. of N. J.	P:	steam
M:	James S. Poche	S:	9
A:	1-4"; 1-3"; 8-20 mm		

On the morning of 16 February, the *Esso Baton Rouge* sailed in Convoy UC-1 en route from Swansea, South Wales, to Curaçao, NWI. The tanker proceeded in station #43 in the thirty-two vessel convoy. Within minutes four ships close to the *Esso Baton Rouge* were torpedoed by the *U-382* and *U-202*. The master sounded the general alarm before a stern shot from the *U-202* (Poser) struck the tanker on the starboard side between the engine room and aft bunkers. The explosion carried away the bulkhead between the tanks and the engine room, filled the latter compartment with burning oil, and stopped the engines. Other parts of the ship including the superstructure tore loose and flew over fifty feet in the air. As the ship started to settle by the stern, her complement of eight officers, thirty-five men, and twenty-five armed guards began mustering at their boat stations. The ship still had headway as the men tried to lower the boats. The men launched three life rafts, but they drifted rapidly astern. Three lifeboats pulled away from the ship and eventually picked up all the men in the water. The escort sloop HMS *Totland* (Y-88) rescued the survivors within ninety minutes. The tanker sank by the stern at 0100. One officer and one man died on watch below; one of the armed guards also perished. The *Totland* treated the injured and put them ashore at Antigua. The other survivors transferred to a Dutch ship and landed in Trinidad.

NSS; WACR; WCSR; *Washington Post*, 24 March 1943. *Ships of the Esso Fleet*, pp. 181-86. The book relates that instead of a four-inch gun there was a five-inch aft. Rohwer, p. 151; *War Action Casualties*, p. 134.

JONATHAN STURGES

D:	2-23-43	YB:	1942
T:	2220	Tn:	7,176
Pos:	46.15 N / 38.11 W	Dr:	14 ft.
Ow:	WSA	C:	1,500 tons sand ballast
Op:	Mississippi Shipping Co.	P:	steam
M:	Thorbjorn Leerberg	S:	9
A:	1-4"; 1-3"; 8-20 mm		

On 11 February, the *Jonathan Sturges* sailed in Convoy ON-166 en route from Liverpool to New York. The vessel straggled from the convoy, and during a

squall the *U-707* (Gretschel) put two torpedoes into the #1 and #2 holds. The watch below secured the engines, and the master ordered the ship abandoned. The ship's eight officers, thirty-six men, and thirty-one armed guards launched three lifeboats and two life rafts. The heavy seas swamped one of the boats, so the known survivors got on the remaining two lifeboats. The *Sturges* was last seen barely above the water with her stern in the air. The #1 boat with nineteen men met a boat from the Dutch SS *Madoera* containing three survivors from that ship. The men shifted so that an equal number was in each boat. The men in the *Madoera*'s boat were rescued by the USS *Belknap* (DD-251) on 12 March and landed in Argentia, Newfoundland. One of these men died of exposure. The nine men in the #3 lifeboat found the chief cook in the #2 boat and also picked up four armed guards found clinging to a capsized lifeboat. After righting the boat, the men also regrouped so that the numbers in the boats were equal. These boats remained close for thirty-six hours but separated in the rough weather. The #2 boat with seven men remained at sea for forty-two days. During this time one man died of hunger and exposure. The *U-336* (Hunger) picked up the six survivors in this boat (four merchant crew and two Navy men) and took them to be interned as POWs near Bremen. The survivors in the #1 and #3 boats were never seen again. Nine of the armed guards, three officers, and twelve men survived the attack.

The survivors' statements are contradictory. NSS; WACR; WCSR; AG; Rohwer, p. 152; Moore, p. 569.

NATHANAEL GREENE

D:	2-24-43	YB:	1942
T:	1355	Tn:	7,176
Pos:	35.56 N / 00.05 E	Dr:	18 ft. 6 in.
Ow:	U.S. Maritime Commission	C:	1,300 tons general and food; 700
Op:	U.S. Lines		tons ballast
M:	George A. Vickers	P:	steam
A:	1-4"; 1-3"; 4-50 cal.	S:	7.5

On 24 February, the Liberty ship *Nathanael Greene*, bound from Mostaganem, Algeria, for Algiers, Algeria, steamed to join the six-vessel Convoy MKS-8. About forty miles northeast of Oran the *U-565* (Franken) torpedoed the vessel. The first torpedo struck the starboard side between the #1 and #2 hatches. A few seconds later a second torpedo struck the engine room on the same side. At the time of the attack the British minesweeper HMS *Brixham* (J-105), on station about a quarter of a mile away, came to her aid. The explosions severely damaged the deck cargo of tanks and trucks, damaged the midships deckhouse, disabled the engines, destroyed the starboard boiler, and completely flooded the forward compartments and the machinery spaces. The ship quickly settled by the head, but before the master could react, enemy planes also attacked the

convoy. A torpedo launched by one of these planes struck the midships section, adding to the damage already incurred. The master gave the alarm to abandon ship. As the *Brixham* came alongside the freighter, twenty-six men jumped directly on board. Other survivors got away in two lifeboats, and the minesweeper picked others from the water. The *Brixham* towed the *Nathanael Greene* until the salvage tug *Restive* took over the tow at 0900. Beached near Oran, the USS *Redwing* (ARS-4) managed to save at least 400 tons of cargo even though the vessel was judged a CTL. The complement of nine officers, thirty-two men, and sixteen armed guards survived, with the exception of one officer and three men on watch in the engine room who died in the initial torpedo explosion.

The ship's complement figures are contradictory. The master's report does not mention the attacking aircraft or any damage by aerial torpedoes. NSS; WACR; WCSR; AG; Rohwer, p. 243.

DANIEL CARROLL

D:	2-28-43	YB:	1942
T:	1723	Tn:	7,176
Pos:	37.05 N / 04.02.30 E	Dr:	24 ft. 6 in.
Ow:	WSA	C:	4,800 tons general
Op:	W. H. Winchester	P:	steam
M:	Kenneth Walker Pratt	S:	8.5
A:	1-5"; 1-3"; 8-20 mm		

The *Daniel Carroll* sailed from New York to Algiers, via Casablanca, Morocco, steaming in station #23 as part of Convoy TE-16. The *U-371* (Mehl) fired a torpedo that struck the freighter's starboard side at the bow. A second torpedo struck the freighter and failed to explode. Even though the explosion extensively damaged the ship, the ten officers, thirty-three men, twenty-seven armed guards, and thirty passengers remained on board. A British tug took the *Daniel Carroll* in tow to Algiers, where she arrived on 1 March. Salvors saved most of the cargo. The ship later went to Gibraltar for intermediate repairs and then to New York. She returned to service in July 1943. All hands survived the attack.

WACR; WCSR; TF; AG; Moore, p. 348; Rohwer, p. 243, places the attack at 37.03 N / 03.58 E.

WADE HAMPTON

D:	2-28-43	YB:	1942
T:	1754	Tn:	7,176
Pos:	59.55 N / 35.55 W	Dr:	27 ft. 11 in.
Ow:	Miss. Shipping Maritime Co.	C:	8,000 tons general, including
Op:	WSA		explosives
M:	John L. Reynolds	P:	steam
A:	1-4"; 1-3"; 8-20 mm	S:	11.75

The Liberty ship *Wade Hampton* left New York en route to Loch Ewe, Scotland, in the seventy-six ship Convoy HX-227. The freighter straggled behind the convoy when the chief mate decided to stop the ship in heavy weather to take in lifeboats hanging overboard. Eight miles astern of the convoy, the *U-405* (Hopmann) fired two torpedoes that struck the ship on the port side at the #4 and #5 hatches. The explosion carried away the entire stern, blew off the hatch covers, broke the shaft, and carried away the propeller and steering gear. The radio operator sent distress signals but never received a reply. The ship's complement of eight officers, thirty-six men, and thirty-one armed guards cleared the ship in four lifeboats and five rafts. The HMS *Vervain* (K-190) picked up most of the survivors three hours after the initial explosions. The chief engineer and master remained on board to see if the vessel could be salvaged, and they were the last to leave. On 3 March, the HMS *Beverly* (H-64) picked up the final survivor from a small raft. Five armed guards and three of the ship's crew died as a result of the attack.

NSS; WACR; WCSR; AG; Rohwer, p. 153, places the attack at 59.49 N / 34.43 W; Moore, p. 289, relates that the survivors were also rescued by the SS *Bayano*.

FITZ JOHN PORTER

D:	3-1-43	YB:	1942
T:	0341	Tn:	7,176
Pos:	12.25 S / 36.55 W	Dr:	14 ft.
Ow:	WSA	C:	ballast
Op:	McCormick SS Co.	P:	steam
M:	Herbert G. Gregg	S:	12
A:	1-3"; 5-20 mm		

On 28 February, the *Fitz John Porter* departed Bahia, Brazil, for Trinidad, BWI, in Convoy BT-6. As the ship traveled in ballast in station #14 in the formation, lookouts spotted a torpedo cross the bow. Some time later a second torpedo missed the stern by thirty yards. A third torpedo fired by the *U-518* (Wißßmann) struck the ship on the port side at the #5 hatch. The explosion blew large holes in the ship at the waterline on both sides, demolished the after gun mount, severed the main shaft, and completely destroyed the #5 hold. Most of the ship's

complement of eight officers, thirty men, and seventeen armed guards abandoned ship in four lifeboats and one raft in good order. The Brazilian mine layer *Carioca* rescued the survivors within two hours of the attack. The men later transferred to a Brazilian freighter and landed in Recife, Brazil. The explosion blew overboard and killed one armed guard asleep on the #5 hatch. The *Porter* sank sometime during the night of 2 March.

The ship's complement figures contrast immensely in the sources. The *U-518* reported six missed shots and eight duds in attacks on the convoys. NSS; WACR; WCSR; AG; Rohwer, p. 153, places the attack at 12.26 S / 36.56 W.

GULFWAVE

D:	3-1-43	YB:	1937
T:	1555	Tn:	7,140
Pos:	22.30 S / 174.45 E	Dr:	20 ft. 9 in.
Ow:	Gulf Oil Corp.	C:	water ballast
Op:	WSA	P:	steam
M:	Hans Sorensen	S:	12
A:	1-4"; 4-50 cal.; 1-20 cal.		

On 27 February, the *Gulfwave* proceeded from Nouméa, New Caledonia, to Suva, Fiji. She sailed from Suva on 2 March, under independent routing instructions from the Navy. A lookout spotted a torpedo fired from the *I-10* (Yamada) just as it struck abaft the bridge on the starboard side. The explosion ripped a hole approximately forty feet square in the ship's side and under the bottom. The pump room and the #4 and #5 tanks flooded, the engines stopped, and compasses and gauges broke and shattered. The ship swung to starboard after sighting a periscope, and the armed guards began firing at it as it disappeared. The helmsman started steering a zigzagging course at nine knots, and the ship arrived in Suva under her own power. The Navy made minor repairs there, and on 26 March, the tanker sailed to Pago Pago, via Tutuila, American Samoa, and then to Honolulu for more repairs. She received permanent repairs in Portland, Oregon, and went back in service in September 1943. None of the ship's eight officers, thirty-one men, or fifteen armed guards were killed or injured during the attack.

The armament figures are contradictory within the sources. NSS; WACR; WCSR; AG; TF; Rohwer, p. 282, places the attack at 20.30 S / 174.45 E; *War Action Casualties*, p. 135.

MERIWETHER LEWIS

D:	3-2-43	YB:	1942
T:	0603	Tn:	7,176
Pos:	62.10 N / 28.25 W	Dr:	28 ft. 10 in. (approximately)
Ow:	WSA	C:	ammunition, tires
Op:	American Mail Line	P:	steam
M:	John Edward Beal	S:	10
A:	1-4"; 1-3"; 8-20 mm		

The *Meriwether Lewis* sailed from New York to the USSR in Convoy HX-227. The freighter straggled from the convoy, and the *U-759* (Friedrich) attacked and missed. The *U-759*, however, led the *U-634* (Dahlhaus) to the freighter, and the latter sank the ship in broad daylight before she could return to the convoy. In a rain storm, the *U-634* maneuvered and fired a torpedo from 800 yards. The U-boat began to maneuver to fire a stern shot when a detonation occurred. The *Lewis* continued as the radio operator sent distress signals. The U-boat closed for a coup de grâce shot from 1,000 yards. This torpedo struck under the bridge and then quickly spread over the entire ship. After about six minutes a "mighty detonation" occurred in the forward part of the vessel, and the *Lewis* sank rapidly by the head. The *U-634* fired another torpedo into the ship an hour later, and the forward section broke off and sank. The U-boat sank the after section with gunfire. The USCG cutter *Ingham* (WPG-35) searched the area for two days and only located a trail of automobile tires that stretched for thirty miles. The entire complement of eight officers, thirty-six men, and twenty-five armed guards died in the attack.

WACR; WCSR; AG; WJ; Rohwer, p. 153.

HARVEY W. SCOTT

D:	3-3-43	YB:	1942
T:	2324	Tn:	7,176
Pos:	31.54 S / 30.37 E	Dr:	27 ft.
Ow:	WSA	C:	8,250 tons high explosives;
Op:	Grace Lines Inc.		gasoline, general
M:	Axel Eichel Uldall	P:	steam
A:	1-4"; 1-3"; 4-20 mm	S:	9

The Liberty ship *Harvey W. Scott* sailed from Durban, South Africa, en route to Bandar Shahpur, Iran, in Convoy DN-21. The convoy consisted of eleven merchant ships, one corvette escort, and two converted whalers. The *Scott* steamed in station #32 in the formation. A torpedo fired from the *U-160* (Lassen) struck the freighter on the port side at the #2 hold. The ship settled slowly as the watch below secured the main engines, and the radio operator sent a distress signal. Eleven minutes after the torpedo struck, the master gave the order to abandon ship. All eight officers, thirty-four men, and nineteen armed guards cleared the ship in four lifeboats. The ship sank just after midnight, plunging bow first. The boats later became separated. The Argentine SS *Ombu* spotted one boat containing sixteen men and took the men to Durban. The other three boats landed at Umtata, Natal, South Africa, on 3, 4, and 6 March. All hands survived.

NSS; WACR; WCSR; AG; Rohwer, p. 267.

STAGHOUND

D:	3-3-43	YB:	1942
T:	1915	Tn:	8,591
Pos:	16.44 S / 36.33 W	Dr:	29 ft.
Ow:	U.S. Lines	C:	5,800 tons dynamite, trucks, gas,
Op:	WSA		steel
M:	Harold Thomas McCaw	P:	diesel
A:	1-5"; 1-3"; 6-20 mm	S:	16.1

On 28 February, the *Staghound* departed New York bound for Rio de Janeiro. The vessel, capable of eighteen knots, proceeded alone. The submarine *Barbarigo* (Rigoli) initially fired two torpedoes that struck the freighter ten seconds apart—one in the #5 hold and the other at the forward portion of the #3 hold. The explosions damaged the ship fatally, knocked down the main antenna, and destroyed the steering gear. The general alarm and whistle sounded to alert the crew to abandon ship. The ship's complement of ten officers, forty-nine men, and twenty-five armed guards left the freighter in two lifeboats and one raft ten minutes after the initial explosion. After the vessel was abandoned, the *Barbarigo* put another torpedo into the *Staghound* amidships and caused the ship to sink rapidly stern first at 1950. Twenty-five hours after the attack the Argentine SS *Rio Colorado* picked up all hands and landed them at Rio de Janeiro on 8 March.

NSS; WACR; WCSR; USMMA; AG; Rohwer, p. 153.

EXECUTIVE

D:	3-5-43	YB:	1920
T:	0928	Tn:	4,600
Pos:	72.45 N / 11.40 E	Dr:	19 ft. 8 in.
Ow:	American Export Lines	C:	1,500 tons potassium chloride
Op:	American Export Lines	P:	steam
M:	James Walden	S:	9
A:	1-4"; 2-50 cal.; 2-30 cal.		

On 1 March, the *Executive* sailed from Murmansk, USSR, to Loch Ewe, Scotland, in the thirty-vessel Convoy RA-53. The "Hog Islander" steamed in station #51 in the formation but later shifted to station #52. At dawn German aircraft began shadowing the convoy and broadcasting its position. Lookouts spotted a torpedo fired by the *U-255* (Reche) crossing the ship's bow at 0926. Two minutes later a second torpedo struck the starboard side between the #4 hatch and the engine room. The explosion blew the hatch covers off the #4 hatch and demolished the booms, the engine, the dynamos, and all the equipment in the immediate area. Water flooded rapidly into the #4 hold, and the ship began to settle slowly by the stern. The eight officers, thirty men, and twenty-four armed guards abandoned ship without orders, getting away in three lifeboats and one raft. The trawlers HMS *St. Elstan* (FY-240) and HMS *Northern Pride* (FY-105) immediately rescued the men and landed them in Iceland. One armed guard, three officers, and five merchant crewmen died. A destroyer sank the *Executive* with gunfire at 1030.

NSS; WACR; WCSR; AG; Rohwer, p. 202.

RICHARD BLAND

D:	3-5-43	YB:	1942
T:	0928	Tn:	7,191
Pos:	72.45 N / 11.40 E	Dr:	22 ft. 6 in.
Ow:	U.S. Maritime Commission	C:	4,000 tons lumber, planes, food,
Op:	American-South African Line		tanks
M:	Lawrence Dodd	P:	steam
A:	1-4"; 1-12 lber.; 8-20 mm;	S:	7.7
	2-50 cal.; 2-30 cal.		

On 1 March, the new Liberty ship *Richard Bland* sailed in Convoy RA-53 bound from Murmansk, USSR, to Loch Ewe, Scotland. Since dawn of the 5th German planes continually circled the convoy. Meanwhile, the *U-255* (Reche) shadowed the convoy and, after maneuvering into a good attacking position, fired a three-torpedo spread. The first one missed the American SS *Executive*, the second hit that freighter, and the third struck the *Bland*. This torpedo struck at the #1 hold on the starboard side, did not explode, and passed through the ship and out the port side. The torpedo cracked the deck on both sides and ruptured the collision bulkhead, flooded the forepeak tank, and created eight-foot holes on either side. The ship listed to starboard but continued on course with only a slightly reduced speed. The master reported the damage to the convoy commodore and remained with the formation. None of the nine officers, thirty-three men, and twenty-six armed guards reported any injuries. Later,

during rough weather the *Bland* dropped from the convoy and proceeded toward Iceland. On 10 March, the *U-255* attacked again. (See attack on 10 March.)

NSS; WACR; WCSR; AG; Butler, pp. 70-71; Rohwer, p. 202, places the attack at 72.44 N / 11.27 E.

JAMES B. STEPHENS

D:	3-8-43	YB:	1942
T:	2218	Tn:	7,174
Pos:	28.53 S / 33.18 E	Dr:	18 ft.
Ow:	WSA	C:	1,086 tons bottles, medicine,
Op:	U.S. Lines		propellers, personal effects
M:	John Edward Green Jr.	P:	steam
A:	1-5"; 1-3"; 4-20 mm	S:	11.5

On 18 February, the *James B. Stephens* sailed independently from Suez en route to Durban, South Africa. The *U-160* (Lassen) spotted the freighter as she steered on a nonevasive course. A torpedo struck the vessel on the port side between the #2 and #3 hatches. The explosion set the fuel oil on fire and created an inferno as the ship settled rapidly by the head. The *U-160* fired a second torpedo about eight minutes later that struck the port side at the #4 hatch and broke the ship in two. After the initial torpedo struck, the ship's complement of eight officers, thirty-five men, and twenty armed guards began to abandon ship in four lifeboats and three rafts. As the men lowered the lifeboats, the second torpedo struck. This explosion overturned the motor lifeboat and threw its occupants into the water; it also blew three men in the #4 boat into the water. The remaining boats picked up all the men with the exception of one armed guard who drowned. On 11 March, a plane spotted one of the boats, and the trawler HMS *Norwich City* (FY-229) rescued nineteen men and landed them in Durban. The cruiser HMS *Nigeria* (60) picked up thirty more on the same day and took them to Durban. A South African Air Force crash boat rescued the remaining thirteen survivors one mile off Durban six days after the attack. Both halves of the vessel remained afloat. A British naval vessel attempted to tow the bow section to Durban, but it sank while under tow in heavy seas. Naval vessels sank the stern half by gunfire.

NSS; WACR; WCSR; AG; Rohwer, p. 267.

GEORGE G. MEADE

D:	3-9-43	YB:	1942
T:	0006	Tn:	7,176
Pos:	07.11 N / 52.30 W	Dr:	unknown
Ow:	WSA	C:	water ballast
Op:	Weyerhaeuser SS Co.	P:	steam
M:	Paul Belden Hyatt	S:	unknown
A:	1-3"; 5-20 mm		

The Liberty ship *George C. Meade* sailed from Bahia, Brazil, to Paramaribo, Dutch Guiana, in Convoy BT-6. The vessel steamed in station #34 in the convoy. During the convoy conference, the *Meade* was designated as one of the rescue vessels. After the *U-510* (Neitzel) torpedoed several ships in the convoy, the *Meade* hove to for two and one-half hours to rescue thirty survivors from other ships. Two hundred miles off Paramaribo the *U-510* (Neitzel) torpedoed the *Meade* and slightly damaged the vessel. The *Meade* was towed to Paramaribo and arrived on 10 March 1943. She later went to New York for further repairs and returned to service. All eight officers, thirty-three men, and twenty-five armed guards on board survived.

WCSR; AG; Sawyer and Mitchell, p. 65; Rohwer, p. 154.

MARK HANNA

D:	3-9-43	YB:	1942
T:	0206	Tn:	7,176
Pos:	07.11 N / 52.30 W	Dr:	17 ft.
Ow:	WSA	C:	ballast
Op:	Moore McCormick SS Co.	P:	steam
M:	Henry Hoeppner	S:	8.5
A:	1-5"; 5-20 mm; 2-30 cal.		

The *Mark Hanna* sailed with Convoy BT-6 en route from Bahia, Brazil, to Paramaribo, Dutch Guiana. The *Hanna* proceeded in convoy station #33. A torpedo fired by the *U-510* (Nietzel) struck the vessel on the port side at the #5 hold. The explosion ripped a forty-foot by thirty-foot hole in the ship's port side and several smaller holes in the starboard side. Booms fell, the deck buckled, the #5 hatch cover flew off, the rudder jammed, and the shaft broke. To add to the peril, it appeared that the damaged ship might collide with the American SS *James Smith* torpedoed just minutes after the *Hanna*. The master ordered those assigned to the port boats to abandon ship and to return after the ships collided. The collision, however, was avoided, but the boats drifted away and the *PC-592* rescued their thirty-three occupants. The remaining crewmen helped to get the ship under tow and arrived in Trinidad on 17 March. The *Hanna* went back in service in September 1943.

NSS; WACR; WCSR; AG; Rohwer, p. 154, places the attack at 07.40 N / 52.07 W.

JAMES SMITH

D:	3-9-43	YB:	1942
T:	0208	Tn:	7,181
Pos:	7.11 N / 52.30 W	Dr:	16 ft.
Ow:	WSA	C:	water ballast
Op:	Matson SS Co.	P:	steam
A:	1-5"; 1-3"; 4-50 cal.; 2-30 cal.	S:	11.5
M:	William H. Aguilar		

The *James Smith* sailed in Convoy BT-6 from Bahia, Brazil, to Paramaribo, Dutch Guiana. She steamed in station #73 as the third ship in the outboard column. The ship began following evasive maneuvers under orders of the convoy commodore. Lookouts spotted the wake of a torpedo fired from the *U-510* (Neitzel) just before it struck the port side at the #5 hold. The explosion occurred nearly at the waterline and blew a large section out of the ship's side and bottom. The explosion also disabled the steering gear, knocked down the radio antenna, and damaged the propeller shaft. After securing the engines, the survivors among the eight officers, thirty-four men, and sixteen armed guards on board calmly left the ship in four lifeboats. Five armed guards and six crewmen sleeping on the tarpaulin cover of the #5 hatch died from the explosion. After daybreak two of the four boats returned to the ship. The *PC-592* picked up the other two boats and at noon pulled beside the *James Smith*, whose bow lay out of the water. On 12 March, convinced the ship was lost, the master boarded the *PC-592*. The *Smith*, however, did not sink, and the master, three crewmen, and the armed guard officer again reboarded and stayed with the ship as the British rescue tug HMS *Zwarte Zee* (W-163) towed her to Trinidad. She returned to service in August 1943.

NSS; WACR; WCSR; AG; TF; The Action Report of the USS *Borie* (DD-215) claims the *Smith*'s convoy position was #32. Rohwer, p. 154, places the attack at 07.40 N / 52.07 W.

THOMAS RUFFIN

D:	3-9-43	YB:	1942
T:	0210	Tn:	7,191
Pos:	07.11 N / 52.30 W	Dr:	16 ft.
Ow:	U.S. Maritime Commission	C:	water ballast
Op:	A. H. Bull Co.	P:	steam
M:	Severin Broadwick	S:	8.75
A:	1-4"; 1-3"; 4-20 mm; 2-30 cal.		

On 6 February, the *Thomas Ruffin* sailed from Cape Town, South Africa, for Georgetown, British Guiana, via Bahia, Brazil. The ship joined Convoy BT-6 and proceeded in convoy station #31. A lookout spotted a torpedo fired from the *U-510* (Neitzel) just before it struck the ship on the port side in the engine room. The explosion disabled the radio, ruptured steam lines and fuel tanks, destroyed the shaft and the engines, and killed those on watch below. The Liberty ship took an immediate list to starboard. Most of the ship's complement of eight officers, thirty-five men, and fifteen armed guards abandoned the ship immediately in two boats and two rafts. The armed guard commander and a seaman remained on board. The boats stayed in the area until the next day when the master and another man reboarded the ship. The USS *Courage* (PG-70) rescued forty of the crew. Three of these men died from steam burns on board the corvette. Fifteen of the forty later transferred to the USS *Borie* (DD-215). All survivors landed in Trinidad. The *PC-592* later removed the master, the armed guard commander, and the two men. The *Thomas Ruffin* was towed to the naval dock in Port-of-Spain, and after some repairs she was towed to Mobile, Alabama, and declared a CTL. Two officers, two men, and two armed guards died in the attack.

NSS; WACR; WCSR; AG; Rohwer, p. 154, places the attack at 07.40 N / 52.07 W.

JAMES K. POLK

D:	3-9-43	YB:	1942
T:	0210	Tn:	7,177
Pos:	07.11 N / 52.30 W	Dr:	10 ft.
Ow:	WSA	C:	water ballast
Op:	American-South African Line	P:	steam
M:	Herbert Vidrian Olson	S:	8.5
A:	1-5"; 1-3"; 4-20 mm		

The Liberty ship *James K. Polk* sailed with Convoy BT-6 from Bahia, Brazil, to Paramaribo, Surinam. Proceeding in station #23 in the convoy, the *Polk* received orders from the convoy commodore to take evasive actions after torpedoes fired by the *U-510* (Neitzel) struck other ships in the convoy. As the ships performed evasive maneuvers, the convoy became unorganized. Five minutes later a torpedo fired by the *U-510* struck the *Polk* on the port side amidships. The explosion knocked out all six sides of the #3 deep tank, extensively damaged the #5 double bottom tank, damaged the engine room, wrecked pumps and piping, carried away the radio antenna, and sprung the carriages of the two large guns. The ship began to settle by the stern until only three feet of freeboard remained. The ship's seven officers, thirty-seven men, eighteen armed guards, and three passengers remained on board. All but the master and seven others transferred to the *PC-592* and landed at Port-of-Spain, Trinidad. The master and the volunteers rigged tarpaulins on the foremast and mizzenmast, and the master sailed the vessel 360 miles. An Allied ship later met the vessel and towed her to Trinidad, where she arrived on 17 March. She was later towed to Mobile, Alabama, and declared a CTL. The only death occurred when the explosion blew the #4 lifeboat from its davits and it crushed one of the armed guards.

NSS; WACR; WCSR; Sawyer, Mitchell, p. 111; Rohwer, p. 154, places the attack at 07.40 N / 52.07 W.

MALANTIC

D:	3-9-43	YB:	1929
T:	1930	Tn:	3,837
Pos:	59.30 N / 24.00 W	Dr:	22 ft.
Ow:	Marine Transport Line	C:	4,300 tons ammunition and
Op:	WSA		general
M:	Peter Hansen Lang	P:	steam
A:	1-4"; 4-20 mm; 2-30 cal.	S:	7.5

On 23 February, the *Malantic* departed New York for Liverpool, England, in Convoy SC-121. As the ship proceeded in convoy station #102, a torpedo fired from the *U-409* (Maßmann) struck her at the #1 hatch on the starboard side. A violent explosion occurred fifteen seconds later, blowing out the wheelhouse windows. The watch below secured the engines, and the radio operator sent distress signals but received no answers. The master ordered the ship abandoned immediately. In a gale, the men launched the two port lifeboats, the starboard boats having been rendered useless by the blast. All eight officers, twenty-five men, thirteen armed guards, and one passenger safely left the ship. The *Melrose Abbey* stood by in rough seas to pick up the survivors. Several men from the #4 boat drowned while trying to get on board the rescue vessel. The #2 lifeboat swamped beside the rescue vessel, drowning several more. In all, three officers, sixteen men, five naval gunners, and the passenger died trying to get on the

British SS *Melrose Abbey*. The survivors landed at Gourock, Scotland, the next day. The *Malantic* gradually settled by the head and sank on the 10th.

NSS; WACR; WCSR; AG; Rohwer, p. 155, and other sources place the attack at 58.37 N / 22.32 W.

PUERTO RICAN

D:	3-9-43	YB:	1919
T:	2200	Tn:	6,076
Pos:	66.44 N / 10.41 W	Dr:	12 ft.
Ow:	U.S. Maritime Commission	C:	3,500 tons ore
Op:	American Hawaiian SS Co.	P:	steam
M:	Ralph Albert Oliver	S:	6
A:	1-5"; 1-3"; 4-20 mm; 4-50 cal.; 2-30 cal.		

On 1 March, the *Puerto Rican* sailed from Molotovsk, USSR, in Convoy RA-53 bound for the United Kingdom. The freighter straggled from the convoy and traveled alone for two days. The *U-586* (von de Esch) spotted the lone freighter and fired a torpedo that struck the ship aft of the #5 hatch. The ship with her dense cargo sank on an even keel in fifteen minutes. The eight officers, thirty-two men, and twenty-five armed guards on board attempted to abandon ship in two lifeboats and two life rafts in rough seas and 30° below zero weather. The boats and rafts unfortunately had frozen in place, and the men managed to free only one boat. This boat capsized when the after fall failed to release and threw all the occupants into the sea. The men in the water and those clinging to the overturned boat quickly froze to death. In the 21° water only eight men eventually managed to swim to a doughnut raft. Six of these men later transferred to a large provisioned raft. During the next two days all these men except one froze to death or washed off the raft. The sole survivor, a fireman wearing a lifesaving suit, was rescued on 12 March by the British trawler HMS *St. Elstan* (FY-240).

NSS; WACR; WCSR; RWCS; AG; Wall, pp. 27-29, 69; Rohwer, p. 202.

VIRGINIA SINCLAIR

D:	3-10-43	YB:	1930
T:	0030	Tn:	6,151
Pos:	20.11 N / 74.04 W	Dr:	24 ft. 8 in.
Ow:	Sinclair Refining Co.	C:	66,211 bbls. aviation gasoline
Op:	WSA	P:	steam
M:	Fred Charles Vosloh	S:	8.5
A:	1-4"; 2-30 cal.		

The *Virginia Sinclair* sailed from Baytown, Texas, to Panama and joined the ten-ship Convoy KW-123. The *U-185* (Maus) fired a torpedo that struck the tanker on the starboard side at the stern. The explosion stopped the engines and damaged the steering gear. Fortunately, the cargo did not ignite as the ship sank rapidly by the stern. The complement of nine officers, twenty-nine men, and six armed guards including two naval signalmen abandoned ship in three lifeboats and one raft. The USS *SC-742* rescued the survivors three and one-half hours later and landed them at Guantánamo, Cuba. One officer and two men died on watch below, while four other men never left the ship. The *Sinclair*'s bow remained fifteen feet above the water, and she had to be sunk by gunfire.

NSS; WACR; WCSR; AG; Rohwer, p. 155, places the attack at 19.49 N / 74.38 W.

JAMES SPRUNT

D:	3-10-43	YB:	1943
T:	0310	Tn:	7,177
Pos:	19.49 N / 74.38 W	Dr:	28 ft. 10 in.
Ow:	WSA	C:	4,000 tons general, explosives
Op:	Black Diamond SS Co.	P:	steam
M:	Elie Constantine Carr	S:	9.5
A:	1-5"; 9-20 mm		

The new Liberty ship *James Sprunt* left Texas via the Canal Zone to Karachi, India, on her maiden voyage. Traveling in Convoy KG-123 in station #42, the freighter had shifted out of position between the third and fourth columns. The *U-185* (Maus) fired a torpedo that struck the vessel and caused her cargo to explode. The blast went straight up and sent debris over the entire convoy, and the Liberty ship completely disappeared in thirty seconds. The blast was so large that a ship forty miles away witnessed it. The ship's complement of eight officers, thirty-six men, and twenty-five armed guards all perished.

NSS; WACR; WCSR; AG; Sawyer, Mitchell, p. 113.

RICHARD BLAND

D:	3-10-43	YB:	1942
T:	1543	Tn:	7,191
Pos:	66.48 N / 14.15 W	Dr:	23 ft. 6 in.
Ow:	U.S. Maritime Commission	C:	4,000 tons lumber
Op:	American-South African Line	P:	steam
M:	Lawrence Dodd	S:	7.3
A:	1-4"; 1-12 lber.; 8-20 mm; 2-50 cal.; 2-30 cal.		

On 1 March, the *Richard Bland* sailed from Murmansk, USSR, to Loch Ewe, Scotland. On 5 March, a dud torpedo fired from the *U-255* (Reche) damaged the freighter. The vessel, however, continued with Convoy RA-53, although with a slightly reduced speed. Gale force winds and rough seas later caused the ship to lose contact and straggle from the convoy. The *U-255* returned to finish the job on the 10th. Three torpedoes were fired. The first struck at the #4 hatch on the port side. After the first attack the freighter developed a slight list, and flooding from the explosion brought the ship back on an even keel. A second torpedo missed astern. The third torpedo hit the port side at the fireroom, and the explosion bent the propeller shaft, flooded the #4 and #5 holds, and broke the ship in two. After the first explosion the master ordered the complement of nine officers, thirty-three men, and twenty-six armed guards to remain on board since the ship did not seem in immediate danger. At 1715, Captain Dodd had two weather boats launched, each carrying four men, and they rode at their painters until time to abandon ship. When the second torpedo hit at 1838, it convinced the master to abandon ship. In attempting to pass these boats around the ship, the painters were lost and the boats drifted astern. The remaining sixty-one crewmen thus had to clear the ship in the other two boats. Launching the overcrowded boats in rough seas became a problem. The #4 boat got away first and quickly filled with survivors. With only inches of freeboard, many clung to the overloaded boat's side until they lost strength, fell in the water, and drowned. The #2 boat is thought to have swamped and was never seen. The eight men in the #1 and #3 boats were rescued the same morning. The destroyer HMS *Impulsive* (I-11) rescued the other twenty-seven in the #4 boat the same day. Apparently none of the crew perished from the explosions; however, seventeen armed guards, six officers, and thirteen crewmen perished from drowning or exposure. The forward section of the ship was eventually towed to Iceland for salvage.

The NSS reports the ship loaded with war cargo, which is unlikely. WACR; WCSR; AG; Rohwer, p. 202, places the attack at 66.53 N / 14.00 W; Bunker, pp. 71-72.

ANDREA F. LUCKENBACH

D:	3-10-43	YB:	1919
T:	1836	Tn:	6,564
Pos:	51.04 N / 29.40 W	Dr:	28 ft. 2 in.
Ow:	Luckenbach SS Co.	C:	11,600 tons general Army
Op:	WSA		equipment and explosives
M:	Rolf Neslund	P:	steam
A:	1-4"; 1-3"; 8-20 mm	S:	9

On 28 February, the *Andrew F. Luckenbach* sailed from New York, en route to Liverpool, England, in Convoy HX-228. At dusk on 10 March, the lead ship in

the *Luckenbach*'s column was torpedoed, and the crew went to general quarters. Minutes later lookouts spotted a periscope and within moments two torpedoes from the *U-221* (Trojer) struck the freighter. The first hit the vessel on the port side about ninety feet forward of the stern post. The combination of the torpedo's explosion and the detonation of the after magazine, blew the after end off. Seconds later another torpedo hit just forward of the first. The master determined that the torpedoes had fatally damaged his ship, and he immediately ordered the ship abandoned. The freighter sank stern first in seven minutes, but the majority of the nine officers, forty-six men, twenty-eight armed guards, and one passenger got away in two lifeboats. Others jumped overboard and swam to the boats, the rafts, and wreckage. In just over an hour the oiler HMS *Orangeleaf* rescued seventeen armed guards, nine officers, thirty-seven men, and the passenger. The survivors landed at Clyde, Scotland. The remaining twenty men died. Ten armed guards on the after gun platform perished when the ship's magazine exploded.

NSS; WACR; WCSR; Rohwer, p. 155, places the attack at 51.20 N / 29.29 W.

RICHARD D. SPAIGHT

D:	3-10-43	YB:	1942
T:	1930	Tn:	7,177
Pos:	28.00 S / 37.00 E	Dr:	16 ft. 6 in.
Ow:	WSA	C:	3,000 tons steel, concrete
Op:	American-West African Line	P:	steam
M:	Russell Hoover Quynn	S:	12
A:	1-5"; 1-3"; 8-20 mm		

On 25 February, the *Richard D. Spaight* sailed from Massaua, Eritrea, bound for Durban, South Africa. The vessel was proceeding alone in the Mozambique Channel when the *U-182* (Clausen) fired a torpedo that struck the starboard side at the #1 hold. Thirty seconds later another torpedo struck between holds #2 and #3. The explosions extensively damaged the ship and showered the deck with debris. The bow immediately submerged and lifted the stern and propeller out of the water. The crew never secured the engines, and the propellers continued turning even after the crew abandoned ship. The eight officers, thirty-five men, and twenty-four armed guards on board left the ship in four boats. The revolving screw made the abandonment perilous and drew one boat containing several men toward the propeller. These men jumped out before the boat passed through the propeller and swamped. After the boats cleared the ship, the *U-182* surfaced and from 2,000 yards fired about thirty-five rounds from its 105-mm gun, hitting her twenty-five times. The vessel sank just over two hours later. The *U-182* came near the boats and the officers questioned the men. They then offered medical supplies, food, and water and left. Two of the boats made Richards Bay, South Africa, in just under three days. Another boat made

landfall at Cape St. Lucia. The fourth boat put in at Cuanalonbi Beach, South Africa, five days after the attack. The only man lost, a messman, was sitting on the #1 hatch when the torpedo struck. The explosion blew this man over the side, and no one saw him afterwards. Another man, also lying atop the hatch on a mattress, survived. The explosion blew him higher than the mast, but fortunately he stayed on the mattress and landed right side up to be rescued by one of the boats.

NSS; WACR; WCSR; RWCS; AG; Rohwer, p. 267.

WILLIAM C. GORGAS

D:	3-10-43	YB:	1943
T:	2340	Tn:	7,176
Pos:	51.35 N / 28.30 W	Dr:	28 ft.
Ow:	WSA	C:	8,000 tons food, cotton, TNT,
Op:	Waterman SS Co.		planes, landing craft
M:	James Calvin Ellis Jr.	P:	steam
A:	1-4"; 1-3"; 8-20 mm	S:	6.5

On 28 February, the Liberty ship *William C. Gorgas* departed New York en route to Liverpool, England, in Convoy HX-228. The *Gorgas* proceeded in station #131 in the convoy. The *U-444* (Langfeld) fired a torpedo that struck the freighter on the starboard side amidships. The explosion ripped a hole fifteen feet in diameter in the side at the engine room and killed the watch below. The crew secured the engines as the machinery spaces flooded. In rough seas and snow, the master ordered the ship abandoned, and the survivors among the eight officers, thirty-five men, and twenty-seven armed guards cleared the ship in four lifeboats. While being lowered, one of the lieboats was lifted upwards by a wave. The wave then suddenly dropped the boat, and it snapped back on the falls, causing the men and equipment to go right through the bottom. The British destroyer HMS *Harvester* (H-19) rescued all the gun crew, six officers, and twenty-seven men. Two torpedoes from the *U-432* (Eckhardt) later struck the *Harvester,* and she sank leaving only eight of the merchant crew and four armed guards alive. The corvette *Aconite* (K-58) rescued these men. The *William C. Gorgas* remained afloat after abandonment, and the *U-757* (Deetz) later sank her with a coup de grâce shot in the #1 hold.

NSS; WACR; WCSR; RWCS; AG; WJ; Rohwer, pp. 155-56, credits the *U-444* with firing the initial torpedo. This is not completely confirmed in the WJs of the two U-boats.

CITIES SERVICE MISSOURI

D:	3-13-43	YB:	1920
T:	0458	Tn:	7,612
Pos:	14.10 N / 74.40 W	Dr:	15 ft. 6 in.
Ow:	Cities Service Oil Co.	C:	24,000 bbls. water ballast
Op:	WSA	P:	steam
M:	John H. B. Morton	S:	8.5
A:	1-5"; 2-50 cal.		

The *Cities Service Missouri* sailed from New York to Aruba, NWI, in Convoy GAT-49. The tanker proceeded in station #23 as the last ship in the second column. A torpedo fired by the *U-68* (Lauzemis) struck the ship at the stem on the starboard side. The explosion ripped a ten-foot hole in the side and vented upward, damaging the bridge and wheelhouse. The master ordered the engines full speed astern and then stopped the vessel to determine the damage. The master and chief engineer concluded that the ship could be saved if they shifted the ballast. After getting the vessel on an even keel, the *U-68* fired a second torpedo that struck the port side in the engine room at 0610 and demolished the engines. With the ship sinking, the submarine surfaced about 1,300 yards from her. The armed guards fired three shots, but all missed the submarine. By this time, water had risen to the base of the gun. The master ordered the ship abandoned at 0640, and all eight officers, thirty-five men, and eleven armed guards left the tanker in three lifeboats and one raft. Three hours later the USS *Biddle* (DD-151) rescued fifty-one of the crew. A boatswain drowned trying to get on the *Biddle*, and a second man died of wounds and burns on board the destroyer. The survivors landed at Curaçao, NWI. At 0740 the ship plunged stern first with her bow straight in the air.

NSS; WACR; WCSR; AG; Rohwer, p. 157, places the attack at 14.50 N / 71.46 W; *War Action Casualties*, p. 138.

KEYSTONE

D:	3-13-43	YB:	1919
T:	1740	Tn:	5,565
Pos:	38.10 N / 37.58 W	Dr:	22 ft.
Ow:	States Marine Corp.	C:	6,000 tons war cargo, planes,
Op:	WSA		tanks, trucks
M:	John Henry Darby	P:	steam
A:	1-4"; 9-20 mm	S:	11.5

On 4 March, the *Keystone* departed New York en route to North Africa in Convoy UGS-6, which consisted of forty-five merchant ships and seven escorts. On 12 March, the *Keystone* developed engine problems and straggled from the convoy. An escort remained with the freighter for some time and then left to

rejoin the convoy. The *U-172* (Emmermann) spotted the lone freighter and fired a torpedo that struck the port side aft of the #5 hatch. The explosion ruptured the hull, destroyed the steering engine and steering gear, buckled the deck, disabled the four-inch gun, and flooded the shaft alley. A fire started five minutes later, and one of the planes lashed to the deck began to burn. The crew immediately secured the engines. Convinced the ship was unsalvageable, the master ordered the crew to abandon ship. Most of the eight officers, thirty-five men, twenty-seven armed guards, and two passengers left the ship in good order in four lifeboats. After the crew cleared the ship, the *U-172* fired a second torpedo that struck at the #3 hold and caused the vessel to break in two and rapidly sink. The initial explosion killed one of the gun crew and a fireman. The Portuguese SS *Sines* rescued seventy-one men and landed them in the Azores.

The operator of the vessel is unclear in the sources. NSS; WACR; WCSR; AG; VSC; Rohwer, p. 157, places the attack at 37.59 N / 37.40 W.

BENJAMIN HARRISON

D:	3-16-43	YB:	1943
T:	1850	Tn:	7,191
Pos:	39.09 N / 24.15 W	Dr:	22 ft.
Ow:	WSA	C:	4,250 tons food, machinery,
Op:	Calmar SS Corp.		ammunition, trucks, tanks
M:	George Hunter Sterne	P:	steam
A:	1-4"; 1-3"; 4-20 mm	S:	8.5

On 4 March, the *Benjamin Harrison* sailed from New York to North Africa in Convoy UGS-6. The freighter proceeded in station #73 in the formation. The convoy had just made an evasive turn when the ship was struck by a torpedo fired from the stern tube of the *U-172* (Emmermann). The torpedo struck the #5 hold on the starboard side. The *Harrison* began to settle slowly and appeared to be in no great danger of sinking quickly. The master did not order the eight officers, thirty-five men, twenty-seven armed guards, and one passenger to abandon ship. Some men shouted this order, creating great confusion, and they began leaving the ship in a chaotic manner. The explosion had damaged one of the ship's boats, and in their haste the crew improperly launched two others. They left them hanging by the falls, causing their occupants to fall into the sea. Only one boat was launched effectively. Fifteen of the men wore life preservers, and sixteen clung to the full lifeboat until rescued. The USS *Rowan* (DD-405) rescued three men and landed them at Casablanca. The SS *Alan A. Dale* rescued the other survivors and landed them in Algeria. The *Rowan* sank the freighter with gunfire at 1930. Only two officers died in the attack and subsequent confusion.

NSS; WACR; WCSR; AG; Rohwer, p. 157.

JAMES OGLETHORPE

D:	3-16-43	YB:	1943
T:	1847	Tn:	7,176
Pos:	50.00 N / 36.00 W	Dr:	26 ft. 8 in.
Ow:	WSA	C:	8,000 tons steel, cotton, food,
Op:	South Atlantic SS Co.		aircraft, tractors
M:	Albert W. Long	P:	steam
A:	1-4"; 1-3"; 8-20 mm	S:	12

On 8 March, the *James Oglethorpe* departed New York bound for Liverpool, England. She traveled in station #93 in the forty-two ship Convoy HX-229. The *U-758* (Manseck) fired a torpedo that struck the starboard side at the forward section of the #2 hold. The vessel began settling by the head with her rudder stuck and a starboard list. A fire started in the #1 hold, and the crew managed to extinguish it in fifteen minutes. The master did not order the engines secured, and as the freighter made large circles to port at eight knots, forty-four of the eight officers, thirty-six men, twenty-six armed guards, and four passengers, abandoned ship in two boats. The #5 boat's fall was cut prematurely and spilled its occupants into the sea, drowning thirteen men. Another man died when he fell into the water while trying to get into the #6 boat. The British corvette HMS *Pennywort* (K-11) rescued the thirty men in boat #6 and landed them in Londonderry, Ireland. The master and the thirty men who remained on the ship perished when the *U-91* (Walkerling) fired a coup de grâce shot on the 17th and sank the ship. Three officers and ten men of the merchant crew, two passengers, and fifteen armed guards survived.

NSS; WACR; WCSR; WJ; Rohwer, p. 157, places the attack at 50.38 N / 36.46 W.

WILLIAM EUSTIS

D:	3-16-43	YB:	1943
T:	2008	Tn:	7,196
Pos:	49.57 N / 37.06 W	Dr:	27 ft. 6 in.
Ow:	WSA	C:	7,000 tons sugar, 600 tons food
Op:	United Fruit Co.	P:	steam
M:	Cecil Desmond	S:	7
A:	1-5"; 1-3"; 8-20 mm		

On 8 March, the *William Eustis* sailed from New York to Scotland in Convoy HX-229. As the Liberty ship proceeded in station #22, the *U-435* (Strelow) fired two torpedoes at her. One struck the *Eustis* on the starboard side at the #2 hatch, and another missed by 200 feet. The explosion blew off the #2 and #3 hatch covers and flooded the #2 hold immediately. A split developed on the starboard side twenty feet from the #2 hold to the bridge. The master decided to abandon

ship about thirty minutes after the explosion. The eight officers, thirty-four men, and thirty armed guards left the ship in one lifeboat and four rafts. Heavy weather had damaged four of the boats, and the torpedo's explosion damaged the fifth. The destroyer HMS *Volunteer* (D-71) rescued all hands four hours later. The freighter remained afloat, and seven hours later the *U-91* (Walkerling) sank her with a coup de grâce shot.

NSS; WACR; WCSR; Rohwer, pp. 157-58, places the attack at 50.34 N / 135.02 W.

HARRY LUCKENBACH

D:	3-17-43	YB:	1919
T:	0030	Tn:	6,399
Pos:	50.38 N / 34.46 W	Dr:	25 ft. 6 in.
Ow:	Luckenbach SS Co.	C:	8,381 tons general
Op:	Luckenbach SS Co.	P:	steam
M:	Ralph McKinnon	S:	9.5
A:	1-4"; 1-3"; 8-20 mm		

On 8 March, the *Harry Luckenbach* sailed from New York en route to the United Kingdom in Convoy HX-229. Assigned station #111 in the convoy, the ship was so exposed that the master had nervously steamed a zigzag course out in front of the convoy until ordered to return to his station. The *U-91* (Walkerling) fired two torpedoes that struck the freighter's starboard side amidships in the machinery spaces. Eyewitnesses in the convoy observed a huge explosion and much smoke. In rough seas, some of the nine officers, forty-five men, and twenty-six armed guards fired distress rockets as they cleared the ship in three lifeboats. The ship sank in three minutes, however, and few managed to survive the sinking and the rough seas. As many as four escort vessels spotted some of the men in the boats. The corvette *Anemone* (K-48) was ordered to find the lifeboats, and the corvette *Pennywort* (K-111) had come across them but could not pick up the men because she already had 108 survivors on board. The other escorts never located any of the men, and all hands perished.

WACR; WCSR; AG; TF; Middlebrook, pp. 184, 186.

IRÉNÉE DU PONT

D:	3-17-43	YB:	1941
T:	0300	Tn:	6,125
Pos:	50.36 N / 34.30 W	Dr:	26 ft. 6 in.
Ow:	International Freighting Corp.	C:	3,200 tons oil, 5,800 tons
Op:	WSA		general, 11 bombers
M:	Christian Simonson	P:	steam
A:	1-5"; 1-3"; 8-20 mm	S:	9.5

On 8 March, the *Irénée Du Pont* departed New York en route to Liverpool, England, in Convoy HX-229. The freighter maintained her station #81 in the convoy until the beginning of the attack. The *U-600* (Zurmühlen) fired a spread of five torpedoes; two hit the *Du Pont* and the others struck two other vessels in the convoy. The two torpedoes struck the starboard side at holds #2 and #3. The explosions knocked out the generators, flooded both holds, and also slowly flooded the engine room and hold #1. The master gave orders to abandon the Liberty ship forty-five minutes after the torpedoes struck. The ten officers, thirty-nine men, twenty-six naval gunners, and nine naval passengers on board abandoned ship in two lifeboats and three rafts. Some men jumped in the water because a third lifeboat fouled a cargo net, and some of the rafts could not be launched. The Dutch SS *Tekoa* rescued fifty-five men. The Royal Canadian Navy destroyer *Mansfield* (G-76) rescued sixteen others. Six armed guards, six of the merchant crew, and one passenger drowned. One other merchant crewman died from shock and was buried at sea from the *Mansfield*. The British corvette *Anemone* (K-48) tried to sink the vessel with four-inch shells and a depth charge, but the ship remained afloat. The *U-91* (Walkerling) sent the ship to the bottom at 0830 with a coup de grâce shot about ten hours after the initial attack.

There is evidence that the master of the *Du Pont* asked to leave the convoy since his ship could steam at sixteen knots. This permission was denied. The casualty figures are contradictory. NSS; WACR; WCSR; AG; Rohwer, pp. 158-59, places the attack at 50.34 N / 35.02 W; Middlebrook, p. 97; Rohwer, *The Critical Convoy Battles*, p. 120.

MOLLY PITCHER

D:	3-17-43	YB:	1943
T:	1815	Tn:	7,176
Pos:	38.21 N / 19.54 W	Dr:	27 ft. 7 in.
Ow:	WSA	C:	5,600 tons sugar, coffee, TNT,
Op:	Prudential SS Co.		coal, vehicles, tanks
M:	David Martin Bailie	P:	steam
A:	1-5"; 9-20 mm	S:	9

On 4 March, the *Molly Pitcher* sailed from New York en route to Casablanca, North Africa, in Convoy UGS-6. As she proceeded in station #82, the *U-167* (Sturm) fired a torpedo that struck the vessel on the port side at the #3 hold. The explosion damaged the forward bulkhead between holds #2 and #3, resulting in the flooding of both compartments. The helmsman deserted the wheel after the explosion, and the ship veered to port toward the center of the convoy. After getting the ship under control, and with great confusion on board, the master and fifty-two of the eight officers, thirty-four men, twenty-seven armed guards, and one passenger on board decided to abandon the ship in three lifeboats, leaving seventeen men on the ship. The engines remained in motion, and the

freighter began making circles while the men launched the boats. Those left on board got the vessel under control and avoided the survivors. The men managed to get the ship under way at ten knots to rejoin the convoy. Compass damage, however, hampered efforts to find the convoy, and at 2130 the seventeen men abandoned the ship on one raft and two other hastily improvised ones. The USS *Champlin* (DD-601), the SS *William Johnson*, and the *Rowan* (DD-405) rescued sixty-six survivors. The master's license was later suspended on a charge of misconduct. The *Champlin* tried to sink the freighter with a torpedo, but a coup de grâce shot by the *U-521* (Bargsten) finally sent her to the bottom. Two officers and two armed guards drowned leaving the ship.

NSS; WACR; WCSR; AG; Rohwer, p. 159.

WALTER Q. GRESHAM

D:	3-18-43	YB:	1943
T:	1256	Tn:	7,191
Pos:	53.39 N / 27.53 W	Dr:	23 ft. 6 in.
Ow:	Standard Fruit & SS Co.	C:	10,000 tons powdered milk and
Op:	WSA		sugar, general
M:	Byron Wade Miller	P:	steam
A:	1-5"; 1-3"; 8-20 mm	S:	9.5

The *Walter Q. Gresham* sailed on her maiden voyage from New York bound for Clyde, England, in Convoy HX-229. The *Gresham* proceeded in station #21 in the convoy. A torpedo fired by the *U-221* (Trojer) struck the port side at the #5 hold. The explosion destroyed the gun crew's after quarters, created a hole thirty feet in diameter, and probably blew the screws off the shaft. The crew immediately secured the engines, and the master ordered the men to their abandon ship stations. At 1311 the eight officers, thirty-four men, twenty-six armed guards, and two passengers mustered at the lifeboat stations. They successfully launched two boats, but a third capsized while being lowered. The remaining men used two rafts to save themselves. Two hours after the attack the HMS *Pennywort* (K-111) and the HMS *Anemone* (K-48) rescued forty-two survivors and landed them in Gourock, Scotland. Five officers, eighteen merchant sailors, and five armed guards perished, most of them from drowning. The *Gresham* sank stern first about an hour after the initial explosion.

NSS; WACR; WCSR; Middlebrook, pp. 248, 250-51; Rohwer, p. 159, places the attack at 53.35 N / 28.05 W.

MATHEW LUCKENBACH

D:	3-19-43	YB:	1918
T:	0854	Tn:	5,847
Pos:	54.20 N / 25.07 W	Dr:	28 ft.
Ow:	Luckenbach SS Co.	C:	8,360 tons steel, grain,
Op:	WSA		ammunition, etc.
M:	Atwood N. Borden	P:	steam
A:	1-4"; 1-3"; 8-20 mm	S:	11.5

On 8 March, the *Mathew Luckenbach* departed New York en route to the United Kingdom in Convoy HX-229. On 18 March, the freighter deliberately left the convoy—the master and the crew thinking the ship had a better chance alone. Unfortunately, the master proceeded into an area near Convoy SC-122, a convoy that the Germans had actively attacked. The new type IX C submarine *U-527* (Uhlig) fired a three-torpedo spread, and two torpedoes hit the *Luckenbach*. The first torpedo struck the port side at the #2 hatch and ripped a hole about nine feet long in the hull at the waterline. The second torpedo struck at the #4 hatch, and the damage could not be ascertained. The master immediately secured the engines. The complement of eight officers, thirty-four men, and twenty-six armed guards began to abandon the ship in three lifeboats and two rafts. The USCG cutter *Ingham* (WPG-35) rescued all hands and landed them in Londonderry, Ireland. Seven hours after the initial attack the *U-523* (Pietzsch) discovered the freighter still afloat and finished her off with a coup de grâce shot.

NSS; WACR; WCSR; AG; Middlebrook, p. 267; Rohwer, p. 159, places the attack at 54.23 N / 23.34 W.

EXAMINER

D:	3-19-43	YB:	1942
T:	2200	Tn:	6,737
Pos:	in Oran Harbor	Dr:	25 ft.
Ow:	WSA	C:	6,000 tons ammunition and
Op:	American Export Lines		gasoline
M:	Willy W. Kuhne	P:	steam
A:	1-4"; 2-3"; 8-20 mm	S:	at anchor

On 14 January, the *Examiner* sailed from New York in convoy to Oran via Gibraltar. As she waited to discharge her cargo, enemy bombers attacked the ships in the harbor. The *Examiner* did not receive any direct hits, but shrapnel from indirect hits put seventy holes in the vessel and damaged the foremast. The gun crew on board claimed the downing of two planes. Of the ten officers, forty-five men, and thirty-six armed guards on board during the attack, shrapnel killed one armed guard and wounded six naval gunners and three merchant crew

members. One armed guard and one merchant sailor attached to the ship also died on shore during the attack. The damage to the ship was listed as slight.

On 21 May, her foremast was slightly damaged by flack. WACR; WCSR; AG; TF; ONF.

WILLIAM PIERCE FRYE

D:	3-29-43	YB:	1943
T:	2050	Tn:	7,176
Pos:	56.57 N / 26.15 W	Dr:	26 ft. 11 in.
Ow:	WSA	C:	7,500 tons general war cargo,
Op:	Mystic SS Line		wheat, explosives, 5 LCTs
M:	Meinhard Scherf	P:	steam
A:	1-3"; 9-20 mm	S:	12.5

On 18 March, the *William Pierce Frye* sailed from New York bound for Liverpool, England, in Convoy HX-230. The freighter developed engine trouble on the 23rd and straggled from the convoy. The master had the ship stopped to make repairs when lookouts spotted a submarine on the surface. The ship immediately got under way at fourteen knots in rough seas and successfully evaded the submarine. The next day the freighter could manage only a speed of just over twelve knots, and the *U-160* (von Freyberg) attacked the crippled Liberty ship. The first torpedo struck the starboard side at the #1 hold. The wheat in this hold cushioned the explosion. A second torpedo hit amidships and extensively damaged the ship, flooded the shaft alley, and knocked down the stack. Previous heavy weather had damaged three of the *Frye*'s lifeboats. The torpedo explosions damaged two more, and the last good boat fouled and swamped when the crew launched it. To make matters worse, all four of the rafts and the two floats drifted away in heavy seas. The ship settled rapidly and sank by the head in ten minutes, forcing the eight officers, thirty-two men, and twenty-four armed guards to jump into the water. Only seven managed to swim to one of the LCTs that had floated free of the vessel. Five days later the British destroyer HMS *Shikari* (D-85) rescued these men and landed them in Londonderry, Ireland. The remaining twenty-two armed guards, six officers, and twenty-nine men died.

NSS states that one lifeboat was launched and was never seen again. Coast Guard Records do not confirm this. WACR; WCSR; AG; Rohwer, p. 160, places the attack 2° farther east.

GULFSTATE

D:	4-3-43	YB:	1923
T:	0310	Tn:	7,216
Pos:	24.22 N / 80.27 W	Dr:	28 ft. 6 in.
Ow:	Gulf Oil Corp.	C:	68,417 bbls. crude oil
Op:	WSA	P:	steam
M:	James Frank Harrell	S:	10.5
A:	1-5"; 4-50 cal.; 2-30 cal.		

On 29 March, the *Gulfstate* sailed independently from Corpus Christi, Texas, to Portland, Maine, via New York. As she steamed a nonevasive course off Key West, Florida, the *U-155* (Piening) fired a torpedo that struck the tanker on the port side directly under the bridge. The explosion ripped a large hole in the hull at the waterline, causing immediate flooding, and the cargo of oil caught fire. Moments later a second torpedo struck the vessel at the engine room. The fire leapt 100 feet in the air and spread from the bridge to the after part of the vessel. The master immediately ordered the engines secured and the ship abandoned. Because the flames spread so quickly and the ship sank bow first in less than four minutes, none of the lifeboats could be launched and all the rafts burned before they could be released. Only a single doughnut raft managed to break free of the ship. The complement of eight officers, thirty-four men, and nineteen armed guards had no choice but to jump in the water and swim through the 600 feet of burning oil surrounding the ship. The few survivors clung to flotsam and the doughnut raft for seven hours before being discovered. A Navy blimp and a Coast Guard plane spotted the survivors and dropped two more rubber life rafts. The Coast Guard plane picked up three of the most seriously wounded two hours later. At 1300 the *YP-351* picked up fifteen more survivors and later transferred some of the wounded to the USS *Noa* (DD-343). The remaining nine armed guards, eight officers, and twenty-six men perished in the attack.

The complement figures for the crew are contradictory within the sources. Navy Records differ on the armament and indicate the vessel carried 78,000 bbls. of oil. NSS; WACR; WCSR; AG; Rohwer, p. 161, places the attack at 24.26 N / 80.18 W.

SUNOIL

D:	4-5-43	YB:	1927
T:	0950	Tn:	9,005
Pos:	58.16 N / 34.14 W	Dr:	28 ft. 4 in.
Ow:	Sun Oil Co.	C:	102,000 bbls. Navy fuel oil
Op:	Sun Oil Co.	P:	motor
M:	Sedolf Berg Heggelund	S:	8
A:	1-4"; 1-3"; 8-20 mm		

On 27 March, the *Sunoil* sailed from New York to the United Kingdom via Halifax in Convoy HX-231. She had traveled in station #45 in the formation but developed engine trouble and straggled from the convoy. While sailing independently, she began a zigzagging course. In snow showers, the *U-563* (von Hartmann) surfaced. Spotting the tanker, the U-boat hit her with a torpedo. The *Sunoil*'s armed guards returned fire and forced the *U-563* to submerge. The radio operator sent a distress signal that the escort commander received. The HMS *Vidette* (I-43) steamed to assist the stricken tanker. Meanwhile the *U-530* (Lange) spotted the *Sunoil* and began to follow. About ten and a half hours after the initial attack the *U-530* put three torpedoes into the crippled tanker, sinking her quickly. None of the ship's ten officers, thirty-three men, and twenty-six armed guards were ever located by the *Vidette*.

WACR; WCSR; AG; WJ; Rohwer, p. 161; *War Action Casualties*, p. 141.

JOHN SEVIER

D:	4-6-43	YB:	1942
T:	0658	Tn:	7,143
Pos:	20.35 N / 74.00 W	Dr:	28 ft. 2 in.
Ow:	WSA	C:	9,060 tons bauxite ore
Op:	Pacific Atlantic SS Co.	P:	steam
M:	Charles Frederick Drury	S:	6.5
A:	1-4"; 2-30 cal.; 4-20 mm		

The *John Sevier* sailed from Guantánamo Bay, Cuba, to Mobile, Alabama, in the four-ship Convoy GTMO-83. The ship proceeded as the lead ship in the port column, station #11. Lookouts spotted the wake of a torpedo fired from the *U-185* (Maus) only seconds before it hit the starboard side at the #5 hold. The torpedo pierced the hull, exploded inside the ship, and caused most of its damage on the port side, flooding the #4 and #5 holds rapidly. With the engines secured, the master ordered the ship abandoned about fifteen minutes after the torpedo struck. The *Sevier* sank stern first in forty minutes. In rough seas, all eight officers, thirty-one men, seventeen armed guards, and one passenger left the ship in good order in four lifeboats and one raft. The USS *Bennett* (DD-473) rescued all hands just over four hours after the attack and landed them at Guantánamo Bay the same day.

NSS; WACR; WCSR; AG; Rohwer, p. 161, places the attack at 20.49 N / 74.00 W.

EDWARD B. DUDLEY

D:	4-10-43	YB:	1943
T:	1430 GWT	Tn:	7,177
Pos:	53.00 N / 38.00 W	Dr:	unknown
Ow:	WSA	C:	4,000 tons munitions, food,
Op:	T. J. Stevenson Co.		cotton
M:	Gibson Douglass Hillary	P:	steam
A:	1-4"; 9-20 mm	S:	unknown

On 4 April, the *Edward B. Dudley* sailed in Convoy HX-232 from New York bound for the United Kingdom. The freighter straggled from the convoy, perhaps because of bent propeller blades. The *U-615* (Kapitzky) fired a dud torpedo on the 10th that hit the ship and failed to explode. The *U-615* followed the freighter and the next day at 0446 GWT put two torpedoes into the vessel amidships. From 800 yards, the *U-615* fired a third torpedo that struck at the stern and ignited the after magazine. At 0516 the U-boat fired a coup de grâce shot from 500 yards that struck under the bridge. The explosion that followed lifted the ship in the air, and the debris damaged the *U-615*'s conning tower. Even though the War Journal mentions that boats were launched, none of the ship's complement of eight officers, thirty-four men, and twenty-five armed guards were ever found.

WACR; WCSR; AG; WJ; Rohwer, p. 162, places the attack at 53.00 N / 39.00 W.

JAMES W. DENVER

D:	4-11-43	YB:	1943
T:	1516	Tn:	7,191
Pos:	28.46 N / 25.40 W	Dr:	26 ft.
Ow:	WSA	C:	6,000 tons sugar, planes,
Op:	Calmar SS Co.		vehicles, acid, flour, bull dozers
M:	Everett William Staley	P:	steam
A:	1-4"; 9-20 mm	S:	11

On 1 April, the *James W. Denver* sailed on her maiden voyage from New York to Casablanca in Convoy UGS-7. Within the first day the freighter's engine bearings overheated and she straggled from the convoy. As she proceeded independently via a straggler route, the coxswain sighted a torpedo's wake only forty yards from the ship. The torpedo, fired from the *U-195* (Buchholz), struck below the waterline on the starboard side between the #2 and #3 holds. The general quarters alarm sounded, and the watch below secured the engines immediately. The master ordered the ship abandoned about twenty minutes after the torpedo struck as the ship took a heavy list and settled by the head, bringing the propeller out of the water. Most of the eight officers, thirty-four men,

twenty-five armed guards, and one passenger on board left the ship in five lifeboats. The #6 port motorboat capsized throwing eighteen men into the sea, but they all managed to get into other boats. The master stayed on board for an hour before leaving the ship. The master's boat stayed in the vicinity of the sinking until the next morning. The other four set sail for the African coast. These four boats stayed together for one day and became separated during the second night. The Spanish SS *Cabo Huertas* rescued eleven men seven days after the attack. The SS *Campana* rescued fifteen others thirteen days after the attack. After twenty-three days at sea the Portuguese steam fishing trawler *Albufeira* rescued another eleven men. The master and thirteen men made landfall seventy miles north of Port Etienne after twenty-five days at sea, and patrol boats landed them at Port Etienne. The last boat remained at sea for thirty-five days. The Spanish sailing vessel *Juan* rescued the eighteen men in this boat and landed them at Lisbon. The second engineer died of exposure and was buried at sea, and an oiler later died in a hospital at Gibraltar.

NSS; WACR; WCSR; RWCS; AG; Rohwer, p. 162, places the attack at 28.52 N / 26.30 W; Bunker, p. 87.

MATT W. RANSOM

D:	4-11-43	YB:	1943
T:	1540	Tn:	7,177
Pos:	33.59 N / 07.51 W	Dr:	25
Ow:	WSA	C:	8,000 tons iron pipe, sugar, vehicles, war materials, road equipment
Op:	Smith & Johnson		
M:	John Metsall		
A:	1-5"; 1-3"; 8-20 mm	P:	steam
		S:	11

On 19 March, the *Matt W. Ransom* sailed on her maiden voyage from New York to Casablanca in Convoy UGS-6A. While steaming in station #32, the vessel struck a mine under the #1 hold. The explosion threw water 100 feet in the air, causing holds #1 and #3 to flood rapidly. The explosion broke the keel, damaged other equipment, and severed some steam lines. The master sent the crew to their abandon ship stations to lower the boats. The crew interpreted this to mean they should abandon ship—an order the master never uttered. Twenty-five minutes after the explosion most of the eight officers, thirty-six men, twenty-eight armed guards, and two passengers had cleared the ship in six lifeboats. One boat swamped because the men mishandled the falls. The master and six men later reboarded the vessel, got her under way, and took her into Casablanca. The *PC-481* and *PC-471* picked up the men in the boats and took them to Gibraltar. The crew reported no injuries. She was later sunk as a

breakwater, one of the "gooseberries," during military operations off the French coast on 8 June 1944.

NSS; WACR; WCSR; USMMA; AG.

THOMAS HARTLEY

D: 4-18-43	YB: 1942
T: 1230	Tn: 7,176
Pos: Murmansk Harbor	Dr: unknown
Ow: WSA	C: unknown
Op: Merchant and Miners Trans. Co.	P: steam
M: Herbert E. Callis	S: anchored
A: 1-5"; 1-3"; 8-20 mm	

The *Thomas Hartley* sailed in convoy to Murmansk, USSR. The vessel remained in the port of Murmansk for two months and went through over sixty bombing raids. Aircraft attacked the Liberty ship at least six times. During one of these attacks an incendiary bomb struck the *Hartley* and started a small fire that the crew quickly extinguished. On the morning of the 18th a German bomber dropped a bomb twenty feet off the port quarter. The concussion broke steam flanges in the engine room and shattered glass throughout the vessel. The crew size is unknown, but no casualties resulted from the attacks.

USMMA; AG; The master of record was Paul Burris. ONF.

MICHIGAN

D: 4-20-43	YB: 1920
T: 0745	Tn: 5,609
Pos: 36.01 N / 01.25 W	Dr: 24 ft.
Ow: States SS Co.	C: 6,300 tons food, ammunition,
Op: States SS Co.	asphalt, vehicles, fuel, lumber
M: Birger Jacobsen	P: steam
A: 1-4"; 1-3"; 6-20 mm	S: 10

On 1 April, the *Michigan* departed New York en route to Oran, Algeria, in Convoy UGS-7. The *Michigan* was proceeding in station #81 forty miles west of Oran when the *U-565* (Franken) fired a torpedo that struck between the #1 and #2 holds with a muffled explosion. The blast caused extensive damage to the hull and minor damage to the deck and superstructure and threw water in the air to the height of the bridge. The ship, however, began to settle rapidly and lost way immediately. The master had the engines secured as the ship settled by the bow. All eight officers, twenty-nine men, twenty-three armed guards, and one passenger left the ship in two lifeboats and three rafts within ten minutes.

Two hours later the escort trawlers HMS *Stella Carina* (FY-352) and HMS *Foxtrot* (T-109) rescued all hands. The men later transferred to the minesweeper HMS *Felixstowe* (J-126) and landed in Oran. The *Michigan* stayed afloat for about an hour before plunging bow first. Some of the crew remained in their lifeboats to rescue Senegalese troops being carried by the torpedoed French army transport *Sidi-Bel Abbes*, which took station behind the *Michigan*. Many of these men drowned, but the assistance of the crew of the *Michigan* prevented a greater loss of life.

NSS; WACR; WCSR; AG; Rohwer, p. 245, places the attack at 35.59 N / 01.25 W.

JOHN DRAYTON

D:	4-21-43	YB:	1942
T:	2119	Tn:	7,177
Pos:	34.00 S / 34.40 E	Dr:	18 ft. 2 in.
Ow:	WSA	C:	250 tons fresh water ballast
Op:	A. H. Bull SS Co.	P:	steam
M:	Carl Norman	S:	11.5
A:	1-5"; 1-3"; 4-20 mm		

On 3 April, the *John Drayton* sailed from Bahrein, en route to Cape Town, South Africa, in Convoy PB-34. The ship departed the convoy on 6 April and proceeded alone. At about 1500, lookouts spotted a torpedo fired by the Italian submarine *Da Vinci* (Gazzana) that seemed to pass about five feet ahead of the bow. The master ordered the helmsman to steer a zigzag course. Forty-five minutes later, a second torpedo passed twenty-five feet aft of the ship. A third torpedo struck the vessel on the starboard side amidships, entering the ship about four feet below the waterline. The explosion damaged the engine, the boilers, and the steam and water lines. The ship's whistle signaled the complement of eight officers, thirty-four men, and fifteen armed guards to abandon ship. Most of the men escaped in two lifeboats and a raft; a third boat capsized when launched. After the crew left, the *Leonardo Da Vinci* surfaced and lit the sky with a red flare. It then fired twenty-three shells at the freighter and scored nineteen hits. The *Da Vinci* came alongside and took on board one of the crew. Officers questioned and then released him. The Swedish SS *Oscar Gorthon* rescued eleven survivors in one boat thirty-eight hours after the attack. The HMS *Relentless* (H-85), six days later, spotted the raft containing the master and thirteen others. The last boat with twenty-four men remained at sea for thirty days before being found. Only eight men were still alive; three merchant men in this boat later died in Durban. A total of five officers, sixteen men, and six armed guards perished.

NSS; WACR; RWCS; AG; Rohwer, p. 111, places the attack at 32.10 N / 34.50 W; Enright, p.9.

ROBERT GRAY

D:	4-23-43	YB:	1942
T:	1500 GWT	Tn:	7,176
Pos:	57.30 N / 43.00 W	Dr:	27 ft. 8 1/2 in.
Ow:	WSA	C:	8,600 tons general war supplies
Op:	Waterman SS Agency	P:	steam
M:	Alfred Rasmussen Lyngby	S:	unknown
A:	1-4"; 1-3"; 8-20 mm		

On 12 April, the *Robert Gray* sailed from New York en route to the United Kingdom in Convoy HX-234. The freighter straggled from the convoy on the night of 13 April. The *U-306* (von Trotha) spotted the ship about 125 miles south of Cape Farewell ten days after she lost the convoy. The U-boat fired four torpedoes from about 4,000 yards. Three struck the freighter. The explosions caused the munitions on board to explode, and the U-boat's war journal records twelve extra explosions. None of the eight officers, thirty-one men, and nineteen armed guards survived the attack.

WACR; WCSR; AG; TF; WJ; Rohwer, p. 163.

SANTA CATALINA

D:	4-23-43	YB:	1943
T:	2056	Tn:	6,507
Pos:	30.59 N / 70.57 W	Dr:	25 ft.
Ow:	Grace Line	C:	6,700 tons airplanes, tanks, steel,
Op:	WSA		tires, gasoline, small arms, etc.
M:	Olaf Berg	P:	steam
A:	1-5"; 9-20 mm	S:	16.5

On 21 April, the *Santa Catalina* sailed independently from Philadelphia, Pennsylvania, to Basra, Iraq. The *U-129* (Witt) attacked the freighter with two torpedoes while she steamed on a zigzag course. The first torpedo struck the freighter at the #1 hold on the starboard side. The second hit nearly the same spot and blew holes in both sides of the ship. Gasoline in this hold caught fire and the ship listed to starboard about 40°, preventing the master from maneuvering the ship. The crew secured the engines, and the radio operator began sending distress signals. The ten officers, forty-seven men, twenty-eight armed guards, and ten passengers on board abandoned ship about twenty minutes after the explosions, clearing the ship in the two starboard lifeboats and four rafts. Ten minutes after the crew left the ship, the fire reached the hold containing powder, causing a huge explosion. The ship sank rapidly bow first at 2120. Twelve hours later the Swedish MV *Venezia* rescued all hands.

NSS; WACR; WCSR; AG; Rohwer, p. 163, places the attack at 30.42 N / 70.58 W.

SAMUEL PARKER

D:	4-25-43	YB:	1942
T:	0500	Tn:	7,176
Pos:	Avola, Sicily	Dr:	unknown
Ow:	WSA	C:	unknown
Op:	American Mail Line	P:	steam
M:	Elmer J. Stull	S:	at anchor
A:	1-5"; 1-3"; 8-20 mm		

On 1 November 1942, the *Samuel Parker* loaded war cargo in Puget Sound and sailed for Sydney, Australia, via San Pedro. She eventually steamed through the Suez Canal and shuttled between Mediterranean ports carrying troops and military supplies. The freighter arrived in Tripoli Harbor in March. During an air attack a nearby vessel loaded with bombs and gasoline caught fire. After burning for five hours it exploded, and debris rained down in the harbor for minutes, damaging the *Parker*'s deck. On Easter morning, 25 April, the vessel had a lighter tied off beside her #4 hatch to load gasoline. During an air raid the lighter caught fire, and the blaze buckled 600 square feet of plating. None of the crew, the armed guards, or the Egyptian stevedores on board were apparently killed in either incident.

USMMA; TF; AG.

LYDIA M. CHILD

D:	4-27-93	YB:	1943
T:	2110	Tn:	7,176
Pos:	33.08 S / 153.24 E	Dr:	23 ft. 6 in.
Ow:	WSA	C:	6,246 tons food, tanks, sheet
Op:	McCormick SS Co.		metal, steel rods, locomotives
M:	Carl Maurits Enstrom	P:	steam
A:	1-3"; 5-20 mm; 4-50 cal.	S:	12

On 3 April, the *Lydia M. Child* sailed on her maiden voyage independently routed from San Francisco, California, to Suez via Sydney, Australia. About 100 miles east of Sydney, lookouts on the zigzagging freighter spotted a torpedo that passed forty feet forward of the bow. A second torpedo, fired by the *I-178* (Utsuki), sped from the port quarter and struck the bulkhead between the #2 and #3 holds, about twelve feet below the waterline. The ship immediately listed to port, both holds flooded rapidly, and the ship sank in nine minutes by the bow. The master reversed the main engines, and the ship lost all headway. The armed guards fired one round from the after three-inch gun in the direction of the submarine. All eight officers, thirty-three men, and twenty-one armed guards abandoned the ship in five lifeboats minutes after the torpedo struck. Fifteen

hours later the Australian minesweepers *Warrnambool* (J-202) and *Deloraine* (J-232) rescued all hands. The ships landed the men at Port Jackson, Sydney, Australia.

NSS; WACR; WCSR; AG; Rohwer, p. 282.

McKEESPORT

D:	4-29-43	YB:	1919
T:	0530	Tn:	6,198
Pos:	60.52 N / 34.20 W	Dr:	18 ft. 3 in.
Ow:	WSA	C:	2,000 tons sand ballast
Op:	U.S. Lines	P:	steam
M:	Oscar John Lohr	S:	7
A:	1-4"; 9-20 mm		

On 21 April, the *McKeesport* departed Liverpool, England, en route to New York in Convoy ONS-5. The freighter had sailed in convoy station #42 but had fallen slightly astern. A torpedo fired from the *U-258* (Mässenhausen) struck the starboard side at the collision bulkhead and the #1 hold. The explosion blew out all beams, hatches, and ballast; put the steering gear out of order; and created a large hole. The ship worked up to full speed, causing a second torpedo to pass astern. The *McKeesport* continued at full speed for forty-five minutes but gradually developed a list of 20° to port and began to sink further by the head. The order to abandon ship was finally passed, and at 0615 the twelve officers, thirty-one men, and twenty-five armed guards left the ship in four lifeboats. Because of the list, the crew experienced difficulty launching the boats, and some of the boats became tangled in the life nets draped over the side. The trawler HMS *Northern Gem* (FY-194) picked up the survivors within thirty minutes and landed the men at St. John's, Newfoundland. One man died of exposure on the escort ship after the rescue. The convoy commodore sent the frigate HMS *Tay* (K-232) back to sink the freighter by gunfire, and she sank at noon.

The *U-258* fired three torpedoes; two exploded outside the convoy. NSS; WACR; WCSR; AG; Moore, pp. 176-77; Rohwer, p. 164.

PHOEBE A. HEARST

D:	4-30-43	YB:	1943
T:	0710	Tn:	7,176
Pos:	19.48 S / 176.44 W	Dr:	27 ft.
Ow:	WSA	C:	3,000 tons munitions and
Op:	American President Lines		gasoline, plane parts
M:	Stephanos Bacoyanis	P:	steam
A:	1-3"; 9-20 mm	S:	12.5

On 27 April, the Liberty ship *Phoebe A. Hearst* sailed independently from Nouméa en route to Pago Pago. About 240 miles southeast of Suva, a lookout heard a humming noise and at 200 yards spotted a torpedo fired from the *I-19* (Kinashi). Because the vessel had no time to maneuver, the torpedo struck the starboard side, creating a hole nine and one-half feet in diameter at the waterline between holds #2 and #3. The explosion threw water and flames into the air as high as the bridge and started a fire in both holds. The freighter remained on an even keel, and the crew of eight officers, thirty-two men, and sixteen armed guards abandoned ship immediately in the #2 and #4 port lifeboats and three rafts. The #3 lifeboat fouled while being lowered and could not be used. The men on the three rafts lashed them together to give a more stable platform in the moderate seas. The ship continued to burn, and nearly twelve hours after the initial attack she blew up and disintegrated, throwing debris 1,500 feet in the air. After thirty-five hours a PBY spotted the eight men on the rafts and took them to Suva, Fiji Islands. The twenty-three survivors in the #4 boat made landfall at Tofua Island after five days at sea, and the USS *YMS-89* took them to Tongatabu. Fourteen days after the attack, the small rescue boat USS *Dash* (AM-88) rescued the remaining twenty-five men in the #2 lifeboat, including the master. All survived the attack and the ordeal in the boats.

NSS; WACR; WCSR; AG; Rohwer, p. 282, places the attack at 20.07 S / 177.35 W.

WILLIAM WILLIAMS

D:	5-2-43	YB:	1942
T:	1454	Tn:	7,182
Pos:	20.10 S / 178.03 W	Dr:	16 ft.
Ow:	WSA	C:	none; ballast
Op:	Isthmian SS Co.	P:	steam
M:	Willie R. Freeman	S:	10
A:	1-3"; 5-20 mm		

On 1 May, the *William Williams* sailed from Suva, Fiji, on independent routing to Tongatabu Island. The *I-19* (Kinashi) fired a torpedo that struck the zigzagging freighter's port side between the #4 and #5 bulkheads. The explosion

tore a hole forty feet long by thirty feet wide in the ship's plating and blasted a hole through the starboard side. The explosion blew the hatch covers and beams off the #4 and #5 hatches, threw debris as high as the mast, and damaged the shaft alley and structural members of the ship. A fire broke out in two compartments and a firefighting party quickly assembled. The crew immediately secured the engines, and the ship lost all headway as the stern settled. With the main deck awash, the master ordered all hands except the gun crew and the firefighting party to abandon ship. After the fires were extinguished, the master, the chief engineer, and a few men reboarded the Liberty ship to restart her engines. The remaining men stayed in the lifeboats made fast to the ship with a painter and trailed astern. Two days later all the crew reboarded the ship except twelve who were taken on a minesweeper standing by. The USS *Catalpa* (AN-10) took the freighter under tow, and with two escorts, including the USS *Dash* (AM-88), and air cover she arrived in Suva on 7 May. All eight officers, sixteen armed guards, and thirty-two men survived, with only one man reporting an injury.

The armed guard numbers conflict within the sources. After repairs and conversion, the *William Williams* reentered service as the U.S. Navy *Venus* (AK-135). NSS; WACR; WCSR; AG; Rohwer, p. 283, places the attack at 20.09 S / 178.04 W; Sawyer, Mitchell, p. 143.

WEST MAXIMUS

D: 5-4-43   YB: 1919
T: 2519   Tn: 5,561
Pos: 55.00 N / 43.00 W   Dr: 18 ft. 6 in.
Ow: WSA   C: 745 tons slag ballast
Op: Moore-McCormack SS Co.   P: steam
M: Earl Elmo Brooks   S: 7
A: 1-5"; 6-20 mm

On 20 April, the *West Maximus* sailed from Milford Haven, Wales, bound for New York in Convoy ONS-5. As the freighter proceeded in convoy station #22 in heavy weather, the formation was attacked by the *U-264* (Looks). The first torpedo struck the port side in the after peak tank and blew off a large section of the stern. Because of a misunderstanding, some of the eight officers, thirty-one men, twenty-one armed guards, and two Army passengers abandoned the ship. The master ordered the men not yet in the boats to return to their stations and allowed the two boats already launched to stand by the freighter. As the vessel settled, she became unmaneuverable, and the master ordered the main engines secured. The crew awaited assistance from another vessel. A second torpedo struck the freighter about two hours later at the #3 hatch on the port side. The explosion demolished the after bulkhead of the #3 hold, blew off the hatch covers, flooded the fireroom, wrecked steam lines, and showered the vessel with fuel oil. On the master's orders, the remaining crew began to abandon ship in four lifeboats. Within minutes of leaving the ship a third torpedo hit the vessel at the #2 hold on the port side. This explosion sent the freighter to the bottom bow first ten minutes later. One officer and four men died from the merchant crew, and one of the armed guards drowned while trying to jump from a life raft to a boat. The trawler HMS *Northern Spray* (FY-129) rescued the survivors three and one-half hours later and landed them at St. John's, Newfoundland.

The number of armed guards given in the sources conflict. NSS; WACR; WCSR; AG; Rohwer, p. 165, places the attack at 55.00 N / 42.58 W.

WEST MADAKET

D:	5-5-43	YB:	1919
T:	1200	Tn:	5,565
Pos:	54.47 N / 44.12 W	Dr:	16 ft.
Ow:	Waterman SS Co.	C:	100 tons sand ballast, 75 tons
Op:	WSA		water
M:	Hans Schroeder	P:	steam
A:	1-4"; 1-3"; 6-20 mm	S:	8.5

The *West Madaket* steamed from Milford Haven on 20 April, en route to New York in Convoy ONS-5. Heavy weather caused the freighter to straggle from the convoy, and more than a day later she joined five other stragglers with the corvette HMS *Pink* (K-137) as an escort. The *U-584* (Deecke) attacked two ships in this group of stragglers south of Cape Farewell. A single torpedo struck the *West Madaket* on the port side between the #5 hatch and the after peak tank. Immediate flooding caused the ship to settle by the stern, and a crack developed amidships, indicating she had broken her back. The explosion also damaged the steam lines aft as well as one in the engine room, and the crew secured the engines immediately. The ship's eight officers, thirty-one men, and twenty-two armed guards began leaving the ship about twenty minutes after the torpedo struck. The merchant crew got off in three lifeboats, while the armed guards stayed behind hoping to get a shot at the submarine. The gun crew eventually left by jumping into the water and by climbing down lines into the boats. The HMS *Pink* rescued all hands. About an hour after the attack she sank the freighter with four depth charges.

NSS; WACR; WCSR; AG; Rohwer, p. 165.

SAMUEL JORDAN KIRKWOOD

D:	5-6-43	YB:	1943
T:	2340	Tn:	7,176
Pos:	15.00 S / 07.00 W	Dr:	15 ft.
Ow:	WSA	C:	water ballast
Op:	A. H. Bull & Co. Inc.	P:	steam
M:	Samuel Olsen	S:	12
A:	1-5"; 1-3"; 8-20 mm		

On 28 April, the *Samuel Jordon Kirkwood* departed Cape Town, South Africa, bound for Bahia, Brazil. At 0315, the *U-195* (Buchholz) fired a torpedo that passed fifteen feet astern of the zigzagging freighter, and it exploded two minutes after passing the ship. A second torpedo fired by the *U-195* crossed the ship's bow twenty minutes later and again exploded two minutes after passing the vessel. Almost exactly twenty hours after sighting the first torpedo lookouts spotted a third torpedo on the port beam. The helmsman put the rudder hard aport, but since the ship had sailed in light ballast with the propeller protruding above the water, she could not be maneuvered well. The torpedo struck about ten feet below the waterline on the port quarter just aft of the #5 hatch. The explosion ripped a twenty-foot hole in the side, demolished the shaft alley and steering gear, and hurled one of the armed guards overboard. The watch below immediately secured the engines, and the six officers, thirty-six men, twenty-five armed guards, and four passengers left the ship in four lifeboats. The Liberty ship sank stern first nearly two hours after the torpedo struck her. Ten days later a U.S. Army crash boat spotted the lifeboats and took the four in tow. All hands were later landed on Ascension Island.

The sources conflict regarding the ship's complement. NSS; WACR; WCSR; AG; Rohwer, p. 166.

PAT HARRISON

D:	5-8-43	YB:	1942
T:	0605	Tn:	7,191
Pos:	Gibraltar Bay	Dr:	16 ft.
Ow:	WSA	C:	sand ballast
Op:	Standard Fruit SS Co.	P:	steam
M:	Karl Harry Kellar	S:	stopped
A:	1-5"; 1-3"; 8-20 mm		

The *Pat Harrison* sailed from Oran to Algeciras Bay, off Gibraltar. As the freighter awaited Convoy GUS-7 at the commercial anchorage in the bay, an Italian mine detonated under the ship near the boiler room. The explosion fractured the vessel across the bottom and on either side, lifted the boilers off their saddles, and immediately flooded the engine room and the #3 hold. Fuel oil sprayed out the stack, coated the amidships portion of the vessel, and partially filled the lifeboats. As the vessel settled, the master ordered the boats readied for lowering. The master stated that at the time of the explosion the ship's complement consisted of forty-two men, twenty-six naval gunners, and two Army security officers. The freighter settled about five or six feet. Under the direction of the officers and the master, several British Admiralty tugs successfully towed her by the stern and put the *Harrison* on the beach. Only three plates on either side of the vessel held her together. British Navy divers found two clamps on the bilge keel, which led them to suspect that a mine had been placed there by a swimmer. She was later declared a CTL. Two other vessels also suffered explosions within minutes of the *Pat Harrison*. Only one man on watch below died from the explosion.

The size of the crew and the casualty figures are contradictory. A second man received severe injuries, but the master in his statement claims he was discharged from the hospital. NSS; WACR; WCSR; AG; Moore, pp. 216, 512.

DANIEL HUGER

D:	5-9-43	YB:	1942
T:	2000	Tn:	7,176
Pos:	docked at Bône, Algeria	Dr:	unknown
Ow:	WSA	C:	7,000 tons drummed gasoline
Op:	Mississippi SS Co.	P:	steam
M:	James B. Adams	S:	at anchor
A:	1-4"; 1-3"; 8-20 mm		

On 1 April, the *Daniel Huger* sailed from New York to Algiers, Algeria, and joined Convoy UGS-7. She arrived in Bône on 8 May. As the freighter unloaded cargo in Bône Harbor, enemy aircraft attacked the anchorage. When the air raid alarm sounded, the crew went to their battle stations. Near misses from bombs sent a hot fragment through the shell plating and ignited the gasoline cargo in the #5 hold. Instead of abandoning the Liberty ship, the master determined he would fight the fire and save his ship. Two cadet-midshipmen and one other man volunteered to go into the hold to fight the fire. For ninety minutes these men battled the inferno. The volunteer party of men eventually had to leave the hold because of small explosions and smoke. The fire, shooting mast high, eventually burned out of control. Most of the eight officers, thirty-seven men, and twenty-seven armed guards left the ship because of the danger of the cargo exploding. Eventually a crew of British firemen came on board with chemical firefighting gear and water pumps. They fought the fire for five hours and flooded completely the #4 and #5 holds. With the fire extinguished, the crew pumped water out of the ship for two days. The vessel was raised and the crew completed discharging her cargo. After temporary repairs the ship proceeded in

Convoy GUS-7A to the United States. The third mate and an armed guard died in the attack.

Cadet-Midshipman Phil Cox Vannais and Elmer C. Donnelly received the Distinguished Service Medal for their roles in the firefighting efforts. WACR; WCSR; AG; USMMA; TF.

CAPE NEDDICK

D:	5-12-43	YB:	1941
T:	0113	Tn:	6,797
Pos:	23.21 S / 01.22 W	Dr:	28 ft.
Ow:	United Fruit Co.	C:	7,100 tons ammunition, tanks,
Op:	United Fruit Co.		locomotives, airplane parts,
M:	Harry Edward Stark		jeeps, etc.
A:	1-4"; 1-3"; 8-20 mm	P:	steam
		S:	13.5

On 28 March, the *Cape Neddick* departed New York en route to Suez via Durban, South Africa, on independent routing. The *U-195* (Buchholz) fired two torpedoes at the zigzagging freighter. The first torpedo struck the vessel aft at the #3 hatch on the bilge keel but did not explode. Nearly simultaneously a second torpedo struck at the #2 hatch. The explosion threw a sheet of flame and a column of water higher than the bridge. The ship rolled first to port, then to starboard, and finally settled on an even keel. The explosion ripped a hole in the ship twenty-five feet by thirty feet. The armed guards began firing all the guns as the freighter headed into the direction of the submarine. As the ship settled by the head and the water reached the foredeck, the master ordered most of the eight officers, forty-three men, and twenty-five armed guards into two boats and three rafts. After the ship lost way, the deck cleared of water and gave the master hope that the ship could be salvaged. Bringing on board a contingent of the engine room crew, the master got the ship under way and proceeded away from the area on a zigzagging course. Just as the vessel got under way, members of the armed guards observed a torpedo pass ahead of the ship. The gun crew fired three salvos, but they never sighted the U-boat. Fifteen hours later the master and the skeleton crew returned to pick up the men in the boats and rafts. The master shifted the ship's cargo and got under way again. The *Cape Neddick* arrived at Walvis Bay, South Africa. All hands survived, and no one reported a serious injury.

NSS; WACR; WCSR; AG; USMMA; Rohwer, p. 268.

NICKELINER

D:	5-13-43	YB:	1938
T:	0328	Tn:	2,249
Pos:	21.31 N / 76.48 W	Dr:	15 ft. 10 in.
Ow:	All Waterways Navigation Corp.	C:	24,000 bbls. aqua ammonia
Op:	WSA	P:	diesel
M:	Julius Fridlef Swensson	S:	8.5
A:	1-3"; 2-30 cal.		

On 13 May, the *Nickeliner* sailed from Nuevitas, Cuba, in convoy to Nicaro, Cuba, with the tanker *Mambi* and three Cuban submarine chasers providing escort. The *U-176* (Dierksen) fired a torpedo that struck the tanker's port bow. The explosion lifted the bow out of the water and threw water and flames 100 feet into the air. Twenty seconds later a second torpedo hit the port side aft of the first and released the ammonia from the cargo tanks. The officer on the bridge rang up full speed ahead. As the ship's bow began to settle, her speed decreased, and after ten minutes the watch below secured the engines. At 0355, the master gave the order to abandon ship as she sank on an even keel. All eight officers, fifteen men, seven armed guards, and one passenger abandoned ship in two lifeboats. The *Nickeliner* sank bow first at 0415. One of the Cuban escort vessels rescued all hands and landed them in Nuevitas.

The *Nickeliner* was specifically reconstructed to carry bulk ammonia water. No other vessel had the capacity to carry this important strategic cargo. NSS; WACR; WCSR; AG; Rohwer, p. 167, places the attack at 21.25 N / 76.40 W; *War Action Casualties*, p. 142.

WILLIAM K. VANDERBILT

D:	5-17-43	YB:	1942
T:	0220	Tn:	7,181
Pos:	18.41 S / 175.07 E	Dr:	12 ft. 6 in.
Ow:	WSA	C:	988 tons water ballast
Op:	Isthmian SS Co.	P:	steam
M:	William Francis Goldsmith	S:	8.0
A:	1-3"; 5-20 mm		

The *William K. Vanderbilt* departed Vila, Efate (New Hebrides), en route to Balboa, Canal Zone, via Suva, Fiji. The Liberty ship proceeded independently on a nonevasive course. The *I-19* (Kinashi) intercepted the vessel and fired a single torpedo that struck the port side of the ship at the #5 hatch. The explosion blew off the hatch cover and either broke the shaft or blew off the screw. The watch below secured the engines immediately when they began to race and vibrate. The ship listed to port as the merchant crew of eight officers and thirty-three men started to leave the ship in three lifeboats. One of these boats overturned while launching, and the men abandoned it. The sixteen men of the armed guard contingent remained on board. Twenty minutes after the initial explosion a second torpedo struck the ship amidships at the engine room. This explosion split the ship and enveloped the bridge with flames, oil, and steam. The armed guards left the ship by raft, by jumping overboard, and by walking off the stern into awaiting boats. The ship sank immediately stern first after the second torpedo struck. The *I-19* approached the survivors with a searchlight and fired at one of the boats, but hit no one. The master went on board the submarine for questioning. The USS *Dash* (AM-88) rescued the survivors the next morning, and they landed at Suva, Fiji. The only death occurred when the second torpedo explosion blew the first assistant engineer clear of the ship as he descended into a lifeboat.

NSS; WACR; WCSR; RWCS; AG; Rohwer, p. 283.

H. M. STOREY

D:	5-18-43	YB:	1921
T:	0239	Tn:	10,764
Pos:	17.30 S / 173.02 E	Dr:	18 ft. 3 in.
Ow:	Standard Oil Co. of California	C:	2,000 tons water ballast
Op:	WSA & USN	P:	steam
M:	Gustaf Adolf Johnson	S:	11.2
A:	1-4"; 2-50 mm; 6-20 mm		

On 15 May, the *H. M. Storey* sailed independently from Nouméa, New Caledonia, bound for San Pedro, California. A torpedo fired by the *I-25* (Tagami) struck the zigzagging tanker in the engine room on the starboard side. The explosion opened the entire after side of the engine room to the sea. The machinery spaces quickly flooded, the engines stopped, and the ship began to settle. Almost forty minutes later, with the ship dead in the water, a second torpedo struck between the #9 and #10 tanks. This explosion threw a column of water 150 feet in the air and tore away more of the hull below the waterline. On the master's orders the survivors among the crew of ten officers, thirty-eight men, fifteen armed guards, and two passengers immediately abandoned ship in lifeboats #1, #2, and #4 and two rafts. The *I-25* surfaced and circled the ship, shelling the tanker and hitting her about eight times. The tanker sank at 0424 stern first. The USS *Fletcher* (DD-445) rescued the survivors and landed them at Vila, Efate, on 20 May. One officer and one crewman lost their lives while on watch below.

The *Story* was also unsuccessfully attacked by the *I-19* (Narahara) on 23 December 1941, but escaped without damage. NSS; WACR; WCSR; AG; Rohwer, pp. 278, 283, places the attack at 17.20 S / 173.30 E; *War Action Casualties*, p. 143.

SAMUEL GRIFFIN

D:	5-19-43	YB:	1942
T:	2145	Tn:	7,176
Pos:	Oran Harbor	Dr:	25 ft.
Ow:	WSA	C:	6,000 tons general, locomotives,
Op:	Seas Shipping Co.		gliders, gasoline
M:	Francis DeSales Gorman	P:	steam
A:	1-5"; 1-3"; 8-20 mm	S:	at anchor

The *Samuel Griffin* sailed from New York to Oran, Algeria, and moored away from the docks. During a full moon, enemy bombers attacked the anchorage, and two bombs damaged the freighter. One bomb struck at the #5 hold and the other landed nearby off the stern. The bomb that struck near the #5 hatch shattered deck plates and started a fire that the crew found difficult to extinguish. The near miss caused minor damage from shrapnel. Thirty-six of the eight officers, thirty-six men, and twenty-six armed guards left the Liberty ship. This number included fifteen injured that remained on board an escort. Because of the extensive damage, the *Samual Griffin* had to be towed for repairs.

WACR; WCSR; AG.

LUTHER MARTIN

D:	5-19-43	YB:	1942
T:	2210	Tn:	7,177
Pos:	Oran, Algeria	Dr:	27 ft.
Ow:	WSA	C:	7,000 tons explosives, gasoline,
Op:	Agwilines		general
M:	Grady Lee Robertson	P:	steam
A:	1-5"; 1-3"; 8-20 mm	S:	docked

On 28 April, the *Luther Martin* sailed from New York in Convoy UGS-8 and docked at Oran, Algeria, on 18 May, to unload her war cargo. During an air raid a bomb exploded off the starboard bow. The shrapnel from the bomb put about 200 holes in the forepeak tank. The Liberty ship received emergency repairs in Oran and sailed on 7 June for final repairs in Hoboken, New Jersey. None of the eight officers, thirty-four men, and twenty-eight armed guards were injured or killed during the attack.

WACR; WCSR; AG; TF.

FLORIDA

D:	5-27-43	YB:	1937
T:	2345	Tn:	8,580
Pos:	03.56 S / 36.43 W	Dr:	18 ft. 8 1/2 in.
Ow:	Texas Co.	C:	water ballast
Op:	Texas Co.	P:	diesel
M:	Magnus Gunderson	S:	8
A:	1-5"; 1-3"; 8-20 mm		

On 27 May, the *Florida* sailed from Natal, Brazil, bound for Trinidad, BWI, in Convoy BT-14. The *U-154* (Kusch) fired six torpedoes and struck two other American ships and the *Florida*. The *Florida* proceeded in convoy station #53. A torpedo struck forward of the after peak tank on the starboard side fifteen feet beneath the waterline. The explosion opened a hole sixteen feet by six feet in the tanker and broke her back. As water filled the engine room, the ship lost way, and water eventually rose to the level of the after five-inch gun. The master ordered the ship abandoned at 0035. The complement of eight officers, forty four men, and twenty-seven armed guards left the ship in three boats. A fourth boat swamped in the moderate seas. The *PC-592* rescued all hands and landed the men at Fortaleza, Brazil. A salvage crew later boarded the vessel, and the corvette USS *Saucey* (PG-65) towed her into Fortaleza. The U.S. Navy salvage ship *Crusader* (ARS-2) later towed the *Florida* to Puerto Rico where she received repairs in dry dock and then returned to service.

NSS; WACR; WCSR; AG; USMMA; Rohwer, p. 167.

CARDINAL GIBBONS

D:	5-27-43	YB:	1942
T:	2346	Tn:	7,191
Pos:	03.56 S / 36.43 W	Dr:	17 ft.
Ow:	WSA	C:	none
Op:	Sword Line Inc.	P:	steam
M:	Donald Dinsmore Fitzpatrick	S:	8
A:	1-5"; 9-20 mm		

On 27 May, the *Cardinal Gibbons* sailed in the twelve-ship Convoy BT-14 bound from Bahia, Argentina, for Trinidad, BWI. The freighter traveled in station #61 in the starboard column. One minute after a torpedo struck the *Florida*, the *Cardinal Gibbons* was hit by a torpedo also fired by the *U-154* (Kusch). The torpedo struck abaft the stem on the starboard side and ripped a hole in the forepeak tank containing fresh water. The eight officers, thirty-five men, and twenty-seven armed guards remained on board and suffered no injuries. The gun crew took no action because they feared the gunfire might

strike their escorts. The ship remained on course and arrived in Trinidad on 5 June.

WACR; WCSR; AG; Rohwer, p. 167.

JOHN WORTHINGTON

D:	5-27-43	YB:	1920
T:	2347	Tn:	8,166
Pos:	03.52 S / 36.48 W	Dr:	16 ft.
Ow:	Standard Oil Co. of N. J.	C:	water ballast
Op:	Standard Oil Co. of N. J.	P:	steam
M:	Gunnar Gjertsen	S:	8
A:	1-4"; 1-3"; 2-50 cal.; 2-30 cal.		

The *John Worthington* sailed from Rio de Janeiro, Brazil, to Trinidad, BWI, via Bahia, Brazil. She joined Convoy BT-14 and proceeded in convoy station #42. A few minutes after torpedoes struck the *Florida* and *Cardinal Gibbons* one of the six torpedoes fired by the *U-154* (Kusch) hit the *Worthington* at the #8 tank. The explosion blew a hole thirty feet by ten feet in her side, buckled the deck, and pushed fragments out the port side. The force of the explosion caused the ship to veer 30° to starboard, but she regained her course and continued on her way. Only a few of the complement of eight officers, thirty-four men, and fourteen armed guards suffered slight injuries. The vessel fell behind the convoy but managed to rejoin it by the following morning. The vessel made temporary repairs in Trinidad and then sailed to Galveston, Texas, for major repairs.

NSS; WACR; WCSR; USMMA; AG; *Ships of the Esso Fleet*, pp. 447-51; Rohwer, p. 167.

AGWIMONTE

D:	5-28-43	YB:	1941
T:	2355	Tn:	6,679
Pos:	34.57 S / 19.33 E	Dr:	27 ft.
Ow:	WSA	C:	8,000 tons war cargo, tanks,
Op:	Agwilines		locomotives
M:	James William Geattie	P:	steam
A:	1-5"; 1-3"; 8-20 mm; 2-30 cal.	S:	7

On 28 May, the *Agwimonte* sailed from Cape Town, South Africa, to Suez via Durban. Proceeding in Convoy CD-20, which was composed of fourteen merchant ships and four escorts, the freighter steamed in station #53 in the formation (last ship in the starboard column). Lookouts spotted the wake of a torpedo fired from the *U-177* (Gysae) about twenty-five feet from the ship. The torpedo struck on the starboard side between the #2 and #3 hatches. The

explosion caused the ship to heel to starboard, and the sea washed over the forward deck and the bridge. The watch below secured the engines as the ship settled on an even keel. When the general alarm sounded, the ten officers, thirty-six men, and twenty-three armed guards began leaving the ship in two boats and three rafts. The #1 boat, however, swamped in the swells when the after fall failed to release. The men on board tumbled into the sea and climbed back on board the *Agwimonte*. Several of these men left the ship in the now overcrowded #2 lifeboat. Just over an hour later the survivors in the lifeboats witnessed a second torpedo strike the vessel in the engine room. This torpedo caused the boilers to explode, and she sank bow first in ten minutes with the general alarm still blaring. Two of the survivors on one of the rafts later transferred into an abandoned lifeboat from a Norwegian vessel. The South African Navy whaler *Vereeniging* (T-72) picked up sixty-one survivors in the #1 boat and two rafts and landed them at Gordon Bay, South Africa. An Army crash boat rescued the occupants of the other two boats eighteen hours after the attack and took the men to Cape Town. All hands survived the sinking.

NSS; WACR; WCSR; RWCS; AG; Rohwer, p. 268.

FLORA MACDONALD

D:	5-30-43	YB:	1943
T:	2107	Tn:	7,177
Pos:	07.20 N / 13.15 W	Dr:	25 ft. 1 in.
Ow:	WSA	C:	6,270 tons cocoa, mahogany,
Op:	Calmar SS Co.		rubber
M:	Ernest Wright Jones	P:	steam
A:	1-5"; 9-20 mm	S:	7.3

On 29 May, the *Flora MacDonald* departed Marshall, Liberia, en route to Freetown, Sierra Leone, escorted by a single trawler, the HMS *Fandango* (T-107). The *U-126* (Kietz) fired a torpedo that struck the freighter on the port side at the engine room. The explosion opened a large hole that immediately flooded the engine room, stopped the engines, and caused the ship to settle by the stern. The blast also started a fire in the #3 hold, and flames quickly trapped some of the men in their quarters. With the flames shooting forty feet in the air, the surviving members of the complement of eight officers, thirty-six men, and twenty-four armed guards, as well as two passengers, immediately abandoned ship in six lifeboats. Five of these men suffered severe burns, and the third assistant engineer and a fireman died in the engine room. The fire raged out of control and later spread to the #2 and #4 holds and the entire midships house. The escort vessel with the badly burned men on board decided to head to Freetown so they could be treated. Three died on the trawler and two died on shore from their burns. The HMS tug *Zwarte Zee* (W-163), escorted by the sloop HMS *Milford* (L-51) and the corvettes HMS *Woodruff* (K-53) and HMS

Tamarisk (K-216), went to tow the vessel, still afire. On 1 June, they beached the freighter in Freetown Harbor where she burned for sixteen days. The damage could not be economically repaired, and she was declared a CTL. One officer and eight men died as a result of the attack.

NSS; WACR; WCSR; RWCS; USMMA; AG; Rohwer, p. 167, places the attack at 07.15 N / 13.20 W.

MONTANAN

D:	6-3-43	YB:	1917
T:	1435	Tn:	4,826
Pos:	17.58 N / 58.09 E	Dr:	17 ft.
Ow:	American Hawaiian Line	C:	fuel oil and water ballast
Op:	WSA	P:	steam
M:	Charles Harry McGahan	S:	10
A:	1-4"; 8-20 mm		

On 29 May, the *Montanan* sailed from Abadan, Iran, en route to Mombasa, Africa. The *I-27* (Fukumura) intercepted the zigzagging freighter about 200 miles east of the Arabian coast and put a torpedo into the forward part of the #2 hold. The explosion caused a sheet of flame to shoot up the foremast and flooded the forward holds rapidly enough to put the foredeck under water in about two minutes. Most of the eight officers, thirty-four men, and twenty-three armed guards on board immediately abandoned ship in four lifeboats, while others jumped in the water. The ship sank by the head, foredeck aflame, five minutes after the torpedo struck. The rough seas prevented the four boats from remaining together. The dhow *Naranpasha* discovered the #2 lifeboat and transferred the survivors to the Royal Indian Navy trawler *Baroda* (T-249). These men landed at Port Okah, India. The other three boats landed on Masirah Island off Oman. Two officers, four of the ship's crew, and two armed guards perished in the attack.

The ship's complement figures are contradictory. NSS; WACR; WCSR; AG; Rohwer, p. 268, places the attack at 17.54 N /58.09 E.

WILLIAM KING

D:	6-6-43	YB:	1942
T:	1340	Tn:	7,170
Pos:	30.34 S / 33.56 E	Dr:	16 ft. 6 in.
Ow:	WSA	C:	18,000 bbls. fuel oil
Op:	Marine Transport Lines Inc.	P:	steam
M:	Owen Harvey Reed	S:	10
A:	1-5"; 9-20 mm		

On 14 May, the *William King* sailed from Bahrein to Durban, South Africa. The *U-198* (Hartmann) fired two torpedoes at the zigzagging tanker as it proceeded in choppy seas. The first torpedo hit the ship on the port side at the #3 hatch. The second passed astern. The first torpedo's explosion opened a large hole in the ship's side, shattered two lifeboats, and exploded the port boiler. The blast stopped the engines, and fire raged in the engine room, the #3 hold, and all through the midships house. The freighter remained on an even keel allowing the ship's complement of eight officers, thirty-four men, and twenty-three armed guards to more easily abandon the ship in two lifeboats and two rafts. After the men abandoned the ship, a second torpedo slammed into the starboard side, shooting flames hundreds of feet into the air. The ship went down stern first about ten minutes later. With the vessel nearly underwater, the *U-198* surfaced and laid down a short burst of machine gun fire to halt the lifeboats and to bring them alongside the U-boat. The Germans took the master on board as a prisoner, and the *U-198* submerged and left. The survivors remained close to the area during the night and tied two of the rafts together. After the attack, the #3 boat, in charge of the second officer, drifted away. The trawler HMS *Northern Chief* (4-34) discovered the rafts after thirty-six hours. This same vessel also rescued the men in the #3 boat. The destroyer HMS *Relentless* (H-85) rescued the men in the #1 boat six days after the attack. All the survivors landed in Durban, South Africa. Two officers and four of the merchant crew died in the attack. The initial explosion killed all three on watch below. The master was placed in a Japanese prison camp and later died while being transferred.

NSS; WACR; WCSR; AG; Rohwer, p. 269, places the attack at 30.25 S / 34.15 E.

ESSO GETTYSBURG

D:	6-10-43	YB:	1942
T:	1500	Tn:	10,173
Pos:	31.02 N / 79.15 W	Dr:	31 ft. 6 in.
Ow:	Standard Oil Co. N. J.	C:	120,120 bbls. crude oil
Op:	Standard Oil Co. N. J.	P:	steam
M:	Pedar A. Johnson	S:	15.5
A:	1-4"; 1-3"; 8-20 mm		

On 6 June, the *Esso Gettysburg* departed Port Arthur, Texas, en route to Philadelphia, Pennsylvania. The zigzagging tanker received a U-boat warning, and shortly thereafter the *U-66* (Markworth) fired two torpedoes at the ship. The first struck the port side between the #6 and #7 tanks. This torpedo ripped up twenty-five feet of deck, blew oil 100 feet into the air, and disabled the steering gear. Seconds later the second torpedo struck on the port side at the engine room, causing an immediate fire as the ship began to settle stern first and listed to port. The two tanks, blown apart by the first explosion, began to spread oil on

the water. Within seconds fire ignited the cargo, and flames spread 100 feet on both sides of the ship while smoke rose over 1,000 feet in the air. The ship's complement of eight officers, thirty-seven men, and twenty-seven armed guards attempted to launch the boats but failed because of the intense flames. Fifteen of these men jumped into the water and swam as fast as they could from the burning oil. They were the only survivors. Five died on the watch below, and the other fifty-two burned to death in the inferno. The survivors managed to get to a badly burned boat and extinguished the fire. The SS *George Washington* rescued these men and landed them in Charleston, South Carolina. Only seven of the gun crew, three officers, and five of the merchant crew lived through the attack.

The armed guard ensign was awarded the Navy Cross. NSS; WACR; WCSR; AG; *Report on Lifeboat and Life Raft Performance*; *Ships of the Esso Fleet*, pp. 454-60; Rohwer, p. 168, places the attack at 31.02 N / 79.17 W.

WILLIAM H. WEBB

D:	6-14-43	YB:	1943
T:	0131	Tn:	7,176
Pos:	39.03 N / 72.10 W	Dr:	25 ft. 4 in.
Ow:	WSA	C:	5,000 tons general
Op:	States Marine	P:	steam
M:	Percy M. Eslick	S:	8
A:	1-5"; 9-20 mm		

On 23 May, the *William H. Webb* sailed from Baltimore, Maryland, to Casablanca, Morocco. As she was en route, a mine struck the ship's port side torpedo streamer. The explosion caused "extensive" damage to the main shaft bearings, the piping systems, and the ship in general, forcing her to return to port. None of the eight officers, thirty-four men, one passenger, and thirty armed guards were injured.

WACR; AG; TF; ONF. Another location listed is 37.38 N / 70.08 W.

HENRY KNOX

D:	6-19-43	YB:	1942
T:	1850	Tn:	7,176
Pos:	00.05 S / 69.50 E	Dr:	27 ft.
Ow:	WSA	C:	8,500 tons food, planes, jeeps,
Op:	Matson Navigation Co.		explosives, tanks
M:	Eugene M. Olsen	P:	steam
A:	1-4"; 1-3"; 8-20 mm	S:	9.2

On 5 June, the *Henry Knox* sailed from Freemantle, Australia, to Bandar Shahpur, Iran, with lend lease goods for the Soviets. At dusk a torpedo launched from the *I-37* (Otani) struck the vessel on the port side between the #1 and #2 hatches. The explosion blew flaming dunnage, tires, and cordite over the entire length of the vessel. The vessel immediately listed to port as fire broke out in both forward holds. The general alarm sounded, and the fire began spreading fore and aft as the ship settled by the head. With the fire out of control, the master ordered the crew to the lifeboats. Most of the eight officers, thirty-four men, and twenty-five armed guards on board managed to launch three of the lifeboats and one raft; the other boat and rafts caught fire. Other crew members jumped overboard to be rescued by the boats. Forty minutes after the torpedo struck, the *I-37* surfaced, and a Japanese officer held a lengthy questioning session with the survivors in the #2 boat. The boats remained in the vicinity during the night, and the survivors watched the vessel sink at 2200. The men later redistributed equally among the lifeboats. The master instructed the survivors to sail for the Maldive Islands 200 miles away. In rough weather they proceeded alone. During the trip, several men in the boats died from their injuries and were buried at sea. All three boats landed on the Maldive Islands, one boat in eight days, one in nine, and the last, eleven days after the attack. Thirteen of the gun crew perished along with two officers and eleven men of the merchant crew. All the survivors eventually went by dhow to Colombo, Ceylon.

WACR; WCSR; AG; Rohwer, p. 269, places the attack at 00.00 N / 70.15 E.

SANTA MARIA

D:	6-20-43	YB:	1942
T:	0705	Tn:	6,507
Pos:	14.34.18 N / 17.28.23 W	Dr:	23 ft. 6 in.
Ow:	Grace Line	C:	450 tons sisal
Op:	WSA	P:	steam
M:	Robert John Twaddell	S:	15.5
A:	1-5"; 1-3"; 8-20 mm		

On 20 June, the *Santa Maria* sailed on independent routing from Dakar, French West Africa, to New York. Five miles offshore, while proceeding in smooth seas, the vessel struck a mine laid by the *U-214* (Graf von Treuberg). The mine exploded in the vicinity of the #1 hatch and caused the forward magazine to explode. The vessel disappeared forward of the #2 watertight bulkhead. The men mustered at their boat stations, and most of the nine officers, forty-eight men, and thirty armed guards cleared the ship in two lifeboats. The lifeboats stood by the freighter for two hours until two French naval towboats arrived. Forty-six men then went ashore, and the rest reboarded the ship to help with the

tow. The ship entered a French naval dry dock in Dakar. The explosion blew one member of the gun crew overboard, and he was never found.

The figures for the ship's complement are radically different within the sources. The Shipping Articles lists ten officers and forty-five men. NSS; WACR; WCSR; AG; Rohwer, p. 168.

EAGLE

D:	6-25-43	YB:	1917
T:	0055	Tn:	6,003
Pos:	22.58 S / 41.54 W	Dr:	19 ft.
Ow:	Socony-Vacuum Oil Co.	C:	2,000 tons water ballast
Op:	Socony-Vacuum Oil Co.	P:	steam
M:	Albert James Beck	S:	10
A:	1-4"; 2-30 cal.		

On 24 June, the *Eagle* sailed from Rio de Janeiro to Bahia, Brazil. Approximately eight miles southeast of Cape Frio, Brazil, the *U-513* (Guggenberger) fired a torpedo that passed under the ship amidships. Three minutes later a second torpedo struck the port forepeak. The explosion flooded the forward pump room and other portions of the ship with water. The master ordered the engines full speed astern and commanded the helmsman to steer hard right rudder. This maneuver caused a third torpedo to pass astern fifteen feet away. The gun crew fired four shots from the four-inch stern gun to keep the submarine submerged. The tanker zigzagged back to Rio de Janeiro where she received temporary repairs and later proceeded to a U.S. port. All eight officers, thirty-three men, and twelve armed guards survived.

NSS; WACR; WCSR; AG; WJ; Rohwer, p. 168, places the attack at 23.07 S / 41.53 W.

SEBASTIAN CERMENO

D:	6-27-43	YB:	1943
T:	1115	Tn:	7,176
Pos:	29.00 S / 50.10 E	Dr:	17 ft. 3 in.
Ow:	WSA	C:	water ballast
Op:	Oliver J. Olsen SS Co.	P:	steam
M:	David Martin Nilsson	S:	10.5
A:	1-5"; 1-3"; 8-20 mm		

On 19 June, the Liberty ship *Sebastian Cermeno* sailed independently from Mombasa, Kenya, to Bahia, Brazil. The *U-511* (Schneewind) fired two torpedoes, both striking the port side five seconds apart. One struck the after part of the #5 hold, and the other struck the forward part of the #4 hold. The explosions destroyed the armed guard's quarters, buckled the gun deck, blew off

the after two hatches, destroyed the shaft, and disabled the engines. The master ordered the eight officers, thirty-four men, twenty-seven armed guards, and five passengers to abandon ship five minutes after the explosions. The men launched five lifeboats, and five minutes after the last boat touched the water the ship plunged stern first. The U-boat surfaced and the Germans questioned the survivors before submerging and leaving. That night the five boats became separated. On 14 July, the SS *Theodore Parker* sighted the #3 boat and took the survivors to Durban, South Africa. A British corvette rescued the men in the #2 boat, and they arrived in Durban on 23 July. A British destroyer rescued the survivors in the #6 boat and landed them on the 27th. The #1 boat landed in Madagascar eleven days after the attack, and the #5 boat was towed into Durban by an Allied ship after sixteen days at sea. A total of five men perished. One officer died of exposure in one of the lifeboats, another officer and two men died on watch below, and the last man, asleep on the #4 hatch when the ship was struck, died of his injuries.

NSS; WACR; WCSR; AG; Rohwer, p. 269.

BLOODY MARSH

D:	7-2-43	YB:	1943
T:	0008	Tn:	10,195
Pos:	32.45 N / 78.45 W	Dr:	30 ft. 6 in.
Ow:	Cities Service Oil Co.	C:	102,500 bbls. Navy fuel oil
Op:	Cities Service Oil Co.	P:	steam
M:	Albert Harrison Barnes	S:	13.5
A:	1-5"; 1-3"; 8-20 mm		

On 28 June, the *Bloody Marsh* sailed from Houston, Texas, bound for New York on her maiden voyage. Just after midnight the ship's torpedo indicator sounded a short blast after detecting the approach of a torpedo fired from the *U-66* (Markworth). The master had the helm swung hard left. Thirty seconds later a torpedo struck the port side at the engine room. The explosion completely destroyed the engine room and flooded that compartment. As the tanker settled by the stern, the after gun crew reported a conning tower but could not open fire because the explosion had jammed the gun. The forward gun did not get into action because it could not be brought to bear. Most of the ten officers, forty men, and twenty-seven armed guards on board left the ship in four lifeboats, with the exception of the armed guard commander and three of his men. Some confused and panicked men lowered boats without orders, while others reported to the wrong boat stations. Nearly twenty minutes after the initial explosion, the *U-66* fired a second torpedo that struck the port side amidships and broke the ship in half. The four armed guards on board remained until water rose to the after gun platform and then dove into the water to be picked up. At 0600 the next morning a Navy blimp sighted the survivors and at 0900 the Navy

submarine chaser *SC-1048* picked them up. An officer and two men died on watch below.

The numbers given for the armed guards are contradictory within the sources. NSS; WACR; WCSR; USMMA; AG; Rohwer, p. 168, places the attack at 31.33 N / 78.57 W; *War Action Casualties*, p. 151.

ELIHU B. WASHBURNE

D:	7-3-43	YB:	1943
T:	1525	Tn:	7,176
Pos:	24.05 S / 45.25 W	Dr:	22 ft.
Ow:	WSA	C:	7,638 tons coffee
Op:	Matson Navigation Co.	P:	steam
M:	George Lambert Mollison	S:	12
A:	1-3"; 9-20 mm		

On 3 July, the *Elihu B. Washburne* sailed from Santos, Brazil, to Rio de Janeiro under independent routing. The *U-513* (Guggenberger) intercepted the freighter, and its first torpedo struck between the after port peak tank and the #5 hatch. The explosion either knocked off the propeller or broke the shaft. It did carry away the rudder, caused the after three-inch gun to discharge, and caused the after 20-mm ammunition magazine to explode. Without control of the ship, the vessel turned 90° to port and gradually lost way. The eight officers, thirty-four men, twenty-five armed guards, and three passengers on board began mustering at their abandon ship stations. The master, eight crewmen, and the armed guards remained on board to attempt to beach the ship. The remaining men abandoned the vessel in three lifeboats. At 1550, twenty-five minutes later, a second torpedo struck the hapless ship at the #3 bulkhead. This explosion lifted the bow out of the water and threw a geyser of water over the ship. At 1600 a third torpedo struck in the engine room. The remaining men on board now left in the fourth lifeboat. The survivors in the four boats last saw the ship still afloat with her bow raised completely out of the water. All hands survived the attack and landed on the island of São Sabastião early the next morning.

NSS; WACR; WCSR; AG; Rohwer, p. 168, places the attack at 24.03 S / 45.11 W.

MALTRAN

D:	7-5-43	YB:	1920
T:	0332	Tn:	3,513
Pos:	18.11 N / 74.57 W	Dr:	21 ft.
Ow:	Solvay Process Co.	C:	3,200 tons general
Op:	Marine Operating Co.	P:	steam
M:	Donovan Floyd Pierce	S:	10
A:	1-4"; 2-50 cal.; 2-30 cal.		

On 4 July, the *Maltran* sailed from Guantánamo Bay, Cuba, to Ponce, Puerto Rico, escorted by the submarine chaser *SC-1279* in Convoy GTMO-134. A lookout on board spotted a torpedo fired from the *U-759* (Friedrich) seconds before it hit the starboard side at the #2 hatch. The explosion blew the hatch cover off and threw portions of the cargo over the deck and into the sea. The watch below secured the main engines as the ship settled rapidly. The armed guards managed to fire one round to indicate the submarine's direction as the ship immediately listed to starboard and then settled on an even keel. In just over ten minutes water rose to the level of the forward deck, and the master ordered the freighter abandoned. The eight officers, twenty-seven men, and twelve armed guards on board cleared the ship in two lifeboats and three rafts. The overboard discharge from the condenser swamped one of the boats. The ship settled beneath the waves by the stern only fifteen minutes after the initial explosion. The *SC-1279* picked up the entire crew about two and a half hours after the attack. All hands survived.

NSS; WACR; WCSR; AG; Rohwer, p. 168.

ALCOA PROSPECTOR

D:	7-5-43	YB:	1941
T:	0810	Tn:	6,797
Pos:	24.26 N / 58.20 E	Dr:	17 ft. 6 in.
Ow:	Alcoa SS Co.	C:	none
Op:	WSA	P:	steam
M:	Ernest Henke	S:	9
A:	1-4"; 1-3"; 8-20 mm; 2-30 cal.		

On 28 June, the *Alcoa Prospector* sailed from Abadan, Iran, in Convoy PA-44 en route to Montevideo, Uruguay. The freighter proceeded in convoy station #41 with thirteen other merchant ships and a two-corvette escort in a formation five ships wide and three deep. The *I-27* (Fukumura) struck the freighter with a torpedo ten feet below the waterline in the starboard side at the #4 hold. The explosion blew the #4 hatch cover off and scattered steel and dunnage aft. The explosion also ruptured the shaft alley and the after engine room bulkhead, as well as demolished the crew's quarters. Fuel from the reserve fuel tanks mixed with escaping steam spewed for nearly three minutes and coated the surface of the ship with oil. The crew stopped the main engines and rang the general alarm. Most of the nine officers, thirty-six men, and twenty-six armed guards on board began to abandon ship in two lifeboats and four life rafts. The gunnery officer and nine men remained on board. The Royal Indian Navy minesweeper *Bengal* (J-243) left her station in the convoy and steamed to the stricken freighter's side. Thirty minutes after the crew cleared the ship, the master and a few men reboarded her to survey the damage. That night all hands slept on board the

Bengal. The next day, after noon, the armed guard officer, twelve of the gun crew, the master, and four merchant crewmen reboarded the ship. The minesweeper stood by the freighter for several days as she drifted. On 9 July, the *Bengal* tried unsuccessfully to tow the vessel. The next day, two Anglo-Iranian oil company tugs towed the freighter into Bandar Abbas, Iran. All hands survived the attack, but one of the merchant crew died on the minesweeper of pneumonia contracted prior to sailing.

NSS; WACR; WCSR; USMMA; AG; Rohwer, p. 269, places the attack at 24.21 N / 59.04 E.

JAMES ROBERTSON

D:	7-7-43	YB:	1943
T:	0110	Tn:	7,176
Pos:	04.00 S / 36.00 W	Dr:	10 ft. 8 in.
Ow:	WSA	C:	1 1/2 tons radio sets, ballast
Op:	American President Lines	P:	steam
M:	Harold Fletcher DeLasaux	S:	8
A:	1-4"; 9-20 mm		

On 3 July, the Liberty ship *James Robertson* sailed in Convoy BT-18 bound from Bahia, Brazil, for Paramaribo, Dutch Guiana. The freighter steamed in station #21 in the convoy. The *U-185* (Maus) attacked the convoy twice. During the first attack the *U-185* fired at least two torpedoes that struck the ship in the #2 and the #3 holds. The explosions ruptured the engine room bulkhead and blew several hatch covers off, littering the deck with bits of metal, rock ballast, and pieces of lifeboats. With the rudder jammed and the engines still running, the ship cut through the columns of the convoy. She collided with the *Alcoa Banner* (convoy station #32), striking at the hole created by the torpedo. Seconds later she struck the *Cotazaloide* (convoy position #33) at the #1 hatch. On orders from the master, part of the complement of eight officers, thirty-six men, and twenty-five armed guards immediately began abandoning the ship in two lifeboats and rafts. One boat swamped during launching, and other men escaped by jumping overboard and swimming to the rafts. The *PC-575* picked up the twenty-one men on the rafts eighteen hours later and landed them at Trinidad. The remainder of the crew later abandoned the freighter in the remaining two good lifeboats and stood by until the following morning in order to reboard her and recover personal effects. A Brazilian vessel rescued the master and twenty-three men, including three survivors of the torpedoed *William Boyce Thompson.* On 9 July, the remaining men in the two boats made port, one at Fortaleza, Brazil, and the other at Cascavel, Brazil. In the chaos one of the armed guards drowned, the only casualty.

NSS; WACR; WCSR; USMMA; AG; Rohwer, p. 169, places the attack at 04.05 S / 05.58 W.

WILLIAM BOYCE THOMPSON

D: 7-7-43   YB: 1921
T: 0110   Tn: 7,061
Pos: 04.00 S / 36.00 W   Dr: 18 ft.
Ow: Sinclair Refining Co.   C: water ballast
Op: WSA   P: steam
M: Fred Charles Vosloh   S: 8.5
A: 1-4"; 2-50 cal.

On 3 July, the *William Boyce Thompson* sailed from Bahia, Brazil, to Trinidad, BWI, in Convoy BT-18 as the convoy commodore's flagship. The *U-185* (Maus), in its initial attack on the convoy, put a torpedo into the ship's starboard side at the engine room as it proceeded in convoy station #41. The explosion destroyed the engine and severely damaged the entire after end of the ship. The *Thompson* began to rapidly settle by the stern. Most of the eight officers, thirty-two men, eleven armed guards, and six passengers on board remained on the ship. Twelve men, however, panicked and abandoned ship without orders in the #4 lifeboat. These men were later picked up by the *James Robertson* (also torpedoed) and the corvette USS *Surprise* (PG-63). The rest of the crew left the ship nearly seven hours later in two lifeboats and were rescued by the *Surprise*. An officer and two men died on watch below. A fourth man later died on shore as a result of the explosion. The tanker remained afloat and had to be sunk with gunfire and depth charges from the escort vessels.

NSS; WACR; WCSR; USMMA; AG; Rohwer, p. 169, places the attack at 04.05 S / 35.58 W; *War Action Casualties*, p. 153.

S. B. HUNT

D: 7-7-43   YB: 1918
T: 0320   Tn: 6,840
Pos: 03.51 S / 36.22 W   Dr: 15 ft. 6 in.
Ow: Standard Oil Co. of N. J.   C: 24,000 bbls. water ballast
Op: WSA   P: steam
M: Henry S. Westmoreland   S: 8
A: 1-5"; 2-50 cal.

On 5 July, the *S. B. Hunt* sailed from Recife, Brazil, en route to Caripito, Venezuela. She joined Convoy BT-18 and proceeded in convoy station #51. In a second attack on the convoy, the *U-185* struck the *Hunt* with a torpedo on the port side at the bulkhead between the pump room and the #4 tank. The explosion ripped open a hole forty-five feet by thirty-five feet. The eight officers, twenty-nine men, and eleven armed guards did not abandon ship. The ship continued on course and did not drop from the convoy. The *Hunt* arrived at

Trinidad for emergency repairs and later steamed to Galveston, Texas, for final repairs. She returned to service in November 1943.

The armament conflicts within the sources. The *Hunt* later became an oil storage ship for the Navy, sporting the name *Flambeau* (IX-192). NSS; WACR; WCSR; AG; Rohwer, p. 169; *Ships of the Esso Fleet*, pp. 466-69; Ship's History Division, NHC.

THOMAS SINNICKSON

D:	7-7-43	YB:	1942
T:	0329	Tn:	7,176
Pos:	03.51 S / 36.22 W	Dr:	18 ft.
Ow:	WSA	C:	700 tons manganese ore, ballast
Op:	Stockard SS Co.	P:	steam
M:	Joseph Linder	S:	8.5
A:	1-4"; 1-3"; 8-20 mm		

On 3 July, the *Thomas Sinnickson* sailed from Bahia, Brazil, in the fourteen-ship Convoy BT-18, en route to Paramaribo, Surinam, Dutch Guiana. The freighter proceeded in convoy station #21, moving from station #22 after the attack on the *James Robertson*. Two hundred and sixty miles northwest of Recife, the *U-185* (Maus) struck the *Sinnickson* with a torpedo on the starboard side at the #1 hold. Three seconds later a second torpedo struck at the #2 hold in one of the fuel bunkers. The later explosion sent flames hundreds of feet into the air when the oil vaporized and exploded. The force of the explosion blew three life rafts clear of the ship and the fourth on top of the after gun tub, and filled the remaining starboard lifeboats with oil and water. The master had the engines secured after twenty minutes. The complement of eight officers, thirty-five men, and twenty-seven armed guards remained on board. The master maneuvered the ship by going astern, in an attempt to bring the vessel to land ninety miles away. While the crew valiantly tried to save the ship, the *Sinnickson* settled by the head. The master instructed the engineers to pump out the flooded compartments. The pumps could not keep ahead of the incoming water, and about thirteen hours after the attack, eighteen men transferred to the USS *Surprise* (PG-63). The *Surprise* radioed for a salvage tug, but the tug did not arrive until 0600 the next day. At daybreak on the 8th the officers ascertained that the vessel could not survive, and the remaining crew abandoned ship with the *Surprise* standing by. The corvette sank the freighter with gunfire at 0930, minutes after the crew abandoned her. The *Surprise* landed the survivors at Recife, Brazil, on 11 July. An armed guard, who died in the attack, constituted the only casualty.

NSS; WACR; WCSR; AG; Rohwer, p. 169.

ELDENA

D:	7-8-43	YB:	1919
T:	0125	Tn:	6,900
Pos:	05.50 N / 50.20 W	Dr:	30 ft.
Ow:	Sea Shipping Co.	C:	7,640 tons general
Op:	WSA	P:	steam
M:	Charles Clinton Bently	S:	7.5
A:	1-4"; 1-3"; 8-20 mm		

On 3 July, the *Eldena* sailed from Trinidad, BWI, to Saldanha Bay, South Africa, in Convoy TJ-1. As the vessel proceeded in convoy station #43, a torpedo fired from the *U-510* (Eick) struck on the port side in the forepeak. The explosion breached the collision bulkhead and flooded the #1 hold. As the *Eldena* settled by the head, the eight officers, thirty-two men, and twenty-six armed guards on board abandoned ship in four lifeboats. Most of the men boarded the escort vessel *PC-495*. An hour after the attack the master and sixteen crewmen in lifeboat #2 reboarded the freighter and started the engines and pumps. While proceeding at just over four knots, the *Eldena* was hit by a second torpedo fired from the *U-510*, this one striking the vessel on the starboard side at the #2 hatch. The explosion threw water thirty-five feet in the air, and the ship sank within minutes. The *PC-495* rescued all hands and landed the men in Recife, Brazil.

NSS; WACR; WCSR; AG; Rohwer, p. 169.

SAMUEL HEINTZELMAN

D:	7-9-43	YB:	1942
T:	unknown	Tn:	7,176
Pos:	09.00 S / 81.00 E	Dr:	24 ft.
Ow:	WSA	C:	5,644 tons ammunition and
Op:	Coastwise (Pacific Far East)		general
	Line	P:	steam
M:	Johann W. G. Wilkie	S:	unknown
A:	1-5"; 1-3"; 8-20 mm		

On 1 July, the *Samuel Heintzelman* departed Freemantle, Australia, for Colombo, India. The *U-511* (Schneewind) attacked the freighter on the 9th. A crew member of the submarine stated that after firing the torpedoes the submarine submerged to a deep depth and heard underwater explosions. The *U-511* surfaced and found no trace of the ship except floating debris. All eight officers, thirty-four men, twenty-seven armed guards, and six passengers on board perished in the attack.

WACR; WCSR; AG; Rohwer, p. 269; Moore, p. 250.

MATTHEW MAURY

D:	7-10-43	YB:	1942
T:	1239	Tn:	7,176
Pos:	37.00 N / 05.00 E	Dr:	12 ft. 8 in.
Ow:	WSA	C:	1,200 tons ballast
Op:	Lykes Bros. SS Co.	P:	steam
M:	Costa Carlson	S:	6
A:	1-4"; 1-3"; 8-20 mm		

On 10 July, the *Matthew Maury* sailed from Philippeville, Algeria, to Algiers, Algeria, in the six-ship Convoy BT-22. The *U-371* (Mehl) fired a torpedo that struck the zigzagging freighter in the stern. The explosion blew off the propeller, bent the shaft, and flooded the #5 hold. The ship careened out of control and gradually lost way. The complement of eight officers, thirty-five men, and twenty-eight armed guards, as well as the seven passengers, went to their boat stations but did not abandon ship. Two British corvettes stood by and towed the vessel to Bougie, Algeria. Two days later tugs towed the Liberty ship to Algiers. After emergency repairs the vessel steamed to Newport News, Virginia, to receive final repairs. All hands survived the attack.

One document relates the owner was the U.S. Maritime Commission. The figures for the ship's complement conflict within the sources. NSS; WACR; WCSR; AG; VSC; Rohwer, p. 247, places the attack at 37.13 N / 05.12 E.

GULFPRINCE

D:	7-10-43	YB:	1921
T:	1240	Tn:	6,560
Pos:	37.13 N / 05.12 E	Dr:	14 ft.
Ow:	Gulf Oil Corp.	C:	1,000 bbls. aviation gasoline,
Op:	Gulf Oil Corp.		salt water ballast
M:	John Lund	P:	steam
A:	1-5"; 1-3"; 8-20 mm	S:	6

On 10 July, the *Gulfprince* sailed from Philippeville, Algeria, to Algiers, Algeria, in Convoy LT-22, which consisted of six merchant vessels and five escorts. The tanker proceeded in convoy station #22. About eight hours out of port, the *U-371* (Mehl) fired a torpedo that struck the ship on the starboard side at the #7 tank. The torpedo penetrated twenty feet into the empty but non-gas-free tank before exploding. The explosion ripped a twenty-foot hole in the side, destroyed the steering engine, brought down the mainmast, and started fires in the tanks carrying fuel. The ship listed to starboard, and the second assistant engineer secured the engines after one minute. Within minutes of the explosion, the complement of eight officers, twenty-eight men, and twenty-eight armed guards began abandoning ship in the #2 and #4 lifeboats and three rafts, and by

jumping overboard. The British trawler *Sir Gareth* (T-227) and the SS *Empire Commerce* rescued the survivors and landed them in Algeria. The only casualty, one of the armed guards, later died from burns on board the *Empire Commerce*. A salvage crew boarded the vessel, and the British tugs *Weazel* (W-120) and *Hudson* (W-02) towed her to Algiers, arriving on the 12th. Rather than declaring the vessel a CTL, WSA bought her and chartered the tanker to the Navy for use as a mobile storehouse in North Africa.

The vessel was allocated to the British Ministry of War Transport. NSS; WACR; WCSR; WCSR; AG; Rohwer, p. 247; *War Action Casualties*, p. 155, relates the *Lotus* rescued the survivors instead of the *Sir Gareth*.

ALICE F. PALMER

D: 7-10-43   YB: 1943
T: 1500   Tn: 7,176
Pos: 26.30 S / 44.10 E   Dr: 15 ft. 6 in.
Ow: WSA   C: water ballast
Op: American President Lines   P: steam
M: George Pederson   S: 11
A: 1-3"; 9-20 mm

On 2 July, the Liberty ship *Alice F. Palmer* sailed from Colombo, Ceylon, en route to Durban with no escort. The *U-177* (Gysae) fired a torpedo that struck the port side at the #5 hold. The explosion destroyed the stern, blew off the prop and rudder, flooded the engine room and the #5 hold, put the after gun out of action, and broke the ship's back. With the stern drooping at a 45° angle, some of the ship's complement of eight officers, thirty-five men, and twenty-five armed guards decided to abandon ship in two of the lifeboats ten minutes after the attack. The order to abandon ship, however, came about twenty minutes later, and the remaining men left the ship in the other two boats. The *U-177* surfaced and signaled the men to come alongside. After questioning the crewmen for twenty minutes, the U-boat took a position off the port side of the vessel and began shelling her. The *U-177* fired about twenty shells into the stricken vessel and left with the freighter burning. The ship slowly sank by the stern and disappeared at about 1700. The four lifeboats became separated as they sailed to Madagascar. A British PBY rescued the survivors in the #3 boat sixty miles southeast of Madagascar three days after the attack. The three remaining boats all landed in Mozambique. Boat #1 landed fifteen days after the attack, boat #2 with twenty-two men landed sixteen days after the attack, and boat #4 landed twenty days after the attack. All hands survived.

Time was also given as 1440. The sources conflict on the number of armed guards. NSS; WACR; WCSR; RWCS; AG; Rohwer, p. 269, places the attack at 26.30 S / 44.20 E.

ROBERT ROWAN

D: 7-11-43   YB: 1943
T: 1545   Tn: 7,176
Pos: Gela Harbor, Sicily   Dr: 24 ft.
Ow: WSA   C: 2,900 tons ammunition, gas,
Op: Isthmian SS Co.   guns, jeeps, troops, equipment
M: Ivar J. H. Rosenquist   P: steam
A: 2-3"; 8-20 mm; 2-40 mm; 2-50   S: at anchor
     cal.

On 6 July, the *Robert Rowan* departed Oran, North Africa, en route to Gela, Sicily. She arrived at Gela on the 11th and anchored to discharge her cargo. Lookouts spotted approximately thirty planes approaching from the northwest and sounded the air alarm. All the ships in the harbor put up a heavy barrage of fire. Bombs fell around the *Rowan*, and at 1545 three struck the ship seconds apart. The first penetrated the main deck at the #1 hatch, passed through the starboard side, and fell into the water unexploded. The second entered the #2 hatch, and the third passed through the #3 hatch. The latter two bombs exploded in the holds, blew the hatch covers off, and started fires. The fires caused the ammunition stored below to explode. The boatswain organized a firefighting party but could not control the fire. The ship's complement of 8 officers, 33 men, 32 armed guards, and the 348 troops on board, including 12 naval personnel, all began abandoning ship thirty-five minutes after the bombs struck. They used the ship's four lifeboats, a raft, and life floats, but most of the Army personnel jumped overboard. A Navy landing craft picked up the men in the water as the ship settled on an even keel. The USS *Orizaba* (AP-24) rescued other members of the crew. The ship settled to the bottom with the superstructure above the water at 1700. The fire had completely burned the boat deck and the bridge, and exploding ammunition had blown the forward end apart. All the ship's complement of 421 survived.

NSS; WACR; WCSR; AG.

JOSEPH G. CANNON

D: 7-11-43   YB: 1943
T: 7905   Tn: 7,181
Pos: Avola Harbor, Sicily   Dr: 19 ft.
Ow: WSA   C: 100 tons general
Op: Weyerhaeuser SS Co.   P: steam
M: Ernest Otto Damzog   S: at anchor
A: 1-4"; 1-3"; 8-20 mm

The *Joseph G. Cannon* received extensive damage while anchored at Avola Harbor, Sicily. On the evening of 11 July, German dive bombers attacked the harbor and sank the British hospital ship *Talamba*. The Liberty ship fortunately received the protection of a British destroyer and was spared any damage. The next morning German aircraft again attacked, and a bomb struck the vessel at the #5 hold, killing a number of British soldiers. The ship's complement of eight officers, thirty-two men, and twenty-five armed guards did not abandon ship and escaped injury. The ship settled until the stern lay aground, and tugs later towed her to Malta for repairs. She returned to service in September.

WACR; WCSR; AG; TF; Moore, p. 366.

AFRICAN STAR

D:	7-12-43	YB:	1942
T:	0158	Tn:	6,507
Pos:	25.46 S / 40.35 W	Dr:	25 ft.
Ow:	WSA	C:	5,500 tons chrome, asbestos,
Op:	American South African Line		wattle extract
M:	John George Waller	P:	steam
A:	1-5"; 1-3"; 8-20 mm	S:	16.5

On 11 July, the *African Star* sailed on independent routing from Rio de Janeiro, Brazil, bound for New York. The *U-172* (Emmermann) intercepted the zigzagging vessel and fired a torpedo that struck the port side at the #4 hold. The explosion blew the hatch covers off the #4 and #5 holds and disabled the generator and the steering controls. As the general alarm sounded, the crew secured the engines, and the ship listed to port, slowly settled, and lost way. The master ordered the ship abandoned, and most of the complement of eight officers, forty-eight men, and thirty-one armed guards cleared the freighter in two lifeboats and a raft. At 0220, with both boats away, the *U-172* fired a second torpedo that struck the ship on the starboard side between the #4 and #5 holds. The *African Star* broke into two pieces and sank within one minute. The *U-172* surfaced about 1,000 yards from the ship and took a few men on board. After questioning the men, the Germans gave directions to the nearest land and returned the men to the boats. Aircraft spotted the boats on the 12th and 13th. Thirty-seven hours after the attack the Brazilian destroyer *Maranhao* picked up the survivors and landed them at Rio de Janeiro. The explosion of the first torpedo blew one armed guard over the side. He was never found and constituted the only casualty.

The ship's complement is contradictory within the sources. NSS; WACR; WCSR; RWCS; AG; Rohwer, p. 169.

TIMOTHY PICKERING

D:	7-13-43	YB:	1942
T:	1145	Tn:	7,181
Pos:	500 yards off Avola Beach	Dr:	23 ft.
Ow:	WSA	C:	5,000 tons army cargo and
Op:	American President Lines		British troops
M:	Gustaf Erick Swanson	P:	steam
A:	1-4"; 1-3"; 8-20 mm	S:	at anchor

On 6 July, the *Timothy Pickering* sailed from Alexandria, Egypt, to Avola, Sicily. The *Pickering* had anchored with the convoy just off the beach. Dive bombers attacked the ship at 1145, and a 500-pound bomb struck at the fore part of the #4 hold, penetrated the deck, and exploded in the engine room and the #4 deep tank. This caused the cargo to explode and created a hole twenty feet square on the starboard side of the #4 hold. Fire broke out and engulfed the entire amidships as the ship settled on her after end. The ship's complement of 8 officers, 35 men, and 23 armed guards, together with the 128 British troops on board, had no time to launch boats. Some jumped into the water; others climbed down ropes and the anchor chain to escape the flames. The craft from other vessels in the convoy rescued most of these men. An invasion barge picked up five men and put them on the SS *O'Henry*. Others went on board the hospital ship HMS *Amra*. The inferno trapped many men below, and several tried to escape through portholes and burned to death. Three officers, nineteen merchant crewmen, sixteen armed guards, and all but one of the British troops died in the attack. A British destroyer sank the vessel with a torpedo at 1330. The *Pickering* broke in two, and her bow rested on the beach above the water.

NSS; WACR; WCSR; AG.

ROBERT BACON

D:	7-14-43	YB:	1943
T:	0235	Tn:	7,192
Pos:	15.25 S / 41.13 E	Dr:	18 ft.
Ow:	WSA	C:	ballast
Op:	R. A. Nicol & Co. Inc.	P:	steam
M:	Clyde Frank Henderson	S:	11
A:	2-3"; 8-20 mm		

On 11 July, the *Robert Bacon* sailed independently from Mombasa, Kenya, to Cape Town, South Africa. Thirty-five miles off the Mozambique Light the *U-178* (Dommes) fired two torpedoes at the freighter. The first crossed the ship's bow, and the second struck the port side at the #2 hatch in one of the fuel bunkers. The ship immediately listed 10° to starboard but appeared not to be

sinking. The explosion blew oil and water into the air, destroyed steam lines, and damaged a great deal of the ship's equipment. The engineer on watch stopped the engines, and the crew of nine officers, thirty-five men, and twenty-seven armed guards mustered at their boat stations. The crew found two of the lifeboats unusable because they were filled with water and oil. They cleared the ship in the three other lifeboats and three rafts. After the crew abandoned the freighter, a second torpedo struck the starboard side. At daybreak the *U-178* fired a third torpedo that hit the starboard side aft, causing the ship to sink ten minutes later, plunging by the bow. The submarine surfaced and the Germans questioned the occupants of the #3 boat, giving them directions to land before leaving. This boat remained in the vicinity of the sinking until the next morning and then headed for Mozambique. On 16 July, the #3 boat, with the master in charge, reached Mozambique Harbor, and a tug towed it to the custom's pier. The British SS *English Prince* rescued fourteen survivors in another boat, and the British tanker SS *Steaua Romana* picked up several more in the last boat on the 27th. One raft stayed at sea for fourteen days, one for twenty days, and the final raft made landfall forty-four days after the attack. Two men never reached the lifeboats, and a third died ashore from exposure.

NSS; WACR; WCSR; RWCS; AG; Rohwer, p. 269.

JOHN H. EATON

D:	7-16-43	YB:	1943
T:	1522	Tn:	7,176
Pos:	Algiers Harbor	Dr:	unknown
Ow:	WSA	C:	unknown
Op:	Lykes Brothers SS Co.	P:	steam
M:	Henry A. Fritz	S:	at anchor
A:	2-3"; 8-20 mm		

On 13 June, the *John H. Eaton* departed New York in Convoy UGS-10 for Algiers, North Africa, and arrived on 9 July. German planes attacked the anchorage and dropped bombs, striking two ships near the *Eaton*. These ships suffered shattering explosions that completely demolished them. Debris rained down on the anchorage, and the *Eaton* suffered damage to her lifeboats, stack, guns, and the Jumbo boom at the #2 hatch. The concussion also blew off ventilators and blew in doors. The abandon ship signal was sounded, but some members of the crew remained on board to assist a tug that towed the Liberty ship out of danger. There were no injuries among the crew (complement unknown). The *John H. Eaton* was able to sail on 26 July for Baltimore, Maryland.

USMMA; AG; TF; ONF.

STEPHEN C. FOSTER

D:	7-16-43	YB:	1943
T:	1530	Tn:	7,176
Pos:	Algiers Harbor	Dr:	unknown
Ow:	WSA	C:	unknown
Op:	Standard Fruit Co.	P:	steam
M:	John J. Carr	S:	moored
A:	1-5"; 1-3"; 8-20 mm		

On 13 June, the *Stephen C. Foster* sailed from New York in convoy to Algiers, North Africa. During an air raid in Algiers Harbor, a bomb from a German aircraft fell near the Liberty ship, which lay moored in the end berth of Quay Francis Number One in Algiers Harbor. An explosion on the quay ripped the bow out of a Norwegian freighter, created a crater about thirty-five feet in circumference, and damaged the *Foster*. The concussion and flying debris caused a large dent in the forward deck on the starboard side. The blast sprung the hatch coamings of the #2 and #5 hatches, damaged the winch, and ripped away doors and glass fittings. None of the crew were injured in the blast.

WCSR; AG.

RICHARD CASWELL

D:	7-16-43	YB:	1942
T:	1615	Tn:	7,176
Pos:	28.10 S / 46.30 W	Dr:	31 ft. 6 in.
Ow:	WSA	C:	9,000 tons manganese ore, hides,
Op:	South Atlantic SS Co.		meat, fertilizers
M:	Solomon A. Suggs	P:	steam
A:	1-4"; 9-20 mm	S:	12

On 12 July, the *Richard Caswell* sailed from Buenos Aires for New York. About 200 miles off Brazil the *U-513* (Guggenberger) fired a torpedo that struck the Liberty ship on the starboard side at the after end of the engine room. The explosion destroyed the engines and killed the three men on watch below. The master ordered the surviving men among the eight officers, thirty-four men, twenty-four armed guards, and two passengers on board to abandon ship. Most of the men left in three lifeboats and two rafts. The master and a small party of men remained on board to ascertain the complete damage. A second torpedo struck the ship at the forward end of the engine room ten minutes after the first. This explosion blew a few men over the side and caused extensive damage to the amidships deck and the superstructure. The *U-513* surfaced as the ship split in two and sank. After questioning the men, the U-boat officers gave the survivors cigarettes and then the submarine disappeared. On 19 July, the

Argentine SS *Mexico* rescued two boats of survivors. On 22 July, the third lifeboat landed at Florianopolis, Brazil. The USS *Barnegat* (AVP-10) rescued the men on the raft and landed them at Rio de Janeiro. Three officers and six merchant crewmen died in the attack.

NSS; WACR; WCSR; RWCS; Rohwer, p. 170.

SAMUEL PARKER

D:	7-19-43	YB:	1942
T:	unknown	Tn:	7,176
Pos:	off Avola, Sicily	Dr:	unknown
Ow:	WSA	C:	unknown
Op:	American Mail Line	P:	steam
M:	Elmer J. Stull	S:	at anchor
A:	1-5"; 1-3"; 8-20 mm		

In November 1942, the *Samuel Parker* sailed from Puget Sound to Sydney, Australia, via San Pedro. Beginning in March, she had shuttled between ports in the Mediterranean carrying troops and cargo. She previously had been damaged in Tripoli Harbor in April. The *Parker* joined the invasion forces off Sicily and anchored off the beachhead for ten days. During her stay, German aircraft attacked the anchorage nightly. On the night of 19 July, two planes attacked the freighter, straddling her with twelve bombs. One struck the port bow hawsehole and ripped the bulwark. After passing through the bulwark, it exploded. The others fell on either side of the ship and punctured the hull with shrapnel. On 22 July, several more near misses damaged the ship again. In this attack strafing runs by aircraft killed two of the armed guards on board. At least six others in the crew reported injuries. After the attacks the *Parker* sailed back to Tripoli in Convoy MKS-198 with over 180 holes in the shell plating.

TF; AG; USMMA; Moore, p. 382.

WILLIAM T. COLEMAN

D:	7-20-43	YB:	1942
T:	0200	Tn:	7,180
Pos:	Syracuse Harbor, Sicily	Dr:	20 ft.
Ow:	WSA	C:	2,000 tons munitions
Op:	J. H. Winchester & Co.	P:	steam
M:	S. J. Reynard	S:	at anchor
A:	1-4"; 9-20 mm		

The *William T. Coleman* sailed from Alexandria, Egypt, to Syracuse, Sicily. While she was at Sicily, German aircraft kept the anchorage under continuous attack, and the crew answered about seventy-five air raid alarms. On the 16th, a bomb fell nearby, causing slight structural damage. Four days later in another air raid a ship tied to the same buoy as the *Coleman* was set on fire by enemy bombs. When the blazing ship began to explode, the *Coleman's* master ordered that the mooring lines be cut. As the ship got under way, she went aground. Meanwhile, the flaming cargo of a nearby blazing tanker had poured into the water and lay burning for 250 yards around the ship. As the blazing oil approached the *William T. Coleman,* three American Liberty ships swung their sterns toward the burning oil and pushed it back with the wash of their propellers. The blazing ship eventually exploded, lifting the *Coleman* from the water, knocking the crew down, and sending up a great deal of debris. A large piece of a 50-ton lighter landed on the *Coleman's* afterdeck and tore up the deck and steam lines. Thinking the ship had been hit by a bomb, the master ordered the eight officers, thirty-five men, seven passengers, and twenty-five armed guards on board to abandon the ship. With two boats in the water, the mate realized what had happened and called the boats back. Two men in the crew suffered injuries during the attacks.

WACR; USMMA; AG; ONF.

CHERRY VALLEY

D:	7-22-43	YB:	1942
T:	0322	Tn:	10,172
Pos:	25.10 N / 68.35 W	Dr:	18 ft. 6 in.
Ow:	Kaymar Tankers Inc.	C:	6,000 tons water ballast, 165
Op:	WSA		tons Army cargo
M:	John H. Rose	P:	steam
A:	1-5"; 1-3"; 8-20 mm	S:	15.5

On 19 July, the *Cherry Valley* sailed on independent routing from New York to Aruba, NWI. The ship constantly steered a zigzagging course during the trip. The *U-66* (Markworth) fired two torpedoes that struck the starboard side in the #6 and #7 tanks. The explosions ripped open the #5, #6, #7, and #8 starboard and center tanks. The engines and steering gear escaped serious damage, so the ship reduced speed to thirteen knots and tried to escape. The *U-66* fired another spread of three torpedoes that all missed. The *U-66* then surfaced to stop the vessel with its deck guns. The tanker's gun crew began firing the three-inch, five-inch, and smaller guns at the *U-66.* The master adjusted the tanker's trim by emptying the #1 starboard tank of ballast. The vessel successfully escaped the U-boat and arrived at San Juan, Puerto Rico, under her own power, escorted into harbor by the Dutch corvette *Jan Van Brakel.* None of the complement of

eleven officers, forty men, and twenty-eight armed guards were killed or injured in the attack.

NSS; WACR; WCSR; AG; Rohwer, p. 170; *War Action Casualties*, p. 156.

JOHN A. POOR

D:	7-28-43	YB:	1943
T:	0630	Tn:	7,176
Pos:	42.51 N / 64.55 W	Dr:	28 ft.
Ow:	WSA	C:	8,500 tons general
Op:	International Freighting Corp.	P:	steam
M:	William J. Uppit	S:	8
A:	2-3"; 8-20 mm		

On 26 July, the *John A. Poor* sailed from Boston for Halifax, Nova Scotia, in Convoy BX-65. She steamed in station #14 in the convoy but lost contact in heavy fog. The ship, streaming her anti-torpedo nets, wandered into mines laid by the *U-119* (von Kameke). When a heavy concussion occurred off the starboard side, the ship suffered only minor damage, and the master continued the voyage. An hour later another explosion occurred off the starboard side, and the master, thinking he saw a U-boat, turned the vessel. Fifteen minutes later a violent explosion rocked the ship and damaged the steam lines, the boilers, and the generators, and cracked the spring bearings. The armed guards fired the guns at a nonexistent enemy. The ship's complement of eight officers, thirty-four men, and twenty-eight armed guards remained at their posts as the ship lay dead in the water. At 1430, patrol boat #123 came alongside, informing the master that tugs were en route. The watch below got one boiler lit, and the crew retrieved the torpedo nets and proceeded at just over four knots. At 1500 the vessel took a tow line from the tug *North Star*. On 30 July, forty-four miles off Sambro Light the tug *Foundation Aramore* towed the vessel to St. George Island, Halifax.

NSS; WACR; WCSR; AG; Rohwer, p. 170, places the incident at 42.51 N / 64.55 W.

WILLIAM ELLERY

D:	7-30-43	YB:	1942
T:	2330	Tn:	7,176
Pos:	32.00 S / 36.00 E	Dr:	16 ft.
Ow:	WSA	C:	25 tons general cargo
Op:	Pope & Talbot, McCormick Div.	P:	steam
M:	David Slater McDonald	S:	11.5
A:	1-4"; 1-3"; 8-20 mm		

On 9 July, the *William Ellery* sailed from Basra, Iraq, to Durban, South Africa. Three hundred miles from Durban the *U-197* (Bartels) fired a torpedo that struck the ship on the port side at the #4 hatch. The explosion caused the ship to swerve to port and created a 450-square-foot hole. The general alarm sounded immediately, and the complement of eight officers, thirty-one men, and twenty-seven armed guards raced to their boat stations. Lookouts spotted a second torpedo that passed along the port side and under the stern. The chief engineer reported that the ship could be kept afloat and running if a damage control party made immediate repairs. As the ship maintained nine knots, the crew helped the chief engineer shore up the bulkhead between the #4 and #5 holds and strengthen the watertight door separating the shaft alley and the engine room. The crew suffered no casualties, and the ship made Durban under her own power on 1 August. On 30 August, the ship went into dry dock and later returned to service.

NSS; WACR; WCSR; Rohwer, p. 270.

YANKEE ARROW

D: 8-3-43   YB: 1921
T: 0705   Tn: 8,046
Pos: 37.10 N / 11.06 E   Dr: 22 ft.
Ow: Socony Vacuum Oil Co.   C: 800 tons water ballast
Op: WSA   P: steam
M: John Belgonen   S: 8.7
A: 1-5"; 1-3"; 8-20 mm

On 2 August, the *Yankee Arrow* traveled with Convoy KMS-20 from Bône, Algeria, to Bizerte, Tunisia. The ship sailed in convoy station #48. The convoy began forming a single column to enter the narrow Bizerte Harbor Channel. Off Cape Bon, a mine struck the tanker about eight feet below the waterline on the port side at the forward deep tank. The explosion drove the ship up and back and blew a large hole in the hull. The blast threw fuel oil over the vessel and started a fire in the forward portion of the ship. The helmsman turned the ship away from the wind, and the crew brought the fire under control about thirty minutes later. The surviving members of the complement of eight officers, thirty-five men, and twenty-five armed guards, along with ten in the Navy communications detail, did not abandon ship. The force of the explosion, however, carried several men overboard. Quick-thinking men on deck released a raft for these men. Two members of the gun crew and five merchant seamen died from the explosions or fire. The ship got under way and steamed into Bizerte Harbor. The mine extensively damaged the ship, and naval engineers judged her too weakened for sea duty. WSA bought the ship and chartered her to the Navy as a storehouse.

The ship's complement figures and casualties conflict within the sources. NSS; WACR; WCSR; AG; TF; *War Action Casualties*, p. 158.

HARRISON GREY OTIS

D:	8-4-43	YB:	1943
T:	0335	Tn:	7,176
Pos:	off Gibraltar	Dr:	13 ft.
Ow:	WSA	C:	ballast
Op:	American Hawaiian SS Co.	P:	steam
M:	Roy Moyes	S:	at anchor
A:	1-3"; 9-20 mm		

The *Harrison Grey Otis* sailed from Tripoli en route to the United States via Gibraltar. After the ship anchored in Gibraltar, a fantail lookout spotted an exhausted swimmer one hundred yards off the stern. A cadet engineer saved the man who proved to be in the Italian Navy. Suspecting an Italian limpet mine, the master had the engines turned over to wash away any bombs or mines. A British lieutenant took the prisoner away and promised to send a diver. However, no diver ever returned to examine the vessel. About three hours after the discovery of the swimmer, a violent explosion rocked the ship on the port side at the #3 hold. The blast damaged the engines and boilers and flooded the engine room and the #3 hold. The ship's crew slipped her anchor cable, and the master beached the vessel. The ten officers, thirty-five men, and twenty-three armed guards on board remained on the ship. The explosion damaged the vessel severely enough for her to be declared a CTL. The owners eventually towed the vessel to Spain to be scrapped. The blast injured eight men and killed one of the ship's crew on watch below.

NSS; WACR; WCSR.

MATTHEW LYON

D:	8-11-43	YB:	1943
T:	1320	Tn:	7,775
Pos:	13.42 S / 165.59 E	Dr:	18 ft. 6 in.
Ow:	WSA	C:	ballast
Op:	Dichman Wright & Pugh	P:	steam
M:	Jean De Reske Dandel	S:	9
A:	1-3"; 9-20 mm		

On 9 August, the *Matthew Lyon* sailed from Guadalcanal, with the SS *J. H. Kincaide* and the escort USS *Crosby* (APD-17), all bound for Espíritu Santo. A torpedo fired from the *I-11* (Tagami) struck the zigzagging Liberty ship on the port side at the #3 hatch. Three strongbacks from the #3 hatch fell on the flying bridge and crippled the steering apparatus. The damage to the steering gear caused the vessel to veer in a large circle to starboard. The crew managed to rig emergency steering gear, and the vessel proceeded toward Espíritu Santo at full speed. The explosion created a hole thirty-five feet square. Only one man in the complement of the eight officers, thirty-three men, and eighteen armed guards reported an injury. In October, the U.S. Navy pressed her into service as a net cargo ship and renamed her *Zebra* (IX-107). Five months later she was redesignated the AKN-5.

NSS; WACR; WCSR; AG; Rohwer, p. 284, lists the attack at 22.30 S / 66.30 E; DANFS, 8:560-61.

M. H. DE YOUNG

D:	8-13-43	YB:	1943
T:	1950	Tn:	7,176
Pos:	21.50 S / 175.10 W	Dr:	23 ft.
Ow:	WSA	C:	3,900 tons construction cargo
Op:	R. A. Nicol & Co.	P:	steam
M:	William Munda	S:	12.8
A:	1-3"; 9-20 mm		

On 29 July, the *M. H. De Young* sailed from Port Hueneme, California, to Espíritu Santo, New Hebrides, on independent routing. Lookouts on the Liberty ship spotted two torpedoes fired by the *I-19* (Kinashi). One torpedo struck the starboard side at the engine room, and the other passed fifty yards astern. The explosion completely demolished the engine room and blew a hole twenty feet by fifteen feet in the starboard side and wrecked the crew's living quarters. The master ordered most of the nine officers, thirty-three men, and twenty-eight passengers on board to abandon ship in two boats. Twenty-five armed guards, the master, the chief engineer, and the boatswain remained on board. The two lifeboats laid by the ship during the night, and the crew and passengers reboarded the *Young* the next morning. The ship remained afloat and would have been difficult to sink because part of the cargo consisted of construction battalion barge pontoons stowed in every hold. On the morning of the 14th, the *SC-67* took the injured on board and then proceeded to Tongatabu. The SS *Quebec* towed the *M. H. De Young* into Tongatabu on the 16th. A passenger and one officer and two men on watch below died.

Figures for the ship's complement are contradictory within the sources. NSS; WACR; WCSR; AG; Rohwer, p. 284.

JONATHAN ELMER

D:	8-13-43	YB:	1942
T:	2045	Tn:	7,191
Pos:	36.07 N / 03.07 W	Dr:	15 ft.
Ow:	WSA	C:	none
Op:	Marine Transport Lines Inc.	P:	steam
M:	Cristen Delphin Anderson	S:	7
A:	1-5"; 1-3"; 8-20 mm		

On 13 August, the *Jonathan Elmer* sailed from Oran to Casablanca in Convoy MKS-21. During the trip about fifty German aircraft attacked the seventy-one ship convoy and repeatedly strafed the ship. The twenty-eight armed guards claimed four enemy planes during the attack, and the attacking planes wounded three of the armed guards. The strafing runs of the enemy planes put numerous holes all over the Liberty ship, but the damage could only be considered slight. None of the remaining ship's crew of eleven officers and thirty-five merchant crew, or the twenty passengers, reported any injuries. The freighter arrived in Gibraltar on 14 August.

WACR; WCSR; AG; TF.

ANNE BRADSTREET

D:	8-13-43	YB:	1942
T:	2000	Tn:	7,176
Pos:	36.19 N / 02.18 W	Dr:	13 ft.
Ow:	WSA	C:	none
Op:	Agwilines	P:	steam
M:	Saamund Saamundsen	S:	7
A:	1-5"; 1-3"; 8-20 mm		

On 13 August, the *Anne Bradstreet* sailed from Oran, Algeria, to Gibraltar in the twenty-eight ship Convoy MKS-21. Enemy aircraft attacked the convoy, and as the torpedo bombers launched their torpedoes, the helmsman expertly maneuvered the Liberty ship, causing one torpedo to pass ahead and another to pass astern. The armed guards maintained a scathing fire on the planes as they raked the decks with machine gun fire. The *Bradstreet* suffered slight damage over her entire length, including some dented hull plates. Only one man from the ship's complement of nine officers, thirty-eight men, and twenty-seven armed guards was injured. The ship arrived safely in Gibraltar on 14 August.

The armed guards claimed they downed four planes. WACR; WCSR; AG; TF.

FRANCIS W. PETTYGROVE

D:	8-13-43	YB:	1943
T:	2100	Tn:	7,160
Pos:	36.08 N / 02.14 W	Dr:	18 ft.
Ow:	WSA	C:	ballast
Op:	American Mail Line Ltd.	P:	steam
M:	Kenneth Seton McPherson	S:	12
A:	2-3"; 8-20 mm		

On 13 August, the *Francis W. Pettygrove* sailed from Oran, Algeria, to Gibraltar in Convoy MKS-21, which consisted of twenty-eight merchant ships and seven British escort vessels. At about 2000 lookouts spotted enemy planes approaching the convoy from ahead. The German bombers and torpedo planes began an attack on the convoy that would last an hour. During this time the *Pettygrove* successfully evaded two torpedoes, one crossing the bow and the other passing astern. A third struck the port side between the engine room and the after bulkhead of the #3 hold. The explosion carried away the main steam lines, ruptured the main deck, and flooded both the engine room and the #3 hold. With a fire reported in the forward magazine, the master ordered most of the eight officers, thirty-two men, and four passengers on board to abandon ship. They cleared the ship in two lifeboats and went on board the British minesweeper *Hythe* (J-194). Some of the twenty-eight armed guards remained on board along with the master and two crewmen. After determining the ship safe, the master allowed some men to return to prepare her for towing. On the following morning the *Hythe* took the freighter in tow to Gibraltar. On 15 August, the *Francis W. Pettygrove* anchored in Gibraltar, and she was beached on 12 October. All hands survived the attack. WSA declared the ship a CTL, and in 1949 she was towed to Spain and scrapped.

NSS; WACR; WCSR; USMMA; AG; Sawyer, Mitchell, p. 126.

BENJAMIN CONTEE

D:	8-16-43	YB:	1942
T:	2323	Tn:	7,176
Pos:	16 mi. N. of Bone, Algeria	Dr:	17 ft.
Ow:	WSA	C:	1,350 tons sand ballast, POWs
Op:	Mississippi Shipping Co.	P:	steam
M:	Even Evensen	S:	6
A:	1-5"; 1-3"; 8-20 mm		

On the night of 16 August, the *Benjamin Contee* steamed from Bône, Algeria, with 1,800 Italian POWs to meet a convoy bound for Oran, Algeria. In a full moon, about sixteen miles west of Bône, a torpedo bomber attacked the small convoy that included one British merchantman and a British corvette. A torpedo plane glided in with its motors off and released a torpedo that struck the *Benjamin Contee* between the #1 and #2 holds in the double bottom tanks. The explosion created a hole fifty feet wide and twenty-one feet high and blew several men over the side. The ship eventually settled by the head with a forty-foot draft. The Italian POWs in the #1 and #2 holds immediately panicked. Breaking past their guards, they seized the lifeboats. The master instructed two Italian-speaking crewmen to tell the POWs that the ship would not sink. The master had the ship trimmed by flooding the #5 hold with fire hoses. The ship had on board 10 officers, 33 men, 27 armed guards, 26 British POW guards, 7 U.S. Army security personnel, and the 1,800 POWs. The explosion killed 264 POWs and injured 142 others. None of the crew, the British POW guards, or the armed guards died in the attack. Other ships in the convoy rescued the men that fell into the water, and these men landed at Bône. The *Benjamin Contee* received temporary repairs in Gibraltar and steamed into New York on 24 January 1944.

The Benjamin Contee was sunk off Normandy to form part of the artificial harbor on 6-8-44. NSS; WACR; WCSR; AG.

CAPE MOHICAN

D:	8-21-43	YB:	1942
T:	2258	Tn:	5,094
Pos:	33.42 N / 16.43 E	Dr:	12 ft.
Ow:	WSA	C:	800 tons chrome ore ballast
Op:	A. H. Bull SS Co.	P:	steam
M:	Homer Ryland Callis	S:	13
A:	1-4"; 1-3"; 8-20 mm		

On 19 August, the *Cape Mohican* departed Alexandria, Egypt, en route to Algiers, Algeria, in Convoy MKF-22. The ship sailed in convoy station #41. A torpedo fired from an unidentified submarine or a mine struck the freighter on the starboard side under the after peak. The explosion flooded the after peak, the #5 hold, and the shaft alley. The engine room flooded up to the floor plates. The explosion broke the main shaft and destroyed the rudder. The master ordered some of the complement of eight officers, thirty-three men, and twenty-four armed guards off the ship directly into a rescue vessel. Only the officers, a few men, and the gun crew remained on board. A British destroyer stayed by the ship during the night while the skeleton crew shored up some of the damage. The next morning more men returned to the *Cape Mohican*, and a British naval tug took the vessel in tow. The ship arrived at Malta on 24 August. All hands survived the explosion, and only two reported slight injuries.

WACR; WCSR; AG; TF.

PIERRE SOULE

D:	8-23-43	YB:	1943
T:	1928	Tn:	7,191
Pos:	38.21 N / 12.50 E	Dr:	18 ft.
Ow:	WSA	C:	sand ballast
Op:	Moore McCormick	P:	steam
M:	Patrick Driscoll	S:	10
A:	1-5"; 1-3"; 8-20 mm		

After discharging cargo, the Liberty ship *Pierre Soule* sailed in escort of three destroyers and one tug from Palermo, Sicily, to Bizerte, Tunisia. A torpedo fired from the *U-380* (Röther) struck the vessel at the rudder post, bodily lifted the vessel out of the water, and threw a column of water 100 feet into the air. The explosion blew off the rudder, damaged the shaft and the engines, wrecked the gun crew's quarters, and partially flooded the engine room and holds #4 and #5. When the ship failed to respond to the wheel, the watch below secured the engines on orders from the bridge. The eight officers, thirty-six men, twenty-eight armed guards, and fifty passengers remained on board. The Navy tug *Nauset* (AT-89) shot a line over to the ship and took her in tow. On 24 August, the *Pierre Soule* dropped anchor in Bizerte. She later went into a dry dock for repairs. All hands survived the attack.

The ship's personnel figures are contradictory within the sources. NSS; WACR; WCSR; USMMA; AG; Rohwer, p. 249, puts the attack at 38.19 N / 12.55 E.

ESSO PROVIDENCE

D:	8-24-43	YB:	1921
T:	0700	Tn:	9,057
Pos:	Port Augusta, Sicily	Dr:	26 ft. 10 in.
Ow:	Standard Oil Co. of N. J.	C:	71,029 bbls. Navy special fuel
Op:	Standard Oil Co. of N. J.	P:	steam
M:	Walter F. Andrews	S:	at anchor
A:	1-5"; 1-3"; 8-20 mm		

The *Esso Providence* sailed from New York to Port Augusta, Sicily, and anchored off the harbor breakwater. Without warning, approximately nine low altitude bombers began attacking the ships in the harbor. Before the watch could sound the general alarm, a bomb struck the water off the starboard beam. A second struck the ship in the #9 starboard tank, and a third struck the water on the port beam. The bomb that struck the ship severely damaged the #8, #9, and #10 port tanks, the #9 starboard tank, and the #4 and #5 summer tanks, leaving a hole forty feet wide. Despite the damage, the tanker managed to deliver the remaining cargo and sailed to Malta, arriving there on 2 December, for emergency repairs. After making temporary repairs at Malta and Gibraltar, she steamed to Staten Island on 26 January. After extensive repairs in dry dock, she returned to service in May 1944. Only two men among the eight officers, thirty-five men, and twenty-eight armed guards on board suffered injuries in the attack.

NSS; WACR; WCSR; AG; *Ships of the Esso Fleet*, pp. 486-91, gives the armed guards' complement at 34.

JOHN BELL

D:	8-26-43	YB:	1943
T:	2115	Tn:	7,226
Pos:	37.11.30 N / 08.21 E	Dr:	26 ft. 5 in.
Ow:	WSA	C:	7,200 tons general
Op:	J. H. Winchester & Co.	P:	steam
M:	David Dunlap Higbee	S:	8.5
A:	2-3"; 8-20 mm		

On 5 August, the *John Bell* departed Hampton Roads, Virginia, as part of the seventy-nine ship Convoy UGS-14. At 1530 the convoy began reforming into four columns to pass through minefields. The *John Bell* steamed from station #52 to station #32 for this maneuver. Catching the convoy at a vulnerable time, the *U-410* (Fenski) fired a torpedo that struck the freighter between the #4 and #5 starboard holds. The torpedo hit a compartment with aviation gasoline, and the explosion ignited the cargo. Flames rose twenty-five feet above the holds and spread rapidly aft and slowly forward. The complement of eight officers, thirty-five men, and twenty-nine armed guards began abandoning ship in five of the ship's six lifeboats. The ship eventually blazed like a torch from stern to stern and continued burning for more than nine hours before sinking stern first the next day. All of the crew managed to escape in the boats except five of the armed guards, who left by diving in the water from the stern. A British minesweeper BYMS-23 and the South African Navy whaler *Southern Maid* (T-27) picked up the survivors within forty-five minutes of the initial explosion. The men landed at Bizerte. An oiler trapped in the shaft alley died—the only casualty in the attack.

NSS; WACR; WCSR; AG; Rohwer, p. 249.

RICHARD HENDERSON

D:	8-26-43	YB:	1943
T:	2120	Tn:	7,194
Pos:	37.12 N / 08.21 E	Dr:	28 ft.
Ow:	WSA	C:	5,000 tons war cargo and
Op:	U.S. Lines		explosives
M:	Lawrence Joseph Silk	P:	steam
A:	2-3"; 8-20 mm	S:	7.5

On 6 August, the *Richard Henderson* sailed in the seventy-nine ship Convoy UGS-14, which consisted of forty-two merchant ships and twenty-eight escorts, from Hampton Roads, Virginia, to the Persian Gulf. The *Henderson* steamed in station #43 in the convoy, but in order to pass through minefields the convoy reformed into four columns with the *Henderson* at convoy station #22. A torpedo fired by the *U-410* (Fenski) struck the freighter on the starboard side, aft of the #5 hatch. The explosion destroyed the gun crew's quarters, blew away the rudder and screw, and flooded the engine room. The chief engineer secured the engines, and the vessel began to settle by the stern. The master ordered the eight officers, thirty-four men, and twenty-eight armed guards to abandon ship. All hands cleared the freighter in six lifeboats. The ship plunged stern first five hours later. Three of the boats, with the master in command, made port at La Calle, Algeria, the next morning. Allied ships rescued the men in the other boats. One of the rescuing ships was the South African Navy armed whaler *Southern Maid* (T-27). All hands survived the attack.

NSS; WACR; WCSR; AG; Rohwer, p. 249, places the attack at 37.15 N / 08.24 E.

W. S. RHEEM

D:	8-31-43	YB:	1921
T:	1535	Tn:	10,872
Pos:	15.51 S / 167.02 E	Dr:	28 ft. 6 in.
Ow:	Standard Oil Co. of California	C:	86,500 bbls. Navy special fuel
Op:	WSA	P:	steam
M:	Gustaf Adolf Johnson	S:	10.2
A:	1-4"; 9-20 mm		

The *W. S. Rheem* sailed from San Francisco to Havannah Harbor, New Hebrides, via Tutuila, Samoa. Leaving Samoa on 24 August, the tanker steamed a zigzag course with one escort and two other ships. The *I-20* (Otsuka) fired three torpedoes, and lookouts spotted the first torpedo on the surface as it approached the ship and crossed the bow. The second torpedo struck the vessel on the port side in the dry cargo hold forward. This explosion created a hole twenty-five feet by twenty feet, broke a cargo boom, and knocked down the main antenna. The third torpedo passed astern. The master ordered several turns and then had the engines secured after ten minutes. Less than an hour later, after surveying the damage and shifting several thousands of barrels of oil, the master had the engines restarted. The vessel steamed to Espíritu Santo on a zigzag course and arrived on the 31st. All ten officers, thirty-nine men, and twenty-five armed guards on board survived.

The armed guard officer mentions a sheet of flame from the first torpedo shooting over the bridge. This is not confirmed in the other sources. NSS; WACR; WCSR; AG; Rohwer, p. 284; *War Action Casualties*, p. 160.

LYMAN STEWART

D:	9-7-43	YB:	1943
T:	0420	Tn:	7,176
Pos:	03.30 N / 75.00 E	Dr:	27 ft. 3 in. aft
Ow:	WSA	C:	7,100 tons ground nuts
Op:	Coastwise Pacific Line	P:	steam
M:	Alfred E. Fuller	S:	10.5
A:	1-4"; 9-20 mm		

On 5 September, the *Lyman Stewart* sailed independently from Colombo, Ceylon, to Durban, South Africa. While the freighter was en route, the *I-27* (Fukumura) attacked. Lookouts spotted a torpedo cross the bow about ten feet from the ship. The general alarm alerted the crew, and the master began maneuvering the freighter. After a second torpedo crossed the stern, a heavy bump was felt throughout the ship caused by a dud torpedo that struck at the #2 hatch. Lookouts sighted two more torpedoes that both missed the freighter. The armed guards fired in the direction of the submarine, and the ship escaped with only slight damage. None of the forty-two men in the merchant crew or the twenty-five armed guards reported any injuries.

NSS; WACR; AG; ONF; Rohwer, p. 270.

WILLIAM B. TRAVIS

D:	9-12-43	YB:	1942
T:	0150	Tn:	7.176
Pos:	37.17 N / 10.30 E	Dr:	18 ft. 4 in.
Ow:	WSA	C:	sand ballast
Op:	Lykes Bros.	P:	steam
M:	Karl Sandberg	S:	7
A:	1-5"; 1-3"; 8-20 mm		

On 11 September, the *William B. Travis* departed Palermo, Sicily, for Bizerte, Tunisia, in a convoy of fourteen ships. She maintained convoy station #41.

About twenty-five miles north of Bizerte an explosion occurred on the port side at the #2 hold. The blast opened a hole thirty-six feet wide, severed the keel, and damaged plates on the starboard side. As the #2 hold flooded, the crew secured the engines. After investigating the damage, the master got the ship under way within five minutes and brought her speed up to eleven knots. The eight officers, thirty-nine men, twenty-seven armed guards, and forty-one passengers on board never abandoned ship. The Coast Guard and master later attributed the explosion to a mine. No Axis records exist to refute this attribution or connect it to a specific submarine. Only one passenger, a man sleeping on the #2 hatch, was killed. The *Travis* anchored in Bizerte the next day.

NSS; WACR; WCSR; AG; Rohwer, p. 250, places the attack at 37.17 N / 109.54 E.

JAMES W. MARSHALL

D: 9-13-43, 9-15-43   YB: 1942
T: 0745   Tn: 7,176
Pos: Gulf of Salerno   Dr: 16 ft.
Ow: WSA   C: 250 tons tanks, guns,
Op: McCormack SS Co.   amphibians, trucks, etc.
M: Ragnar Wm. Roggenbihl   P: steam
A: 2-3"; 8-20 mm   S: at anchor

On 9 September, the *James W. Marshall* sailed from Bizerte, Algiers, in a convoy for the Gulf of Salerno. At Salerno the vessel anchored 1.5 miles off shore and offloaded most of her cargo. In the early afternoon on the 13th, planes attacked the anchored vessel. At 1440 one 250-pound bomb struck a 20-mm gun shield on the starboard side of the bridge, glanced off, pierced the deck, and exploded in the master's quarters and office. The explosion caused a small fire, but the crew quickly extinguished it. The crew suffered no casualties. Two days later planes attacked again. During the attack a glide bomb penetrated the boat deck and exploded near the crew's mess room and the engine room. Fire broke out, and the engine room and the #3 hold flooded. Two LCTs loaded with gas lay on the port side of the ship and caught fire, adding to the inferno. Tugs later got this blaze under control. As the fire raged, most of the 8 officers, 38 men, 29 armed guards, and 100 stevedores on board tried to abandon ship. They used two lifeboats and two rafts to escape. Others climbed down cargo nets to be taken off in nearby landing craft. The seaplane tender *Biscayne* (AVP-11) took many of the survivors on board. The loss of life during the second attack was tragic. One officer, twelve men, and fifty Army stevedores died. The British SS *Empire Perdita* later towed the *Marshall* to Bizerte. She ended her career as a breakwater off France on 8 June 1944.

The figures for the number of armed guards are contradictory. NSS; WACR; WCSR; AG.

BUSHROD WASHINGTON

D: 9-14-43
T: 1422
Pos: at anchor in Gulf of Salerno
Ow: WSA
Op: American South African Line
M: Jonathan M. Wainwright
A: 1-5"; 1-3"; 8-20 mm

YB: 1943
Tn: 7,191
Dr: 17 ft.
C: 2,000 tons war cargo,
      ammunition, aviation gasoline
P: steam
S: at anchor

On 3 September, the Liberty ship *Bushrod Washington* sailed in convoy from Oran, en route to Salerno, Sicily. The ship arrived at Salerno on 11 September and dropped anchor three miles off the beach. The vessel later shifted anchorage to three-fourth miles off the beach. Enemy aircraft kept the entire anchorage under attack for three days while the Liberty ship discharged her cargo into landing craft. On the afternoon of the 14th, a plane dove out of the sun and released two 500-pound bombs. One bomb struck about 150 feet from the ship, and the second struck on the boat deck, penetrated through the crew's mess room, and exploded in the ice machine room. The explosion moved the ship's engines to the starboard side, destroyed the port boiler, and ignited the gasoline cargo in the #4 hold. The ship had on board 8 officers, 34 men, 33 armed guards, and 200 stevedores (men from the port battalion). The fire pumps proved to be useless, and the fire quickly consumed the vessel as flames shot mast high. The master gave the order to abandon ship. The men launched two lifeboats, but most of them went overboard on nets and awaiting landing craft rescued them. The USS *Hopi* (ATF-71) towed the lifeboats ashore. One armed guard, one ship's officer, three men, and ten stevedores died as a result of the explosion and fire. At 1500 a fireboat came alongside the freighter but could not get the fire under control. The *Bushrod Washington* exploded and sank the following day when the fire reached the cargo of 500-pound bombs stored in the forward holds.

NSS; WACR; WCSR; AG.

WILLIAM BRADFORD

D: 9-15-43
T: 1815
Pos: in Salerno Bay
Ow: WSA
Op: American South African Line
M: James Fay Logan
A: 1-5"; 1-3"; 8-20 mm

YB: 1942
Tn: 7,176
Dr: 20 ft.
C: general
P: steam
S: at anchor

While at anchor in Salerno Bay the *William Bradford* suffered slight damage from enemy aircraft. German aircraft kept the anchorage under attack for days. During the many attacks the *Bradford* suffered twenty-nine near misses. The worst damage occurred on the 15th when enemy planes strafed the vessel and left her slightly damaged over her entire length. None of the eight officers, thirty-three men, or thirty-three armed guards on board suffered any injuries.

WACR; AG; ONF.

EDWARD P. COSTIGAN

D:	9-16-43	YB:	1943
T:	2000	Tn:	7,194
Pos:	off Bizerte	Dr:	21 ft.
Ow:	WSA	C:	2,000 tons general
Op:	American President Lines	P:	steam
M:	Robert Sweetser	S:	at anchor
A:	1-5"; 1-3"; 8-20 mm		

The *Edward P. Costigan* sailed from Algiers, Algeria, to Bizerte, Tunisia. German planes attacked the vessels in the harbor as she lay at anchor. One near miss struck fifteen feet off the starboard side at the #4 hatch. The concussion broke shaft bearings and damaged the auxiliary condenser and some electrical gear. The bomb also sprung some of the hull plates, and the ship's bilge tanks leaked at the rate of five inches of water an hour. The 8 officers, 34 men, 28 armed guards, and 333 passengers on board did not abandon the ship. No one on board reported an injury after the attack.

WACR; AG; ONF.

WILLIAM PEPPERELL

D:	9-18-43	YB:	1943
T:	1642	Tn:	7,176
Pos:	55.02 N / 29.27 W	Dr:	27 ft. 8 in.
Ow:	WSA	C:	9,000 tons wheat, lumber,
Op:	Calmar SS Co.		general
M:	John Fabricius	P:	steam
A:	1-5"; 1-3"; 8-20 mm	S:	7

On 6 September, the *William Pepperell* steamed from St. Johns, Newfoundland, en route to the United Kingdom in Convoy HX-256. During the trip, the ship deployed its torpedo streamers. On 18 September, in foggy weather and rough seas, the ship suffered an explosion off the port side near the #4 hatch.

Fortunately, the ship had its torpedo nets employed, and the torpedo detonated before it reached the hull. The master could not find any damage to the hull and only slight damage to the machinery and pumps. According to German records, the *U-260* (Perkhold) had fired a torpedo that struck the torpedo streamer. Two days later the *U-260* tried again with the same results. A second and similar explosion occurred on the starboard side, again at the #4 hatch. This time a column of water rose about twenty-five feet. Again the explosion caused only slight damage to the engine and disabled one of the dynamos. After putting the ship in dry dock an indentation three inches deep and about five feet long was discovered. None of the complement of eight officers, thirty-four men, and twenty-six armed guards reported any injuries.

WACR; WCSR; AG; Rohwer, p. 171.

FREDERICK DOUGLASS

D:	9-20-43	YB:	1943
T:	0536	Tn:	7,176
Pos:	57.03 N / 28.08 W	Dr:	20 ft.
Ow:	WSA	C:	sand ballast
Op:	Luckenbach SS Co.	P:	steam
M:	Adrian Richardson	S:	9.5
A:	1-5"; 9-20 mm		

On 14 September, the *Frederick Douglass* sailed from Avonmouth, England, and joined the fifty-four ship Convoy ON-202 at the Clyde River bound for New York. The ship was proceeding in convoy station #11 when a torpedo from the *U-238* (Hepp) struck the vessel on the port side bulkhead between the #4 and the #5 holds. The explosion made only a relatively small hole in the ship's side but blew off the hatch covers and strongbacks. The ship began to settle slowly. About seven minutes after the explosion and without orders from the master, some of the officers and crew began launching the #1 and #3 lifeboats. The remaining officers and crew left in boats #2 and #4 at 1036. By this time water had covered the engines. The British rescue ship *Rathlin* rescued all eight officers, thirty-two men, twenty-nine armed guards, and one woman stowaway and landed them at Halifax. The *Douglass* remained afloat, and a coup de grâce shot from the *U-645* (Ferro) sank her at about 1700.

NSS; WACR; WCSR; AG; Rohwer, p. 171.

THEODORE DWIGHT WELD

D: 9-20-43   YB: 1943
T: 0538   Tn: 7,146
Pos: 57.03 N / 28.12 W   Dr: 20 ft.
Ow: WSA   C: 1,200 tons sand ballast
Op: Sea Shipping Co. - Robin Line   P: steam
M: Michael Formanack   S: 7.5
A: 1-3"; 9-20 mm

On 15 September, the *Theodore Dwight Weld* sailed from Liverpool, England, to join Convoy ON-202 en route to New York. As the vessel proceeded in the convoy on station #21, the *U-238* (Hepp) fired a torpedo that struck the port side in the settling tanks opposite the #3 hold. About twenty seconds later the engine room exploded and broke the ship into two pieces just forward of the bridge. The stern sank almost immediately, trapping men below and washing others into the sea. The eight officers, thirty-four men, and twenty-eight armed guards on board had no time to launch any of the boats or trip the life rafts. Three doughnut rafts managed to float free of the wreckage. One of the armed guards remained on the bow and was later saved by the British rescue ship *Rathlin*. Several men managed to cling to the rafts until their rescue. The *Rathlin* saved two officers, twenty men, and fifteen of the armed guards. The majority of those men who lived left the ship wearing a life jacket. The survivors landed in Halifax, Nova Scotia, on 28 September.

NSS; WACR; WCSR; AG; Rohwer, p. 171, puts the attack at 57.03 N / 28.12 W.

WILLIAM W. GERHARD

D: 9-21-43   YB: 1943
T: 0930   Tn: 7,176
Pos: 40.07 N / 14.43 E   Dr: 21 ft.
Ow: WSA   C: 1,440 tons army cargo, guns,
Op: American South African Line   gasoline, ammunition
M: Olof J. Anderson   P: steam
A: 1-5"; 1-3"; 8-20 mm   S: 8

On 14 September, the *William W. Gerhard* sailed from Oran, Algeria, to Salerno, Italy, in convoy. The *Gerhard* proceeded in convoy station #13. The *U-593* (Kelbling) fired a torpedo that struck the Liberty ship on the port side in the middle of the #1 hold. The explosion raised the bow out of the water, buckled the deck forward of the bridge, and broke steam and water lines. The vessel began to shake, and the watch below immediately secured the engines. A large crack appeared on each side of the ship as the #1 and #3 holds rapidly flooded and the ship settled by the head. Because 191 soldiers were on board, the master gave the order to abandon ship. The eight officers, thirty-eight men, thirty armed guards, and the soldiers utilized four lifeboats, four rafts, and fifteen floats. While in the lifeboats, the escort commander ordered the crew to return to the ship and stand by for a tow if steam could not be raised. The salvage tug USS *Moreno* (ATF-87) took the freighter in tow at 1300. Nearly three hours later fire broke out in the #1 hold, and the USS *Narrangansett* (ATF-88) and the rescue tug HMS *Weazel* (W-120) helped to battle the flames. After two hours of fighting the fire, they secured the hoses; the crew then abandoned the ship and went on board the *Moreno*. During the night, while the ship blazed, explosions broke the vessel in two. The forward section sank at once, and the tugs sank the other section by gunfire at 1055 the next day. Of the 267 on board, only 2 armed guards died. One died instantly from the torpedo explosion. The second died on board the HMS hospital ship *Vita*. The survivors landed in Salerno on 22 September.

NSS; WACR; WCSR; AG; Rohwer, p. 250.

CORNELIA P. SPENCER

D:	9-21-43	YB:	1943
T:	0803	Tn:	7,176
Pos:	02.08 N / 50.10 E	Dr:	23 ft.
Ow:	WSA	C:	2,910 tons steel, 300 tons gum arabic
Op:	A. L. Burbank & Co. Inc.		
M:	Elmer H. Kirwan	P:	steam
A:	2-3"; 8-20 mm	S:	8

On 16 September, the *Cornelia P. Spencer* sailed from Aden, Arabia, for Durban, South Africa. The *U-188* (Lüdden) fired a torpedo that struck the Liberty ship on the port side at the #5 hold, as she was steaming a nonevasive course. The explosion blew off the hatch cover, flooded the hold, broke the shaft, and rendered the engines useless. The master sounded the general alarm, and moments later the *U-188* surfaced 100 yards off the port quarter. The armed guards manned their guns and fired about seventy-five rounds from the three-inch guns to force the submarine to submerge. A second torpedo struck the vessel on the port side at the after peak about thirty minutes later. The second torpedo ignited the after magazine, killed two men, and blew the after gun crew into the water. The blast also carried away the ship's rudder and propeller. The *Spencer* now began to settle rapidly, and the master ordered the ship abandoned. The surviving men of the complement of eight officers, thirty-three men, and twenty-seven armed guards left the ship in four lifeboats and two rafts. Some of the armed guards jumped into the water. The four boats picked up all the survivors. At 0915 a third torpedo struck amidships on the port side and the vessel sank, plunging stern first ten minutes later. The four boats set sail on a westerly course, and the next afternoon the destroyer HMS *Relentless* (H-85)

discovered two boats, one with sixteen survivors and another with eighteen men. The SS *Sandown Castle* rescued the survivors in a third boat that contained sixteen men. All these men landed at Aden. The fourth boat with sixteen men landed on the coast of Somalia fifteen days after the attack. The only casualties were the two merchant crewmen killed by the second torpedo.

NSS; WACR; WCSR; USMMA; AG; Rohwer, p. 271.

RICHARD OLNEY

D:	9-22-43	YB:	1943
T:	0755	Tn:	7,191
Pos:	37.25 N / 09.54 E	Dr:	23 ft.
Ow:	WSA	C:	4,000 tons ammunition, trucks, vehicles
Op:	Marine Transport Lines		
M:	Erich Richter	P:	steam
A:	1-5"; 1-3"; 8-20 mm	S:	9

On 19 September, the *Richard Olney* sailed from Oran, North Africa, to Salerno via Malta. The Liberty ship traveled in Convoy KMS-26 with two other Liberty ships, two British corvettes, and a trawler. Within sight of Bizerte, the ship ran over a mine that struck the starboard side and exploded outside the engine room. The explosion blew a hole about thirty-six feet in diameter in the starboard side and a smaller hole in the port side. The explosion destroyed the engines and fireroom and flooded the #5 hold. The armed guards fired to attract the other escorts, which returned in thirty minutes. The 8 officers, 35 men, 31 armed guards, and 143 Army passengers remained on the ship. The cutter HMS *Landguard* (Y-56) towed the *Olney* into Bizerte where the vessel was declared a CTL. Two men died on watch below.

NSS; WACR; WCSR; AG; Rohwer, p. 250.

STEEL VOYAGER

D:	9-23-43	YB:	1920
T:	0435	Tn:	6,198
Pos:	53.30 N / 40.40 W	Dr:	18 ft.
Ow:	Isthmian SS Co.	C:	2,500 tons sand ballast
Op:	WSA	P:	steam
M:	John Joseph Brady	S:	7
A:	2-3"; 8-20 mm		

On 13 September, the *Steel Voyager* departed Liverpool en route to New York in Convoy ONS-18. The freighter proceeded in convoy station #11. On 20 September, the convoy merged with Convoy ON-202, and the *Steel Voyager*

took convoy station as the fourth in line in the port outboard column. The *U-952* (Curio) maneuvered into a favorable position and fired two torpedoes at the freighter. One struck the vessel at the collision bulkhead on the starboard side. The explosion blew the windlass and forecastle deck upward and the hatch covers off the #1 hatch. The survivors reported only one explosion but lookouts in other nearby ships and German records reveal there were two. The second torpedo struck in the vicinity of the #2 hatch, given the description of the damage. Without orders, about seven of the merchant crew launched a lifeboat and lay by the ship's side. The master, meanwhile, had the engines stopped while his men inspected the damage. As the ship sank by the head, the propeller raised out of the water, and the master decided to abandon ship. The nine officers, the remnants of the thirty-man crew, and twenty-seven armed guards cleared the ship in the remaining three boats and stood by the vessel. When the Canadian corvette *Morden* (K-170) and the French corvette *Renoncule* came to their assistance, the master and crew reboarded the vessel. A committee from the *Renoncule* boarded the freighter and declared her unseaworthy. The escort commander advised the master that the escorts had to return to the convoy and that unless his ship could immediately get under way she should be abandoned. With the bow down and the *Steel Voyager*'s prop out of the water, the master realized it could not be done and had his men abandon the ship for a second time. Thirty-five men boarded the *Renoncule* and thirty-one boarded the *Morden*. They landed in St. Johns, Newfoundland, on 26 September. All hands survived the attack.

NSS; WACR; WCSR; AG; McNee, p. 134, states that the *Rathlin* picked up the survivors. Rohwer, p. 172, places the attack at 53.18 N / 40.24 W.

ELIAS HOWE

D:	9-24-43	YB:	1942
T:	0320	Tn:	7,176
Pos:	11.40 N / 44.35 E	Dr:	28 ft. 4 in.
Ow:	WSA	C:	9,259 tons bulk nitrate
Op:	Pacific Atlantic SS Co.	P:	steam
M:	Joseph Warren Dickover	S:	9
A:	1-5"; 5-20 mm		

On 17 July, the *Elias Howe* sailed from Antofagasta, Chile, to Durban, South Africa. After picking up a convoy at Durban, she traveled near Madagascar and then took an independent route to Alexandria, Egypt. The *I-10* (Tonozuka) intercepted the freighter seventy-five miles southeast of Aden and fired a torpedo that struck the port side in the engine room. The explosion completely destroyed the engines and hurled red hot fire brick through the engine room skylight. The ship began to flood immediately. Five minutes later, as the Liberty ship settled with a slight port list, the master gave the order to abandon ship. The

survivors of eight officers, thirty-four men, and eighteen armed guards left the ship in one lifeboat (two having been wrecked by the torpedo) and four rafts. The *I-10* then put another torpedo into the *Howe* near the #3 hatch. Flames shot to the sky, and the freighter disappeared beneath the water within three minutes. The *I-10* surfaced and cruised within 200 yards of the survivors before leaving the area. In the morning the forty-seven survivors on the four rafts secured them together. The motor lifeboat with twelve men including the master proceeded toward Aden to get help. A PBY sighted the lifeboat and picked up these men, and they landed at Aden on 25 September. The rafts, however, later became separated. A Royal Air Force plane rescued two rafts with twenty men and landed them the same day. The British trawler HMS *Aiglon* (FY-1841) rescued the remaining twenty-six men and landed them at Aden on the 26th. One officer and one man died on watch below.

The nitrite cargo might have caused the second explosion. NSS; WACR; WCSR; USMMA; AG; Rohwer, p. 271, places the attack at 11.37 N / 45.46 E.

METAPAN

D:	10-1-43	YB:	1909
T:	1320	Tn:	4,736
Pos:	37.20 N / 10.35 E	Dr:	21 ft.
Ow:	United Fruit Co.	C:	1,100 tons frozen meat and
Op:	United Fruit Co.		Army rations
M:	Christian Dahlgaard	P:	steam
A:	1-4"; 8-20 mm	S:	8

On 30 September, the *Metapan* sailed from Palermo, Sicily, to Bizerte, Tunisia. The ship joined Convoy UGS-15, which consisted of eleven merchant ships and three escorts. While steaming in station #23, the *Metapan* ran over an acoustic mine. The ship suffered a small shock followed immediately by a tremendous explosion that raised the stern and pushed the ship forward. The blast at once flooded the after part of the ship, damaged the steering gear, and blew the hatch cover off the #4 hold. The master had the engines secured, and ten minutes later the seven officers, forty-three men, twenty-three armed guards, and one passenger abandoned ship in four lifeboats. The barge USS *Syncline* (YO-63) rescued all hands and landed them at Bizerte. The ship sank by the stern at 1345.

NSS; WACR; WCSR; AG; TF.

HIRAM S. MAXIM

D:	10-4-43	YB:	1943
T:	1815	Tn:	7,179
Pos:	36.42 N / 01.17 E	Dr:	26 ft.
Ow:	WSA	C:	7,200 tons war cargo
Op:	Pacific Far East Line	P:	steam
M:	Alfred Sandvig	S:	6
A:	1-5"; 1-3"; 8-20 mm		

On 11 September, the *Hiram S. Maxim* departed Hampton Roads, Virginia, bound for the Persian Gulf via the Suez Canal. The ship proceeded in station #36 at the rear of Convoy UGS-18. About nine German aircraft attacked the formation twelve miles northwest of Cape Tenes, Algeria. During the attack a bomb exploded fifteen feet off the port side of the *Maxim* and abreast of the machinery spaces. The concussion damaged the main injector and the overboard discharge pumps, causing the engine room to flood. The watch below secured the engines as the crew surveyed the damage. The master feared that the bulkheads would not hold, and thirty minutes after the explosion he orally ordered the ship abandoned. The eight officers, thirty-two men, and twenty-eight armed guards left the ship in five lifeboats. The master, six of the crew, and six armed guards stood by the ship during the night. The SS *Leslie M. Shaw* and the SS *Harry Lane* picked up the rest of the crew and landed them at Cape Tenes. The master and his skeleton crew remained with the ship, and later a British salvage tug towed the vessel into Algiers. All hands survived. After repairs the *Hiram S. Maxim* sailed from Algiers on 30 January 1944.

NSS; WACR; WCSR; AG.

COTTON MATHER

D:	10-5-43	YB:	1942
T:	1830	Tn:	7,160
Pos:	36.00 N / 01.00 E	Dr:	25 ft.
Ow:	WSA	C:	7,000 tons ammunition and
Op:	American Export Lines		vehicles
M:	Willie F. Kuhne	P:	steam
A:	1-5"; 8-20 mm	S:	6

On 15 September, the *Cotton Mather* sailed in Convoy UGS-18 from Lynhaven Roads, Virginia, to Khorramshahr, Persian Gulf. While sailing fifteen miles north of Cape Tenes, the convoy was attacked by enemy aircraft. One aircraft dropped a bomb that landed within one hundred feet of the vessel off the port beam. The concussion damaged the reversing engines and broke a steam pipe that caused the engines to lose their vacuum. The eight officers, forty-five men,

and twenty-seven armed guards on board remained on the ship, and she arrived in Algiers later that day under her own power. The crew suffered no casualties.

WACR; WCSR; TF; ONF.

YORKMAR

D:	10-9-43	YB:	1919
T:	0535	Tn:	5,612
Pos:	56.48 N / 20.30 W	Dr:	28 ft. 1 in.
Ow:	Calmar SS Corp.	C:	8,740 tons, food, grain, truck
Op:	WSA		parts, ammunition
M:	William Augustus DePuey	P:	steam
A:	1-4"; 1-3"; 8-20 mm	S:	8.5

On 24 September, the *Yorkmar* sailed in Convoy SC-143 from Boston, Massachusetts, to Barry Roads, Scotland. In overcast weather, the *U-645* (Ferro) fired a torpedo that struck the ship on the starboard side between the #4 and #5 holds, as she steamed in convoy station #111. The explosion blew off both hatch covers, knocked down the mainmast, and damaged some machinery. The helmsman turned the ship's wheel hard to starboard, and the watch below secured the engines. With the general alarm sounding, the ship's complement of eight officers, thirty-one men, and twenty-eight armed guards abandoned the ship immediately in great confusion as she quickly sank by the stern. Most of the crew suffered from inexperience and went to the #2 lifeboat instead of evenly distributing themselves among the three good boats. Only two men put the #3 boat in the water, and the last boat was never launched. The fully loaded #2 boat swamped in the rough seas after hitting the water. Other men jumped from the ship and swam to two released rafts. The *Yorkmar* sank by the stern in five minutes. The men stayed in the water about one hour before being rescued by the Canadian corvette *Kamloops* (K-175) and the frigate HMS *Duckworth* (K-351). Two armed guards, one officer, and ten men drowned. The survivors landed in Londonderry and Belfast on the 9th and 11th.

NSS; WACR; WCSR; AG; Rohwer, p. 173, places the attack at 56.38 N / 20.30 W.

GEORGE H. HIMES

D:	10-11-43	YB:	1943
T:	0145	Tn:	7,176
Pos:	Koli Point, Guadalcanal	Dr:	25 ft.
Ow:	WSA	C:	7,000 tons lumber, shells, bombs
Op:	Shephard SS Co.	P:	steam
M:	Charles Arthur Treanor	S:	at anchor
A:	2-3"; 8-20 mm		

The *George H. Himes* sailed from Espíritu Santo and arrived at Koli Point, Guadalcanal. As she unloaded her cargo, a torpedo plane approached from the west, launched a torpedo, and veered astern. The torpedo struck the Liberty ship between the #4 and #5 holds. The lumber stowed there absorbed a great deal of the force of the blast. The explosion ripped a sixteen-foot by twenty-foot hole in the side of the ship and flooded the engine room and the shaft alley along with the two holds. The eight officers, thirty-three men, twenty-seven armed guards, and twenty construction battalion stevedores on board remained on the ship. The USS *Menominee* (ATF-73) beached the *Himes* to save the ship and her cargo. All hands survived the attack.

NSS; WACR; WCSR; AG.

JOHN H. COUCH

D:	10-11-43	YB:	1943
T:	0150	Tn:	7,176
Pos:	Koli Point, Guadalcanal	Dr:	26 ft. 1 in.
Ow:	WSA	C:	5,056 tons grease, gas, kerosene,
Op:	Weyerhaeuser SS Co.		diesel oil
M:	David Newton Welch	P:	steam
A:	2-3"; 8-20 mm	S:	at anchor

On 24 August, the *John H. Couch* sailed from San Francisco to Guadalcanal via Nouméa. A torpedo plane circled the ship while she was discharging cargo into lighters off Koli Point. The plane then dropped a torpedo 2,000 feet from the ship off the port beam. The torpedo struck the #2 hold, and the explosion blew several men over the side and threw flames, hatch covers, and drums of fuel above the masts. The cargo of gas and oil stored below immediately caught fire. Firefighting parties could not control the flames, and the fire spread to the #1 and #3 holds. Two destroyer escorts also helped fight the flames, using foam equipment but to no avail. With the fire still spreading and threatening the cargo of explosives, the master gave the order to abandon ship. Survivors among the 8 officers, 35 men, 26 armed guards, 28 Army passengers, and 100 construction battalion stevedores on board launched two lifeboats, but nearby landing craft rescued most of the men. A Navy destroyer attempted to sink the stern by firing eighteen shells into the *Couch*, but they had no effect. The ship burned for four days while water was pumped on board to extinguish the fire. On 13 October, the USS *Pawnee* (ATF-74) towed the vessel two miles east of Koli Point where she rolled on her side. The cargo in the after two holds remained undamaged. One member of the gun crew, one merchant seaman, and one stevedore died in the attack.

NSS; WACR; WCSR; USMMA.

JAMES RUSSELL LOWELL

D:	10-15-43	YB:	1942
T:	1140	Tn:	7,176
Pos:	37.18.15 N / 07.10.30 E	Dr:	18 ft. 6 in.
Ow:	WSA	C:	1,200 tons sand and gravel
Op:	McCormick SS Co.		ballast
M:	Richard Newton Forman Jr.	P:	steam
A:	1-4"; 1-3"; 8-20 mm	S:	8

The *James Russell Lowell* sailed on 14 October in Convoy GUS-18 from Bizerte, Tunisia, to the Virginia Capes. The ship maintained station #85 in the convoy. The *U-371* (Mehl) fired a torpedo that struck the Liberty ship on the rudder, carrying it and the rudder post away. A second torpedo struck an instant later on the port side at the #3 hold, and a third struck at the #1 hold. The second torpedo blew off the #3 hatch cover, created cracks in the hull on both sides of the #3 hold, and flooded the #3 hold and the engine room. The third torpedo blew the hatch cover off the #1 hold and flooded that space. The men below secured the engines in about two minutes. Because the vessel had a slight port list, the master ordered the complement of eight officers, thirty-eight men, and twenty-eight armed guards to abandon ship. The men used four lifeboats to clear the vessel. The boats lay by the *Lowell,* and an hour later the British whaler *Southern Sea* (FY-326) appeared. The master went on board for a conference, and the escort's commander ordered the merchant crew back on board about thirty minutes later. The whaler took the Liberty ship in tow. During the night the wind freshened to force five, and the ship's list increased. The crew, with the exception of the master and two mates, left the ship again at approximately 2100. A British naval tug later took over the tow and beached the *Lowell* at Colla, Algeria, on 16 October. Two weeks later the vessel broke in two and sank. All hands survived the attack. The WSA considered the vessel a CTL.

The NSS documents the convoy as HR-303. NSS; WACR; WCSR; USMMA; AG; TF; Rohwer, p. 251, places the attack at 37.22 N / 07.08 E; Sawyer, Mitchell, p. 120.

DELISLE

D:	10-19-43	YB:	1919
T:	1835	Tn:	3,478
Pos:	47.19 N / 52.27 W	Dr:	19 ft.
Ow:	A. H. Bull & Co.	C:	3,000 tons zinc concentrate,
Op:	WSA		machinery, vehicles, asphalt
M:	William Watts Clendaniel	P:	steam
A:	1-3"; 1-6 lber.; 2-30 cal.	S:	stopped

On 19 October, the *Delisle* sailed from St. Johns, Newfoundland, to New York with Convoy WB-65, which consisted of seven merchant ships and two

Canadian corvettes. While steaming in convoy station #22, the freighter received permission to pick up survivors of the *Penolver*, which had run into a mine set out by the *U-220* (Barber). Fifteen miles out of St. Johns, with the *Delisle* hove to, and the ship's crew amidships and aft throwing lines to survivors, another mine laid by the same U-boat struck the *Delisle* forward of the bridge. The explosion lifted the bow in the air, the foremast collapsed, and the ship bounced several times before righting herself on an even keel. The blast virtually blew the bow off and collapsed the wheelhouse and the after gun platform. The seven officers, twenty-five men, seven armed guards, and three crew members from the *Penolver* abandoned ship without orders into two lifeboats and two rafts. All the men on the American ship survived. The trawler HMS *Miscou* (T-277) picked them up within thirty minutes and landed them at St. Johns. The ship sank forty minutes after striking the mine, plunging bow first.

NSS; WACR; WCSR; Rohwer, p. 173.

TIVIVES

D:	10-21-43	YB:	1911
T:	1845	Tn:	4,596
Pos:	36.50 N / 01.39 E	Dr:	24 ft. 6 in.
Ow:	United Fruit Co.	C:	1,900 tons meat, butter
Op:	WSA	P:	steam
M:	Einor C. Peterson	S:	7.8
A:	1-3"; 8-20 mm		

On 21 October, the *Tivives* sailed from Norfolk, Virginia, and later joined the fifty-seven ship Convoy MKS-28 bound for Oran from Algiers. At dusk, fifteen miles off Cape Tenes, approximately twenty-three planes attacked the convoy. As the escorts laid down a smoke screen, the formation of planes, one behind the other, began attacking the ships. The leading planes strafed the *Tivives* with machine gun fire, and one plane coming from the port quarter released a torpedo that struck the port side at the #4 hatch. The explosion shook the ship violently, buckled the deck, broke the shaft, damaged the steering gear, and flooded the engine room through the shaft alley. The ship immediately began sinking by the stern. The torpedo so severely damaged the ship that water reached the deck in five minutes. The ship sank stern first about twenty minutes later. After the explosion the master immediately gave orders to abandon ship. The eight officers, forty men, twenty-five armed guards, six of the convoy commodore's staff, and one passenger had time to launch only two of the four lifeboats. Most of the men jumped into the water and swam to three rafts. The ex-French corvette HMS *La Malouine* (K-46) picked up the survivors and transferred them

to the sloop HMS *Bryony* (K-192), which took them to Oran the following day. One armed guard and one of the merchant crewmen drowned.

NSS; WACR; WCSR; USMMA; AG.

JAMES IREDELL

D:	10-23-43	YB:	1942
T:	1845	Tn:	7,177
Pos:	off Naples, Italy	Dr:	26 ft.
Ow:	WSA	C:	5,500 tons shells, armored
Op:	Agwilines Inc.		vehicles, gas, land mines, etc.
M:	Alfred Leon Jones	P:	steam
A:	1-5"; 1-3"; 8-20 mm	S:	at anchor

On 4 September, the *James Iredell* sailed from New York to Palermo, Sicily, in Convoy UGS-17. On 22 October, she sailed from Palermo bound for Naples. Flares lit the sky as German aircraft bombed and strafed the vessels anchored in the harbor, including the *Iredell*, for about thirty-five minutes. During this time a bomb penetrated the #2 hold loaded with gasoline and electric wire. Fire broke out immediately in this hold. Within five minutes two more bombs fell down the hatchway as the crew fought the fire. The firefighting parties battled the blaze for an hour, while drums of gasoline exploded intermittently. At 1945 the master ordered his men to abandon ship. The eight officers, thirty-six men, twenty-eight armed guards, and thirty-eight passengers left the ship in three lifeboats. British salvage firefighters boarded the ship in the master's absence. At midnight the master, two officers, and the armed guard officer returned. The fire burned for sixty-four hours, and a tug later towed the *Iredell* alongside a dock in Naples where the remaining cargo was discharged. All hands survived the attack. She sailed in damaged condition for Bizerte on 23 December and returned to the United States. The *Iredell* ended her career as part of the "gooseberry" at Normandy on 7 June 1944.

NSS; WACR; WCSR; AG.

SANTA ELENA

D:	11-6-43	YB:	1933
T:	1856	Tn:	9,135
Pos:	37.13 N / 06.21 E	Dr:	15 ft.
Ow:	Grace Line	C:	200 tons Army supplies and
Op:	Grace Line		troops
M:	William C. Renaut	P:	steam
A:	1-4"; 1-3", 8-20 mm	S:	12

On 28 October, the *Santa Elena* departed Liverpool, England, in Convoy KMF-25A en route to Naples, Italy. The convoy, with the *Santa Elena* steaming in station #24, began shifting into four columns when enemy aircraft attacked the formation about twenty-seven miles from Philippeville, Algeria. The first warning of the attack came when the escort vessels began firing their guns and laying a smoke screen. In the confusion, a torpedo plane flew through the screen and directly over the ship. Moments later a torpedo struck the ship on the port side between the engine room and the #4 hold. The explosion created a hole twenty feet in diameter, disabling the engines and steering gear. The hole caused the ship to flood rapidly, and she took a 20° list as she lay dead in the water. The ship had on board 8 officers, 125 men, 44 armed guards, and 1,870 Canadian troops and nurses. For four hours beginning at 1900, the troops safely left the ship in the nine lifeboats. The SS *Monterey* took them all on board. The crew also left the ship, but most returned at 2300. At 0220 the following morning, with the *Santa Elena* still powerless, the damaged Dutch transport SS *Marnix Van St. Aldegonde* under tow at the time came across the bow of the *Santa Elena* and struck forward of the bridge on the starboard side. This caused more damage to the *Santa Elena* and increased the flooding. At 0730 a small British tug took the *Santa Elena* in tow. During the journey the master realized his ship could not reach port and signaled the tug to take his vessel into seven fathoms of water. The tug's captain disregarded this request. At 1811 the bow lifted and the ship heeled to port, sinking quickly in thirty fathoms. Many of the merchant crew and armed guards did not have time to get off the ship and jumped into the water. Four merchant seamen drowned while abandoning ship.

NSS; WACR; WCSR; AG.

CAPE SAN JUAN

D:	11-11-43	YB:	1943
T:	0530	Tn:	6,711
Pos:	28.08 S / 178.06 W	Dr:	23 ft.
Ow:	WSA	C:	2,000 tons general cargo and
Op:	American Hawaiian SS Co.		troops
M:	Walter Mervyn Strong	P:	steam
A:	1-4"; 4-3"; 8-20 mm	S:	15

On 28 October, the *Cape San Juan* sailed from San Francisco en route to Townsville, Australia. Lookouts spotted a torpedo fired by the *I-21* (Inada) that missed the stern by twenty yards. Seconds later another torpedo struck the zigzagging ship on the starboard side at the after end of the #2 hold. The explosion raised the ship's bow, and the ship took an immediate starboard list and settled by the head. The watch below secured the engines, and the ship lost way and lay dead in the water. Shortly after the torpedo struck, the master

sounded the general alarm and blew the steam whistle signaling the 12 officers, 48 men, 42 armed guards, and 1,348 Army troops on board to abandon ship. The ship gradually settled as the men left the vessel in fairly good order. The crew launched five lifeboats, four rafts, and thirty-six doughnut rafts. The overfilled motor lifeboat swamped when it touched the water. Many of the troops just jumped into the water and swam to the rafts. All the boats picked up survivors until they could hold no more. Some of the merchant crew and the officers stayed with the ship until about 1900. Apparently, shortly after 0800 the *I-21* fired another torpedo that struck the ship, but it failed to explode. The *Edwin T. Meredith* arrived at 1100 to pick up men out of the water and those in the boats. Allied aircraft, the USS *McCalla* (DD-488), the USS *Dempsey* (DE-26), and the USS *YMS-241* rescued other survivors. All of the merchant crew survived, but 16 Army troops died in the explosion and another 114 drowned. The SS *Edwin T. Meredith* fired twelve shells into the *Cape San Juan* vessel to hasten her sinking, but she remained afloat for forty-eight hours. The survivors landed at Suva, Fiji, and Nouméa, New Caledonia.

The ship's personnel figures are contradictory. NSS; WACR; WCSR; USMMA; AG; Rohwer, p. 284.

ELIZABETH KELLOGG

D:	11-22-43	YB:	1920
T:	0330	Tn:	5,189
Pos:	11.10 N / 80.43 W	Dr:	26 ft. 6 in.
Ow:	Spencer Kellogg & Sons	C:	55,000 bbls. bunker "C" oil
Op:	WSA	P:	steam
M:	Norman Thomson Henderson	S:	9
A:	1-4"; 2-50 cal.; 2-30 cal.		

The *Elizabeth Kellogg* sailed independently from Curaçao, NWI, to Puerto Barrios, Guatemala, via Cristobal, Canal Zone. The *U-516* (Tillessen) fired a torpedo that struck the tanker on the port side at the #4 tank. The explosion ruptured the #2, #3, and #4 port tanks and threw burning oil all over the ship. Fire immediately consumed the ship from the bridge aft to the poop deck and killed all the deck officers. Flames shot through the ventilators into the engine room and prevented the watch below from throttling down the engines. The survivors from the complement of seven officers, twenty-nine men, and twelve armed guards cleared the ship in the #3 and #4 lifeboats and two rafts; others jumped into the water. The blazing tanker with engines at full speed astern and her rudder hard aport made large circles around the survivors. Nearly six hours after the attack the fire reached the after magazine. A plane spotted the tanker dead in the water, with a broken back and the fire extinguished. The tug USS *Favorite* (IX-45) and several escort vessels unsuccessfully attempted to find the ship to salvage her. Presumably the vessel sank three days after the attack. On the 24th, the tanker USAT *Y-10* and the *SC-1017* rescued the survivors and landed them all in Cristobal the same day. Five officers, three men, and two armed guards died in the attack.

The ship's complement figures are contradictory within the sources. NSS; WACR; WCSR; AG; Rohwer, p. 174; *War Action Casualties*, p. 162.

MELVILLE E. STONE

D:	11-24-43	YB:	1943
T:	0012	Tn:	7,176
Pos:	10.29 N / 80.20 W	Dr:	31 ft. 6 in.
Ow:	WSA	C:	10,538 tons copper, coffee,
Op:	Norton-Lilly & Co.		balsa, vanadium
M:	Lawrence J. Gallagher	P:	steam
A:	1-4"; 1-3"; 8-20 mm	S:	12

On 23 November, the *Melville E. Stone* sailed independently from Cristobal, Canal Zone, to New York. Less than seven hours into the trip, one of the forward lookouts spotted two torpedoes fired from the surface by the *U-516* (Tillessen) moments before they struck the vessel. The first hit the freighter in the settling tank, and the second struck ten seconds later near the #4 hold. The explosions opened large holes in the side of the vessel and extensively damaged the main and auxiliary machinery. The chief engineer stopped the engine with the emergency stop valve, as the ship rapidly settled on an even keel. In choppy seas, the ten officers, thirty-two men, twenty-three armed guards, and twenty-three passengers immediately began abandoning ship. The ship sank in eight minutes. Two of the boats capsized from the suction created by the rapidly sinking vessel and dragged several men to their deaths, including the master. Three boats got away from the ship and picked up men off rafts and those clinging to debris in the water. Planes located the survivors and dropped flares so that the rescue crafts *SC-1023* and *SC-662* could find and pick them up. Five officers, seven of the merchant crew, two armed guards, and one passenger died in the attack.

The figures given for the ship's personnel are contradictory within the sources. NSS; WACR; WCSR; USMMA; AG; Rohwer, p. 174, places the attack at 10.36 N / 80.19 W.

SAMUEL J. TILDEN

D:	12-2-43	YB:	1942
T:	1910	Tn:	7,176
Pos:	Bari, Italy	Dr:	22 ft.
Ow:	WSA	C:	2,300 tons gasoline,
Op:	A. H. Bull SS Co.		ammunition, trucks, troops
M:	Joseph Lumpkin Blair Jr.	P:	steam
A:	1-5"; 1-3"; 8-20 mm	S:	at anchor

The *Samuel J. Tilden* sailed on 1 December from Taranto, Italy, to Bari, Italy, and anchored about two miles off the city. German aircraft attacked the numerous vessels anchored at Bari beginning at 1910. A spotlight from the entrance to the mole illuminated the ship to allow a pilot to come on board. This light remained on for several minutes after the attack began, making the ship an easy target. Ten minutes after the first appearance of enemy aircraft, a bomb fell through the skylight and exploded in the engine room, completely demolishing the engine and starting a blaze. A second bomb struck the deck, forward of the bridge, and started a fire in the #3 hold. The 209 troops on board began abandoning ship just after the attack began. Many jumped into the water and were taken on board PT boats. Others used three of the ship's four lifeboats and four rafts. The armed guards and the merchant crew stayed at their posts for about an hour until the fire burned completely out of control. The last men left the ship at 2300. The ship's complement consisted of eight officers, thirty-three men, and twenty-eight armed guards. Three officers, seven of the merchant crew, and seventeen passengers perished. The ship burned for nearly seven hours, and at 0110 on 3 December, she was sunk by two torpedoes from British vessels.

NSS; WACR; WCSR; USMMA; AG; Infield, pp. 76-77.

GRACE ABBOTT

D:	12-2-43	YB:	1942
T:	1924	Tn:	7,191
Pos:	Bari, Italy	Dr:	18 ft.
Ow:	WSA	C:	250 tons general
Op:	Calmar SS Co.	P:	steam
M:	Carl H. Deal	S:	at anchor
A:	1-5"; 1-3"; 8-20 mm		

The *Grace Abbott* sailed from Baltimore, Maryland, to Bari, Italy, via Augusta, Sicily. On 19 November she sailed from Augusta in Convoy AN-9A for Bari. As she lay at anchor in Bari, German aircraft attacked. The bombs devastated many ships in the anchorage, but only a single bomb struck the *Abbott* forward of the bridge in the #1 hatch. Fortunately the bomb did not explode. Although the Liberty ship suffered slight shrapnel damage from numerous close explosions, only one officer was injured in the complement of eight officers, thirty-three men, and twenty-eight armed guards.

WACR; AG; TF; ONF.

JOHN M. SCHOFIELD

D:	12-2-43	YB:	1942
T:	1925	Tn:	7,181
Pos:	Bari, Italy	Dr:	unknown
Ow:	WSA	C:	general
Op:	Sudden & Christenson Inc.	P:	steam
M:	Karl Edwin Katlas	S:	docked
A:	1-4"; 1-3"; 8-20 mm		

The *John M. Schofield* sailed from New York to perform cargo shuttle service in the Mediterranean. While docked at Bari, Italy, the freighter suffered minor damage from a near miss that exploded on the starboard side between the ship and the quay at the #1 hold. A concussion parted the lines, and the ship smashed into the quay. A large fragment passed through the side into the bulkhead between the #1 and #2 holds. The fragment created a hole in the side of the ship nearly four feet in diameter. The *Schofield* later sailed to another port for repairs and went back into service. None of the eight officers, thirty-six men, twenty-eight armed guards, and an undetermined number of British Army stevedores on board reported any injuries during the attack.

WACR; WCSR; AG.

LYMAN ABBOTT

D:	12-2-43	YB:	1943
T:	1930	Tn:	7,176
Pos:	Bari, Italy	Dr:	26 ft.
Ow:	WSA	C:	6,018 tons war supplies
Op:	International Freighting Co.	P:	steam
M:	Carl Peter Richard Dahlstrom	S:	at anchor
A:	2-3"; 8-20 mm		

On 4 November, the *Lyman Abbott* sailed from Norfolk, Virginia, via Baltimore, Maryland, to Bari, Italy. As the ship lay at anchor about a mile offshore, German planes attacked. The bombs never directly struck the *Lyman Abbott*, but the many near misses damaged the ship. One particular near miss bent the rudder post 18° to starboard. At 1914 the nearby *John L. Motley* exploded and

blew debris all over the *Abbott*, started a fire in the #1 hold, set the deck on fire in several places, and damaged all the lifeboats. The *John Harvey*, also nearby, released her cargo of mustard gas in the carnage and affected many of the eight officers, thirty-four crewmen, twenty-nine armed guards, and one passenger on board the *Abbott*. Nearly the whole crew suffered from mustard gas burns and had to be taken to a local hospital. One merchant crewman, one officer, one armed guard, and the passenger died, three from shrapnel wounds and the fourth from inhaling mustard gas.

WACR; WCSR; AG.

JOSEPH WHEELER

D:	12-2-43	YB:	1942
T:	1930	Tn:	7,176
Pos:	Bari, Italy	Dr:	30 ft. 2 in.
Ow:	WSA	C:	8,000 tons general and
Op:	South Atlantic SS Co.		ammunition
M:	Patrick Morrissey	P:	steam
A:	1-5"; 1-3"; 8-20 mm	S:	at anchor

The Liberty ship *Joseph Wheeler* sailed from New York to Bari, Italy. The freighter lay berthed at a jetty when German aircraft attacked the anchorage. During this attack a bomb pierced the deck near the #3 hatch and ignited the cargo of ammunition. With a tremendous roar the ship exploded, leaving only a burned out hulk. The freighter's complement consisted of eight officers, thirty-three men, twenty-eight armed guards, and one passenger. The only survivors were the fifteen men of the gun crew, six officers, and twenty men who happened to be ashore when the air raid occurred.

WACR; WCSR; AG.

JOHN HARVEY

D:	12-2-43	YB:	1943
T:	1930	Tn:	7,177
Pos:	Bari, Italy	Dr:	31 ft.
Ow:	WSA	C:	8,000 tons ammunition
Op:	Agwilines	P:	steam
M:	Elwin Foster Knowles	S:	at anchor
A:	1-5"; 1-3"; 8-20 mm		

On 20 November, the *John Harvey* departed Oran, North Africa, bound for Bari, Italy. Arriving on the 28th, she tied up stern first to the jetty in berth #30. The *Joseph Wheeler* lay close to the port side, and the *John L. Motley* lay on her

starboard side. During the attack on Bari the *Harvey* was showered by burning debris from vessels that exploded nearby. The freighter caught fire, broke her mooring lines, and began to drift in the harbor, where she exploded. Tragically, part of the cargo contained mustard gas. Once released it injured and killed hundreds of people in Bari. The master had permitted half the men to go ashore each evening. When the air raid occurred, however, only seven of the eight officers, forty-two men, twenty-eight armed guards, and nine passengers had gone ashore. The six merchant crew and a U.S. Merchant Marine cadet ashore were the only survivors.

WACR; WCSR; USMMA; AG; Infield, pp. 69-70.

JOHN L. MOTLEY

D:	12-2-43	YB:	1943
T:	1940	Tn:	7,176
Pos:	off Bari, Italy	Dr:	27 ft.
Ow:	WSA	C:	8,000 ammunition and gasoline
Op:	American Export Lines	P:	steam
M:	Constantine Tsimenis	S:	at anchor
A:	1-5"; 1-3"; 8-20 mm		

On 21 October, the *John L. Motley* sailed from Norfolk, Virginia, to Bari, Italy. Docked sternmost to the jetty with anchors out, the *Motley* lay there with the *John Bascom* on the starboard side and the *Joseph Wheeler* to her port side. German aircraft attacked the ships in the harbor beginning about 1930. At 1940 the *Motley* took hits on the #5 hatch, down the stack, and in the deep tanks at the #1 hold. The cargo in the #5 hold, including cyanide, caught fire, and five minutes later the ship exploded, raining burning debris over the entire anchorage. The ship's complement included eight officers, thirty-eight men, and twenty-nine armed guards. The only survivors were the four armed guards and seven merchant crewmen ashore at the time.

NSS of *John Bascom*; WACR; WCSR; AG; Infield, pp. 55, 57.

JOHN BASCOM

D:	12-2-43	YB:	1943
T:	2000	Tn:	7,176
Pos:	Bari, Italy	Dr:	26 ft. 6 in.
Ow:	WSA	C:	8,300 tons Army cargo, gasoline, acid
Op:	Moore McCormick SS Co.		
M:	Otto Heitman	P:	steam
A:	2-3"; 8-20 mm	S:	at anchor

On 25 November, the Liberty ship *John Bascom* sailed from Augusta, Sicily, and arrived at Bari, Italy, on 1 December. Moored to the seawall stern first, the *Bascom* and the other ships in the harbor came under attack from German aircraft at about 1930. Bombs struck the *Bascom* near the #1, #2, and #3 holds and in the machinery space. The explosions caused fires in holds #1, #3, and #5. The crew remained with the ship for forty-five minutes battling the blaze and firing on the attacking aircraft. At 2045 the master gave the order to abandon ship owing to the fires and explosions on the nearby ammunition ship *John L. Motley*. These explosions damaged three lifeboats, and the eight officers, thirty-six men, twenty-eight armed guards, and one passenger had only one usable lifeboat to leave the ship. The wounded filled this lifeboat, and the other survivors had to cling to the sides to escape. Two officers, two men, and ten armed guards died as a result of the bombs and injuries they received. After abandonment, the fire burned the mooring lines, and the ship began to drift directly toward the *John L. Motley*. When fifty feet away, the *Motley* exploded and caved in the port side of the *Bascom*, causing her to sink immediately.

The ship's casualty and complement numbers are contradictory within the sources. NSS; WACR; WCSR; USMMA; AG; Infield, p. 56.

TOUCHET

D:	12-3-43	YB:	1943
T:	0230	Tn:	10,172
Pos:	25.15 N / 86.15 W	Dr:	30 ft. 10 in.
Ow:	WSA	C:	120,000 bbls. heating oil
Op:	American Petroleum Corp.	P:	steam
M:	Jesse Field Bird	S:	16.5
A:	1-5"; 1-3"; 8-20 mm		

On 1 December, the *Touchet* sailed on independent routing from Galveston, Texas, to New York. The ship's torpedo indicator warned the bridge of a torpedo fired by the *U-193* (Pauckstadt) approaching the port side. The general alarm sounded and the helmsman swung the ship to port. The torpedo struck the port bow ten feet aft of the stem and blew a hole twenty feet long in the vessel, flooding the forward hold. The watch below secured the engines for a short period while the ship turned in the opposite direction. The master then ordered full speed ahead, but the ship, being down by the head, began driving her bow under. He thus changed the order to full speed astern. Just as the ship reversed direction, the anti-torpedo device sounded once more, indicating a torpedo again coming from the port side. The crew felt a thud amidships but no explosion, denoting a dud. With the main deck forward nearly under water, the master ordered the ship abandoned. Most of the complement of ten officers, forty men, and nineteen of the thirty armed guards began leaving the ship in six lifeboats.

The armed guard officer and ten of his men remained on board to man the after five-inch gun. At 0330 a third torpedo struck the ship at the engine room and caused a tremendous explosion. Ten of the armed guards jumped over the side and swam to a raft. The suction created by the ship's sinking began pulling at the raft, so the men tried to swim away and nine drowned. The armed guard officer left last and presumably drowned. The ship sank stern first at about 1800. All the survivors redistributed themselves evenly in the six boats. After fifty-four hours at sea, the Norwegian SS *Lillemor* rescued forty-three survivors in four boats and landed them at Pensacola, Florida. Two hours later the USS *Falgout* (DE-324) picked up eleven more survivors. On 6 December, the USS *Raven* (AM-55) rescued the remaining sixteen survivors in the last boat and landed them in Galveston, Texas. The ten armed guards who drowned constituted the only casualties.

NSS; WACR; WCSR; USMMA; AG; Rohwer, p. 175, places the attack at 25.50 N /86.30 W.

WILLIAM WHIPPLE

D:	12-5-43	YB:	1942
T:	1230	Tn:	7,177
Pos:	Kiddercor Dock, Calcutta	Dr:	23 ft.
Ow:	WSA	C:	3,500 tons general
Op:	Isthmian Line	P:	steam
M:	R. A. Cousins	S:	docked
A:	1-5"; 1-3"; 8-20 mm		

The *William Whipple* sailed from Charleston, South Carolina, to Calcutta, India, via Egypt. While in Calcutta the vessel tied up to Kiddercor Dock. Enemy aircraft appeared shortly after noon and began attacking the ships in the harbor. A stick of bombs straddled the *Whipple* and sprayed the hull with shrapnel. The bomb put at least thirty holes in the ship's hull, stretching from the #2 hold to the #4 hold. The Liberty ship underwent repairs in Calcutta and did not sail until 16 December. Only one of the armed guards in the ship's complement of seven officers, thirty-five men, and twenty-eight armed guards reported an injury.

WACR; WCSR; AG; ONF.

JOHN S. COPLEY

D:	12-16-43	YB:	1942
T:	1515	Tn:	7,176
Pos:	33.55.59 N / 00.54.30 W	Dr:	18 ft.
Ow:	WSA	C:	sand ballast, 5 LCMs
Op:	American Mail Line Ltd.	P:	steam
M:	Arthur Dowell	S:	6
A:	2-3"; 8-20 mm		

On 16 December, the *John S. Copley* sailed from Arzeu, Algeria, to the United States. As the Liberty ship steamed to take station #21 in Convoy GUS-24, the *U-73* (Deckert) fired a torpedo that struck the starboard side in the empty #2 hold. The blast created a hole eighteen feet long and threw oil and water in the air and all over the ship. Four of the five LCMs secured to the deck also went skyward and fell back on the deck. The #2 hold flooded quickly, causing an 8° list. The steering engines failed and the engineering officer secured the main engines. The freighter's complement consisted of eight officers, thirty-six men, twenty-eight armed guards, and one Army security officer. The master ordered thirty-four of the merchant crew and twelve armed guards into four boats to stand by the vessel. The remaining skeleton crew surveyed the damage. After determining the damage was not fatal, the master ordered some of the crew and gunners back on board and had the engines restarted. Three harbor tugs came to the ship's assistance off Oran, and the rescue tug *ATR-47* took the *Copley* in tow. The USS *PC-546* and USS *SC-977* picked up thirty-eight men just outside the harbor and landed them in Oran. All hands survived the attack, and only two men reported injuries.

The escorts sank the *U-73* shortly after the attack on the *Copley*. NSS; WACR; WCSR; USMMA; AG; Rohwer, p. 253, places the attack at 35.54 N / 00.53 W.

BLUE JACKET

D:	12-16-43	YB:	1943
T:	0145	Tn:	6,180
Pos:	46.00 N / 22.16 W	Dr:	26 ft.
Ow:	WSA	C:	4,200 tons frozen meat
Op:	United Fruit Co.	P:	steam
M:	John Shiell	S:	16
A:	1-4"; 2-3"; 8-20 mm		

On 22 November, the *Blue Jacket* sailed from Buenos Aires en route to Cardiff, Wales. Just before 0200, as the *Blue Jacket* steamed toward her destination, lookouts spotted three ships. They were three British frigates that perhaps mistook the *Blue Jacket* for a German blockade runner. One frigate lay about two miles off the port quarter, one directly ahead, and one on the starboard

quarter. Moments after the general alarm rang, the frigate off the port quarter fired dozens of flares. At this point the other two ships opened fire. The first shell hit the flying bridge, the second struck the radio room, and two more hit the crew's quarters. The master did not know that his attackers were friendly and decided to use the ship's speed to escape. A running battle began, with the three ships pursuing the freighter for two and one-half hours. The *Blue Jacket* maintained full speed while returning the fire at a range of from 600 to 3,000 yards. During the gun battle, a fire started in the #2 hold, but the crew quickly put it out. The *Blue Jacket* began signaling the British ships after a member of the crew picked up a shell fragment with British markings. The British vessels stopped firing and provided the refrigerator ship with a doctor to treat the seven men wounded during the attack. All eight officers, forty-eight men, and thirty-three armed guards survived. The *Blue Jacket* fired 43 rounds of four-inch and 168 rounds of three-inch ammunition at the frigates. The armed guards were praised for their gunnery, which "prevented three HM frigates from closing, and . . . undoubtedly saved her from a severe mauling." Extensively damaged, the ship made Liverpool on 19 December.

WACR; WCSR; TF; AG; ONF.

McDOWELL

D:	12-16-43	YB:	1943
T:	0528	Tn:	10,195
Pos:	13.08 N / 70.02 W	Dr:	21 ft.
Ow:	WSA	C:	water ballast
Op:	Marine Transport Lines Inc.	P:	steam
M:	Henry David Barrow	S:	15
A:	1-5"; 1-3"; 8-20 mm		

On 10 December, the *McDowell* sailed independently from New York City bound for Aruba, NWI. The *U-516* (Tillessen) spotted the tanker in the light of the third quarter moon. Firing a single torpedo, it struck the port side at the screw. The explosion demolished the propeller and shaft, disabled the main and auxiliary engines, and damaged the steering gear. The ship began to settle rapidly by the stern as the general alarm mustered the crew to their stations and guns. At sunrise, about one hour after the first explosion, a second torpedo struck at the #7 port wing tank, and the master ordered the ship abandoned. As the men assembled to leave the ship, a third torpedo struck at the #4 tank. This caused the ship to sink stern first in five minutes. The survivors among the ten officers, thirty-five men, and twenty-eight armed guards got away in five lifeboats and a raft. A plane spotted the survivors at 0710, and the tanker SS *Fairfax* picked up sixty-three survivors and landed them at Aruba. At 1015 the USS *YMS-56* picked up the remaining eight survivors, and they also landed at

Aruba. Two men in the merchant crew drowned, and the chief cook later died from injuries ashore.

The ship's torpedo detector failed to warn of the approaching torpedo. NSS; WACR; WCSR; USMMA; RWCS; AG; Rohwer, p. 175; *War Action Casualties*, p. 165.

CHAPULTEPEC

D: 12-26-43	YB: 1943
T: 0725	Tn: 10,195
Pos: 10.33 N / 79.10 N	Dr: 31 ft. 3 in.
Ow: WSA	C: 101,176 bbls. fuel oil
Op: Barber Asphalt Corp.	P: steam
M: Allen L. Remick Jr.	S: 14.5
A: 1-5"; 1-3"; 8-20 mm	

On 24 December, the *Chapultepec* sailed independently from Aruba, NWI, to Cristobal, Canal Zone. In sight of a small convoy, she proceeded on a zigzag course. At daybreak, in hazy weather, the *U-530* (Lange) spotted the vessel. The tanker's acoustic torpedo detector warned of an approaching torpedo, and seconds later one struck just abaft the stem. The explosion destroyed the forepeak tank and damaged nearby compartments. The ship immediately began a series of short zigzags and then returned to the normal pattern after ten minutes. The tanker settled by the head, but the master shifted cargo and brought the vessel back on an even keel. The ship made full speed to Cristobal, arrived on the afternoon of the 26th, and discharged her cargo the next day. Only two of the ten officers, forty-three men, and twenty-eight armed guards reported any injuries. The ship later steamed to Galveston for dry docking and repairs.

NSS; WACR; WCSR; Rohwer, p. 176, places the attack at 10.30 N / 78.58 W; *War Action Casualties*, p. 167.

ESSO BUFFALO

D: 12-26-43	YB: 1943
T: 0730	Tn: 11,349
Pos: 10.25 N / 78.28 W	Dr: 30 ft.
Ow: Standard Oil Co. of N. J.	C: 156,840 bbls. Navy fuel, aircraft on deck
Op: WSA	
M: Maurice W. Carter	P: steam
A: 1-5"; 1-35"; 8-20 mm	S: 16

On 26 December, the *Esso Buffalo* sailed from Aruba, NWI, to Melbourne, Australia. As the ship steered a zigzag course, her torpedo indicator gave warning of an approaching torpedo, and lookouts spotted a wake across the

ship's bow. The master ordered the wheel hard right, and three minutes later a second torpedo passed the ship 250 feet off the starboard side. Moments later the crew felt a heavy jar from the area of the bow. Following this they heard a muffled explosion and scraping noises. The damage could not be ascertained at sea, but in port they discovered cracked and dented plates almost the entire length of the vessel. The damage was attributed to a dud torpedo. None of the twelve officers, thirty-five men, or twenty-eight armed guards reported any injuries.

WACR; AG; *Ships of the Esso Fleet*, pp. 424-25, relates the attack occurred on the 29th.

JOSE NAVARRO

D: 12-27-43   YB: 1943
T: 0412   Tn: 7,244
Pos: 08.20 N / 73.35 E   Dr: 22 ft.
Ow: WSA   C: 3,000 tons Army cargo, mules,
Op: Grace Lines   fodder, pipes, landing mats
M: Ernest Wesley MacLellan   P: steam
A: 1-4"; 2-3"; 8-20 mm   S: 10

On 19 December, the *Jose Navarro* sailed independently from New Orleans, Louisiana, to Calcutta, India, via Aden. The *U-178* (Spahr) fired a torpedo that struck on the starboard bow, forward of the torpedo streamer, between the #1 and #2 holds at the foremast. The blast threw the ship to port, and she then rapidly settled by the bow. The explosion destroyed the bulkhead separating the first two holds and damaged the bulkhead separating holds #2 and #3. All three spaces flooded quickly. As the ship settled by the bow, the propeller came halfway out of the water. At 0445 the master ordered the engines secured and the ship abandoned by blowing one blast on the ship's whistle. The gun crew fired two errant shots at lights on two life rafts that had been released. The eight officers, thirty-eight men, thirty-four armed guards, and eighty-six troops on board cleared the ship in eight lifeboats. Just over three hours later, thirty men volunteered to reboard the ship in an attempt to salvage her. After working for three hours the men gave up and abandoned the ship again. A second torpedo struck the vessel at 1915, sending her immediately to the bottom. The Indian Navy minesweeper *Rajputana* (J-197) rescued the survivors the next day and landed them at Cochin, India. Only one man reported an injury.

NSS; WACR; WCSR; AG; Rohwer, p. 272.

ROBERT F. HOKE

D:	12-28-43	YB:	1943
T:	0705	Tn:	7,178
Pos:	20.05 N / 59.58 E	Dr:	24 ft.
Ow:	WSA	C:	2,000 tons general, empty oil
Op:	American Export Lines		drums, dates, bitumen
M:	Frederick Nicholas MacLean	P:	steam
A:	2-3"; 8-20 mm	S:	10

On 23 December, the *Robert F. Hoke* sailed independently from Abadan, Iran, to Mombasa, Kenya. As the *Hoke* steered a zigzag course, lookouts spotted a torpedo fired by the *I-26* (Kusaka). The torpedo passed aft of the torpedo streamer and struck on the port side between the #4 and #5 holds. The explosion demolished the bulkhead between these two holds, and they flooded immediately. The blast distorted the propeller shaft, and the watertight door to the shaft alley failed and emitted water into the engine room. After twenty minutes the master gave the order to abandon ship. The crew of eight officers and thirty-three men left the ship in four lifeboats and three rafts. The twenty-seven armed guards remained with the Liberty ship and fired at the *I-26*'s periscope to keep the submarine submerged. Two hours after the attack the master and several officers reboarded the vessel with hopes of salvage. The watch below, however, had not secured the boilers, and they had burned out. The officers could not raise steam, and they and the armed guards abandoned the ship together. The ship settled by the stern but did not sink. The crew left the crippled ship and set sail for land. A Royal Air Force crash boat picked up the crews of two lifeboats on 28 December and took them to Masirah Island. The next day the other two lifeboats also reached Masirah Island. The *Hoke*'s cargo of empty oil drums kept the ship afloat, and the rescue tug HMS *Masterful* (W-20) later took the Liberty ship in tow to Aden. The SS *Mark Keppell* towed her to Suez in a sinking condition, where the WSA declared her a CTL. There were no injuries or casualties among the crew.

The Liberty ship was never used again as a cargo vessel. Her last use before being scrapped was to train stevedores in Bombay. NSS; WACR; WCSR; USMMA; AG; Rohwer, p. 272, places the attack at 20.00 N / 59.25 E. Washington *Post*, 6 September 1844; Sawyer, Mitchell, p. 114.

ALBERT GALLATIN

D:	1-2-44	YB:	1942
T:	0852	Tn:	7,176
Pos:	21.21 N / 59.58 E	Dr:	26 ft. 6 in.
Ow:	WSA	C:	7,954 tons war cargo
Op:	American Hawaiian Line	P:	steam
M:	Cyrus Lee Brown	S:	9.2
A:	1-4"; 1-3"; 8-20 mm		

On 28 December, the *Albert Gallatin* sailed independently from Aden en route to Bandar Shahpur, Iran. The *I-26* (Kusaka) intercepted the zigzagging freighter sixty miles off the coast of Arabia. A torpedo struck the vessel on the starboard side under the #3 hold. The explosion started a fire in the #3 hold, and the ship slowly settled by the head. The armed guards fired over fifty rounds from the deck guns at a periscope but never struck the submarine. The master gave the order to abandon ship at 0920. The crew of eight officers and thirty-five men left the ship in three lifeboats and two rafts. The twenty-eight armed guards remained until they had to jump overboard. About an hour after the crew abandoned the ship, a violent explosion rocked the vessel on the port side. The master later attributed this to a second torpedo. The ship settled at a more rapid pace and split in two when water reached the main deck. The survivors remained in the water only two hours before being picked up by the Norwegian tanker *Britannia*. All hands survived the attack.

NSS; WACR; WCSR; USMMA; AG; Rohwer, p. 272.

WILLIAM S. ROSECRANS

D:	1-6-44	YB:	1942
T:	1245	Tn	7,176
Pos:	40.40 N / 14.15 E	Dr:	16 ft.
Ow:	WSA	C:	ballast
Op:	American President Lines	P:	steam
M:	Elmer Paul Barstow	S:	drifting
A:	1-5"; 1-3"; 8-20 mm		

The *William S. Rosecrans* lay anchored about eight miles south of Naples, Italy, awaiting orders to join Convoy NV-14. A northeast gale caused the ship to drag her anchor while riding out the storm. As the *Rosecrans* drifted at an unknown rate, an explosion caused by a mine occurred on the starboard side at the #2 hold. The explosion blew off the hatch cover and scattered portions of the ship's permanent sand ballast and the hatch beams. It also damaged the bulkhead to the #3 hold and started a fire in the waste dunnage and oil-soaked sand ballast. The crew secured the engines immediately. Within three minutes of the first explosion the ship struck a second mine on the starboard side at the #4 hold. This explosion blew off the hatch cover and again threw ballast sand and hatch beams in the air. The #2, #3, and #4 holds flooded, and the ship slowly settled on an even keel. At 1253 the master gave the order to abandon ship. The crew of eight officers, thirty-five men, and twenty-seven armed guards cleared the ship in four lifeboats. British naval craft rescued all hands and took them to Naples. The *Rosecrans* sank at 1500.

The armed guard figures are contradictory. NSS; WACR; WCSR; USMMA; AG. The NSS also lists an Army cargo security officer.

DANIEL WEBSTER

D:	1-10-44	YB:	1943
T:	1835	Tn	7,176
Pos:	36.04 N / 00.14 W	Dr:	27 ft.
Ow:	WSA	C:	7,000 tons Army cargo, vehicles
Op:	Sprague SS Co.	P:	steam
M:	Addison Roebuck	S:	7
A:	1-5"; 1-3"; 8-20 mm		

On 9 January, the *Daniel Webster* sailed from Gibraltar in Convoy KMS-37 en route to Augusta and Naples. The freighter proceeded in convoy station #91, the first ship in the starboard column. Escorts ahead of the formation began laying a smoke screen at 1825, and other vessels lit smoke pots. With most ships still visible, lookouts on the *Daniel Webster* spotted enemy torpedo planes. As the planes attacked the convoy, the Liberty ship successfully avoided two torpedoes launched from one plane. As she swung back into her convoy position, a second plane released torpedoes off the port bow. The ship was unable to maneuver quickly enough, and one of the torpedoes hit her between the #1 and #2 holds in the double bottoms. Both holds above the explosion flooded in twenty-five minutes, and cracks appeared on the main deck. The ship settled by the head until only three feet of freeboard remained. The engineering officer below secured the engines, but after the master appraised the danger, he proceeded to Oran under escort of the frigate HMS *Barle* (K-289). On 11 January, at 0250 the Navy tug *ATR-47* pulled the vessel into Oran and beached her two miles from the breakwater. The next day lighters discharged the cargo, reducing the draft so the *Webster* could get into Mers-el-Kabir. The WSA later declared the ship a CTL. Only one injury occurred among the eight officers, thirty-three men, twenty-nine armed guards, and three passengers on board.

The armed guard figures conflict within the sources. NSS; WACR; WCSR; Sawyer, Mitchell, p. 104.

SUMNER I. KIMBALL

D:	1-16-44	YB:	1943
T:	2202 GWT	Tn	7,176
Pos:	52.35 N / 35.00 W	Dr:	27 ft. 9 in.
Ow:	WSA	C:	unknown
Op:	Eastern Gas & Fuel Associates	P:	steam
M:	Harry Atkins	S:	approximately 10
A:	2-3"; 8-20 mm		

On 9 January, the *Sumner I. Kimball* sailed from the United Kingdom to New York in Convoy ON-219. On the morning of 16 January, during bad weather, the freighter straggled from the convoy. The freighter maintained a zigzag course in her effort to catch the convoy. The *U-960* (Heinrich) sighted the ship through a rain cloud and from about 800 yards hit her with its first torpedo. The *Kimball* tried to escape at seven knots with the *U-960* in pursuit. About thirty minutes later, at 2202 (GWT), the U-boat missed with two single shots. The U-boat momentarily lost the freighter but soon found her again and fired two more torpedoes from a distance of just over 2,000 yards. Both struck the *Kimball*; she stopped and the radio operator began sending distress signals. The U-boat dove to reload and fired another single shot from 400 yards and again struck the ship. After reloading again, the U-boat fired another shot from the port side at 400 yards and hit the freighter amidships. The *U-960* dove one more time to reload. When it came up, the freighter had broken apart amidships, with the stern and forecastle moving quickly away from each other. The U-boat's war journal mentions that they saw no survivors. None of the crew of eight officers, thirty-two men, and twenty-nine armed guards lived through the attack.

The figures for the crew and armed guards conflict. The Mystic SS Co. was also a co-operator. WACR; WCSR; AG; TF; WJ; Rohwer, p. 177.

F.A.C. MUHLENBERG

D:	1-24-44	YB:	1942
T:	0236	Tn	7,176
Pos:	Naples, Italy	Dr:	22 ft. 3 in.
Ow:	WSA	C:	3,000 tons Army cargo, gas,
Op:	Luckenbach SS Co.		ammunition
M:	Kristian Tobias Kristiansen	P:	steam
A:	1-4"; 1-3"; 8-20 mm	S:	at dock

On 10 January, the *F.A.C. Muhlenberg* departed Oran, Algeria, en route to Naples, Italy, and joined Convoy VN-16. On 18 January, the freighter anchored in Naples at berth 6-W and began discharging her cargo. Five days later enemy aircraft attacked the vessels in the harbor. During the attack a plane approached from seaward and dropped bombs on the dock and on the ship. One bomb

exploded close off the ship's bow, and a second struck the port gun on the after part of the bridge. The second bomb pierced the bridge deck, passed through the boat deck, and exploded in the galley. Fire broke out immediately and damaged much of the midships house, particularly the officers' quarters and the crew and armed guards' mess rooms. Firefighting parties from the crew fought the fire, and the port fire department brought pumps from shore. An hour later they had the fire under control. The crew of eight officers, thirty-eight men, thirty-one armed guards, and four Army passengers remained on board during the blaze. Three officers, three men, and one of the armed guard officers died. The Liberty ship was towed to berth forty-two, docked, and repaired.

NSS; WACR; WCSR; AG; TF.

PENELOPE BARKER

D:	1-24-44	YB:	1942
T:	2015	Tn	7,176
Pos:	72.23 N / 23.10 E	Dr:	26 ft.
Ow:	WSA	C:	8,000 tons steel, vehicles,
Op:	North Atlantic & Golf SS Co.		locomotives, planes, tanks
M:	John Paul Kounce	P:	steam
A:	1-5"; 1-3"; 8-20 mm	S:	10

The *Penelope Barker* sailed from New York to Murmansk, USSR, via Akureyri, Iceland. The eighteen-ship and twelve-escort Convoy JW-56A left Iceland on 21 January, and the *Barker* proceeded in convoy station #12. In snow squalls, approximately 115 miles from North Cape, Norway, the *U-278* (Franze) fired a spread of three torpedoes. Two of these torpedoes struck simultaneously on the port side. One struck the #5 hold and the other in the engine room. The explosion aft blew off the hatch cover and beams to the #5 hold, and knocked the port machine guns out of their tub. The other torpedo toppled the stack, damaged the bridge area, and filled the engine room with live steam. With the engines secured, the survivors of the eight officers, thirty-five men, twenty-eight armed guards, and one passenger (Royal Navy doctor) left the ship either in the two remaining starboard lifeboats or by jumping in the water. The ship steadily sank, plunging stern first ten minutes after the initial explosions. The explosions accounted for most of the men killed—one officer, nine men, and five armed guards. The destroyer HMS *Savage* (G-20) rescued the survivors forty minutes later and took them to Murmansk.

Figures for the crew and armed guards conflict within the sources. NSS; WACR; WCSR; USMMA; AG; Rohwer, p. 204, places the attack at 73.22 N / 22.30 E.

JOHN MUIR

D:	1-24-44	YB:	1942
T:	2040	Tn	7,176
Pos:	06.32.08 S / 147.53.05 E	Dr:	14 ft. 6 in.
Ow:	WSA	C:	500 tons lumber and vehicles
Op:	Alaska Packers, Inc.	P:	steam
A:	1-5"; 5-20 mm	S:	docked
M:	Sven Ericksen		

On 23 January, the *John Muir* sailed from Finschhafen, New Guinea, to Dreger Bay, New Guinea. During an enemy air attack, at least four bombs struck near the *John Muir*, causing 126 dents and fragmentation holes in the #1, #2, and #3 holds. Another bomb struck at the #2 hatch. Fortunately, the bombs only slightly injured the vessel. The Liberty ship had to be patched before sailing to the United States for permanent repairs. The eight officers, thirty-four men, twenty-eight armed guards, and forty construction battalion stevedores remained on board. One officer, one merchant seaman, and one man from the gun crew reported injuries. The bombs injured thirteen of the CBs, and some later died ashore.

WACR; WCSR; AG.

JOHN BANVARD

D:	1-26-44	YB:	1943
T:	1815	Tn	7,191
Pos:	Anzio Beach, Italy	Dr:	20 ft.
Ow:	WSA	C:	1,800 tons explosives, gas,
Op:	Seas Shipping Co., Inc.		machinery, troops
M:	John Lind	P:	steam
A:	1-5"; 3-3"; 8-20 mm	S:	at anchor

The *John Banvard* sailed from the United States to Anzio, Italy, arriving and anchoring on 22 January, four miles southwest of the breakwater. On the 26th the Liberty ship shifted her anchor to 2.5 miles off the beach. Just over an hour after shifting her anchorage six enemy aircraft attacked the ship. One glide bomb hit the water fifteen yards off the ship's stern. The concussion from this near miss sprung watertight doors, cracked frames, and damaged equipment and steam and water lines throughout the vessel. On board the ship were eight officers, thirty-five men, twenty-seven armed guards, one passenger, and twenty men of the port battalion. The master blew the abandon ship signal on the ship's whistle, and all but twenty-three of the men abandoned the *Banvard* (chief engineer, third assistant engineer, naval communications officer, an Army major, and nineteen of his Army port battalion). The men in the four boats later reboarded the ship. The crew used dunnage to raise steam in the boilers and got her under way. The WSA later declared the ship a CTL. She was eventually towed to Jacksonville, Florida, and scrapped. All hands survived the attack.

NSS; WACR; WCSR; AG; Sawyer, Mitchell, p. 43.

HILARY A. HERBERT

D:	1-26-44	YB:	1943
T:	1645	Tn	7,176
Pos:	off Nettuno, Italy	Dr:	16
Ow:	WSA	C:	ammunition, gas, vehicles, field
Op:	Cosmopolitan Shipping Co.		pieces
M:	Percey Harold Hauffman	P:	steam
A:	1-4"; 1-3"; 8-20 mm	S:	at anchor

On 24 January, the *Hilary A. Herbert* sailed from Naples, Italy, and anchored about two miles off Nettuno, Italy. The ship had shifted her anchorage several times because of enemy attacks. At 1645 during an air attack a German fighter crashed into the starboard side slightly forward of the bridge and just below the waterline. Seconds later a bomb struck the water on the starboard side only twenty feet from the ship and threw water and airplane parts all over the deck. Within moments a second bomb exploded on the port side about thirty-five feet from the ship. This explosion lifted the ship out of the water and heeled her over 15°. The explosions separated hull seams and carried away the condenser intake. With the Liberty ship's engine room flooding rapidly, the master decided to beach her. The ship's pumps had the water under control in thirty minutes, and at 1900 the master put the ship gently on the beach. The *Herbert* had on board 8 officers, 33 men, 8 British military passengers, 250 Army troops, and 31 armed guards. Three men from the merchant crew, the military passengers, and the 250 Army troops went ashore in landing barges. The armed guards debarked later. The following day only a skeleton crew remained on the ship to make repairs. On 2 February, the British tug *Prosperous* (W-96) towed the freighter to Naples. After repairs the ship went back in service. All hands survived the attack.

The complement numbers conflict within the sources. NSS; WCSR; AG.

ANDREW G. CURTIN

D:	1-26-44	YB:	1943
T:	0020	Tn	7,200
Pos:	73.25 N / 25.16 E	Dr:	23 ft. 6 in.
Ow:	WSA	C:	9,000 tons steel, locomotives,
Op:	Calmar SS Co., Inc.		general
M:	Jacob Olai Jacobson	P:	steam
A:	1-5"; 1-3"; 8-20 mm	S:	9

On 21 January, the *Andrew G. Curtin* sailed from Akureyri, Iceland, to Murmansk, USSR. While the freighter proceeded in station #61 in Convoy JW-56A, the *U-716* (Dunkelberg) fired a spread of three torpedoes. One of the torpedoes struck the freighter on the starboard side between the #2 and #3 holds. The watch below secured the engines as the ship settled by the head and listed to starboard. The deck cracked forward of the #3 hold and extended across the vessel. As the *Curtin* sank, the crack widened and the bow soon hogged about 25°. The Liberty ship's complement of eight officers, thirty-five men, and twenty-eight armed guards abandoned ship in some confusion in one raft and the four lifeboats aft of the crack. The destroyer HMS *Inconstant* (H-49) rescued the survivors in less than an hour. Two men from the merchant crew drowned, and one armed guard died after being hurled over the side. The survivors observed the *Curtin* breaking in two before sinking. The survivors landed at Murmansk.

NSS; WACR; WCSR; USMMA; AG; Rohwer, p. 204.

WALTER CAMP

D:	1-26-44	YB:	1943
T:	0427	Tn	7,176
Pos:	10.00 N / 71.40 E	Dr:	26 ft.
Ow:	WSA	C:	6,100 tons food, barges,
Op:	American President Lines		vehicles, cranes, earth movers
M:	Henry Alfred Shutz	P:	steam
A:	1-5"; 1-3"; 8-20 mm	S:	12.3

On 19 January, the *Walter Camp* sailed independently from Aden for Calcutta, India, via Colombo. In the darkness, the *U-532* (Junker) torpedoed the zigzagging Liberty ship. The U-boat fired a torpedo that struck the vessel on the starboard side at the #3 hold. The explosion caused both the #2 and the #3 holds to flood, ruptured steam lines, and damaged the steering engine, which caused the ship to swing hard right. The ship took a 30° list and began to settle by the bow. The watch below secured the engines, and the master ordered the complement of eight officers, thirty-two men, and twenty-eight armed guards,

and the one passenger, to abandon ship. With both starboard boats gone, the crew left safely in the two port boats and three rafts. About fifteen minutes after the first explosion and with all hands off the ship, a second torpedo struck the vessel in the engine room, and she sank stern first. The survivors remained at sea for four and a half days before being rescued and landed at Aden by the light cruiser HMS *Danae* (I-44).

NSS; WACR; WCSR; AG; Rohwer, p. 272, places the attack at 10.00 N / 71.49 E.

SAMUEL HUNTINGTON

D:	1-29-44	YB:	1942
T:	1800	Tn	7,149
Pos:	Nettuno Beach, Italy	Dr:	24 ft.
Ow:	WSA	C:	4,000 tons ammunition, vehicles,
Op:	Oliver J. Olson		gasoline, TNT
M:	Richard Stenman	P:	steam
A:	1-4"; 1-3"; 8-20 mm	S:	at anchor

On 28 January, the *Samuel Huntington* departed Naples and anchored a quarter of a mile off Nettuno Beach, Italy. While the ship lay there waiting to be unloaded, enemy planes attacked the anchorage at 1705 and again at 1800. The ship suffered no harm during the first attack. During the second attack one bomb struck the port side aft of the flying bridge. It penetrated the superstructure and exploded in the engine room. Two more bombs struck on the port side below the waterline amidships. These explosions blew off the #3 and #4 hatches, blew out the engine room skylights, and caused several vehicles and men to go over the side. The engine room and holds #3 and #4 flooded, and fires started in the #3 hold and the #2 tween deck. The ship listed 10° to port and settled on the bottom. The ship had on board eight officers, thirty-seven men, thirty-nine armed guards, and eighteen passengers (five U.S. Army and thirteen British Navy). The injured men left in lifeboats and rafts and transferred to waiting landing craft. The remaining crew fought the flames for an hour and then abandoned ship. After searching for members of the crew, the master left at 2000. Three men of the merchant crew died from the explosions, and another man died ashore nearly two weeks later. The *Samuel Huntington* smoldered for hours after the attack, and at 0230 and 0340 explosions rocked the freighter and left her ablaze from stem to stern. The WSA later judged her a CTL.

NSS; WACR; WCSR; AG.

GEORGE STERLING

D:	1-29-44	YB:	1943
T:	1557	Tn	7,176
Pos:	06.41 S / 147.52 E	Dr:	18 ft.
Ow:	WSA	C:	8,000 tons gasoline, landing
Op:	Waterman SS Co.		mats, ammunition, general
M:	Jens Jensen	P:	steam
A:	2-3"; 8-20 mm	S:	at anchor

The *George Sterling* sailed from Brisbane, Australia, to Milne Bay, Finschhafen. The Liberty ship anchored 100 yards from shore at Cape Cretin and began discharging cargo into DUKWs. Starting after noon, enemy bombers began attacking the anchorage. One bomb struck thirty feet from the vessel on the port side, amidships. This explosion damaged the ship with shrapnel and put numerous holes in the shell plating, particularly in the after section. Dunnage in the #4 hold caught fire, but a firefighting party quickly extinguished it. The shrapnel also nearly cut the #4 and #5 booms in half. The crew of eight officers, thirty-six men, and twenty-six armed guards remained on the ship. Shrapnel killed two Marines in the DUKWs, and three men on board reported slight injuries.

WACR; AG; ONF.

ALEXANDER MARTIN

D:	1-29-44	YB:	1942
T:	1930	Tn	7,176
Pos:	off Anzio Beach, Italy	Dr:	18 ft.
Ow:	WSA	C:	2,000 tons general
Op:	American South African Line	P:	steam
M:	Morgan A. Rock	S:	at anchor
A:	1-5"; 1-3"; 8-20 mm		

The *Alexander Martin* sailed from Naples to Anzio, Italy, and anchored one and a half miles off Anzio Beach. During an enemy air attack the freighter suffered slight damage from strafing runs by enemy aircraft. The damage was concentrated on the starboard side at the superstructure. At the time of the attack 8 officers, 33 men, 24 armed guards, 29 passengers, and 250 stevedores were on board. Only three of these men reported injuries.

WACR; AG.

STEPHEN CRANE

D:	1-31-44	YB:	1943
T:	1420	Tn:	7,176
Pos:	06.32.08 S / 147.53.05 E	Dr:	19 ft.
Ow:	WSA	C:	2,000 tons U.S. Army Engineer
Op:	Isthmian SS Co.		supplies
M:	William Edward Green	P:	steam
A:	1-5"; 1-3"; 8-20 mm	S:	docked

The *Stephen Crane* steamed from San Francisco to Langemak Bay, New Guinea. The freighter arrived in the bay on 30 December and tied up to the dock. The following day a high altitude bomber dropped a bomb that glanced off the ship's stack and exploded several yards off the port side. The blast hurled water and shrapnel over the decks. The fragments put about fifty holes in the shell plating of the vessel and also damaged cargo booms, the superstructure, two lifeboats, and other equipment and fittings about the ship. The eight officers, twenty-five men, twenty-nine armed guards, and forty Army passengers remained on the ship. The explosion killed one of the Army passengers and injured twenty-two others, including one of the armed guards and one of the merchant seamen. The freighter departed Milne Bay on 18 February.

The armed guard report claims a captured P-38 dropped the bomb. WACR; WCSR; AG; Washington *Post*, 4 June 1944.

RICHARD P. HOBSON

D:	2-1-44	YB:	1943
T:	1900	Tn	7,176
Pos:	36.40 N / 01.10 E	Dr:	unknown
Ow:	WSA	C:	general
Op:	Ibrandtsen SS Co.	P:	steam
M:	George Henry Snyder	S:	9
A:	2-3"; 8-20 mm		

On 14 January, the *Richard P. Hobson* sailed from Norfolk, Virginia, to Calcutta, India. As the vessel traveled in the seventy-ship Convoy UGS-30, in station #11, a torpedo plane approached from the ship's starboard side. The plane released two torpedoes; one crossed the Liberty ship's bow and the second slammed into her trailing torpedo streamer at the after part of the #3 hatch. The ship suffered minor damage in the engine room, to the forward three-inch gun and to the ship's hull. She maintained station and arrived at Port Said, Egypt, on 10 February. There were no casualties among the armed guards or the crew.

WCSR; AG.

EDWARD BATES

D:	2-1-44	YB:	1943
T:	1900	Tn	7,891
Pos:	36.34 N / 01.14 E	Dr:	25 ft.
Ow:	WSA	C:	8,000 tons flour, mail
Op:	Hammond SS Co.	P:	steam
M:	Leo H. Luksichl	S:	5
A:	4-3"; 8-20 mm		

On 14 January, the *Edward Bates* sailed from Norfolk, Virginia, to Naples, Italy, in the fifty-five ship Convoy UGS-30. The Liberty ship maintained station #81 at the head of the convoy. At 1800, sixty-five miles from Oran, an air alarm sounded, and four German torpedo bombers appeared off the port bow an hour later. One plane approached from the port bow and dropped a torpedo. The helmsman attempted to turn the ship, but at convoy speed she did not answer the helm quickly. The torpedo struck the port side just forward of the #4 hold in the deep tanks laden with fuel. The cargo of flour contained the explosion to some degree, but the explosion and water flowing into the engine room crippled the engines. The ship initially began to sink quickly and she took a port list, but the pace of flooding gradually slowed. An hour after the torpedo struck, the master gave the order to abandon ship. The eight officers, thirty-eight men, thirty-eight armed guards, and seven passengers cleared the ship in four lifeboats and two rafts. A British tug and a British destroyer rescued the men within an hour. A patrol boat later carried the master, three deck officers, two engine room officers, the gunnery officer, and five other men back to the *Bates* to salvage her. The patrol boat came within a mile of the ship when an explosion at 0800 broke her in two and she sank immediately. An oiler who died on watch below was the only death among the crew. On 2 February, the survivors landed in Algiers.

The ship's complement figures are contradictory within the sources. NSS; WACR; WCSR; AG.

ELIHU YALE

D:	2-15-44	YB:	1942
T:	1810	Tn	7,176
Pos:	1/2 mi. off Anzio	Dr:	20 ft.
Ow:	WSA	C:	1,500 tons general, gas,
Op:	McCormick SS Co.		ammunition, machinery
M:	Thure W. F. Ekstrom	P:	steam
A:	1-4"; 1-3"; 8-20 mm	S:	at anchor

On 12 February, the *Elihu Yale* departed Naples, Italy, for the Anzio beachhead. After reaching Anzio, the Liberty ship discharged 40 percent of her cargo and

began unloading ammunition. After an air raid alert sounded, the ship received warning that lookouts had spotted eight enemy planes approaching the beachhead. A short time later a glide bomb dropped by one of the aircraft penetrated through the main deck into the #4 hatch. The explosion in the empty hold blew out both sides of the ship down to the waterline. The explosion also brought down masts, destroyed deck machinery, and burst piping about the ship. The ship settled by the stern until the stern came to rest on the bottom. The explosion also started a fire in the #4 hold, and it spread to an LCT tied alongside, to the superstructure, and later to the ammunition in the #5 hold. The USS *Hopi* (ATF-71) helped fight the fire throughout the night. Just an hour after the initial explosion, the master gave the order to abandon ship. The 8 officers, 37 men, 40 armed guards, and 182 stevedores left the ship in only one lifeboat and some rafts. Many were picked up by naval craft and taken to the beach. The master and some of his crew later returned to fight the fire. At 0430 the *Hopi* finally extinguished the flames. The stevedores later managed to save some of the cargo in holds #1, #2, and #3. The WSA later judged the ship a CTL. Two armed guards, three of the merchant crew, and seven stevedores perished in the attack.

NSS; WACR; WCSR; AG.

PETER SKENE OGDEN

D:	2-22-44	YB:	1942
T:	1218	Tn	7,176
Pos:	37.18 N / 06.59 E	Dr:	24 ft.
Ow:	WSA	C:	1,750 tons obsolete tanks
Op:	W. R. Chamberlin & Co.	P:	steam
M:	William Petit Magann	S:	9
A:	1-5"; 1-3"; 8-20 mm		

On 21 February, the *Peter Skene Ogden* sailed from Bizerte, Tunisia, en route to the east coast of the United States. The Liberty ship took station #111 in Convoy GUS-31. Fifteen miles off the coast of Algeria, the *U-969* (Dobbert) maneuvered into a favorable position and fired a torpedo that struck the vessel at the #5 hold on the starboard side. The blast threw sand ballast, hatch beams, and covers into the air; blew one of the after booms over the side; damaged the shaft; and caused the propeller to drop off. The stern began to settle immediately, and at about 1400 the master ordered the eight officers, thirty-three men, twenty-eight armed guards, and the convoy commodore and his seven aides to abandon ship. Using four lifeboats and four rafts, all safely cleared the ship. A British escort vessel picked up most of the survivors at 1630. The master and ten volunteers returned to the ship to facilitate her salvage. The Royal Navy tug *Hengist* (W-110) towed the freighter to Herbillon and beached

her at 1800 on the 23rd. The WSA later declared the vessel a CTL. All hands survived the attack.

The complement figures are contradictory within the sources. NSS; WACR; WCSR; USMMA; AG; Rohwer, p. 255, places the attack at 37.22 N / 07.17 E.

GEORGE CLEEVE

D: 2-22-44   YB: 1943
T: 1220   Tn 7,176
Pos: 37.18 N / 06.59 E   Dr: 20 ft.
Ow: WSA   C: 1,002 tons scrap iron, rubber
Op: American Export Lines   P: steam
M: Daniel Livingston MacDonald S: 9.9
A: 1-4"; 1-3"; 8-20 mm

On 21 February, the *George Cleeve* sailed from Tunis, Tunisia, to Hampton Roads, Virginia, in the eighty-ship Convoy GUS-31. The Liberty ship proceeded in station #121 (first ship second column) on the starboard side of the convoy. The *Peter Skene Ogden*, one column over, was struck by a torpedo at 1218. Two minutes later another torpedo fired from the *U-969* (Dobbert) struck the starboard side amidships and exploded in the engine room, creating a hole twenty-one feet long. The explosion destroyed the engine and turned it over on its side. The blast forced its way into the #4 hold, blew scrap iron through the deck, and enveloped the superstructure in steam and oil. A large crack appeared in the vessel amidships and the master thought the ship would break in two. The ship listed 20° to port, and as she settled, water rose to the after deck and the bow rose out of the water. The master ordered the eight officers, thirty-three men, twenty-eight armed guards, and one passenger on board to abandon ship. At 1315 they began leaving the ship in two boats and a raft. The SS *William T. Barry* picked up the survivors after thirty minutes and landed them in Oran. The explosion killed the second assistant engineer on watch below. A salvage crew boarded the *Cleeve* and had her towed to Bône and beached. The port authorities discharged her cargo, and after an examination the WSA declared her a CTL. The *Cleeve* was later scrapped in Italy.

NSS; WACR; WCSR; USMMA; AG; Rohwer, p. 255, places the attack at 37.22 N / 07.17 E; Sawyer, Mitchell, p. 99.

E. G. SEUBERT

D:	2-23-44	YB:	1918
T:	0330	Tn	9,181
Pos:	13.45 N / 48.56 E	Dr:	30 ft.
Ow:	Standard Oil Co. of N. J.	C:	79,000 bbls. Admiralty fuel
Op:	Standard Oil Co. of N. J.	P:	steam
M:	Ivar Boklund	S:	9
A:	1-4"; 1-3"; 8-20 mm		

On 13 February, the *E. G. Seubert* sailed from Abadan, Iran, to Suez via Aden. The vessel traveled with Convoy PA-69 in station #21. About 200 miles from Aden, a torpedo fired from the *U-510* (Eick) struck the tanker on the port side in the #10 tank and the cross bunkers. The explosion blew one of the after machine guns over the side and started a small fire. The steam smothering line quickly put out the flames. The ship listed to port, and the master ordered the engines stopped as the vessel settled rapidly. Only the #3 boat could be launched before the ship suddenly capsized to port and sank by the stern; just twelve minutes had elapsed since the torpedo struck. The survivors among the complement of eight officers, thirty-five men, and twenty-seven armed guards swam through fuel oil several inches thick. Most climbed on three rafts that had been released as the ship went down. Men in the #3 boat searched and rescued many others from the water. The Australian minesweeper *Tamworth* (J-181) and Royal Indian Navy corvette *Orissa* (J-200) rescued other survivors and landed them in Aden. One officer, two men, and three armed guards including the commanding officer died.

NSS; WACR; WCSR; AG; *Ships of the Esso Fleet*, pp. 496-502. Rohwer, p. 273, places the attack at 13.50 N / 48.49 E; *War Action Casualties*, p. 169.

VIRGINIA DARE

D:	3-6-44	YB:	1942
T:	0812	Tn	7,177
Pos:	approx. 37.18 N / 10.22 E	Dr:	29 ft. 8 in.
Ow:	WSA	C:	8,240 tons general, war supplies
Op:	South Atlantic SS Co.	P:	steam
M:	Vernon Albert Davis	S:	8.5
A:	1-4"; 1-3"; 8-20 mm		

On 9 February, the *Virginia Dare* sailed from New York to Alexandria, Egypt, in Convoy UGS-33. While off Tunis, the convoy commodore ordered a change in formation, and the *Virginia Dare* took station #85. Eight miles offshore the convoy strayed into an Allied minefield. A mine struck the vessel on the port side at the #3 hold, and the hold filled immediately. The master, thinking the ship had been torpedoed, sounded the general alarm, increased the vessel's speed

to 11.5 knots, and began a zigzagging course. Thirty minutes after the explosion a British escort directed the master to take his ship to Tunis. The eight officers, thirty-seven men, twenty-eight armed guards, and three passengers on board all survived the explosion. On 8 March, after discharging 1,200 tons of cargo into the SS *David Burnett*, the vessel proceeded to Bizerte. During the trip, with wind and sea increasing, cracks extending below the waterline began to appear on both sides of the ship at the #3 hatch. The master brought the ship back to Tunis and tried to beach her. The vessel, with the British rescue tug *Charon* (W-109) standing by, broke in two across the after end of the #3 hatch. The after part drifted into deep water and was towed to Bizerte. Salvors also saved the cargo in the forward end. The WSA declared the vessel a CTL.

WACR; WCSR; RWCS; AG.

DANIEL CHESTER FRENCH

D:	3-6-44	YB:	1942
T:	0820	Tn	7,200
Pos:	37.18 N / 10.22 E	Dr:	29 ft. 6 in.
Ow:	WSA	C:	8,200 tons general, munitions,
Op:	Stockard SS Corp.		troops, vehicles, tires
M:	Malcolm R. McClintock	P:	steam
A:	1-5"; 1-3"; 8-20 mm	S:	10

On 13 February, the *Daniel Chester French* sailed from Newport News, Virginia, bound for Bandar Shahpur, Iran, in the nearly ninety-ship Convoy UGS-33. Off Tunisia, the convoy commodore ordered a change in formation, and the convoy strayed into an Allied minefield. As the Liberty ship steamed in convoy station #93, two mines struck her on the starboard side within seconds. The explosions opened large holes in the #2 and #3 holds and buckled the ship eight feet at the after hold. The blasts threw oil and water over the entire ship and filled the #3 and #5 lifeboats. The ship listed first to port and then to starboard and began settling by the head. Five minutes after the explosions the chief engineer reported the engine room flooding. The master gave the order to abandon ship at 0835. In rough seas, the freighter's eight officers, thirty-six men, twenty-eight armed guards, and eighty-six U.S. Army troops abandoned ship in six lifeboats and four rafts. The seas swept across the foredeck of the ship, carrying the #2 lifeboat and several crewmen into the sea. The half-filled boats later capsized and spilled men into the water. Four armed guards, one officer, eight seamen, and twenty-four passengers drowned on board or while trying to abandon ship. The British rescue tug *Charon* (W-109) picked up some of the survivors, while the British SS *Thelma* and an English tug the HMS

Rescue later stood by to rescue others. The *Daniel Chester French* plunged by the head at 0900.

NSS; WACR; WCSR; USMMA; AG.

CLARK MILLS

D:	3-9-44	YB:	1942
T:	0635	Tn	7,176
Pos:	37.18 N / 10.13 E	Dr:	17 ft.
Ow:	WSA	C:	none
Op:	Waterman SS Co.	P:	steam
M:	Charles Bernard Raeburn	S:	9
A:	1-5"; 3-3"; 8-20 mm		

On 8 March, the *Clark Mills* sailed independently from Tunis bound for Bizerte, Tunisia. As the vessel was en route, a mine struck in the fuel tank between the #2 and #3 holds. The explosion threw oil over the ship and blew off the #2 and #3 hatch covers. The ship flooded quickly and immediately listed to port. The master gave the order for all eight officers, thirty-eight men, forty-two armed guards, and four passengers to abandon ship. Using four lifeboats and two rafts, all hands cleared the ship safely. Down by the head and with her screw out of the water, a British tug began towing the freighter to Bizerte. An hour later the tug stopped, and the master and a group of volunteers reboarded the ship and anchored her. The remaining survivors boarded a British submarine chaser and landed in Bizerte. Port authorities beached the ship off Bizerte, and the WSA later considered the vessel a CTL.

The armament indicated in the armed guard files is not conclusive. NSS; WACR; WCSR; AG.

WILLIAM B. WOODS

D:	3-10-44	YB:	1943
T:	1621	Tn	7,176
Pos:	38.43 N / 13.50 E	Dr:	21 ft. 6 in.
Ow:	WSA	C:	ammunition, troops, general, army vehicles
Op:	A. H. Bull SS Co.		
M:	Edward Ames Clark	P:	steam
A:	2-3"; 8-20 mm	S:	10

On 10 March, the *William B. Woods* sailed from Palermo to Naples, Italy, escorted by the Italian destroyer escort *Aretusa*. About forty-seven miles off Palermo, the *U-952* (Curio) fired a torpedo that struck the freighter on the port side in the #5 hold. The explosion opened a hole twelve feet wide, blew off the hatch cover, threw cargo from the hold over the deck, and broke the shaft.

Fortunately, the bombs stowed in the #5 hold did not explode. As the ship slowly settled by the stern, the watch below secured the engines. The master initially believed the vessel could be saved but had to order the ship abandoned after twenty-five minutes. Most of the ship's 9 officers, 34 men, 28 armed guards, and 407 Army troops began leaving in four lifeboats and about fourteen rafts. Seventy men remained on board after all the boats and rafts cleared the ship's side. The remaining men started to construct makeshift rafts but eventually had to jump into the water, with the master leaving last. The *Aretusa* never launched any boats or came alongside to help the men. Later two small British vessels arrived to pull men out of the water. One of the armed guards and fifty-one troops died. At 1940, the bulkhead between the #4 and #5 holds gave way and the ship plunged by the stern.

The figures for the ship's complement are contradictory within the sources. NSS; WACR; WCSR; USMMA; AG; Rohwer, p. 255, places the attack at 38.36 N / 13.45 E.

H. D. COLLIER

D:	3-13-44	YB:	1938
T:	1320	Tn	8,298
Pos:	21.30 N / 66.11 E	Dr:	29 ft. 10 in.
Ow:	Standard Oil Co. of CA.	C:	103,000 bbls. gasoline, kerosene
Op:	WSA - Caltex Oil Co. Ltd.	P:	steam
M:	Joseph Fox	S:	13
A:	1-4"; 1-3"; 8-20 mm		

On 9 March, the *H. D. Collier* sailed independently from Abadan, Iran, to Bombay, India. The *I-26* (Kusaka) fired a single torpedo that struck the port side of the zigzagging tanker between the #7 and #8 tanks. A flash extended mast-high as the gasoline vapors ignited. Fire immediately engulfed these two tanks, enveloped everything astern, and spread fifty feet forward. The blast damaged the steering gear and the ship swung hard right, bringing her into the wind. The *I-26* surfaced, but the forward three-inch gun could not be trained on the submarine and fire had engulfed the after four-inch gun. The *I-26* opened fire on the vessel and hit her several times before leaving. With the tanker still making several knots and with no formal order given by the master, the complement of ten officers, thirty-three men, and twenty-eight armed guards began abandoning ship. The #2 boat swamped and drifted aft through the flames. Twelve men managed to swim back to the ship and release a raft. Another fourteen men launched the motor lifeboat, but they could not start the motor for two hours. This boat stayed in the vicinity looking for survivors until the next morning. On 16 March, after nearly seventy hours in the water, the fourteen men in the motor lifeboat were picked up by the British SS *Empire Raja*, which landed them at Karachi. The twelve men on the raft rescued a man clinging to a float, and they remained long enough to watch the ship sink by the stern on the 16th. These

men spotted an empty burned out lifeboat and transferred into it. The master meanwhile had remained behind on the raft, but when the crew came back to pick him up, they could not find him. The SS *Karagola* rescued the survivors in the last boat over ninety hours after the attack and landed them in Bombay. Twelve armed guards, five officers, and twenty-eight merchant crewmen lost their lives.

NSS; WACR; WCSR; AG; Rohwer, p. 274; *War Action Casualties*, p. 171.

CHINA MAIL

D:	3-15-44	YB:	1942
T:	0120	Tn	8,616
Pos:	Naples, Italy	Dr:	23 ft.
Ow:	WSA	C:	2,500 tons ammunition
Op:	American Mail Line	P:	diesel
M:	Byron P. Stone	S:	docked
A:	1-5"; 1-3"; 8-20 mm		

The *China Mail* sailed from Philadelphia, Pennsylvania, to Naples, Italy. While the ship was docked in Naples, enemy aircraft attacked the anchorage. The aircraft dropped flares around the vessels and lit up the harbor. One flare dropped down the #2 hatch but fortunately did not ignite the cargo. During the attack six bombs fell near the freighter. One of these bombs heavily damaged the British tug *Empire Ace* astern. Another bomb landed forty feet off the port beam, spraying the ship with shrapnel and knocking holes in the port side superstructure. The ship suffered slight damage over her entire length from the bomb fragments. None of the ten officers, fifty-three men, thirteen armed guards, and one passenger on board reported any injuries.

WACR; WCSR; AG; ONF.

JAMES GUTHRIE

D:	3-17-44	YB:	1942
T:	2300	Tn	7,191
Pos:	Naples, Italy	Dr:	27 ft.
Ow:	WSA	C:	8,000 tons general war supplies
Op:	Agwilines, Inc.	P:	steam
M:	Grady Lee Robertson	S:	docked
A:	2-3"; 8-20 mm		

On 9 February, the *James Guthrie* sailed from New York to Naples, Italy. As the ship was discharging cargo during the night of 17 March, enemy aircraft attacked the anchorage. One bomb dropped into the #2 hold, and the explosion

damaged the magnetic compass on the bridge, blew the hatch coaming away, and opened a hole eight feet square in the main deck. The bomb did little else except ruin two tons of soap. The ship's eight officers, thirty-four men, twenty-eight armed guards, and one passenger reported no injuries. An unknown number of stevedores were on board, and four of these men were hospitalized for shock.

This ship was also slightly damaged in an air raid two days earlier. The vessel was subsequently mined. See entry for 17 April 1944. WACR; WCSR.

MAIDEN CREEK

D: 3-17-44
T: 0920
Pos: 37.08 N / 05.27 E
Ow: WSA
Op: Isthmian SS Co.
M: Oscar Pedersen
A: 2-3"; 8-20 mm

YB: 1944
Tn 6,156
Dr: 19 ft. 6 in.
C: water ballast
P: steam
S: 13.5

On 15 March, the *Maiden Creek* sailed from Naples, Italy, in Convoy SNF-17 for Oran, Algiers. The ship proceeded in convoy station #52 among nine transports, three cargo vessels, and three British escorts. About thirty miles north northeast of Bougie, Algeria, the formation shifted its zigzag pattern, and the *U-371* (Mehl) attacked the convoy. A torpedo fired by the U-boat struck the freighter forward of the #4 hatch. The explosion broke the shaft and the ship's back, and filled the #4 hold and the engine room with water. As the vessel slowly settled by the stern, the master gave the order to abandon ship. The ship's eight officers, forty men, twenty-nine armed guards, and one passenger cleared the ship in two lifeboats and a raft. The boats stood by the vessel for two hours until an escort appeared. The escort commander ordered the men back on the vessel to prepare her to be towed. They tied their boats to the stern and climbed on board. As the freighter awaited a tug, the *U-371* put another torpedo into the *Maiden Creek* directly under the stern on the port side. The explosion lifted the vessel out of the water and destroyed the boats. The crew abandoned the ship, this time by jumping into the water, and the survivors all swam to a single raft. Motor launches from a British destroyer rescued the men thirty minutes later. One officer, two armed guards, and five merchant seamen died; all these deaths are attributed to the second torpedo. On the morning of 18 March, the ship was towed into Bougie and beached. Several days later heavy weather rolled her off the rocks; she then broke in half and sank.

Most survivors reported a third explosion simultaneously with the second torpedo. There is no conclusive evidence that a third torpedo struck the freighter. NSS; WACR; WCSR; USMMA; AG; Rohwer, p. 255.

SEAKAY

D:	3-18-44	YB:	1942
T:	1010	Tn	10,342
Pos:	51.10 N / 20.20 W	Dr:	28 ft. 10 in.
Ow:	Keystone Tankship Corp.	C:	110,000 bbls. kerosene, aircraft
Op:	Keystone Tankship Corp.	P:	steam
M:	Alfred Kristian Jorgensen	S:	14.5
A:	1-5"; 1-3"; 8-20 mm		

On 10 March, the *Seakay* sailed from New York to Avonmouth, England, in Convoy CU-17. As the tanker proceeded in convoy station #51, the convoy commodore ordered an emergency turn to port. The *U-311* (Zander) fired a torpedo that struck the tanker's starboard bow at the after bulkhead of the forward dry cargo hold. Flames shot twenty-five feet above the deck, fire broke out in the forward pump room, and the deck cargo of aircraft caught fire. As the tanker rapidly sank, the crew began battling the blaze but had to abandon the effort. About five minutes after the torpedo struck, the master ordered the ten officers, forty-six men, twenty-eight armed guards, and one Army security officer passenger off the ship. Using four lifeboats and a raft, all hands cleared the ship. One of the boats overturned and caused the death of one of the armed guards. The ship rolled over within eighteen minutes but remained afloat. The USS *Reeves* (DE-156) rescued the survivors and took them to Londonderry. At 1220 escort vessels sank the tanker with forty-five shells and depth charges.

NSS; WACR; WCSR; USMMA; AG; Rohwer, p. 179.

ORIENTAL

D:	3-19-44	YB:	1944
T:	1131	Tn	6,214
Pos:	15.31.36 S / 167.17.49 E	Dr:	26 ft.
Ow:	WSA	C:	6,000 tons general and oil in
Op:	Seas Shipping Co.		drums
M:	Johannes Bryde	P:	steam
A:	1-5"; 4-3"; 8-20 mm	S:	12

On 3 March, the *Oriental* sailed from San Francisco, California, to Espíritu Santos, New Hebrides. East of the island a mine detonated beneath the ship's keel. The blast created an elliptical-shaped hole fifteen feet long by four feet wide forward of the bridge at the #2 hold. The ship's starboard deep tanks and the #2 hold flooded. The freighter took a 5° list but made Espíritu Santo under her own power on 19 March. None of the crew of eight officers, forty-five men, twenty-eight armed guards, and five passengers reported any injuries.

WACR; WCSR; AG.

JOHN A. POOR

D:	3-19-44	YB:	1943
T:	2245	Tn	7,160
Pos:	13.58 N / 70.30 E	Dr:	26 ft.
Ow:	WSA	C:	8,400 tons nuts, jute, hides,
Op:	International Freight Corp.		ilmenite, scrap
M:	Francis Wallace Dulac	P:	steam
A:	2-3"; 8-20 mm	S:	12

On 17 March, the *John A. Poor* sailed in a coastwise convoy from Cochin, India, to Aden, Arabia. On 18 March, the Liberty ship left the convoy and traveled independently. The *U-510* (Eick) fired a torpedo that struck the zigzagging freighter's starboard side between the #4 and #5 holds. The explosion blew off the #4 hatch cover and created a hole about twelve feet in diameter in the deck. A second torpedo struck the ship seconds later in the #5 hold, and the ship immediately listed to starboard and settled rapidly. Because of the nature of the cargo the ship sank in ninety seconds. None of the boats could be launched, but the four rafts cleared the ship. Nearly half of the complement of eight officers, thirty-five men, and thirty armed guards, did not survive. Only one officer, twenty-one armed guards, and seventeen merchant seamen reached the rafts. The survivors later lashed three of the rafts together and rigged a sail. The British freighter SS *Fort Worth* rescued the survivors the following day and landed them at Colombo, Ceylon.

The Armed Guard Reports mention a passenger lost in the sinking. NSS; WACR; WCSR; AG; Rohwer, p. 274.

RICHARD HOVEY

D:	3-29-44	YB:	1943
T:	1630	Tn	7,176
Pos:	16.40 N / 64.30 E	Dr:	23 ft.
Ow:	WSA	C:	4,500 tons tea, jute, Army cargo
Op:	Sprague SS Co.	P:	steam
M:	Hans Thorsen	S:	9.5
A:	2-3"; 8-20 mm		

On 27 March, the *Richard Hovey* sailed independently from Bombay, India, for Aden, Arabia. Lookouts spotted the wakes of two torpedoes fired from the *I-26* (Kusaka). With about ten seconds to react, the helmsman put the wheel over hard right, causing one of the torpedoes to pass fifty feet astern and the other to hit the starboard side in the engine room. A third undetected torpedo struck the starboard side at the #4 hatch. The torpedoes came through or under the trailing torpedo streamer. The explosions jammed the rudder in a half-right position, wrecked the bridge and main steering house, caused the port boiler to explode,

and buckled a large portion of the shell plating. At 1650 most of the nine officers, thirty-two men, twenty-eight armed guards, and two passengers on board began leaving the ship in three lifeboats. The armed guards and a few officers and men remained behind. At 1700 a third torpedo struck the ship on the starboard side near the #3 hold. This explosion blew off the hatch cover, threw cargo over the deck, and broke the ship's back. With bow and stern rising, and the ship sinking rapidly, the armed guards and remaining merchant crew jumped into the water and swam to three rafts. The *I-26* surfaced at 1715 and began shelling the ship until she was aflame. The *I-26* then turned its guns on the lifeboats and rafts and later rammed and capsized the #2 boat. The men in this boat jumped into the water and tried to avoid the gunfire. The submarine pulled beside the #1 boat and took four prisoners, including the master, before leaving. After eighty hours at sea the #4 lifeboat containing twenty-five survivors was sighted by the British SS *Samcalia*. The survivors were picked up and landed at Karachi, Pakistan. Sixteen days after the attack the British SS *Samuta* spotted the #1 boat with thirty-eight survivors and landed them at Cochin, India. The four prisoners survived the POW camp and were repatriated to the United States in 1945. Miraculously, in the hail of gunfire aimed at the lifeboats and rafts, only one armed guard died. One officer and two merchant seamen on watch below died when the torpedo hit the engine room.

NSS; WACR; WCSR; RWCS; AG; Rohwer, p. 275.

JARED INGERSOLL

D:	4-1-44	YB:	1942
T:	0412	Tn	7,191
Pos:	36.46 N / 01.44 E	Dr:	28 ft.
Ow:	WSA	C:	7,140 tons lend lease material
Op:	American West African Line	P:	steam
M:	Sigurd Dahl	S:	10.5
A:	1-5"; 1-3"; 8-20 mm		

On 10 March, the *Jared Ingersoll* sailed from Charleston, South Carolina, to Bizerte, Tunisia, in Convoy UGS-36. The ship proceeded in convoy station #93. Just after 0400 flares dropped from aircraft illuminated the merchantmen through the smoke screen laid down by the escorts. Within minutes a lookout spotted a torpedo's wake off the port side, and the torpedo struck the vessel in the #1 hold. The explosion started a fire among the oil drums in the #1 hold and damaged the hold's after bulkhead. The forward hold flooded rapidly, while the #2 hold flooded more slowly. The master ordered the ship abandoned fifteen minutes after the explosion. The ship's eight officers, thirty-two men, twenty-nine armed guards, and one passenger cleared the freighter in four lifeboats. The USS *Mills* (DE-383) and the British rescue tug *Mindful* (W-135) rescued all hands. At 0615, with the vessel still afire, the merchant crewmen then on the

The *Irénée Du Pont* had geared turbines and was built similarly to the U.S. Maritime Commission's C2 design. The *Irénée Du Pont* was sunk by the *U-600* while traveling in Convoy HX-229. The freighter is shown here in her neutral colors before America's entry into the war.

The Liberty ship *Richard Hovey*, shown here with a deck load of trucks and tanks. Brailed to the after mast are her torpedo streamers. Two torpedoes fired by the *I-26* traveled under her deployed torpedo streamers and sank her.

Mills reboarded the freighter to prepare her for towing. These men had to abandon the ship again at 0800 when the fire looked as if it would consume the vessel. At 0930 the *Mills* put her firefighting crew on board. With acetylene torches they burned holes in the deck to lead fire hoses into the #1 hold. The crew jettisoned her anchors to get the bow up. The *Mills* and *Mindful* took the vessel in tow and beached her off Algiers. In Algiers workers strengthened the forward bulkhead of the #2 hold, and after discharging her cargo, the vessel left on 18 May. All hands survived the attack.

NSS; WACR; WCSR; AG. The NSS relates that the *Talbot* also helped with the tow. The British vessel by this name had been changed to the *Medway II* in 1943, confusing the issue. Lenton, Colledge, p. 308.

CHARLES PIEZ

D: 4-11-44   YB: 1943
T: 2335   Tn 7,171
Pos: 37.10 N / 03.45 E   Dr: 27 ft. 11 in.
Ow: WSA   C: 6,000 tons ammunition
Op: Duchman Wright & Pugh   P: steam
M: Philip Moore   S: 8.5
A: 1-5"; 1-3"; 8-20 mm

The Liberty ship *Charles Piez* sailed from Hampton Roads, Virginia, to Naples, Italy, in convoy. As the formation of ships steamed through the Mediterranean Sea, fourteen bombers and torpedo planes attacked the convoy. The vessel managed to avoid damage from bombs but suffered negligible damage over the entire length of the ship from the strafing runs of the aircraft. The nine officers, thirty-five men, twenty-eight armed guards, and one passenger on board suffered no injuries in the attack. On 15 April, the freighter safely arrived in Augusta, Italy.

WACR; AG; TF; ONF.

HORACE H. LURTON

D: 4-12-44   YB: 1943
T: 2330   Tn 7,176
Pos: west of Algiers   Dr: 23 ft.
Ow: WSA   C: general Army cargo and troops
Op: Cosmopolitan Shipping Co.   P: steam
M: Alton M. Bowen   S: 9
A: 1-4"; 1-3"; 8-20 mm

On 10 April, the *Horace H. Lurton* sailed with a large convoy from Oran, Algeria, to Naples, Italy. Just as the complement of eight officers, thirty-six men, and twenty-eight armed guards went to their battle stations, a shell from an Allied ship struck the freighter on the bridge. The explosion injured five men but only slightly damaged the ship. A doctor from the USS *Breckenridge* (DD-148) came on board the Liberty ship to treat the wounded. The *Lurton* continued with the convoy to Naples.

WACR; AG; ONF.

PAN PENNSYLVANIA

D:	4-16-44	YB:	1943
T:	0805	Tn	10,017
Pos:	40.05 N / 69.40 W	Dr:	31 ft. 3 in.
Ow:	National Bulkcarriers Inc.	C:	140,000 bbls. gasoline and
Op:	WSA		airplanes
M:	Delmar Melum Leidy	P:	steam
A:	1-5"; 1-3"; 8-20 mm	S:	13

On 15 April, the *Pan Pennsylvania* sailed from New York en route to the United Kingdom in the thirty-ship Convoy CU-1. The commodore signaled for the convoy to form 150 miles east of Ambrose Light, and the tanker steamed to station #72 (second ship in the port column). The *U-550* took advantage of the momentary confusion and put a torpedo into the *Pan Pennsylvania*'s port side #8 tank. The explosion blew a large hole in the side of the ship, ruptured the #7 tank, and disabled the steering gear. The vessel immediately listed to port about 30°. The master sounded the general alarm and tried unsuccessfully to communicate with the engine room to stop the engines. Some of the ship's nine officers, forty-one men, and thirty-one armed guards panicked and tried to launch the #1 and #3 lifeboats with the tanker still making thirteen knots. The master halted those at the #1 boat, but the #3 boat capsized when it touched the water, throwing all the men into the sea. After ascertaining the damage and finding gas in the bilges on fire, the master blew the torpedo warning on the ship's whistle and put the engines in reverse. At 0820 with the ship nearly dead in the water, the remaining crew began to abandon ship. Only two usable lifeboats remained, and the crew launched these and three rafts. The USS *Joyce* (DE-317) and USS *Peterson* (DE-152) rescued the survivors and landed them in Londonderry. Ten armed guards, two officers, and thirteen men died in the attack. Three of these men were crushed trying to launch the #2 boat on the weather side, and some drowned after jumping overboard. The greatest number died while attempting to launch the #3 boat. The ship later capsized, and two days later Allied planes sank her at 40.24 N / 69.37 W.

The escorts successfully brought the *U-550* to the surface and sank her. Eleven Germans survived. NSS; WACR; WCSR; AG; Rohwer, p. 180, places the attack at 40.07 N / 69.24 W; *War Action Casualties*, p. 172.

MEYER LONDON

D:	4-16-44	YB:	1944
T:	1826	Tn	7,210
Pos:	32.51 N / 23.00 E	Dr:	25 ft. 6 in.
Ow:	WSA	C:	7,800 tons general military
Op:	T. J. Stevenson & Co.		stores, aircraft
M:	Fred Harry Rylander	P:	steam
A:	1-5"; 1-3"; 8-20 mm	S:	8.5

On 24 March, the *Meyer London* departed Norfolk for Abadan, Iran, in Convoy UGS-37. The ship proceeded in convoy station #12. About seventeen miles off Derna, Libya, the *U-407* (Korndörfer) fired a torpedo that struck the port side at the #5 hatch below the after magazine. The explosion blew a large column of oil and water over the stern, demolished the aft gun crew quarters, blew off the rudder and the screw, and left the fantail drooping 15°. With no rudder, the ship went out of control. The *U-407* also torpedoed the *Thomas G. Masaryk* a minute later and the two vessels nearly collided, missing by only twenty feet. The eight officers, thirty-seven men, and twenty-seven armed guards left the ship in four lifeboats. The British corvette *La Malouine* (K-46) rescued all hands an hour later and landed them in Alexandria, Egypt. The *Meyer London* sank by the stern at 1935.

NSS; WACR; WCSR; USMMA; AG; Rohwer, p. 256.

THOMAS G. MASARYK

D:	4-16-44	YB:	1943
T:	1827	Tn	7,176
Pos:	32.51 N / 23.00 E	Dr:	24 ft.
Ow:	WSA	C:	5,000 tons drummed acetone,
Op:	Seas Shipping Co.		planes, general
M:	Robert Harrison Sloan	P:	steam
A:	2-3"; 8-20 mm	S:	9

On 21 March, the *Thomas G. Masaryk* sailed from New York to the Persian Gulf in Convoy UGS-37 and maintained convoy station #23. At 1825 the *U-407* (Korndörfer) fired a torpedo that struck the *Meyer London*, steaming in convoy station #12. A minute later the *U-407* struck the *Masaryk* with a torpedo on the port side at the #3 hatch, blowing a hole twenty-six feet in the side. This hold, loaded with drums of acetone, caught fire immediately. Flames shot over the bridge and ignited the 20-mm magazine, causing the ammunition to explode in all directions. The flames drove everyone from the bridge, and the orders to abandon ship were passed before the damage to the machinery could be determined. The ship began to circle to starboard out of control and missed the

Meyer London by only twenty feet. The complement of eight officers, thirty-five men, and twenty-seven armed guards left in one lifeboat and three rafts. An escort vessel rescued all hands and landed them in Alexandria, Egypt. The rescue tug HMS *Captive* (W-148) towed the freighter into Maneloa Bay, Libya, and beached her in water twenty-eight feet deep, still afire. In order to extinquish the fire, the escort vessel shelled the vessel and sank her. Salvors eventually saved about 50 percent of the cargo, but the WSA declared the ship a CTL.

NSS; WACR; WCSR; AG; Rohwer, p. 256.

JAMES GUTHRIE

D:	4-17-44	YB:	1942
T:	1030	Tn:	7,191
Pos:	40.34.10 N / 14.16.50 E	Dr:	27 ft. 9 in.
Ow:	WSA	C:	1,700 tons sand ballast
Op:	Agwilines Inc.	P:	steam
M:	Grady Lee Robertson	S:	6
A:	2-3"; 8-20 mm		

On 17 April, the *James Guthrie* departed from Naples, Italy, en route to the United States, traveling in Convoy NV-33. The convoy had just formed up north of the Isle of Capri with the *Guthrie* steaming in station #64. The Liberty ship struck an Allied mine on the port side between the #2 and #3 holds, and both holds flooded rapidly. Fifteen minutes later a second explosion occurred aft at the #5 hold. The blasts blew sand and fuel oil on the deck and broke steam lines. The #5 hold and the engine room flooded immediately, and the ship went dead in the water. The master blew the ship's whistle to give the signal to abandon ship, but the whistle jammed for several minutes, making it difficult to pass any orders. The eight officers, thirty-four men, twenty-eight armed guards, and one passenger on board abandoned the ship in three lifeboats after the second explosion. The port command harbor craft *Charles McIver* picked up the survivors and transferred them to a British corvette, which took them to Naples. At 1330 the USS *Weight* (ARS-35) began towing the vessel to Naples and beached her in forty-two feet of water. The WSA later declared the vessel a CTL. All hands survived the incident.

The *Guthrie* had also suffered considerable damage while anchored in Naples. See entry for 3-17-43. NSS; WACR; AG; Sawyer, Mitchell, p. 135.

ALEXANDER GRAHAM BELL

D:	4-17-44	YB:	1942
T:	1047	Tn	7,160
Pos:	40.34.15 N / 14.17.20 E	Dr:	13 ft. 6 in.
Ow:	WSA	C:	150 tons sand ballast
Op:	Weyerhaeuser SS Co.	P:	steam
M:	George N. Axiotes	S:	8.5
A:	3-3"; 8-20 mm		

On 17 April, the Liberty ship *Alexander Graham Bell* sailed from Naples, Italy, in Convoy NV-33 en route to the United States. As the convoy began to form, the *Bell* steamed to convoy station #24 and struck an Allied mine at the #2 hold on the port side. The #2 hold flooded and the #1 hold also began to leak. The master had the engines secured, and the vessel drifted for nearly forty-five minutes until receiving orders from the convoy commodore to return to Naples. Most of the complement of eight officers, thirty-five men, and forty-two armed guards remained on board. Six men lowered the #2 boat, and after thirty minutes a harbor vessel picked these men up. The explosion injured two of the crew. The vessel returned to Naples for temporary repairs and departed on 7 July 1944.

NSS; WACR; WCSR; USMMA; AG.

JOHN STRAUB

D:	4-18-44	YB:	1943
T:	2358	Tn:	7,176
Pos:	54.15 N / 163.30 W	Dr:	27 ft. 8 in.
Ow:	WSA	C:	7,737 tons diesel oil, gasoline
Op:	Alaska SS Co.	P:	steam
M:	Axel Wilhelm Westerholm	S:	10.5
A:	2-3"; 8-20 mm		

On 12 April, the *John Straub* sailed independently from Seattle, Washington, for Attu via Dutch Harbor, Alaska. In smooth seas off Sanak Island in the Aleutians, the ship suffered a violent explosion on the port side at the machinery spaces. A whitish flame and a pillar of smoke engulfed the midships section. The Coast Guard attributed the explosion to a mine. The Liberty ship broke in two aft of the midships house. The forward half sank in one minute. The after section remained afloat for nearly sixteen hours. The seven officers, thirty-five men, twenty-seven armed guards, and one passenger had no time to launch any of the boats. Those that could, jumped into the water. Eight men managed to board the capsized #1 lifeboat. These men and six others taken from one raft and a float were the only men saved from the water. One man remained on the after end of the ship and climbed in the boat six hours later. The USAT *FP-41*

rescued all the survivors and took them to Cold Bay, Alaska. Six officers, thirty-four men, the passenger, and fourteen armed guards perished. The *Albuquerque* (PF-7) later found the stern half still afloat and sank it with her three-inch guns.

There were no Japanese submarines operating this far east in 1944. WACR; AG; *Washington Post*, 24 April 1944.

PAUL HAMILTON

D:	4-20-44	YB:	1942
T:	2111	Tn:	7,177
Pos:	36.55 N / 03.54 E	Dr:	24 ft. approx.
Ow:	WSA	C:	explosives, troops
Op:	Black Diamond SS Co.	P:	steam
M:	Robert Govett Winans	S:	9
A:	1-5"; 1-3"; 8-20 mm		

On 3 April, the *Paul Hamilton* sailed from Hampton Roads, Virginia, for Italy via Bizerte, Tunisia, in Convoy UGS-38. As the Liberty ship steamed in convoy station #66 or #76, German torpedo planes attacked the convoy. A torpedo struck the *Hamilton*, and she suffered a tremendous explosion as the cargo detonated. Flames from the blast reached almost 1,000 feet into the air. The remnants of the Liberty ship sank in thirty seconds. On board were 8 officers, 39 men, 29 armed guards, and 504 troops. None of these men survived the violent explosion.

WACR; WCSR; AG; NSS for *Stephen F. Austin*.

STEPHEN F. AUSTIN

D:	4-20-44	YB:	1942
T:	2105	Tn:	7,165
Pos:	37.02 N / 03.38 W	Dr:	27 ft. 6 in.
Ow:	WSA	C:	5,027 tons general, troops,
Op:	Lykes Bros. SS Co.		trucks, flat cars
M:	Ernest Ban	P:	steam
A:	1-5"; 1-3"; 8-20 mm	S:	9

On 3 April, the *Stephen F. Austin* sailed from Hampton Roads, Virginia, in the large Convoy UGS-38 en route to the Persian Gulf. The freighter traveled in convoy station #96, the last ship in the ninth column. Twenty miles east of Algiers, the *Paul Hamilton*, two or three columns over, began firing her guns and immediately exploded. With the whole sky lit from the *Hamilton*'s explosion, lookouts spotted a torpedo plane making a run on the *Austin*, and the master ordered hard right rudder. The torpedo passed twenty feet under the

stern. The ship suffered two other near misses before a torpedo struck the starboard side at the #2 hold. The explosion ripped a hole forty feet by thirty feet below the waterline. The ship immediately listed and began settling by the head. The watch below secured the engines, and the ship's eight officers, thirty-eight men, twenty-seven armed guards, and seventy-two troops began abandoning ship in four lifeboats. After ascertaining the freighter would not capsize, the master, the armed guards, the chief engineer, and the first assistant engineer reboarded the vessel. The rest of the crew boarded the Liberty ship an hour later. At daybreak, the rescue tug HMS *Hengist* (W-110) placed salvage officers on board. The ship steamed to Algiers under her own power and arrived the afternoon of the 21st. All hands survived the attack.

The ship's complement figures are contradictory within the sources. NSS; WACR; WCSR; AG.

JOHN ARMSTRONG

D:	4-21-44	YB:	1943
T:	1708	Tn:	7,196
Pos:	41.12 N / 12.32 E	Dr:	25 ft. 3 in.
Ow:	WSA	C:	100 empty drums and shell
Op:	Grace Line		casings
M:	George E. Strom	P:	steam
A:	1-5"; 1-3"; 8-20 mm	S:	7.5

On 21 April, the *John Armstrong* sailed from Anzio, to Naples, Italy, escorted by an LST and an LCI. During the journey, the Liberty ship struck a mine at the bow on the starboard side. Shortly thereafter, a second mine struck at the #1 hold on the port side. The explosions raised the ship out of the water, buckled the deck and sides, twisted the stern, and damaged the forward booms. The #2 hold flooded slowly, but the ship's pumps managed to keep ahead of the water. The ship had on board 9 officers, 33 men, 29 armed guards, and 154 port battalion stevedores. All the stevedores transferred to a British corvette and landed in Anzio. One armed guard died as a result of the explosion, and twelve more men reported injuries. The Liberty ship proceeded under her own power to Naples.

The NSS document refers to only one explosion. NSS; WACR; WCSR; AG.

GEORGE POPHAM

D: 4-22-44
T: 1542
Pos: 51.11.20 N / 01.48.40 E
Ow: WSA
Op: Luckenbach SS Co.
M: Einar Marsdahl
A: 2-3"; 8-20 mm

YB: 1943
Tn: 7,176
Dr: 26 ft. 10 in.
C: 8,200 general
P: steam
S: 7

The *George Popham* sailed from Methel, Scotland, to London, England, in Convoy FS-28. In clear weather and calm seas a mine exploded near the stern of the ship. Extensively damaged, the *Popham* managed to steam to the Thames River, exhibiting only a slight list. The blast caused no injuries among the complement of eight officers, thirty-four men, and twenty-nine armed guards. The *Popham* remained in London for three weeks for repairs and sailed on 27 May.

WACR; WCSR; AG; ONF.

WILLIAM S. THAYER

D: 4-30-44
T: 2005
Pos: 73.46 N / 19.10 E
Ow: WSA
Op: A. L. Burbank & Co.
M: Daniel A. Sperbeck
A: 1-5"; 1-3"; 8-20 mm

YB: 1943
Tn: 7,176
Dr: 20 in.
C: 950 tons sand ballast
P: steam
S: 10

On 28 April, the *William S. Thayer* sailed from Murmansk, USSR, en route to Loch Ewe, Scotland, in Convoy RA-59. The *U-711* (Lange) caught the convoy fifty miles south of Bear Island. The *Thayer* was struck by two torpedoes while in convoy station #33. The first torpedo struck the starboard side between the #1 and #2 hatches. A second torpedo struck at the #4 hatch, starboard side. The explosions broke the shaft, knocked out the engines, and split the ship across the #4 hatch and across the #1 hatch, causing the freighter to separate into three parts. The forward part listed to starboard and sank in about thirty seconds. The midships section sank in two minutes, and the after section floated for three hours. The 8 officers, 33 men, 28 armed guards, and 165 Russian naval passengers on board never had time to launch any boats owing to the rapid flooding and extreme list. Only six small square floats could be utilized. The Russians stayed on the ship's stern and a rescue ship took most of them off. All the other men jumped into the water and swam to the floats. The SS *Robert Eden* and the destroyer HMS *Whitehall* (I-94) picked up the survivors and landed them in Glasgow, Scotland. Six officers, seventeen men, seven armed guards, and twenty Russians died in the attack. Escorts later sank the after section with gunfire.

NSS; WACR; WCSR; RWCS; AG; Rohwer, p. 207, places the attack at 73.52 N / 18.26 E.

FRANCIS C. HARRINGTON

D:	6-7-44	YB:	1943
T:	0735	Tn:	7,176
Pos:	50.10 N / 00.40 W	Dr:	26 ft.
Ow:	WSA	C:	1,500 tons general, ammunition
Op:	International Freighting Corp.	P:	steam
M:	James Hassell	S:	4
A:	1-5"; 1-3"; 8-20 mm		

The *Francis C. Harrington* sailed from Newport, England, to Omaha Beach, France, in Convoy EMB-2. Within five miles of the beach the freighter struck two mines, one under the #5 hold and the second at the stern. The explosions caused extensive damage to the ship and flooded the shaft alley and the engine room. The crew made emergency repairs so that the cargo could be discharged and the troops disembarked. The *Harrington* returned to England under tow on 17 June. The ship had on board 8 officers, 35 men, 28 armed guards, and 515 troops. Six of the troops lost their lives in the explosion. There were no other deaths.

WACR; WCSR; AG; Moore, 355.

EZRA WESTON

D:	6-9-44	YB:	1943
T:	1330	Tn:	7,176
Pos:	off Normandy Beach	Dr:	21 ft.
Ow:	WSA	C:	general, vehicles, and 600 troops
Op:	International Freight Corp.	P:	steam
M:	Joseph Tatocka	S:	at anchor
A:	2-3"; 8-20 mm		

On 5 June, the *Ezra Weston* sailed from Cardiff, Wales, to the beachhead at Normandy, France. As the ship lay off the beachhead, three German shells struck the superstructure. The vessel caught fire and the crew quickly extinguished the blaze, limiting the damage. The ship had on board 8 officers, 34 men, 26 armed guards, and 600 troops. These men remained on the vessel.

The explosion and fire killed five and wounded eleven of the troops. She returned to Belfast, arriving on 8 August.

WACR; WCSR; AG; TF.

CHARLES MORGAN

D:	6-10-44	YB:	1943
T:	0400	Tn:	7,244
Pos:	Utah Beach, France	Dr:	19 ft.
Ow:	WSA	C:	1,700 tons sand ballast
Op:	United Fruit Co.	P:	steam
M:	William Adams	S:	at anchor
A:	2-3"; 8-20 mm		

On 6 June, the *Charles Morgan* sailed from Newport, South Wales, in Convoy EBM-3 and anchored about three-fourths mile off Utah Beach. The *Morgan* had completely discharged all of her Army cargo when a German dive bomber dropped a 500-pound bomb that struck the ship in the center of the #5 hatch. The explosion blew off the hatch covers and strong backs, buckled the deck, ruptured the bulkhead between the #4 and #5 holds, and fractured steam lines. A fire started immediately in the after two holds, but sea water and fire hoses extinguished the flames in five minutes. The vessel settled by the stern and touched bottom just as the crew extinguished the fire. The eight officers, thirty-seven men, twenty-seven armed guards, six passengers, and sixty-four men from the port battalion remained on the ship for nearly eight hours before leaving the ship at 1145. All the survivors transferred to the USS *Kiowa* (ATF-72). The master and eleven men reboarded the vessel at 1730 to attempt to salvage the ship, or to have her towed to form a breakwater with the aid of naval tugs. At 1700 the next day the effort to save the *Morgan* ended, and the crew abandoned the ship again. The ship was declared a derelict and later a CTL. The explosion killed seven of the Army stevedores and one merchant seaman.

NSS; WACR; WCSR; USMMA; AG.

TARLETON BROWN

D:	6-10-44	YB:	1943
T:	2400	Tn:	7,191
Pos:	Anzio Beachhead	Dr:	unknown
Ow:	WSA	C:	4,368 tons explosives, gasoline,
Op:	Mississippi SS Co.		troops
M:	Willy R. G. Blum	P:	steam
A:	1-4"; 3-3"; 8-20 mm	S:	at anchor

The *Tarleton Brown* sailed from Naples, Italy, to the Anzio beachhead. At midnight, while the vessel lay off the beach, enemy aircraft attacked the anchorage. The smoke screen laid by the small craft had blown clear of the *Brown*, exposing her to the attacking planes. Two bombs fell near the freighter, one off the port bow and one off the #1 hold. Both bombs sent fragments into the side of the ship, causing slight damage. The ship had on board 9 officers, 31 men, 44 armed guards, and 501 passengers. Four men reported slight injuries.

WACR; AG; TF; ONF.

LARK

D:	6-13-44	YB:	1922
T:	0230	Tn:	148
Pos:	42.54 N / 65.25 W	Dr:	14 ft. 6 in.
Ow:	O'Hara Vessels	C:	50 tons fish
Op:	O'Hara Vessels	P:	diesel
M:	James Abbott	S:	8
A:	unarmed		

On 5 June, the *Lark* sailed from Boston, Massachusetts, to La Havre Banks off Nova Scotia. After loading the holds with fish, the *Lark* began her return trip. A lookout spotted a vessel off the starboard quarter thirty-two miles from the Cape Sable Light. Ten minutes later the lookout identified it as a submarine. The *U-107* (Simmermacher) came up on the port quarter and at about 650 feet fired a warning shot over the vessel. The master immediately secured the engines. The crew of two officers and twenty-five men abandoned ship in five dories, with the exception of the master and the cook who remained behind. The U-boat began shooting at the vessel's rigging and her deck and hull. After running through the dories full of men, the submarine turned around and again raked the vessel with machine gun fire. The U-boat did not depart until daybreak. The master and the cook got the ship under way and at 0930 began picking up the dories. By 1030 the fishing vessel had rescued all hands.

NSS; WACR; WCSR; Rohwer, p. 181.

CYRUS H. K. CURTIS

D:	6-22-44	YB:	1943
T:	1145	Tn:	7,176
Pos:	off Sword Beach, France	Dr:	18 ft. 6 in.
Ow:	WSA	C:	2,500 tons general cargo and
Op:	American Export Lines, Inc.		troops
M:	Thomas A. McGirr	P:	steam
A:	1-4"; 1-3"; 8-20 mm	S:	at anchor

The *Cyrus H. K. Curtis* sailed from Southend, United Kingdom, to Normandy. As the *Curtis* anchored off Sword Beach, a mine exploded off the port side at the #5 hold. The explosion caused slight damage to the ship, and the crew continued discharging the cargo. With 1,500 tons of ballast the vessel steamed from Sword Beach to Juno Beach and anchored. On 25 June, at 0430, a second mine exploded off the port quarter and damaged the ship, again only slightly. None of the 8 officers, 35 men, 27 armed guards, and 350 American troops on board were injured in either of the explosions.

WACR; AG; ONF.

CHARLES W. ELIOT

D:	6-28-44	YB:	1943
T:	0750	Tn:	7,176
Pos:	4 mi. off Juno Beach, France	Dr:	19 ft.
Ow:	WSA	C:	1,800 tons sand and shale ballast
Op:	Sprague SS Co.	P:	steam
M:	Walter O'Brien	S:	4
A:	2-3"; 8-20 mm		

The *Charles W. Eliot* sailed to Juno Beach and arrived off Normandy, France, on the 26th. The vessel discharged all cargo and troops by the following day. The freighter had just begun to shift into convoy formation, and five vessels preceded the *Eliot* in line ahead. A mine struck the vessel at the after end of the #3 hold, and the explosion lifted the vessel out of the water. Three seconds later a second mine exploded under the stern. The first mine cracked open hull plates from the bulwark to the waterline on both sides of the ship. The second explosion broke the shaft, ignited the after magazine, and blew the hatch covers and beams off the #4 and #5 holds. The hatch beams, sand, and water flew 350 feet into the air. The vessel broke in two just aft of the #3 hatch, and holds #3, #4, and #5 filled with water. The master ordered all eight officers, thirty-four men, thirty-one armed guards, and one passenger to abandon ship. A first aid boat came alongside the vessel and took the most seriously wounded ashore. Using three lifeboats, all the remaining crew left the Liberty ship. Two British motor boats later picked up these men and transferred them to the SS *George W. Woodward*. They later went on board the LCT-527 and landed in Gosport, England, on 29 June. Salvage tugs towed the vessel to deeper water, but the stern settled on the bottom and she was declared a CTL. German bombers later attacked the floating part of the bow and sent her to the bottom. Four men reported injuries, but all hands survived.

NSS; WACR; WCSR; AG; Sawyer, Mitchell, p. 99.

EDWARD M. HOUSE

D:	6-29-44	YB:	1943
T:	1530	Tn:	7,240
Pos:	50.07 N / 00.47 W	Dr:	19 ft.
Ow:	WSA	C:	1,000 tons Army equipment and
Op:	A. L. Burbank Co. Ltd.		troops
M:	Austin Stuart Fithian	P:	steam
A:	2-3"; 8-20 mm	S:	2

On 29 June, the *Edward M. House* sailed from Southampton, England, to Utah Beach, Normandy, France, via Omaha Beach. The *House* proceeded as the third or fourth ship in the port column of Convoy EMC-17. The *U-984* (Sieder) attacked the convoy thirty miles south of the Isle of Wight. A single torpedo struck the cargo ship under the stern. The explosion threw up a column of water several hundred feet in the air, stove in the forepeak, flooded the #1 port and starboard deep tanks, and buckled the shell plating and the collision bulkhead. The master stopped the engines briefly and then continued in the convoy. The ship had on board 9 officers, 33 men, 28 armed guards, and 587 troops. The explosion only injured one armed guard and one crewman. The Liberty ship discharged her troops and equipment at the Normandy beachhead. The ship returned to the United Kingdom on 1 July, and received repairs at Newcastle-on-Tyne beginning on 9 July. With repairs complete on 31 October, the vessel sailed to New York.

NSS; WACR; WCSR; AG; Rohwer, p. 182.

H. G. BLASDEL

D:	6-29-44	YB:	1943
T:	1538	Tn:	7,176
Pos:	50.07 N / 00.47 W	Dr:	unknown
Ow:	WSA	C:	vehicles, troops
Op:	American President Lines, Inc.	P:	steam
M:	Roman J. Wank	S:	7.5
A:	2-3"; 8-20 mm		

The *H. G. Blasdel* sailed from Southampton on 29 June in Convoy EMC-17 en route to Utah Beach, Normandy. The *Blasdel* steamed in convoy station #12. Thirty miles south of St. Catherine Point, the *U-984* (Sieder) attacked the convoy. The U-boat fired a spread of two torpedoes—one hit the *Edward M. House* and the second struck the *Blasdel* on the port side at the #5 hold. The explosion extensively damaged the interior of the vessel. The entire stern section sagged, leaving the after gun platform laying partially submerged. The ship did not answer the helm, and the watch below secured the engines. The #5 hold and shaft alley immediately flooded, and the engine room filled with water until the top of the cylinders lay submerged. The gasoline in the jeep and command cars stowed in the #5 hold caught fire, and firefighting parties from the crew extinguished the fire. The crew anchored the vessel to keep her from drifting into a minefield and to await tugs. On board at the time of the attack were 8 officers, 36 men, 28 armed guards, and 436 troops. The explosion killed 76 of the troops and wounded 180 others. All of the merchant crew and armed guards survived. At 1615 a British corvette came alongside to remove the wounded, and at 1630 a British buoy tender arrived to help with the injured. At 1700 the *LST-326* arrived alongside to take off the remaining troops. At 2300 as the *Blasdel's* stern threatened to break off, two tugs made fast to the Liberty ship and towed her to Southampton, England. The ship was declared a CTL.

NSS; WCSR; USMMA; AG; Rohwer, p. 182.

JOHN A. TREUTLEN

D:	6-29-44	YB:	1944
T:	1530	Tn:	7,176
Pos:	50.11.50 N / 00.45.35 W	Dr:	27 ft.
Ow:	WSA	C:	6,800 tons engineering
Op:	S. Atlantic & Savannah SS Co.		equipment, machinery
M:	Gustave Anderson	P:	steam
A:	1-5"; 1-3"; 8-20 mm	S:	9

On 28 June, the *John A. Treutlen* departed Falmouth, England, to join Convoy EMC-17 bound for the Normandy beachhead. As the convoy formed thirty miles off the Isle of Wight, the *U-984* (Sieder) struck the freighter on the port side with a single torpedo. The torpedo hit the ship between the #5 hold and the after peak tank and blew a huge hole in the side of the ship. The explosion forced its way forward and is thought to have set off the after magazine. This second explosion blew another huge hole in the port side. The initial explosion lifted the vessel's stern out of the water, and flames and water shot into the air. The blast broke the shaft, wrecked the steering gear, and cracked the vessel athwartships, leaving the stern hanging several feet lower. The master ordered most of the complement of eight officers, thirty-five men, and thirty-one armed

guards off the ship. Three boats cleared the ship while a skeleton crew of twelve men and the master remained on board. The Canadian corvette *Buctouche* (K-179) and the *LST-336* picked up the men in the boats and took them to Southampton. At 0930 the tug *WSA-2* arrived and took the vessel in tow. Salvors saved the cargo, but the ship was declared a CTL. The explosion injured nine armed guards and one of the merchant crew, but all hands survived the attack.

The figures for the ship's crew are widely contradictory. The Armed Guard Report also lists two British passengers. NSS; WACR; WCSR; Rohwer, p. 182.

JAMES A. FARRELL

D:	6-29-44	YB:	1943
T:	1540	Tn:	7,176
Pos:	50.07 N / 00.47 W	Dr:	29 ft.
Ow:	WSA	C:	1,200 tons Army vehicles and
Op:	American South African Line		troops
M:	Michael E. Martin	P:	steam
A:	1-5"; 1-3"; 8-20 mm	S:	8

The *James A. Farrell* became the fourth victim of the *U-984* (Sieder) while en route from Southampton, England, to Omaha Beach, Normandy. As the *Farrell* steamed in Convoy EMC-17 in the port column, the *U-984* torpedoed the vessel ahead of her. The Liberty ship took a 40° turn to avoid the vessel, and moments later a torpedo struck the *Farrell* just forward of the stern post on the starboard side. The explosion threw water mast high, tore a large hole in the hull plating, blew off the propeller and stern tube, blew off the #5 hatch cover, and buckled the main deck. The #3, #4, and #5 holds flooded, and the watch below secured the engines as the vessel slowly settled by the stern. The ship's 8 officers, 34 men, 31 armed guards, and 421 troops all went directly on board the *LST-50* standing by to port. The LST landed all the survivors at Portland, United Kingdom. Four soldiers died in the #5 hold, and forty-five more were injured when the hatch cover and beams collapsed into the hold. A British tug towed the vessel to Spithead, and she arrived there on 30 June. The ship was declared a CTL and scrapped in place.

The casualty figures are contradictory within the sources. NSS; WACR; WCSR; AG; Rohwer, p.182.

JEAN NICOLET

D:	7-2-44	YB:	1943
T:	1907	Tn:	7,176
Pos:	03.00 S / 74.30 E	Dr:	23 ft. 2 in.
Ow:	WSA	C:	7,000 tons Army cargo, trucks,
Op:	Oliver J. Olsen SS Co.		steel, landing barges
M:	David Martin Nilsson	P:	steam
A:	2-3"; 8-20 mm	S:	10.5

On 12 May, the *Jean Nicolet* sailed independently from San Pedro, California, to Colombo, Ceylon, via Fremantle, Australia. The cargo ship departed Fremantle on 21 June. South southwest of Ceylon, the *I-8* (Ariizumi) fired two torpedoes, both striking at the #3 hold, starboard side. The ship immediately listed 30° to starboard, and the watch below secured the engines and the fires. The master issued orders to abandon ship less than fifteen minutes after the explosions. The ship's eight officers, thirty-three men, twenty-eight armed guards, and thirty (twelve civilians, eighteen Army) passengers began abandoning the ship in four lifeboats and two rafts. Forty-five minutes after the torpedoes struck, the *I-8* surfaced and began randomly shelling the ship from 2,000 yards. The submarine fired twelve rounds at the freighter, setting her on fire, and she sank the following morning. The Japanese ordered most of the survivors on board the submarine. The Japanese searched the men, tied their hands behind their backs, beat and questioned some, and made others run through a gauntlet. They shot at least one man. As the crew was brutalized, the Japanese gun crews riddled the lifeboats with machine gun fire. Finally the *I-8* submerged with the men still on deck and their hands tied. Fortunately, some men escaped and swam back to the burning vessel and launched life floats. The next day, at 1330, a Catalina dropped some life preservers, a raft, and food rations. On 4 July, at 1100 the Royal Indian naval trawler *Hoxa* (T-16) rescued ten armed guards, one officer, nine men, and three passengers on this raft and took them to the Maldive Islands. The Japanese took Captain Nilsson, the radio operator, and a civilian passenger as prisoners. The civilian Frank O'Gara is the only one among the three who survived the internment.

NSS; WACR; WCSR; RWCS; Rohwer, p. 275, places the attack at 03.28 S / 74.30 E; Riesenberg, pp. 259-62.

KITTANNING

D:	7-4-44	YB:	1943
T:	0935	Tn:	10,195
Pos:	09.50 N / 79.40 W	Dr:	24 ft.
Ow:	Paco Tankers Inc.	C:	water ballast
Op:	Keystone Shipping Co.	P:	steam
M:	Raymond J. S. Chambers	S:	14.5
A:	1-5"; 1-3"; 8-20 mm		

On 4 July, the tanker *Kittanning* sailed from Cristobal, Canal Zone, to Aruba, NWI. The ship left port at about 0600, but the third assistant engineer fell and seriously injured himself and the master decided to return to Cristobal. The order to turn around had just been issued when the *U-539* (Lauterbach-Emden) torpedoed the tanker. Two torpedoes struck the starboard side, one in the #6 tank and the second in the #7 tank. The explosions left a hole sixty-five feet long and twenty feet high and flooded five tanks. The tanker swung hard right after the torpedoes struck, and she listed to starboard about 45°. The master ordered the ship abandoned at 1000. The complement of ten officers, thirty-nine men, and twenty-five armed guards cleared the ship in four lifeboats. Two of the boats swamped in the choppy seas and squally weather. The *U-539* put a coup de grâce shot into the port side at the #4 tank, but instead of sinking, the tanks flooded and the vessel righted herself. The USCG cutters *Marion* (WPC-145) and *Crawford* (WPC-134) arrived; the former picked up the survivors and landed them at Cristobal. With the ship righted and the cutters on the scene, the master and five men reboarded the vessel. The *Crawford* began towing the tanker, but when the tow line parted, the operations halted for the night. The next morning the Navy tug *Woodcock* (ATO-145) arrived and began towing the tanker. The *Woodcock*, however, suffered engine trouble and had to drop the tow. At 1800 the Panama Canal tug *Tavernilla* took the tanker in tow, and the Panama Canal tug *Cardenas* later arrived and rendered assistance. Finally the Maritime Commission tug *Jupiter Inlet* helped the ship moor at Cristobal, Canal Zone. All hands survived the attack.

One document mentions that the ship was under bareboat charter to WSA. NSS; WACR; WCSR; USMMA; AG; Rohwer, p. 182, places the attack at 09.55 N / 79.27 W; *War Action Casualties*, p. 175.

SEA PORPOISE

D: 7-5-44
T: 2115
Pos: 49.37 N / 00.51 W
Ow: WSA
Op: U.S. Lines
M: Nils Leknes
A: 1-4"; 4-3"; 8-20 mm

YB: 1943
Tn: 10,584
Dr: 22 ft. 4 in.
C: 1,400 tons ballast
P: steam
S: 8

On 5 July, the *Sea Porpoise* sailed from Utah Beach to Southampton, England, in convoy. The convoy formed into two columns, with the *Sea Porpoise* as the last ship in the starboard column. A torpedo fired from the *U-390* (Geissler) struck the vessel on the starboard side amidships. The explosion threw the shaft out of line, damaged the main turbine, and cracked some hull plating. The nine officers, eighty-one men, forty-five armed guards, and twenty-four passengers remained on the ship. The ship listed 10° to starboard because of flooding in the evaporator room. The master corrected the list by shifting fuel oil to tanks on the port side. At 0100 on the 6th, the freighter was taken in tow to the Omaha Beachhead and on the 9th was towed to Spithead, England. The *Sea Porpoise* received temporary repairs at New Castle-on-Tyne. On 16 September, she left under tow in a slow convoy for the United States and after further repairs returned to service in May 1945. The explosion injured twelve men but caused no deaths.

It is possible that the ship was damaged by a mine. However, the *U-390* was in the area and claimed two ships. NSS; WACR; WCSR; USMMA; AG; Rohwer, p. 183; The ship's complement figures are contradictory.

ESSO HARRISBURG

D: 7-6-44
T: 1930
Pos: 13.56 N / 70.59 W
Ow: Standard Oil Co. of N. J.
Op: WSA
M: Ernest C. Kelson
A: 1-4", 1-3"; 8-20 mm

YB: 1942
Tn: 9,670
Dr: 30 ft. 11 in.
C: 110,000 bbls. crude oil
P: steam
S: 13.5

On 5 July, the *Esso Harrisburg* sailed from Cartagena, Colombia, to New York. The ship had just stopped her zigzag course when a lookout spotted a torpedo fired by the *U-516* (Tillessen). The lookout notified the bridge, and the master ordered the helmsman to put the helm over hard left. The tanker managed to turn 90° when the acoustic torpedo struck under the stern. The blast demolished the four-inch gun and damaged the rudder and screw. The ship lost headway and began to settle slightly by the stern. Ten minutes after the explosion, the master had one long blast sounded on the ship's whistle—the signal to lower the boats. The complement of eight officers, thirty-six men, and twenty-eight armed guards began lowering four boats and tripped two rafts in the heavy seas. Most of the men got away before a second torpedo struck the tanker at 1940. This torpedo hit in the cross bunkers on the starboard side, aft of the #8 tank. At 1955 a third torpedo struck the #6 tank on the starboard side. The vessel sank by the stern within one minute after the last torpedo exploded. At dawn the #1, #2, and #3 lifeboats gathered and evenly distributed the survivors. The #4 boat had drifted out of sight. On 8 July, the USS *SC-1299* picked up five survivors on a raft and an hour later thirteen more in the #4 boat. The same day, the Netherlands escort vessel *Queen Wilhelmina* rescued thirty-one survivors in the #1 and #3 boats. The #2 boat with fifteen men made landfall five days later in Colombia. A Navy blimp landed the next day and took the men to Barranquilla, Colombia. The master, three men, and four armed guards died in the attack.

NSS; WACR; WCSR; USMMA; AGG; Rohwer, p. 183, puts the attack at 13.26 N / 72.11 W; *Ships of the Esso Fleet*, pp. 506-10; *War Action Casualties*, p. 176.

WILLIAM GASTON

D:	7-23-44	YB:	1942
T:	2230	Tn:	7,177
Pos:	26.37 S / 46.13 W	Dr:	27 ft. 4 in.
Ow:	WSA	C:	9,038 tons corn
Op:	American West African Line	P:	steam
M:	Harry W. Chase	S:	10
A:	1-5"; 1-3"; 8-30 cal.		

On 19 July, the *William Gaston* sailed independently from Buenos Aires for Baltimore, Maryland. In heavy seas, the *U-861* (Mahrholz) fired a torpedo that struck the starboard side between the #4 and #5 holds. The explosion blew through the port side, knocked off the #5 hatch cover, ruptured steam lines, and blasted corn all over the deck. About fifteen minutes later a second torpedo hit just forward of the stern post. This caused the ship to roll over and sink stern first about three minutes later. The complement of eight officers, thirty-three men, and twenty-six armed guards had begun to abandon ship when the second torpedo struck. Heavy seas destroyed the #1 boat as it went into the water. The crew successfully launched the other three boats and a raft. A plane later spotted some wreckage and the boats, and at 2000 on 25 July, the seaplane tender USS *Matagorda* (AVP-22) rescued the survivors, saving all hands. They landed in Florianopolis, Brazil, the same day.

NSS; WACR; WCSR; AG; Rohwer, p. 183, places the attack at 26.42 S / 46.12 W.

ROBIN GOODFELLOW

D:	7-25-44	YB:	1920
T:	0212 (GWT)	Tn:	6,885
Pos:	20.03 S / 14.21 W	Dr:	31 ft.
Ow:	Seas Shipping Co.	C:	8,602 tons chrome ore
Op:	WSA	P:	steam
M:	Bjarne Bjornsgaard	S:	unknown
A:	1-4"; 1-3"; 5-20 mm		

On 16 July, the *Robin Goodfellow* sailed from Cape Town, South Africa, to New York. The *U-862* (Timm) torpedoed the ship. The steamer *Priam* received the distress signal, but none of the crew of eight officers, thirty-three men, and twenty-seven armed guards survived the attack.

The *U-862* was lost on patrol and never filed a written report of the incident. WACR; WCSR; AG; TF; Rohwer, p. 184.

DAVID STARR JORDAN

D:	7-25-44	YB:	1943
T:	0120	Tn:	7,176
Pos:	Utah Beach, France	Dr:	19 ft. 8 in.
Ow:	WSA	C:	250 tons vehicles, troops
Op:	General Steamship Corp.	P:	steam
M:	Jacob Bernhard Wihlborg	S:	anchored
A:	2-3"; 8-20 mm		

The *David Starr Jordan* sailed from Southampton, England, to Utah Beach, France. In overcast skies, while the vessel was anchored off the beach, high level enemy bombers attacked the anchorage. The vessel was bombed and strafed and suffered damage from several near misses. Numerous hits over the length of the ship, however, left her only slightly damaged. The ship's complement was nine officers, thirty-four men, and twenty-six armed guards. In addition, the ship had on board 500 U.S. troops. The bombs killed two soldiers and wounded thirteen other men.

WACR; AG; ONF.

EXMOUTH

D:	7-31-44	YB:	1919
T:	0715	Tn:	4,979
Pos:	56.33 N / 01.38 W	Dr:	20 ft.
Ow:	American Export Lines	C:	1,500 tons slag ballast
Op:	WSA	P:	steam
M:	James J. Casey	S:	10.2
A:	1-4"; 1-3"; 8-20 mm		

On 29 July, the *Exmouth* sailed from Hull, England, to Loch Ewe, Scotland. She joined a northbound convoy for a while and then proceeded independently. In dense fog, about sixty miles off the coast of Scotland, the ship struck two mines. The first hit at the #1 hold on the starboard side, and a minute later a second mine struck the #2 hold, port side. The #1 hold filled quickly, and the freighter began to settle by the head. The second explosion broke the "Hog Islander" in two, forward of the bridge. The complement of eight officers, thirty-five men, and twenty-seven armed guards abandoned ship in four lifeboats as the foredeck settled beneath the water. The vessel sank at 0820. The boats remained in the vicinity, and the fog lifted at 1030. At 2120 the Royal Air Force rescue launch #2731 saved all hands and landed them at Dundee, Scotland, at 2300.

WACR; WCSR; AG; RWSA.

EXTAVIA

D:	8-1-44	YB:	1941
T:	1117	Tn:	6,551
Pos:	Solomon Islands	Dr:	23 ft.
Ow:	American Export Lines Inc.	C:	400 tons general and troops
Op:	American Export Lines Inc.	P:	steam
M:	Wenzel Habel	S:	17
A:	1-4"; 4-3"; 8-20 mm		

The *Extavia* sailed from New Georgia Island en route to the Treasury Islands. During the trip an explosion occurred near the stern but damaged the *Extavia* only slightly. The vessel proceeded under her own power to her destination. None of the ship's complement of 9 officers, 64 men, 81 armed guards, and 845 troops were killed or injured.

WACR; AG; ONF.

WILLIAM L. MARCY

D: 8-7-44   YB: 1943
T: 0445   Tn: 7,176
Pos: 49.23.42 N / 00.26.36 W   Dr: 18 ft.
Ow: WSA   C: none
Op: American Hawaiian Lines   P: steam
M: Albert E. Bamforth   S: at anchor
A: 2-3"; 8-20 mm

The Liberty ship *William L. Marcy* anchored off Juno Beach awaiting a convoy to London. The ship had discharged all cargo and lay swinging at ebb tide. A torpedo, thought to have been launched by an E-boat, struck the ship and caused a shattering explosion on the starboard side at the #5 hatch. The blast created a hole thirty feet by thirty-eight feet in the side of the vessel. It also blew off the #5 hatch covers, blew holes in the deck, ripped a hole in the port side, and demolished all the quarters in the after part of the ship. The ship settled by the stern, and the master ordered the vessel abandoned. Most of the ship's eight officers, thirty-nine men, twenty-eight armed guards, and one passenger left in four lifeboats at about 0545. A landing craft towed the lifeboats to the Liberty ship *George W. Woodward.* Two tugs later towed the *William L. Marcy* to Falmouth, and she arrived on 17 August. On 21 August, she was towed to Swansea, Wales, put on a beach, and later declared a CTL. The only casualty was the death of the passenger.

One source mentions that another possible cause of the explosion was a human torpedo. NSS; WACR; WCSR; AG.

EZRA WESTON

D: 8-8-44   YB: 1943
T: 2127   Tn: 7,176
Pos: 50.42 N / 05.02 W   Dr: 28 ft. 3 in.
Ow: WSA   C: 5,800 tons Army cargo, trucks,
Op: International Freighting Corp.   acid, flour
M: Joseph Patoka   P: steam
A: 2-3"; 8-20 mm   S: 7

On 7 August, the *Ezra Weston* sailed in Convoy EBC-66 from Avonmouth, England, to Falmouth. The cargo ship proceeded in the starboard column third in line. The *U-667* (Lange) fired a torpedo that struck the port side at the #1 hold. The explosion lifted the ship out of the water, blew off the covers of the #1 and #2 hatches, and ruptured the hull on both sides. A column of water and deck cargo flew mast high. The ship flooded slowly, possibly due in part to the flour in the #1 hold, seen trailing on both sides of the ship. The master tried to beach the ship and for forty-five minutes steamed toward the coast of England seven miles away. At 2212 with the forecastle head awash the master ordered the engines secured. The vessel cracked forward of the bridge shortly after the explosion and had now broken nearly in two. The English LCT #24 came alongside and removed most of the nine officers, thirty-four men, twenty-six armed guards, and two Army passengers on board. The master, two mates, and the armed guard officers all left by a lifeboat five minutes later and went on board the French trawler *Jackues Morgand*. The Canadian corvette *Regina* (K-234) stood by the *Weston*, and the *U-667* put a torpedo into her, causing her to blow up and sink in thirty seconds. At 2322 the *Weston* broke in two and sank. All hands survived and landed in Padstow Bay, England.

NSS; WACR; WCSR; AG; Rohwer, p. 184, places the attack one minute farther west.

TARLETON BROWN

D:	8-15-44	YB:	1943
T:	2100	Tn:	7,191
Pos:	off St. Raphael, France	Dr:	unknown
Ow:	WSA	C:	Army rolling equipment
Op:	Mississippi SS Co.	P:	steam
M:	Willy R. G. Blum	S:	at anchor
A:	1-4"; 3-3"; 8-20 mm		

The *Tarleton Brown* sailed from Oran, Algeria, to St. Raphael, France, in convoy. While anchored, the vessels in the harbor were attacked by enemy aircraft. The freighter suffered damage from a near miss and also from a bomb that struck amidships on the superstructure. The damage to the vessel, however, was considered negligible. The ship had on board nine officers, thirty-one men, forty-four armed guards, and eighty-five passengers. Two officers and two of the merchant crew reported injuries.

WACR; AG.

ALBERT A. MICHELSON

D:	8-18-44	YB:	1943
T:	2120	Tn:	7,176
Pos:	St. Tropez	Dr:	16 ft. 8 in.
Ow:	WSA	C:	general cargo and troops
Op:	R. S. Nicol & Son	P:	steam
M:	Hans R. Bieneman	S:	at anchor
A:	2-3"; 8-20 mm		

On 12 June, the *Albert A. Michelson* sailed from Naples to St. Tropez, France, and anchored 500 yards offshore. During her stay the crew responded to

frequent air raids. On the 8th at 2055 the air raid alarm sounded as German aircraft began attacking the vessels. Shortly afterwards a small bomb hit the after part of the boat deck on the starboard side. Fortunately, the nearly seventy troops on board had disembarked minutes before the bomb struck. The explosion damaged two of the lifeboats and left a large dent in the deck. All nine officers, thirty-four men, twenty-seven armed guards, and one Army security officer survived the attack. The explosion, however, injured five of the crew. The Liberty ship sailed on the 19th leaving the five men in the hospital ashore.

WACR; WCSR.

LOUIS KOSSUTH

D:	8-23-44	YB:	1943
T:	1237	Tn:	7,176
Pos:	50.16 N / 01.41.30 W	Dr:	20 ft. 6 in.
Ow:	WSA	C:	vehicles and troops
Op:	A. H. Bull & Co. Inc.	P:	steam
M:	Carl Norman	S:	9
A:	1-5"; 1-3"; 8-20 mm		

The *Louis Kossuth* sailed from Southampton, England, to the Utah Beachhead. The *U-989* (Rodler von Roithberg) fired a torpedo that struck the vessel in the stern on the starboard side. The explosion caused extensive structural damage to the Liberty ship, but she did not sink. The 8 officers, 32 men, 28 armed guards, and 334 troops remained on the ship. The explosion injured thirteen of the troops. The British tug *Empire Winnie* towed the *Louis Kossuth* back to Cowes, England, the next day.

WACR; WCSR; AG; Rohwer, p. 184, places the attack at 50.14 N / 01.41 W.

JOHN BARRY

D:	8-28-44	YB:	1941
T:	2200	Tn:	7,172
Pos:	15.10 N / 55.18 E	Dr:	26 ft. 3 in.
Ow:	WSA	C:	8,200 tons general cargo and
Op:	Lykes Bros.		$26,000,000 in silver bullion
M:	Joseph Ellerwald	P:	steam
A:	1-4"; 1-3"; 8-20 mm	S:	12

On 26 August, the *John Barry* sailed from Aden to Ras at Tanura, Persian Gulf. The *Barry* had maintained a zigzagging course since leaving Aden, and the helmsman had just changed course when a torpedo fired from the *U-859*

(Jebsen) struck the ship on the starboard side between the #2 and #3 hatches. The forward portion of the ship immediately sank. The watch below secured the engines, and the crew began climbing into the lifeboats before the master ordered the ship abandoned. The explosion tossed the #3 lifeboat onto the after deck and blew the forward starboard boat overboard. The complement of ten officers, thirty-one men, and twenty-seven armed guards began launching the other two lifeboats and tripped three of the four rafts. The #2 lifeboat capsized while being launched and spilled the occupants into the water. Most of these men swam to the rafts and to the #4 boat. At 2230 the *U-859* put another torpedo into the engine room, causing the vessel to break in two and sink. The men remained in the swamped #2 boat during the night and bailed it out the next day. Within fourteen hours the Dutch SS *Sanetta* rescued the survivors on the two rafts and in the #4 boat and landed them at Aden. The SS *Benjamin Bourn* rescued the survivors in the #2 boat about the same time and landed them at Khorramshahr, Iran. The only men lost were the chief officer and a seaman who drowned when the #2 boat swamped.

The rescue accounts differ slightly within the sources. NSS; WACR; WCSR; AG; Rohwer, p. 276.

JACKSONVILLE

D:	8-30-44	YB:	1944
T:	1515	Tn:	10,448
Pos:	55.30 N / 07.30 W	Dr:	30 ft.
Ow:	WSA	C:	141,000 bbls. gasoline
Op:	Deconhil Shipping Co.	P:	steam
M:	Edgar Winter	S:	14
A:	1-5"; 1-3"; 8-20 mm		

On 19 August, the *Jacksonville* departed New York for Loch Ewe, Scotland, in Convoy CU-36. On 30 August, five ships split from the convoy to continue their course to Loch Ewe. The *Jacksonville* took station as the last ship in the single column breaking away from the formation. As the column completed its turn, the *U-482* (Graf von Matuschka) fired a torpedo that struck the tanker's starboard side at the #7 tank. The cargo of gas immediately ignited, and flames covered the ship from stem to stern and leapt 300 feet in the air in a matter of seconds. A second explosion broke the vessel in two. The complement of eight officers, forty-one men, and twenty-nine armed guards virtually had no chance to get off the ship, nor time to launch any of the lifeboats or life rafts. A few men escaped the ship, some with life preservers, only to die in the flames on the water's surface. Only one man from the gun crew and a fireman survived. The USS *Poole* (DE-151) rescued both of these men after they spent ninety minutes in the water. Both sections of the ship remained afloat. Escort vessels sank the

after section with depth charges and shellfire. The forward section sank fifteen hours later.

NSS; WACR; WCSR; AG; Rohwer, p. 185; *War Action Casualties*, p. 177.

GEORGE ADE

D:	9-12-44	YB:	1944
T:	0020	Tn:	7,171
Pos:	33.30 N / 75.40 W	Dr:	29 ft.
Ow:	WSA	C:	8,250 tons cotton, steel,
Op:	American-West African Lines		machinery
M:	Torlief C. Selness	P:	steam
A:	1-5"; 1-3"; 8-20 mm	S:	13.5

On 10 September, the *George Ade* sailed from Mobile, Alabama, to New York, via Key West, Florida. The Liberty ship proceeded on a nonevasive course during her journey. The *U-518* (Offermann) fired an acoustic homing torpedo that struck the ship on the starboard side near the rudder. The explosion threw a column of water twenty-five feet into the air, buckled the deck and the stern plating, demolished the steering engine, destroyed the rudder, broke steam lines, and flooded the shaft alley and the after peak tank. Minutes later, as the general quarters alarm sounded, another torpedo passed under the ship. The gun crew fired two shots from the five-inch gun at an object thought to be the submarine. The ship lay dead in the water with all her after compartments flooded. The watch below found that the blast had knocked the engines out of line enough to make them difficult to use. The complement of eight officers, thirty-three men, and twenty-seven armed guards did not abandon ship and tried to rig a jury rudder. The USS *Barton* (DD-722) contacted the ship, and at 1400 the USS *Escape* (ART-6) took the Liberty ship in tow. An approaching hurricane caused the tow line to break on 14 September, and the ship anchored in 100-knot winds and 50-foot seas. The tow was again resumed the next day. The ship entered the Chesapeake Bay on 16 September and arrived at Hampton Roads, Virginia. All hands survived the attack. The ship was later repaired and returned to service.

NSS; WACR; WCSR; AG; Rohwer, p. 185, mistakenly claims the ship sank.

ELIHU THOMPSON

D:	9-26-44	YB:	1942
T:	0830	Tn:	7,182
Pos:	22.22.10 S / 166.34 E	Dr:	16 ft.
Ow:	WSA	C:	2,000 tons general, explosives,
Op:	De La Rama SS Co.		troops
M:	Frank C. Waters	P:	steam
A:	1-4"; 1-3"; 8-20 mm	S:	11

The *Elihu Thompson* sailed from Efate, New Hebrides, to Nouméa, New Caledonia. On 26 September, the freighter ran into a minefield south of Porcupine Island, off Nouméa Harbor. Two mines struck the Liberty ship; one exploded on the port side at the #1 hold and the second on the same side at the #2 hold. The ship sank by the head as both compartments flooded. The 8 officers, 34 men, 33 armed guards, and 211 troops on board began abandoning ship within minutes after the initial explosion. They used four lifeboats, three rafts, and eighteen floats. The USS *Apache* (ATF-67) laid alongside to pick up survivors. After the vessel was beached, the crew reboarded her at 1900. The *Apache* towed the *Elihu Thompson* to Nouméa and put her stern on the beach. The cargo was later discharged and the water pumped out of the compartments. Crews worked to shore up bulkheads and plug holes so that she would be seaworthy to be towed for repairs. Thirty-two troops on board died from the explosion. The Coast Guard cancelled the master's license until a hearing could be held in the states. The *Thompson* sailed from Espíritu Santo on 4 January 1945.

WACR; WCSR; AG; *Apache* War Diary, NHC.

EDWARD H. CROCKETT

D:	9-29-44	YB:	1944
T:	1635	Tn:	7,176
Pos:	73.00 N / 24.32 E	Dr:	20 ft.
Ow:	WSA	C:	1,659 tons chrome ore
Op:	American Export Line Inc.	P:	steam
M:	Albert Baldi	S:	11
A:	1-5"; 1-3"; 8-20 mm		

On 26 September, the *Edward H. Crockett* sailed from Archangel, USSR, in Convoy RA-60 bound for Scotland. The cargo ship proceeded in convoy station #102. The *U-310* (Ley) fired a torpedo that struck the starboard side forward of the #4 hatch. The explosion broke the shaft, wrecked the engine, and damaged the hold's forward bulkhead. The master ordered the four lifeboats to be lowered while the men stood by their abandon ship stations. An hour later he ordered

three of the boats to the British rescue ship *Zamalek*. The remaining lifeboat took the master, the second and third mates, and the chief officer to the rescue ship. A British destroyer sank the *Crockett* with gunfire after the last boat left the ship's side. The complement consisted of eight officers, thirty-three men, and twenty-seven armed guards. The first assistant engineer died in the engine room and was the only casualty.

NSS; WACR; WCSR; AG; Rohwer, p. 209, places the attack at 72.59 N / 24.26 E.

CARL G. BARTH

D:	9-30-44	YB:	1944
T:	1844	Tn:	7,212
Pos:	at Morotai Island	Dr:	17 ft. 8 in.
Ow:	WSA	C:	3,000 tons general
Op:	Olympic SS Co.	P:	steam
M:	William R. Cleasby	S:	at anchor
A:	1-5"; 1-3"; 8-20 mm		

The *Carl G. Barth* was attacked by enemy aircraft while anchored off Morotai Island, Admiralty Group. The attacking aircraft strafed the Liberty ship, causing slight damage over the length of the vessel. The ship had on board 7 officers, 45 men, 26 armed guards, and 118 passengers. The attacking aircraft wounded six of the passengers.

WACR; AG; ONF.

JOHNS HOPKINS

D:	10-2-44	YB:	1943
T:	0150	Tn:	7,200
Pos:	43.16 N / 05.08.28 E	Dr:	21 ft. 6 in.
Ow:	WSA	C:	1,534 tons general, vehicles,
Op:	North Atlantic & Gulf SS Co.		troops
M:	Frank A. Middleton	P:	steam
A:	1-4"; 1-3"; 8-20 mm	S:	3.5

On 26 September, the *Johns Hopkins* sailed from Oran, Algeria, in convoy to Marseilles, France. She arrived three days later and received orders to proceed alone to Toulon, France. Before she could clear the harbor, a gale swept the area and the freighter began dragging her anchor. The master steered the ship in the middle of the cleared channel to wait until the weather moderated. During the move a mine struck the vessel in the settling tank between the #3 hold and the engine room. The Liberty ship took a 25° list as the #3 hold, and the engine room flooded. The shaft alley also began to fill with water and leaked into holds

#4 and #5. The engines were immediately secured, and the 7 officers, 34 men, 28 armed guards, and 466 U.S. and French troops on board swung the boats out in case they needed to be launched. Two hours after the explosion, several rescue vessels and the USS *Hobson* (DD-464) came to aid the stricken ship. Later the Navy rescue tug *ATR-127* towed the ship to Marseilles. At 0800 on 3 October, she arrived off the breakwater, and the troops and cargo were discharged. There were no casualties with the exception of a major who broke a leg when he fell into the #3 hold.

NSS; WACR; WCSR; AG.

ELINOR WYLIE

D:	10-6-44	YB:	1944
T:	1430	Tn:	7,207
Pos:	42.57.30 N / 05.49.30 E	Dr:	16 ft. 6 in.
Ow:	WSA	C:	none
Op:	McCormack SS Co.	P:	steam
M:	David Slater McDonald	S:	8
A:	2-3"; 8-20 mm		

The *Elinor Wylie* sailed from Marseille to Toulon, France. While en route the ship struck a mine at the #2 hold on the port side. The explosion caused a great deal of structural damage to the ship, but the complement of eight officers, thirty-two men, and twenty-nine armed guards remained on board. The *Wylie* was towed into Toulon Harbor and after she discharged her cargo, a Navy tug towed the ship to Oran, Algeria. After receiving further repairs and conversion at Pearl Harbor, the Navy took her over under a "bare boat" charter basis, renamed her *Triana* (IX-223), and used her as a floating storage ship.

WACR; WCSR; AG; TF; DANFS, 7:274.

GEORGE POPHAM

D:	10-6-44	YB:	1943
T:	1900	Tn:	7,176
Pos:	off Normandy Beachhead	Dr:	23 ft.
Ow:	WSA	C:	5,000 tons general
Op:	Luckenbach SS Co.	P:	steam
M:	Einar Marsdahl	S:	at anchor
A:	2-3"; 8-20 mm		

The *George Popham* sailed from New York to the Normandy beachhead. As the ship anchored in a gale, a mine struck her anchor chain. The ship was only slightly damaged, and none of the nine officers, thirty-three men, twenty-six armed guards, or seventy stevedores on board reported any injuries.

WACR; ONF.

AUGUSTUS THOMAS

D:	10-24-44	YB:	1943
T:	0840	Tn:	7,176
Pos:	San Pedro Bay, Leyte, PI	Dr:	22 ft. 3 in.
Ow:	WSA	C:	5,500 tons ammunition, general
Op:	Coastwise Line		military equipment, 1,000 bbls.
M:	Alfred A. Pedersen		gasoline and diesel oil
A:	2-3"; 8-20 mm	P:	steam
		S:	anchored

On 22 October, the *Augustus Thomas* entered San Pedro Bay, Leyte Gulf. The following day a Japanese bomber strafed the freighter and wounded one of the armed guards. On 24 October, the ship's general alarm sounded at 0545. Just under three hours later, Japanese aircraft attacked the ships in the harbor. At 0840 a Japanese bomber bore down on the ship abaft the beam. The armed guards on the *Augustus Thomas* set the plane on fire about one-half mile from the ship. The plane continued toward the ship, and one wing struck the stack of the USS *Sonoma* (AT0-12). Then it crashed on the starboard side of the *Thomas* just aft of amidships. The plane's bombs fell between the two ships and detonated. The exploding plane set the *Sonoma* on fire, and she began burning from stem to stern. The explosions also blew in the side of the *Augustus Thomas* and flooded the engine room and the #4 and #5 holds. The 7 officers, 34 men, 27 armed guards, and 480 U.S. troops on board all survived the attack. The *Thomas* was ordered beached, and on 3 November the Navy tugs USS *Chowanoc* (ATF-100) and USS *Whippoorwill* (ATO-169) towed her near the Polo River. Here they filled the forepeak storeroom and the chain locker with water to hold the vessel on the beach.

Another small antipersonnel bomb struck the ship on 17 November causing minimal damage. NSS; WCSR.

DAVID DUDLEY FIELD

D: 10-24-44	YB: 1943
T: 0900	Tn: 7,176
Pos: 1 1/2 mil off Tacloban, Leyte	Dr: 22 ft.
Ow: WSA	C: 4,500 tons gasoline, vehicles,
Op: Isthmian SS Co.	ammunition, troops
M: Albion M. Burbank	P: steam
A: 2-3"; 8-20 mm	S: at anchor

The *David Dudley Field* sailed from Hollandia, New Guinea, to Leyte, Philippine Islands. While the ship was anchored in San Pedro Bay, Japanese bombers attacked the anchorage. During the attack, a Japanese plane intentionally dove into the *Field*'s bridge amidships on the starboard side. The plane initially struck the #7 gun tub, which ripped off the plane's wing. The plane cartwheeled over the ship, taking off ventilators and starting a fire at the #6 gun tub. Firefighting parties brought the fire under control quickly. All nine officers, thirty-one men, thirty armed guards, fifty stevedores, and ten Army passengers remained on the ship. Only 4 of the 130 men on board reported injuries. The ship suffered extensive damage but after repairs went back in service.

See also the attack on 12 January 1945. WACR; AG; TF; ONF.

ADONIRAM JUDSON

D: 10-25-44	YB: 1943
T: 1250	Tn: 7,194
Pos: Tacloban, Leyte, PI	Dr: 15 ft. 1 in.
Ow: WSA	C: 1,400 tons general
Op: W. R. Chamberlin & Co.	P: steam
M: Charles A. Jarvis	S: at anchor
A: 2-3"; 8-20 mm	

The *Adoniram Judson* sailed from Finschhafen, New Guinea, to Leyte Island in the Philippines. While the freighter was en route, Japanese aircraft attacked. The armed guards on board maintained a murderous fire on the enemy aircraft and claimed six kills. One bomb struck the water just off the port side of the bow and sprayed the ship with shrapnel, causing slight structural damage. The ship had on board ten officers, thirty-three men, twenty-eight armed guards, and an undetermined number of stevedores. The shrapnel injured two of the stevedores and killed two other men on the dock.

WACR; AG; ONF.

JOHN W. FOSTER

D:	10-25-44	YB:	1943
T:	1815	Tn:	7,176
Pos:	San Pedro Bay, Leyte, PI	Dr:	21 ft. 4 in.
Ow:	WSA	C:	4,000 tons general, troops
Op:	Interocean SS Corp.	P:	steam
M:	James P. Hansen	S:	at anchor
A:	2-3"; 8-20 mm		

On 18 October, the *John W. Foster* sailed from Hollandia, New Guinea, to Leyte, Philippines. A Japanese plane attacked the *Foster* from the port beam as she lay at anchor in San Pedro Bay. After making this pass, the plane circled and made another pass, strafing the ship. The attack caused only slight damage over the entire length of the vessel. All 8 officers, 33 men, 27 armed guards, 30 stevedores, and 170 U.S. Army troops remained on board. The attacking planes wounded seven of the armed guards, three of the troops, and one officer.

WACR; AG; ONF.

BENJAMIN IDE WHEELER

D:	10-27-44	YB:	1942
T:	1000, 1845	Tn:	7,176
Pos:	Leyte Island, PI	Dr:	15 ft.
Ow:	WSA	C:	1,200 tons general, gasoline,
Op:	American-Hawaiian SS Co.		vehicles, troops
M:	Daniel J. Coughlin	P:	steam
A:	2-3"; 8-20 mm	S:	at anchor

On 18 October, the *Benjamin Ide Wheeler* departed Hollandia, New Guinea, for Leyte, Philippines, and anchored one-half mile offshore. On 26 October, a Japanese plane approached from the west with no warning and dropped at least two bombs that struck the water twenty feet off the port side amidships. The explosions sent water over the ship and drenched the gun crews. Shrapnel pierced the ship's hull all along the side, damaged the lifeboats and other gear, and wounded three Army passengers. The following day a flaming Japanese bomber appeared from four miles away and headed directly toward the ship. The armed guards kept up an intense fire and shot off the plane's wing, causing it to swerve and miss the bridge, striking instead the ship just above the waterline at the #5 hold. The plane and its bombs exploded on contact and ripped out a section 300 feet square off the side of the ship and made many smaller holes. The plane's engine continued through the hold and passed out the port side. Fire broke out immediately in the #5 hold, containing 400 barrels of gasoline. The crew fought the fire amid the exploding gasoline drums and

flooded the #4 hold to prevent the fire from spreading. Several smaller craft came to help fight the fire. At 0915, the USS *Cable* (ARS-19) came alongside, and using her foam equipment, she extinguished the fire just after midnight. Some of the 8 officers, 35 men, 27 armed guards, and 500 troops on board temporarily boarded the USS *Wasatch* (AGC-9). The ship slowly settled by the stern and eventually rested on the bottom. In this attack three of the troops reported injuries. One of the armed guards and a merchant crewman died. On 22 December, the ship moved to the inner harbor at Tacloban.

See also 17 November 1944. NSS; WACR; WCSR; AG.

CAPE ROMANO

D:	10-28-44	YB:	1942
T:	0415	Tn:	5,106
Pos:	Leyte Island, PI	Dr:	22 ft. 10 in.
Ow:	WSA	C:	none
Op:	Lykes Bros. SS Co.	P:	steam
M:	Edward Tomti	S:	at anchor
A:	1-4"; 1-3"; 8-20 mm		

On 10 September, the *Cape Romano* sailed from San Francisco, California, to San Pedro Bay, Leyte, Philippine Islands. The ship anchored 1,500 yards from the beach and discharged all her cargo. Japanese aircraft attacked the ships in the bay early in the morning, and during the attack three bombs fell near the freighter. One exploded 500 yards off the starboard quarter. A second bomb fell within twenty yards, and a third fell about seventy-five yards off the port bow. The shrapnel from the bombs put thirty-five holes and numerous gouges and dents on the port side from the bow to the #2 hatch. The starboard side suffered damage from the bow to the engine room. The bombs punctured forty holes in the superstructure, the deck, and the stack and also damaged the cargo gear. The ship had on board eleven officers, thirty-six men, twenty-six armed guards, and two passengers at the time of the attack. Shrapnel injured two of the armed guards and two of the crew.

NSS; WACR; WCSR; AG; TF.

UNITED VICTORY

D:	10-28-44	YB:	1944
T:	0440	Tn:	7,608
Pos:	07 N / 134.15 E	Dr:	27 ft.
Ow:	WSA	C:	1,800 tons ammunition
Op:	American President Lines	P:	steam
M:	J. E. Murphy	S:	2
A:	1-5"; 1-3"; 8-20 mm		

On 12 August, the *United Victory* sailed from Gray's Harbor, Washington, to Peleliu Island. Off Peleliu, Japanese surface craft strafed the vessel, causing only slight damage. There were no casualties to the ship's complement of 11 officers, 46 men, 27 armed guards, and 100 stevedores.

WACR; AG; TF; ONF.

JOHN A. JOHNSON

D:	10-29-44	YB:	1943
T:	2105	Tn:	7,176
Pos:	29.36.30 N / 141.43 W	Dr:	28 ft. 4 in.
Ow:	WSA	C:	7,000 tons provisions,
Op:	American Mail Lines, Ltd.		explosives, trucks
M:	Arnold Herman Beeken	P:	steam
A:	2-3"; 8-20 mm	S:	8.9

On 25 October, the *John A. Johnson* sailed independently from San Francisco, California, en route to Honolulu, Hawaii. The *I-12* (Kudo) intercepted the freighter 1,000 miles northeast of Oahu in rough weather. As the ship made a heavy roll to port, a torpedo struck the starboard side forward of the bridge and underneath the #3 hold. A second torpedo passed seventy-five yards astern. The explosion blew a hole twelve feet square in the ship's side and broke her back, but the damage seemed to be mainly contained within the #3 hold packed with canned provisions. The watch below secured the engines as the ship began to split, and within ten minutes the *Johnson* broke in two but remained afloat. The order to abandon ship was sounded on the ship's whistle, and the vessel's complement of eight officers, thirty-three men, and twenty-eight armed guards, as well as the one U.S. Army security officer, began leaving in three lifeboats and by jumping overboard. Because water was breaking over the bow, the forward lookouts had been positioned on the bridge, so all hands left from the after section. The port lifeboats, #2 and #4, got away safely. The #1 boat could not be used owing to damage from the explosion, and the #3 boat swamped on contact with the rough water. The *I-12* surfaced after thirty minutes and began shelling the Liberty ship, and after eight shots both ends lay ablaze. The *I-12*

then bore down on the #2 boat and its twenty-eight occupants. The survivors jumped out of the boat before the *I-12*'s bow brushed by. The Japanese began firing their 20-mm guns at the boat, while a man on deck fired a pistol at the boat, its occupants, and the men in the water. The *I-12* turned about and repeated the action. The Japanese also strafed seventeen men on a raft. The submarine later attempted to ram the raft, missing the first time but succeeding on the second try. Before leaving, the *I-12* unsuccessfully tried to ram the #4 lifeboat, which had about twenty-four men on board. The *I-12* caused the deaths of the Army security officer, five armed guards, and four of the merchant crew. At 0105 the forward half of the ship blew up and sent flames 700 feet in the air. The after section was last seen burning on the horizon by the survivors. A Pan American Airways plane sighted the sixty survivors, and the USS *Argus* (PY-14) rescued them the next day and took them to San Francisco.

NSS; WACR; WCSR; RWCS; AG; Rohwer, p. 286, places the attack at 29.55 N / 141.25 W.

FORT LEE

D:	11-2-44	YB:	1943
T:	2002	Tn:	10,198
Pos:	27.35 S / 83.11 E	Dr:	31 ft.
Ow:	WSA	C:	93,000 bbls. fuel oil
Op:	Bernuth Lembcke Co.	P:	steam
M:	Ottar Marius Andersen	S:	15.5
A:	1-5"; 1-3"; 8-20 mm		

On 21 October, the *Fort Lee* sailed independently from Abadan, Iran, to Brisbane, Australia. The *U-181* (Freiwald) intercepted and torpedoed the tanker as she proceeded on a nonevasive course. A torpedo struck the port side in the fireroom about twelve feet below the waterline. The ship's torpedo warning device did not sound until after the torpedo struck. The explosion likely caused the port boiler to explode; the power failed and the engines stopped. As the ship settled by the stern, the boiler room and the engine room filled with water and the crew's mess filled with smoke and steam. When the ship began to lose headway, the master passed the word to prepare the boats for lowering. Some of the men misunderstood his orders and lowered the #3, #5, and #6 boats. As the men lowered these boats, a second torpedo struck the starboard side between the engine room and the #9 tank. This explosion shattered the #3 and #5 lifeboats, threw the men into the water, and sent a ball of flame 200 feet in the air. The ship caught fire for ten seconds, but a wave washed over the well deck and put the fire out. The complement consisted of ten officers, thirty-nine men, and twenty-six armed guards—sixty-six of these men successfully abandoned the ship in four boats. The *U-181* surfaced and officers questioned the men in the #4 boat before leaving. The survivors picked men from the water and cannibalized the provisions from the four rafts that floated free of the wreck. The tanker sank

stern first at about 2110. The four boats sailed in company for three days and then became separated during strong winds that lasted for forty-eight hours. On 7 November, the British MV *Ernebank* rescued the sixteen survivors in the #2 boat and landed them in Fremantle. On 9 November, the American tanker SS *Tumacacori* rescued the seventeen men in the #6 lifeboat and landed them at Albany, Australia. On 16 November, the American SS *Mary Ball* fired on the #1 lifeboat with seventeen survivors. Twelve rounds landed near the boat before it could be identified. All these men landed at Colombo, Ceylon. The #4 boat with ten merchant crewmen and six armed guards on board was never seen again. Three officers, twelve men, and ten armed guards perished.

NSS; WACR; WCSR; USMMA; AG; Rohwer, p. 277; *War Action Casualties*, p. 178.

MATTHEW P. DEADY

D:	11-3-44	YB:	1942
T:	0545	Tn:	7,176
Pos:	Tacloban, Leyte, PI	Dr:	19 ft.
Ow:	WSA	C:	5,000 tons general, gasoline,
Op:	American-Hawaiian SS Co.		acid, acetylene, troops
M:	K. D. Frye	P:	steam
A:	1-4"; 1-3"; 8-20 mm	S:	at anchor

On 29 October, the *Matthew P. Deady* sailed from Hollandia, New Guinea, in convoy and arrived at Tacloban Bay, Leyte, on 2 November. The next day an air raid alert sounded just before daybreak, and several Japanese planes began attacking the nearly 100 ships in the harbor. One of the planes dropped bombs about 100 yards astern of the Liberty ship and then strafed her as it passed over the stern. The armed guards maintained an intense fire as this plane returned, passed over the stern, and swerved and crashed into the #2 gun tub. Part of the plane also hit the #1 gun tub. An explosion ignited gasoline, acetylene, and oxygen tanks stowed under the #2 gun. A second explosion set fire to the cargo of gasoline range fuel for Army mess stoves and 300 acetylene tanks on board. The explosion blew some of the crew overboard; others jumped into the water to avoid the flames. The fire spread forward and threatened the three-inch ammunition magazine. The master ordered the men to their abandon ship stations in order to assemble the crew. He then ordered the remaining 7 officers, 30 men, 27 armed guards, and 300 troops on board to their fire stations. The firefighting parties brought the fire under control in about one hour. The burning acetylene accounted for most of the deaths. Two of the gun crew and twenty-six of the troops died. Another seventy-seven men reported injuries. The ship returned to Hollandia under her own power and arrived on 27 November.

NSS; WACR; WCSR; AG.

FRANK J. CUHEL

D:	11-4-44	YB:	1944
T:	0430	Tn:	7,176
Pos:	Tacloban, Leyte, PI	Dr:	22 ft.
Ow:	WSA	C:	1,500 tons general, vehicles,
Op:	Black Diamond SS Co.		troops
M:	James McCubbin	P:	steam
A:	1-5"; 1-3"; 8-20 mm	S:	at anchor

The *Frank J. Cuhel* sailed from Hollandia, New Guinea, to Tacloban, Leyte, Philippine Islands. While anchored off Tacloban, the ship was struck by a shell on the #6 port gun tub. The damage to the vessel was slight. The explosion injured one of the Army passengers and two armed guards from the total of 8 officers, 34 men, 28 armed guards, and 500 troops on board.

WACR; AG; ONF.

CAPE CONSTANCE

D:	11-4-44	YB:	1943
T:	0520	Tn:	6,711
Pos:	Tacloban, Leyte, PI	Dr:	20 ft.
Ow:	WSA	C:	3,500 tons general
Op:	Grace Lines	P:	steam
M:	A. E. Uldall	S:	at anchor
A:	2-3"; 8-20 mm		

On 14 October, the *Cape Constance* sailed from Hollandia, New Guinea, to Leyte, Philippine Islands. She arrived at Leyte on 24 October, and for several days the Japanese kept the ships in the harbor under attack. A lone enemy bomber approached the vessel as she anchored in a large group of merchantmen and LSTs in Tacloban Bay. The plane started its dive toward the midships house under a scathing fire maintained by the armed guards; however, it hit the starboard boom at the #3 hatch. The plane exploded; scattered wreckage over the bridge, the boat deck, and the after deck; and then crashed in the water on the port side. Small fires started on the after deck, but the crew quickly extinguished them. The ship had on board eight officers, forty-three men, twenty-eight armed guards, and one passenger. Only the armed guard officer received a slight wound. The damage to the ship was listed as slight in this close call.

WACR; USMMA; AG; TF; ONF.

LEE S. OVERMAN

D:	11-11-44	YB:	1943
T:	1100	Tn:	7,176
Pos:	Le Havre Harbor, France	Dr:	26 ft. 6 in.
Ow:	WSA	C:	14,000 tons, explosives, etc.
Op:	Bildberg-Rothchild	P:	steam
M:	Creston Clarke Jenkins	S:	1.5
A:	2-3"; 8-20 mm		

On 10 October, the *Lee S. Overman* sailed from New York in Convoy HX-313 to Le Havre, France, via Southampton, England. The freighter reached the entrance to the harbor on the 6th and anchored to await a pilot. On the 11th, the pilot boarded the Liberty ship, and she proceeded to Le Havre. Five hundred yards off the Le Havre breakwater she struck a mine. The explosion occurred under the #3 hold on the port side and broke the ship's back. The ship settled on the bottom rapidly, not allowing her to clear the channel. The master rang the general alarm, and several men launched the #1 lifeboat. The majority of the eight officers, thirty-one men, twenty-seven armed guards, and one passenger left the ship in Army barges that pulled alongside and took them to La Havre. Only one man in the merchant crew reported an injury. The WSA declared the ship a CTL.

WACR; WCSR; AG.

LEONIDAS MERRITT

D:	11-12-44	YB:	1943
T:	1125	Tn:	7,176
Pos:	Dulag, Leyte, PI	Dr:	18 ft. 2 in.
Ow:	WSA	C:	2,000 tons bridge parts
Op:	U.S. Lines	P:	steam
M:	Douglas E. Wiltshire	S:	at anchor
A:	2-3"; 8-20 mm		

On 7 December, the *Leonidas Merritt* sailed from Hollandia, New Guinea, to Leyte and anchored off Dulag. During an air attack, several Japanese planes appeared and headed directly toward the ships. One Japanese plane chose the *Merritt* as a target and began strafing the vessel from 400 yards and then crash dived onto the forward deck between the #2 and #3 hatches. The single bomb under the plane's wing exploded on contact. Fire broke out in holds #1, #2, and #3 and on the bridge. The explosion destroyed cargo booms, holed tanks and compartments, and damaged and destroyed a great deal of the deck gear. The eight officers, thirty-five men, twenty-eight armed guards, and fifty stevedores on board were at general quarters when the plane struck the ship. The men

managed to get the fire under control in about thirty minutes. At 1725 eight more planes attacked the anchorage. One of the enemy planes singled out the *Leonidas Merritt* and strafed the freighter as it crashed into the #2 hatch, again causing severe damage. The port boiler, hatch covers, steam lines, and deck gear were damaged or destroyed. Fire broke out in the forward half of the ship, but the crew extinguished it quickly. During the attacks, one armed guard, one merchant crewman, and one stevedore lost their lives. Thirty-six others reported injuries. The freighter returned to Astoria, Oregon, for repairs on 5 January 1945.

NSS; WACR; WCSR; AG; TF.

THOMAS NELSON

D:	11-12-44	YB:	1942
T:	1127	Tn:	7,176
Pos:	10.58 N / 125.04 E	Dr:	18 ft. 5 in.
Ow:	WSA	C:	1,850 tons general, ammunition,
Op:	Calmar SS Co.		gas, troops, vehicles
M:	Axel Michael Michelson	P:	steam
A:	1-4"; 1-3"; 8-20 mm	S:	at anchor

The *Thomas Nelson* sailed from Hollandia, New Guinea, in convoy to Leyte, arriving there on 29 October. The freighter lay anchored 3,000 yards off the city at Dulag and had discharged half of her cargo. Three planes suddenly appeared over the anchorage and immediately attacked the ships. One of the planes strafed the *Nelson* as it dove into the vessel, striking the jumbo boom at the #4 hatch. The derrick sheared off part of the plane, which continued on through the bulwark on the port side. There were two distinct explosions, one when the plane struck the boom and a second caused by the bomb carried by the plane. Fires started on the after decks, in the tween deck of the #5 hold, in the gun crew's quarters, and in the steering engine room. Immediately firefighting parties began to fight the flames. The fire in the #5 hold threatened gasoline and bombs stowed there. A Navy LCT brought some expert firefighters who helped get the fire under control at about 1400. The ship had on board 8 officers, 30 men, 28 armed guards, and 578 Army troops. The explosions and fire tragically killed 3 armed guards and 133 of the troops, and injured 88 more. The ship returned to San Francisco without repairs.

NSS; WACR; WCSR; AG; TF.

JEREMIAH M. DAILY

D:	11-12-44	YB:	1943
T:	1420	Tn:	7,177
Pos:	Leyte, PI	Dr:	16 ft. 1 1/2 in.
Ow:	WSA	C:	1,367 tons Army gear, troops,
Op:	American South African Line		trucks
M:	Harry J. Manwaring	P:	steam
A:	1-5"; 1-3"; 8-20 mm	S:	at anchor

On 5 November, the *Jeremiah M. Daily* sailed in convoy from Hollandia, New Guinea, to Leyte, Philippine Islands. The ship arrived on 12 November and anchored in berth number thirty among the approximately 100 ships in the harbor. Lookouts on board reported the approach of four Japanese aircraft, and the general alarm sounded. Two of these planes headed for the *Daily*, but one changed course and crashed into another vessel. The second dropped bombs on a nearby merchant ship and continued toward the *Daily*. This second plane swerved and crashed into the forward starboard corner of the wheelhouse. The plane destroyed the wheelhouse, the chartroom, the master's office and quarters, the chief mate's quarters, and the cadet quarters. Flaming gasoline and parts of the plane ignited fuel stowed near the #3 hatch. The fire at this hatch fueled fires throughout the deckhouse and caused a great loss of life among the 9 officers, 30 men, 29 armed guards, and 557 troops on board. The fire raged until after 1800 and was extinguished with the help of a Navy fireboat. A total of 3 officers, 1 crew member, 2 armed guards, and 100 troops died. The fire injured another forty-three men. At least fifty of the soldiers jumped into the water and were picked up by patrol boats. The crew later made emergency repairs, and on 27 November, she departed Leyte Gulf, for San Francisco.

NSS; WACR; WCSR; AG.

WILLIAM A. COULTER

D:	11-12-44	YB:	1943
T:	1745	Tn:	7,176
Pos:	10.57 N / 125.04 E	Dr:	18 ft. 2 in.
Ow:	WSA	C:	3,500 tons general
Op:	Hammond Shipping Co.	P:	steam
M:	H. D. McLeod	S:	at anchor
A:	1-4"; 1-3"; 8-20 mm		

The *William A. Coulter* sailed from Hollandia, New Guinea, to Dulag, Leyte, Philippine Islands. Several Japanese planes attacked the anchorage as the ship lay off Dulag. One plane dove toward the after end of the *Coulter*, strafing her as it approached. The plane struck the flag staff and sheared off the top of the ammunition locker davit. The plane then broke up in flames, slammed into the splinter shield of the #2 gun tub on the port side, and tumbled into the sea. A fire started on the after end of the ship, and as it burned a second aircraft tried to crash onto the forward deck. This plane's right wing struck the #2 gun tub and then careened into the ship's side at the #1 hatch and exploded. The plane's bomb went off under water and lifted the ship up but did no serious damage. Later inspections revealed only indentations in the hull at the #1 hatch. Five of the eight officers, thirty-three men, twenty-seven armed guards, and four passengers reported injuries, but no one died as a result of the attacks. The overall damage was considered light, and only a shaft alley leak required any pumping.

WACR; WCSR; AG.

MORRISON R. WAITE

D:	11-12-44	YB:	1942
T:	1829	Tn:	7,182
Pos:	off Dulag, Leyte, PI	Dr:	15 ft.
Ow:	WSA	C:	1,050 tons vehicles, troops
Op:	Costwise Pac-Far East Line	P:	steam
M:	Frank Fishbourne Boyd Jr.	S:	at anchor
A:	1-4"; 1-3"; 8-20 mm		

The *Morrison R. Waite* sailed from Hollandia, New Guinea, in convoy and arrived at San Pedro Bay, Leyte, on 29 October. After shifting anchorages several times, the ship anchored about 2,700 yards off Dulag, Leyte Island. During an air raid, a Japanese plane dove on the ship, strafing the vessel as it closed. The plane cleared the stern by fifty feet, flew down the port side, and crashed into the ship's side at the #1 hatch. The plane exploded, leaving a huge hole in the ship and causing a fire in the #1 hold. The hatch covers, life jackets, and bedding began burning in this hold containing 140 men. Firefighting parties from the 8 officers, 31 men, 29 armed guards, and 600 Army troops on board began to battle the flames. They flooded the forward magazine and brought the fire under control in fifteen minutes. LCMs and DUKWs took the most seriously injured ashore. The explosion and fire killed about twenty-one and wounded forty-one of the troops and two of the armed guards. On 23 December, the Liberty ship steamed back to San Francisco for repairs.

The casualty figures are contradictory within the sources. The Japanese pilot was decapitated during the crash, and reports indicate that one of the Air Corps troops on board scalped the skull. NSS; WACR; WCSR; AG; TF.

ALEXANDER MAJORS

D: 11-12-44
T: 1832
Pos: 11.03.15 N / 125.03.30 E
Ow: WSA
Op: Isthmian SS Co.
M: John Michael Griffin
A: 1-5"; 1-3"; 8-20 mm

YB: 1944
Tn: 7,176
Dr: 21 ft.
C: 1,222 tons trucks, tractors, oil, gas, troops
P: steam
S: at anchor

On 29 October, the *Alexander Majors* sailed from Hollandia, New Guinea, in convoy and arrived at Dulag Harbor, Leyte, in the Philippines on 4 November. The ship lay at anchor 3,500 yards offshore. Throughout the day on the 12th, enemy suicide planes attacked the anchorage. As the sun began setting, ten Japanese planes appeared. One of these aircraft headed for the *Alexander Majors*. A blast from the ship's five-inch gun lifted the plane and altered its course slightly upwards. The plane cleared the starboard wing of the bridge and struck the mainmast. The plane and the bomb it carried exploded, showering gasoline, plane parts and bomb fragments over the forward portion of the ship. The explosion shook the entire ship and blew off the #2 and #3 hatch covers, igniting fuel stowed on the deck. Flames engulfed the forward deck as many of the seven officers, thirty-four men, twenty-six armed guards, and thirteen Army passengers on board began fighting the fire. Shrapnel damaged one of the forward fire mains, forcing the men to run the fire hoses from the after part of the ship. The armed guards on the forward three-inch and 20-mm guns had to jump overboard. The flames eventually spread to the #2 and #3 tween decks. A Navy LCI fireboat came alongside and brought the fire under control with foam within an hour. Two of the merchant crew died and sixteen others reported injuries. The *Alexander Majors* returned to San Francisco for repairs on 15 March.

The ship's complement figures are contradictory within the sources. NSS; WACR; WCSR; TF.

FLOYD B. OLSON

D: 11-14-44
T: 0900
Pos: off Leyte, PI
Ow: WSA
Op: Oliver J. Olson Co.
M: H. Norby
A: 2-3"; 8-20 mm

YB: 1943
Tn: 7,176
Dr: 25 ft. 2 in.
C: 10,400 tons lumber and steel
P: steam
S: at anchor

The *Floyd B. Olson* sailed from Hollandia, New Guinea, to Leyte, Philippine Islands, and on 30 September the vessel anchored off Leyte to discharge her cargo. During a Japanese air raid, six bombers attacked the anchorage. Six bombs straddled the ship, and a single bomb struck on the bow, port side. The damage to the ship was considered slight. The eight officers, thirty-five men, twenty-eight armed guards, and forty stevedores on board escaped unhurt.

WACR; AG; TF; ONF.

THEODORE PARKER

D:	11-16-44	YB:	1942
T:	1215	Tn:	7,176
Pos:	53.33 N / 00.39 E	Dr:	21 ft.
Ow:	WSA	C:	3,000 tons steel plates
Op:	Agwilines Inc.	P:	steam
M:	Robert Vagner	S:	6
A:	2-3"; 8-20 mm		

On 16 November, the *Theodore Parker* sailed from Hull, England, to the United States in convoy. Just over two hours into her trip, the *Parker* struck a mine about twelve miles east of the Humber River. The explosion occurred under the #1 hold on the starboard side. The vessel returned to Hull under her own power for repairs. There were no casualties among the complement of eight officers, thirty-four men, and twenty-seven armed guards.

WACR; WCSR; AG; TF.

BENJAMIN IDE WHEELER

D:	11-17-44	YB:	1942
T:	0700	Tn:	7,176
Pos:	Red Beach, Leyte, PI	Dr:	26 ft.
Ow:	WSA	C:	none
Op:	American Hawaiian SS Co.	P:	steam
M:	Daniel J. Coughlin	S:	at anchor
A:	2-3"; 8-20 mm		

On 18 October, the *Benjamin Ide Wheeler* sailed from Hollandia, New Guinea, to Leyte, Philippine Islands, and arrived on 25 October. On 26 and 27 October, Japanese air attacks damaged the ship. On 17 November, the freighter lay moored beside the *Augustus Thomas* when three shots sounded from shore indicating an air raid. A few minutes later a plane approached and dropped about fifty small antipersonnel-type bombs. Most of these bombs fell into the water, but two struck the ship, causing minimal damage. On 27 October, most of the armed guards had left the ship and none of the eight officers, thirty-four

crewmen, and the rest of the armed guards on board reported any injury from the bombs.

NSS; WACR.

NICHOLAS J. SINNOTT

D:	11-18-44	YB:	1943
T:	0725	Tn:	7,176
Pos:	11.15.45 N / 125.02.45 E	Dr:	21 ft. 2 in.
Ow:	WSA	C:	4,000 tons general and troops
Op:	James Griffith & Sons	P:	steam
M:	A. Larson	S:	at anchor
A:	2-3"; 8-20 mm		

On 7 October, the *Nicholas J. Sinnott* sailed from Hollandia, New Guinea, and arrived at Leyte, Philippine Islands, on 12 November. While the ship lay at anchor in the harbor, Japanese aircraft attacked. One of the planes attempted to crash dive onto the freighter but struck a glancing blow and fell into the water. The Liberty ship escaped with only slight damage. The eight officers, thirty-two men, twenty-six armed guards, and eighty Army troops on board reported no injuries.

WACR; AG.

GILBERT STUART

D:	11-18-44	YB:	1943
T:	0724	Tn:	7,176
Pos:	off Tacloban, Leyte, PI	Dr:	15 ft.
Ow:	WSA	C:	500 tons general, 6,000 bbls.
Op:	American Mail Line		gasoline, troops
M:	John Baer Kiehl	P:	steam
A:	1-4"; 1-3"; 8-20 mm	S:	at anchor

On 29 October, the *Gilbert Stuart* sailed in convoy from Hollandia, New Guinea, and arrived in San Pedro Bay, Leyte, on 4 November. The ship had discharged troops and tons of equipment and lay in berth number eighteen about three miles offshore to unload her cargo of gasoline. During the morning about twelve enemy planes appeared and began attacking the ships in the harbor. One Japanese plane dove on the Liberty ship from dead ahead, strafing the ship as it closed. When the plane passed over the deck, the armed guards shot off the tail and caused the plane to strike the funnel and the starboard side gun tub. The plane crashed on the freighter's after end, scattering antipersonnel and incendiary bombs and spraying the plane's gasoline all over the midships

section. The plane dropped down the #4 hatch, exploded, and spread gasoline, shrapnel, and debris all the way aft. Small fires started over the entire deckhouse. Luckily the plane did not start a fire in the #4 hold where 2,000 barrels of gasoline were stowed. The *Stuart* suffered damage over a large portion of the deck and in the crew's quarters. The eight officers, thirty-one men, twenty-nine armed guards, and approximately twenty-three stevedores on board put out the fires within four hours with help from the USS *Chickasaw* (ATF-83). Two officers, three men, and one armed guard died. Eleven others reported injuries. After provisional repairs the ship left Leyte on 22 November.

NSS; WACR; WCSR; AG.

ALCOA PIONEER

D:	11-19-44	YB:	1941
T:	0710	Tn:	6,711
Pos:	San Pedro Bay, Leyte	Dr:	19 ft. 3 in.
Ow:	Alcoa SS Co.	C:	1,200 tons gasoline
Op:	Alcoa SS Co.	P:	steam
M:	Andrew William Gavin	S:	at anchor
A:	1-4"; 1-3"; 8-20 mm		

The *Alcoa Pioneer* sailed from Hollandia, New Guinea, to Leyte and anchored in San Pedro Bay in berth number sixteen. Shots from shore warned the ships of approaching enemy aircraft. Three aircraft flew toward the anchorage, and each selected a merchant vessel as a target. One of the planes attacked the *Alcoa Pioneer* from dead astern at a 45° angle. The plane crash dived into the port side of the flying bridge, exploded, and inflicted great damage on the midships section of the ship. The deckhouse and the forward deck immediately caught fire. The freighter appeared in great danger because the three forward holds contained gasoline. The merchant crew, however, swiftly responded and had the fire out in five minutes. The ship had on board ten officers, thirty-six men, twenty-eight armed guards, and two passengers. Six armed guards died and thirteen others reported injuries. The USS *PCE-851* removed many of the wounded. After making repairs the *Pioneer* sailed from Leyte to San Francisco. The *Alcoa Pioneer* broke down south of Guadalcanal, and the Navy tug *ATR-33* towed her to Espíritu Santo. She eventually arrived in San Francisco in February 1945.

The ship's complement numbers conflict within the sources. NSS; WACR; WCSR; AG.

CAPE ROMANO

D:	11-19-44	YB:	1942
T:	0715	Tn:	5,106
Pos:	off Leyte, PI	Dr:	22 ft. 10 in.
Ow:	WSA	C:	none
Op:	Lykes Bros. SS Co.	P:	diesel
M:	Edward Tonti	S:	at anchor
A:	1-4"; 1-3"; 4-20 mm		

On 18 October, the *Cape Romano* sailed from Hollandia, New Guinea, in convoy to Tacloban, Leyte, Philippine Islands. The vessel had just been attacked three weeks earlier, and on 18 November, she suffered slight damage from a bomb exploding off the starboard side at the #2 hatch. On the morning of 19 November, three Japanese planes appeared from dead astern. One plane crashed on board the *Alcoa Pioneer*, and a second struck the Norwegian MV *General Fleischer*. The third plane approached the *Romano*, and the armed guards took it under fire. The plane veered sharply to port and struck the port side of the bridge, shearing off two feet of the plane's right wing. The plane careened into a gun tub station and a life rail, shearing off six feet more of the wing. The plane then crashed off the side of the ship next to the #3 hatch and exploded, throwing debris over the deck and blowing eleven holes in the port side. None of the eleven officers, thirty-six men, twenty-six armed guards, and two passengers on board suffered injuries in this or any of the latter attacks. The ship returned to San Francisco for repairs and arrived on 4 January.

NSS; WACR; WCSR; TF.

FORT DEARBORN

D:	11-20-44	YB:	1943
T:	1500	Tn:	10,448
Pos:	12 N / 155 E	Dr:	21 ft.
Ow:	WSA	C:	142,000 bbls. water ballast
Op:	Deconhil Shipping Co.	P:	steam
M:	Gordon O. Robinson	S:	14.5
A:	1-5"; 1-3"; 8-20 mm		

The *Fort Dearborn* sailed from Ulithi, Caroline Islands, on 18 November en route to Eniwetok, Marshall Islands. The tanker sailed in consort with the SS *Ball's Bluff* and the SS *Mission Buenaventura*. The three vessels proceeded in a "V" formation, with the *Mission Buenaventura* taking the position astern. Japanese planes attacked the three vessels for ninety minutes and made about fifteen attempts to bomb and strafe the ships. The near misses and enemy machine gun fire, however, caused only slight damage. Four of the eight officers, forty-two men, twenty-seven armed guards, and five passengers on board reported minor injuries. The *Fort Dearborn* arrived at Eniwetok on 22 November.

The complement figures conflict within the sources. NSS; WACR; ONF; *War Action Casualties*, p. 179.

WILLIAM D. BURNHAM

D:	11-23-44	YB:	1943
T:	1520	Tn:	7,176
Pos:	49.34 N / 01.15 W	Dr:	22 ft. 2 in.
Ow:	WSA	C:	4,083 tons food, vehicles
Op:	American-Hawaiian SS Co.	P:	steam
M:	Emil Rosol	S:	11
A:	1-4"; 1-3"; 8-20 mm		

On 22 November, the *William D. Burnham* sailed from Cowes, England, to Cherbourg, France. The freighter was to rendezvous with another convoy, but it never appeared. The *Burnham* proceeded on with the escort drifter HMS *Fidget* (FY-551). The *U-978* (Palst) attacked the Liberty ship five miles off the beach at Barfleur, France. A torpedo struck under the stern, and the explosion lifted the ship out of the water, threw water over each side of the ship, blew off the rudder, damaged the propeller, and broke the shaft. The #5 hold flooded immediately, and the ship began settling by the stern. The master ordered all lifeboats to be readied for lowering. At this point the *U-978* fired a second torpedo that struck at the #3 hold just forward of the bridge on the port side. This explosion threw up a large column of water, created a hole forty feet in diameter, and demolished the #2 lifeboat still in the falls. Eighteen of the nineteen men in the boat and standing beside it died. The remaining three boats got away and headed toward the beach. The *Fidget* picked up most of the men and later transferred the majority of the survivors to the USS *PT-461*. Several of the injured went on board the destroyer HMS *Vesper* (D-55) to Portsmouth, England. The ship had on board eight officers, thirty-three men, twenty-six armed guards, and one passenger. Two officers, six men, and ten armed guards died when the torpedo exploded under the #2 boat. The Navy tug *ATR-3* towed the ship and beached her west of Cherbourg. She was later declared a CTL.

NSS; WACR; WCSR; AG; Rohwer, p. 187.

GUS W. DARNELL

D:	11-23-44	YB:	1944
T:	1920	Tn:	7,247
Pos:	off Samar Island, PI	Dr:	18 ft.
Ow:	WSA	C:	5,000 tons vehicles, gas, troops,
Op:	J. H. Winchester Co.		ammunition, war cargo
M:	George Robert Parsons	P:	steam
A:	1-5"; 1-3"; 8-20 mm	S:	at anchor

The *Gus W. Darnell* sailed from British New Guinea and arrived in San Pedro Bay, Philippines, on 15 November. During the next week over 300 troops had disembarked, but the cargo still remained on board. As the *Darnell* anchored five miles off Samar Island, a Japanese torpedo bomber glided over the anchorage and released its torpedo. The torpedo struck the freighter on the starboard side at the after end of the #2 hold. The plane then flew over the ship at mast height but did not strafe the ship. The explosion blew a hole nineteen feet by thirty-one feet in the ship's side and threw hull plates, debris, and shrapnel into the air. The explosion buckled hull plates on the port side and started a fire in the #2 hold. The Army cargo and trucks on top of the hold turned into a molten inferno as the gasoline tanks exploded and spread the fire. Firefighting parties from the eight officers, thirty-three men, twenty-seven armed guards, and fifteen Army troops on board began to combat the flames, but thick smoke complicated the firefighting efforts. A Navy fireboat and a tug brought hose lines and chemical agents on board to fight the fire. The ship gradually began to settle by the head and listed to port as the firefighters pumped water into the forward holds. The master ordered those not fighting the fire to abandon the ship. The ship's list did not improve, and to keep her from rolling over, a tug towed her to the beach. The fires could not be brought under control until noon the next day. All hands survived the attack, but seventeen men reported injuries. The WSA declared the ship a CTL and on 6 January, the *Darnell* moved to an anchorage off Tacloban, Leyte, and transferred to the Army to be used for storage. The ship was later towed to San Francisco and scrapped.

NSS; WACR; WCSR; AG; E. C. Lucas is the master of record. ONF.

HOWELL LYKES

D: 11-26-44   YB: 1940
T: 2235   Tn: 8,252
Pos: San Pedro Bay, Leyte, PI   Dr: 21 ft. 10 in.
Ow: WSA   C: 85 tons fresh water
Op: Lykes Bros. SS Co.   P: steam
M: William Henderson   S: at anchor
A: 1-4"; 4-3"; 8-20 mm

On 6 September, the *Howell Lykes* sailed from San Francisco to Leyte, Philippine Islands. Japanese bombers attacked the vessels anchored in San Pedro Bay, and several bombs fell near the *Lykes*. Two of these bombs hit the water on the port side abreast the #1 and #2 holds. Shrapnel holed the hull and caused slight damage to the freighter. On board were eleven officers, sixty-eight men, forty-one armed guards, and fifty-eight Army passengers. Two of the ship's officers reported injuries during the attack.

WACR; TF; ONF.

WILLIAM C. C. CLAIBORNE

D: 11-29-44   YB: 1942
T: morning   Tn: 7,176
Pos: off Leyte, PI   Dr: 20 ft.
Ow: U.S. Maritime Commission   C: 5,000 general, gasoline in drums
Op: Mississippi Shipping Co.   P: steam
M: Benjamin Alexander   S: at anchor
A: 1-4"; 1-3"; 8-20 mm

On 15 November, the *William C. C. Claiborne* sailed from Hollandia, New Guinea, to Leyte, Philippine Islands. While at anchor off Leyte, the ship was struck by a shell on the superstructure, port side. It is conjectured that the shell came from an Allied vessel. The explosion caused only slight damage to the Liberty ship, but it injured three of the gun crew and one merchant seaman. On board at the time were eight officers, thirty-four men, twenty-eight armed guards, and one passenger.

WACR; AG; TF; ONF.

ARIZPA

D:	12-1-44	YB:	1920
T:	0710	Tn:	5,437
Pos:	51.23 N / 03.18 W	Dr:	23 ft.
Ow:	WSA	C:	general
Op:	Waterman SS Co.	P:	steam
M:	George S. Hancock	S:	5
A:	1-4"; 1-3"; 8-20 mm		

On 16 September, the *Arizpa* sailed from New York to Antwerp, Belgium, in Convoy HX-309 via Southend, England. Between buoy numbers thirteen and fourteen in the Schelde River, the freighter struck a mine. The explosion occurred on the starboard side underneath the #5 hold. The explosion buckled thirty shell plates and caused extensive structural damage to the vessel. A British destroyer and two smaller craft stood by with lines until the crew could make repairs. None of the eight officers, thirty-three men, twenty-eight armed guards, and one passenger on board reported any injuries. The ship proceeded to Antwerp under her own power escorted by two salvage tugs.

WACR; WCSR; AG; TF.

FRANCIS ASBURY

D:	12-3-44	YB:	1943
T:	0522	Tn:	7,176
Pos:	51.22 N / 03.53 E	Dr:	28 ft. 6 in.
Ow:	WSA	C:	6,000 tons general
Op:	A. H. Bull Lines	P:	steam
M:	Jean Virgil Patrick	S:	7
A:	2-3"; 2-30 cal.; 8-20 mm		

The *Francis Asbury* sailed from the Downs, England, to Antwerp, Belgium, in Convoy TAM-6. The convoy had proceeded into the Schelde River in two columns, with the *Asbury* the second ship in the starboard column. One-half mile past Buoy NF 10 the vessel struck a mine. The explosion occurred under the engine room and broke the ship's back, blew parts of the engines through the decks, destroyed the boilers, and filled the vessel with live steam. Within two minutes water had reached to within two feet of the boat deck. On the master's orders, the survivors among the nine officers, thirty-two men, and twenty-eight armed guards immediately abandoned ship in three of the four lifeboats and four rafts. British trawlers rescued many of the men. Two officers, seven men, and six of the armed guards perished on the ship. The explosion also injured forty-six other men. The chief engineer and an armed guard later died ashore. The vessel went aground near Ostend, and escort vessels sank her so she would not be a menace to navigation. The survivors landed in Antwerp.

WACR; WCSR; AG.

ANTOINE SAUGRAINE

D:	12-5-44	YB:	1943
T:	1220	Tn:	7,176
Pos:	09.42 N / 127.05 E	Dr:	17 ft.
Ow:	WSA	C:	3,000 tons Army gear and troops
Op:	Agwilines	P:	steam
M:	Anthony Van Cromphaut	S:	7
A:	1-4"; 1-3"; 8-20 mm		

On 5 November, the *Antoine Saugraine* sailed from Humbolt Bay, New Guinea, in convoy to Leyte, Philippines. The Liberty ship proceeded in convoy station #25 in the formation of thirty-five ships and six escorts. A Japanese torpedo plane attacked the freighter and released a torpedo about 2,000 yards off the port side. Lookouts did not sight the track of the torpedo until it had traveled to within 500 yards of the freighter. The master ordered hard right rudder and full speed, but the ship did not answer fast enough and the torpedo struck the stern under the counter. The explosion lifted the stern out of the water, broke the shaft and the propeller, and blew off the rudder. With the engines still engaged, the ship began to vibrate and water entered the engine room through the shaft alley. The ship lost way and soon lay dead in the water. The master ordered the 8 officers, 34 men, 26 armed guards, and 376 troops on board to stand by their abandon ship stations. At 1231 another torpedo plane approached the ship as the *Saugraine* fell astern of the convoy. The plane dropped a torpedo at 1,600 yards, and it struck at the #2 hold, port side. The vessel heeled to starboard and then to port and began sinking by the head. At 1300 the master ordered the ship abandoned. All hands left by the four lifeboats, the four rafts, or by jumping overboard. The frigates USS *San Pedro* (PF-37) and the USS *Coronado* (PF-38) and the Army tug *LT-454* rescued all hands and landed them at Leyte. The master inspected the ship three times to make sure she would float. The Army tug began to tow the freighter stern first at nearly six knots, with the *Coronado* escorting the two. Later the destroyer USS *Halford* (DD-480) relieved the *Coronado*. The USS *Quapaw* (ATF-110) arrived on the 6th and stood by to help tow the vessel if necessary. The next day planes again attacked the Liberty ship, but several bombing runs failed to damage her. At 1410 a Japanese torpedo plane succeeded in striking the ship with a torpedo in the #3 hold. The ship rapidly sank by the head at 1500.

The number of troops differs slightly among the sources. WACR; WCSR; Action Report USS *Coronado*, NHC; AG; TF.

MARCUS DALY

D:	12-5-44	YB:	1943
T:	1500	Tn:	7,167
Pos:	09.34 N / 127.35 E	Dr:	14 ft. 6 in.
Ow:	WSA	C:	4,000 tons general, gas, vehicles,
Op:	Sudden & Christensen		troops
M:	Alvin William Opheim	P:	steam
A:	2-3"; 8-20 mm	S:	8

On 29 November, the *Marcus Daly* sailed from Hollandia in a forty-ship convoy to San Pedro Bay, Leyte. During most of the day on the 5th, the Japanese subjected the ships in the convoy to dive bombing and torpedo attacks. On one attack, a dive bomber approached the convoy from astern and dove directly toward the *Marcus Daly*. All guns fired on the approaching plane and damaged the tail section so severely that the pilot lost control. The plane continued to strafe the ship, passed over the stern, and swung down the ship's port side. The plane's wing struck the shrouds of the foremast, turning the plane into the ship. The plane crashed through the main deck into the forepeak area. The plane's bomb exploded, throwing flames, plane parts, and other debris over 100 feet into the air. A fire broke out in the forepeak locker used to stow paint. The crew battled the flames for seven hours to bring the blaze under control. The explosion opened holes in both sides of the ship large enough to "drive a train through," the upper deck "ripped like paper," and the whole bow twisted. All 8 officers, 32 men, 27 armed guards, and 1,200 troops remained on board except 34 troops who jumped overboard. A raft was released for these men, and an Allied ship picked them up. The casualties, however, were heavy. One armed guard, two of the merchant crew, and sixty-two of the troops died. The explosion and fire wounded another forty-nine men. The ship made the harbor of Tarragona only to be attacked again on 10 December.

See entry for 10 December. NSS; WACR; AG.

JOHN EVANS

D:	12-5-44	YB:	1943
T:	1510	Tn:	7,176
Pos:	09.34 N / 127.35 E	Dr:	unknown
Ow:	WSA	C:	3,190 tons, deckload of
Op:	General Steamship Corp.		amphibious craft
M:	George Brimble	P:	steam
A:	1-5"; 1-3"; 8-20 mm	S:	unknown

On 29 November, the *John Evans* sailed from Hollandia, New Guinea, to Leyte Gulf. The ship proceeded in a convoy of thirty-four vessels and escorts in

convoy station #22. Throughout the day on 5 December, Japanese aircraft attacked the convoy seven times. During one of the attacks a plane singled out the *John Evans* and appeared to make a bombing run. The armed guards maintained an intense fire on the enemy aircraft and set the plane's cockpit afire, causing the plane to swerve out of control. The plane missed the ship but carried away the top mast at the #3 hatch and struck the funnel before cartwheeling into the sea. The plane's bomb detonated, showering the entire ship with water and shrapnel. The main damage to the ship was to the mast, cargo booms, and radio antenna in the area of the #3 hatch. Two of a merchant crew of forty-three and two of the twenty-six armed guards reported injuries from the shrapnel.

NSS; AG reports the ship in convoy station #12; ONF.

DAN BEARD

D:	12-10-44	YB:	1943
T:	1350	Tn:	7,176
Pos:	51.56 N / 05.28 W	Dr:	20 ft. 6 in.
Ow:	WSA	C:	2,100 tons ballast
Op:	Stockard SS Co.	P:	steam
M:	William Robert Wilson	S:	9
A:	1-4"; 1-3"; 8-20 mm		

On 10 December, the Liberty ship *Dan Beard* sailed from Barry, Wales, to Belfast, Ireland, to join a convoy to the United States. In rough seas the *U-1202* (Thomsen) fired a torpedo that struck the stern of the Liberty ship. The explosion caused the vessel to rise out of the water and blew off the rudder and broke the propeller. The motion of the ship rising in the stern caused her to split into two pieces. The complement of eight officers, thirty-two men, and twenty-seven armed guards immediately abandoned ship. Some of the men abandoned the ship by jumping in the water, but most left in the four lifeboats. The #4 boat swamped and the #3 boat capsized in the thirty-foot seas. The #2 boat with sixteen men landed at Dwll-Deri Bay, South Wales. The #1 boat made landfall with nine men. Coastal craft picked up thirteen others. Three officers, fourteen men, and twelve armed guards perished in the abandonment of the ship.

The Coast Guard records noted that a plate had been welded over a crack at the #3 hold in December 1943, and left the vessel in a weakened state. WACR; WCSR.

MARCUS DALY

D: 12-10-44   YB: 1943
T: 1700   Tn: 7,176
Pos: Tarragona Gulf, Leyte   Dr: 13 ft. 6 in.
Ow: WSA   C: 3,300 tons general, gasoline
Op: Sudden & Christensen   P: steam
M: Alvin William Opheim   S: .5
A: 2-3"; 8-20 mm

On 29 November, the *Marcus Daly* departed Hollandia, New Guinea, en route to San Pedro Bay. A Japanese aircraft crashed into the freighter and severely damaged her on the 5th, but she arrived at her destination. The previous damage made it impossible for her to anchor, yet the crew managed to discharge a good deal of the cargo into landing craft. While drifting in the harbor, the ship came under air attack again. The ship had an LCT alongside and the beach lay off the bow one-half mile. Late in the day three planes appeared over the harbor. One of these planes made a crash dive toward the bridge but struck the #3 port side cargo boom and broke it in half "like a match stick." The plane crashed into the #4 gun tub and demolished the 20-mm gun. Another part of the plane sheared off both port side lifeboats and struck the LCT, discharging cargo from the #5 hold. The disintegrating plane showered the entire ship with shrapnel and plane parts. A small fire started among the gasoline drums in hold #4, but the crew quickly extinguished it. The number of casualties among the remaining crew of 7 officers, 31 men, 26 armed guards, 60 stevedores, and 124 troops on board was lighter than the earlier attack. The attack wounded eight men but killed no one. On 28 January 1945, the ship returned to San Francisco under her own power.

NSS; WACR; WCSR; AG.

WILLIAM S. LADD

D: 12-10-44   YB: 1943
T: 1703   Tn: 7,176
Pos: South of Dulag, Leyte, PI   Dr: 12 ft.
Ow: WSA   C: 600 tons explosives, gasoline in
Op: Weyerhaeuser SS Co.   drums
M: Nels F. Anderson   P: steam
A: 2-3"; 8-20 mm   S: at anchor

On 29 November, the *William S. Ladd* sailed from Hollandia, New Guinea, to an anchorage eleven miles south of Dulag, Leyte. By 10 December, the crew had finished unloading most of the cargo. At 1658 lookouts spotted three tracers from shore indicating an air raid. Five minutes later four Japanese planes approached from the south. Gunfire brought down two planes, the third struck the *Marcus Daly*, and the fourth approached the *Ladd* from astern. This plane dove through a hail of gunfire and struck the mizzenmast, shearing it off a few feet below the crosstrees. The plane then struck the after part of the midships house and fell into the #4 hatch. The plane and its bomb load exploded in the #4 hold. The explosion blew out the forward bulkhead of the #4 hold, destroyed the engines, and started a fire among the 500 barrels of gasoline in the hold. The eight officers, thirty-three men, twenty-nine armed guards, and fifty stevedores on board battled the fire for about two and a half hours. They never managed to get the gas fire under control, and the barrels began exploding, blowing large holes through the bulkheads. The midships house eventually caught on fire and threatened the 150 tons of ammunition in the #5 hold. With this threat the master ordered all hands off at 1940. All hands escaped by boarding the ship's four boats or the ship's rafts; boarding the four LCIs laying beside the *Ladd* fighting the fires; or boarding other ships. The *Ladd* eventually settled by the stern, and the fire gutted the freighter from the second hold aft. All hands survived, but six men reported injuries.

The complement conflicts among the sources. NSS; WACR; WCSR; AG.

STEEL TRAVELER

D:	12-18-44	YB:	1922
T:	1700	Tn:	7,681
Pos:	Schelde River	Dr:	26 ft. 6 in.
Ow:	WSA	C:	1,500 tons ballast
Op:	Isthmian SS Co.	P:	steam
M:	Savilion Huntington Chapman	S:	6
A:	1-4"; 1-3"; 8-20 mm		

On 18 December, the *Steel Traveler* sailed in the eight-ship Convoy ATM-16 from Antwerp, Belgium, to the Downs, England. The ships proceeded down the Schelde River in single column. In mid-channel, two cable lengths east of buoy NF 14, the freighter struck a mine. The explosion occurred under the #3 hold on the starboard side. Immediately after the explosion, the ship broke in half—split between the #3 hatch and the fireroom. The ship began to flood and sink rapidly. Most of the eight officers, thirty-seven men, twenty-six armed guards, and one passenger on board cleared the ship in two lifeboats and two rafts. Within minutes of the explosion the water had reached the bridge with bow and stern in the air. The French destroyer *La Combattante* rescued all the survivors from the rafts and the boats and landed them at Birkenhead. One officer and one of the merchant crew died.

WACR; WCSR.

JUAN DE FUCA

D:	12-21-44	YB:	1943
T:	1720	Tn:	7,176
Pos:	off Panay Island	Dr:	18 ft.
Ow:	WSA	C:	1,500 tons machinery, lumber,
Op:	Weyerhaeuser SS Co.		rations
M:	Charles S. Robbins	P:	steam
A:	2-3"; 8-20 mm	S:	6.5

On 19 December, the *Juan De Fuca* sailed from Leyte, Philippine Islands, in a thirty-ship convoy to Mindoro, Philippines. While the convoy was off Panay, Japanese aircraft attacked. All hands went to general quarters at 1700, and lookouts spotted about ten enemy planes. One plane approached the Liberty ship from the stern, port quarter, and attempted to crash dive amidships. The armed guard sustained an intense fire on the plane as it approached the ship. Struck many times, the plane veered off course and crashed into the #2 hold. The plane's single bomb exploded on contact and created a hole six feet by three feet on the port side at the waterline. The explosion started a fire in this hold loaded with lumber, concrete pilings, and troops berthed in the tween deck area. The fire alarm brought the eight officers, thirty-three men, twenty-seven armed guards, and sixty-five troops to their stations. Fire parties put the fire out in forty-five minutes, and the ship proceeded to Mindoro. The explosion and fire killed two of the troops and wounded fourteen others as well as three armed guards. The vessel continued on her trip, only to be attacked again on 31 December.

The figures for the armed guards and troops are contradictory. NSS; WACR; WCSR; AG.

TIMOTHY BLOODWORTH

D:	12-24-44	YB:	1943
T:	1410	Tn:	7,191
Pos:	docked at Antwerp	Dr:	13 ft. forward
Ow:	WSA	C:	none
Op:	Lykes Bros. SS Co.	P:	steam
M:	Arthur C. Story	S:	docked
A:	2-3"; 8-20 mm		

The *Timothy Bloodworth* lay anchored in Antwerp, Belgium, waiting to sail in a convoy to New York, when a German V-1 or V-2 rocket exploded overhead and showered the ship with shrapnel. A second rocket hit nearby, and fragments struck the starboard side at the #1 hold. The damage was considered slight, and none of the ship's eight officers, thirty-three men, twenty-six armed guards, and one passenger were killed or injured.

WACR; AG; ONF.

ROBERT J. WALKER

D:	12-25-44	YB:	1942
T:	0230	Tn:	7,180
Pos:	36.35 S / 150.43 E	Dr:	17 ft.
Ow:	WSA	C:	none
Op:	McCormick SS Co.	P:	steam
M:	Murdock D. MacRae	S:	10.8
A:	1-5"; 1-3"; 8-20 mm		

On 15 December, the *Robert J. Walker* sailed independently from Fremantle to Sydney, Australia. The *U-862* (Timm) intercepted the zigzagging freighter and put a torpedo into the starboard side near the rudder. The explosion blew off the rudder, created a hole three feet by six feet, bent the shaft, and destroyed the steering gear. The master turned the ship south, but she could not be maneuvered. Lookouts spotted a second torpedo at 0420, 1,000 yards off the starboard side. One of the armed guards opened fire with a 20-mm gun and exploded the torpedo 100 yards from the ship. After this explosion, the crew threw smoke floats over the side, and they effectively screened the Liberty ship for about forty-five minutes. At 2200 lookouts spotted another torpedo 1,000 yards off the starboard side. Gunfire failed to explode this torpedo, and it struck at the #4 hold. The explosion in the empty hold was tremendous and created a hole ten feet by twenty feet on the starboard side and six feet by eight feet on the port side. The explosion also ruptured the #3 deep tank and showered the ship with oil and water. The master ordered the ship abandoned one minute after the second torpedo struck. The survivors among the ten officers, thirty-two men, twenty-six armed guards, and one passenger lowered the three good boats. The men also tripped four of the rafts but used only two. After the survivors were in the water for twenty-four hours, the Australian destroyer *Quickmatch* (G-92) rescued them and landed them at Sydney. Two of the merchant crew died in the attack. The freighter remained afloat and was later sunk by gunfire.

The complement figures are contradictory within the sources. NSS; WACR; WCSR; AG; Rohwer, p. 287, places the sinking at 36.45 S / 150.43 E.

JAMES H. BREASTED

D:	12-26-44	YB:	1943
T:	2000	Tn:	7,176
Pos:	anchored off Mindoro	Dr:	23 ft.
Ow:	WSA	C:	2,000 tons autos, rations,
Op:	American President Lines		gasoline
M:	Anton Henry Barnhard Kummel	P:	steam
A:	1-5"; 1-3"; 8-20 mm	S:	anchored

On 19 December, the Liberty ship *James H. Breasted* cleared Leyte Gulf in a convoy for Mindoro, Philippine Islands. The ship arrived on 22 December and disembarked her troops. The Japanese sent two cruisers and six destroyers to disrupt the landing. With this knowledge, Allied naval authorities instructed the *Breasted* to take cover in Ilin Straight. At 1000 on 26 December, the ship moved to Ilin Channel and anchored. Beginning at 2000 a Japanese naval bombardment commenced. Shells rained down all around the vessel causing numerous shrapnel holes. Paratroopers also landed on the island, and small arms fire from shore added to the damage to the ship. At 2230 a Japanese plane dropped a bomb in the #3 hold. The gasoline stored in this hold caught fire, and a heavy wind helped spread the flames to the #2 hold, also containing gasoline. The master gave the order to abandon ship at 2240. All hands, eight officers, thirty-five men, and twenty-seven armed guards, left the ship in three lifeboats. As the boats were lowered, machine gun fire from shore struck around them, but fortunately caused no further casualties. PT boats towed the lifeboats safely to shore. Only one man from the merchant crew had to be hospitalized. The fire completely gutted the ship, and she later sank and was declared a CTL.

The complement figures conflict within the sources. NSS; WACR; WCSR; AG; Morison, 13: 37-43, postulates that an Allied plane may have dropped the bomb on the *Breasted*.

WILLIAM SHARON

D:	12-28-44	YB:	1943
T:	1022	Tn:	7,176
Pos:	Surigao Straits	Dr:	26 ft.
Ow:	WSA	C:	7,000 tons food, beer, pontoons,
Op:	United Fruit Co.		trucks, gasoline
M:	Edward Macaughey	P:	steam
A:	2-3"; 8-20 mm	S:	6.5

On 27 December, the *William Sharon* sailed from Dulag, Leyte, en route to Mindoro, Philippine Islands. The freighter proceeded in a convoy of five merchant ships, about thirty LSTs, and other amphibious craft, escorted by nine destroyers and about fifteen PT boats. The *Sharon* steamed in convoy station #21. During an air attack, a Japanese plane singled out the freighter and began a

dive from the starboard quarter. The plane strafed the ship as it approached; however, the armed guards returned the fire and set the aircraft on fire. The plane dove for the bridge but struck the #4 gun tub and crashed into the flying bridge on the port side, setting the ship on fire. The fire raged out of control and completely gutted the midships house. The crew fought the flames for four hours and finally extinguished them with help from the USS *Wilson* (DD-408). With the fire extinguished, the survivors among the eight officers, thirty-two men, twenty-nine armed guards, and one passenger left by directly boarding the *Wilson*. The USCG cutter *Spencer* (WPG-36) later found the vessel drifting and removed the dead. The salvage tug USS *Grapple* (ARS-7) from Leyte towed the Liberty ship to San Pedro Harbor. After temporary repairs, the ship steamed to San Francisco for permanent repairs. Four officers, two men, four armed guards, and the passenger died. Eleven others reported injuries.

The complement figures conflict within the sources. NSS; WACR; WCSR; AG; Sawyer, Mitchell, p. 138; Morison, 13:45.

JOHN BURKE

D:	12-28-44	YB:	1942
T:	1024	Tn:	7,180
Pos:	Surigao Straits	Dr:	unknown
Ow:	WSA	C:	explosives
Op:	Northland Transportation Co.	P:	steam
M:	Herbert August Falk	S:	7
A:	2-3"; 8-20 mm		

The *John Burke* sailed from Seattle, Washington, and arrived in the Surigao Straits off Mindoro Island. As the ship lay at anchor, the Japanese attacked. A suicide plane crashed between the #2 and #3 hatches, and the ensuing explosion set off the cargo of ammunition. With a tremendous roar the ship exploded and disappeared. All nine officers, thirty-one men, and twenty-eight armed guards died in the explosion. The debris from this ship killed and wounded over two dozen men on other ships nearby. The explosion likewise sank a small Army transport steaming astern with the loss of all but one man.

WACR; WCSR; AG; AG report of *William Sharon*; Moore, p. 152.

ARTHUR SEWALL

D:	12-29-44	YB:	1944
T:	1435	Tn:	7,176
Pos:	50.28 N / 02.28 W	Dr:	20 ft.
Ow:	WSA	C:	1,833 tons ballast
Op:	Eastern SS Co.	P:	steam
M:	Harold C. Jessen	S:	9.5
A:	1-5"; 1-3"; 8-20 mm		

The *Arthur Sewall* sailed from Southampton, England, en route to Mumbles, Wales, traveling in the two-column Convoy TBC-21 as the fourth ship in the port column (listed as station #18). The convoy consisted of about ten ships and two British corvettes as escorts. Seven miles southeast of Portland Bill Lighthouse, the *U-772* (Radenmacher) attacked the convoy, firing a torpedo into the port side of the freighter's engine room. The torpedo entered the machinery space and traveled over ten feet before exploding. The blast demolished the engines and the port boilers and created a hole twenty feet long. The keel remained as the only structural member holding the ship together. The complement of eight officers, thirty-two men, and twenty-nine armed guards did not abandon ship. The vessel settled by the stern four feet and remained on an even keel. The tug *Pilot* took the vessel in tow, and she arrived at Weymouth, England, at 2345. The explosion injured five men and killed one officer on watch below. A fireman died the next day. Authorities later declared the ship a CTL.

The complement figures are contradictory within the sources. NSS; WACR; WCSR; AG.

BLACK HAWK

D:	12-29-44	YB:	1943
T:	1437	Tn:	7,191
Pos:	50.28 N / 02.28 W	Dr:	14 ft. forward
Ow:	WSA	C:	none
Op:	United Fruit Co.	P:	steam
M:	William Leroy Bunch	S:	9
A:	1-5"; 1-3"; 8-20 mm		

The *Black Hawk* sailed in Convoy TBC-21 en route from Cherbourg, France, to Fowey, England. The ship proceeded as the last ship in the starboard column of ten merchantmen and two British corvettes. The *U-772* (Radenmacher) torpedoed the *Arthur Sewall* about 500 yards off the *Black Hawk*'s starboard bow, and two minutes later the *U-772* fired a torpedo that struck the *Black Hawk* at the #5 hatch. The torpedo set off the after magazine, completely destroyed the after section of the ship, and shot flames and smoke 150 feet into the air. The crew immediately secured the engines as the ship sank by the stern. A crack appeared at the #3 hatch, and water entered the #3 and #4 holds and the engine room until only the forward two compartments kept the ship afloat. The seven officers, thirty-four men, twenty-seven armed guards, and one Army security officer on board began to abandon ship thirty minutes after the initial explosion. The survivors left in four boats and made use of two rafts. The HMS corvette *Dahlia* (K-59) rescued the men and landed them at Brixham, England, at 1930. The blast injured four men, and the ship's cook later died ashore in a hospital. A salvage crew later boarded the vessel to prepare her to be towed to Warboro Bay. She was beached there and declared a CTL.

The ship's complement figures are contradictory within the sources. NSS; WACR; WCSR.

FRANCISCO MOROZAN

D: 12-29-44   YB: 1944
T: 1930   Tn: 7,176
Pos: off Mindoro, PI   Dr: 28 ft.
Ow: WSA   C: none
Op: Isthmian SS Co.   P: steam
M: John J. Brady   S: 9
A: 1-5"; 1-3"; 8-20 mm

On 27 December, the Liberty ship *Francisco Morozan* sailed from Leyte to Mindoro Island in the Philippines in convoy. Earlier in the day, a Japanese plane crash dove into the *John Burke*, and she blew up 100 yards off the *Morozan*'s starboard beam, wounding three of the *Morozan*'s men. These men transferred to the USS *Philip* (DD-498). On 30 December, after arriving and anchoring off Mindoro, an American fighter plane shot down a Japanese plane as it dove for the ship. The enemy plane passed just over the freighter, exploded, and left portions of the tail and flaming fragments on the deck. During the air attacks the ship suffered many other minor incidences of damage from shrapnel. The largest hole was made by a three-inch shell that passed through the stack. There were no further injuries to the crew of seven officers, thirty-one men, twenty-nine armed guards, and one security officer.

WACR; WCSR; AG.

HOBART BAKER

D:	12-30-44	YB:	1943
T:	0115	Tn:	7,176
Pos:	12.17.55 N / 121.04.47 E	Dr:	19 ft.
Ow:	WSA	C:	2,500 tons steel landing mats
Op:	General SS Corp.	P:	steam
M:	Joseph A. Stevens	S:	at anchor
A:	2-3"; 8-20 mm		

The *Hobart Baker* sailed from Port Hueneme, California, to Mindoro, Philippine Islands, via Leyte. On 22 December, the ship anchored off the southern coast of Mindoro, three-quarter mile offshore. During an air raid eight days later a Japanese plane approached the ship out of the dark, flying at mast height, and dropped two bombs over the vessel. One bomb fell into the #3 hold and the second fell in the water abreast of the hold. The first bomb destroyed the bulkhead between the engine room and the #3 hold, blew out steam lines in the engine room, and caused a large V-shaped crack in the hull. Smoke, flames, and steam filled the fireroom, engine room, and the midships quarters. As the ship flooded and settled by the head, the survivors among the complement of nine officers, twenty-nine men, and twenty-six armed guards abandoned ship in four lifeboats. As they cleared the ship, the amidships section burst into flame. The boats made landfall on Mindoro forty minutes after leaving the ship. The chief engineer died on watch below, and two armed guards and one other member of the crew reported injuries. The ship settled on the bottom the next day, leaving only the portion of the ship from the #4 hatch to the stern showing. The Liberty ship eventually lay completely submerged—a total loss.

Casualty numbers conflict in the sources. A steward was ashore at the time of the attack. NSS; WACR; WCSR.

JUAN DE FUCA

D:	12-31-44	YB:	1943
T:	0330	Tn:	7,176
Pos:	off Ambulong Island	Dr:	19 ft.
Ow:	WSA	C:	2,500 tons machinery, gasoline,
Op:	Weyerhaeuser SS Co.		troops, lumber
M:	Charles S. Robbins	P:	steam
A:	2-3"; 8-20 mm	S:	7.0

On 19 December, the *Juan De Fuca* sailed from Leyte, Philippine Islands, to Mindoro, Philippines, in convoy. A Japanese suicide plane extensively damaged the ship on the 21st, but the freighter proceeded on her way with a 5° list to prevent water from entering a hole in the side of the ship. On 22 December, the ship arrived at Mangarin Bay and began unloading her cargo. On 31 December,

as the *De Fuca* cruised about twenty miles off Mindoro, a Japanese torpedo bomber circled the ship and attacked from the port side. The torpedo struck at the #2 hatch, and the explosion showered the entire ship with oil and water and created a hole "large enough to drive 2 trucks through." The ship kept moving and tried to hide in one of the small coves in the area but went aground off Ambulong Island at 0600. Meanwhile, the forward holds flooded, and the ship began to split at the #4 hold. The master ordered his men to abandon ship just after midnight. Most of the complement of eight officers, thirty-three men, and twenty-seven armed guards left the ship in three of the ship's boats and rowed to Ambulong Island. The master and one of his men, along with the armed guard officer and two of his men, remained on the ship. Six hours later they also went ashore. The ship was refloated on 24 February and towed to Subic Bay. The Navy took over the ship on bare boat charter from WSA and renamed her the *Araner* (IX-226).

See also the attack on 21 December 1944. Originally the *John C. Fremont* was to be called the *Araner*, but she was replaced with the *Juan De Fuca*. NSS; WACR; WCSR; AG; *Araner* file, Ship's History Division, NHC; "Steady" *The Mast*, vol. 3, no. 5 (May 1946) pp. 14-17, 42-43.

JOHN M. CLAYTON

D:	1-1-45	YB:	1943
T:	2340	Tn:	7,184
Pos:	off Blue Beach, Mindoro	Dr:	20 ft.
Ow:	WSA	C:	75 tons general
Op:	American-Hawaiian SS Co.	P:	steam
M:	Nels Emanuel Nelson	S:	anchored
A:	2-3"; 8-20 mm		

On 19 December, the *John M. Clayton* sailed from Tacloban, Leyte, to Mindoro in convoy. Arriving in Mangarin Bay on 22 December, she anchored 2,000 yards off the beach and discharged 401 Army troops and 1,300 tons of vehicles. In the darkness a Japanese plane approached with its motors cut off. The plane strafed the *Clayton* and dropped a single bomb that skipped on the water and struck the port side at the #3 tank. The bomb passed through the shell plating and exploded inside. The hole was only fourteen inches in diameter, but the explosion blew a large hole in the port side of the hold and another hole ten feet in diameter in the ship's bottom through the double-bottom tanks. The oil in these tanks ignited and blew off the hatch covers, showering flaming oil over the bridge, gun tubs, deck house, and aft to the #5 hatch. Firefighting parties formed from the nine officers, thirty-three men, twenty-six armed guards, and twenty-one passengers on board. They managed to put the fire out in about ten minutes. Shore authorities never acknowledged the ship's call for medical assistance. Beginning at 0400 on 2 January, the ship's steam whistle sounded an SOS every fifteen minutes. Finally Army LCMs arrived and removed the

wounded and the survivors. On 2 January 1945, the master beached his ship to prevent further damage. The Navy Salvage Division patched up the *Clayton*, and the Navy took her into service as the *Harcourt* (IX-225). One officer, one of the merchant crew, and four armed guards died from burns, and eight other men reported injuries.

Two torpedoes struck the vessel, one on 26 December and one on 30 December. Neither exploded or caused any serious damage to the ship. NSS; WACR; WCSR; USMMA; AG; TF; DANFS, 3:241.

HENRY MILLER

D:	1-3-45	YB:	1943
T:	1803	Tn:	7,207
Pos:	35.51 N / 06.24 W	Dr:	27 ft. 9 in.
Ow:	WSA	C:	1,000 tons iron ore ballast
Op:	Moore-McCormick SS Co.	P:	steam
M:	Charles William Spear	S:	8.5
A:	2-3"; 8-20 mm		

The *Henry Miller* left Gibraltar on 3 January, en route to Hampton Roads, Virginia, in Convoy GUS-63. The convoy sailed in twelve columns of seventy-nine ships. The *Miller* proceeded as the leading ship in the fifth column, station #51. The *U-870* (Hechler) attacked the convoy twenty-two miles southwest of Cape Spartel. A torpedo struck the freighter at the bulkhead between the #2 and #3 holds. The crew secured the engines immediately, and the general alarm sounded. A fire started in the #3 hold, but as water filled the two damaged holds it extinguished the flames. The ship rapidly lost way and drifted aft of the convoy. Although the ship was down by the head and listing to port, the master decided to make Gibraltar fifty miles away. The eight officers, thirty-six men, twenty-seven armed guards, and one Armed security officer initially remained on board. At 1840 the master ordered lifeboats #3 and #4 to take twenty-five of the merchant crew, twenty-four armed guards, and the security officer off the ship in case a bulkhead failed. Fifteen minutes later they boarded the Coast Guard-manned frigate USS *Brunswick* (PF-68) and landed in Gibraltar the next day. The skeleton crew brought the *Miller* into Gibraltar at 0300 on 4 January, under her own power. All hands survived the attack. The vessel was later declared a CTL.

The complement figures are contradictory within the sources. NSS; WACR; WCSR; AG; Sawyer, Mitchell, p. 74; Rohwer, p. 189.

LEWIS L. DYCHE

D:	1-4-45	YB:	1943
T:	0820	Tn:	7,176
Pos:	off Mindoro	Dr:	unknown
Ow:	WSA	C:	bombs and fuses
Op:	InterOcean SS Co.	P:	steam
M:	John Warren Platt	S:	anchored
A:	2-3"; 8-20 mm		

The Liberty ship *Lewis L. Dyche* had shuttled around the Pacific Islands for several months prior to January 1945. On 14 December, she sailed from Leyte to Mindoro, Philippine Islands. Off Mindoro a Japanese suicide plane approached the ship flying twenty feet above the water and struck the *Dyche* amidships. The explosion that followed caused the cargo of bombs to ignite, and the ship disintegrated. The debris from the *Dyche* showered the other ships in the harbor, killing or wounding a number of crewmen. The ship's complement of eight officers, thirty-three men, and twenty-eight armed guards all perished.

WACR; WCSR; AG.

ISAAC SHELBY

D:	1-6-45	YB:	1944
T:	1545	Tn:	7,200
Pos:	41.10 N / 13.21 E	Dr:	14 ft. 6 in.
Ow:	WSA	C:	none
Op:	Smith & Johnson	P:	steam
M:	John Henry Lanctot	S:	7.5
A:	1-5"; 1-3"; 8-20 mm		

On 5 January, the *Isaac Shelby* sailed from Piombino, to Naples, Italy, in Convoy NV-90, composed of four ships and an Italian escort. Later that day, in bad weather, the vessel straggled from the convoy and ran into a minefield, striking three mines. The first explosion occurred under the bow on the port side. Thirty seconds later a second explosion rocked the ship under the #2 hold. The last mine exploded under the bow, starboard side. All the explosions threw water over forty feet in the air. The explosions ripped out the Liberty ship's double bottoms, flooded the #1 and #2 holds rapidly, and blew the hatch covers off both holds. A crack appeared at the after part of the #2 hatch coaming aft to the coaming of the #3 hatch. After the third explosion the master stopped the ship, and the crew put out small fires caused by fuel oil from the double bottoms that ignited. The ship lost way and began settling by the head, causing the screw and rudder to rise out of the water. The eight officers, thirty-five men, twelve armed guards, and one Army security officer abandoned the ship in three boats

and one raft. Those on the raft later transferred to the boats. All three boats made landfall the next day. One boat landed at San Felice, another landed at Cape Circeo, and the last boat came ashore on Isola Di Ponza. A U.S. destroyer removed those on the island. The *Shelby* eventually drifted and beached herself during the night of the 6th. Salvage crews reboarded her on 10 January, got up steam on 12 January, and beached her near San Felice. She eventually broke in two at the #2 hatch, and the WSA Total Loss Committee declared her a CTL. All hands survived the incident.

NSS; WACR; WCSR; AG; TF.

BLENHEIM

D:	1-8-45	YB:	1923
T:	1615	Tn:	5,097
Pos:	Antwerp, Belgium, Pier 123	Dr:	23 ft. 6 in.
Ow:	WSA	C:	4,000 tons general
Op:	Waterman SS Co.	P:	motor
M:	Axel Carl G. Lindgren	S:	docked
A:	1-4"; 8-20 mm		

On 17 November, the *Blenheim* sailed from New York to Antwerp, Belgium. On 3 January, the freighter tied up to Pier 123 in Antwerp and began discharging her cargo. While she was still moored at the pier, a German V-2 rocket exploded on the quay about fifty feet off the starboard side. The concussion broke and cracked all the bulkheads in the cabins and forecastle, blew off or damaged the doors, broke water pipes, and ripped radiators and bunks from the bulkheads. The concussion also blew in all the port holes, both port and starboard, wrecked the armed guards' quarters and every cabin on the starboard side, and destroyed three of the four lifeboats. The blast injured twenty of the eight officers, thirty-six men, twenty-five armed guards, and the one passenger on board. The crew made temporary repairs, and on 2 February, the ship sailed from Antwerp in convoy for England.

NSS; WACR; WCSR; AG.

JONAS LIE

D:	1-9-45	YB:	1944
T:	1720	Tn:	7,198
Pos:	51.43 N / 05.25 W	Dr:	21 ft. 8 in.
Ow:	WSA	C:	none
Op:	Agwilines Inc.	P:	steam
M:	Carl Lionel Von Schoen	S:	6
A:	1-5"; 1-3"; 8-20 mm		

On 9 January, the *Jonas Lie* departed Milford Haven, Wales, in Convoy ON-277 bound for New York. The ship proceeded with twenty other ships in convoy station #35. The *U-1055* (Meyer) attacked the convoy at the entrance to Bristol Channel. The U-boat fired a torpedo that struck the vessel in the #3 deep tank, starboard side, and ripped open the bulkhead between the engine room and the #4 hold. The blast created a hole twenty-five feet long at the waterline and broke steam and electrical connections. The ship listed over 10° to port as she lost way. At 1745 the master ordered the majority of the crew to abandon ship. All hands except the master, chief officer, boson, and one seaman left the ship in three lifeboats. The current swept these men away from the freighter, and the British trawler *Huddlersfield Town* (FY-197) picked them up. The master and his skeleton crew remained on board until the British Admiralty officials ordered them off at 2030. All these men landed at Milford Haven at 2300. The Norwegian MV *Fosna* rescued one survivor, which the torpedo explosion had blown overboard, and landed him in New York. Two men on watch below perished. On 10 January, the master and thirteen men departed on the sea-going tug HMS *Storm King* (W-87) to board the *Jonas Lie*. Overnight the vessel had drifted into a minefield. They got on board on the 11th and attached a tow line to the tug. On 12 January, the cable parted in heavy seas, and the tug HMS *Empire Sprite* assisted but to no avail. At 1210 on 13 January, a lifesaving boat took the crew off and landed them at St. Mary's Island. The vessel sank on the 14th.

NSS; WACR; WCSR; AG; Rohwer, p. 189, places the attack at 51.45 N / 05.27 W.

PONTUS H. ROSS

D:	1-11-45	YB:	1944
T:	0615	Tn:	7,247
Pos:	02.33.07 S / 140.06.01 E	Dr:	23 ft.
Ow:	WSA	C:	5,200 tons trucks, ammunition,
Op:	Moore-McCormick SS Co.		gasoline, rations
M:	Joseph E. Gibbons	P:	steam
A:	1-5"; 1-3"; 8-20 mm	S:	at anchor

The *Pontus H. Ross* sailed from New Orleans, Louisiana, to Hollandia, New Guinea. As the *Ross* anchored off Hollandia, the Japanese submarine *I-47* (Orita) released four Kaiten suicide craft nearby. Apparently only one reached the Liberty ship. It struck the port side at the #3 hold, scraped along the ship traveling forward, and exploded off the port bow. The blast only slightly damaged the freighter. It dented inward only seventy-five feet of hull plates beginning at the #3 hold forward. None of the crew of eight officers, thirty-four men, twenty-seven armed guards, and one passenger on board reported any injuries.

The *I-47* claimed four successful explosions. Another Kaiten torpedo may account for a second explosion observed nearby. WACR; AG; ONF; Rohwer, p. 287, places the attack at 01.33 S / 140.46 E; Campbell, p. 211.

ELMIRA VICTORY

D:	1-12-45	YB:	1944
T:	0800	Tn:	7,607
Pos:	16.11 N / 120.20 E	Dr:	28 ft. 3 in.
Ow:	WSA	C:	7,542 tons ammunition and 75
Op:	Alaska SS Co.		torpedoes on deck
M:	Christen Ellingsen Trondsen	P:	steam
A:	1-5"; 1-3"; 8-20 mm	S:	at anchor

The *Elmira Victory* sailed from Kossol Road, Palau, to Luzon in convoy. At 0740 the general alarm rang, and shortly afterwards lookouts spotted a plane flying through the smoke screen surrounding the vessels. A suicide plane struck the ship's cargo gear at the #5 hatch but caused only slight damage. Shortly thereafter, a second plane attacked through the smoke screen. Many of the ships in the anchorage took this plane under fire. The gunfire struck the plane, and it seemed to fly out of control and plunged into the water against the ship's side just aft of the superstructure. The plane's bomb exploded and scattered debris over the forward part of the ship and holed the vessel. It also destroyed and damaged the starboard boats. The plane's fuel or the gasoline from the motor lifeboat started a small fire on deck. Another small fire started in the #4 hold filled with bombs, but the crew quickly extinguished it. The Victory ship was further damaged by shells fired from a U.S. destroyer. The ship's twelve officers, forty-four men, twenty-seven armed guards, and six passengers all survived. The exploding plane injured two officers and four of the crew.

WACR; AG, ONF.

OTIS SKINNER

D:	1-12-45	YB:	1943
T:	1253	Tn:	7,176
Pos:	14.42 N / 119.35 E	Dr:	21 ft. 5 1/2 in.
Ow:	WSA	C:	7,000 tons explosives, gasoline,
Op:	American-Hawaiian SS Co.		vehicles
M:	G. H. Blackett	P:	steam
A:	2-3"; 8-20 mm	S:	8.5

The *Otis Skinner* sailed from Hollandia, New Guinea, to Lingayen Gulf, Luzon, in convoy. Japanese aircraft attacked the convoy as it proceeded to its destination. A suicide plane crashed on the *Skinner*, striking the starboard side at the #2 hatch. An explosion and fire damaged the ship and some of the cargo. The explosion put a hole in the shell plating at the tween decks that spanned from two to seven feet wide. The explosion also damaged other structural members and equipment throughout the ship. The vessel's cargo in the tween deck caught fire, and the flames destroyed and damaged trucks, PX supplies, and pontoons. The flames leapt to the bridge and drove the men there to the boat deck. The explosion also damaged a DUKW and an LCM on deck. Firefighting parties assembled from the ship's ten officers, thirty-three men, twenty-seven armed guards, and one passenger and quickly extinguished the fire. On 13 January, she steamed into Lingayen Gulf with a 7° list caused by water entering the #2 hold. After repairs she went back in service. The fire injured two crew members.

WACR; WCSR; AG.

EDWARD N. WESTCOTT

D:	1-12-45	YB:	1943
T:	1800	Tn:	7,176
Pos:	West Coast Luzon	Dr:	24 ft.
Ow:	WSA	C:	3,600 tons vehicles, gasoline,
Op:	Agwilines Inc.		troops
M:	Lars Hanson	P:	steam
A:	2-3"; 8-20 mm	S:	8

On 3 January, the *Edward N. Westcott* sailed in convoy from Hollandia, New Guinea, to Lingayen Gulf, Philippine Islands. Off the coast of Luzon eight enemy planes attacked the convoy from astern. One aircraft, after being hit by defensive gunfire, headed straight for the *Westcott* at boat deck level with its guns pouring fire into the ship. The after guns of the Liberty ship maintained an intense fire on this plane. Thirty yards from the ship the three-inch gun landed a direct hit that blew the plane apart. The exploding plane showered the ship with debris and damaged the whole after part of the freighter. The engine sheared off the binnacle and landed on the after part of the starboard boat deck. The plane's tail sheared off the #4 and #5 starboard booms and other gear on the starboard quarter. All 8 officers, 33 men, 25 armed guards, and 365 U.S. troops on board survived. Flying debris, however, injured ten armed guards and one merchant crewman.

WACR; WCSR; AG.

KYLE V. JOHNSON

D:	1-12-45	YB:	1944
T:	1830	Tn:	7,176
Pos:	15.12 N / 119.30 E	Dr:	17 ft. 5 in.
Ow:	WSA	C:	2,500 tons vehicles, gasoline,
Op:	Waterman SS Co.		troops
M:	Carl W. Moline	P:	steam
A:	1-5"; 1-3"; 8-20 mm	S:	9

On 3 January, the *Kyle V. Johnson* sailed in convoy from Hollandia, New Guinea, to Lingayen Gulf, Philippine Islands. The convoy totaled 100 ships, including 40 merchant ships, 40 LSTs, and 20 PT boats. Nine destroyer escorts and destroyers provided escort. With the *Johnson* in convoy station #51, about eight Japanese planes attacked. The ship's armed guards took two planes under fire. One of these planes dove onto the ship and crashed on the starboard side through the hull, passing through the tween deck and into the #3 hold. An explosion blew the steel hatch beams above the bridge. The cargo in this hold caught fire, and flames swept over the bridge. The ship slowed and dropped from the convoy while a destroyer escort stood by. The crew broke out seven fire hoses to flood the hold. They had the fire under control in fifteen minutes and extinguished it in an hour. The Liberty ship had on board 8 officers, 35 men, 29 armed guards, and 506 U.S. troops. The merchant crew lost only 1 man, but 129 troops quartered in the tween deck section died. The initial explosion blew nine men overboard and escorts rescued these men. The ship arrived with the convoy in Lingayen Gulf on 13 January.

The ship's complement figures and Army deaths conflict within the sources. NSS; WACR; WCSR; AG.

DAVID DUDLEY FIELD

D:	1-12-45	YB:	1943
T:	1830	Tn:	7,176
Pos:	Subic Bay, PI	Dr:	22 ft.
Ow:	WSA	C:	4,000 tons Army supplies,
Op:	Isthmian SS Co.		pontoons
M:	Albion M. Burbank	P:	steam
A:	2-3"; 8-20 mm	S:	9

The *David Dudley Field* sailed from Hollandia, New Guinea, to Lingayen Gulf, Philippines. A Japanese suicide plane dove toward the Liberty ship while she was in convoy. The armed guards successfully defended the ship and caused the Japanese plane to swerve and hit the freighter with only its wing tip. The plane's bomb exploded off the port side at the #4 hold, throwing a sheet of water over the after guns and washing one man overboard. The concussion caused only slight damage. All nine officers, thirty-one men, thirty armed guards, ten passengers, and fifty stevedores on board survived. Eight men reported injuries.

WACR; AG.

MARTIN VAN BUREN

D: 1-14-45	YB: 1943
T: 1045	Tn: 7,176
Pos: 44.27.30 N/ 63.26 W	Dr: 27 ft. 1 in.
Ow: WSA	C: 6,000 tons provisions,
Op: West India SS Co.	locomotives, vehicles
M: James Howard Hiss Jr.	P: steam
A: 1-5"; 1-3"	S: 10.5

On 12 January, the *Martin Van Buren* cleared Boston, Massachusetts, en route to Halifax, Nova Scotia, in Convoy BV-141. The convoy reached the Sambro Light Vessel and reduced from eight columns to one. The *Van Buren* wore pennant #71, and she took station #4 after the convoy formed into one column. At 1330 the *U-1232* (Dobratz) torpedoed the *British Freedom* dead ahead of the *Van Buren*, and the *Van Buren*'s helmsman steered to starboard to avoid the disabled tanker. As the *Van Buren* swung back to port to regain her station, a torpedo struck near the stern post slightly to port. The explosion blew off the rudder and propeller. The crew secured the engines immediately. The hull cracked abreast of the #3 hatch across the deck and extended down both sides below the waterline. A second crack appeared on the after deck between the #4 and #5 hatches on the port side, and the strain caused the hull to bulge on the starboard side. The vessel began settling slowly by the stern and listed sharply to port. She eventually righted herself and took a slight starboard list. At 1110 the ship's surviving eight officers, thirty-three men, twenty-seven armed guards, and one passenger began to abandon ship in four lifeboats and three rafts. The explosion blew four members of the five-inch gun crew overboard. Three of these men were never found. The Canadian trawlers *Comox* (J-64) and *Fundy* (J-88) and one other Canadian escort rescued all hands with the exception of the armed guards and landed them at Halifax on the 14th. An escorting tug later took the ship in tow. However, a naval vessel disregarded the tug's lights and cut across the towing hawser. With no other lines available, the ship drifted upon the rocks near Sambro and broke in two. The WSA declared the vessel a CTL, and salvors scrapped her in place.

NSS; WACR; WCSR; AG; Rohwer, p. 189, places the attack at 44.28 N / 63.28 W; Sawyer, Mitchell, p. 53.

MICHAEL DE KOVATS

D:	1-14-45	YB:	1944
T:	1717	Tn:	7,240
Pos:	Antwerp, Belgium	Dr:	17 ft. 6 in.
Ow:	WSA	C:	1,000 tons general U.S. Army
Op:	Polarus SS Co. Inc.		cargo
M:	Armand A. Veilleux	P:	steam
A:	1-5"; 1-3"; 8-20 mm	S:	docked

The *Michael De Kovats* departed Boston, Massachusetts, and arrived in Antwerp, Belgium, on 1 January and anchored in berth 218. During her stay, a V-2 bomb hit the dock off the starboard quarter. Bomb fragments damaged the superstructure and rigging, cracked the #1 tween deck, and ripped doors and fixtures from the bulkheads. The ship's complement consisted of nine officers, thirty-three men, twenty-seven armed guards, and one passenger. The explosion injured one officer and two men and reportedly killed one soldier ashore.

WACR; AG; ONF.

MARINA

D:	1-16-45	YB:	1941
T:	1119	Tn:	5,068
Pos:	49.30.20 N / 00.04.12 W	Dr:	22 ft.
Ow:	WSA	C:	2,500 tons general U.S. Army
Op:	A. H. Bull & Co.		cargo
M:	Charles Hendrickx	P:	steam
A:	1-4"; 1-3"; 8-20 mm	S:	10

On 3 January, the *Marina* left New York in Convoy CU-53 bound for Le Havre, France. Before proceeding into port, the vessel stopped outside the harbor to pick up a pilot. Because of the important nature of the cargo, the ship was given clearance to be docked first. The pilot tried to swing ahead of two other ships by cutting inside the entrance buoy—but outside of the mine-swept channel. While navigating outside the swept channel, the vessel struck a mine at the stern. Water flooded through the open shaft alley door into the engine room, and the ship settled by the stern. The British tug *Empire Rodgers* put a tow line on board, and shortly thereafter a U.S. Army tug also made fast alongside. The tugs beached the *Marina* outside the breakwater at La Havre. Thirty men left the vessel by stepping over the side into an escort vessel, and the remaining men left after the tugs beached the ship. All eight officers, thirty-seven men, twenty-nine armed guards, and twenty-seven passengers on board survived the explosion.

On 18 February, the freighter received temporary repairs and then days later went into dry dock in Rouen, France.

NSS; WACR; WCSR; AG; ONF.

GEORGE HAWLEY

D:	1-21-45	YB:	1944
T:	1438	Tn:	7,176
Pos:	49.53.24 N / 05.44 W	Dr:	14 ft. 9 in.
Ow:	WSA	C:	none, 73 bags of mail
Op:	Sprague SS Co.	P:	steam
M:	Charles Paul John Muhle	S:	6
A:	1-5"; 1-3"; 8-20 mm		

On 19 January, the *George Hawley* left Cherbourg, France, en route to Mumbles, Wales. The *Hawley* arrived off the Isle of Wight on the morning of 20 January, where she joined Convoy TBC-43. The convoy steamed in two columns, and the *Hawley* took station as the second ship in the starboard column. The *U-1199* (Nollmann) fired a torpedo that struck the starboard side amidships. The explosion demolished the engines, flooded the engine room immediately, and started a small fire in the galley. The Liberty ship began to list slightly to port as the British coastal tug *TID-74* and the SS *Wiley Wakeman* stood by. The ship's complement of eight officers, thirty-three men, and twenty-seven armed guards abandoned ship at 1500 in the vessel's four lifeboats. The British tug and the *Wakeman* rescued the men and landed them at Cardiff. One officer and one crewman died on watch below. The master, the chief officer, the boson, and another man returned to the *Hawley* at 1700. They passed a line to a tug, but she did not have the power to tow the freighter. The salvage tug HMS *Allegiance* (W-50) arrived at 2200 and took the ship in tow to Falmouth, arriving there on 22 January. The *Hawley* lay beached until June 1946. Authorities loaded her with obsolete chemical ammunition and scuttled her at sea in October 1946.

NSS; WACR; WCSR; AG; Rohwer, p. 190; Sawyer, Mitchell, p. 100.

ALCOA BANNER

D:	1-24-45	YB:	1917
T:	0815	Tn:	5,035
Pos:	Antwerp, Belgium	Dr:	unknown
Ow:	Alcoa SS Co.	C:	general
Op:	WSA	P:	steam
M:	Magnus Emanuel Wiklund	S:	docked
A:	1-4"; 8-20 mm		

The old "Hog Islander" *Alcoa Banner* sailed from the Downs to Antwerp, Belgium, and docked at berth 166. While she was alongside the dock, German bombers attacked the anchorage and struck the freighter with two bombs. They both exploded in the #3 hold and extensively damaged the ship. The explosions started a fire that gutted the deep and settling tanks, the boiler room, the engine room, and the midships quarters. The fire also destroyed most of the ship's cargo. As the ship began to sink at the dock, a salvage vessel attempted to save her. Water filled holds #2, #3, and #4 and eventually rose to deck level as the ship sank on an even keel. The ship's eight officers, thirty-two men, twenty-seven armed guards, and one passenger remained on the freighter as she sank. The chief engineer and a fireman died in the boiler room. The *Alcoa Banner* went into dry dock on 27 January, and the remaining salvagable cargo was discharged. The WSA later declared the vessel a CTL.

WACR; WCSR; AG.

RUBEN DARIO

D:	1-27-45	YB:	1944
T:	1237	Tn:	7,198
Pos:	52.27.30 N / 05.21 W	Dr:	27 ft.
Ow:	WSA	C:	8,026 tons grain and gliders
Op:	International Freight Corp.	P:	steam
M:	Ernest Frederick Carlsson	S:	9.5
A:	1-5"; 1-3"; 8-20 mm		

On 13 January, the *Ruben Dario* sailed from New York in Convoy HS-332 bound for the Mersey. The convoy later split, and the remaining ships formed two columns and proceeded into Saint George's Channel. The *Ruben Dario* took the sixth position in the port column (#16). At noon the commodore alerted the convoy to watch for the enemy. Two German U-boats, the *U-825* (Stökler) and the *U-1051* (von Holleben), stalked the convoy. A torpedo, probably from the *U-825*, struck the Liberty ship on the starboard side in the #2 hold. The explosion burst the bulkhead between the #1 and #2 holds. The #2 hold flooded rapidly, and the forward hold leaked at a slower rate. As the ship settled by the head, the watch below secured the engines. After making a survey of the damage, the master had the engines restarted and the ship proceeded at nine knots, joining the convoy at 1600. None of the nine officers, thirty-two men, twenty-seven armed guards, and five passengers on board perished, but the explosion did injure one merchant seaman lying on the #2 hatch. The ship arrived at Liverpool the next day with a forty-foot draft forward.

The figures for the armed guards are contradictory within the sources. NSS; WACR; WCSR; AG; Rohwer, p. 190, places the attack at 52.35 N / 05.18 W.

HENRY B. PLANT

D:	2-6-45	YB:	1944
T:	0445	Tn:	7,240
Pos:	51.19.24 N / 01.42.30 E	Dr:	26 ft.
Ow:	WSA	C:	8,000 tons iron landing strips,
Op:	A. L. Burbank & Co.		general
M:	Charles James Ward	P:	steam
A:	1-5"; 1-3"; 8-20 mm	S:	6

On 8 January, the Liberty ship *Henry B. Plant* sailed from New York on her maiden voyage to the United Kingdom. After several changes of port the vessel sailed from Margate Roads on 6 February, in the ten ship Convoy TAM-71 en route to Antwerp, Belgium. As the *Plant* steamed in convoy station #19 (last ship in the starboard column), lookouts spotted a submarine 300 yards off the starboard side. The master ordered the helmsman to steer hard left, but the *U-245* (Schumann-Hindenberg) had already fired a torpedo and moments later it struck at the #4 hold. The force of the explosion ruptured the main deck, severed steam lines, blasted the hatches and beams overboard, and probably set off the after magazines. The watch below secured the engines as the vessel rapidly sank. Most of the eight officers, thirty-three men, twenty-eight armed guards, and an Army security officer on board jumped into the water. The ship sank stern first in five minutes. The men managed to launch only one lifeboat but did trip four of the rafts and used two of them. The minesweeper HMS *Hazard* (N-02) and the trawler *Sir Lancelot* (T-228) picked up the survivors. One officer, eight men, and seven armed guards drowned trying to leave the ship.

NSS; WACR; WCSR; AG; Rohwer, p. 190, puts the attack at 51.22 N / 02.00 E.

PETER SILVESTER

D:	2-6-45	YB:	1942
T:	1540	Tn:	7,176
Pos:	34.19 S / 99.37 E	Dr:	19 ft. 7 in.
Ow:	WSA	C:	2,700 tons Army cargo, 317
Op:	Pacific Far East Line		mules, troops
M:	Bernard C. Dennis	P:	steam
A:	1-4"; 1-3"; 8-20 mm	S:	11.7

The *Peter Silvester* left Melbourne, Australia, on 28 January and sailed independently to Colombo, Ceylon. The *U-862* (Timm) intercepted the freighter while patrolling off the southeast coast of Australia. The *U-862* fired two torpedoes, both striking the ship on the starboard side at the #3 hold. One of the torpedoes was seen entering the starboard side and exiting the port side. The other exploded in the hold, ruptured the deck forward of the bridge, blew off the

#3 hatch cover, and flooded the hold and the engine room. As the bow settled, the ship lost way but stayed on an even keel. At 1610 two more torpedoes struck the starboard side at the transverse bulkhead between holds #2 and #3 and fatally damaged the ship. As the bow began to sink rapidly, the master ordered the 8 officers, 34 men, 26 armed guards, and 107 U.S. Army troops to abandon ship. They cleared the freighter in four lifeboats and six life rafts. As they left, two final torpedoes struck the freighter. Both struck the #1 hold, and this caused the Liberty ship to break in two just forward of the superstructure. The forward end sank immediately and the after section remained afloat. Fifty-seven hours after the attack the SS *Cape Edmont* rescued the fifteen survivors in the #2 boat and landed them in Fremantle, Australia. The USS *Corpus Christi* (PF-44) picked up all six of the rafts with ninety survivors after six days at sea. The same day she rescued twelve survivors in the #4 lifeboat. All these men landed in Fremantle. The escort carrier HMS *Activity* (D-94) picked up twenty survivors in another boat after twenty-one days at sea and landed these men in Fremantle. The USS *Rock* (SS-274) rescued the fifteen survivors in the last boat after thirty-one days at sea and landed them at Exmouth Rock. A total of 142 men survived. One merchant seaman died along with seven armed guards and twenty-five troops. (One of the Army men died in the #3 boat from injuries.)

NSS; WACR; WCSR; RWCS; AG; Rohwer, p. 277.

HORACE GRAY

D:	2-14-45	YB:	1943
T:	1510	Tn:	7,200
Pos:	69.21 N / 33.43 E	Dr:	22 ft. 6 in.
Ow:	WSA	C:	2,500 tons potash
Op:	American Export Lines	P:	steam
M:	Charles Fox Brown	S:	9
A:	1-5"; 1-3"; 8-20 mm		

On 9 February, the *Horace Gray* sailed from Molotovsk, USSR, in convoy to Murmansk. The convoy comprised nine ships traveling in two columns. The *Horace Gray* steamed in the starboard column behind two other ships. As the convoy approached Kola Inlet, the *U-711* (Lange) torpedoed the Norwegian tanker *Noffell* directly ahead of the *Grey*. The American ship took the station vacated by the torpedoed ship. Minutes later another torpedo fired by the *U-711* struck the Liberty ship on the port side at the bulkhead, separating the #4 and #5 holds. The explosion blasted the #4 and #5 hatch covers off and opened one hole twenty feet by sixty feet in the port side and another hole twenty feet by twenty feet in the starboard side. The ship settled rapidly by the stern until water reached the after deck. At 1530 the master gave the orders to abandon ship. The complement of eight officers, thirty-three men, and twenty-eight armed guards used all four of the ship's lifeboats to clear the ship. A Russian submarine chaser

picked up the survivors in boats #2 and #4 about fifteen minutes after abandoning ship. A Russian escort vessel rescued the survivors in boats #1 and #3. The master and the men from boats #2 and #4 reboarded the vessel at 1610. After raising steam, a small Russian tug towed her to Kola Inlet. While under tow a crack appeared on the starboard side and the vessel began to sink. The master beached the *Horace Gray* on the 15th, and the WSA later declared her a CTL. All hands survived the attack.

The ship's complement figures are contradictory within the sources. NSS; WACR; WCSR; AG; Rohwer, p. 211, places the attack at 60.23 N / 33.47 E.

THOMAS SCOTT

D: 2-17-45   YB: 1942
T: 1150   Tn: 7,176
Pos: 69.30 N / 34.42.30 E   Dr: 19 ft. 11 in.
Ow: WSA   C: none
Op: Waterman SS Co.   P: steam
M: Jack Alvin Teston   S: 3
A: 1-4"; 1-3"; 8-20 mm

On 17 February, the *Thomas Scott* left her anchorage in Kola Inlet to steam into her assigned station #34 in the thirty-six ship Convoy RA-64. The freighter was bound to Gourock, Scotland, and as the convoy formed, the *U-968* (Westphalen) attacked. A torpedo struck the ship on the starboard side at the #3 hatch and the *Scott* immediately took a 25° starboard list. As the ship careened out of control, she broke in two and hung together only by deck plates on the well deck. The crew secured the engines from the boat deck. At 1200 the master passed the order to abandon ship. The vessel's eight officers, thirty-four men, twenty-seven armed guards, and forty Norwegian refugees cleared the ship in four boats and one raft. The British escort carrier HMS *Fencer* (D-64) rescued the survivors after about forty minutes in the water. Two hours later the merchant crew and armed guards transferred to the Russian destroyer *Zhestkij* and the tug *M-12*. The tug and the destroyer took the Liberty ship in tow stern first. During the trip she broke in half and the after part sank immediately. The destroyer tried to salvage the forward end, but it sank at 2100. Eight men reported injuries, but all hands survived the attack. The Americans landed in Murmansk, and the Norwegians continued their passage in the *Fencer*.

WACR; WCSR; Rohwer, pp. 211-12.

MICHAEL J. STONE

D:	2-17-45	YB:	1942
T:	1055	Tn:	7,176
Pos:	35.55 N / 05.53 W	Dr:	27 ft.
Ow:	WSA	C:	7,705 tons landing mats, oil,
Op:	Lykes Bros. SS Co.		jeeps, asphalt
M:	Guy Earnest Parker	P:	steam
A:	1-4"; 1-3"; 8-20 mm	S:	8

On 2 February, the *Michael J. Stone* sailed from Norfolk, Virginia, in Convoy UGS-72 bound for Calcutta, India. The *Stone* proceeded in station #43 in the convoy of eighty-six ships. Twenty-seven miles from Gibraltar, the *U-300* (Hein) fired a torpedo that struck the freighter on the starboard side at the bulkhead, separating the #4 and #5 holds. The blast damaged 650 square feet of the hull. The vessel began to slowly settle by the stern as water rushed into the two holds. The steering room also flooded, but the ship maintained way. Even though the ship was damaged, the master maintained his determination to save his vessel. As the ship limped to Gibraltar, the bridge steering control failed and the crew steered the ship manually. She arrived in Gibraltar at 1800, drawing forty feet aft but under her own power. The salvage tug HMS *Behest* (W-174) took the freighter in tow outside the port. All eight officers, thirty-four men, twenty-seven armed guards, and four passengers survived the explosion.

NSS; WACR; WCSR; AG; Rohwer, p. 191, places the attack at 35.56 N / 05.45 W.

JANE G. SWISSHELM

D:	2-23-45	YB:	1943
T:	0715	Tn:	7,176
Pos:	Dock 187, Antwerp, Belgium	Dr:	16 ft.
Ow:	WSA	C:	approximately 1,500 tons war
Op:	Olympic SS Co.		supplies
M:	Harold Svantemann	P:	steam
A:	2-3"; 8-20 mm	S:	docked

On 2 February, the *Jane G. Swisshelm* sailed from New York to Antwerp, Belgium. The freighter arrived and docked in Antwerp on 20 February and began discharging her cargo. On the 23rd, the Germans attacked the town with rockets. A V-2 rocket landed about twelve feet off the port side at the #1 hatch. The explosion caused the Liberty ship to dip into the water so deep that a large wave washed over her bow. The blast blew a ventilation cover off and caused minor damage throughout the ship. Bomb shrapnel also caused minor damage and put holes and dents in the vessel. Only three of the eight officers, thirty-six

men, twenty-seven armed guards, and one passenger on board reported minor injuries from the explosion.

The times and crew figures are contradictory among the sources. WACR; WCSR; AG.

HENRY BACON

D:	2-23-45	YB:	1942
T:	1420	Tn:	7,176
Pos:	67.00 N / 07.00 E	Dr:	18 ft.
Ow:	WSA	C:	5,500 tons sand ballast
Op:	South Atlantic	P:	steam
M:	Alfred Carini	S:	10
A:	1-5"; 1-3"; 8-20 mm		

On 17 February, the *Henry Bacon* left Murmansk, USSR, bound for Gourock, Scotland. She sailed in Convoy RA-64. Two days later she encountered heavy weather and straggled from the convoy. The Liberty ship later rejoined the convoy but lost contact once again. On the 22nd, the master thought he had steamed ahead of the convoy and turned his vessel back. At 1400, while the ship was on a reverse course, lookouts spotted twenty-three enemy torpedo bombers. The armed guards skillfully protected the ship as the planes reportedly launched forty-six torpedoes. Several times the helmsman expertly avoided the torpedoes by turning the ship. At 1420 a torpedo struck the starboard side at the #5 hatch. The explosion blasted a large hole in the hull, blew off the hatch covers, damaged the rudder and propeller, and ruptured steam lines, causing the ship to settle by the stern quickly. The ship carried four lifeboats, but the eight officers, thirty-two men, twenty-six armed guards, and nineteen Norwegian refugees on board only made use of two. Heavy weather had damaged the #4 boat, and the #3 boat capsized while being lowered. The refugees and a few of the crew climbed into boat #1 shortly after the torpedo struck. At about 1500, fifteen of the merchant crew and seven armed guards launched the #2 lifeboat. The ship sank stern first minutes later. None of the rafts could be used, and several men, remaining on the freighter, jumped into the water and swam to a doughnut raft that floated free of the ship. Some of the survivors later transferred to this raft because of overcrowding in the boats. Four British destroyers quickly arrived on the scene. The HMS *Opportune* (G-80) picked up the survivors in the boats about three hours after the sinking. The HMS *Zest* (R-02) rescued eleven men on the raft, and the destroyer HMS *Zambesi* (R-66) rescued the other survivors. The survivors landed in Scapa Flow and Gourock, Scotland. Seven armed guards died along with six merchant officers and nine men.

The complement figures are contradictory within the sources. NSS; WACR; WCSR; RWCS; AG.

NASHABA

D:	2-26-45	YB:	1921
T:	0846	Tn:	6,054
Pos:	51.22.18 N / 02.55.25 E	Dr:	22 ft. 6 in.
Ow:	Lykes Bros.	C:	2,600 tons crane parts, barbed
Op:	Lykes Bros.		wire
M:	Albert Lee Newsome	P:	steam
A:	1-4"; 1-3"; 8-20 mm	S:	6

On 22 February, the *Nashaba* cleared Cardiff, Wales, en route to Ghent, Belgium, in Convoy TAM-91. While proceeding in the Schelde Estuary in convoy station #7, the vessel struck a mine one mile north of Buoy NF 7. The explosion occurred at the keel under the #4 hold. The blast broke the ship's back, carried away the hatch covers, and blew cargo through the hatches. Initially the master did not consider the damage serious, but as the vessel sank slowly by the stern with a 15° port list the master had the engines secured. At 0905 he ordered the complement of ten officers, thirty-one men, twenty-seven armed guards, and the Dutch river pilot to abandon ship. A British corvette and a Norwegian ship rescued the men from the four lifeboats and landed them in Ostend and Antwerp. The second mate died in the explosion.

The merchant crew figures are contradictory within the sources. NSS; WACR; WCSR; AG.

ROBERT L. VANN

D:	3-1-45	YB:	1943
T:	1920	Tn:	7,176
Pos:	51.22 N / 02.53 E	Dr:	20 ft.
Ow:	WSA	C:	ballast
Op:	United Fruit Co.	P:	steam
M:	Lars Ostervold	S:	8
A:	2-3"; 8-20 mm		

On 1 March, the *Robert L. Vann* sailed in the twelve-ship Convoy ATM-76 from Antwerp, Belgium, to the Thames River. While proceeding through the swept channel in a single column, the ship struck a mine one and one-half miles north of Buoy NF 8 off Ostend. The explosion occurred on the starboard side of the #3 hold, and the blast broke the ship's back aft of the #3 hatch. The ship began sinking at a slow rate with bow and stern raised. The eight officers, thirty-three men, twenty-seven armed guards, one Army security officer, and the Belgian pilot abandoned ship in three lifeboats and two rafts. All hands survived the sinking. One of the merchant crew and four armed guards reported slight injuries. A British escort vessel rescued twenty-six survivors and landed them at Sheerness. An Army tug picked up twenty-five survivors and landed them at

Ramsgate. A British PT boat rescued the remaining nineteen and took them to Ostend. The ship eventually settled on the bottom of the channel with only the stack above the water.

The shipping articles record the master as Daniel L. Burns, but Ostervold was listed as the master during the attack. NSS; WACR; WCSR; AG.

OLIVER KELLEY

D:	3-17-45	YB:	1943
T:	1030	Tn:	7,176
Pos:	Surigao Strait, PI	Dr:	27 ft.
Ow:	WSA	C:	6,000 tons explosives, vehicles,
Op:	McCormick SS Co.		machinery
M:	H. E. Clever	P:	steam
A:	2-3"; 8-20 mm	S:	8.5

On 27 January, the *Oliver Kelley* sailed from Port Townsend, Washington, to Lingayen Gulf, Philippine Islands. On 13 March, the vessel departed Kossel Roads en route to Palau. While proceeding through Surigao Strait, the ship suffered a severe jar. It was blamed on a dud torpedo that struck between the #4 and #5 holds on the port side. There were no casualties among the eight officers, thirty-four men, twenty-eight armed guards, and one passenger on board. The master recorded slight damage to his vessel.

WACR; AG; TF; ONF; Rohwer, p. 219, notes the Japanese submarines reported three transports sunk in this area in March.

HADLEY F. BROWN

D:	3-19-45	YB:	1944
T:	1345	Tn:	7,176
Pos:	51.22 N / 02.53 E	Dr:	23 ft. 5 in.
Ow:	WSA	C:	4,124 tons Army Engineers'
Op:	Mystic SS Co.		supplies
M:	Edward Walter Hutchinson	P:	steam
A:	1-5"; 8-20 mm	S:	7

The Liberty ship *Hadley F. Brown* sailed from Barry, Wales, to Ghent, Belgium, in Convoy TAG-12. At the entrance to the Schelde River Estuary near Buoy NF 9, the vessel struck a mine. The explosion occurred on the starboard side under the machinery spaces, and threw water over the flying bridge, flooded the engine room, and disabled the engines. The complement of eight officers, thirty-three men, and twenty-seven armed guards remained on the ship. A salvage vessel later towed the freighter first to Flushing and then to Antwerp on the 21st.

The ship received repairs for eight weeks at Antwerp and later returned to service. Eight men reported injuries from the blast.

WACR; WCSR; AG.

HORACE BUSHNELL

D:	3-20-45	YB:	1943
T:	0915	Tn:	7,176
Pos:	69.23 N / 35.17 E	Dr:	27 ft.
Ow:	WSA	C:	6,500 tons locomotives, tires,
Op:	R. A. Nicol & Co.		ammunition, machinery, trucks
M:	William John Lacey	P:	steam
A:	1-5"; 1-3"; 8-20 mm	S:	10

The *Horace Bushnell* left Gourock, Scotland, on 10 March, en route to Murmansk, USSR, in the twenty-six ship Convoy JW-65. The ship traveled in convoy station #11 in the port column. Twenty-four miles east of the North Kilden Light, the *U-995* (Hess) fired a torpedo that struck the port side in the engine room. The blast created a hole thirty-three feet by twenty-six feet, cracked the main deck, and completely destroyed the ship's engines. The explosion also blew the engine room skylight over the side, cut off the ship's power, destroyed one lifeboat, and filled another with oil. The ship settled with a slight list by the stern till water reached thirty-four feet, and then she steadied and began taking on water at a slower rate. The master passed word that the ship should be prepared for abandonment at a moment's notice. He had hoisted the flags x-ray and fox indicating the ship had been torpedoed. The complement of eight officers, thirty-four men, and twenty-seven armed guards remained on board to take a tow line from the destroyer HMS *Orwell* (G-98) standing by. The master hoped to beach the Liberty ship, but the heavy seas prevented the destroyer from making any headway. The destroyer's captain advised the crew of the *Bushnell* to abandon ship. At 1150 all hands went directly on board the escorting destroyer except the officer and three men who died on watch below. The chief engineer died of shock on the escort vessel. Two Russian salvage tugs later beached the vessel at Teriberski, and the WSA declared the ship a CTL. The survivors landed at Murmansk, USSR.

The *Bushnell* was eventually salvaged and converted into a Russia fish carrier and renamed the *Pamyati Kirova*. Complement figures conflict within the sources. NSS; WACR; WCSR; AG; Rohwer, p. 212; Sawyer, Mitchell, p. 50.

THOMAS DONALDSON

D:	3-20-45	YB:	1944
T:	1215	Tn:	7,210
Pos:	68.26.30 N / 33.44.20 E	Dr:	27 ft. 8 in.
Ow:	WSA	C:	6,000 tons ammunition,
Op:	American Export Lines		locomotives on deck
M:	Robert Headden	P:	steam
A:	1-5"; 1-3"; 8-20 mm	S:	10.5

On 11 March, the *Thomas Donaldson* sailed in Convoy JW-65 from Gourock, Scotland, to Murmansk, USSR. The convoy formed into one column to enter Kola Inlet, and the *Donaldson* steamed behind nineteen other ships in the column of twenty-six ships. About five miles off Kilden Island, the *U-968* (Westphalen) fired a torpedo that struck the starboard side in the engine room and demolished the engines. Since the ship carried ammunition, the master gave the order to abandon ship at 1230. Many among the complement of eight officers, thirty-four men, and twenty-seven armed guards launched the two port lifeboats and a raft, while others jumped into the water. The British corvette HMS *Bamborough Castle* (K-412) rescued the men in the boats and raft. The British corvette *Oxlip* (K-123) rescued those in the water. The master and eight of the crew temporarily remained behind and later boarded the British corvette HMS *Honeysuckle* (K-27), which towed the *Donaldson* toward Kola Inlet. At 1530 a Russian tug took over the tow, but the ship sank stern first at 1645, one-half mile from Kilden Island. The officer and two men on watch below perished. A fourth man died on board an escort vessel, and the remaining men survived.

NSS; WACR; WCSR; AG; Rohwer, p. 212.

JOHN R. PARK

D:	3-21-45	YB:	1942
T:	1445	Tn:	7,194
Pos:	49.56 N / 05.26 W	Dr:	17 ft. 9 in.
Ow:	WSA	C:	none
Op:	Luckenbach SS Co.	P:	steam
M:	Oho Leiner Bortfeld	S:	7
A:	2-3"; 8-20 mm		

On 20 March, the *John R. Park* left Southampton, England, en route to Mumbles, Wales, in Convoy TBC-102. The *Park* carried the convoy commodore and proceeded as the first ship in the port column of the two-column convoy. In a heavy fog, the *U-399* (Buhse), one of three subs attacking the convoy, put a torpedo in the freighter on the port side at the #4 hold just forward of the bulkhead separating the #5 hold. The blast threw a column of

water, sand ballast, and oil over the bridge and onto the main deck. The explosion ruptured the main deck between the after two hatches, caused a large crack that extended across the ship, destroyed the after life rafts, and damaged the shaft. As the Liberty ship's bow swung to port, she lost way and began to settle by the stern. The eight officers, thirty-three men, twenty-eight armed guards, and the commodore and his staff of five left the ship at 1500 in the ship's six lifeboats. The master and ten men later reboarded the ship to determine if she could be salvaged. They could not save the ship, and the *Park* sank stern first at 2040. The SS *American Press* rescued the men in five of the boats and landed them at Swansea. An RAF crash boat towed the master's boat to Newland, England. All hands survived.

The ship's complement figures are contradictory within the sources. NSS; WACR; WCSR; RWCS; AG; Rohwer, p. 193. According to Rohwer, p. 193, the attacks also could have been made by the *U-246* and *U-1195*.

JAMES EAGAN LAYNE

D:	3-21-45	YB:	1944
T:	1440	Tn:	7,176
Pos:	50.13 N / 04.14 W	Dr:	22 ft. 10 in.
Ow:	WSA	C:	4,500 tons Army Engineers'
Op:	U.S. Navigation Co.		equipment
M:	William Albert Sleek	P:	steam
A:	1-5"; 1-3"; 8-20 mm	S:	7

On 20 March, the *James Eagan Layne* sailed from Barry, Wales, en route to Ghent, Belgium, in Convoy BTC-103. The ship steamed as the lead ship in the starboard column, station #21. Three U-boats attacked the convoy, and it is likely that the *U-1195* (Cordes) fired the torpedo that struck the starboard side just aft of the bulkhead between the #4 and #5 holds. The explosion threw water twenty feet over the main deck, blew off the #5 hatch cover, and damaged the shaft and the steering gear. When the engines began to race, the watch below secured them. The after two holds flooded, and the after bulkhead of the engine room gave way and flooded the machinery spaces. The master gave orders to abandon ship by the ship's whistle at 1455. The complement of eight officers, thirty-four men, and twenty-seven armed guards left the freighter in four lifeboats and two rafts. The British SS *Monkstone* picked up some of the survivors, and others later went on board the rescue tug HMS *Flaunt* (W-152). The master, fourteen of the crew, and four armed guards reboarded the ship at 1530 and prepared the freighter to be towed. About seven miles from the Plymouth breakwater, the tug *Flaunt* began towing the vessel to Whitesand Bay, aided by the tug *Atlas*. They beached her at 1800, where she eventually settled

on the bottom with only her masts and stack showing. The WSA later declared the freighter a CTL.

The other U-boats attacking the convoy were the *U-399* and the *U-246*. NSS; WACR; WCSR; AG; Rohwer, p. 193.

CHARLES D. McIVER

D:	3-22-45	YB:	1943
T:	1430	Tn:	7,176
Pos:	31.22.35 N / 03.05.50 E	Dr:	19 ft. 9 in.
Ow:	WSA	C:	sand ballast
Op:	Marine Transport Lines, Inc.	P:	steam
M:	Julius Palu	S:	9.5
A:	1-4"; 1-3"; 8-20 mm		

On 20 March, the *Charles D. McIver* departed Antwerp, Belgium, for Southend, United Kingdom, in Convoy ATM-100. The convoy, steaming in a single column, began to form a double column. The *McIver* had just taken station #19 near Buoy NF 11, when she struck a mine. The explosion occurred on the starboard side at the #4 hold. The blast threw oil and sand mast high and all over the ship. The ship immediately listed to starboard and began settling by the stern. The explosion blew off the #4 hatch cover, damaged the steering gear and fittings, smashed furniture all about the ship, ruptured steam pipes, and damaged the deep tanks, causing oil to flow into the engine room. With his ship unmaneuverable, the master ordered the vessel abandoned at 1455. The complement of eight officers, thirty-four men, and twenty-seven armed guards left the ship in four lifeboats. The minesweeper *BYMS-2279* rescued the men in the #2 boat and landed them in Ostend. A PT boat picked up the survivors in the other three boats and placed them on board the *LST-430*. These men landed in Antwerp. Within twenty-five minutes the *McIver* settled stern first on the bottom and came to rest with water up to her boat deck. The WSA later declared her a CTL. All hands survived.

NSS; WACR; WCSR; AG.

RANSOM A. MOORE

D:	3-22-45	YB:	1944
T:	2340	Tn:	7,176
Pos:	Lingayen Gulf, PI	Dr:	13 ft.
Ow:	WSA	C:	none
Op:	G. H. Winchester	P:	steam
M:	George D. Millman	S:	at anchor
A:	1-5"; 1-3"; 8-20 mm		

On 25 February, the *Ramsom A. Moore* sailed from Leyte Gulf to Lingayen Gulf, Philippine Islands. As she lay at anchor, an attacking plane drew the fire of a number of ships in the anchorage. The *Moore* was caught in the crossfire and was damaged by friendly fire. The gunfire hit the #2 topping lift on the port side and runners on the Jumbo Boom, parting a few wires. The master registered the damage as slight; nevertheless, the ship had to be ordered back to Hollandia. None of the eight officers, thirty-one men, and twenty-seven armed guards on board reported injuries.

WACR; AG.

OKLAHOMA

D:	3-28-45	YB:	1940, rebuilt 1942
T:	0204	Tn:	9,298
Pos:	13.52 N / 41.17 W	Dr:	29 ft. 1 in.
Ow:	Texas Oil Co.	C:	103,199 bbls. gasoline, kerosene
Op:	WSA	P:	steam
M:	Alfred Mathesen	S:	14.5
A:	1-5"; 1-3"; 8-20 mm		

On 23 March, the *Oklahoma* sailed independently for Dakar, French West Africa. As the ship steamed on a nonevasive course, the *U-532* (Junker) fired a torpedo that struck the starboard side between the #6 and #7 tanks aft of the pump room. The ship suffered two muffled explosions as the torpedo exploded, and then the cargo exploded and caught fire. The survivors reported the ship ablaze on both sides and from the bridge to the stern. Fortunately, the wind and the ship's speed kept the flames aft for some time. The master immediately gave orders to abandon ship. Many of the complement of eight officers, thirty-eight men, and twenty-six armed guards did not have a chance to escape. Only the two forward boats could be launched in the rough seas and force four winds. The fire consumed all the other boats and rafts. The #1 boat caught fire before it could clear the side of the ship, and its occupants had to jump into the water. The #2 boat rowed around the flaming hulk looking for more survivors. Flames surrounded the vessel for a distance of 500 feet, and the flaming cargo blazed on the water a mile astern. Only four officers, six men, and twelve armed guards survived the inferno. A plane and a blimp both failed to see the boat on 11 April, but a Navy plane diverted another Texas oil company ship to the boat. On 14 April, the SS *Delaware* rescued the men in the #2 boat and landed them in Aruba. The ship was last seen ablaze from stem to stern, and the Navy Department declared her sunk.

The times of the attack conflict within the sources. NSS; WACR; WCSR; RWCS; Rohwer, p. 193, places the attack at 13.37 N / 41.43 W; *War Action Casualties*, p. 180.

O. B. MARTIN

D:	3-29-45	YB:	1944
T:	1200	Tn:	7,247
Pos:	35.45 N / 06.46 W	Dr:	27 ft.
Ow:	WSA	C:	8,258 tons general, cased lube,
Op:	American Foreign SS Co.		engine oil
M:	Ralph H. Edwards	P:	steam
A:	1-5"; 1-3"; 8-20 mm	S:	unknown

On 14 March, the *O. B. Martin* sailed from Norfolk, Virginia, to Calcutta, India. As the *Martin* proceeded with Convoy UGS-80, twenty-five miles west of Gibraltar, the escort vessels believed they detected a submarine directly ahead of her. They began throwing depth charges ahead of the freighter, and one of them exploded close to the starboard bow, slightly damaging the ship and some of her cargo. None of the ship's eight officers, thirty-three men, twenty-nine armed guards, or five passengers reported any injuries.

The master of record was E. C. Lucas. WACR; TF; ONF.

JOHN C. FREMONT

D:	3-31-45	YB:	1942
T:	0858	Tn:	7,176
Pos:	south of Pier 7, Manila Bay	Dr:	18 ft. 8 in.
Ow:	WSA	C:	300 tons Army equipment
Op:	American President Lines	P:	steam
M:	Ludwig J. Yttergaard	S:	2
A:	1-4"; 1-3"; 8-20 mm		

The *John C. Fremont* moved from berth 89 in Manila Bay on the last day of March 1945. While moving to pier 7, the freighter struck a mine 700 yards south of the pier. The explosion opened a hole ten feet by seven feet in the starboard side at the #5 hold. The master beached the extensively damaged vessel as the #5 hold and machinery space flooded. Most of the ship's complement of seven officers, twenty-six men, twenty-seven armed guards, and a pilot were signed off the ship, but the explosion did injure five men. The tug *Bayou St. John* towed the ship to Guiuan Bay. The Navy considered using the *Fremont* for a self-propelled floating storage of lubricants and drummed petroleum at Eniwetok. The poor condition of the vessel changed the department's mind and instead they used the *Juan De Fuca*.

WACR; WCSR; *Araner* File, Ship's History Division, NHC.

ATLANTIC STATES

D:	4-5-45	YB:	1943
T:	1830	Tn:	8,537
Pos:	42.07 N / 70.00.42 W	Dr:	18 ft.
Ow:	Atlantic Refining Co.	C:	ballast
Op:	WSA	P:	steam
M:	Edgar Leroy Lindenmuth	S:	14.4
A:	1-5"; 1-3"; 8-20 mm		

On 5 April, the *Atlantic States* sailed on independent routing from Boston, Massachusetts, to Las Piedras, Venezuela. Only about two hours out of port, the *U-857* (Premauer) attacked the tanker off Cape Cod and fired a torpedo that struck the starboard side at the stern. The explosion blew the screw and the rudder off and wrecked the steering engines. The ship settled rapidly by the stern, and the watch below secured the engines as water began to enter the engine room. Without a means to steer the ship, the master ordered most of the nine officers, thirty-six men, and twelve armed guards to the four lifeboats. The master, the mate, the armed guard officer, and two other men stayed on board and opened valves in the pump room to trim the vessel. At 1900 the armed guards left as the seas began breaking over the well deck. At 2200 the USS *Guinevere* (IX-67) rescued all hands with the exception of the five men who remained on board. The USS *Richard S. Bull* (DE-402) stood by to assist the tanker. The rescue tugs *ATR-14* and *ATR-89*, with the help of the USS *Wandank* (ATO-26), towed the ship back to Boston for repairs. All hands survived.

NSS; WACR; WCSR; AG; Rohwer, p. 194.

LOGAN VICTORY

D:	4-6-45	YB:	1945
T:	1647	Tn:	7,607
Pos:	26.10 N / 127.16 E	Dr:	24 ft. 6 in.
Ow:	WSA	C:	9,033 tons explosives and
Op:	American Hawaiian SS Co.		drummed oil
M:	Edson Baxter Cates	P:	steam
A:	1-5"; 1-3"; 8-20 mm	S:	at anchor

On 21 February, the *Logan Victory* sailed from San Francisco to Okinawa via Eniwetok and Ulithi. The vessel had only been at anchor for twenty minutes when approximately eight Japanese planes appeared. Lookouts spotted one of the planes two miles away zigzagging about 100 feet above the water. Most of the ships in the anchorage took this plane under fire, but it managed to get through the hail of gunfire and crash dived onto the freighter's midships house. The plane exploded, showering flaming debris and gasoline over the decks. The

#4 and #1 hatches as well as the after section of the midships house burst into flames immediately. The fires soon raged out of control over much of the ship. At 1700, most of the eight officers, forty-eight men, twenty-seven armed guards, fifteen stevedores, and an Army security officer abandoned ship. Because of the intense flames, the men could launch only one boat and four life rafts. Many others dove overboard to escape the flames. Within twenty minutes the USS *Strategy* (AM-308), the *YMS-86*, and other ships and naval craft rescued the survivors. Five officers, six men, three armed guards, and the security officer died. The master was severely wounded by a 20-mm shell set off by the burning ship and later died ashore. Owing to the nature of the cargo, naval vessels sank the *Logan Victory* with gunfire to prevent a harbor disaster.

NSS; WACR; WCSR; USMMA; AG.

HOBBS VICTORY

D:	4-6-45	YB:	1945
T:	1850	Tn:	7,607
Pos:	26.05 N / 125.14 E	Dr:	24 ft. 6 in.
Ow:	WSA	C:	6,500 tons ammunition
Op:	Sudden & Christenson Inc.	P:	steam
M:	Kenneth Folsom Izant	S:	15
A:	1-5"; 1-3"; 8-20 mm		

The *Hobbs Victory* sailed from Ulithi to Okinawa in convoy. Arriving on 6 April, the vessel steamed directly to her anchorage and dropped anchor. The *Logan Victory*, anchored nearby, was the victim of a suicide plane at about 1645. After this attack, the *Hobbs Victory* raised anchor and began to move northwest of the harbor and outside the harbor nets. While she was under way two Japanese planes attacked. The armed guards shot down one of the planes; however, the second plane continued toward the ship even though under a hail of gunfire. The naval gun crew shot off a portion of the plane's wing. It began smoking but remained under control and struck the port side forward of the #4 lifeboat at the boat deck level. The tremendous explosion blew the #6 gun tub into the water, blew out the entire port side of the midships house and boat deck, and covered the deck with flames. Tragically, the port boiler also exploded killing those on watch below. Without hesitation the master ordered the ship abandoned. Survivors among the ten officers, forty-six men, twenty-seven armed guards, fifteen Navy stevedores, and one passenger had to leave the ship through a mass of fire. The crew utilized two lifeboats and three rafts. The watch below had secured the engines just before the plane struck, but the ship still had headway and the boats could not be launched until the ship slowed to five knots. The USS *Success* (AM-310) picked up the survivors and transferred them to the USS *Gosper* (APA-170). A fireboat fought the fire for four hours but could never get it under control The ship blew up the next morning at 0300. One officer, ten men, one armed guard, and one of the Navy stevedores died.

NSS; WACR; WCSR; USMMA; AG; ONF.

CAPTAIN NATHANIEL B. PALMER

D:	4-6-45	YB:	1942
T:	1430	Tn:	36
Pos:	9 mi. SSE of Block Island, RI	Dr:	7 ft.
Ow:	John B. Bindloss	C:	5 tons fish
Op:	John B. Bindloss	P:	motor
M:	Robert Moran	S:	stopped
A:	unarmed		

The *Captain Nathaniel B. Palmer*, while hauling in a fishing net off Block Island, unknowingly snagged a depth charge. Realizing that the net seemed exceedingly heavy, the crew of one officer and three men continued to pull it toward the trawler. As the depth charge came to the surface, it exploded and demolished the fishing vessel. The explosion killed the master and two men. The fishing vessel *Mandalay* picked up the sole survivor and took him to Block Island.

WACR; WCSR.

JAMES W. NESMITH

D:	4-7-45	YB:	1942
T:	1725	Tn:	7,176
Pos:	53.23 N / 04.53 W	Dr:	23 ft.
Ow:	WSA	C:	3,325 tons tobacco, fertilizer,
Op:	McCormick SS Co.		plane parts, lumber
M:	Reginald Stanley Rossiter	P:	steam
A:	1-4"; 3-3"; 8-20 mm	S:	10

On 24 March, the *James W. Nesmith* left New York in Convoy HX-347 for the Mersey. The ship proceeded as the fourth ship in line in the port column. Off Holyhead, United Kingdom, the *U-1024* (Gutteck) fired a torpedo that struck the port side at the #5 hold. The explosion damaged the steering gear, flooded the #4 and #5 holds, and damaged the ship's machinery as water came through the shaft alley into the engine room and fireroom. The nine officers, thirty-one men, forty-one armed guards, and one passenger remained on the ship. The Canadian corvette *Belleville* (K-332) towed the Liberty ship and beached her off Holyhead on the night of the 8th. Salvage vessels later refloated the *Nesmith* and

towed her to Liverpool. After repairs she returned to service. The crew suffered no casualties from the attack.

NSS; WACR; WCSR; AG; Rohwer, p. 194, places the attack at 53.24 N / 04.48 W.

SOLOMON JUNEAU

D:	4-9-45	YB:	1943
T:	2126	Tn:	7,176
Pos:	50.53.15 N / 01.03.45 E	Dr:	18 ft. 6 in.
Ow:	WSA	C:	ballast
Op:	Weyerhaeuser SS Co.	P:	steam
A:	1-5"; 2-3"; 8-20 mm	S:	7
M:	Samuel Bascom Jennings		

On 7 April, the *Solomon Juneau* sailed from Ghent, Belgium, to Cherbourg, France. While the Liberty ship proceeded with the twelve-ship Convoy TBC-123, a German midget submarine attacked three and a half miles off Dungeness. A torpedo struck on the starboard side at the stern, and the explosion threw tons of water on the deck, destroyed the rudder, disabled the steering gear, and blew a hole nine feet in diameter in the hull. The Liberty ship swung hard right, and the crew quickly secured the engines. The ship's complement of eight officers, thirty-three men, and forty-one armed guards remained on the ship, with the exception of one of the armed guards blown overboard by the explosion. An hour after the explosion a tug arrived to tow the *Juneau* to the Downs. The ship anchored in the Downs and then proceeded to dry dock in London on 16 April. The armed guard blown overboard was never found, and a second armed guard later died of internal injuries. These two constituted the only deaths.

The armed guard complement figures contradict within the sources. There was also a report of small boats in the area, possibly E-boats. NSS; WACR; WCSR.

MORGANTOWN VICTORY

D:	4-11-45	YB:	1945
T:	0115	Tn:	7,607
Pos:	49.46 N / 00.21 E	Dr:	19 ft. 6 in.
Ow:	WSA	C:	386 tons Army mail
Op:	States Marine Corp.	P:	steam
M:	Nils Peter Bjornsgaard	S:	14
A:	1-5"; 1-3"; 8-20 mm		

On 10 April, the *Morgantown Victory* sailed independently from Rouen, France, to La Havre, and then sailed to join Convoy VWP-21 to Southampton, United

Kingdom. While steaming to join the convoy, the vessel strayed outside the swept channel and struck a mine one-half mile from Buoy HD 1, eleven miles from La Havre. The explosion occurred off the port side at the #5 hold and damaged all the ship's generators and the midships quarters. The #5 hold and the shaft alley flooded quickly, while water slowly leaked into the engine room through the damaged shaft alley. The master ordered the crew to swing out the lifeboats and lower them to within a few feet of the water in case they had to abandon ship. A Navy patrol craft took several wounded off the ship about two hours after the explosion. At 0400 a Navy salvage tug arrived and towed the vessel into the dock at La Havre, arriving at 1030. On 30 April, the ship arrived at Antwerp, Belgium, for dry docking. The explosion injured three men among the ten officers, forty-five men, and fourteen armed guards on board.

NSS; WACR; WCSR; USMMA; AG.

MINOT VICTORY

D:	4-12-45	YB:	1945
T:	1455	Tn:	7,607
Pos:	26.18.30 N / 127.43.15 E	Dr:	22 ft. 9 in.
Ow:	WSA	C:	3,895 tons military supplies
Op:	American Mail Line	P:	steam
M:	A. Jensen	S:	at anchor
A:	1-5"; 1-3"; 8-20 mm		

The *Minot Victory* sailed from San Francisco, California, to Okinawa, arriving there on 11 April. The freighter discharged cargo for two weeks. While the ship anchored at Okinawa, a Japanese plane attempted to crash dive onto her. However, scathing fire from the armed guards brought down the plane, and it missed the ship, striking the #4 king post aft of the boat deck. The plane disintegrated and wreckage fell all along the deck. Fuel from the plane engulfed one of the gun tubs, but the men at the gun escaped injury. Other small fires slightly damaged the vessel and the lifeboats, but the vessel's damage was listed as slight. The attack injured five of the ten officers, forty-seven men, twenty-seven armed guards, and nine other men on board.

The armed guard figures conflict within the sources. WACR; WCSR; RWCS; AG.

WILL ROGERS

D: 4-12-45   YB: 1942
T: 1400   Tn: 7,200
Pos: 53.45 N / 04.44 W   Dr: 24 ft. 8 in.
Ow: WSA   C: 4,995 tons landing mats, flour,
Op: Merchants & Miners Trans. Co.   general
M: Thomas Manford Lewis   P: steam
A: 1-5"; 1-3"; 8-20 mm   S: 7

On 12 April, the *Will Rogers* sailed from Liverpool, England, in local Convoy BB-80 for Antwerp, Belgium. The *Rogers* took the van in the starboard column of the seven-ship convoy. The *U-1024* (Gutteck) attacked the convoy thirty miles southwest of Holyhead, United Kingdom. A torpedo struck the freighter on the starboard side at the #1 hold near the forepeak bulkhead, causing the #1 hold and the forepeak to flood. The vessel was taken in tow and under her own power beached off Holyhead. There were no casualties among the nine officers, thirty-four men, twenty-seven armed guards, and one passenger on board. The Liberty ship was later refloated, and on 23 April, she arrived in Liverpool under tow. After repairs she returned to service.

The merchant crew figures conflict within the sources. NSS; WACR; WCSR; AG; Rohwer, p. 194. Other sources place the attack at 53.48 N / 04.46 W.

HARRINGTON EMERSON

D: 4-13-45   YB: 1943
T: 1400   Tn: 7,176
Pos: 05.03 N / 119.44 E   Dr: 17 ft. 6 in.
Ow: WSA   C: 300 tons gasoline in drums
Op: Pacific Far East Line   P: steam
M: Otto J. Jaeger   S: 2
A: 1-5"; 1-3"; 8-20 mm

On 9 April, the *Harrington Emerson* sailed from Jolo Island to Sanga Sanga, Philippine Islands. Off the coast of Borneo, an American bomber mistook the freighter for an enemy vessel. The bomber circled the ship and began strafing her. It then released two bombs that struck off the port side. Two corsairs flew to escort the plane away minutes after the attack. The bomb's concussions and the plane's gunfire only slightly injured the vessel, and she arrived under her own power at her destination. Six of the nine officers, thirty-one men, twenty-nine armed guards, seventeen passengers, and twenty stevedores on board reported injuries.

WACR; AG; The master of record was Edward A. Mortensen. ONF.

CYRUS H. McCORMICK

D: 4-18-45
T: 1211
Pos: 47.47 N / 06.26 W
Ow: WSA
Op: W. R. Chamberlain Co.
M: Heinrich Herman Kronke
A: 1-3"; 9-20 mm

YB: 1942
Tn: 7,181
Dr: 27 ft.
C: 6,384 tons cranes, engineering
      equipment, locomotives, trucks
P: steam
S: 8

On 2 April, the *Cyrus H. McCormick* sailed from New York with Convoy HX-348 for the Downs, United Kingdom. The *McCormick* steamed in station #101 in the twelve-column convoy. About seventy miles southwest of Brest, France, the *U-1107* (Parduhn) attacked the convoy. A torpedo struck the starboard side of the Liberty ship between the #1 and #2 holds. Both holds flooded rapidly, and the ship settled by the head and sank in less than four minutes. The bridge immediately rang the abandon ship signal, but the eight officers, thirty-two men, twelve armed guards, and one Army security officer had little time to leave the ship. The men did not successfully launch any of the lifeboats and only managed to trip two of the four rafts. The survivors swam to the rafts, and twenty-three hung onto floating dunnage. An hour later the British rescue ship SS *Gothland* rescued the survivors and landed them at Gourock, Scotland. One officer, three men, and two armed guards perished.

The ship's complement figures conflict within the sources. The naval report relates that the vessel was struck on the port side. The Coast Guard report and the master both say it was the starboard side. NSS; WACR; WCSR; AG; Rohwer, p. 194.

SWIFTSCOUT

D: 4-18-45
T: 0925
Pos: 37.30 N / 72.45 W
Ow: Swiftscout SS Corp.
Op: Marine Transport Lines Inc.
M: Peter Katsaris
A: 1-4"; 1-3"; 8-20 mm

YB: 1921
Tn: 8,300
Dr: 21 ft. 6 in.
C: 40,000 bbls. salt water ballast
P: steam
S: 8.5

On 16 April, the *Swiftscout* sailed independently from Philadelphia, Pennsylvania, to Puerto La Cruz, Venezuela. About 145 miles northeast of Cape Henry the *U-548* (Kremel) fired a torpedo that struck the port side at the #6 tank just abaft amidships. The explosion broke the ship's back at the #6 tank, the main deck buckled, and the bow and stern rose into the air. The armed guards manned the guns and fired on the *U-548* cruising about 650 yards away. The *U-548*, however, dove and fired a second torpedo that struck the ship at 0935 on the port side abaft the previous spot. This explosion threw water into the air and blew the after hatch covers off. The vessel buckled in the center into a "V" shape with bow and stern raised above the water. The master had ordered the ship abandoned just before the second torpedo struck. The complement of nine officers, twenty-eight men, and ten armed guards got away in four boats, and minutes later the ship sank stern first. The bow sank and reappeared several times before finally disappearing. About seven hours later the SS *Chancellorsville* rescued the survivors and transferred them to a Coast Guard boat at Lynnhaven Roads, and they landed at Little Creek, Virginia. The chief engineer drowned trying to reach one of the lifeboats.

NSS; WACR; WCSR; AG; Rohwer, p. 194. Other sources place the attack at 37.30 N / 73.03 W.

BENJAMIN H. BRISTOW

D:	4-22-45	YB:	1943
T:	1623	Tn:	7,191
Pos:	51.24.30 N / 03.22 E	Dr:	19 ft. 10 in.
Ow:	WSA	C:	none
Op:	American-West African Line	P:	steam
M:	Francis Costello Pollard	S:	6
A:	1-4"; 1-3"; 8-20 mm		

On 22 April, the *Benjamin H. Bristow* sailed from Antwerp, Belgium, to Southend, England, in Convoy ATM-123. A mine struck the ship in the #5 hold starboard side as she was off the coast of Flushing, two and one-half miles from Knocke Lighthouse. The crew of eight officers, thirty-four men, twenty-six armed guards, and a channel pilot remained on the Liberty ship. Salvage tugs towed her to Terneuzen, Holland, the same day. She remained in shipyard for repairs for six weeks and sailed on 14 June. Only one man reported an injury.

WACR; WCSR; AG.

CANADA VICTORY

D:	4-27-45	YB:	1944
T:	2145	Tn:	7,711
Pos:	26.23.15 N / 127.41.47 E	Dr:	29 ft.
Ow:	WSA	C:	7,000 tons ammunition
Op:	Alaska SS Co.	P:	steam
M:	William MacDonald	S:	at anchor
A:	1-5"; 1-3"; 8-20 mm		

On 7 March, the *Canada Victory* sailed from San Francisco, California, to Okinawa via Eniwetok and Ulithi. At 2000, while at anchor off Okinawa, the ship received notification of enemy planes in the area. A small craft circled the

The tragic end of the Liberty ship *Paul Hamilton* after an aerial torpedo struck her cargo of explosives. Note the splashes from the debris in the water.

The tanker *Swiftscout* is representative of many of the pre-war tankers that served and carried cargoes worldwide. She met her end 145 miles northeast of Cape Henry after being torpedoed by the *U-548*.

anchorage laying down a smoke screen, but the smoke pots ran out of fuel and the smoke soon drifted away revealing the ship. A Japanese plane spotted the vessel and dove into the stern. The plane crashed at the five-inch gun mount and skidded forward to the #4 hold on the port side. An explosion blew off the hatch covers and split the bulwark between the #4 and #5 holds. The damaged after holds began filling with water, and the ship rapidly sank by the stern with a 44° port list. At 2200 the master ordered the ten officers, thirty-three men, twenty-seven armed guards, and fifteen Navy stevedores to abandon ship. The crew managed to launch only one boat, and most of the men went over the side and swam to the USS *Lauderdale* (APA-179). The *Canada Victory* sank with a heavy port list in about fifteen minutes. The blast injured five of the crew and killed one officer and two armed guards.

The ship's complement figures conflict within the sources. It appears that two of the armed guards were off the ship at the time. NSS; WACR; WCSR; AG; USMMA.

BOZEMAN VICTORY

D:	4-28-45	YB:	1945
T:	0210	Tn:	7,612
Pos:	1,500 yds. off Okinawa	Dr:	26 ft. 3 in.
Ow:	WSA	C:	6,000 tons ammunition
Op:	Alaska Steamship Co.	P:	steam
M:	Hugh M. Campbell	S:	at anchor
A:	1-5"; 1-3"; 8-20 mm		

The *Bozeman Victory* sailed from Mukilteo, Washington, to Okinawa. While the ship was anchored 1,500 yards off Okinawa, a Japanese small craft attacked. This small craft zigzagged through a smoke screen and dropped a depth charge off the port side at the #4 hold. The armed guards had no time to train the guns on the small boat before the attack. The explosion damaged the hull plates, broke bearings, and extensively damaged the ship. The ten officers, forty-nine men, twenty-seven armed guards, and thirteen stevedores remained with the ship. The explosion injured six of these men.

WACR; AG.

S. HALL YOUNG

D: 4-30-45   YB: 1943
T: 0345   Tn: 7,176
Pos: Nago Bay, Okinawa   Dr: 17 ft.
Ow: WSA   C: 1,400 tons machinery,
Op: American Hawaiian SS Co.   explosives, gasoline
M: Peter Francis Butler   P: steam
A: 2-3"; 8-20 mm   S: at anchor

The *S. Hall Young* sailed from Saipan to Okinawa and anchored in Nago Bay. A Japanese aircraft crash dived onto the ship at the #5 hatch port side. The plane put a hole twelve feet by fifteen feet in the port side of the ship and passed through to the starboard side. The plane's bomb exploded in the hold and started a fire that firefighting parties quickly extinguished. Only one man among the eight officers, thirty men, twelve armed guards, and twenty-five passengers on board reported an injury. The *Young* remained twenty-three days in Okinawa for repairs.

WACR; WCSR; RWCS; AG.

HENRY L. ABBOTT

D: 5-1-45   YB: 1943
T: 0829   Tn: 7,176
Pos: 14.35 N / 120.58 E   Dr: 25 ft. 2 in.
Ow: WSA   C: 6,005 tons Army general cargo
Op: Alaska Transportation Co.   P: steam
M: Malcolm Neill MacLaren   S: 2
A: 2-3"; 8-20 mm

The Liberty ship *Henry L. Abbott* sailed from Kossol Passage, Palau Islands, to Manila, Philippine Islands. While proceeding to her anchorage inside the breakwater in Manila Harbor, the ship struck a mine 1,000 yards from Pier 7. The explosion put a hole eight feet by ten feet in the ship under the engine room. The eight officers, thirty-five men, twenty-seven armed guards, and the harbor pilot remained on the ship. With the engine room flooded, she was towed to Pier 3 and anchored. Two of the ship's engineering officers on watch below died in the explosion.

WACR; WCSR; AG.

EDMUND F. DICKENS

D: 5-3-45   YB: 1943
T: 0157   Tn: 7,176
Pos: Manila Bay   Dr: 25 ft.
Ow: WSA   C: 5,000 tons general
Op: Pacific Atlantic SS Co.   P: steam
M: John Newton Ferree   S: at anchor
A: 2-3"; 8-20 mm

The *Edmund F. Dickens* sailed from New Orleans, Louisiana, to Manila, Philippine Islands. The Liberty ship anchored inside the Manila Bay breakwater, and while she was discharging cargo, a mine struck the vessel under the stern. The explosion bent the shaft and damaged the hull. The ship's pumps managed to contain the flooding, and the crew discharged the ship on schedule. The complement of eight officers, thirty-five men, and twenty-seven armed guards suffered no injuries. The mine caused an estimated $100,000 damage to the vessel.

WACR; WCSR.

SEA FLASHER

D: 5-3-45   YB: 1943
T: 1500   Tn: 8,008
Pos: off Okinawa   Dr: 22 ft.
Ow: WSA   C: 2,000 tons general and troops
Op: Isthmian SS Co.   P: steam
M: Gust E. Jonsson   S: at anchor
A: 1-5"; 4-3"; 8-20 mm

The *Sea Flasher* sailed from San Francisco, California, to Okinawa and arrived on 3 May. As the ship anchored off Okinawa and discharged the troops on board, one of the gun crews on the USS *New Mexico* (BB-40) accidentally fired the 40-mm gun during exercises. Eight high explosive incendiary shells struck the starboard side between the #2 and #3 holds and started a small fire. The crew quickly extinguished the flames, and overall the ship suffered only slight damage to her hull, winches, and rafts. The ship's complement consisted of 11 officers, 50 men, 43 armed guards, and 1,609 troops. The shells injured forty-seven men and killed seven of the troops.

WACR; AG; ONF; Action Report, *New Mexico*, NHC.

BLACK POINT

D: 5-5-45	YB: 1918
T: 1740	Tn: 5,353
Pos: 41.19.02 N / 71.25.01 W	Dr: 27 ft. 10 in.
Ow: Sprague SS Co.	C: 7,759 tons coal
Op: Sprague SS Co.	P: steam
M: Charles E. Prior	S: 8
A: 1-6 lber.; 2-30 cal.	

On 2 May, the *Black Point* sailed from Newport News, Virginia, for Weymouth, Massachusetts. In fog, about five miles southeast of Point Judith, Rhode Island, the *U-853* (Frömsdorf) fired a torpedo that struck the stern of the vessel. The explosion carried away the aftermost forty feet of the ship aft of the #5 hold. The vessel quickly began to sink by the stern. The eight officers, thirty-three men, and five armed guards lowered the #1 and #2 boats and released a life raft. Most of the crew left in the two boats, and the few that jumped overboard were picked up by the boats. The *Black Point* capsized, and all but the bow disappeared beneath the water twenty-five minutes after the torpedo struck. The Yugoslavian SS *Karmen* and the Norwegian SS *Scandanavia* picked up some of the survivors and later transferred them to a Coast Guard patrol boat that took them to Point Judith, Rhode Island. Crash boats from Quonset Point, Rhode Island, rescued other men and landed them at Newport. One of the armed guards and eleven of the merchant crew died.

This was the last American-flagged ship torpedoed by a German U-boat. Other records indicate that the WSA chartered the vessel. NSS; WACR; WCSR; AG; Rohwer, p. 195, places the attack at 111.19 N / 71.23 W.

HORACE BINNEY

D: 5-8-45	YB: 1942
T: 1145	Tn: 7,191
Pos: 51.21 N / 02.27 E	Dr: 24 ft. 10 in.
Ow: WSA	C: 4,000 tons Army general cargo
Op: American Export Lines	P: steam
M: Cecil Douglas Davies Jr.	S: 7
A: 1-5"; 3-3"; 8-20 mm	

On 3 May, the *Horace Binney* left Avonmouth, England, for Ghent, Belgium, in the twenty-ship Convoy TAM-62. The ship maintained convoy station #41 (the last ship in the starboard column). Fifteen miles off Ostend the vessel struck a mine at the #3 hold near the keel. The explosion broke the ship's back, split the double bottom, broke steam lines, damaged equipment throughout the ship, and caused a loss of power. As holds #1, #2, #3, and #4 all became tidal, the ship lost way, and the crew dropped anchor. Most of the eight officers, thirty-four

men, thirty-six armed guards, and one passenger abandoned the ship in two of the lifeboats. The master and four others remained on board. The British motor launch *ML-1456* took the five men on board and landed them at Dover, England. A British naval tug began towing the *Binney* stern first at 1330. The salvage tug HMS *Lincoln Salvor* also came alongside. At 1030 on 9 May, the freighter anchored in the Downs. The next day the crack widened and tugs beached her at Deal. The explosion injured twenty men but caused no deaths. The WSA declared the *Horace Binney* a CTL.

The numbers listed for the crew radically differ within the sources. NSS; WACR; WCSR; AG.

CORNELIUS VANDERBILT

D:	5-18-45	YB:	1944
T:	2251	Tn:	7,212
Pos:	Ie Shima, Okinawa	Dr:	20 ft.
Ow:	WSA	C:	1,000 tons gasoline, explosives, general
Op:	Alaska SS Co.		
M:	Roland R. Flaherty	P:	steam
A:	1-5"; 1-3"; 8-20 mm	S:	at anchor

On 4 May, the *Cornelius Vanderbilt* sailed from Saipan to Ie Shima, Okinawa. While riding at anchor the vessel was bombed by an enemy aircraft. A bomb fell and exploded nearby, blowing fragments all over the after deck and starting small fires. Firefighting parties assembled from the 8 officers, 30 men, 27 armed guards, and 108 stevedores to put the fires out quickly. One man died when he accidentally fell into an open hatch while running out a fire hose.

WACR; AG; TF.

WILLIAM B. ALLISON

D:	5-25-45	YB:	1943
T:	0305	Tn:	7,176
Pos:	Buckner Bay, Okinawa	Dr:	18 ft. 3 in.
Ow:	WSA	C:	1,400 tons lumber, steel, general
Op:	Waterman SS Co.	P:	steam
M:	Robert Hubert Sonneman	S:	at anchor
A:	2-3"; 8-20 mm		

On 15 May, the *William B. Allison* departed Ulithi Atoll for Okinawa and anchored in Buckner Bay on the 21st. The crew had worked steadily to unload cargo until the air alert sounded. In cloudy, squally weather a Japanese torpedo bomber located the ship and launched a torpedo that struck the port side at the engine room. The explosion put a hole eighteen feet long and thirty feet high in

the ship's side, demolished the engines, and caused the port boiler to explode. The engine room bulkheads held and contained the flooding, which enabled the 8 officers, 32 men, 28 armed guards, and 150 stevedores to remain with the ship and finish unloading the cargo. The three officers and two men on watch below died. The explosion and escaping steam also killed a stevedore and a member of the merchant crew. The WSA abandoned the vessel as a CTL. The USS *Tenino* (ATF-115) took the vessel in tow and towed her to Kerama Retto for repairs and conversion for the Navy.

The Navy acquired the vessel and renamed her *Gamage* (IX-227). The Navy used the vessel as a mobile storehouse for lubricants and drummed petroleum products at Ulithi. NSS; WACR; WCSR; AG; DANFS, 3:14.

JOHN WOOLMAN

D:	5-27-45	YB:	1943
T:	0900	Tn:	7,176
Pos:	off Dunkirk	Dr:	21 ft.
Ow:	WSA	C:	ballast
Op:	American West African Line	P:	steam
M:	Jacob Harrison Carter	S:	7
A:	1-5"; 1-3"; 8-20 mm		

The *John Woolman* sailed from Antwerp, Belgium, to La Havre via the Downs in Convoy ATM-167. While steaming in convoy station #35, sixteen miles northeast of Dunkirk, and off Buoy NF 5, the ship struck a mine. The explosion occurred under the engine room on the starboard side and ruptured the ship's intakes and steam pipes. The engine room immediately flooded to sea level, but all the other compartments remained dry. The complement of seven officers, thirty-four men, and twenty-six armed guards remained with the vessel until midnight and then abandoned ship in three lifeboats. A British destroyer rescued all hands within twenty minutes. The master and crew reboarded the vessel several hours later and prepared her for towing. The HMS *Lincoln Salvor* and two other tugs towed the ship to the Thames River, where she arrived on 31 May.

WACR; WCSR; AG; TF.

MARY A. LIVERMORE

D:	5-28-45	YB:	1943
T:	0515	Tn:	7,176
Pos:	26.12 N / 127.46 E	Dr:	18 ft.
Ow:	WSA	C:	1,200 tons cement, lumber,
Op:	Isthmian SS Co.		machinery
M:	James Alfred Stewart	P:	steam
A:	1-4"; 1-3"; 8-20 mm	S:	at anchor

On 5 May, the *Mary A. Livermore* left Ulithi and arrived at Okinawa and later anchored in Buckner Bay. Early in the morning lookouts sighted a Japanese float plane taking off from the water. The plane rapidly approached and then dove onto the ship. It struck the #3 boom and careened to starboard, crashing into the chart room and the captain's quarters. The plane's bomb exploded and extensively damaged the entire area. Firefighting parties from the eight officers, thirty-three men, twenty-seven armed guards, seven passengers, and seventy-five CBs on board put out the fire in the midships house. The explosion and fires killed the master, six men, and four armed guards and injured six other men. The Liberty ship received temporary repairs at Okinawa and on 5 June, sailed in convoy for Saipan. She returned to service after undergoing permanent repairs in San Francisco.

NSS; WACR; WCSR; AG; Sawyer, Mitchell, pp. 153-54.

BROWN VICTORY

D:	5-28-45	YB:	1945
T:	0745	Tn:	7,606
Pos:	off Ie Shima	Dr:	18 ft. 6 in.
Ow:	WSA	C:	1,000 tons gasoline and trucks
Op:	Alaska Packers, Inc.	P:	steam
M:	Terje Andreas Johannsen	S:	at anchor
A:	1-5"; 1-3"; 8-20 mm		

The *Brown Victory* sailed from Seattle, Washington, to Ie Shima, Ryukyu Islands. The ship anchored off the island and began discharging her cargo. During an air attack, a Japanese bomber carrying two bombs singled out the ship and dove from the port quarter. The Japanese plane hit the after mast fifteen feet below the crosstrees and carried away all the after cargo booms. One-half of the plane fell on the starboard side, the bombs exploded, and the plane burst into flames, showering the vessel with shrapnel. Fires started aft of the superstructure and in the #4 hold. Firefighting parties assembled from the nine officers, forty-seven men, twenty-seven armed guards, and one passenger on board. The steam smothering system and fire hoses had the fires controlled by 0805. The master listed the damage to the ship as slight—the principal damage being done to the masts and booms struck by the plane. Two armed guards died immediately, and the flames and explosion injured eighteen others. One merchant crewman and another armed guard later died ashore from their injuries.

WACR; WCSR; AG.

JOSIAH SNELLING

D:	5-28-45	YB:	1943
T:	0801	Tn:	7,176
Pos:	off Okinawa	Dr:	16 ft. 10 in.
Ow:	WSA	C:	1,200 tons cement and lumber
Op:	Sudden & Christenson	P:	steam
M:	Peter Grimstad	S:	at anchor
A:	2-3"; 8-20 mm		

On 7 May, the *Josiah Snelling* departed Saipan and arrived off Okinawa on 14 May, anchoring at the northeast edge of the harbor. In hazy and cloudy weather a Japanese plane approached the anchorage from the northeast. The armed guards defended the ship with her 20-mm and the after three-inch guns. The plane dove for the midships house, but the concentrated gunfire damaged it enough to cause it to veer and hit the freighter between the two forward winches. The plane sheered off booms, a ventilator, and gear, and went through the deck, exploding in the #1 hold full of cement and 12 x 12 timbers. This cargo absorbed the shock but sent a flame mast high and threw five men from the #1 and #2 gun tubs onto the main deck. The crew quickly extinguished the fire in the #1 hold. All the ship's eight officers, thirty-one men, fourteen armed guards, thirty-two passengers, and ninety stevedores remained on board. The explosion and fire slightly injured about twenty-five men, but no one died as a result.

NSS; WACR; WCSR; AG.

COLIN P. KELLY JR.

D:	6-4-45	YB:	1942
T:	0850	Tn:	7,176
Pos:	51.22.48 N / 02.35 E	Dr:	26 ft. 5 in.
Ow:	WSA	C:	5,356 tons Army foodstuffs
Op:	Waterman SS Co.	P:	steam
M:	Oscar Clinton Sones	S:	8.5
A:	1-5"; 3-3"; 8-20 mm		

On 4 June, the *Colin P. Kelly Jr.* sailed from the Downs in the thirty-two ship Convoy TAM-89 en route to Antwerp, Belgium. Steaming in station #28, about 700 yards from Buoy NF 6, the *Kelly* struck a mine. The explosion occurred on the starboard side amidships and threw up a large column of black smoke and water mast high. The master hoisted flags to indicate the ship had struck a mine. The blast split the deck and damaged equipment and gear throughout the Liberty ship. The engine room and the #3 and #4 holds flooded rapidly. In some places the butt strap remained as the only structural member holding the ship together. The mate on watch sounded the general alarm, and the engines were secured from the deck. The British tug *TID-91* tried to tow the vessel out of the channel but could not make headway. At 0945 the U.S. Army tug *Hughes* took a forward line and shifted to the stern. A third tug, the British *Empire Jane*, arrived at noon to help with the tow. The blast injured four of the *Kelly*'s eight officers, thirty-nine men, thirty-seven armed guards, and four passengers. At 1230 fifteen men of the merchant crew boarded the *TID-91* and later transferred to the escort trawler HMS *Herschell* (T-289). At 1315 the tug took fourteen more of the merchant crew off. Eventually all the crew but sixteen went on board the escort vessel. At 1615 the tug HMS *Lincoln Salvor* made fast to the *Kelly*'s port side at the stern. The skeleton crew on board jettisoned the deck cargo and brought more pumps on board. At 1915 the tug *L. Brassey* took an additional line forward to help move the ship. The next day the tugs *King Lear* and HMS *Sun VIII* also made fast to the *Kelly*. The tugs towed the vessel to Tillsbury Docks, London, arriving the following afternoon. After examination, the WSA later declared the vessel a CTL.

NSS; WACR; WCSR; RWCS; AG; Sawyer, Mitchell, p. 34.

NEW BERN VICTORY

D:	6-4-45	YB:	1945
T:	1514	Tn:	7,607
Pos:	off Odessa, USSR	Dr:	21 ft.
Ow:	WSA	C:	none
Op:	Prudential SS Co.	P:	steam
M:	Eric Sodergren	S:	16
A:	1-5"; 1-3"; 8-20 mm		

On 4 June, the *New Bern Victory* sailed from Odessa, Russia, to Constanta, Romania. About six miles off Odessa, the ship struck a floating mine in the channel. A bow lookout spotted the mine only forty feet from the vessel, and no evasive action could be taken. The explosion blew a wall of water over the bridge and created a hole about twelve feet square in the port side at the #2 hold. With emergency repairs and counterflooding she sailed from Odessa about three days later. There were no casualties among the complement of twelve officers,

forty-four men, and twelve armed guards. The vessel steamed to Istanbul, Turkey, and went in dry dock for temporary repairs. She departed Istanbul on 7 July and went back in service in November.

WACR; WCSR; RWCS; AG; ONF.

WALTER COLTON

D:	6-11-45	YB:	1942
T:	1915	Tn:	7,181
Pos:	off Okinawa	Dr:	25 ft.
Ow:	WSA	C:	5,233 tons general
Op:	Williams Dimond SS Co.	P:	steam
M:	R. N. Mendenhall	S:	at anchor
A:	1-5"; 1-3"; 8-20 mm		

On 23 May, the *Walter Colton* sailed from Ulithi and arrived off Okinawa on 29 May. After the *Colton* anchored off Okinawa, a plane dove toward the Liberty ship while under a terrific fire from the ships in the anchorage. It flew past the bow, circled, and made a second dive toward the ship's bridge. The plane, however, missed and struck the #3 boom, careening into the water beside the ship. Fortunately, the *Colton* escaped serious injury from the plane, but gunfire from the Allied ships in the anchorage also slightly damaged the vessel. Three men from the eight officers, thirty-three men, twenty-nine armed guards, and eleven CBs on board reported injuries.

The sources conflict on the number of armed guards. WACR; AG.

ATTLEBORO VICTORY

D:	6-14-45	YB:	1945
T:	2357	Tn:	7,607
Pos:	44.59 N / 30.54 E	Dr:	16 ft.
Ow:	WSA	C:	19 tons general
Op:	Stockard SS Corp.	P:	steam
M:	W. Hope	S:	16.5
A:	1-5"; 1-3"; 8-20 mm		

The *Attleboro Victory* sailed from Odessa, Russia, to Constanta, Romania. In the Black Sea, the vessel struck a mine, and the explosion blew a hole sixteen feet by fourteen feet in the port side at the #2 hold. The master stopped the vessel and lowered a lifeboat to survey the damage. Satisfied that the ship would not

sink, he proceeded to Constanta for repairs. There were no casualties among the
ten officers, forty-four men, twelve armed guards, and seven passengers on
board.

WACR; WCSR; RWCS; AG; ONF.

CALVIN COOLIDGE

D:	6-19-45	YB:	1942
T:	1030	Tn:	7,176
Pos:	49.50 N / 04.57 W	Dr:	20 ft. 10 in.
Ow:	WSA	C:	troops, ballast
Op:	Sprague SS Co.	P:	steam
M:	H. E. Andersen	S:	11.5
A:	1-5"; 1-3"; 8-20 mm		

On 18 June, the *Calvin Coolidge* sailed from Le Havre, France, to Boston,
Massachusetts. A magnetic mine exploded 100 feet off the starboard bow,
shaking the Liberty ship violently. The ship suffered only slight injury. There
were no casualties among the 8 officers, 48 men, 31 armed guards, and 457
troops on board.

WACR; RWCS; AG; ONF.

PIERRE GIBAULT

D:	6-22-45	YB:	1943
T:	1820	Tn:	7,176
Pos:	36.04.30 N / 23.06.30 E	Dr:	18 ft.
Ow:	WSA	C:	669 tons tobacco, licorice root,
Op:	Shepard SS Co.		fuel oil
M:	Albert G. Hokins	P:	steam
A:	1-5"; 1-3"; 8-20 mm	S:	12

On 21 June, the *Pierre Gibault* sailed from Ismir, Turkey, bound for Oran,
Algeria. Off Kýthera Island, at the edge of a swept channel, the *Gibault* struck a
mine. The explosion occurred under the #2 hatch on the port side and threw oil
and debris over the deck. The #2 and #3 holds filled with water, and the vessel
began to settle by the head. The explosion sprayed oil from the #2 hold
containing fuel oil over the entire ship. Fire broke out in this hold and spread aft
to the #4 hold, engulfing the bridge and midships house. The eight officers,
thirty-two men, twelve armed guards, and three women passengers did not
abandon ship. The crew fought the fire all night and brought it under control at
0500 the next day. Three hours after the explosion, the Greek escort destroyer
Thermistocles arrived and removed the wounded and killed. At 0730 on

25 June, the South African Navy whaler *Southern Maid* (T-27) arrived with salvage gear and a Greek salvage crew. The following day the HMS salvage ship *Prince Salvor* (W-05) arrived, and a salvage officer had the ship beached at Kapsali Bay on the Island of Kýthera. As a result of the explosion and fire one officer and one merchant crewman died. Two of the armed guards also perished, and seven others reported injuries. The salvors cut the bow off and towed the stern to Piraeus, Greece. The WSA later declared the ship a CTL.

WACR; WCSR; AG; Sawyer, Mitchell, p. 125.

JOHN H. HAMMOND

D:	7-17-45	YB:	1944
T:	2213	Tn:	7,198
Pos:	42.55.30 N / 10.08.00 E	Dr:	27 ft.
Ow:	WSA	C:	6,484 tons general, flour,
Op:	William J. Roundtree Co., Inc.		ordinance equipment
M:	John Wooten Niemeyer	P:	steam
A:	1-5"; 1-3"; 8-20 mm	S:	7

On 16 July, the *John H. Hammond*, sailed from Naples, Italy, to Leghorn, Italy. Off Elba a mine struck the starboard side at the engine room and created a hole twenty-five feet in diameter. The engine room and holds #2 and #3 filled rapidly with water and forced the crew to abandon ship at 2330. The survivors among the eight officers, thirty-two men, three armed guards, and one passenger left the ship in two boats and a raft. An RAF crash boat picked up the survivors at 0200 the next day and landed them at Leghorn. On 19 July, the British tug *Griffin* embarked fifteen men of the crew to return to the ship. Six men and a British salvage officer boarded the *Hammond* at 2130 the next day and prepared the Liberty ship to be towed. On 20 July, the *Griffin* and another tug towed the *Hammond* into Piombino, with five feet of freeboard forward and six feet aft. By this time, water had entered all the holds. The mine killed the officer and two men on watch in the engine room and injured four others.

WACR; WCSR; RWCS; AG.

JOHN A. RAWLINS

D:	7-27-45	YB:	1942
T:	2323	Tn:	7,182
Pos:	Naha Harbor, Okinawa	Dr:	22 ft.
Ow:	WSA	C:	3,000 tons cased oil, general
Op:	Matson Navigation Co.	P:	steam
M:	Emil Hrubik	S:	at anchor
A:	1-4"; 1-3"; 8-20 mm		

On 27 April, the *John A. Rawlins* sailed from San Francisco, California, to Okinawa. While the ship was at anchor in Naha Harbor, a Japanese torpedo bomber attacked through an opening in the anchorage's protective smoke screen. An aerial torpedo struck the ship on the port side at the #3 hold and blew a hole twenty feet by thirty feet in the ship's side. The cargo in the #3 hold caught fire and burned for forty hours. At the time of the attack the ship had 8 officers, 31 men, 28 armed guards, and 191 CBs on board. The explosion wounded only three men. The damage to the ship was considered extensive. As the ship awaited repairs in Buckner Bay, Okinawa, a typhoon drove her on a reef, and the WSA declared the *Rawlins* a CTL.

WACR; WCSR; AG; Stindt, p. 120.

PRATT VICTORY

D:	7-27-45	YB:	1945
T:	2255	Tn:	8,230
Pos:	South of Ie Shima	Dr:	26 ft.
Ow:	WSA	C:	general, asphalt in drums
Op:	Waterman SS Corp.	P:	steam
M:	Reese A. Broadus	S:	at anchor
A:	1-5"; 1-3"; 8-20 mm		

On 27 May, the *Pratt Victory* sailed from San Francisco to Ie Shima, Okinawa, and arrived on 12 July. The freighter anchored in berth M-38, two miles offshore, and had discharged over one-third of her cargo. An air alert sounded at 1242, and an enemy torpedo plane approached from the starboard side of the ship. About 1,500 yards away the plane dropped a torpedo that struck at the #2 hold. The explosion blew asphalt through the hatch and 150 feet into the air and created a hole thirty feet high by thirty-five feet wide. The explosion ruptured the deep tanks and flooded the #1 and #2 holds, causing the ship to slowly settle by the head. When the plane attacked, the *LCT-1050* lay tied along the starboard side discharging cargo. The explosion blew the landing craft twenty feet into the air, and the LCT sank beside the freighter. Five of the *Pratt Victory*'s eight officers, forty-seven men, twenty-seven armed guards, and twenty-eight other men stayed on the ship and had her remaining cargo discharged. She left for Buckner Bay on 8 August. The Navy surveyed the vessel, and repairs began on 10 September.

The figures for the armed guards conflict within the sources. NSS; WACR; WCSR; USMMA; AG.

WILLIAM J. PALMER

D:	8-4-45	YB:	1943
T:	1245	Tn:	7,176
Pos:	45.34.15 N / 13.36.15 E	Dr:	22 ft.
Ow:	WSA	C:	4,000 tons forage, clothing,
Op:	South Atlantic SS Co.		horses
M:	Joseph Innes Moody	P:	steam
A:	2-3"; 8-20 mm	S:	12

On 17 July, the *William J. Palmer* sailed from New York bound for Yugoslavia via Trieste, Italy. The vessel struck a mine five miles out of Trieste and about two miles from shore. The explosion occurred on the starboard side at the #4 hold, causing a 5° list. The Liberty ship began to sink by the stern, and when the bulkhead separating the engine room gave way, the master ordered the ship abandoned. The complement of eight officers, thirty-five men, three armed guards, and eighteen workaways, who were signed on to take care of the horses, left the ship in four lifeboats. Ten minutes after the explosion all hands safely left the ship. The master boarded a British cutter that circled the *Palmer* but could not save the horses. Only six of the horses, those tethered on the deck, were saved by local fishermen. A tugboat towed the four lifeboats into Trieste. The *Palmer* rolled over on her starboard side and sank at 1300.

WACR; WCSR; AG.

CASIMIR PULASKI

D:	8-8-45	YB:	1943
T:	1140	Tn:	7,176
Pos:	Pier 13, Manila, PI	Dr:	24 ft.
Ow:	WSA	C:	6,000 tons trucks, jeeps,
Op:	United Fruit Co.		kerosene, beer
M:	Stanley Widden	P:	steam
A:	2-3"; 8-20 mm	S:	docked

The *Casimir Pulaski* sailed from New Orleans, Louisiana, to Manila, Philippine Islands. On 18 April, the *Pulaski* docked at Pier 13 in Manila Harbor. During dredging operations a mine or bomb exploded seventy-five feet off the port bow. The concussion of the explosion damaged the shell plating from the stern to the after bulkhead of the #1 hold. The damage, however, did not require any substantial repairs. The Liberty ship's complement consisted of eight officers, thirty-four men, and twenty-eight armed guards. The blast injured two of the armed guards.

WACR; AG.

JACK SINGER

D:	8-10-45	YB:	1944
T:	2305	Tn:	7,207
Pos:	off Naha, Okinawa	Dr:	22 ft.
Ow:	WSA	C:	3,500 tons trucks, airplanes,
Op:	American West African Lines		machinery
M:	Julius M. Jacobson	P:	steam
A:	2-3"; 8-20 mm	S:	at anchor

The *Jack Singer* sailed from Calcutta, India, to Naha, Okinawa, with a Navy tanker and four escorts. While the *Singer* was anchored off Okinawa, a Japanese torpedo plane attacked and put a torpedo into the starboard side at the #3 hold. The explosion blew water over the bridge and created a hole forty feet by twenty-seven feet in the shell plating. The vessel listed to starboard immediately, but the master did not order the eight officers, thirty-one men, and twenty-nine armed guards to abandon ship. Instead, he beached the vessel on a reef, and she was later refloated but grounded during a typhoon. She was abandoned as a CTL by the WSA. Only one man in the crew reported an injury.

WACR; AG.

WILLIAM D. BYRON

D:	8-15-45	YB:	1944
T:	0453	Tn:	7,210
Pos:	44.00 N / 09.00 E	Dr:	13 ft. 7 in.
Ow:	WSA	C:	none
Op:	Dickmann, Wright, & Pugh Inc.	P:	steam
M:	Michael E. Martin	S:	7
A:	1-5"; 1-3"; 8-20 mm		

On 15 August, the *William D. Byron* sailed from Savona to Naples, Italy. While off Savona, the vessel struck two mines at the #2 hold on the port side. The #1, #2, and #3 holds immediately flooded, and the ship took a 17° port list. The vessel was towed back to Savona with a thirty-six foot draft forward and thirty-three foot draft aft. The eight officers, thirty-three men, and four armed guards stayed with the Liberty ship until she returned to her anchorage. The crew then left in two lifeboats without orders from the master. Only one of the armed guards reported an injury.

WACR; WCSR; AG; TF.

PETER WHITE

D:	8-30-45	YB:	1943
T:	1450	Tn:	7,176
Pos:	14.37 N / 122.26 E	Dr:	15 ft. 10 in.
Ow:	WSA	C:	400 tons copra
Op:	Seas Shipping Co.	P:	steam
M:	Ernest N. Kettenhofen	S:	10.5
A:	2-3"; 8-20 mm		

The *Peter White* sailed independently from Mauban, Luzon, to San Francisco, California, via Homonhon Island. About fifty miles from Mauban, the vessel struck a mine at the #3 hold, port side. The explosion blew a large hole in the ship's side and started a fire that the crew quickly extinguished. The eight officers, forty-four men, seventeen armed guards, and one passenger remained on board. Naval vessels stood by the ship, and under her own power and by tow she arrived at Leyte. The four men injured by the blast were transferred to one of the naval vessels for treatment. The ship went into dry dock in Guiuan, Philippines, on 15 September.

The master listed in the Shipping Articles is C. D. Wells. WACR; WCSR; AG; ONF.

JOSEPH CARRIGAN

D:	8-31-45	YB:	1945
T:	1305	Tn:	7,176
Pos:	Brunei Bay, Borneo	Dr:	unknown
Ow:	WSA	C:	general, whiskey, beer, troops
Op:	U.S. Navigation Co.	P:	steam
M:	Karl Emil Knudson	S:	unknown
A:	1-5"; 1-3"; 8-20 mm		

On 27 August, the *Joseph Carrigan* left Morotai, en route to Australia, with two Australian corvettes as escorts. While in Victoria Harbor off Labuan Island, Borneo, the vessel struck a mine 200 yards off the #2 buoy. The explosion occurred on the port side amidships. The Liberty ship immediately listed to port but within minutes righted herself. The explosion broke the main steam line and stopped the engines and caused the engine room and the #3 hold to flood. After an unsuccessful attempt to tow the *Carrigan* on the night of the 31st, one of the escorts managed later to successfully tow the ship to Labuan, and she dropped anchor at noon on 1 September. All eight officers, thirty-one men, and the twenty-seven armed guards survived the explosion, and only one of the merchant crew suffered a minor injury. The *Carrigan* also had on board a large number of Australian troops. The explosion jarred one of the lifeboats loose, and it struck and killed an Australian major standing on the deck. The ship

discharged some of her cargo in Labuan, and the tug *Point Judith* towed the vessel to Manila, arriving on 11 November. After repairs the *Carrigan* went back in service.

WCSR; AG; Sawyer, Mitchell, p. 103.

BENJAMIN F. COSTON

D:	10-27-45	YB:	1944
T:	1306	Tn:	7,176
Pos:	43.32 N / 09.37 E	Dr:	30 ft. 5 in.
Ow:	WSA	C:	9,247 tons coal
Op:	Union Sulphur Co.	P:	steam
M:	Edward Michael Larner	S:	10
A:	1-5"; 1-3"; 8-20 mm		

The *Benjamin F. Coston* sailed independently from Port Said, Suez, to Genoa, Italy. North of Corsica the *Coston* struck a mine. The explosion occurred off the stern and blew off part of the rudder and cracked the hull. The blast extensively damaged the Liberty ship, and she had to be towed to port. None of the eight officers, thirty men, five armed guards, and four passengers on board reported any injuries.

WACR; AG; ONF.

ABBOT L. MILLS

D:	11-10-45	YB:	1943
T:	0945	Tn:	7,176
Pos:	42.34.7 / 18.08.3 E	Dr:	28 ft. 11 in.
Ow:	WSA	C:	8,063 tons wheat
Op:	Pacific Far East Line	P:	steam
M:	David Bowman	S:	5.5
A:	2-3"; 8-20 mm		

On 16 October, the *Abbot L. Mills* sailed from Galveston, Texas, to Dubrovnik, Yugoslavia. In rough weather, five miles off Dubrovnik, the *Mills* struck a mine on the starboard side at the #1 hold. The master had the engines stopped, rang the general alarm, and ordered the ship's complement of eight officers, twenty-nine men, and three armed guards to swing out the lifeboats in preparation for abandoning ship. Two lifeboats with men left the ship, but because of the ship's heavy rolling the master decided to bring the Liberty ship into the anchorage at Dubrovnik. The chief engineer sounded the #1 hold and found eighteen feet of

water, but the #2 hold remained dry. At 1300, after anchoring, the men in the boats came back on board. All hands survived.

WACR; WCSR; AG.

WILLIAM HUME

D:	11-12-45	YB:	1943
T:	1011	Tn:	7,176
Pos:	45.36.18 N / 13.41.18 E	Dr:	unknown
Ow:	WSA	C:	6,500 tons grain
Op:	Weyerhaeuser SS Co.	P:	steam
M:	Richard William Harrison	S:	unknown
A:	2-3"; 8-20 mm		

On 21 October, the *William Hume* sailed from Baltimore, Maryland, to Trieste, Italy. South of the #8 buoy off Point Salvore, as the Liberty ship proceeded through a swept channel into Trieste, she struck a mine at the #1 hold, port side. The explosion shook the ship and sent a column of water high into the air. The master stopped the ship's engines and had his crew and the armed guards muster at their boat stations. As the ship sank rapidly by the bow, the crew swung the boats out. The master restarted the engines and proceeded slowly ahead to keep the bow from submerging. The master signaled a British minesweeper and requested tugs to come to his assistance. At about 1130 the vessel lost steerageway, and the stern rose into the air. The master ordered some of the eight officers, thirty-one men, and two armed guards to abandon ship but to stay close to the vessel. The rest of the men abandoned the ship at 1203, and all went on board the minesweeper. At 1340 a tug arrived. The master and five men reboarded the freighter and secured a tow line from the stern of the *Hume* to the tug. The ship managed to get about one-half mile from land when at 1540 she began to sink rapidly, rolled over, and disappeared at 1552. All hands survived the sinking and landed in Trieste.

WCSR; AG.

JESSE BILLINGSLY

D:	11-19-45	YB:	1943
T:	1140	Tn:	7,244
Pos:	45.23.48 N / 13.19.20 E	Dr:	26 ft. 7 in.
Ow:	WSA	C:	8,140 tons flour in sacks
Op:	William J. Rountree & Co.	P:	steam
M:	Gustav H. Larsen	S:	11.2
A:	unarmed		

The *Jesse Billingsly* sailed from Ancona, Italy, to Trieste, Italy. During the voyage the vessel struck a mine between the #1 and #2 holds along the keel. The explosion blew a hole twenty-two feet square in the ship's bottom. The ship flooded rapidly until her draft forward rose to forty-five feet. The crew of eight officers and thirty men abandoned ship within ten minutes. The master and his men later reboarded the Liberty ship and beached her under her own power. All hands survived the incident. After repairs the ship returned to service.

WACR; AG; ONF.

CEDAR MILLS

D:	11-19-45	YB:	1943
T:	1141	Tn:	10,172
Pos:	Ancona Harbor	Dr:	23 ft. 7 in.
Ow:	WSA	C:	5,000 tons Navy special fuel oil
Op:	American Petroleum Trans. Co.	P:	steam
M:	Robert L. Hartsfield Jr.	S:	10
A:	unarmed		

On 19 November, the *Cedar Mills* sailed from Ancona, Italy, en route to Taranto, Italy. The vessel discharged most of her cargo in Ancona and then proceeded to Taranto. About 100 yards northeast of the North Jetty an explosion occurred under the boilers. The explosion almost broke the vessel in two at the after end of the midships housing. Only two plates on the starboard side held the ship together. The complement of eight officers, thirty-four men, and two armed guards abandoned ship within ten minutes. About seven of the crew used one lifeboat; the rest stepped off the stern into the Italian tugs that immediately came to the damaged tanker's assistance. The master and five crew members later reboarded the ship and helped the tugs to tow her to the beach. A fireman on watch died, and fifteen others reported injuries. The WSA later declared the *Cedar Mills* a CTL.

WACR; WCSR.

NATHANIEL BACON

D:	12-19-45	YB:	1942
T:	0630	Tn:	7,176
Pos:	42.21 N / 11.29 E	Dr:	24 ft.
Ow:	WSA	C:	5,995 tons food and medical
Op:	International Freighting Corp.		supplies
M:	Harvey Lee Huff	P:	steam
A:	unarmed	S:	7

On 19 November, the *Nathaniel Bacon* sailed from Savannah, Georgia, to Civitavecchia, Italy. She sailed unescorted under British Admiralty routing instructions. Because of rough weather the freighter waited outside the port during the night of the 18th. The next day, eight miles southeast of the breakwater at Civitavecchia, the *Bacon* struck a mine underneath the ship at the #1 hold. Fire broke out and a firefighting party put it out in twenty minutes. The master ordered the boats swung out so they could be quickly launched if necessary. Because of the weather, the master did not get under way, and the Liberty ship began to drift. At 0930, after drifting three miles, two more mines exploded underneath the #2 hold. The ship broke in two at the forward end of the #3 hatch, and the forward end sank. At 1005, with seas breaking over the midships house, the master ordered the ship abandoned. The eight officers, thirty-two men, four passengers (three Army), and a woman stowaway left the ship in three lifeboats and a raft. The weather prevented a rescue vessel from coming to the *Bacon*'s assistance. The three boats and the raft made landfall on the coast of Italy that afternoon. The ship drifted aground seventeen miles northwest of Civitavecchia. Salvors saved portions of the cargo and the stern half. The WSA declared the ship a CTL. Two men from the merchant crew drowned while abandoning ship.

The stern half was eventually joined to the forepart of the *Bert Williams*. The sources conflict concerning the personnel on board. WACR; WCSR; AG; Sawyer, Mitchell, p. 34.

DUNCAN L. CLINCH

D:	12-23-45	YB:	1944
T:	1222	Tn:	7,198
Pos:	49.27 N / 00.03 E	Dr:	22 ft. 6 in.
Ow:	WSA	C:	6,368 tons general
Op:	American Export Lines	P:	steam
M:	John L. Paterson	S:	10.5
A:	1-5"; 1-3"; 8-20 mm		

On 23 December, the *Duncan L. Clinch* left Le Havre, France, en route to Rouen, France. Two miles west of La Havre the freighter struck a mine under the #1 hatch, port side. The explosion rapidly flooded the #1 hold, and the ship settled quickly by the head. When the vessel split forward of the engine room, the master gave the order to abandon ship. The eight officers, thirty-two men, two armed guards, and two pilots on board left the ship in four lifeboats at about 1300. Two U.S. Coast Guard cutters and two salvage tugs came out of the harbor to give assistance. All hands boarded the Coast Guard vessels and one of the tugs and went ashore at Le Havre. The master, several crewmen, and a WSA representative took a cutter to the vessel on the 26th. They could not board her, and they realized the ship could not be salvaged because of the heavy seas. By

the end of the day she had settled to the bottom with only her masts and stacks above water—a total loss.

WACR; WCSR; AG.

ANTIETAM

D:	1-30-46	YB:	1919
T:	0856	Tn:	6,273
Pos:	off Blaye, France	Dr:	24 ft.
Ow:	WSA	C:	45,000 bbls. road tar
Op:	Keystone Shipping Co.	P:	steam
M:	Walter E. Schroeder	S:	2
A:	1-4"; 1-3"; 8-20 mm		

The *Antietam* sailed from New York to Blaye, France. The vessel was about to take the pilot on board for the Gironde River when a mine struck the vessel on the starboard side at the machinery space. The stern of the vessel settled on the bottom within twenty minutes. The complement of eight officers, thirty men, and two Navy enlisted men remained on board the tanker until 1245, and the ship sank about ten minutes later. The survivors left the vessel in two lifeboats and one raft and were taken on board a French pilot boat. The blast killed one of the merchant crewmen and injured four other men.

WACR; AG; ONF.

NATHAN HALE

D:	2-5-46	YB:	1942
T:	1005	Tn:	7,176
Pos:	43.23.45 N / 09.31 E	Dr:	16 ft.
Ow:	WSA	C:	none
Op:	Coastwise Line	P:	steam
M:	George W. Tuttle Jr.	S:	10
A:	unarmed		

The *Nathan Hale* sailed from Genoa to Leghorn, Italy. In hazy, rough weather the freighter struck a mine about twenty-five miles north of Corsica. The explosion occurred at the #2 hold, port side, and ripped a hole thirty-four feet by twenty-five feet in the side of the vessel. Both the #1 and the #2 holds flooded. The crew of eight officers and thirty men managed to bring the *Hale* into Leghorn at seven knots. The damage was extensive enough for the WSA to declare the vessel a CTL. There were no casualties.

WACR; ONF; Sawyer, Mitchell, p. 62.

SEA SATYR

D:	2-22-46	YB:	1945
T:	1602	Tn:	7,886
Pos:	off Makassar Breakwater	Dr:	16 ft.
Ow:	WSA	C:	3,000 tons rice
Op:	Matson Navigation Co.	P:	steam
M:	Charles H. Morgan	S:	5
A:	unarmed		

The *Sea Satyr* sailed from Makassar, Celebes, to San Francisco, California. The freighter struck a mine 500 yards off the breakwater in Makassar Harbor. The explosion occurred at the after part of the ship near the #4 hold. The blast extensively damaged the freighter, causing about $400,000 of damage. The crew of eight officers and forty-three men brought the ship back into Makassar for repairs. The explosion injured four of the crew.

WACR; ONF.

CYRUS ADLER

D:	2-26-46	YB:	1944
T:	2210	Tn:	7,176
Pos:	51.24 N / 02.32 E	Dr:	27 ft.
Ow:	WSA	C:	7,102 tons casein and lumber
Op:	West India SS Co.	P:	steam
M:	Harmer H. Van Catt	S:	4
A:	unarmed		

On 20 January, the *Cyrus Adler* sailed from Long View, Washington, to Antwerp, Belgium, via the Downs. Off the Belgium coast the freighter struck a mine on the port side at the #1 hold. This hold flooded and brought the forward draft of the Liberty ship four feet lower. The crew of eight officers and thirty men remained on the ship. The *Adler* was later towed to port, repaired, and put back in service. There were no injuries among the crew.

WACR; TF; ONF.

OSHKOSH VICTORY

D:	3-2-46	YB:	1945
T:	0422	Tn:	7,607
Pos:	31.00 N / 122.32 E	Dr:	22 ft.
Ow:	WSA	C:	4,711 tons Army signal
Op:	Mississippi Shipping Co.		equipment
M:	B. Alexander	P:	steam
A:	unarmed	S:	at anchor

The *Oshkosh Victory* sailed from Yokohama, Japan, to the Yangtze River, China. In overcast weather and moderate seas the ship lay at anchor in the Yangtze River Estuary. A mine struck the ship at the stern and damaged the rudder, the stern frame, and the thrust bearing. The eight officers, forty-two men, and one passenger remained with the ship while she was towed to port. The men reported no injuries.

WACR; ONF.

MINOR C. KEITH

D:	3-3-46	YB:	1944
T:	2118	Tn:	7,247
Pos:	off Weser Lt. Vessel	Dr:	27 ft.
Ow:	WSA	C:	8,331 tons grain
Op:	United Fruit Co.	P:	steam
M:	R. Desmond	S:	11
A:	unarmed		

The *Minor C. Keith* sailed from Baltimore, Maryland, to Bremerhaven, Germany. The vessel strayed out of the cleared channel and struck a mine one and one-quarter miles from the Weser Light Vessel. The explosion occurred under the #5 hold but only slightly damaged the ship. The eight officers, thirty men, and a pilot remained on the Liberty ship. The vessel was repaired and put back in service. The crew suffered no injuries.

WACR; ONF.

LORD DELAWARE

D:	3-9-46	Tn:	7,200
T:	1839	Dr:	26 ft.
Pos:	54.36.06 N / 11.03.06 E	C:	8,094 tons coal and United
Ow:	WSA		Nations Relief and
Op:	International Freight Corp.		Rehabilitation Administration
M:	Willard L. Headly		cargo
A:	unarmed	P:	steam
YB:	1942	S:	11

The *Lord Delaware* sailed from New York to Abo, Finland. Off Fehmarn Island, Germany, the Liberty ship struck a mine. The explosion occurred on the starboard side at the machinery spaces. The blast damaged the machinery and holed the vessel. Since the blast did not cause the ship to leak extensively, the crew of eight officers and thirty men as well as the one passenger remained on the vessel. After being towed to port and repaired, she went back in service. The crew suffered no injuries.

UNRRA–United Nations Relief and Rehabilitation Administration WACR; ONF.

JEAN LYKES

D:	3-23-46	YB:	1943
T:	2332	Tn:	6,711
Pos:	off Kattegat Lt. Ship	Dr:	21 ft.
Ow:	Lykes Bros. SS Co.	C:	4,898 tons general
Op:	Lykes Bros. SS Co.	P:	steam
M:	Edward Tomti	S:	unknown
A:	unarmed		

The *Jean Lykes* sailed from Göteborg, Sweden, to Copenhagen, Denmark. One mile south southeast of the Kattegat Light Vessel, the freighter struck a mine. The explosion occurred at the stern and caused only slight damage to the ship. The crew of eight officers and thirty-eight men, along with one Danish advisor, remained with the ship, and she made Copenhagen harbor under her own power. There were no casualties.

WACR; ONF.

PARK VICTORY

D:	4-30-46	YB:	1945
T:	0706	Tn:	6,707
Pos:	38.09 N / 21.06 E	Dr:	unknown
Ow:	WSA	C:	livestock and feed
Op:	Seas Shipping Co. Inc.	P:	steam
M:	Robert Laws Fairbairn	S:	17
A:	unarmed		

The *Park Victory* sailed from Larnaca, Cyprus, to Patras, Greece. While proceeding through the Gulf of Patras, the ship struck a mine. The explosion occurred under the keel at the #1 hold and caused extensive damage. It blew holes in the hull on both the starboard and port sides and cracked and buckled plates. The eight officers, thirty-seven men, and thirty-four passengers got the ship to port under her own power. Fortunately, none of those on board suffered an injury.

WACR; ONF.

FITZHUGH LEE

D:	7-3-46	YB:	1943
T:	0335 (GMT)	Tn:	7,244
Pos:	off Italy	Dr:	28 ft. 6 in.
Ow:	WSA	C:	8,000 tons corn
Op:	Smith & Johnson	P:	steam
M:	William S. MacFarlane	S:	11
A:	unarmed		

The *Fitzhugh Lee* sailed from Baltimore, Maryland, to Naples, Italy. A mine struck the vessel on the port side at the #1 hold. The explosion blew a twenty-foot hole in the Liberty ship's side. The crew of eight officers and thirty men took the vessel safely into port. There were no injuries associated with the explosion.

The coordinates 45.05 N / 12.40 E in the reports are faulty, given the destination of the vessel. WACR; ONF.

NIELS POULSON

D:	9-14-46	YB:	1944
T:	0358	Tn:	7,198
Pos:	43.27 N / 09.50 E	Dr:	23 ft.
Ow:	U.S. Maritime Commission	C:	4,514 tons coal
Op:	Dichmann, Wright & Pugh, Inc.	P:	steam
M:	Adolph G. Miller	S:	13.6
A:	unarmed		

The *Niels Poulson* sailed from Genoa to Leghorn, Italy. North of Corsica the vessel struck a mine at the #1 hold on the port side. This hold flooded, but the crew of eight officers and thirty men brought the vessel into port under her own power. The blast injured one merchant seaman.

WACR; ONF.

SIGNAL HILLS

D:	10-8-46	YB:	1945
T:	0602	Tn:	10,441
Pos:	43.30.05 N / 09.34 E	Dr:	20 ft. 8 in.
Ow:	U.S. Maritime Commission	C:	none
Op:	Pacific Tankers. Inc.	P:	steam
M:	Andrew John Poydock	S:	13
A:	unarmed		

The *Signal Hills* sailed from Vado Liguire, Italy, to the Persian Gulf. Off Cape Corse, the tanker struck a mine. The explosion occurred on the starboard side at the #9 tank and blew a hole six feet by nine feet in the ship's side. The explosion extensively damaged the ship, requiring her to be towed to port. The crew of eight officers and thirty-nine men reported no injuries.

WACR; ONF.

CASSIUS HUDSON

D:	10-16-46	YB:	1944
T:	0330	Tn:	7,167
Pos:	45.32 N / 13.12 E	Dr:	28 ft. 10 in.
Ow:	WSA	C:	8,000 tons coal
Op:	Standard Fruit	P:	steam
M:	Howard C. Forbes	S:	stop
A:	unarmed		

The *Cassius Hudson* sailed from Norfolk, Virginia, to Venice, Italy. While steaming through the northern Adriatic Sea, the vessel wandered into a minefield and struck two mines within a twelve-hour period. One mine exploded on the starboard side at the #3 hold and disabled the ship. While under tow, another mine exploded underneath the Liberty ship at the #4 hold. The crew of eight officers and twenty-five men abandoned ship in four lifeboats at 1500 and were taken on board a British minesweeper within three hours. All hands survived the explosions, but the *Hudson* sank on 18 October.

WACR; ONF; Sawyer, Mitchell, p. 87.

APPENDIX

POORLY DOCUMENTED U.S. MERCHANT VESSEL LOSSES

DATE	VESSEL	OWNER	YEAR BUILT	TONNAGE	CARGO	PROPULSION	REMARKS
11-19-41	Del Pidio[1]	unknown	unknown	unknown	unknown	unknown	struck a mine at the entrance to Manila Bay; 12 crew on board, 6 survived
12-10-41	Cetus	Madrigal & Co.	1904	943	unknown	steam	scuttled at Aparri, Cagayan River; believed to be renamed Hokuhi Maru
mid-Dec.	Vizcaya	Madrigal & Co.	1890	1,249	unknown	steam	scuttled
12-17-41	Corregidor	Compania Maritima	1911	1,881	unknown	steam	struck a mine, 500 lost
12-24-41	Si Kiang[1]	unknown	unknown	7,014	gasoline	unknown	while in Manila, attacking aircraft set her on fire; had been confiscated by Americans

[1]This vessel is documented in Lloyd's but cannot be documented in any other source.

DATE	VESSEL	OWNER	YEAR BUILT	TONNAGE	CARGO	PROPULSION	REMARKS
12-25-41	*Argus*	Madrigal & Co.	1901	1,025	unknown	steam	captured in Hong Kong, renamed *Hongkong Maru*
12-25-41	*Hirondelle*	Madrigal & Co.	1911	1,243	unknown	steam	captured in Hong Kong, renamed *Gyonan Maru*
12-26-41	*Paz*	Madrigal & Co.	1914	4,260	coal	steam	bombed and set on fire in Manila, salvaged by Japanese, renamed *Hatsu Maru*
12-27-41	*Taurus*	Madrigal & Co.	1911	1,251	unknown	steam	scuttled in the Pasig River, Luzon
12-27-41	*Ethel Edwards*	Smith Navigation Co., Inc.	1919	334	unknown	motor	set on fire by Japanese aircraft in Manila
12-28-41	*Mauban*	Compania Generale de Tabacos de Filipinas	1900	1,253	unknown	steam	sunk in Manila and raised by the Japanese, renamed *Manbo Maru*
12-29-41	*Palawan*	Madrigal & Co.	1927	522	unknown	motor	scuttled in Manila Bay, refloated by Japanese and renamed *Paran Maru*

DATE	VESSEL	OWNER	YEAR BUILT	TONNAGE	CARGO	PROPULSION	REMARKS
12-31-41	*Magallanes*	Gutierrez Hermanos	1880	1,375	unknown	steam	scuttled in Manila
12-31-41	*Montanes*	Gutierrez Hermanos	1880	1,236	unknown	steam	scuttled in Manila
12-31-41	*Dos Hermanos*	Gutierrez Hermanos	1882	838	unknown	steam	scuttled in Manila, refloated by Japanese and renamed *Himeno Maru*
12-41	*Bicol*	Madrigal & Co.	1901	367	unknown	steam	damaged by aircraft at Manila, Allied engineers blew up hulk on 12-28-41
12-41	*Churruca*	Manila SS Co., Inc.	1878	788	unknown	steam	scuttled in Hong Kong
12-41	*Aloha*	North Negros Sugar Co., Lim.	1926	328	unknown	motor	scuttled in Manila Bay
1-2-42	*Latouche*	Madrigal & Co.	1910	2,156	unknown	steam	captured in Manila, renamed *Azuchi Maru*

DATE	VESSEL	OWNER	YEAR BUILT	TONNAGE	CARGO	PROPULSION	REMARKS
1-2-42	*Anakan*	Manila SS Co., Inc.	1938	795	unknown	motor	sunk in the Philippines and raised by the Japanese, renamed *Anan Maru*
1-2-42	*Luzon*[2]	Compania Maritima	1905	1,679	unknown	steam	sunk at Luzon, refloated by the Japanese, renamed *Ruson Maru*
1-2-42	*Bisayas*	Manila SS Co., Inc.	1912	2,832	unknown	steam	sunk at 16.37 N / 120.19 E by aircraft, salvaged and renamed *Hisigata Maru*
2-10-42	*Mindanao*	Cia Maritima	1918	5,236	unknown	steam	captured by Japanese at 14.35 N / 120.55 E, renamed *Palembang Maru*
2-28-42	*Compagnia de Filipinas*	Compania Generale Tabacos de Filipinas	1890	784	unknown	steam	captured by Japanese destroyer in the vicinity of Fortune Island, renamed *Hoei Maru*
End of Feb. 1942	*Surigao*	La Naviera Filipina, Inc.	1938	797	unknown	motor	stranded in the East Indies

[2]This vessel may have been under some type of charter arrangement with the army.

DATE	VESSEL	OWNER	YEAR BUILT	TONNAGE	CARGO	PROPULSION	REMARKS
3-1-42	*Legazpi*[2]	La Naviera Filipina, Inc.	1937	1,200	unknown	motor	shelled and then beached and scuttled by the crew near Puerto Calera
3-1-42	*Lepus*[2]	Madrigal & Co.	1906	1,936	unknown	steam	captured by the Japanese near Cavite, renamed *Reian Maru*
3-16-42	*Princess of Negros*	Negros Navigation Co., Inc.	1933	522	unknown	motor	captured by Japanese torpedo boats in the Sulu Sea, renamed *Toyohime Maru*
March 1942	*Regulus*[2]	Madrigal & Co.	1911	1,160	unknown	steam	captured at Mindoro Island by Japanese, renamed *Syotai Maru*
4-19-42	*Elcano*[2]	Philippine Steam Navigation Co.	1938	1,435	unknown	motor	shelled and sunk off Corregidor
April 1942	*Escalante R*[1]	unknown	unknown	96	unknown	motor	scuttled by order of U.S. Army in early April

[1]This vessel is documented in Lloyd's but cannot be documented in any other source.

[2]This vessel was under some type of charter arrangement with the army.

DATE	VESSEL	OWNER	YEAR BUILT	TONNAGE	CARGO	PROPULSION	REMARKS
April 1942	*Kanlaon II*	De La Rama SS Co., Inc.	1931	477	unknown	motor	scuttled by order of U.S. Army in early April
5-6-42	*Sarangani*[1]	unknown	unknown	2,691	unknown	unknown	presumably captured in the Philippines, renamed *Samraku Maru*
Sept. 1942	*Seminole*	unknown	unknown	unknown	unknown	unknown	seized by Germans at Trouville, France

[1]This vessel is documented in Lloyd's but cannot be documented in any other source.

Sources:

The data in the Appendix come from *Lloyd's War Losses, The American Bureau of Shipping*, and data gleaned from the 10th Fleet Records in the NHC.

GLOSSARY

BAREBOAT CHARTER: A charter agreement made that makes the charterer practically the owner of the ship. The charter appoints the master, engages the crew and pays the wages, provisions the ship, and pays all expenses. The principal obligations to the owner are to pay the owners an agreed rate for the ship's use, to reimburse the owner if the vessel is lost, and to redeliver her in the same condition when chartered, excluding ordinary wear and tear.

BILGE KEEL: A longitudinal fin fitted to the hull on each side of the ship at the turn of the bilge. It provides resistance in the water and reduces the rolling of the ship in a seaway.

BOAT FALL: The ropes by which a ship's boats are lowered or hoisted.

BOILER SADDLE: A semicircular support built of plates and angles on which cylindrical boilers are seated.

BULKHEAD: A vertical partition that separates compartments or spaces from one another.

BULWARK: The raised plating or woodwork that runs along the side of the vessel that helps keep heavy seas from washing over the deck and cargo and persons on board from washing overboard.

BUNKER: A compartment for storing fuel oil below decks. This is fuel for the use of the vessel and separate from that loaded as cargo.

BUTT JOINT: Two hull plates held together with strap (butt strap) that overlaps both pieces.

BUTT STRAP: Strip of plating that connects the plates of a butt joint.

CATWALK: A series of connecting gangways between the forward and after bridges, commonly found on tankers to allow the crew to freely move above the piping on the tanker's main deck.

COAMING: The raised lip that frames hatches and scuttles and prevents water on deck from running below. It also serves as the framework for hatches to which strong backs and hatch covers are fitted.

COLLISION BULKHEAD: An extra strong watertight bulkhead in the fore part of the ship to keep water out of the forward hold in case of a collision.

COUNTER: The underside of the stern that hangs above the waterline.

CROSS BUNKER: A bunker that stretches across the width of the ship and is formed by partitioning forward of the fireroom bulkhead.

CROSSTREE: A spreader fixed athwartship with a slot at each end over which shrouds are led fore and aft.

DEEP TANKS: Part of the vessel's hold partitioned off to carry water ballast and sometimes extra fuel. Often at either end of the machinery space and fireroom extending from side to side of the vessel. The deep tanks provided additional ballast.

DOUBLE BOTTOM: General term for all watertight spaces between the outer skin on the bottom of the ship and the plating over the floors. The double bottom serves to protect the ship's watertight integrity if she runs aground and stows liquid for ballast or fuel.

DOUGHNUT RAFT: Oval raft made of balsa wood.

DUNNAGE: Loose wood or blocks used in the hold to secure the cargo above the floors and away from the sides. This protects the cargo from sweating on the plates and wedges it so that it does not move with the motion of the ship.

FLOAT: Same as a life float.

FOREPEAK: The space between the collision bulkhead and the stem. Sometimes used as a trimming tank.

GARBOARD STRAKE: The strake of plating next to the keel in steel ship construction.

GLIDE BOMB: A German air to ship missile launched by aircraft some distance from the target. It was usually guided by high-frequency radio signals, but in some instances had wire links to the mother plane. Booster rockets accelerated the missiles ahead of the planes and bombardiers guided them to their targets with a small joystick.

HATCH BEAM: A beam placed across a hatch to support the covers. Also called a strongback.

HUMAN TORPEDO: A device whereby two torpedoes were attached, one suspended from the other. An operator sat on the upper torpedo in a watertight casing with a plastic dome to con the weapon to the target. The upper torpedo served to provide the propulsion and could propel the device at four knots.

JUMBO BOOM: A steel derrick usually rigged abaft the foremast on the centerline of a ship for handling heavy weights.

KAITEN TORPEDOES: Kaiten is a Japanese word meaning "the turn toward heaven." First designed in spring 1944, these manned torpedoes were carried by the Japanese on the decks of conventional submarines and ships. Launched close to the intended target, they could reach forty knots and packed an explosive charge of as much as 1,800 kg of TNT. They had crews of one or two men.

KING POST: A short heavy mast that serves to support a boom.

LIBERTY SHIP: A single-screw cargo steamer built by the U.S. Maritime Commission. These were emergency built vessels designed to minimize cost and building time. These vessels had two complete decks and five cargo holds with simple steam reciprocating engines.

LIFE FLOAT: A lifesaving device designed to be equally useful floating either side up. It has an elliptical frame usually made of balsa wood covered with canvas. It is usually stowed so it can be launched quickly by the crew or will float freely from the sinking ship.

LIFE RAFT: Raft-like construction designed to carry at least fifteen persons and stowed so that it could be launched or float free of the sinking ship. The life rafts were stocked with emergency rations, water, and other equipment and provisions to enable the occupants to survive at sea for several days and longer periods with careful rationing.

LIMPET MINE: An explosive device planted by swimmers. These mines could be clamped to the keel of a ship or placed near the condenser intakes to be sucked into the vessel.

MAIN INJECTOR: Large valve fitted to the sea chest to control the intake of water for the engine.

PAINTER: A length of rope made fast to a boat and used to hold the boat in place.

PEAK TANK: A ballast tank in the extreme bow or stern used to trim the ship.

PELICAN HOOK: A quick release hook used to secure the lifeboats.

POOP: A short raised deck on the after end of the ship.

RAFT: See life raft.

SALOON DECK: The deck where the passengers' quarters are situated in passenger steamers.

SETTLING TANK: A small tank in the engine room of ships using oil burning boilers. This tank received oil contaminated with water and with the use of heating coils separated and discharged the water. The pure oil then returned to a service tank.

SHAFT ALLEY: The watertight passage from the engine room to the stern tube that provides access to the shaft.

SMOKE POT: A device that made smoke to screen the ship from attacking aircraft and enemy vessels.

SPRING BEARINGS: The bearings that support the shafting in the stern tube and the immediate area.

STEAM SMOTHERING LINE: A pipe system that leads live steam from the boilers into each cargo hold. This can be used for firefighting purposes or for freeing tank spaces of gas.

STEM: The foremost structural member forming the bow of a vessel and joined to the keel.

STERN POST: The aftermost structural member at the stern, joined to the keel. It sometimes serves as the frame for connecting the ends of the shell plating.

STRAKE: A range of plates that run the length of the ship's hull.

STRONGBACK: See hatch beam.

SUMMER TANK: A tank within a tank vessel where additional oil can be carried during the summer months when freeboard regulations permit increased drafts. These tanks are sometimes used when a vessel is carrying light oil or sometimes carries fuel oil for the use of the ship.

TIME CHARTER: A form of charter whereby the vessel is chartered for a specific period of time. The owner usually manned and provisioned the ship while the charterer paid for the fuel and all the port expenses.

TOPPING LIFT: A wire rope used to take the weight of a boom to enable it to be "topped" at the desired angle. It leads from the end of the boom through a masthead block.

TORPEDO INDICATOR: A torpedo detection device that employed a hydrophone on either side of the hull and gave an audible warning and a visual indication of the direction of the torpedo's approach. These devices were too sensitive and picked up many different noises, causing merchant vessels to discontinue their use.

TORPEDO STREAMER: A mesh steel net secured away from the side of the vessel with booms. They were designed to stop torpedoes from striking the side of the ship and were streamed along the side of the vessel when under way. They could not, however, be used in rough seas or in fast convoys. These were used with varying success and could be brailed up when not in use.

TWEEN DECKS: A deck below the upper deck and above the lowest deck.

VICTORY SHIP: A standardized single screw cargo ship designed by the U.S. Maritime Commission as a faster and more efficient ship than the Liberty ship. These vessels were the same size but faster and had turbine engines.

WEATHER DECK: An uncovered deck exposed to the weather. Usually refers to the uppermost continuous deck, exclusive of the poop, bridge, and forecastle decks.

WELL DECK: The open deck that spans between the forecastle and the bridgehouse and the bridgehouse and the sternhouse.

WING TANK: Ballast tanks located outboard usually just under the weather deck.

WORKAWAY: A person who works his passage on a ship, distinguishable from a stowaway because he signs the articles.

ZIGZAG: A series of short straight line variations from a base course to confuse submarines. The merchant ships employed many different plans, each designed for specific circumstances.

BIBLIOGRAPHY

For convenience, many of the manuscript sources were abbreviated in the notes. These abbreviations can be found on page xiii. There are also numerous government and shipping company publications in this bibliography. Most of these works have no formal author. In order to keep the notes within the body of the text brief, I only cited their titles.

Manuscript Sources

Armed Guard Officer Voyage Reports to CNO, National Archives, Record Group 38, National Archives, Washington, DC.

Bureau of Naval Personnel, Ships Logs, Record Group 24, National Archives, Washington, DC.

Correspondence of the War Shipping Administrator, Records of the War Shipping Administration, Record Group 248, National Archives, Washington, DC.

Official Number Files, Records of the Bureau of Customs, Record Group 36, National Archives, Washington, DC.

Official Number Files, Records of the Bureau of Marine Inspection and Navigation, Record Group 41, National Archives, Washington, DC.

Official Number Files, Records of the Coast Guard, Record Group 26, National Archives, Washington, DC.

Records Relating to Applicants for Ship Warrants, Records of the War Shipping Administration, Record Group 248, National Archives, Washington, DC.

Records of the Department of Commerce, Record Group 40, National Archives, Washington, DC.

Records of the Department of State, Record Group 59, National Archives, Washington, DC.

Ship's Action Reports, Operational Archives, Naval Historical Center, Washington, DC.

Ship's History Files, Operational Archives, Naval Historical Center, Washington, DC.

Summaries of Statements by Survivors. Operational Archives, Naval Historical
    Center, Washington, DC.
Tenth Fleet Records, Operational Archives, Naval Historical Center,
    Washington, DC.
U.S. Coast Guard Vessel Documentation Records, U.S. Coast Guard
    Headquarters, Washington, DC.
U.S. Coast Guard, Records of the War Casualty Section, Record Group 26,
    National Archives, Washington, DC.
U.S. Coast Guard, War Action Casualty Reports, Coast Guard Historian's
    Office, Washington, DC.
U.S. Coast Guard, War Casualty Shipping Records 1941-45, Record Group 26,
    National Archives, Washington, DC.
U.S. Maritime Administration, Merchant Vessel Status Cards, Washington, DC.
U.S. Merchant Marine Academy Cadet Voyage Reports 1941-1945, U.S.
    Merchant Marine Academy, King's Point, New York.
War Journals of U-boats and U-boat Commands, Record Group 242, National
    Archives, Washington, DC.

Published Sources

Newspapers
    Albany Times Union
    Herald (Melbourne)
    Herald (New York)
    New Orleans Daily States
    Herald Tribune (New York)
    New York Times
    Pilot (Virginia Beach)
    Post (Washington)
    Star (Washington)
    The Evening Star (Washington)
    Times Herald (Washington)
American Bureau of Shipping. *Record of the American Bureau of Shipping.*
    American Bureau of Shipping, Chicago: Lakeside Press, 1941–1945.
Bagnasco, Ermino. *Submarines of World War Two.* Annapolis, MD: Naval
    Institute Press, 1977.
Bunker, John Gorley. *Liberty Ships.* New York: Arno Press, 1980.
Bunker, John Gorley. *Liberty Ships, The Ugly Ducklings of World War II.*
    Annapolis, MD: Naval Institute Press, 1972.
Cameron, Frank. "Last Minutes of the *President Coolidge.*" *The Mast Magazine*
    3(5) (May 1946):18–20.
Campbell, John. *Naval Weapons of World War II.* London: Conway Maritime
    Press, 1985.

Carse, Robert. *The Long Haul, The United States Merchant Service in World War II*. New York: W.W. Norton and Company, Inc., 1965.

Charles, Roland W. *Troopships of World War II*. Washington, DC: The Army Transportation Association, 1947.

Chesneau, Roger, ed. *Conway's All the World's Fighting Ships 1922-1946*. London: Conway Maritime Press, 1992.

Colledge, J. J. *Ships of the Royal Navy*. (2 vols.) Annapolis, MD: Naval Institute Press, 1987, 1989.

Connell, Edwin T. "Steady." *The Mast Magazine* 3(5) (Jan. 1946):14-17, 42-43.

Cook, Seabury. "The Voyage of the Wing Ding." *Seapower* 4(1) (Jan. 1944):21-25.

Cremer, Peter. *U-Boat Commander: A Periscope View of the Battle of the Atlantic*, in collaboration with Fritz Brustat-Noval, trans. by Lawrence Wilson. Annapolis, MD: Naval Institute Press, 1984.

de Kerchove, René. *International Maritime Dictionary*. New York: Van Nostrand Reinhold Company, 1961.

Dictionary of American Naval Fighting Ships. 8 vols., 1959-1981. Washington: DC: Naval History Division.

Dierdorff, Ross A. "Pioneer Party—Wake Island." *U.S. Naval Institute Proceedings* 69(4) (April 1943):498-508.

Dowling, Edward J. *The "Lakers" of World War I*. Detroit: University of Detroit Press, 1967.

Engle, Eloise, and Arnold S. Lott. *America's Maritime Heritage*. Annapolis, MD: Naval Institute Press, 1975.

Enright, Marc E. "His First Command." *The King's Pointer* (Winter 1993) p. 9.

Gannon, Michael. *Operation Drumbeat*. New York: Harper and Row Publishers, 1990.

Gibson, Charles Dana. *Merchantman or Ship of War. A Synopsis of Laws; U.S. State Department Position; and Practices Which Alter the Peaceful Character of U.S. Merchant Vessels in Time of War*. Camden, ME: Ensign Press, 1986.

Grover, David H. *U.S. Army Ships and Watercraft of World War II*. Annapolis, MD: Naval Institute Press, 1987.

Guides to the Microfilmed Records of the German Navy 1850-1945: No. 2. Records Relating to U-boat Warfare 1939-1945. Washington, DC: National Archives and Records Administration, 1985.

Infield, Glenn B. *Disaster at Bari*. London: Robert Hale & Company, 1974.

Irving, David. *The Destruction of Convoy PQ-17*. New York: St. Martin's Press, 1987.

James, Marquis. *The Texaco Story: The First Fifty Years 1902-1952*. The Texas Co., 1953.

Lenton, H. T., and J. J. Colledge. *British and Dominion Warships of World War II*. Garden City, New York: Doubleday and Company, Inc., 1968.

Levine, Daniel, and Sarah Ann Platt. "The Contribution of U.S. Shipbuilding and the Merchant Marine to the Second World War" from Robert A. Kilmarx, (ed.), *America's Maritime Legacy*. Boulder, CO: Westview Press, 1979.

Lloyd's Register of Shipping, 1941-1945.

Lloyd's of London. *Lloyd's War Losses, The Second World War, 3 September 1939-14 August 1945, vol. 1, British, Allied and Neutral Merchant Vessels Sunk or Destroyed by War Causes*. London: Lloyd's of London Press, 1989.

Matson Navigation Company. *Ships in Gray, The Story of Matson in World War II*. San Francisco: Matson Navigation Co., 1946.

McCoy, Samuel Duff. *Nor Death Dismay: A Record of Merchant Ships and Merchant Mariners in Times of War*. New York: Macmillian and Co., 1944.

Middlebrook, Martin. *Convoy*. New York: William Morrow and Co., 1977.

Ministry of Defense (Navy). *The U-Boat War in the Atlantic 1939-1945*. London: Her Majesty's Stationary Office, 1989.

Moore, Arthur R. *A Careless Word . . . A Needless Sinking*. Kings Point, NY: American Merchant Marine Museum, 1988.

Morison, Samuel Eliot. *History of United States Naval Operations in World War II*. 15 vols. Boston: Little, Brown and Co., 1947-1962.

Morrell, Robert W. *Oil Tankers*. New York: Simmons-Boardman Publishing Co., 1931.

Morton, Louis. *The Fall of the Philippines*. United States Army in World War II Series. Washington, DC: Office of the Chief of Military History, 1953.

Muggenthaler, August Karl. *German Raiders of World War II*. Englewood Cliffs, NJ: Prentice-Hall, Inc., 1977.

Mullins, Wayman C., ed. *1942: "Issue in Doubt" Symposium on the War in the Pacific by the Admiral Nimitz Museum*. Austin, Texas: Eakin Press, 1994.

National Defense Research Committee. *Summary Technical Report of the National Defense Research Committee: Underwater Sound Equipment I Listening System*. Washington, DC, 1946.

Niven, John. *The American President Lines and Its Forebearers: 1848-1984*. Newark, DE: University of Delaware Press, 1987.

Riesenberg, Jr., Felix. *Sea War: The Story of the U.S. Merchant Marine in World War II*. New York: Rinehart & Co. Inc., 1956.

Rohwer, Jürgen. *The Critical Convoy Battles of March 1943: The Battle for HX 229/SC 122*. Annapolis, MD: Naval Institute Press, 1977.

Rohwer, Jürgen. *Axis Submarine Successes 1939-1945*. Annapolis, MD: U.S. Naval Institute, 1983.

Sawyer, L. A., and W. H. Mitchell. *From America to United States, In Four Parts: The History of the Long-Range Merchant Shipbuilding Programme of the United States Maritime Commission*. Kendal, England: World Ship Society, 1979-1986.

Sawyer, L. A., and W. H. Mitchell. *The Liberty Ships: The History of the "Emergency" Type Cargo Ships Construction in the United States During the Second World War*. London: Lloyd's of London Press, 1985.

Scheina, Robert. *U.S. Coast Guard Cutters and Craft of World War II*. Annapolis, MD: Naval Institute Press, 1982.

Schofield, B. B., and L. F. Martyn. *The Rescue Ships*. Edinburgh: William Blackwood and Sons, 1968.

Silverstone, Paul H. *U.S. Warships of World War II*. Annapolis, MD: Naval Institute Press, 1989.

Smith, J. R., and Anthony L. Kay. *German Aircraft of the Second World War*. London: Putnam & Co., 1972.

Standard Oil Company. *Ships of the Esso Fleet in World War II*. New Jersey: Standard Oil Company, 1946.

Sternhell, Charles M., and Alan M. Thorndike. *Antisubmarine Warfare in World War II*. Washington, DC: Office of the Chief of Naval Operations, 1946.

Stindt, Fred A. *Matson's Century of Ships*. Kelseyville, CA: F. A. Stindt, 1982.

Terrell, Edward. *Admiralty Brief: The Story of Inventions That Contributed to the Battle of the Atlantic*. London: George G. Harrap & Co., 1958.

Texas Company. *History of the Texas Company's Marine Department*. nd.

U.S. Coast Guard. *Coast Guard at War*. 30 vols., *Assistance*, vol. XIV, pt. 2. Washington, DC: Public Information Division, 1947.

U.S. Coast Guard. *Light Lists: Atlantic and Gulf Coasts of the United States*. Washington, DC: Government Printing Office, 1943, 1944, 1945.

U.S. Coast Guard. *Proceedings of the Merchant Marine Council*.

U.S. Coast Guard. *Report on Lifeboat and Liferaft Performance for U.S. Tank Vessels Suffering War Casualties. 1 July 1944*. Washington, DC.

U.S. Coast Guard. *Statistical Analysis of 167 Torpedo Hits on 104 U.S. Tankers*. Washington, DC, 1944.

U.S. Coast Guard. *Summary of Merchant Marine Personnel Casualties: World War II*. Washington, DC: Government Printing Office, 1950.

U.S. Coast Guard. *The Sinking of the Escanaba*. Washington, DC: Statistical Division, U.S. Coast Guard, 1943.

U.S. Coast Guard. *War Action Casualties Involving Merchant Tank Vessels*. Washington, DC: Merchant Vessel Inspection Division, nd.

U.S. Coast Guard. *Wartime Safety Measures for Merchant Marine*. Washington, DC: Government Printing Office, 1944.

U.S. Department of Commerce. *Merchant Vessels of the United States*. Government Printing Office, 1941-45.

U.S. Navy. *Current Tactical Orders and Doctrine, U.S. Fleet*. United States Fleet, Headquarters of the Commander in Chief, 1945.

U.S. Navy. *History of Convoy and Routing*. U.S. Navy Department, Washington, DC, 1945.

Wall, Carl B. "Torpedoed in the Arctic." *Liberty*, 24 June 1944, pp. 27-29, 69.

Walls, Anthony J., and Brian G. Gordon. *The Imperial Japanese Navy*. Garden City, NY: Doubleday & Co., Inc., 1971.

War Shipping Administration. *The United States Merchant Marine at War; Report of the War Shipping Administration to the President*. Washington, DC, 1946.

Waters, John M. Jr. *Bloody Winter*. Annapolis, MD: Naval Institute Press, 1987.

Watts, Anthony J., and Brian G. Gordon. *The Imperial Japanese Navy*. Garden City, NY: Doubleday and Co., Inc., 1971.

Webster's Geographical Dictionary. A Dictionary of Names and Places with Geographical and Historical Information and Pronunciations. Springfield, MA: G. & C. Merriam Co., 1969.

Winslow, W. G. *The Fleet the Gods Forgot: The U.S. Asiatic Fleet in World War II*. Annapolis, MD: Naval Institute Press, 1984.

Woodbury, David D. *Builders for Battle: How the Pacific Naval Air Bases Were Constructed*. New York: E.P. Dutton and Company, Inc., 1946.

Woodward, David. *The Secret Raiders. The Story of the German Armed Merchant Raiders in the Second World War*. New York: W.W. Norton and Co., Inc., 1955.

INDEX

The Naval Institute Press is the book-publishing arm of the U.S. Naval Institute, a private, nonprofit society for sea service professionals and others who share an interest in naval and maritime affairs. Established in 1873 at the U.S. Naval Academy in Annapolis, Maryland, where its offices remain, today the Naval Institute has more than 100,000 members worldwide.

Members of the Naval Institute receive the influential monthly magazine *Proceedings* and discounts on fine nautical prints and on ship and aircraft photos. They also have access to the transcripts of the Institute's Oral History Program and get discounted admission to any of the Institute-sponsored seminars offered around the country.

The Naval Institute also publishes *Naval History* magazine. This colorful bimonthly is filled with entertaining and thought-provoking articles, first-person reminiscences, and dramatic art and photography. Members receive a discount on *Naval History* subscriptions.

The Naval Institute's book-publishing program, begun in 1898 with basic guides to naval practices, has broadened its scope in recent years to include books of more general interest. Now the Naval Institute Press publishes more than seventy titles each year, ranging from how-to books on boating and navigation to battle histories, biographies, ship and aircraft guides, and novels. Institute members receive discounts on the Press's nearly 400 books in print.

For a free catalog describing Naval Institute Press books currently available, and for further information about subscribing to *Naval History* magazine or about joining the U.S. Naval Institute, please write to:

Membership & Communications Department
U.S. Naval Institute
118 Maryland Avenue
Annapolis, Maryland 21402-5035
Or call, toll-free, (800) 233-USNI.